ISBN 978-1-331-43606-5
PIBN 10189930

THE
LAW AND PRACTICE
WITH REGARD TO
HOUSING IN ENGLAND AND WALES

BY

SIR KINGSLEY WOOD, M.P.
SOLICITOR OF THE SUPREME COURT

WITH A PREFACE BY

RT. HON. CHRISTOPHER ADDISON, M.D., M.P.
MINISTER OF HEALTH

LONDON
HENRY FROWDE   HODDER & STOUGHTON
OXFORD UNIVERSITY PRESS   WARWICK SQUARE, E.C.
1921

PRINTED IN GREAT BRITAIN
BY HAZELL, WATSON AND VINEY, LD.,
LONDON AND AYLESBURY.

PREFACE

THE National Housing Problem is to-day in a most acute form, and it will long continue to occupy the attention of our citizens. When sufficient houses have been built to make up the grave War shortage, we have still to take up the equally important task of clearing the slums and the insanitary areas, which are so wasteful and so detrimental both to the physical and commercial interests of the Country.

In this book controversial topics have been avoided, and it may be that, on such a matter as the method that has been adopted to deal with our housing situation, a true verdict can only be given by our succeeding generation. Suffice it to say that nearly every Country has had to deal with a similar situation and has been driven to State intervention. So far as our own progress is concerned, it is at the present time in advance of that attained by any other Nation.

There are many Acts on the Statute Book concerning Housing, and a clear and concise explanation of legislation, such as is afforded by this work, will be of great value to the thousands of Housing administrators and workers which the Country possesses, and to whom it owes so much.

It would obviously be impossible for me to express agreement with all the opinions —legal

v

462622

or otherwise—which this book contains, but it certainly comprises a comprehensive and careful collection of all that is necessary for a proper examination and understanding of this important subject, and I heartily commend it.

CHRISTOPHER ADDISON.

MINISTRY OF HEALTH
January 1921

AUTHOR'S NOTE

MUCH of the matter for this volume was prepared over twelve months ago, and one of the difficulties of its production has been that of frequent revision in consequence of legislative and other changes. For a time publication was withheld in order to incorporate changes proposed to be effected by the Ministry of Health (Miscellaneous Provisions) Bill, which Bill was rejected by the House of Lords in December last. One of the chief objects of the housing provisions of that Bill was the extension, by twelve months, of the period during which the State subsidy was payable to private persons building houses—for the conditions see page 114—and subsequently to its rejection the Government gave a promise that such extension would be the subject of further legislation at an early date. But this volume has been so long promised, so long in hand and in type, that it has not been thought proper to delay its appearance until that legislation was effected.

The subject dealt with in this volume is a very comprehensive one, and I feel I cannot have avoided errors and omissions. I shall welcome corrections.

I have been assisted by the works of eminent legal authorities who have contributed to this subject prior to 1919, and the various official publications of the Health Ministry.

I desire also to express my warmest thanks to my friend Mr. T. A. Rushton for much valuable assistance.

KINGSLEY WOOD.

15, WALBROOK,
LONDON, E.C.4
January 1921

vii

CONTENTS

LIST OF OFFICIAL PUBLICATIONS

31st December 1920

ACTS

	Date.	Title.
53 & 54 Vict. c. 70	18 Aug. 1890	Housing of the Working Classes Act, 1890.
53 & 54 Vict. c. 16	25 July 1890	Working Class Dwellings Act, 1890.
57 & 58 Vict. c. 55	25 Aug. 1894	Housing of the Working Classes Act, 1894.
62 & 63 Vict. c. 44	9 Aug. 1899	Small Dwellings Acquisition Act, 1899.
63 & 64 Vict. c. 59	8 Aug. 1900	Housing of the Working Classes Act, 1900.
3 Edw. 7. c. 39	14 Aug. 1903	Housing of the Working Classes Act, 1903.
9 Edw. 7. c. 44	3 Dec. 1909	Housing, Town Planning, &c., Act, 1909.
4 & 5 Geo. 5. c. 31	10 Aug. 1914	The Housing Act, 1914.
4 & 5 Geo. 5. c. 52	10 Aug. 1914	The Housing Act (No. 2), 1914.
9 & 10 Geo. 5. c. 35	31 July 1919	Housing, Town Planning, &c., Act, 1919.
9 & 10 Geo. 5. c. 99	23 Dec. 1919	Housing (Additional Powers) Act, 1919.
9 & 10 Geo. 5. c. 57	19 Aug. 1919	Acquisition of Land (Assessment of Compensation) Act, 1919.
9 & 10 Geo. 5. c. 59	19 Aug. 1919	Land Settlement (Facilities) Act, 1919 (see section 22 as to appropriation of land).
10 & 11 Geo. 5. c. 17	2 July 1920	Increase of Rent and Mortgage Interest (Restrictions) Act, 1920.
10 & 11 Geo. 5. c. 61	23 Dec. 1920	Public Works Loans Act, 1920 (s. 5.).
10 & 11 Geo. 5. c. 57	3 Dec. 1920	Unemployment (Relief Works) Act, 1920.

STATUTORY RULES AND ORDERS, &C.

S.R. & O. No.	Ministry Order No.	Date.	Title.
2	54,930	11 Jan. 1910	Forms for use in connection with sections 15, 17 and 18 of the Housing Town Planning, &c., Act, 1909 (repealed except as to forms under section 15, by S.R. & O., 1919, No. 1424).

S.R. & O. No.	Ministry Order No.	Date.	Title.
801	55,475	29 July 1910	The County Medical Officers of Health (Duties) Order, 1910.
	55,763	2 Sept. 1910	Regulations as to land in neighbourhood of Royal Palaces and Parks.
919	55,578	2 Sept. 1910	Housing (Inspection of District) Regulations, 1910.
	55,916	19 Nov. 1910	Forms under Part I of the Housing of the Working Classes Act, 1890.
1175	65,408	29 Aug. 1919	The Housing Acts (Compulsory Purchase) Regulations, 1919 (amended by order 65,605).
1556	65,605	23 Oct. 1919	The Housing Acts (Compulsory Purchase) Amendments Regulations, 1919.
167		6 Feb. 1920	The Housing Acts (Compulsory Purchase) Amendments Regulations, 1920.
336	65,815	5 Mar. 1920	The County Councils (Assisted Schemes for the Housing of Employees) Regulations, 1920.
1465	66,495	12 Aug. 1920	The Housing (Loans by County Councils) Order, 1920.
1424	65,480	10 Oct. 1919	The Housing Acts (Forms of Orders and Notices) Order, 1919.
1423	65,473	10 Oct. 1919	The Housing Acts (Appeal Procedure) Rules, 1919.
2128		12 Nov. 1920	The Ministry of Health (Temporary Relaxation of Building Byelaws) Regulations, 1920.
Treasury Minute		1 Nov. 1920	Rates of Interest on Local Loans.
2047	65,736	31 Dec. 1919	The Local Authorities (Assisted Housing Schemes) Regulations, 1919.
56	65,788	22 Jan. 1920	The Housing (Regulation of Building) Order, 1920.
57	65,789	22 Jan. 1920	The Regulation of Building (Appeal Procedure) Rules, 1920.
1428	65,242	6 Oct. 1919	The Public Utility Societies (Financial Assistance) Regulations, 1919.
107	65,704	28 Jan. 1920	The Public Utility Societies (Sale of Houses) Regulations, 1920.
134	65,798	30 Jan. 1920	The Public Utility Societies (Financial Assistance) Regulations, 1920.
1429	65,243	6 Oct. 1919	Housing Trusts (Financial Assistance) Regulations, 1919.
135	65,796	30 Jan. 1920	Housing Trusts (Financial Assistance) Regulations, 1920.
683		4 May 1920	The Housing Accounts Order (Societies and Trusts), 1920.

S. R. & O. No.	Ministry Order No.	Date.	Title.
1836		2 Dec. 1919	The Acquisition of Land (Assessment of Compensation) Rules, 1919.
285		24 Feb. 1920	The Acquisition of Land (Assessment of Compensation) Fees Rules, 1920.
690		5 April 1920	The Acquisition of Land (Assessment of Compensation) Fees (No. 2) Rules, 1920.
197	65,811	25 Feb. 1920	The Housing (Local Bonds) Regulations, 1920.
487	66,165	31 Mar. 1920	The Housing Accounts Order (Local Authorities), 1920.
560	66,017	12 April 1920	The Prohibition of Demolition (Appeal Procedure) Rules, 1920.

MISCELLANEOUS PAPERS, MANUALS, FORMS, &C.

No.	Date.	Title.
First issued	19 July 1919	*Housing*, a fortnightly journal issued by the Ministry.
	Feb. 1920	Housing by Public Utility Societies: The Government proposals (re-issue).
(D. 107)	Sept. 1919	Assisted Scheme (Public Utility Society) Statement of Annual Income and Expenditure.
(D. 106)		Assisted Scheme (Local Authority) Statement of Annual Income and Expenditure.
	17 April 1914	Draft Regulations as to underground rooms as sleeping places.
	April 1920	Draft Model By-laws, Series XIII *b* (section 26 of the Housing, Town Planning, &c., Act, 1920).
(D. 70)		Procedure to be adopted: submission of house tender to Ministry.
(D. 76)		Procedure to be adopted: submission of street and sewerage tender.
(O. 37) (8654)	Aug. 1919	Housing, Town Planning, &c., Act, 1919 (brief explanatory statement of Act).
	Sept. 1919	Housing, Powers and Duties of Local Authorities (full explanatory statement of Act).
	8 April 1919	Manual on the preparation of State-aided Housing Schemes (including Forms D.48 (site proposals); D.49 (proposals for general lay-out, &c.); D.50 (application for approval); D.51 (estimate of street and sewerage works); D.52 (statement of estimated annual receipts and expenditure), &c.

No.	Date.	Title.
(S.O.P. 384)	Sept. 1919	Manual on the Conversion of Houses into Flats for the Working Classes (including D.81 (a), (b) and (c) (schedules) ; D.94 (application by owner) ; D.95 (documents to be forwarded, &c.) ; D.96 (application for acquisition) ; D.97 (statement of estimated annual receipts and expenditure), &c., &c., &c.
	Dec. 1919	Manual on Unfit Houses and Unhealthy Areas, Vol. I (including Housing (Inspection of District) Regulations, 1910 ; Form of Application by owner for loan ; Documents to be forwarded, &c., &c.)
	Jan. 1920	Manual on Unfit Houses and Unhealthy Areas, Vol. II (Legal Powers, &c.).
	June 1920	Type, plans and elevations of cottages designed by the Ministry in connection with State-Aided Housing Schemes.
	Nov. 1919	Report prepared in the Intelligence Department of the Local Government Board on the Housing Problem in Germany.
	Jan. 1920	Memorandum setting out the main provisions of the Housing (Additional Powers) Act, 1919. (Memo. 8/D.)
	Jan. 1920	Memorandum as to conditions governing Grants made to private persons or bodies of persons constructing houses under the Housing (Additional Powers) Act, 1919.
	Mar. 1920	Memo. 109.—Notes on Special Points in connection with the keeping of Assisted Housing Accounts by Local Authorities.
	Sept. 1920	Memorandum setting out the Increases made in the Grants to private persons constructing houses under the Housing (Additional Powers) Act, 1919. (D. 194, Revised).
	July 1920	Summary of the Principal Provisions of the Increase of Rent and Mortgage Interest (Restrictions) Act, 1920.
	Sept. 1920	Pamphlet.—*How to get a House of Your Own.*
	Sept. 1920	Particulars of Systems of House Construction Approved up to April 1920.
(D. 89)	July 1919	Form of Survey of Housing Needs.
(D. 82)	Aug. 1919	Standard Specification for Cottages.
(D. 91)	Sept. 1919	Standard Specification for Roads and Sewers.
		Bills of quantities and estimates for houses of different types, sizes and aspects.

Date.	Title.
Mar. 1920	Standard Specifications for Cottages of Timber Construction.
Mar. 1920	Model Form of Agreement for Purchase by a Local Authority of Working Class Dwellings under Section 12 (3) of the Housing Act, 1919.
May 1920	Model Forms of Tender and Contract, Contract No. 1 (D88 A), revised May 1920.
June 1920	Specifications for Cement Concrete Buildings approved by the Standardisation and Construction Committee of the Ministry of Health.

CIRCULARS TO LOCAL AUTHORITIES, &C.

Date.	Subject.
2 May 1919	Land for Housing Schemes.
11 June 1919	Delegation of Work to Committee: Quantities and Materials.
13 June 1919	Land for Housing Schemes.
29 July 1919	Conversion of Houses into Flats.
25 Aug. 1919	Accompanying Form of Survey (Explanation of 1919 Act).
30 Aug. 1919	County Medical Officers of Health, Assistance by (to County Councils).
7 Oct. 1919	Explanatory leaflet to County Councils, &c.
11 Oct. 1919	Accompanying Appeal Rules, &c.
31 Oct. 1919	Accompanying Compulsory Purchase Amendment Regulations, 1919.
3 Dec. 1919	Co-option of Women on Housing Committees.
21 Nov. 1919	Provision of Houses, with Enclosures A. & B.
Mar. 1920	With Housing Accounts Order (Local Authorities), 1920, and an explanatory Memorandum.

GENERAL HOUSING MEMORANDA

Date.	Form No.	Subject.
18 July 1919	D. 80	Procedure in submission of housing schemes.
Aug. 1919	D. 85	Expenditure of local authorities in connection with the preparation and execution of Housing Schemes by their own staff.
Aug. 1919	D. 90	Standard Specification for Cottage.
Sept. 1919	D. 92	Fees payable to architects and quantity surveyors, &c.

No.	Date.	Form No.	Subject.
5	15 Sept. 1919	D. 93	The provision of temporary housing accommodation by the use of army huts or State-owned hostels.
6	15 Sept. 1919	D. 98	Compulsory Acquisition of Land for Housing (see p. 515).
7	15 Sept. 1919	D. 99	Standard Specification for Roads and Sewers.
8	Oct. 1919	D. 103	Financial Assistance to Local Authorities.
9	Oct. 1919	D. 104	Financial Assistance to Public Utility Societies and Housing Trusts.
9a	Jan. 1920	D. 104a	To replace General Housing Memorandum, No. 9.
10	Sept. 1919	D. 105	Model Form of Contract
11	Nov. 1919	D. 109	Compulsory Purchase (see p. 519).
12	Oct. 1919	D. 111	Relaxation of Building Bylaws.
13	Oct. 1919	D. 115	Expenditure of Local Authorities.
14	Oct. 1919	D. 121	Building Materials to private persons.
15	25 Nov. 1919	D. 124	Quantity Surveyors.
16	Feb. 1920		Enclosing Model Form of Agreement under s. 12 (3)/19.
17	16 Dec. 1919	D. 131	Expenditure of Local Authorities in respect of Administrative work in connection with the erection of houses under Assisted Housing Schemes.
18	16 Dec. 1919	D. 132	Assisted Housing Schemes.
19	20 Jan. 1920	D. 134	With Orders, 65,788, 65,789 (Regulation of Building, and Appeals).
20	20 Jan. 1920	D. 137	*Re* Grants under section 1, Additional Powers Act, 1919.
21	Feb. 1920		Enclosing copies of the Housing (Local Bonds) Regulations, 1920, and outlining procedure of Local Authorities thereunder.
22	Feb. 1920		Setting out the means by which Production Committees of Local Authorities can overcome difficulties arising out of the shortage of labour and materials and delays in transport.
23	Mar. 1920		Applications for payments on account of Exchequer Subsidy for the year ending March 31, 1920.
24	Mar. 1920		Enclosing Standard Specification for Cottages of Timber Construction.
25	Mar. 1920		Ministry of Health decisions in regard to points raised in connection with the conditions governing the payment of Grants to private persons constructing houses under the Housing (Additional Powers) Act, 1919.
26	April 1920		Purchase of certain building materials independently of the Director of Building Materials Supply.

Subject.

Sale of Houses built by Local Authorities.

Enclosing copies of revised model form of contract, No. 1, prepared for use of Local Authorities, &c.

Increase of Grants to private persons under the Housing (Additional Powers) Act, 1919.

Enclosing Standard Specifications for Cement Concrete Building.

Revision of Scales of Fees payable to Architects and Quantity Surveyors in connection with State-aided Housing Schemes.

Payment of Exchequer Subsidy in respect of Local Authorities Assisted Housing Schemes.

Conditions to be observed in drawing up schemes for the Sale of ·Houses included in Assisted Schemes on the Plan of Payment by Instalments.

Loans to Local Authorities from Proceeds of Sales of National Savings Certificates.

Fire Insurance of Houses included in Local Authorities Assisted Housing Schemes.

State-aided Housing Schemes : Preparation and Submission of Final Accounts and Contractors' Statements.

Smoke Abatement.

Grants to Private Builders : Issue of " Λ " Certificates to be discontinued.

COMMAND PAPERS

Title.

Building Construction : Report of Committee (Tudor Walters').

First Report of Committee on the Acquisition and Valuation of Land for Public Purposes.

Second Report of Committee on the Acquisition and Valuation of Land for Public Purposes.

Third Report of Committee (Mines and Minerals).

Fourth Report of Committee (Transfer of Land in England and Wales).

Position of the Building Industry after the War (Building Materials Supply Committee).

Housing : Memorandum by the Advisory Panel on the Emergency Problem (3d.).

Building Construction Contracts (Colwyn Committee).

Women's Housing Sub-Committee First Interim Report (1d.).

No.	Date.	Title.
Cd. 9232	17 Jan. 1919	Women's Housing Sub-Committee Final Report (3d.).
Cd. 9213	13 Nov. 1918	Building Bylaws: Report of Local Government Board Committee on
Cd. 9214	13 Nov. 1918	Building Bylaws : Minutes of Evidence, Appendices and Index.
Cd. 9223	29 Oct. 1918	Financial Assistance Committee : Interim Report on Public Utility Societies (2d.).
Cd. 9238	5 Feb. 1919	Financial Assistance Committee : Final Report (3d.).
Cd. 9235		Report of Committee on Increase of Rent, &c., Legislation.
Cmd. 89	24 Mar. 1919	Financial Assistance to Public Utility Societies and Housing Trusts.
Cmd. 128	28 April 1919	Financial Assistance to Public Utility Societies and Housing Trusts.
(H.C. 957)	April 1919	Housing by Public Utility Societies and Housing Trusts.
Cmd. 542		Housing Schemes submitted to the Ministry of Health (the most recent return of a series).
Cmd. 124	28 April 1919	Statutory Enactments proposed to be extended &c., by the Housing, Town Planning, &c., Bill, 1919.
Cmd. 125	28 April 1919	Estimate of probable Expenditure.
Cmd. 126	28 April 1919	Statement showing existing procedure, &c., and effect of Bill.
Cmd. 127	28 April 1919	Financial Assistance to Local Authorities.
Cmd. 426	Nov. 1919	New Methods of Construction.
Cmd. 444	27 Nov. 1919	Interim Report of Treasury Committee on Housing Finance.
Cmd. 453		Housing (Additional Powers) Bill, 1919. Estimate of probable Expenditure, Conditions Governing Grants to Private Builders.
Cd. 9157	Nov. 1918	Forty-seventh Annual Report of Local Government Board, 1917–18.
Cmd. 413		Forty-eighth Annual Report of Local Government Board, 1918–19.
Cmd 509		Changes in Prices of Building Materials (London).
Cmd. 599	Mar. 1920	Statement showing the names of donors of sites which have been approved by the Ministry of Health for the erection of houses for the Working Classes.
Cmd. 611	Mar. 1920	List of Changes in the Prices of the Principal Building Materials.
Cmd. 658	April 1920	Report of the Committee on the Increase of Rent and Mortgage Interest (War Restrictions) Acts.
	June 1920	Minutes of Evidence of the Committee on the Increase of Rent and Mortgage Interest (War Restrictions) Acts.

RECONSTRUCTION PROBLEMS

Pamphlets on—

(2) Housing in England and Wales.
(4) Housing in Scotland.
(25) Town Planning.

LAW AND PRACTICE WITH REGARD TO HOUSING IN ENGLAND AND WALES

CHAPTER I

INTRODUCTION

THE legislation relating to housing is voluminous and almost chaotic. Besides the Housing Acts, 1890 to 1919, as defined by section 40 of the Housing, Town Planning, &c., Act, 1919, there are seven Acts printed or referred to in this volume which closely affect housing (see the table of contents), and there are references therein to many other Acts which deal with aspects of the problem or some of the questions arising out of it.

This voluminous legislation will perhaps appal the layman, but, though there is ample need for the promised consolidation, the legislation is not quite so difficult as it would appear. It falls readily under certain headings, and, once these are grasped, the subject is much clearer. These headings are :—

Unhealthy Areas (Part I)
Unhealthy Dwelling Houses (Part II)
Housing of the Working Classes (Part III)
Town Planning.

The principal housing Act (1890) is divided into Parts I, II, III . . . and these terms are in common use, often as abbreviations, e.g. " a Part III scheme."

Parts I and II are dealt with fully in Chapter III, and Part III in Chapter II ; and it is not necessary to refer further to them here than to say that while the provision of houses (Part III) is the problem of the moment, the removal of unhealthy housing conditions (Parts I and II) was the problem for many years previously, and may be the problem for many years after the present shortage of houses disappears, though the provision of new houses of the type approved under the Housing, Town Planning, &c., Act, 1919, should materially lessen the future difficulties—as it is designed to do.   Town planning is dealt with in Chapter V.

THE LEGISLATION BRIEFLY REVIEWED

The Housing of the Working Classes Act, 1890 (the principal Act) is the first of the present Housing Acts. It repealed the following Acts :—

A difficult problem—previous attempted solutions.

Session and Chapter.	Short Title.	Extent of Repeal.
14 & 15 Vict. c. 34	The Labouring Classes Lodging Houses Act, 1851	The whole Act
18 & 19 Vict. c. 88	The Dwelling Houses (Scotland) Act, 1855	The whole Act
29 & 30 Vict. c. 28	The Labouring Classes Dwelling Houses Act, 1866	The whole Act
29 & 30 Vict. c. 44	The Labouring Classes Lodging Houses and Dwellings Act (Ireland), 1866	The whole Act
30 & 31 Vict. c. 28	The Labouring Classes Dwelling Houses Act, 1867	The whole Act
31 & 32 Vict. c. 130	The Artizans and Labourers Dwellings Acts, 1868	The whole Act
38 & 39 Vict. c. 36	The Artizans and Labourers Dwellings Improvement Act, 1875	The whole Act
38 & 39 Vict. c. 49	The Artizans and Labourers Dwellings Improvement (Scotland) Act, 1875	The whole Act
42 & 43 Vict. c. 63	The Artizans and Labourers Dwellings Improvement Act, 1879	The whole Act
42 & 43 Vict. c. 64	The Artizans and Labourers Dwellings Act (1868) Amendment Act, 1879	The whole Act
42 & 43 Vict. c. 77	The Public Works Loans Act, 1879	Section six
42 Vict. c. 2	The Artizans and Labourers Dwellings Improvement (Scotland) Act, 1880	The whole Act

Session and Chapter.	Short Title.	Extent of Repeal.
43 Vict. c. 8	An Act to explain and amend the twenty-second section of the Artizans and Labourers Dwellings Act (1868) Amendment Act, 1879	The whole Act
45 & 46 Vict. c. 54	The Artizans Dwellings Act, 1882	The whole Act
48 & 49 Vict. c. 72	The Housing of the Working Classes Act, 1885	The whole Act except sections three and seven to nine, and except section ten so far as it relates to by-laws authorised by those sections

Its chief purpose was the removal of unhealthy housing conditions (Parts I and II). Its Part III powers were adoptive only. By the 1909 Act they took effect without adoption; and by the 1919 Act the powers became duties.

In 1894 there was a short Act dealing with the borrowing powers under a reconstruction scheme (Part II).

In 1900 there was another short Act, only four sections of which now remain in force. These are: Exercise of powers outside district; Provisions as to Metropolitan Borough Councils; Accounts, and Short Title.

In 1903 there was a longer Act dealing with general Amendments, Amendments as to Schemes, Amendments as to Closing Orders, Demolition, and the like.

The 1909 Act was, and is, of considerable importance. The problem of providing houses was emerging, and, as stated, Part III of the principal Act was to take effect without adoption. Powers of enforcing the Acts were extended and there were drastic amendments with regard to Closing and Demolition Orders. Amendments were also made with regard to Parts I and II schemes, and to financial matters. But the matter perhaps of most importance was the introduction of town-planning provisions, which provisions are still largely in force.

Legislation, 1890 to 1919.

In 1914, following the outbreak of war, two war Acts (the Housing Act, 1914 and the Housing (No. 2) Act, 1914) were passed.

The 1919 and 1920 Acts. In 1919 four Acts were passed affecting housing :—

> The Housing, Town Planning Act, 1919.
> The Housing (Additional Powers) Act, 1919.
> The Land Settlement (Facilities) Act, 1919.
> The Acquisition of Land (Assessment of Compensation) Act, 1919.

The first, which is the only one included in " the Housing Acts, 1890 to 1919," is of great importance. It effects considerable amendments in previous Acts and largely provides the machinery for the present housing campaign. It is discussed fully in this volume, and is referred to as " the 1919 Act."

The Housing (Additional Powers) Act, 1919 made provision for a subsidy to private builders who erected houses during 1920 ; for the prohibition of luxury building ; for the issue of housing bonds and for minor matters. It is discussed in Chapter VII, and remarks on its proposed extension are also made in the preface.

The Land Settlement (Facilities) Act, 1919, deals with the powers of county councils (see Chapter IV) in connection with the settlement of soldiers on the land and the provision of the necessary houses. On the whole, however, it is outside the scope of the present volume, and short extracts only are given on page 85.

The Acquisition of Land (Assessment of Compensation) Act, 1919, deals (*inter alia*) with the machinery for the assessment of compensation for land taken compulsorily for the purposes of the housing Acts. It is printed in full on page 495.

The Unemployment (Relief Works) Act, 1920, with the object of finding immediate work for the unemployed, enables local authorities and the appropriate Government department to acquire land compulsorily for the construction or improvement of roads, the construction of sewers and the like (see page 488).

With much the same object, the Public Works Loan Commissioners are empowered by the Public Works Loans Act, 1920, to make temporary advances for building purposes to local authorities (see page 487).

The Small Dwellings Acquisition Acts, 1899 and 1919, Other which enable local authorities to lend money so that legislation persons may acquire their houses (see also section 15 (1) (d) of the 1919 Act) are dealt with on page 241.

Of the other Acts affecting housing, the chief are the Public Health Acts. Those sections thereof which are within the scope of this volume are dealt with in Chapter III.

For some years prior to the outbreak of war there Events had been a falling off in the provision of houses for to the 1919 the working classes. legislation.

With the outbreak of war house building further diminished, and, in time, practically ceased except for Government (war) purposes. Before the termination of the war the Government was well aware that the position necessitated special measures.

On 28th July 1917 the Local Government Board issued a circular letter to the 1,806 borough, urban and rural district councils requesting a return as to housing conditions and needs. 1,660 replied indicating an immediate need for some 400,000 working-class dwellings.

The conditions prevented private enterprise from Offers of meeting this demand, and the Government decided financial assistance to to encourage local authorities to build by offering to local meet 75 per cent. of the annual loss accruing. The authorities. offer, however, was felt to be insufficient in the case of certain local authorities.

On 18th March 1918 the Government, through a circular letter issued by the Local Government Board, made its first amended offer: the Board had discretion to increase the grant beyond 75 per cent. of the loss, provided that the local authority's share of the loss was *not less* than the product of a 1*d*. rate. Many accepted the offer, but a considerable number still hesitated to commit themselves to a financial burden which they could not very well measure.

When the Armistice was signed it was necessary to obtain more definite information, and on 14th November 1918, a further circular letter was issued. 1,300 local authorities replied. 1,150 were prepared to build; 1,080 of them on the terms of the 18th March letter; but only 450 stated when their schemes would be ready, and of these only 400 specified the number of houses which their schemes would provide —the aggregate number being 100,000.

On 6th February 1919, therefore, the Government made its final offer, namely that the burden on the local authority should, on the conditions therein named, be *not more* than the product of a 1*d*. rate—the balance being met by the State. Subsequently there were some modifications as to the period during which the financial assistance should operate, the final result being shown in the regulations printed on page 537.

While the above negotiations were taking place several committees were studying other very practical aspects of the question.

The 1918 Bill.

While these committees were still sitting the Government prepared a short Bill, as an instalment of its housing policy, for it was definitely stated, during the discussion of the estimates in May 1918, that it intended to propose comprehensive legislation. The Bill was introduced on 17th October 1918. Its two main clauses dealt with the borrowing powers of county councils in connection with the housing of their employees, and in connection with the transference to such councils of the housing powers of local authorities who had not used those powers to provide houses for the working classes.

The Bill was not proceeded with after the Armistice

was signed, and on 19th November 1918 was withdrawn.

After the General Election the Government decided The 1919 Bill. to proceed with its comprehensive Bill, and following the before-mentioned circular of 6th February 1919, Dr. Addison, then President of the Local Government Board (now Minister of Health) introduced on 18th March 1919, what is now the Housing, Town Planning, &c., Act, 1919.

The second reading of the Bill was moved in the House of Commons on 7th and 8th April 1918. It was sent to Grand Committee 14th April, reported 15th May, sent to the House of Lords on 28th May, and after further extended debate and "negotiations," received the Royal Assent on 31st July 1919.

For the better understanding of the housing problem, Other points of interest. however, it should be appreciated that for several years before the war, many prominent politicians (including the present Prime Minister) had constantly discussed it, and that private members' Bills had been presented to Parliament with the object of dealing with at least some portions of it. Bad housing had, in fact, become a "burning question," and it was clearly realised that such measures as the National Insurance Act, 1911, were, to some extent, necessitated by it.

The last of such Bills received a second reading on 20th March 1914, on the motion of Sir Arthur Griffith-Boscawen (now Parliamentary Secretary to the Ministry of Agriculture and Fisheries). But it did not go further, the then President of the Local Government Board (the Right Hon. Herbert Samuel, M.P.) saying that the Government was about to prepare its own Bill, and was taking the preliminary steps.

Nor is it correct to think that the idea of a Govern- A housing subsidy not new. ment housing subsidy is a new one. Housing has been subsidised in Ireland for several years. Up to 1914, 52,000 cottages had been built by Irish local authorities at a cost of £8,500,000, and there was an annual loss upon them. The reason for this subsidy, in the words of Mr. Herbert Samuel, in the debate mentioned, was : "It can be truly urged that, before this was effected, cottage building had absolutely ceased in Ireland, and there was no other course to be taken to provide private houses for people, but at the cost of the rates and taxes " (*Hansard*, 20th March 1914, col. 2454).

Further, certain local authorities had been subsidising housing out of the local rates. The report of the Local Government Board for 1912-13 shows that loans had been sanctioned to District Councils for housing in forty-two villages, in twenty-one of which there would be a deficit to be met by the rate-payer. In Liverpool, too, people displaced from slums had been re-housed at less than an economic rent.

The Local Government Board was stimulating local authorities to take action under their existing powers, with the result that such authorities had increased their output of houses.

Housing loans sanctioned.

The Forty-eighth Annual Report of the Local Government Board for 1918–1919 (Cd. 413) contains, on page 183, a statement showing the loans sanctioned to local authorities for the purchase of land and the erection of houses under Part III of the 1890 Act from the passing of the 1909 Act to 31st March 1919 :—

Year ended 31st March.	No. of Authorities.	Total amount of Loans Sanctioned.	No. of Houses to be Erected.
		£	
1911 . . .	13	101,210	464
1912 . . .	45	229,011	1,021
1913 . . .	68	395,432	1,880
1914 . . .	123	750,497	3,291
1915 . . .	181	1,124,621	4,408

After the outbreak of war, the totals necessarily decreased.

At the same time, it should be understood that the housing problem of 1914 was not of exactly the same nature as that of 1919. In 1914 it was more commonly urged, in regard to the provision of new houses, as a rural problem, while in the urban districts the chief complaint was not that the people could not get houses, but that many of the houses were unfit.

There is a great mass of evidence on this point; the *Housing and* following from a summary of the Report for 1918 of *health.* the Medical Officer of Health for Birmingham, Dr. J. Robertson, being typical :—

"In 1913 there were 43,366 back to back houses in Birmingham, housing 200,000, a population equal to that of the City of Cardiff. In six wards, all in the central area, from 51 to 76 per cent. of the houses were of this kind. During the period 1914–18 four of these wards had a general death-rate of more than 19 per 1,000 ; five an infant mortality greater than 134 per 1,000 births ; three a measles death-rate above 0.56 ; five a death-rate from pneumonia and bronchitis above 3.63 ; five a phthisis death-rate above 1.63 ; and five a mortality rate of over 29 per 1,000 births for deaths at ages under two from diarrhœa and enteritis. As a control we may take King's Norton, with less than 8 per cent. of back-to-back houses. The death-rate here from all causes is less than 10.9, the infant mortality less than 78, the measles mortality less than 0.12, the bronchitis and pneumonia rate below 1.62, the phthisis rate below 0.89, the diarrhœa and enteritis figure below 9. Some of the inhabitants may be shiftless and criminal, unfit to thrive in any environment ; but ' it is impossible to imagine a rising generation of young people being able to improve in health or self-respect, even if the best of educational facilities are provided, when everything they come in contact with is sullied by dirtiness and squalor.' "

To-day the difficulty is that 100,000 houses, approxi- *The present* mately, which were required each year, have not been *problem.* built since 1912. Up to 1912 that number, roughly, was provided. Then it dropped to 45,000 a year, and during the war it ceased almost completely.

It has been found from figures returned by local authorities that about 800,000 houses are required at the present time. The question is threefold :—

1. The problem of new houses.
2. The problem of slum clearances.
3. The town planning for the future.

These are the three chief directions of action to be taken by bodies responsible for housing in the next few years.

England is not alone in this matter. All over the world similar problems are facing the Governments of other nations. To-day this country is, as a matter of fact, further advanced with its schemes than any other country in the world.

The latest figures.

Much of the land required has already been acquired. During 1919 sufficient land, reckoning on the basis of ten houses to the acre, to erect 600,000 houses, was approved. To 17th November 1920, 52,857 houses had been commenced by local authorities, in addition to 28,000 public utility society and private builder (subsidy) houses. £86,500,000 had been raised in Housing Loans, including over £13,000,000 by Housing Bonds.

On 1st November 1920, the number of houses built by local authorities and public utility societies was 9,171, including 424 flats, but excluding Army huts converted into dwellings ; and 3,106 had been built by private builders (subsidy houses).

On 1st December 1920, 16,187 houses had been completed, of which 11,122 were provided by local authorities and public utility societies and 5,065 under the private builders' subsidy scheme ; 52,396 other houses were in various stages of construction by local authorities and public utility societies ; and preliminary certificates had been issued in respect of a further 21,448 houses under the private builders' subsidy scheme. The total number of houses included in signed contracts on 11th December by local authorities was 133,301.

CHAPTER II

By sections 1 and 2 of the Housing, Town Planning, Chief powers.
&c., Act, 1919 (referred to subsequently as the 1919
Act, or the Act of 1919) local authorities are required
to provide houses for the working classes in ·accordance
with the needs of their areas ; and, notably by sections 12
and 15, their Part III (1890) powers are enlarged to that
end. Further, by section 7, a large proportion of their
financial losses and expenses, arising out of such provision,
is met out of moneys provided by Parliament, con-
ditionally upon the provision being made within a specified
period.

The local authorities for the provision of these houses Definitions.
(see the 1890 Act, 1st schedule) are :—

    Town Councils,

    Urban District Councils, and

    Rural District Councils (see also section 1 of the
       1900 Act).

And in London :

    The Common Council of the City (for the City), and

    The London County Council, and

    The Metropolitan Borough Councils (for the remainder
      of the Administrative County of London) (see also
      the 1919 Act, section 41).

The position in London differs from that in the country London.
generally, because of the special position of the London
County Council. Excluding the City, in which the
Common Council is the housing authority, the powers

11

and duties in housing matters are divided between the London County Council and the Metropolitan Borough Councils. Section 41 contains a provision defining their powers and duties.

The provision of additional accommodation is a matter for the Metropolitan Borough Councils, if it is to be made to meet a shortage within the borough, and also on land within the borough.

The provision of new houses becomes a matter for the London County Council if the new houses are to be provided outside the county. In certain circumstances, the London County Council may submit a scheme to the Ministry of Health for the use of land in a Metropolitan Borough to meet the needs of districts outside the borough.

The London County Council and the Common Council of the City of London are empowered to enter into agreements with one another for carrying out any schemes for new houses or for slum clearances (section 41).

No. of local authorities.   The number of local authorities required to submit schemes under the 1919 Act is as follows:—

Metropolitan boroughs	.	29
County boroughs	. .	82
Boroughs	. . .	246
Urban districts	. .	799
Rural districts	. .	649

In certain circumstances county councils may be empowered to exercise the housing powers of local authorities (see Chapter IV, which deals with the powers and duties of county councils).

The schemes mentioned are Part III schemes, that is schemes for the provision of housing for the working classes under the provisions of Part III of the principal (1890) Act, as amended. Those at present in operation are also referred to as " assisted schemes," because the loss thereon is being chiefly met by moneys provided by Parliament.

In Part III of the principal Act, sections 53 to 59 give powers to local authorities to acquire and appropriate land (see also section 2, 1909 Act, and section 22 of the Land Settlement (Facilities) Act, 1919) and to erect, convert, alter, &c., buildings suitable for lodging houses for the working classes—which phrase has the same meaning as " houses for the working classes " used in the 1919 Act, see section 40 thereof. These powers are greatly enlarged by the 1919 Act (sections 12 and 15, see also section 11, 1903).

Sections 61 and 62 deal with the management of such houses, including the making of by-laws—as to which, see now section 25 of the 1919 Act.

Sections 65 and 66 deal with the expenses and borrowing powers of local authorities for Part III purposes; see also sections 3 (1900), 1 and 15 (1903), 3 and 31 (1909), and 7 (Additional Powers Act, 1919).

Sections 67–71 deal with loans to and powers of companies, societies and individuals to provide houses : see also sections 20 and 21 (1919). Water and gas companies can make supplies free or on favourable terms to Part III houses (section 69), which must be open for inspection by the local authority (section 70).

By section 74 land may be sold, &c., for working-class dwellings at lower prices than could be otherwise obtained, by companies and tenants for life under the Settled Land Acts, see also sections 7 (1909) and 31 (1919).

By section 80 separate accounts have to be kept by the local authority, and audited : see also section 4 (1900).

By section 81 housing committees may be formed and persons co-opted thereto.

Section 82 deals with the application of the purchase-money when land is sold.

By section 88 persons interested are prohibited from voting as members of the local authority, and section 89 provides the penalty for obstructing the execution of the Act.

Provisions of subsequent Acts.

By section 1 of the 1900 Act, a local authority, other than a rural district council, may acquire land for Part III purposes outside their district. As to the special cases of London, see now section 41 (1919).

Section 1 of the 1909 Act provides that Part III shall take effect without adoption. Previously it could be put into operation only after adoption. Section 5 (1909) deals with the payment of purchase or compensation money which would otherwise be paid into court.

By section 8 (1909) a local authority may accept donations of land or money : see also section 31 (1919).

Sections 10–13 (1909) deal with the powers of enforcing the Act : see now sections 3 and 4 (1919).

Section 34 (1909) makes it unnecessary for local authorities to make good the deficiency in land tax and poor rate, resulting from their acquiring land for housing purposes and putting it temporarily out of rating.

Other provisions of the 1909 Act include power of entry (section 36) ; power of Ministry to obtain report on any crowded area (section 37) ; joint action by local authorities (section 38, see also section 1 (6) 1919) ; appeals to Ministry (section 39) ; sale and disposal of buildings (section 40) ; power of Ministry to prescribe forms and to dispense with advertisements (section 41) ; power to revoke unreasonable by-laws (section 44, see now, however, section 24 of the 1919 Act) ; saving of sites of ancient monuments (section 45, see also section 1 (3) of the 1919 Act) ; provisions as to commons and open spaces (section 73) and to land in the neighbourhood of Royal palaces or parks (section 74).

A more extended reference to some of the powers under the 1919 Act is made below.

By section 10 of the Housing (Additional Powers) Act, 1919, the Minister may acquire land for the purpose of garden cities or town-planning schemes on behalf of local authorities and others.

Re-housing.

By sections 6, 11, 12 and 40 of the 1890 Act, local

authorities may be required to erect houses for the working classes, to re-house persons displaced by the clearance of slums, and, by section 3 of the 1903 Act, re-housing may be required when people are displaced by land being taken under local or private Acts.

In the House of Commons on 27th May 1919 Dr. Addison (Minister of Health) spoke on the subject of the definition of the " Working Classes " as follows :—

Definition of " Working Classes."

" The reason I did not put a definition of the working classes into the Bill, was because I found myself unable satisfactorily to provide one, and that is the plain truth of it. . . . I did not find it possible to frame a definition that was good enough. I think that was sound policy. We had a number of people, very eminent people, amongst them Mr. Hobhouse, who tried their best to frame it, and gave it up. This is the policy I propose to adopt. What is the type of house which we are going to encourage and assist under this scheme ? The type, of course, under the scheme is fairly general, and such a type of house as you would expect to include in the scheme. Having provided this type of house, we must expect the public authorities and public utility societies to secure that they are let to the persons for whom they are intended. The persons for whom they are intended are the persons whose housing needs emerge in that locality. Because the first principle of the Bill proceeds from this, that the local authority is called upon to provide a scheme, which scheme must be designed to meet the housing needs of their locality. It all arises out of that, and begins from that scheme. When we approve the scheme, then it becomes binding on the authority. So the House will see that the whole scheme is related, from the first Clause of the Bill to the needs of the locality, that is, the people who live there, and not people who may want to take a country cottage or anything like that. We must expect local authorities and others to see to it, or else assure ourselves, in framing a scheme, that the scheme is designed to meet the needs of the locality for people who want to or can inhabit this type of house generally. Then, after the scheme is sanctioned, we proceed from that beginning. I think a practical working application, relating to the type of house you are going to provide, rather than trying to frame some arbitrary definition of the working classes, which will break down within a month—I am perfectly certain of that, whatever the definition is, once you try to work it—is the right line of proceeding. I came to this decision because after having tried to frame a definition, and having employed a number of people to try to frame one for me, I found it impossible to get a definition that would form a working basis for this Act."

THE 1919 ACT

An important point of the new (1919) Act is that local authorities are required to ascertain how many houses are needed and to endeavour to provide them, as far as they will not be provided by other agencies (sections 1 and 2).

The problem attacked by the 1919 Act is, however, not only that of the provision of houses, but of houses of a better kind, more conveniently arranged, and more healthily situated and circumstanced.

When, therefore, the Ministry of Health (then the Local Government Board) grappled with the problem of the shortage of houses, it kept before it certain principles. Houses were needed, but the opportunity was to be taken of improving the health of the people by bettering the conditions under which they lived. The standard of accommodation and equipment had been rising, and this tendency was to be encouraged. More air-space was to be provided about each house. There was to be no building of dreary, unbroken rows of " brick boxes with slate lids," to use the phrase of Mr. John Burns, a former President of the Board. In short, the houses to be built were to be adequate in size, equip-ment and amenity. As the State (through the Ministry) was to provide financial assistance towards the provision of the houses, it was able to secure the due observance of the above principles.

To do the work falling upon the Ministry, the central staff was materially strengthened, and to secure the best results, particularly promptitude, as much of the Ministry's work as possible was de-centralised. District offices under the charge of Commissioners, assisted by expert staffs, were established. These Commissioners are particularly charged to assist local authorities in regard to housing schemes at all stages—not waiting to be asked for advice and help, but seeking, by personal inter-course and round-table conferences, to get the best out of everybody and everything, and in the shortest possible time. *The machinery.*

In addition to many other efforts, the Ministry have regularly issued useful circulars, manuals, and memo-randa to local authorities and others (see the list on page xi), and since 19th July 1919, they have published a fortnightly journal—*Housing*—as a further means of communicating with and helping all concerned.

The Government has bought considerable quantities of building materials and standardised fittings for sale to local authorities and private persons (see also page 131).

Section 1 (1) of the 1919 (Housing) Act makes it the duty of every local authority " to consider the needs of their area with respect to the provision of houses for the working classes," and to prepare and submit a housing scheme within three months, namely by 31st October 1919. *Needs of their areas*

There are no statutory rules for the calculation of these needs, the only reference being section 1 (7), which says that the proposals of others to provide housing accommodation must be taken into account.

But the local authority may be superseded if their scheme does not fulfil their obligations (sections 3 and 4). Nor is the matter one for the moment only—the pre-paration of schemes will be required " as often as occasion arises ": section 1 (1).

Are the obligations those existing at the time of

2

consideration ? Probably not; for instance, when work
which is of a temporary nature is ended, there may be
an exodus from the area. Again, the needs to be considered on 31st October 1919 were not those of that
day only, when the houses could not be built before,
say, 31st October 1922. Further, regard must be
had to the ever-improving " public conscience " ; and
houses gradually falling below this standard indicate
a need.

Form of
survey.

The local authority have to *satisfy* the Ministry, which
laid down in the " Form of Survey of Housing Needs "
(D. 89), and circular 8, a method of arriving at the needs.
At the first survey (scheme due by 31st October 1919)
a house-to-house census of the houses was not expected,
main reliance being placed on information in the possession of the Medical Officer of Health, supplemented
by information which might be supplied by various local
committees and organisations, and large employers of
labour.

The 10th May 1920 issue of *Housing* gives the result
of the first survey : 800,000 new houses are required ;
968 satisfactory schemes have been received ; a further
747 are " satisfactory as instalment " ; 40 are not satisfactory ; 40 are doubtful, and in 9 cases schemes have
not been received.

The scheme.

Having discovered the needs of their area, the local
authority proceed with the preparation of an outline
scheme, showing the approximate number and nature of
the houses to be erected, the approximate area and the
locality of the land to be acquired, the average number
of houses per acre, and the time within which the scheme
or part of it is to be completed. If the outline scheme
is satisfactory, the Ministry grant provisional approval,
and the work can go forward. Before the Ministry
finally approve a scheme the local authority must
furnish to them estimates of its cost and of the rents
expected to be obtained : section 1 (4).

If the Ministry consider that a scheme submitted to them is not adequate, they are to take steps to secure an adequate scheme. They may approve the scheme submitted on the condition that a further scheme is to be prepared ; or they may require an amended scheme to be submitted within a time fixed by them : section 1 (3).

If the local authority do not prepare a scheme, or, when a scheme is prepared, do not carry it out, or if it seems better that the county council should prepare and carry out a scheme, the Ministry of Health may transfer the obligations of the local authority to the county council. Further, the Ministry may act themselves on default of a local authority or a county council. In all cases of default the expenses incurred by the Ministry or the county council, as the case may be, may be recovered from the local authority : sections 3 and 4.

Where the circumstances of adjoining districts are such that a combined housing scheme is desirable, two or more authorities may agree to combine in a scheme. If they do not do so where clearly necessary, the Ministry of Health may insist on a joint scheme. A county council may also combine in a joint scheme, with the Ministry's consent : section 1 (6).

Should the local authorities neglect to carry out a joint scheme when required, the Ministry of Health may authorise the county council to proceed, or may proceed themselves : sections 3 and 4.

Local authorities are required to submit certain *Procedure.* documents to the Ministry of Health either directly or to its local representatives, the Housing Commissioners, to secure assent to the proposals in the scheme (section 1), their nature being indicated in the following statement :—

D. 48. *Site proposals :* Situation ; area ; houses to be built thereon, immediately and eventually ; tenure, &c.

D. 49. *Proposals for general lay-out, streets, and sewers.*
D. 50. *Application for approval of house plans.*
D. 51. *Estimate of street and sewerage works :* Various details including cost.
D. 107. *Assisted scheme (local authority) statement of annual income and expenditure :* Full details (estimated), including cost and rental per house.

Where the local authority does not possess the necessary land (as to the appropriation of such land, see page 210, and note the power in the Land Settlement (Facilities) Act, 1919, section 22, page 85), arrangements have to be made for its acquisition, such arrangements being provisional until the approval of the Ministry has been obtained.

Valuation of land.   *The arrangements :* With a view to providing a check on the prices paid for land for housing, the Ministry made arrangements with the Board of Inland Revenue that the services of their Valuation Office should be placed at the disposal of the local authorities, and in accordance with circulars issued by the Ministry the local authorities now avail themselves of the advice of the district valuers in respect of all land proposed to be acquired.

For the purposes of the Inland Revenue the country is divided into over 100 valuation districts in charge of district valuers, who are supervised by superintending valuers and the chief valuer. The district valuers not only have local knowledge of the values, but they are in a unique position to advise on the value of land, owing to the experience gained in the valuation of the country under the Finance (1909-10) Act, 1910, for estate duty purposes and the records kept in connection therewith. But for this organisation it would have been most difficult to deal with such a large number of valuations in so short a time.

To 31st December 1919, purchase negotiations had been completed in respect of 2,500 sites comprising nearly 12,500 acres, the price agreed being approximately £2,200,000.

There is a known saving effected by such negotiations amounting to £759,810, without regard to 540 cases in which the saving cannot be definitely ascertained. For later figures see Cmd. 917, page 15.

The average price paid for land is slightly in excess of £180 per acre, which on the basis of 10 houses to the acre shows a. cost of £18 per house. The whole of the services rendered by the Valuation Office have been free of cost to the local authorities. *Price of the land.*

There have been many cases where landowners have been prepared to sell their land for housing purposes at lower figures than the values placed upon it by the valuers. Some have given land—sections 8 (1909) and 31 (1919).

On occasion, however, it has been necessary to resort to the compulsory purchase powers, given in section 57 of the 1890 Act, and section 2 and the first schedule 1909 Act—as amended. The official circulars and regulations on the subject deal with the powers and procedure, and are given in Appendix I.

To avoid delay, section 10 of the 1919 Act enables local authorities to take early possession of land which is to be compulsorily purchased. This may be done at any time after the Order has been confirmed and notice to treat served, provided that not less than fourteen days' notice is given to the owner and to the occupier of the land (see also page 389). *Early possession of land.*

A similar power of entry on fourteen days' notice is given where land is acquired by agreement, and the land is in the possession of a person who has no greater interest in it than that of a tenant for a year or from year to year.

Under section 15 (1) (b) of the 1919 Act, local authorities will be able to sell or to lease land to other bodies or persons for the erection of working-class dwellings or of dwellings for other classes, or of factories or business premises, or for any purpose incidental to its development as a building estate. This power may be found especially useful where the local authority have, for instance, bought an estate containing more land than is needed for their own housing scheme, because by buying the whole estate they may have been able to obtain the land more easily and cheaply.

Redemption of land tax.

The land tax charged on sites purchased for housing schemes should be redeemed.

There are no special provisions as to land tax in the Housing Acts, and consequently the local authority should communicate in the ordinary way with the appropriate Commissioner of Land Tax, who will require them to fill in a form headed " Redemption of Land Tax." Immediately after this form has been completed and delivered, they can proceed to build houses without danger of reassessment of the land tax on the improved value.

The cost of redeeming the land tax can be charged to the capital cost of the scheme, and will rank for financial assistance.

The great need for economy in the preparation of schemes.

The Minister of Health has not been able to approve, without examination, any and every project or scheme submitted by local authorities. He has a responsibility to Parliament and the country which would be serious enough in normal times, but is doubly so in present circumstances.

Speaking at Plymouth in December 1919, Viscount Astor, Parliamentary Secretary to the Minister of Health, said that the Ministry had by that date saved £578,000 on tenders submitted by local authorities for approval. This represented over 8 per cent. on the original sum. They had also saved £570,000 on land, or 26 per cent. of the original sum asked, or provisionally agreed to, by local authorities. The average saving per acre in over 1,500 cases was £64.

Speaking on 4th February 1920, Dr. Addison, Minister of Health, mentioned a case in which a re-adjustment of the lay-out had resulted in a saving of £2,000 on roads, and another case in which a saving was effected of £10,000 on a scheme for 300 houses.

The Ministry has pointed out that there must, neces- sarily, be differences between schemes for urban and rural areas. In particular, houses in urban areas should not generally exceed twelve to the acre (gross area), and in rural areas eight to the acre (nett area). But here there is no hard and fast rule. In the special case contemplated in the Housing (Additional Powers) Act, 1919, twenty houses to the acre may be allowed (see page 120), and, generally, special cases will be met, especially if the greater local density is compensated for by the provision of suitable open spaces in the neigh- bourhood. Number of houses to the acre.

" Gross area " refers to the acreage of the site including the area of roads on the site and minor open spaces, but excluding any sites reserved for buildings other than dwellings, and also excluding large open spaces, although these latter may be taken into account to the extent to which they effectively contribute to the open space about the dwellings.

"Nett area " means the land devoted to sites for dwelling houses, gardens, and such minor open spaces as may be provided by dividing such land into separate gardens. The land occupied by the necessary roads, sites for other buildings or by large or detached open spaces is excluded.

It is not possible to provide in by-laws with regard to new streets and buildings, for limiting the density of houses per acre, but it is open to a local authority to make a town-planning scheme under which this limitation could be enforced.

If the plans and specifications for a housing scheme, as approved by the Ministry of Health, do not comply with Relaxation of by-laws.

the local building by-laws, these by-laws are to that extent superseded : section 24 (1919).

Where the Ministry of Health have approved plans and specifications which are in any respect inconsistent with the building by-laws in force in the district in which the works are to be executed, any private builder will have the privilege, in that district, of departing from the provision of local by-laws to the same extent, and subject to the same conditions.

The house itself. In the *Manual on the Preparation of State-aided Housing Schemes*, the Ministry has given many particulars and plans of the types of houses which it recommends, and to which the State financial assistance (section 7, 1919 Act) would be applicable. These plans are offered as suggestions, and local authorities and public utility societies are recommended to employ competent architects who are acquainted with the mode of life and requirements of the people for whom the houses are intended.

Special cases. While the Ministry have certain standards in regard to approved houses, they recognise that local conditions and requirements have to be considered, and they do not want monotony. The following decisions of the Ministry will give an indication of the way in which special cases are met :—

Accommodation

Four bedroom houses in seaside towns. Higher proportion may sometimes be allowed. In seaside towns where the working classes practically all take in visitors the Ministry propose to insist on four bedrooms as the maximum, but in special circumstances they might agree to a higher proportion of houses with four bedrooms than they would otherwise regard as proper.

From a financial point of view the Ministry would expect in such cases to secure better rents than are ordinarily obtainable.

Baths

Provision of baths in houses bought in order to repair : The Ministry is not prepared to lay down a rule applicable to all cases, but where there is an adequate water supply and the structure of the house makes it practicable, the Ministry consider that baths should be provided.

Baths in rural cottages : Where there is no proper water supply, provision of baths should not be insisted on, but a space should be left for a bath so that one can be added later. It does not necessarily follow that a well and hand-pump to a cistern would not provide a sufficient water supply, though care will have to be taken in connection with the hot water supply, which might in such cases have to be provided from the copper.

Buildings

Sanitary conveniences : The Ministry refused to agree to the provision of privy middens in a Part III/90 scheme, but consented to the provision of earth closets.

Materials

Thatched roofs : Owing to the scarcity of slates and tiles, thatch should be encouraged for use as a roof covering in rural areas, but should not be used in districts which are urban in character owing to the risk from fire. The thatch should be protected from damage by birds and vermin by galvanised chicken wire.

Land

Recreation grounds : Where a site forms part of land acquired for, and used as, a recreation ground, the Ministry are advised that the local authority have no power to appropriate it for a building scheme under the Housing Acts.

Allotments and open spaces : Provided that open space is secured about the houses, and that there is sufficient distance between rows of houses to give plenty of air space and sunlight, discretion must be exercised as to whether the area of ground remaining will be more

welcome in the form of individual gardens, allotments
or open spaces.

Width of streets : The width of carriage-ways and foot-
ways should be determined in relation to the probable
traffic.   An arbitrary limitation would involve expenditure on roads wider' or more expensively constructed
than necessary for the traffic.

Local authorities may agree with a contractor to
purchase from him, on completion, houses which he
proposes to build.   In such cases, plans and specifications
have to be approved by the Ministry, as in the case of
the scheme of a local authority.   When local authorities are fully occupied with details of their own schemes,
they may find that, by making use of these powers, a
number of houses might be completed at an earlier date
than would otherwise be possible.   Such houses will
rank for the State subsidy.

New
methods of
construction.
New materials and methods of construction have been
sanctioned, and, in view of the high cost of the usual
materials and methods, the Ministry have given the
matter careful and sympathetic attention, and urged it
strongly upon the attention of local authorities.   Speaking on 4th February 1920, Dr. Addison referred with
satisfaction to a statement made by a daily newspaper,
which had been one of his freest critics, to the effect
that more progress had been made with regard to new
and improved methods of housing in the last six months
than had previously been made in this country since the
time of the cave dwellers.   *Housing* gives particulars
of these new methods, from time to time.

Other pro-
jects to meet
the high
prices.
In addition to the above, many interesting suggestions
and projects have been put forward to overcome other
difficulties, notably in connection with the high tenders
received for the building of houses.   The Ministry has
accepted proposals in suitable cases for the erection of
houses by labour employed directly by local authorities.
There has also been a number of experiments in Guild

Socialism—members of trade unions connected with building undertaking contracts for the erection of houses ; and H.M. Office of Works has carried out schemes.

Tenders are to be advertised for, with rare exceptions in the case of rural district councils, and the lowest tender should be accepted unless there is some good ground for refusal, e.g. that the firm were not substantial or of good reputation.

In August 1919, the Ministry issued a " Standard Specification for Cottages " (D. 82). It is to be adapted to local conditions, and to the requirement of the particular works. It describes materials and modes of construction which the Ministry consider should generally be adopted for State-aided housing schemes. *Standard specifications.*

In September 1919, the Ministry issued a " Standard Specification for Roads and Sewers " (D. 91). It is to be adapted to local conditions. It is intended to apply only to residential roads, on which heavy traffic is not anticipated. For roads, carrying heavy traffic, a more substantial construction may, be necessary.

The Ministry pointed out in the covering circulars that every scheme which had not then gone to tender should comply with the above standard forms, and stated that it would not be prepared to approve schemes which showed deviations, except in so far as they were rendered desirable by local circumstances and conditions.

Subsequently other specifications were issued.

Where quantities are supplied, there is no need to send specifications to builders for tendering, as the quantities contain all the necessary information, in addition to the amount of each item required. Printed quantities and estimates have been supplied by the Ministry.

The Ministry have also issued for the general guidance of local authorities and public utility societies model contracts for State-aided housing schemes. Subject to any modifications to suit local conditions, the forms should, wherever possible, be adopted. *Model Form of Contract.*

Owing to the uncertainty as regards costs of labour and materials, it was deemed desirable to include in the conditions of contract provisions for adjustment of the contract price in the event of changes in rates of labour or costs of materials during the currency of the contract.

Cost of houses.

Below are given two statements showing the cost of houses of different types for which the Ministry had approved tenders. The figures are exclusive of the cost of land, road-making and sewering. The first statement covers the period from the commencement to the middle of October 1919, and the second the period from the commencement to 19th June 1920.

STATEMENT ISSUED ON 25TH OCTOBER 1919

Cost as approved.	Non-Parlour Types.					Parlour Types.			Total Number of Houses.
	Living-room, Scullery, and				Average cost per House.	Parlour, Living-room, Scullery, and		Average cost per House.	
	1 Bed-room.	2 Bed-rooms.	3 Bed-rooms.	4 Bed-rooms.			3 Bed-rooms.	4 Bed-rooms.	
					£			£	
£400 to £500	4	—	185	—	453	24	—	449	213
£501 to £600	—	187	529	—	570	216	—	573	932
£601 to £700	—	68	1,303	—	656	51	22	654	1,444
£701 to £800	—	55	624	—	733	1,311	48	760	2,038
£801 to £900	—	—	118	4	817	988	81	832	1,191
£901 and over	—	—	—	—	—	—	6	1,057	6
Totals	4	310	2,759	4	£647	2,590	157	£768	5,824
		3,077				2,747			

Average cost of the 5,824 houses £704.

Of the 5,824 houses :—

5,250 houses were in urban districts, and cost on the average £705 each.

574 houses were in rural districts, and cost on the average £695 each.

STATEMENT FROM COMMENCEMENT TO 19th JUNE 1920

Cost as Approved.	Non-Parlour Types.					Parlour Types.				Total Number of Houses.
	Living-room, Scullery, and				Average cost per House.	Parlour, Living-room, Scullery, and			Average cost per House.	
	1 Bed-room.	2 Bed-rooms.	3 Bed-rooms.	4 Bed-rooms		2 Bed-rooms	3 Bed-rooms.	4 Bed-rooms.		
					£				£	
£500 and under	4	—	134	—	442	—	32	—	462	170
£501 to £600 .	—	199	737	—	571	13	174	—	574	1,123
£601 to £700 .	—	241	2,278	6	660	—	648	2	674	3,175
£701 to £800 .	—	183	7,300	30	765	—	3,727	89	761	11,329
£801 to £900 .	—	244	1,941	19	833	81	11,423	345	859	14,053
£900 and over .	—	5	450	—	962	11	5,391	674	971	¹6,531
Totals	4	872	12,840	55	£747	105	21,395	1,110	£864	36,381
		13,771					22,610			

¹ Excluding seven shops, with cellar, living-room, parlour and three bedrooms, costing £1,390 each.

Average cost of the 36,381 houses   .   . £820
  ,,   ,,   ,,   13,771 non-parlour houses £747
  ,,   ,,   ,,   22,610 parlour houses   . £864

Of the 36,381 houses :—

28,287 were in urban districts, and cost on the average £826 each.

8,094 were in rural districts, and cost on the average £798 each.

This cost includes all the expenses of erection, drainage and interior fittings. It does not include the making of roads or sewers, or the purchase of land. The average cost of road-making and sewering is from £40 to £50 per house. The cost of land per house may be estimated on the average at about £18.

The houses included in the table are divided into two principal groups :—

(a) The non-parlour types, consisting of living-room, scullery and bedrooms ; and (*b*) the parlour types, consisting of a parlour, living-room, scullery, and bedrooms.

Most of the houses contain three bedrooms. The parlour type includes a considerable number of houses with four bedrooms.

Rent for the houses.

The question of the rent to be charged by local authorities for the new houses has been the subject of much discussion. House rents are now at an artificially low level because of the Rents Restriction legislation. Dr. Addison has clearly stated that higher rents will have to be charged initially, and that increases will have to be imposed, year by year, until an economic rent is reached. The State subsidy is intended to help to cover some of the difference between the present cost of building and the normal. It is not the intention of the Government to subsidise rents permanently. On 1st June 1920, the average officially approved rent of the new houses was 12s. 3d. per week, exclusive of rates. 1·5 per cent. were under 6s., and 1·5 per cent. over 20s. The Increase of Rent, &c. (Restrictions) Act, 1920, does not apply to new houses or flats (completed after 2nd April 1919), but though, therefore, the rents are not limited the rates are—see section 12 (9) thereof.

Tenants for the houses.

The Leeds Corporation have decided that the tenants shall be chosen in the following order :—(1) Men who have served in H.M. Forces, wives and mothers of men serving, or widows or mothers and children of deceased soldiers or sailors ; (2) families who have outgrown their accommodation or are residing in apartments ; (3) newly-married couples not at present occupying houses ; (4) persons under notice to quit owing to property having been sold ; (5) former Leeds residents who have had to give up houses during the war (other than service or ex-service men) ; (6) persons living out of Leeds, but employed within the city ; (7) people desiring a change ; and (8) people desiring to live in the city but now residing outside.

Other local authorities have adopted similar rules.

The local authorities choose the tenants and fix the rents, but the latter are subject to the approval of the Minister, or in the absence of such approval to settlement by an impartial tribunal.

A local authority may, with the consent of the Ministry, lease or sell any land or houses bought or erected by them, and may agree to the price being paid by instalments or to the payment of part of the price being secured by mortgage of the premises, but any house so leased or sold may not be used by any person having an interest in it to house his employees. Having regard to any condition imposed, the best price or rent must be obtained (section 15, 1919 Act). Full information on this subject is given in General Housing Memoranda, Nos. 27 and 33. *Local authorities may sell houses bought or erected by them.*

Under the Small Dwellings Acquisition Act, 1899, as amended (see page 241), a local authority may lend money to any person resident in the district to assist him to buy the house in which he lives or intends to live. They may lend on houses up to the value of £800 each ; and the amount which may be lent may be 85 per cent. of the value. The rate of interest and the terms of repayment of the loan are, subject to certain conditions, a matter for agreement between the local authority and the borrower. *Loans under the Small Dwellings Acquisition Act.*

CONVERSION OF HOUSES INTO FLATS

With a view to enabling local authorities to obtain an immediate increase in the amount of accommodation available to relieve overcrowding, powers were conferred upon them by the 1919 Act to acquire houses themselves and convert them into flats (section 12, page 394), and to lend money to owners desirous of undertaking the conversion (section 22). The Act also assists in the modification of restrictive covenants by enabling the county court, upon an application from the local authority or lessee, to make an Order varying the terms of the lease so as to permit of conversion (section 27, see page 429).

Temporary housing accommodation by army huts or hostels.

On 15th September 1919 the Ministry of Health issued General Housing Memorandum No. 5, stating that they had under consideration measures to secure the early provision of housing accommodation in places where the immediate needs were acute. After referring to the possibilities of converting large houses into working-class flats, the Ministry said the conversion of huts or hostels into temporary houses was another way in which such accommodation could be provided. They notified the arrangements to facilitate the action of local authorities in this direction.

The Ministry were prepared to consider proposals from a local authority for the provision of temporary accommodation, whether by the use of army huts or State-owned hostels, and, if they approved, the proposals would be regarded as part of the local authority's housing scheme under section 1 of the Housing, Town Planning, &c., Act, 1919, and rank for financial assistance accordingly.

Where necessary, the Ministry were prepared to sanction loans for the acquisition and adaptation of huts and hostels for housing purposes. The periods for which such loans would be sanctioned were, of course, shorter than those applicable to permanent houses, the maximum being fixed at fifteen years.

Speaking of the results of this policy Dr. Addison said, in the House of Commons on 13th December 1919, that up to that date 1,621 huts and 26 hostels had been taken over by local authorities, and in addition 631 huts had been offered to such authorities. The huts would provide accommodation for 3,217 families, and the hostels for 536 families. 88 local authorities had applied for such buildings.

The provisions which cover the subject of these huts are contained in section 25 of the 1919 Act, page 419. No huts can be converted after 31st July 1922 if they would transgress the local building by-laws.

Section 7 of the 1919 Act provides for a grant out of moneys provided by Parliament being paid to local authorities towards the loss resulting from schemes involving the provision of houses for the working classes. Towards making good this loss the local authority have to find the product of a 1*d*. rate, and the State finds the remainder, subject to conditions. The conditions and the machinery for arriving at the figures are given in the Local Authorities' (Assisted Housing Schemes) Regulations, 1919, printed on page 537, which constitute the second attempt to deal with this difficult subject. The conditions are discussed in General Housing Memos. Nos. 8 and 18. As to accountancy matters, see the Housing Accounts Order (Local Authorities), 1920 (page 550).

Financial assistance to local authorities —the State grant.

3

CHAPTER III

As already explained, the primary purpose of the Housing
Acts prior to 1919 was public health, principally slum
clearances (Part I Unhealthy Areas ; Part II Unhealthy
Dwelling-houses).

The local authorities for this purpose (First Schedule
1890 Act) are :—

    For Parts I and II :
        Borough Councils.
        Urban District Councils.
        The Common Council of the City of London.
        The County Council of London.
    For Part II :
        The Metropolitan Borough Councils.
        Rural District Councils.

That is, Rural District Councils and the Metropolitan
Borough Councils have no Part I powers. The London
County Council do not usually exercise Part II powers, but
may contribute or may be required by the Minister of
Health to contribute towards the expenses incurred
under a Part II scheme by a Metropolitan Borough
Council ; or if the London County Council carry out a
Part II scheme the Metropolitan Borough Council
concerned may, or may be required to, contribute to
the expenses (section 46 of 1890 Act, section 14 of the
1903 Act, and section 33 of the 1909 Act).

The problem of the Housing Acts prior to 1919 was
almost solely connected with public health (though in

the 1909 Act town planning was also dealt with). Necessarily so ; in 1909 there was a building boom : too many houses were being built, and it was the following slump which discouraged builders, and produced to some extent the present shortage. The public health powers conferred under these earlier Acts were supplementary to those of the Public Health Act, 1875, and to appreciate the full powers of local authorities with regard to matters affecting housing it is necessary to consider certain of the provisions of the Act, as amended, or in London, the Public Health (London) Act, 1891.

The Ministry of Health has published an admirable summary of these latter provisions, and also of the whole of the Parts I and II Housing Acts provisions—*Manual on Unfit Houses and Unhealthy Areas*, volume II. It would be an affectation to attempt to supply a similar summary here, in merely different language, and the following numbered paragraphs are a reproduction thereof with a few minor alterations principally caused by the enactment, since the issue of that Manual, of the Housing (Additional Powers) Act, 1919 (section 6).

1. Under the Public Health Acts it is the duty of every local authority to inspect their district in order to abate nuisances.

General powers and duties under the Public Health Acts.

Any premises in such a state as to be a nuisance or injurious to health and any pool, ditch, gutter, watercourse, privy, urinal, cesspool, drain or ashpit, so foul or in such a state as to be a nuisance or injurious to health, and any house or part of a house so overcrowded as to be dangerous or injurious to the health of the inmates are to be deemed to be nuisances liable to be dealt with summarily under the Act (sections 91–111, Public Health Act, 1875).

The corresponding provisions in London are contained in sections 2–16 of the Public Health (London) Act, 1891.

2. The following matters also may be dealt with under

the Public Health Acts; the sections of the Public Health Act, 1875, here referred to are summarised on page 60 :—

Any house without sufficient drainage (section 23) ;

Any house without sufficient closet accommodation, or a sufficient receptacle for refuse (section 36) ;

Examination of drains, privies, &c., on complaint of nuisance (section 41) ;

Any house without a proper water supply (section 62 and, as regards rural districts, the Public Health (Water) Act, 1878).

As regards the Metropolis, provisions are contained in the Public Health (London) Act, 1891, as to closets, ashpits, drains and cesspools (sections 37–43), and as to water supply (sections 48–50).

3. The provisions restricting or prohibiting the letting or occupation of cellar dwellings and the use of underground rooms as sleeping places, are summarised on page 65.

4. The following additional powers are available to local authorities where the respective sections of the Public Health Acts Amendment Act, 1907, have been put in force by an order of the Local Government Board, or are put in force by an order of the Minister of Health :—

Special power to require the paving and drainage of yards (section 25) ;

Special power to require the provision of water closets in place of other forms of closet accommodation (section 39) ;

Special power as to testing drains (section 45) ;

Special power to require the provision of sinks and drains for carrying off refuse water (section 49) ;

Power to deal with the following defects summarily as nuisances :—

Any cistern for the supply of water for domestic purposes so placed constructed or kept as to render

the water therein liable to contamination causing
or likely to cause risk to health ; or

Any gutter, drain, shoot, &c., causing dampness in a
building (section 35).

5. Under sections 23, 36, 41 and 62 of the Public
Health Act, 1875, and sections 25, 45 and 49 of the
Public Health Acts Amendment Act, 1907, the local
authority may, in default of the owner, do the necessary
works and recover the expenses from him. Any person
deeming himself aggrieved by the decision of the local
authority may appeal to the Minister of Health under
section 268 of the Public Health Act, 1875, the effect
of which is set out on page 63.

1. It is the duty of the local authority to cause a **Powers and duties under the Housing Acts.**
thorough inspection of the dwelling houses or localities
in their district to be carried out from time to time by
the medical officer of health, or by an officer designated
by the local authority but acting under the medical
officer's direction and supervision, in order to ascertain
whether any dwelling house in the district is in a state
so dangerous or injurious to health as to be unfit for
habitation (section 17 (1) /09 and Housing (Inspection
of District) Regulations, 1910) ; these Regulations are
printed on page 570.

The necessary power to enter any premises for the
purpose of survey and examination is contained in
section 36 /09.

2. Full records are to be kept giving information
under prescribed headings as to the inspection under
the Housing Acts and action taken on it ; and the local
authority are, as far as may be necessary, to consider
the records at each of their ordinary meetings, and to
take all necessary action in regard to any dwelling house
to which the records relate (Housing (Inspection of
District) Regulations, 1910).

It is the duty of the medical officer of health, in the
case of any dwelling house which appears to him to be

in a state so dangerous or injurious to health as to be unfit for human habitation, to make a written representation to the local authority, stating that the dwelling house appears to him to be in such a state (sections 30 /90 and 79 (2) /90).

3. *Complaint of Justice of Peace or four householders.* It is also the duty of the medical officer forthwith to inspect and, if necessary, to represent to the local authority, any house in regard to which complaint in writing has been made to him by any Justice of the Peace, or any four householders, that it is in a condition so dangerous or injurious to health as to be unfit for human habitation (sections 31 /90 and 39 /19).

Where it appears to the Minister of Health that the local authority have failed to carry out the inspection of their district as required by the Act of 1909, he may, by order, require them to remedy the default within a time fixed by the order. The order may be enforced by proceedings in the High Court (section 11 /09).

Repairs.   4. *Notices requiring repairs.* Under section 15 of the Housing, Town Planning, &c., Act, 1909, the local authority may serve a notice on the landlord of a house which is not in all respects reasonably fit for human habitation requiring him to execute any necessary works.

This section applies only to houses let since the 3rd December 1909, and of which the rental does not exceed certain limits. There is an appeal to the Minister of Health against notices served under it and the landlord may instead of repairing the house declare it to be closed (see, however, the next paragraph (5) and section 6 of the Housing (Additional Powers) Act, 1919).

If the landlord does not do the works and does not declare the house to be closed the local authority may do the works and may, subject to an appeal to the Minister of Health, recover the expenses from him.

5. Fuller powers for securing that an unfit dwelling shall be rendered in all respects reasonably fit, whether

the defects are dangerous or injurious to health or not, are now given by section 28 of the Act of 1919.

This section provides that, if the owner of any house suitable for occupation by persons of the working classes fails to make and keep it in all respects fit for human habitation, the local authority may serve notice on the owner requiring him within a reasonable time, not being less than twenty-one days, to execute such works as may be necessary; the prescribed form of notice is given on page 612. If the house is not capable, without reconstruction, of being rendered fit for human habitation, the owner may within twenty-one days after the receipt of the notice, by written notice to the local authority, declare his intention of closing the house for human habitation. The house is then to be treated as if a closing order had been made and become operative in respect of it. Any question arising in this matter is, in case of difference between the owner and the local authority, to be determined by the Minister of Health. In this section " owner " has the same meaning as in the Public Health Act, 1875 (see page 423).

6. *Power of local authority to execute repairs.* If the owner does not comply with the requirements and does not give notice declaring the house to be closed, the local authority may, at the expiration of the period specified in the notice requiring the execution of works, themselves do the work and recover the expenses from him.

In a case in which the owner has given notice declaring the house to be closed, but the Minister of Health has determined that the house can be made fit for habitation without reconstruction, if then the owner fails to carry out the required repairs within twenty-one days of the date when the Minister gave his decision, the local authority may step in and do the work, as stated above.

Any expenses incurred by the local authority in doing the work may be recovered from the owner, together with interest at a rate not exceeding 5 per cent., in a court of summary jurisdiction, and until recovery are to be a charge on the premises.

The local authority may by order declare the expenses to be payable by monthly or annual instalments within a period not exceeding thirty years, with interest at a rate not exceeding 5 per cent., and any such instalments or interest may be recovered in a summary manner from the owner or occupier. If recovered from the occupier, the amount may be deducted by him from the rent.

By section 6 of the Housing (Additional Powers) Act, 1919, there is prohibited the demolition, in whole or in part, or the use otherwise than as a dwelling house, of any house which on 23rd December 1919, was in the opinion of the local authority reasonably fit or reasonably capable without reconstruction of being rendered fit for human habitation. The local authority may, however, grant permission to demolish, and if they refuse there is an appeal to the Minister. The section remains in force until 23rd December 1921.

Closing
orders.

7. *Closing Orders.* If on the representation of the medical officer of health, or of any other officer, or other information given (see page 47 as to representations by county medical officers of health), any dwelling house appears to the local authority to be in a state so dangerous or injurious to health as to be unfit for human habitation, the authority are required to make a closing order.

Any owner aggrieved by the order may appeal to the Minister of Health within fourteen days after the service of the notice of the order (section 17 (2) /09).

If no appeal is made, or if an appeal is made and is dismissed or abandoned, the closing order becomes operative.

Nothing in the Increase of Rent and Mortgage Interest (War Restrictions) Act, 1915, and the enactments amending that Act (see page 710) is to affect the right of a local authority to make and enforce a closing order (section 35 /19).

8. Where a closing order has become operative, the local authority are required to serve notice of it on the occupier of the dwelling house ordering him to quit it within a specified period, not being less than fourteen days.

Unless the dwelling house has been made unfit by the wilful act or default of the tenant, the local authority may pay him a reasonable allowance on account of his expense of removing, and the allowance is recoverable from the owner (section 17 (4) (5) /09).

If any owner of a house in respect of which a closing order is in force or any other person lets or attempts to let, or occupies or permits to be occupied, that house or any part of it as a dwelling house, he is liable on summary conviction to a fine not exceeding £20 (section 32 /19).

9. If a house is rendered fit for habitation after a closing order has been made, the local authority are required to determine the order, and it then ceases to be in force. If they refuse to do so, the owner may appeal to the Minister against their refusal (section 17 (6) /09).

A repairing notice under section 28 of the 1919 Act cannot be served on the owner of a house in respect of which a closing order has become operative.

10. *Demolition Orders.* Where a closing order has remained operative for a period of three months, the local authority are to take into consideration the question of the demolition of the dwelling house, and are to give every owner of the dwelling house notice of the time (which must not be less than one month after service of the notice) and place at which the question will be considered. Any owner is entitled to be heard when the question is considered. *(marginal note: Demolition orders.)*

If upon such consideration the local authority are of opinion that the dwelling house has not been rendered fit, and that the necessary steps are not being taken with all due diligence to render it fit, or that the continuance of the dwelling house, or any part of it, is a nuisance or dangerous or injurious to the health of the public, or of the inhabitants of the neighbouring dwelling houses, they are to order the demolition of the building.

If any owner undertakes to execute forthwith the works necessary to render the dwelling house fit for human habitation, the local authority may postpone the operation of the order for a period not exceeding six months ; and, if the necessary works are completed, they are to determine the Closing and Demolition Orders relating to the dwelling house (sections 18 (1) (2) (3) /09, 39 (1) /19).

11. Notice of an order for the demolition of a building is to be served forthwith on every owner of the building, and any owner aggrieved may appeal to the Minister of Health within twenty-one days after the notice is served on him, or, where the operation of the order has been postponed for any period, within fourteen days after the expiration of that period (sections 18 (4) /09, 39 (1) /19).

If a demolition order has become operative and the owner fails within three months to demolish the building, the local authority may do so, and may sell the materials to pay expenses and may recover any deficiency from the owner (sections 34 /90, 9 /03 and 46 /09).

Conversion into tenements.

12. *Conversion of houses into tenements.*   A number of houses now remain unoccupied because, owing to changes in the character of the neighbourhood, they can no longer be let as single tenements.   In some cases the houses are held under a lease containing provisions which prevent them from being converted into two or more tenements. In such cases application may now be made, by the local authority or the lessee, to the county court who may authorise the conversion of the houses (section 27 /19).

Where there are provisions in a lease which would prevent compliance with by-laws which will apply if the house is converted into two or more tenements, the local authority may apply to the county court for the provisions to be relaxed so as to make it possible to comply with the by-laws. Application may also be made, where the local authority consider that the whole or part of the expenses of complying with the by-laws should be borne by the lessor or the superior landlord, for a charging order, charging on the premises an annuity to repay the expenses properly incurred. Where a local authority have themselves acquired a leasehold interest in any house, the Minister of Health may, on the application of the local authority, make a similar order relaxing the provisions of the lease or charging an annuity on the premises (section 26 /19).

13. *Owners—Powers and Loans.* The enforcement of necessary repairs has frequently been rendered difficult by the fact that the immediate landlord had little interest in the property, and was unwilling or unable to do what was required. This difficulty is met by section 30 of the Act of 1919, under which if the premises are or are likely to become dangerous or injurious to health or unfit for human habitation the court may authorise the superior landlord if his interests are prejudiced to enter and execute any necessary works.

14. A local authority may lend money to the owner of a house or building for works of reconstruction, enlargement or improvement, which will render the house or building in all respects fit for habitation as a house or houses for the working classes.

The loan is not to exceed one-half of the estimated value of the property mortgaged unless some collateral security is given.

Full particulars of the works are to be submitted to the local authority, and they must satisfy themselves that the works have been efficiently carried out before they make any loan.

The local authority may borrow for the purpose of

such loans in the same manner as for the purposes of Part III of the Act of 1890 (section 22 /19).

15. *Requirements as to tenement houses.* A common evil is the letting of a house in lodgings to more families or lodgers than can be decently accommodated in it. The power under section 90 of the Public Health Act, 1875 to make by-laws as to houses let in lodgings for the working classes has now, by section 26 [1] of the Act of 1919, been extended, so that in the case of houses intended or used for occupation by the working classes proper accommodation for each person or family may be more effectually secured.

A form of model by-laws to deal with these matters is given on page 637.

In the County of London, any such by-laws are to be made by the County Council, and are to be observed and enforced by each Metropolitan Borough Council with the exception that by-laws for securing stability and the prevention of and safety from fire are to be enforced by the County Council.

In the City of London by-laws of this kind are to be made and enforced by the Common Council, with the same exception as stated above.

As regards the water supply of tenement houses in London special powers are contained in section 78 of the London County Council (General Powers) Act, 1907, which is summarised on page 64.

16. A local authority may, under Part III of the Act of 1890 as extended by section 12 /19, buy houses and alter, enlarge, repair and improve them so as to render them in all respects fit for habitation as houses for the working classes.

A separate manual has been issued by the Ministry dealing with the purchase of houses under this section for conversion into tenements.

---

[1] Some provisions of this section have been referred to above, under the heading " Conversion of houses into tenements."

17. *Obstructive buildings.* Under section 38 of the Housing Act of 1890 it is the duty of the medical officer of health to make the necessary representation to the local authority for the pulling down of a building, if he finds that the building, by reason of its proximity to or contact with any other buildings—

(*a*) stops or impedes ventilation, or otherwise makes or conduces to make the other buildings to be in a condition unfit for human habitation, or dangerous or injurious to health ; or

(*b*) prevents proper measures from being carried into effect for remedying any nuisance injurious to health or other evils complained of in respect of those other buildings.

A similar representation may be made by any Justice of the Peace acting for a district, or any four or more inhabitant householders.

18. The local authority, on receiving such a representation, are to cause a report to be made to them as to the circumstances of the building and the cost of pulling it down and acquiring the land. If they decide to proceed, they may, after hearing any objections which the owner has to make, order the obstructive building to be pulled down. The owner has the same right of appealing against the order as against a demolition order.

If no appeal against the order is made, or an appeal is made and either fails or is abandoned, the local authority may purchase the lands on which the obstructive building is erected either by agreement or compulsorily.

The owner may, within one month after notice to purchase the land is served on him, declare that he desires to retain the site of the obstructive building, and undertake either to pull down or to permit the local authority to pull down the obstructive building. In such case the owner is to retain the site and to receive compensation for the pulling down of the building.

19. The amount of compensation to be paid for the

such loans in the sane manner as for the purposes of Part III of the Act o 1890 (section 22 /19).

Requirements as to tenements.

15. *Requirements aso tenement houses.* A common evil is the letting of a hose in lodgings to more families or lodgers than can be ecently accommodated in it. The power under section 0 of the Public Health Act, 187£ to make by-laws as o houses let in lodgings for th working classes has ow, by section 26[1] of the Act c 1919, been extended,so that in the case of houses ir tended or used for ccupation by the working class proper accommodatia for each person or family m£ be more effectually scured.

A form of model bylaws to deal with these matters given on page 637.

In the County of Lndon, any such by-laws are to made by the County Guncil, and are to be observed ; enforced by each Mcropolitan Borough Council v the exception that byaws for securing stability and prevention of and safcy from fire are to be enforced the County Council.

In the City of Lonon by-laws of this kind are tc made and enforced b the Common Council, with same exception as staed above.

As regards the watr supply of tenement house London special powel are contained in section 7· the London County Cuncil (General Powers) Act, l which is summarised n page 64.

16. A local authorit may, under Part III of the of 1890 as extended by ection 12 /19, buy houses and · enlarge, repair and imrove them so as to render · in all respects fit for hbitation as houses for the wo classes.

A separate manual 1as been issued by the Mi dealing with the purchse of houses under this sect conversion into tenemots.

---

[1] Some provisions of this >ction have been referred to above, the heading " Conversion of ouses into tenements."

purchase of the land or for the pulling down of the building is, in case of difference, to be settled by arbitration.

Where part only of a holding is proposed to be taken as obstructive, and the arbitrator considers that it can be severed from the remainder without material detriment thereto, the owner cannot insist on the entire holding being taken, but the arbitrator may award compensation in respect of the severance.

Where, in the opinion of the arbitrator, the demolition of an obstructive building adds to the value of the other buildings, the arbitrator is to apportion so much of the compensation to be paid for the demolition of the obstructive building as may be equal to the increase in value of the other buildings amongst the other buildings.

20. Where the lands are purchased by the local authority, they are to pull down the obstructive building and to keep the whole site, or so much of it as is necessary, as an open space. They may, with the assent of the Minister of Health, sell any portion of this site which is not required as an open space.

The local authority may dedicate any land acquired by them under the section as a highway or other public place.

(Sections 38/90, 28/09, 46/09 and 39/19.)

IMPROVEMENT SCHEMES

1. Improvement schemes for the clearance or reconstruction of slum areas may be made under Part I or Part II (section 39) of the Housing of the Working Classes Act, 1890, as amended by subsequent Acts. Schemes under Part II (section 39) of the Act are referred to in the Acts as reconstruction schemes, but as there is generally no practical difference, except in size, between such schemes and improvement schemes under Part I, the two kinds of scheme are both referred to as " Im-

provement Schemes " and are distinguished as "Part I" and "Part II" schemes respectively.

Both kinds of scheme usually provide for—

(a) the purchase, compulsorily or by agreement, of the whole of an area ;

(b) the demolition of buildings on the area which are themselves insanitary or which would interfere with the re-development of the area on satisfactory lines ;

(c) the proper laying out of the area with convenient streets and any necessary open spaces ;

(d) the erection on the area, or elsewhere, of sufficient dwelling accommodation in respect of persons of the working classes displaced by the scheme ;

(e) the disposal of any surplus lands.

Financial assistance from the State will be available for both classes of schemes. . . .

3. It is the duty of the medical officer of health, in a district other than a rural district, to make a written representation (known as an "official representation") to the local authority in regard to any area which appears to him to be an area of the character described in section 4 of the Act of 1890. Such an area is one within which either— Part I schemes.

(a) any houses, courts or alleys are unfit for human habitation, or

(b) the narrowness, closeness, and bad arrangement or bad condition of the streets and houses, or groups of houses, or the want of light, air, ventilation or proper conveniences, or any other sanitary defects, or one or more of such causes, are dangerous or injurious to the health of the inhabitants of the buildings in the area or of the neighbouring buildings.

A further condition required to justify an "official representation," is that the most satisfactory method of dealing with the evils is an improvement scheme for the re-arrangement and reconstruction of the streets and houses in the area, or some of them (section 22/09).

In London, any medical officer of health, whether appointed by the London County Council or by a Metropolitan Borough Council, may make such a representation to the London County Council. If a representation is made to the London County Council in regard to an area comprising not more than ten houses they are to direct the medical officer of health to represent the case to the Metropolitan Borough Council, who are to deal with it under Part II. (Sections 5/90 and 72/90.)

4. If any Justice of the Peace acting within the district or any six ratepayers complain to the medical officer of health of the unhealthiness of any area, it is the duty of the latter forthwith to inspect the area and make a report on it.

Where in any district (other than a rural district) a complaint of this kind has been made to the medical officer of health and the medical officer has failed to inspect the area, or has reported to the effect that in his opinion the area is not an unhealthy area, the complainant (or complainants) may appeal to the Minister of Health. The Minister may appoint a person to inspect the area, and to make a representation to him stating the facts of the case. The representation is to be transmitted by the Minister to the local authority, and if it states that the area is an unhealthy area, the local authority are to proceed as if it were an official representation made to them. (Sections 5 (2)/90, 16/90, 26/09 and 39/19.)

5. Where an " official representation," as described above, has been made to a local authority (not being a Metropolitan Borough Council or a Rural District Council), the local authority, if satisfied of the truth of the representation, and of the sufficiency of their resources,[1] are to pass a resolution to the effect that the area is an

---

[1] The financial assistance from the State which is now available must be borne in mind in this connection.

unhealthy one and that an improvement scheme ought to be made in respect to it (section 4/90).

6. Where an official representation under Part I is made to the local authority with a view to their passing a resolution in favour of an improvement scheme, and they fail to pass a resolution, or pass a resolution that they will not proceed with a scheme, the local authority are required to send a copy of the official representation and their reasons for not acting upon it to the Minister of Health.

The Minister may direct a local inquiry to be held, and, where necessary, may order a scheme to be made, either under Part I or under Part II of the Act of 1890. (Sections 10/90 and 4/03.)

7. A Part I scheme must be accompanied by maps, particulars and estimates, and :—

(a) may exclude any part of the area included in the official representation ;

(b) may include any neighbouring lands for the purpose of making the scheme efficient ;

(c) may provide for widening any existing approaches to the unhealthy area or otherwise for opening out the same for the purposes of ventilation or health ;

(d) must provide such dwelling accommodation, if any, as is necessary for persons of the working classes who are displaced ;

(e) must provide for proper sanitary arrangements ;

(f) may provide for any other matter (including the closing and diversion of highways) for which it seems expedient to make provision with a view to the improvement of the area or the general efficiency of the scheme.

The scheme must distinguish the lands proposed to be taken compulsorily.

Provision may also be made for the scheme, or any part of it, to be carried out by any person having such interest in any property comprised in the scheme as may be sufficient to enable him to carry out the same under the supervision and control of the local authority and on such terms and conditions (which must be embodied in the scheme) as may be agreed upon between him and the local authority.

.(Sections 6/90, 23 (1)/09 and 39/19.)

Part II
schemes. 8. It is the duty of the local authority to make a Part II scheme in either of the two following sets of circumstances :—

(a) Where an order for the demolition of a building has been made under Part II of the Act of 1890, and it appears to the authority that it would be beneficial to the health of the inhabitants of the neighbouring houses if the land were :—

(1) dedicated as a highway or open space ; or

(2) appropriated, sold or let for the erection of dwellings for the working classes ; or

(3) exchanged with other neighbouring land which is more suitable for the erection of such dwellings ; or

(b) Where it appears to the local authority that the closeness, narrowness, and bad arrangement or bad condition of any buildings, or the want of light, air, ventilation, or proper conveniences, or any other sanitary defect in any buildings is dangerous or prejudicial to the health of the inhabitants of the said buildings, or of the neighbouring buildings, and that the demolition or the reconstruction and re-arrangement of the said buildings, or of some of them is necessary to remedy the evils, and that the area comprising those buildings and the yards, out-houses, and appurtenances thereof, and the site thereof, is too small to be dealt with as an unhealthy area under Part I of the Act.

(Section 39 (1)/90.)

9. There is no provision in the Acts prescribing the minimum size of an area for a Part I scheme or the maximum size of an area for a Part II scheme.

In London, as mentioned above, any unhealthy area comprising not more than ten houses is to be dealt with under Part II (section 72/90). Part II schemes may, however, be made for considerably larger areas.

10. Provision may be made in a Part II scheme for any matters for which provision may be made in a Part I scheme (section 7/03 and 23 (2)/09).

11. Both Part I and Part II schemes may provide for the erection, either within the area of the scheme or elsewhere, of dwellings for persons of the working classes who are displaced. The Minister of Health in confirming or sanctioning a scheme may require provision of this kind to be made. (Sections 11 (2)/90, 40/90 and 46/09.) *Part I and Part II schemes.*

In these respects the position in London is now the same as elsewhere (section 33/19).

12. *Duty of Local Authority to execute Improvement Schemes.* When an improvement scheme under Part I or Part II has been confirmed or sanctioned, it is the duty of the local authority to proceed to execute it as soon as practicable.

It is not obligatory upon them to purchase any leasehold interest which can be allowed to expire without unduly delaying the execution of the scheme.

It is also open to them, instead of acquiring all the lands in the scheme, to contract with any person having sufficient interest in any land to carry out the scheme so far as it relates to such land.

(Sections 12/90, 39 (8)/90 and 39/19.)

13. On application from the local authority, the Minister of Health has power, where an improvement can be made in the details of a Part I or Part II scheme, to permit the local authority to modify it (sections 15/90, 39/90 and 25/09).

14. As soon as a local authority have passed a resolution

to make a Part I or Part II scheme, they may proceed, if they obtain the consent of the Minister of Health, to purchase by agreement any land in the area of the proposed scheme (section 13/19).

Powers of compulsory purchase are available as soon as the Part I or Part II scheme is confirmed or sanctioned, subject to the provisions of the Confirming or Sanctioning Order (sections 20 and 39/90).

Valuation of land.

15. *Valuation of Land.* The Acquisition of Land (Assessment of Compensation) Act, 1919, has altered the law with regard to the method of determining any question of disputed compensation where land is authorised to be acquired compulsorily by any local or public authority. The Act sets up a panel of official arbitrators, by one of whom the question is ordinarily determined. It also makes provision for reference, by consent, of any such question to the Commissioners of Inland Revenue, or to an arbitrator agreed upon between the parties.

The Acquisition of Land Act also contains important rules for determining the compensation to be paid for land which is compulsorily acquired, such as, that the value of the land, subject to certain conditions, is to be the amount which the land, if sold in the open market by a willing seller, might be expected to realise ; that consideration is to be paid in determining the value to any return or assessment of capital value for taxation which has been made or acquiesced in by the claimant ; that no allowance is to be made because of the fact that the acquisition is compulsory ; that the special suitability of the land for any purpose is not to be taken into account if that purpose is a purpose to which it could be applied only in pursuance of statutory powers ; and that no account is to be taken of any increase in the value of the land due to its use, or the use of premises upon it, in a manner which can be restrained by any court, or is contrary to law, or is detrimental to the health of the inmates of the premises or to the public health.

Section 7 of the Act provides that nothing in the Act relating to the rules for assessing compensation is to affect any special provisions (in so far as the provisions are inconsistent with these rules) as to the assessment of the value of land acquired for the purposes of Part I or Part II of the Housing Act of 1890 and contained in that Act or any amending Act.

(Sections 1, 2, 7 and 8 of the Acquisition of Land (Assessment of Compensation) Act, 1919.)

16. There are a number of special conditions in section 9 of the Housing Act of 1919 relating to the compensation to be paid for land in an unhealthy area which is acquired compulsorily.

In the first place payment is to be made only for the land as a cleared site ; nothing is to be paid in respect of the buildings on it. Subject to what is said in the next paragraph, the value of the land is to be its value as a cleared site available for development in accordance with any by-laws or local Acts in force in the district as to new streets or buildings.

In the second place if the land (or a part of it) is required under the improvement scheme to be used for rehousing of the working classes or as an open space the amount of compensation payable by the local authority in respect of the unhealthy area is to be reduced. The Act contains provisions under which the reduction of value is to be spread over all the owners of land in the unhealthy area.

The rules laid down by the Act in this matter are to be found on page 455.

The following example will give an indication of the operation of these rules. If the value of the whole of the land included in the scheme (whether land added to make the scheme efficient or land included in the unhealthy area) is by reason of the intended use of any part of it for housing or as an open space reduced from £5,000 to £3,000, then each owner of land in the unhealthy area will receive only three-fifths of the compensation to which he would have been entitled if the value of the area as a whole were not reduced on account of the restriction on its use.

As already explained, full compensation is to be paid for any land, and buildings on it, which is included in an improvement scheme only in order to make the scheme efficient, and not as part of the unhealthy area.

Default powers. 17. *Default Powers.* If it appears to the Minister of Health that owing to the density of population, or any other reason, it is expedient to inquire into the circumstances of any area, in order to determine whether any powers of the Housing Acts should be put into force in that area, he may require the local authority to make a report to him containing such particulars as he directs (section 37 /09).

Where a representation is made to the Minister as respects any county district that the local authority have failed to exercise their powers under Part I or Part II of the Act of 1890, he may direct the county council to instruct the county medical officer of health to inspect the district and to report to the Minister as to the exercise of their powers by the local authority (section 6/19).

18. Particulars have already been given (page 49) of the power of the Minister of Health, where an official representation has been made by a medical officer of health and the local authority do not proceed to make a scheme, to direct an inquiry and, if he thinks this necessary, to order a scheme to be made.

Where the Minister is satisfied that any area within the district of a local authority is an area in respect of which the local authority ought to exercise their powers under Part I or Part II of the Act of 1890, the Minister may require the local authority to make an improvement scheme and to carry it into execution. In case of default, he may either authorise the county council to make and carry out a scheme, or may himself do so (section 5/19).

Further on this subject, see Chapter IV, on the powers and duties of county councils.

PROCEDURE

1. In making a Part I or Part II scheme, it is important that the statutory requirements should be carefully observed in order that no question may arise as to the validity of the proceedings.

The stages in the procedure are summarised below. In connection with this summary, reference should be made to the forms and instructions given on page 580.

2. The representation must be made in writing to the local authority by the medical officer of health of the local ,authority (in London by that officer or by any medical officer of health in London). Part I schemes

The representation should follow the exact words of section 4 of the Act of 1890, as amended by section 22 of the Act of 1909, so far as the words apply to the particular case, and the medical officer of health should furnish the local authority with sufficient facts to enable the members properly to consider the representation. A form of official representation is given on page 580.

3. The local authority then take the representation into consideration and, if satisfied of the truth of it and of the sufficiency of their resources,[1] pass a resolution declaring that the area referred to is an unhealthy area and that an improvement scheme ought to be made in respect of it, and giving the necessary directions for the preparation of the scheme.

Any number of areas may be included in one improvement scheme.

4. After passing the resolution the local authority must in due course proceed to make the scheme.

The nature of the provisions which may be inserted in the scheme is indicated on page 584.

---

[1] As previously mentioned, the financial assistance which may be received in respect of improvement schemes should be borne in mind.

The scheme must be accompanied by maps, particulars and estimates.

5. When the scheme has been duly made under seal, the local authority must forthwith publish an advertisement of it in a newspaper circulating in their district and deposit a copy of the scheme for inspection in or within the vicinity of the area. One advertisement is sufficient. A form of advertisement is given on page 586.

They must also serve a notice on owners or reputed owners, lessees or reputed lessees, and occupiers (except tenants for a month or less period than a month) of any land proposed to be taken compulsorily. The Act contains provision as to the manner in which a notice may be served (sections 7/90, 5/03 and 39/19). Forms of notice are given on pages 587 and 588.

6. When the advertisement has been published and the notices have been served the local authority must present a petition under their seal to the Minister of Health praying that an order may be made confirming the scheme. The petition must state the names of the owners or reputed owners, and lessees or reputed lessees who dissent in respect of the taking of their land (section 8/90). A form of petition is given on page 590.

Part II schemes. 7. No " official representation " is expressly required in the case of a Part II scheme. But it is desirable that the local authority should have some such representation or report from the medical officer of health before them.

8. The local authority pass a resolution in the terms indicated in section 39 (1) (a) or (b) of the Act of 1890 (see page 184), directing a scheme to be prepared for the improvement of the specified area. A form of resolution is given on page 592.

9. The same course in the making of a scheme should be followed as in the case of a Part I scheme.

10. When the scheme is made notices must be served on every owner, &c., in the same way as in the case of a Part I scheme. No advertisement is necessary (section

39 (2)/90). Forms of notice are given on pages 593 and 595.

11. After the service of the notices, the local authority must apply to the Minister of Health, by a petition under their seal, for an order sanctioning the scheme (section 39 (3)/90). A suggested form of petition is given on page 596.

12. *Proceedings after a Scheme has been made.* Before deciding to confirm or sanction a Part I or Part II scheme, the Minister of Health will hold a local inquiry. At this stage the following matters will be considered :— the area of the scheme ; the delimitation of the unhealthy. area ; the amount of re-housing to be provided ; the manner in which re-housing operations and demolitions are to be co-ordinated ; how far re-housing is to be effected within the area of the scheme (and on what part of the area) ; the accommodation to be provided ; what roads and open spaces are to be provided, and where, in the area of the scheme ; and the appropriation or disposal of lands not required for re-housing.

Subsequent proceedings.

13. *Purchase of Land.* When a scheme is confirmed or sanctioned the local authority should proceed as soon as possible to purchase, by agreement or compulsorily, any land which they will require to purchase under the scheme. The powers of compulsory purchase will lapse on the expiration of three years after the confirmation or sanction of the scheme (section 20 and 39 (7)/90).

Purchase of land.

It will, however, be necessary for the local authority to obtain the consent of the Minister of Health before incurring any expenditure, whether in connection with the acquisition of land, the clearance of the area or any other matter, if the expenditure is to be brought into account in an application for financial assistance from the State.

Before purchasing any land or any interest in land by agreement, whether under section 13 of the Act of 1919 before the scheme is confirmed or after confirmation of the scheme, the local authority should obtain a valuation from the District Valuer and should consult the Ministry. The Ministry have arranged with the Board of Inland Revenue that the District Valuers shall be at the service of local authorities for negotiating the purchase of land or of any interest therein ; and local authorities will find it to their advantage to avail themselves of this arrangement.

The new provisions as to assessment of compensation on the compulsory purchase of land in an unhealthy area should be borne in mind.

14. When the local authority have ascertained what lands they will have to acquire compulsorily, they should follow the procedure laid down for the purpose by the Ministry.

Before making any application to the Reference Committee under the Acquisition of Land (Assessment of Compensation) Act, 1919, for the appointment of an official arbitrator, the local authority must, in the case of a Part I scheme, cause to be made out maps and schedules of all lands proposed to be taken compulsorily, with the names of all persons interested in such lands as owners or reputed owners, lessees or reputed lessees, or occupiers (except tenants for a month or a less period than a month). The maps should be on the scale of $\frac{1}{500}$, or on a scale approximating to this, and should show, by figures referring to the schedules, the lands of all the several owners and, by distinctive colours, each of the separate properties proposed to be taken compulsorily for the purposes of the improvement scheme.

One copy of the maps and schedules should be sent to the Ministry of Health, and one copy deposited in the office of the local authority. (Second schedule /90 and section 39/19.)

Re-housing.   15. *Re-housing.* The displacement of tenants from occupied buildings in the area of the scheme must, of

course, be deferred until any necessary accommodation
is available. The scheme as confirmed often provides
for the re-housing and clearance to be carried out in
sections.

Where re-housing accommodation is to be provided
on a site outside the area of the improvement scheme,
the procedure in regard to the selection of sites, submission of plans, &c., for Part III schemes set out in the
Manual on State-aided Housing Schemes should be
followed.

16. *Loans.* Application to the Minister of Health for   Loans.
sanction to loans may be made from time to time when
the local authority are in a position to supply a statement showing how the sums required to be borrowed
are made up.

A Metropolitan Borough Council carrying out a Part II
scheme should apply to the London County Council for
sanction to any loan required by them.

Some proposals have recently been brought before   Purchase of
the Ministry where the local authority have contem-   unfit houses.
plated the purchase under their Part III powers of houses
in areas which should apparently be dealt with as
" unhealthy " under Part I or Part II of the Act of 1890.

If an area is " unhealthy," within the meaning of
the Housing Acts, it is the duty of the local authority
to deal with it as such ; and the Ministry would not be
justified in approving the purchase, under Part III of
houses in such an area. To do so would be to throw
away the advantages of the special powers granted by
Parliament for the acquisition of slum areas, and to
cast an unnecessarily heavy charge on the Exchequer.

District Valuers. Arrangements have been made with
the Inland Revenue, by which the services of their
district valuers will be available to local authorities in
cases such as these mentioned, in the same manner as
in the purchase of sites for the houses. Before approving
of any purchase, the Ministry will require to know the

valuation of the district valuer. Where negotiations are necessary, local authorities are advised to have them carried out by the district valuers.

SUMMARY OF THE PROVISIONS IN THE PUBLIC HEALTH ACTS, &c., AFFECTING UNHEALTHY HOUSES AND AREAS

1—HOUSE WITHOUT A DRAIN SUFFICIENT FOR EFFECTUAL DRAINAGE
(Section 23, Public Health Act, 1875.)

Where any house is without a drain sufficient for effectual drainage, the local authority are, by written notice, to require the owner or occupier, within a reasonable time to be specified in the notice, to make a drain or drains emptying into a sewer if there is one available not more than one hundred feet from the site of such house, or otherwise into a suitable cesspool or other place.

If the notice is not duly complied with, the local authority may do the work required and may recover the expenses incurred by them in so doing from the owner.

2—CLOSET ACCOMMODATION AND RECEPTACLE FOR REFUSE
(Section 36, Public Health Act, 1875.)

If a house appears to a local authority by the report of their surveyor or inspector of nuisances to be without a sufficient water-closet, earth-closet, or privy and an ashpit furnished with proper doors and coverings, the local authority are, by written notice, to require the owner or occupier of the house to provide a sufficient water-closet, earth-closet, or privy and an ashpit, or either of them, as the case may require.

If the notice is not duly complied with the local authority may do the work and recover the expenses incurred by them in so doing from the owner.

DEFINITION OF ASHPIT
(Section 11 (1), Public Health Acts Amendment Act, 1890.)

The expression " ashpit " in the Public Health Acts is, for the purposes of the execution of those Acts, to include any ashtub or other receptacle for the deposit of ashes, fæcal matters, or refuse.

3—NUISANCE FROM DRAIN, CLOSET, ASHPIT OR CESSPOOL

(Section 41, Public Health Act, 1875.)

On the written application of any person to a local authority stating that any drain, water-closet, earth-closet, privy, ashpit or cesspool on or belonging to any premises within their district is a nuisance or injurious to health, the local authority may, by writing, empower their surveyor or inspector of nuisances, after twenty four hours' written notice to the occupier of the premises, or in case of emergency without notice, to enter the premises, with or without assistants, and cause the ground to be opened, and examine the drain, water-closet, earth-closet, privy, ashpit or cesspool.

If the drain, water-closet, earth-closet, privy, ashpit or cesspool on examination appears to be in bad condition, or to require alteration or amendment, the local authority are forthwith to cause notice in writing to be given to the owner or occupier of the premises requiring him to do the necessary works. If the notice is not complied with, the person to whom it is given is liable to a penalty for default; and the local authority may execute the works and recover the expenses incurred by them in so doing from the owner.

Similar provisions with regard to London are contained in sections 40 and 41 Public Health (London) Act, 1891.

4—WATER SUPPLY

(Section 62, Public Health Act, 1875.)

Where, on the report of the surveyor of a local authority, it appears to them that any house is without a proper supply of water, and that such a supply of water can be furnished at a cost not exceeding the water rate authorised by any local Act in force within the district, or, where there is not any local Act in force, at a cost not exceeding 2d. a week, or at such other cost as the Minister of Health may, on the application of the local authority, determine to be reasonable, the local authority are to give notice in writing to the owner requiring him to obtain such supply, and to do any necessary works for that purpose.

If the notice is not duly complied with the local authority may do the works and obtain the supply, and for that purpose may enter into any contract with any water company supplying water within their district ; and water rates may be made and levied on the premises by the authority or company which furnishes the supply and may be recovered as if the owner or occupier of the premises had demanded a supply of water and were willing to pay water rates for the same. Any expenses incurred by the local authority in doing any such works may be recovered by them from the owner.

5—PAVING AND DRAINAGE OF YARDS

(Section 25, Public Health Acts Amendment Act, 1907.)

If any yard in connection with, and exclusively belonging to, a dwelling house shall not be so formed, flagged, asphalted, or paved, or shall not be provided with such works on, above, or below the surface of the yard, as to allow of the effectual drainage of the subsoil or surface of the yard by safe and suitable means to a proper outfall, the local authority may, by notice in writing, require the owner of the dwelling house, within twenty-one days after the service of the notice, to execute all such works as are necessary for the effectual drainage of the subsoil or surface of the yard to a proper outfall.

If, within the period of twenty-one days, the owner has failed to complete the execution of the works specified in the notice, the local authority may execute the works, and may recover the expenses from the owner.

6—APPLICATION OF SMOKE TEST OR OTHER TESTS TO DRAINS

(Section 45, Public Health Acts Amendment Act, 1907.)

If the medical officer, surveyor or inspector of nuisances reports to the local authority that he has reasonable grounds for believing that any drains of any building are so defective as to be injurious or dangerous to health, the local authority may authorise their medical officer, surveyor or inspector of nuisances to apply the smoke or coloured water test, or other similar test (not including a test by water under pressure) to the drains, subject to the condition that either the consent of the owner or the occupier of the building must be given to the application of the test, or an order of a court of summary jurisdiction in the place where the building is situated must be obtained, authorising the application of the test.

If the drains are found to be defective, the local authority may, by notice, require the owner to remedy the defect, and if the owner does not comply with the notice, the local authority may themselves do the work, and recover the expense from the owner.

7—SINKS AND DRAINS FOR REFUSE WATER

(Section 49, *Public Health Acts Amendment Act,* 1907.)

In addition to all other powers vested in a local authority, the local authority, if it appears to them, on the report of the surveyor, medical officer, or inspector of nuisances, that any building is not provided with a proper sink or drain or other necessary appliance for carrying off refuse water, may give notice in writing to the owner or occupier of the building requiring him to provide such sink, drain, or other appliances.

If the owner or occupier fails to comply with the notice, he is liable to penalties, and the local authority may themselves provide the sink, drain, or other appliances, and recover the expenses incurred by them from the owner or occupier.

8—APPEAL TO MINISTER OF HEALTH

(Section 268, *Public Health Act,* 1875.)

Where any person deems himself aggrieved by the decision of the local authority in any case in which the local authority are empowered to recover in a summary manner any expenses incurred by them, or to declare such expenses to be private improvement expenses, he may, within twenty-one days after notice of the decision, address a memorial to the Minister of Health, stating the grounds of his complaint. He must deliver a copy of any such memorial to the local authority.

The Minister of Health may, on any such complaint, make such order as seems to him equitable.

9—WATER SUPPLY TO TENEMENT HOUSES IN LONDON

As to the water supply of tenement houses in London, section 78 of the London County Council (General Powers) Act, 1907, provides that, for the purposes of section 48 (which contains provisions as to houses without a proper water supply) of the Public Health (London) Act, 1891, a tenement house is to be deemed a house without a proper and sufficient supply of water unless there is provided on the storey or one of the storeys in which the rooms or lodgings in the separate occupation of each family occupying the house are situate a sufficient provision for the supply of water for domestic purposes.

In the case of a building existing and in use as a tenement house on the 28th August 1907, the section does not apply where the only storey or storeys on which a proper and sufficient supply of water is not provided is or are a storey or storeys (i) constructed at a height exceeding that to which the Metropolitan Water Board may for the time being be required to furnish a supply of water for domestic purposes, and (ii) to which a supply of water for such purposes was not, on the 28th August 1907, being furnished by the Water Board by agreement.

The section does not apply to any tenement house in respect of which it can be shown that the provision of a supply of water as above is not reasonably necessary.

10—WATER SUPPLY IN RURAL DISTRICT

(*Section 6, Public Health (Water) Act*, 1878.)

In a rural district it is not lawful for the owner of any dwelling house erected after the 25th March 1879, or of any dwelling house which after that date may be pulled down to or below the ground floor and rebuilt, to occupy the same, or cause or permit the same to be occupied, unless he has obtained from the local authority a certificate that there is provided, within a reasonable distance of the house, such an available supply of wholesome water as may appear to the authority, on the report of their inspector of nuisances or of their medical officer of health, to be sufficient for the consumption and use for domestic purposes of the inmates of the house.

The owner may appeal to a court of summary jurisdiction against the refusal of a certificate by the local authority, and the court may make an order authorising the occupation of the house.

Any owner who contravenes the section is liable to a penalty not exceeding ten pounds.

11—CELLAR DWELLINGS AND UNDERGROUND ROOMS

(*Sections* 71–75, *Public Health Act*, 1875.)

The provisions in force outside London are to the following effect :—

It is not lawful to let or occupy or suffer to be occupied separately as a dwelling, any cellar, vault or underground room built or rebuilt since the 31st August 1848, or which was not so let or occupied before that date.

It is not lawful to let or occupy or suffer to be occupied separately as a dwelling any cellar whatsoever (*a*) unless it is at least seven feet in height, and is to the extent of at least three feet of its height above the surface of the street or ground adjoining or nearest to it, and fronts on an area which complies with certain specified conditions ; and (*b*) unless it is effectually drained and is provided with sufficient closet accommodation, and an ashpit, and with a fireplace and an external window made to open.

Any cellar in which any person passes the night is to be deemed to be occupied as a dwelling.

(*Sections* 96–98, *Public Health* (*London*) *Act*, 1891.)

In London an underground room (that is, a room of which the floor is more than three feet below the level of the adjoining street or ground) may not be let or occupied separately as a dwelling unless it is at least seven feet in height, and unless at least three feet of its height are above ground level (but where the width of the area on which the room fronts is equal to the height of the room from the floor to ground level a height of one foot above ground suffices).

The walls of the underground room must have a damp-proof course, and the floor, if hollow, must be ventilated.

5

The room must front on a paved and drained area at least four feet wide, must be provided with proper closet accommodation, a receptacle for refuse, a fire-place and one or more windows opening externally, and must be properly drained and ventilated.

In the case of an underground room which was occupied separately as a dwelling before 5th August 1891, the sanitary authority have a limited power of dispensing with these requirements, and the owner may appeal to the Minister of Health against a refusal on their part to exercise it.

Where two convictions against the provisions of any Act relating to the occupation of a cellar as a separate dwelling place have taken place within three months, a court of summary jurisdiction may direct the closing of the premises.

(See also sections 17 (7) *of the Housing, Town Planning, &c., Act,* 1909, *and* 39 *of the Housing, Town Planning, &c., Act,* 1919.)

12—DEFINITIONS OF " OWNER "

1. For the purposes of Part II of the Housing of the Working Classes Act, 1890, generally, " owner " is defined by section 49 (2) of the Housing, Town Planning, &c., Act, 1909 (see page 333).

2. For the purposes of sections 26 and 28 of the Housing, Town Planning, &c., Act, 1919, the definition of " owner," contained in section 4 of the Public Health Act, 1875, is applicable (see page 423).

CHAPTER IV

THE direct housing powers and duties of county councils (excepting the London County Council) arise under section 8 of the Housing, Town Planning, &c., Act, 1919 (housing of their employees), and section 12 of the Land Settlement (Facilities) Act, 1919, and the Acts amended by that Act (housing for small holders and for ex-soldiers settling on the land). This latter legislation is beyond the scope of this volume, though extracts from the Land Settlement (Facilities) Act, 1919, are printed on page 85.

The indirect housing powers are mainly those arising under sections 3–6 of the Housing, Town Planning, &c., Act, 1919. They are indirect in that they have to be, almost wholly, transferred specially by order of the Minister of Health, and chiefly where the local authority is in default.

There are, however, several other powers arising under the Housing Acts which, if they have not a great deal to do with the provision of houses, are, nevertheless, of importance. The whole of the references in the Acts will be taken in order.

By section 45 of the 1890 Act, the London County Council as regards a Metropolitan area, and other county councils as regards rural districts, are entitled to copies of representations and complaints about unhealthy dwelling houses, to copies of closing orders and to particulars respecting any proceedings thereunder taken by the district authority. And where the county council are

Copies of representations, &c.

67

of opinion that closing, demolition or " obstructive building " orders ought to be enforced or made they may, after giving not less than one month's notice to the district authority, resolve that such authority are in default and thereupon exercise that authority's statutory (Part II) powers—except in respect of an improvement scheme, as to which see section 5 of the 1919 Act—and may recover their expenses.

Section 69 of the 1909 Act requires the clerk of the rural district council to forward copies of the above representations to the county medical officer of health ; requires the district medical officer of health to give to the county medical officer information reasonably required ; and provides that the Minister of Health shall settle any disputes arising under that section.

Report to local authority by county medical officer.

By section 52 of the 1890 Act, a representation from a county medical officer of health submitted to the county council and by that council forwarded to the district council shall, for the purposes of Part II, have the like effect as a representation from the district medical officer of health.   Such representations precede closing and demolition orders and improvement schemes, and are aimed at unhealthy and obstructive houses and buildings (see sections 30 and 38 of the 1890 Act and section 17 of the 1909 Act). This provision does not apply to boroughs.

Local authority's default— 1909 Act.

By section 10 of the 1909 Act, if the Minister of Health, following complaint, is satisfied that a rural district council, or the council of a non-county borough, or other urban district, have failed to exercise their powers under Part II (unhealthy dwelling houses) or Part III (provision of houses) he may make an order against that authority. And where such an order is made and is not complied with, the Minister may, with the consent of the county council, direct the county council to carry out the necessary works : see also section 5 of the 1919 Act.

By section 12 of the 1909 Act, where complaint is made to the .county council in the manner specified, the county council may cause a public local inquiry to be held, and if satisfied that the rural district council has failed to exercise their Part III (housing) powers may take over those powers or any of them. Powers transferred.

By section 13 of that Act a county council may, in the circumstances specified, have the Part III (housing) powers of a rural district council transferred to them by the Minister of Health, though the rural district council is not in default : see also section 3 of the 1919 Act.

Section 56 is altered as explained in a note on section 42 of the 1919 Act, see below.

Section 68 of the 1909 Act provides that every county council shall appoint a (full-time) medical officer of health, and gives powers for the Local Government Board (now the Minister of Health) to prescribe his duties.   Such duties are prescribed in the County Medical Officers of Health (Duties) Order, 1910, which is printed on page 74. County medical officers of health.

Section 69 of the 1909 Act (which deals with the clerk of the rural district council forwarding copies of representations, &c., to the county medical officer) is referred to on page 68.

Section 70 thereof excepts Scotland and (excluding one small point) the Administrative County of London from the provisions relating to county medical officers of health.

Section 71 requires every county council (except the London. County Council) to establish a public health and housing committee, to which health and housing matters shall stand referred, and to which the council may delegate its public health and housing powers (except the power of raising a rate or borrowing money, and any power of resolving that the powers of a district council in default should be transferred to the council).

Section 3 of the 1919 Act gives the Minister of Health power to authorise county councils to act in the place of local authorities in respect of Part III schemes (provision The powers of county. councils under the 1919 Act.

of houses for the working classes), not only where local authorities are in default but where for any reason it is desirable.   But both the local authority and the county council concerned are first to have an opportunity of being heard.   Provision is also made in the section for expenses and disputes.

Section 4 provides that if the local authority and the county council are in default the Minister of Health may act in their place, and again provision is made for expenses.

Default provisions.   Section 5 provides that the Minister may by order require a local authority to make and carry out an improvement scheme under Part I (unhealthy areas) or Part II (unhealthy dwelling houses) ; and if the local authority fail within the time fixed the Minister may empower the county council to act, or may himself act, at the expense of the local authority.

Section 6 provides that where a representation is made to the Minister as respects any county district that the local authority have failed to exercise their Part I or Part II powers, he may direct the county council to instruct their medical officer of health to ·inspect the district and to make a report to him as to the exercise of the power by the local authority— whereupon the Minister may take the necessary steps under section 5.

The Exchequer grant.   Section 7 provides for State subsidies to county councils (1) to whom the powers of local authorities have been transferred as above mentioned, and (2) who carry out approved schemes for housing persons in their employment, viz. the provision of *new* houses.   The details of the latter subsidy are given in the County Councils (Assisted Schemes for the Housing of Employees) Regulations, 1920, which are printed on page 76.

Borrowing: housing of employees.   Section 8 deals with the borrowing powers of county councils in connection with the housing of their employees, and extends the maximum period for the repayment of loans to eighty years. It provides that loans to county councils by the Public Works Loan Commissioners shall be on the same terms and conditions as those to local authorities. It also provides that county councils shall have power and shall be deemed always to have had the power to provide houses for persons in their employment, and for that purpose may be authorised to acquire land in like manner as a local authority for Part III (housing) purposes: see section 12 and notes thereto, page 394.

Where a county council build houses for their employees on land belonging to them, the fair value of the land may be brought into account for the purpose of estimating the amount of the Exchequer grant.

A county council can, but a local authority cannot, provide "tied" houses for their employees, and a local authority could not sell houses to a county council with a view to their becoming tied houses (section 15).

Section 14 gives power to county councils to acquire water rights for houses provided under the Housing Acts, subject to conditions.

Section 18 authorises county councils to promote and assist public utility societies (as to which societies, see Chapter VI), and where the local authority are unwilling to acquire the land required by such societies for houses for the working classes, the county council may do so on the application of such societies, and for this purpose may exercise the powers of local authorities. County councils may hold shares in public utility societies, and are not restricted to an interest of £200. The county council's expenses herein are to be defrayed as expenses for general county purposes, and the council may borrow —the maximum period for repayment being fifty years. *Public utility societies—assistance.*

Building schemes made by a county council obtain advantages in regard to the relaxation of building by-laws: see section 24 (3) and (4). *Sundry points.*

Section 29, which provides for information being

given to tenants, is of importance to county councils who provide houses.

Section 34, which provides for arrangements between the Ministry of Health and other government departments for the exercise of powers under the Housing Acts, is also to be noted.

Section 36 provides for compensation in cases of subsidence notwithstanding the Brine Pumping (Compensation for Subsidence) Act, 1891.

Section 41 deals with the special case of the London County Council, which throughout the Acts is dealt with, in certain respects, as a local authority.

Town planning.   Section 43 makes an addition to section 56 of the 1909 Act, by requiring that the council of the county in which any land proposed to be included in a town-planning scheme is situated shall be furnished with notice of any proposal to prepare or adopt such a scheme, and with a copy of the draft scheme before the scheme is made. The county council will be entitled to be heard at any public local inquiry held by the Ministry in regard to the scheme.

Section 47 provides that if a local authority fails to provide a town-planning scheme as therein mentioned, the Minister of Health may empower the county council to act in the place and at the expense of a borough or other urban district the population of which is less than 20,000, or of a rural district.

The Housing (Additional Powers) Act, 1919.   Section 4 of the Housing (Additional Powers) Act, 1919, increases the amount of the State subsidy to county councils in respect of schemes for the housing of persons in their employment. The regulations giving effect to this appear on page 76. Briefly stated there is an extra 20 per cent. of the loan charges for the period up to 31st March 1927.

Local bonds.   Section 7 authorises county councils, with the consent of the Minister of Health, to borrow any sums which they have power to borrow for the purposes of the Housing

Acts, 1890 to 1919 (see page 477) by the issue of "local bonds." A county council may also lend to any local authority within their area any money which that local authority have power to borrow for the said purposes, and may with the sanction of the Minister, and irrespective of any limit of borrowing, raise the money required either by the issue of local bonds or by a loan under any of their powers. On the subject of these bonds, &c., see page 477.

Section 9 makes into trustee securities local bonds and future mortgages of any fund or rate.

Section 10 authorises the Minister of Health to acquire land for the purpose of garden cities or town-planning schemes " if satisfied that any local authority (including a county council) . . . are prepared to purchase and develop that land for that purpose."

It will be understood that the foregoing statements of the statutory provisions are offered merely as a guide to the Acts : the sections named should be read for fuller details.

County councils may provide houses for their employees, but are not required so to do. But county councils are the authorities for the provision of housing accommodation for small-holders, and for the settlement of ex-soldiers on the land. Rural district councils are primarily responsible for the housing of the working classes in their areas. Where it is desirable to group labourers' cottages near a colony of small-holders, there should be co-ordination of effort as far as possible.

Many of the documents issued by the Ministry of Health have been forwarded to county councils, so that they should be aware of the provisions of the Acts and the procedure adopted.

The Unemployment (Relief Works) Act, 1920 (10 & 11 Geo. 5. c. 57) facilitates the acquisition of, and entry on, land required for works of public utility, and for purposes connected therewith (see page 488).

STATUTORY RULES AND ORDERS, 1910. No. 801

MEDICAL OFFICER OF HEALTH, ENGLAND

The County Medical Officer of Health (Duties) Order, 1910
Dated 29th July 1910

55,475

To the County Council of every Administrative County
in England and Wales other than London ;—
And to all others whom it may concern.

Whereas it is enacted by subsection (2) of section 68
of the Housing, Town Planning, &c., Act, 1909 (hereinafter referred to as " the Act of 1909 "), that the duties of
a medical officer of health of a county shall be such
duties as may be prescribed by general order of the
Local Government Board and such other duties as may
be assigned to him by the county council ;

And whereas by virtue of section 70 of the Act of 1909
the above cited subsection does not apply to the Administrative County of London :

Now therefore, we, the Local Government Board, in
pursuance of the powers given to us in that behalf, by this
order prescribe the following duties as the duties of
every medical officer of health of a county other than the
Administrative County of London ; that is to say :—

(1) The medical officer of health of the county shall
inform himself as far as practicable respecting
all influences affecting or threatening to affect
injuriously the public health in the county. For
this purpose he shall visit the several county
districts in the county as occasion may require,
giving to the medical officer of health of each
county district prior notice of his visit, so far
as this may be practicable.

(2) The medical officer of health of the county shall
from time to time inquire into and report upon
the hospital accommodation available for the
isolation of cases occurring in the county—

(*a*) of small-pox, and
(*b*) of other infectious diseases,
and upon any need for the provision of
further hospital accommodation.

(3) The medical officer of health of the county shall
communicate to the medical officer of health
of a county district within the county any

information which he may possess as to any danger to health threatening that district.

(4) The medical officer of health of the county shall consult with the medical officers of health of county districts within the county whenever the circumstances may render this desirable.

(5) If the annual or special reports of the medical officer of health of a county district in the county shall not contain adequate information in regard to

    (a) the vital statistics of the district,

    (b) the sanitary circumstances and administration of the district, and

    (c) the action taken in the district for putting in force the provisions of the Housing of the Working Classes Acts, 1890 to 1909,

the medical officer of health of the county shall obtain from the medical officer of health of the county district such further information on those matters as the circumstances may demand.

(6) The medical officer of health of the county shall, when directed by us, or by the county council, or as occasion may require, make a special report to the county council on any matter appertaining to his duties under this order.

(7) The medical officer of health of the county shall as soon as practicable after the 31st day of December in each year make an annual report to the county council up to the end of December on the sanitary circumstances, the sanitary administration and the vital statistics of the county.

In addition to any other matters upon which the medical officer of health may consider it desirable to report, his annual report shall contain the following sections :—

    (a) A digest of all annual and special reports made by the medical officers of health of all county districts within the county ;

    (b) a section as to the isolation hospital accommodation available for each county district and as to the steps which should be taken to remedy any deficiencies which may exist;

    (c) a section on the administration of the Housing of the Working Classes Acts, 1890 to 1909, within the county ;

(d) a section on the water supply of the several
county districts within the county ;

(e) a section on the pollution of streams within
the county and as to the steps for the
prevention of pollution taken :—
(i) by the local authorities, and
(ii) by the county council :

(f) a section on the administration within the
county of the Midwives Act, 1902 ; and

(g) a section on the administration of the
Sale of Food and Drugs Acts, 1875 to
1907, within that part of the county in
which the county council have jurisdiction
for the purposes of those Acts.

(8) The medical officer of health of the county shall
send to us two copies of his annual report and
two copies of any special report ; he shall also
send one copy of his annual report to the council
of every county district in the county and shall
send three copies of any special report to the
council of every such county district affected by
the special report.

This Order may be cited as the County Medical Officers
of Health (Duties) Order, 1910.

Given under the seal of office of the Local Government
Board, this Twenty-ninth day of July, in the year
One thousand nine hundred and ten.

JOHN BURNS,
(L.S.)   *President.*
H. C. MONRO,
Secretary.

STATUTORY RULES AND ORDERS, 1920.   No. 336

HOUSING, ENGLAND

*The County Councils (Assisted Schemes for the Housing
of Employees) Regulations, 1920, dated 5th March
1920*

65,815

To the councils of the several administrative counties in
England and Wales ;—

And to all others whom it may concern.

Whereas by subsection (1) of section 7 of the Housing,

Town Planning, &c., Act, 1919,[1] it is enacted (amongst other things) that if it appears to the Local Government Board that the carrying out of any scheme approved by the Board for the provision of houses for persons in the employment of, or paid by, a county council, or a statutory committee thereof, has resulted or is likely to result in a loss, the Board shall, if the scheme is carried out within such period after the passing of that Act as may be specified by the Board with the consent of the Treasury, pay or undertake to pay to the county council, out of moneys provided by Parliament, such part of the loss as may be determined to be so payable under regulations made by the Board with the approval of the Treasury, subject to such conditions as may be prescribed by those regulations ;

And whereas by subsection (2) of the said section 7, as altered by section 4 of the Housing (Additional Powers) Act, 1919,[2] it is enacted that the regulations shall provide that the amount of any annual payment to be made under the section shall, in the case of a scheme for the provision of houses for persons in the employment of, or paid by, a county council, or a statutory committee thereof, be an amount equivalent during the period ending on the 31st day of March 1927, to 50 per centum and thereafter to 30 per centum of the annual loan charges as calculated in accordance with the regulations on the total capital expenditure incurred by the county council for the purposes of the scheme :

Now, therefore, the Minister of Health, in pursuance of his powers under the recited enactments and under any other Statutes in that behalf, hereby makes the following regulations :—

ARTICLE I—(1) These regulations may be cited as " The County Councils (Assisted Schemes for the Housing of Employees) Regulations, 1920."

(2) The County Councils (Assisted Schemes for the Housing of Employees) Regulations, 1919,[3] are hereby revoked, without prejudice to any right, privilege or liability acquired, accrued or incurred thereunder.

ARTICLE II—(1) In these regulations, unless the contrary intention appears :—

---

[1] 9-10 Geo. 5. c. 35.   [2] 9-10 Geo. 5. c. 99.
[3] S.R. & O., 1919, No. 1430.

(a) The expression " the Minister " means the Minister of Health ;

(b) The expression " the Act of 1919 " means the Housing, Town Planning, &c., Act, 1919 ; and

(c) The expression " County Council " includes a statutory committee of a county council, the Lancashire Asylums Board, the West Riding of Yorkshire Asylums Board, and any other body constituted for the purpose of the administration of the Lunacy Acts on behalf of any combination of county councils and county borough councils.

(2) The Interpretation Act, 1889,[1] applies to the interpretation of these regulations as it applies to the interpretation of an Act of Parliament.

ARTICLE III—Subject to the provision of Article IV of these regulations :—

(1) An annual contribution out of moneys provided by Parliament (hereinafter referred to as " the Exchequer subsidy ") shall be made by the Minister towards the cost of carrying out a scheme submitted by a county council, and approved by the Minister, for the provision of houses for persons in the employment of, or paid by, the county council.

(2) The Exchequer subsidy shall be an amount equivalent during the period ending on the 31st day of March 1927, to 50 per centum and thereafter to 30 per centum of the annual charges, for interest and repayment of principal, in respect of the aggregate amount of the loans raised by the county council for the purposes of the approved scheme :

Provided that the Minister may reduce the amount of the Exchequer subsidy in any case in which he is satisfied that the capital expenditure incurred by the county council has been excessive.

(3) The Exchequer subsidy shall be payable in two half-yearly instalments or in such other manner as the Minister may think fit during the periods allowed for the repayment of the loans raised by the county council for the purposes of the

[1] 52-3 Vict. c. 63.

approved scheme, and shall be reduced by the Minister so far as may be necessary as and when the period allowed for the repayment of any one of the said loans expires.

(4) For the purposes of this Article the annual charges in respect of the aggregate amount of the loans raised by the county council shall be ascertained by calculating the total amount which would be annually payable in respect of the several loans for principal and interest if the loans were repayable by equal annual instalments of principal and interest combined :

Provided that, save with the consent of the Minister, the rate of interest shall not for the purposes of this paragraph exceed the rate for the time being in force for loans advanced by the Public Works Loan Commissioners for the purposes of schemes to which section 7 of the Act of 1919 applies.

(5) The foregoing provisions of this Article shall apply to accumulated funds or capital moneys belonging to a county council and used by them for the purposes of an approved scheme as though such funds or moneys were loans, and for the purpose of the last preceding paragraph the rate of interest in respect of such funds or moneys shall be deemed to be—

(i) where moneys have been borrowed for the purposes of the scheme from sources other than funds or moneys belonging to the county council, the rate of interest payable in respect of the moneys last previously so borrowed ; and

(ii) where no moneys have been borrowed for the purposes of the scheme from such sources as aforesaid, the rate in force for loans advanced by the Public Works Loan Commissioners for the purposes referred to in the last preceding paragraph at the date when the funds or moneys were so used.

ARTICLE IV—(1) The Exchequer subsidy shall cease ꞏ be payable—

(a) in any case in which the Minister is not satisfied

that reasonable progress has been made with the carrying into effect of the scheme within twelve months from the passing of the Act of 1919, or such later date as the Minister may allow, regard being had to the supplies of labour and material available from time to time and all other local or general circumstances affecting the carrying into effect of the scheme ; and

(b) in respect of any scheme or part of a scheme not carried into effect before the expiry of a period of three years from the passing of the Act of 1919, or such later date as the Minister may allow, regard being had to the supplies of labour and material available from time to time and all other local or general circumstances affecting the carrying into effect of the scheme.

(2) For the purposes of these regulations a scheme or part of a scheme shall be deemed to have been carried into effect when all the houses to be provided thereunder are let or available for letting.

Given under the official seal of the Minister of Health, this Fifth day of March, in the year One thousand nine hundred and twenty.

(L.S.)   CHRISTOPHER ADDISON,
                              Minister of Health.

We approve these regulations—

JAMES PARKER,

J. TOWYN JONES,

Lords Commissioners of His Majesty's Treasury.

STATUTORY RULES AND ORDERS, 1920.   No. 1465

HOUSING, ENGLAND

The Housing (Loans by County Councils) Order, 1920, dated 12th August 1920, made by the Minister of Health under section 7 (2) of the Housing (Additional Powers) Act, 1919 (9 & 10 Geo. 5. c. 99)

66,495.

The Minister of Health, in exercise of the powers conferred on him by subsection (2) of Section 7 of the Housing (Additional Powers) Act, 1919, and of all other powers enabling him, hereby makes the following Order :

1. This Order may be cited as the Housing (Loans by County Councils) Order, 1920.

2.—(1) In this Order, unless the context otherwise requires,—

"The Minister" means the Minister of Health;

"The Act" means the Housing (Additional Powers) Act, 1919;

"Housing Loan" means a loan raised by a county council for the purpose mentioned in Section 7 (2) of the Act, or, where a loan is raised partly for that purpose and partly for other purposes, such portion of the loan as is declared by the Minister to have been raised for the purpose of the said Section 7 (2).

(2) The Interpretation Act, 1889,[1] shall apply to the interpretation of this Order as it applies to the interpretation of an Act of Parliament.

3. Where the proceeds of a Housing Loan have been lent to local authorities, the county council shall discharge or provide for repayment of such part of the loan as represents the money lent to each local authority within a term ending not later than one year after the date at which that local authority is required to pay off the money lent to it.

4. Money lent to a local authority shall be repayable by it to the county council by equal half-yearly instalments of principal and interest combined within the period for which the local authority has power to borrow:

Provided that where the money lent to a local authority has been raised by the issue of stock, the local authority shall repay to the county council not less than six months before the expiration of the maximum period of the currency of the stock any outstanding balance of the amount borrowed from the county council.

5. All sums received by the county council from a local authority representing repayment of principal shall be applied in or towards discharge of the Housing Loan, or where the Housing Loan was raised by the issue of stock, in or towards redemption of such stock.

6. All sums which under the last preceding Article are required to be applied in or towards redemption of stock

[1] 52–3 V. c. 63.

6

shall be transferred to the fund or account to which, under the provisions of the Acts or Regulations for the time being governing the issue and redemption of stock by the county council, sums required to be applied in redemption of stock are to be paid, and notwithstanding anything in those provisions the county council shall not be under any obligation to transfer to that fund or account in any year any greater sum than the aggregate of the sums received during that year and required by this Article to be so transferred.

7. The rate of interest at which money may be lent by the county council to a local authority shall be subject to the approval of the Minister and shall be calculated so as to cover the interest payable by the council in respect of such money together with all expenses incurred by the council in raising the same, and all expenses incurred or to be incurred by them in connection with the management or redemption of any stock or local bonds by means of which the money was raised, including any loss incurred by the council by reason of the rate of interest received in respect of any portion of the proceeds of the Housing Loan and not immediately required for loans to local authorities or in respect of any investments of moneys standing to the credit of any fund or account for the redemption of the Housing Loan falling short of the rate at which interest is payable by the council upon the Housing Loan :

Provided that where the Housing Loan was raised by the issue of stock, the rate of interest payable by the local authority may, with the consent of the Minister, be the same as that payable by the county council on such stock, but in that event the mortgage to be entered into by the local authority shall, in addition to securing the repayment of principal and interest as provided in Article 4 of this Order, include the provisions specified in the Schedule to this Order.

8. This Order shall not apply to the London County Council.

SCHEDULE

The following provisions shall apply to every mortgage made between a county council and a local authority for securing repayment of a loan where the rate of interest charged is the same as that payable on the stock issued by the county council, and the mortgage shall include such covenants and conditions as may be necessary to give effect to such provisions.

(a) The local authority shall pay to the county council by means of an annuity of an amount to be specified in the mortgage payable half-yearly during a period to be similarly specified not exceeding the maximum period of currency of the stock, a sum equal to the amount, if any, by which the nominal amount of that part of the stock of which the proceeds were applied in making the loan to the local authority exceeded the net proceeds of such nominal amount of stock with interest on that sum at the rate payable under the mortgage in respect of the principal money secured thereby. In ascertaining net proceeds for the purpose of this paragraph a proportionate part of the expenses of the issue of the stock and of any unaccrued interest payable under the terms of issue at the date of the first payment of interest shall be deducted from the proceeds.

(b) The local authority shall pay annually to the county council on a date to be specified in the mortgage a proportionate part of the expenses incurred by the council during the previous year in connection with the management of the stock, including any composition for stamp duties and any remuneration payable to the registrar of the said stock and other establishment charges in connection therewith.

(c) At a date within one year from the commencement of the loan to be specified in the mortgage and thereafter at the end of each year from that date during the continuance of the loan and until the redemption of the stock, the amount, if any, by which the total interest paid by all the local authorities (i) in respect of loans made to them out of the proceeds of the Housing Loan, and (ii) under paragraph (a) of this Schedule, together with any interest received by the county council either upon any portion of the proceeds of the Housing Loan which has not for the time being been lent to any local authority, or upon moneys representing principal previously repaid by any such local authority and forming part of the council's redemption fund account relating to the Housing Loan, exceeds or falls short of the amount required to pay interest on the Housing Loan shall be ascertained, and in the case of any excess a proportionate part thereof shall be set off against any sum payable by the local authority under paragraphs (a), (b) or (d), of this Schedule, and in the case of any deficiency a proportionate part thereof shall be paid by the local authority to the county council.

(d) (i) If upon the realisation of any investments standing to the credit of the county council's redemption fund account relating to the Housing Loan the net proceeds of the sale of such investments represent a profit or loss to the council, a proportionate part of the amount of such profit or loss shall in the case of a profit be set off against the sums payable by the local authority to the county council, and in the case of a loss be paid by the local authority to the county council.

(ii) If the county council redeem or purchase and extinguish stock at less than its nominal value by the application of any part of the money carried to the said redemption fund account, the difference between the price at which the stock is so redeemed or purchased and its nominal value shall be treated for the purposes of this Article as a profit made on the realisation of an investment.

(iii) The necessary adjustments between the county council and the local authority for the purpose of this paragraph shall be made annually upon a date to be specified in the mortgage.

(e) Upon the redemption by the county council of any stock issued for the purposes of the Housing Loan the local authority shall repay to the council a proportionate part of any expenses incurred by the council in connection with such redemption.

(f) All powers and remedies of the county council for securing and recovering payment of the principal and interest payable under the mortgage shall be exercisable in respect of any payment to be made by the local authority to the council under the foregoing provisions of this Schedule.

(g) For the purposes of this Schedule a proportionate part of any expenses, profit, loss or other amount shall mean as regards any local authority a part of such expenses, profit, loss or other amount bearing the same proportion to the whole as the nominal amount of stock represented by the moneys lent to that local authority bears to the total nominal amount of the stock representing the amount lent to local authorities issued for the purpose of Housing.

Given under the Official Seal of the Minister of Health this Twelfth day of August, in the year One thousand nine hundred and twenty.

(L.S.)   E. R. FORBER,
Assistant Secretary, Ministry of Health.

LAND SETTLEMENT (FACILITIES) ACT, 1919
[9 & 10 GEO. 5. CH. 59.]

An Act to make further provision for the acquisition of land for the purposes of small holdings, reclamation, and drainage, to amend the enactments relating to small holdings and allotments, and otherwise to facilitate land settlement. [19th August 1919.]

12. (1) Subject to the consent of the Board of Agriculture and Fisheries in cases where their consent is required under this section or under regulations made by the Board, a county council shall have power in any case where in the opinion of the council it is necessary or expedient so to do for the better carrying into effect of the principal Act— *Extension of powers of councils in relation to land acquired under principal Act.*

  (a) to erect, repair, or improve dwelling houses and other buildings on any land acquired by the council under the principal Act, or to execute any other improvement on or in connection with and for the benefit of any such land, or to arrange with the tenant of any such land for the execution of any such improvement of such terms as may be agreed :

20. (1) Subject to the provisions of this section, a county council may provide a holding of less than one acre if it is not less than half an acre and has a cottage erected thereon, and such a holding shall be deemed to be a small holding for the purposes of the principal Act. *Provisions as to small holdings of less than one acre.*

(2) As respects holdings to which this section relates provided by a county council during such period after the passing of this Act as may be specified by the Board

of Agriculture and Fisheries with the consent of the Treasury, the county council shall keep separate accounts of all receipts and expenditure in respect thereof, and at the end of each financial year ending on the 31st day of March the excess of the expenditure over the receipts or of the receipts over the expenditure during that year shall be paid to the county council by the local authority, for the purposes of Part III of the Housing of the Working Classes Act, 1890, of the district in which the holdings are situate, or to that authority by the county council, as the case may be, and any amount so paid or received by the local authority shall be treated as if it was expenditure or receipts of the authority in carrying out a scheme for the exercise of their powers under that Part approved by the Local Government Board.

(3) As respects holdings to which this section relates provided by a county council after the expiration of the period so specified, the local authority, for the purposes of Part III of the Housing of the Working Classes Act, 1890, of the district in which the holdings are situate may contribute or agree to contribute to the expenses of providing such holdings, and any sums so payable to the county council by the local authority shall be treated as expenses of the local authority under Part III of that Act.

(4) Any question as to the amount payable to or by a local authority under this section may be determined by the Local Government Board.

(5) Any receipts and expenditure of the council of a county borough in respect of the provision of holdings to which this section relates shall be treated as if they were receipts and expenditure of the council in carrying out such a scheme as aforesaid.

Power of
appropria-
tion of land.

22. (1) A council of a borough, urban district, or parish may, in a case where no power of appropriation is otherwise provided, with the consent of the Board of Agriculture and Fisheries and the Local Government Board, and subject to such conditions as to the repayment of any loan obtained for the purpose of the acquisition of land or otherwise as the last-mentioned Board may impose—

(a) appropriate for the purpose of allotments any land held by the council for other purposes of the council ; or

(b) appropriate for other purposes of the council land acquired by the council for allotments.

(2) This section shall apply, in the county of London, to the council of the county and to any Metropolitan borough council.

CHAPTER V

TOWN PLANNING

General observations. THE legislation affecting town planning is contained in Part II of the Housing, Town Planning, &c., Act, 1909, as amended by Part II of the Housing, Town Planning, &c., Act, 1919—see pages 324 and 447.

By section 10 of the Housing (Additional Powers) Act, 1919, provision is made as to the acquisition of land for the purpose of garden cities and town-planning schemes.

Before sanctioning a housing scheme, the Minister of Health requires to be satisfied not only that the site is a good one for building purposes, but also that it is in a locality which, having regard to the district as a whole, will be suitable for working-class dwellings. He requires a well-considered lay-out plan, which will secure that the houses shall be advantageously placed on the site and that the streets shall be arranged with due regard to the needs of through traffic and to the development of the surrounding area. To this extent the new housing schemes include town planning.

It is, however, very important to ensure not only that any development of the land around the sites of the housing schemes shall be in harmony with the lay-out plans of the housing schemes, but that all future building development shall be properly controlled. It is essential, therefore, that local authorities should proceed as quickly as possible to prepare town-planning schemes. By means of such schemes all future development may be regulated in accordance with definite plans, which will prevent the faulty street planning and congestion of buildings which mar so many existing towns and villages. Provision may be made by such schemes for arterial and other roads, for fixing building lines, limiting the number of buildings per acre, reserving sufficient land for open spaces, and assigning suitable areas for industrial, commercial, and residential purposes respectively.

By the 1919 Act the procedure for making town-planning schemes has been simplified. A local authority may now by resolution decide to prepare a town-planning scheme, and it is not necessary for them to obtain authority from the Ministry of Health to do so, except where the area to be town-planned extends to land outside the district of the local authority (section 42). *New procedure.*

Additional powers have been given to the Ministry to make regulations as to the preparation of town-planning schemes and for securing that schemes shall be prepared with all reasonable speed (section 43).

In order that there may be no unnecessary holding up of development during the preparation of schemes, the Minister of Health is empowered to make an order, or orders prescribing the conditions under which any proposed development may be permitted to proceed pending the making and approval of the scheme (section 45).

Any local authority may at any time be required by the Ministry of Health to prepare a town-planning scheme for any area for which the Ministry are satisfied that a scheme ought immediately to be prepared (section 47). After the 1st January 1923, the preparation of town-planning schemes will be compulsory on all boroughs or urban districts with a population exceeding 20,000. The scheme will have to be prepared within three years of that date (section 46).

Further, if a local authority fail to carry out their duties as regards town planning, the Ministry of Health may themselves act, or in the case of a borough or other urban district with a population of less than 20,000, or of a rural district, may empower the county council to do so, in either case charging the expense to the local authority (section 47 (3)).

Doubtless progress will be made in town planning before 1923, and many local authorities have the subject well in mind, but at present energy is being concentrated on the provision of houses, and big town-planning schemes are often more involved than many people imagine.

The resolution. A resolution deciding to prepare a town-planning scheme should include a reference to section 42/19, and should define the area by reference to a map on the scale of 25·344 inches to the mile and marked Map No. 1.

The following resolution has been considered by the Ministry " too vague to be effective " :—

" That a town-planning scheme be prepared to include all land in the urban district of X, on the eastern side of the High Road, in respect of which a town-planning scheme may be made under the above Act."

No portion of the costs in connection with the preparation and carrying out of a town-planning scheme may be included in the expenditure on a housing scheme ranking for financial assistance. The scope of such assistance is indicated in section 7 (1)/19.

The 1909 Act as amended. The land which can be town-planned is land which is in course of development or appears likely to be used for building purposes (section 54/09), but the definitions are wide—see notes to section 54/09. Land already built upon and land not likely to be used for building purposes can be included in the scheme in certain circumstances, and the scheme can provide for demolition or alteration of the buildings—section 54 (1)/09.

Joint schemes may be prepared or adopted by two or more local authorities.

In addition to preparing schemes, local authorities have power to adopt, with or without modifications, schemes proposed by land-owners. A scheme may be varied or revoked by a subsequent scheme, and the Ministry may make modifications in any scheme and impose conditions, or even revoke it.

Section 55 of the 1909 Act deals with the contents of town-planning schemes and refers to the Fourth Schedule in which matters of detail are set out.

Section 56 deals with procedure regulations, as to which see page 93. Co-operation on the part of the local authority and the owners and other persons interested is to be secured, and county councils are given certain rights by an extension by section 43 of the 1919 Act, i.e. the right to a notice of the proposal for a scheme, copy of the draft scheme before the scheme is made, and the right to be heard at any public local inquiry.

Section 57 deals with " power to enforce scheme." If any question arises whether any building or work contravenes the scheme it is referred to the Ministry, which determine it as arbitrators.

Section 58 deals with " compensation in respect of property injuriously affected by scheme." Any person whose property is injuriously affected is entitled to compensation on making a claim within due time ; but not on account of any building erected, or contract made, after the date of the resolution of the local authority to prepare or adopt the scheme, or after certain other times—but see below.

Compensation.

If property is increased in value by the scheme the local authority may recover one half of the amount of the increase from its owner.

Any question on these points is to be determined by a single arbitrator appointed by the Ministry unless the parties otherwise agree. Compensation may be payable where a scheme is revoked.

By section 45 of the 1919 Act, the above was extended

to enable the Minister of Health to make an order permitting any proposed development to proceed pending the making and approval of the scheme, and where such permission has been given, the person concerned may be entitled to compensation on account of any building erected on, or contract made or other thing done with respect to, land included in a scheme after the date of the resolution of the local authority to prepare or adopt the scheme.

Section 59 deals with " exclusion or limitation of compensation in certain cases." No compensation is payable if the injurious affection would have resulted from by-laws made by the local authority ; or if the scheme prescribes the space about buildings or limits the number of buildings, or prescribes the height or character of buildings, if the Ministry consider the provisions reasonable. If a person is entitled to compensation under any other Act as well as under the present Act, he cannot get it twice, nor can he get greater compensation under this Act than under the other Act.

Acquisition of land.

Section 60 deals with " acquisition by local authorities of land comprised in a scheme," as to which reference should also be made to sections 12 and 15 of the 1919 Act, and section 10 of the 1919 (Additional Powers) Act. Land may be acquired voluntarily or (if authorised) compulsorily, subject to the same conditions as a local authority may acquire land for Part III purposes—see Chapter II.

Default.

By section 61 of the 1909 Act the Ministry, in case of default of local authority to make or execute a town-planning scheme, may hold a public local inquiry and make an order on the local authority, which it may enforce by mandamus. But extended powers in this direction are conferred on the Ministry by sections 46 and 47 of the 1919 Act, as already explained.

Sundry points.

By section 62 the Ministry may determine certain matters in dispute as arbitrators or otherwise ; by section 63 it may hold inquiries affecting town planning as under section 85 of the 1890 Act. By section 64 its " general provisions " have to be laid before Parliament. Section 65 defines " local authority " and deals with expenses and the borrowing of money. Section 66 deals with " application to London."

The new Town Planning Regulations have not been issued up to the time of printing this volume, but if available before binding will be found on page 739.

CHAPTER VI

The
statutory
provisions.

SECTION 19 of the Housing, Town Planning, &c., Act,
1919, provides that where a public utility society or a
housing trust, as defined by˙ section 40 thereof, has
submitted to the Local Government Board (now the
Minister of Health) an approved scheme for the provision
of houses for the working classes then, if the scheme is
carried out within a specified time (see page 99), the
Minister may contribute towards the cost of carrying
out the scheme. Section 18 gives powers to local authorities and county councils to promote and assist public
utility societies (not housing trusts), and section 20 provides that the Public Works Loan Commissioners may
make loans to such societies.

The sections above mentioned cover the provisions
affecting public utility societies and housing trusts now
in force in the Housing Acts, but there is an amendment
affecting finance made by section 4 of the Housing
(Additional Powers) Act, 1919.

Public
utility
societies.

A public utility society is essentially a co-operative
society. It is defined by section 40 of the Housing,
Town Planning, &c., Act, 1919, as " a society registered
under the Industrial and Provident Societies Acts, 1893
to 1913, the rules whereof prohibit the payment of any
interest or dividend at a rate exceeding 6 per cent. per
annum." (This dividend is non-cumulative.)

A society which may be registered under the Industrial and Provident Societies Acts (the Act under which

co-operative societies are registered) is defined by section 4
of the Industrial and Provident Societies Act, 1893, as
" a society for carrying on any industries, businesses or
trades specified in or authorised by its rules, whether
wholesale or retail, and including dealings of any description with land." The section also provides that no
member other than a registered society shall have or
claim any interest in the shares of the society exceeding
two hundred pounds ; but this is amended by section
18 (2) of the Housing, Town Planning, &c., Act, 1919,
which provides that where a local authority or county
council assist a public utility society under that subsection, the local authority or council shall not be prevented from having or claiming an interest in the shares
of the society exceeding two hundred pounds.

A public utility society must consist of at least seven The rules.
persons with a secretary. Application for registration
must be made to the Registrar of Friendly Societies,
17, North Audley Street, W.1, who provides forms for the
purpose. The application for registration must be signed
by seven members and the secretary, and must be accompanied by two printed copies of the rules. These rules
must cover provisions required by or under the Industrial
and Provident Societies Acts and sections 18 and 19 of
the Housing Town Planning, &c., Act, 1919.

Certain very useful organisations have drawn up
model rules which cover these provisions ; and these
organisations will supply copies and give all guidance
and help. Amongst them are the following :—

> The Garden Cities and Town Planning Association,
> 3 Gray's Inn Place, W.C. ;
> The Welsh Town Planning and Housing Trust,
> Ltd., 32 Park Place, Cardiff ; and
> The Agricultural Organisation Society, 40 Broad-
> way, S.W.1.

The rules of these organisations have a further advantage : the Registrar of Friendly Societies has the power

when model rules, accepted by him, are adopted, to reduce the registration fee from £5 to £1.

The rules and any amendment require the approval of the Minister of Health, and this should be obtained before the rules or amendments are submitted to the registrar.

The registration of a society renders it a body corporate, with perpetual succession and a common seal, and with limited liability.

Assistance by local authority. Under section 18 (2) of the 1919 Act, a local authority or county council, with the consent of, and subject to any regulations or conditions which may be made or imposed by, the Minister of Health, may :—

(a) Make grants or loans to the society ;

(b) Subscribe for any share or loan capital of the society ; or

(c) Guarantee or join in guaranteeing the payment of interest on money borrowed by the society or of any share or loan capital issued by the society ;

on such terms and conditions as to rate of interest and repayment or otherwise, and on such security, as the local authority or council think fit.

Any assistance which they may give to a public utility society will be outside the arrangement by which the financial obligations of the local authority under an assisted housing scheme are limited to a penny rate. In future years it may be found that the whole of the housing needs of a district can be suitably provided for by a public utility society, and in such cases the local authority would no doubt be willing to render financial assistance. In any case the local authority may be willing to take up a portion of the share capital of the society. By so doing they would secure a voice in the management of the society, and it may be expected that both the authority and society would welcome the measure of co-operation which would follow from the participation of the local authority in the society's affairs.

In some cases a public utility society may find it difficult to acquire a site at a reasonable cost. Under section 12 (2) of the Act of 1919, a local authority may assist the society by acquiring a site compulsorily and selling or leasing it to the society. Section 18 provides that where a society is desirous of erecting houses for the working classes which, in the opinion of the Minister of Health, are required, and the local authority of the area in which the houses are proposed to be built are unwilling to acquire land with a view to selling or leasing the same to the society, the county council may, on the application of the society, acquire the land and sell or lease it to the society.

Acquisition of land.

Under section 67 of the Housing of the Working Classes Act, 1890, as amended by section 4 of the Housing, Town Planning, &c., Act, 1909, the Public Works Loan Commissioners were empowered to make loans to public utility societies, for a period of forty years, up to two-thirds of the value (not cost) of the land or houses to be mortgaged. Under the 1919 Act the period for the maximum period for repayment is extended to fifty years, and loans may be made, during a period to be specified by the Minister of Health, with the consent of the Treasury, up to 75 per cent. of the cost of the land and houses.

Loans.

Advances of the loan may be made by instalments as the building progresses. The loans and advances may be made by the Commissioners, on the recommendation of the Minister, and it is important that the information which the Commissioners will require before deciding whether they can make a loan, should be forwarded to them at an early stage, and the society should obtain from the local Housing Commissioner, well in advance, a note of the information which the Loan Commissioners will require.

The State subsidy.

In addition to the loan, an annual subsidy may be paid by the Minister of Health to the public utility society during a maximum period of fifty years. The amount of the subsidy (see section 19 of the 1919 Act, as amended by section 4 of the Housing (Additional Powers) Act, 1919) will be equivalent, during the period ending on 31st March 1927, to 50 per cent. and thereafter to 30 per cent. of the loan charges (including interest and the payments for redemption of principal) on the whole of the capital borrowed under the approved scheme ; and for the purpose of the calculation of the amount of the subsidy it will be assumed that loan charges are payable on the annuity system (i.e. by equal half-yearly instalments of principal and interest combined) on the whole of the capital at the same rate as the charges fixed in the case of loans to public utility societies by the Public Works Loan Commissioners. It is immaterial for this purpose whether loans have in fact been made to the society by the Commissioners. This is an important point. A society may be able to borrow from others at a lower rate of interest than the State charges (see the Treasury Minute on page 536), but it will get its annual subsidy from the Minister of Health as though it had borrowed three-quarters of its capital from the State and were paying the full Government rate of interest.

The payment of the subsidy is conditional upon the society complying with the financial regulations (see page 650).

The State subsidy is an emergency measure due to the temporary disturbance of normal economic conditions, and it is not contemplated that housing should permanently be placed on a subsidised footing. The intention of the subsidy is to encourage building during the present emergency period, by placing the societies who build during this period in a not less favourable position than those who defer building until more normal conditions are established. Accordingly, the subsidy is available only for those who commence building forthwith. Article III of the 1919 Regulations (page 653) provides that financial assistance will cease (a) unless reasonable progress is made with carrying the scheme into effect within one year from the passing of the Act, and (b) in respect of any scheme, or part, not completed within three years from that date ; or, in each case, within such further period as the Minister may allow. The Act was passed on 31st July 1919.

The site, lay-out, house plans and cost of the scheme will be subject to the approval of the Ministry, and before the scheme is finally approved the society must submit a statement in Form D.107 (see page 657), showing the estimated income and expenditure under the scheme (Article IV of the 1919 Regulations). Professional charges must not exceed 5 per cent. of the total capital approved expenditure (Article V). The rents will be subject to the approval of the Ministry (Article VI). The plans must also be passed by the local authority in the usual way (under section 167 of the Public Health Act, 1875, and the by-laws), but the by-laws may be relaxed (see page 416).

Houses provided under an approved scheme must not be sold except on conditions laid down by the Ministry (Article VII). These conditions form the subject of the Sale of Houses Regulations, printed on page 663. Under them a tenant may buy his house outright, in which connection the provisions of the Small Dwellings Acquisition Act, 1899, as to loans from the local authority (see page 258), may be read. Or of course he can borrow (if necessary) from any other source. The alternative method of purchase by instalments, in addition to the rent, presents many practical difficulties, notably in regard to the custody of the instalments and the safeguarding of the interests of the tenant-purchaser in the possible event of the bankruptcy of the society, and is not recommended.

Sale of houses, &c.

Other points in the regulations. The accounts of the society will be subject to audit by the district auditor, in addition to the audit prescribed by the Industrial and Provident Societies Acts (Article VIII, page 654).

In the event of the dissolution of the society before the Exchequer subsidy has ceased to be payable, the State will be a creditor for the amount of the subsidies actually paid (Article IX). The society will be required to enter into an agreement to give effect to this regulation. A form of agreement for this purpose is obtainable from the Housing Commissioner.

The objects of the society must include the provision of houses for the working classes, and it is only the provision of working class houses (with the necessary land, street works, &c.) which will rank for the Government subsidy. The scheme may include larger houses, or such buildings as factories, shops, clubs, or places of worship, or additional land for the purpose of small holdings, but the additional expenditure for these purposes will not be subsidised by the Government. There is no statutory definition of "the working classes" which is applicable to housing by public utility societies, and it is intended that this term should be generously interpreted. Certain types of houses have, however, come to be regarded, by accepted usage, as working-class houses. Such types of houses are instanced in the *Manual on State-Aided Housing Schemes* (see page xiii), and the local housing commissioner will be prepared to advise as to the standard of accommodation which can be approved.

Societies may be formed for acquiring large empty houses and converting them into flats for the working classes. Where this is contemplated the promoters should refer to the *Manual on the Conversion of Houses into Flats for the Working Classes* (see page xiii).

Housing trusts. The expression "housing trust" is defined by section 40 of the Act of 1919 as "a corporation or body of persons which, by the terms of its constituent instrument, is required to devote the whole of its funds, including any surplus which may arise from its operations, to the provision of houses for persons the majority of whom are in fact members of the working classes, and to other purposes incidental thereto."

The definition is intended to apply mainly to trustees who have the administration of trust funds, and will not ordinarily require to borrow. Accordingly no provision is made for State assistance towards the capital expenditure, but an annual subsidy may be granted on the same terms as in the case of public utility societies. In other words it will be calculated as though the trust were a public utility society and had borrowed for the purposes of the approved scheme an amount equivalent to the trust funds used for those purposes. The subsidy will then be calculated as per the regulations, "The Housing Trusts (Financial Assistance) Regulations, 1919 and 1920"), printed on pages 669 and 673. These regulations contain many other matters of importance, and should be read.

Public utility societies are of comparatively recent introduction as far as housing purposes are concerned. Though recognised by the Act of 1890 and encouraged by the Act of 1909, it is only during the past ten or eleven years that they have had much construction to their credit. To some extent their rise has coincided with the decline in private enterprise. *General remarks on public utility societies.*

One hundred and six societies were in active operation before the war and at the date of the armistice. They had built rather less than 8,000 houses. Nevertheless, they were seen to be a new force, particularly at Letchworth, Bournville, Hampstead, &c. Better still, they were often possessed of ideals which promised much in the matter of improving the worker's house, its architecture, arrangement, and surroundings.

Though essentially co-operative associations, there was an element of commerce about them, within the limits of the legislation—in a few cases a strong element.

Their founders in some cases were working men wanting houses, and in other cases housing reformers; and occasionally a philanthropist or an employer of labour was interested in them.

It may here be mentioned that, in the past, quite a large number of houses have been built by co-operative societies, and that several of such societies, by a small addition to their rules, have become public utility societies, as the term is here used.

Private capital.

The money needed by the societies came from several sources: (1) the Public Works Loan Commissioners; (2) the tenants; (3) philanthropists; (4) employers; and (5) public companies and societies, which usually lent on mortgage but occasionally subscribed for loan stock. It is still intended that they should raise as much money as possible in this way, but the Public Works Loan Commissioners may lend up to the 75 per cent. of the cost, as already explained. If, in the opinion of these Commissioners, there is a special risk that it may at some future date, during the currency of the loan, be impossible to secure tenants for a large proportion of the houses, owing to changes in the industrial circumstances of the locality, it will be open to them to require collateral security. Though the loan from the Commissioners is the first charge on the premises, the money lent on mortgage or the loan stock can, by arrangement, rank first after the loan has been repaid to the Commissioners. Land and materials, subject to the valuation thereof being officially approved, can be subscribed for loan stock instead of cash. In the case of leaseholds the Ministry will accept terms of not less than sixty years, but prefers ninety-nine years.

Dr. Addison touched on some of the above points when moving the second reading of the Housing (Additional Powers) Bill. He said: "There has been already built a goodly number of houses by public utility societies on the experimental plan adopted in the early stages.

Some of them have very big enterprises in front of them, but they are nearly all, though not quite all, great employers of labour for great firms which must have the houses anyhow. They are iron companies, steel companies, engineering companies, and so forth, and they have frankly recognised that under the existing terms for public utility societies they will get very little or no return on their share of the capital. It was evident that, in order to bring in the aid of public utility societies and to make the best use of them, we must, at any rate for the first few years, improve the terms to them " (*Hansard*, 8th December 1919, cols. 563–4).

A special department was set up at the Ministry of Health to deal with public utility societies and housing trusts, and it has supplied, by means of circulars and the like, much useful information to them, while the Housing Commissioners and their staffs have been anxious to give assistance and advice. *Departmental help.*

The following is a list of the official publications dealing specially with public utility societies and housing trusts :

Cd. 9223.   Financial Assistance Committee : Interim Report.

S.R. & O., 1919, No. 1428.   The Public Utility Societies (Financial Assistance) Regulations, 1919, dated 6th October 1919.

S.R. & O., 1920, No. 134.   The Public Utility Societies (Financial Assistance) Regulations, 1919, dated 30th January 1920.

S.R. & O., 1920, No. 107.   The Public Utility Societies (Sale of Houses) Regulations, 1920, dated 28th January 1920.

S.R. & O., 1919, No. 1429.   The Housing Trusts (Financial Assistance) Regulations, 1919, dated 6th October 1919.

S.R. & O., 1920, No. 135.   The Housing Trusts (Financial Assistance) Regulations, 1920, dated 30th January 1920.

S.R. & O., 1920, No. 683. Housing Accounts Order (Societies and Trusts), 1920, dated 4th May 1920.

D. 107. Assisted Scheme (Public Utility Society) Statement of Estimated Annual Income and Expenditure.

D. 104a. General Housing Memorandum, No. 9a.

April 1919. Housing by Public Utility Societies, The Government proposals.

Cmd. 89. Financial Assistance to Public Utility Societies.

Cmd. 128. Financial Assistance to Public Utility Societies and Housing Trusts.

In addition the Ministry's fortnightly journal, *Housing*, and the valuable manuals and other documents have been available.

Another form of assistance took the form of the provision by the Government, at an early stage, of certain building materials and standardised fittings.

Some difficulties. It would, however, be idle to deny that public utility societies have had difficulties. In the initial stages, at least, there is a considerable amount of work falling upon committee men and other officers of such societies, in making the thousand and one arrangements which have to be made, including interviews with the Housing Commissioner, and the landowner, framing the rules, instructing the architect (the societies have been advised to employ architects), agreeing to the plans, and so forth. Not only so, the Ministry, through its Housing Commissioner, has had to go into many matters carefully so as to protect the interests of the taxpayer. The price provisionally agreed to with the landowner has possibly been found to be too high, when the valuation of the Inland Revenue District Valuer has come to hand. The plans have been wasteful, possibly, in some respects.

It may be added that the State allowance to public utility societies is larger than the subsidy to private builders—some one-third of the cost per house, against the maximum subsidy to the private builder of £260.

CHAPTER VII

THE HOUSING (ADDITIONAL POWERS) ACT, 1919

GENERAL SUMMARY

THE Housing (Additional Powers) Act, 1919, confers certain powers which supplement those contained in the Housing, Town Planning, &c., Act, 1919. The Government scheme, which was brought into force by the latter Act, inevitably threw a severe strain on the machinery of local government. By the new Act that machinery has been strengthened and relieved of a part of its burden.

Its most notable feature was that of authorising grants to private builders (averaging £250 per house) for the construction of houses. The houses must comply with the conditions prescribed by the Minister of Health (section 1) (see page 114) ; they must be in material accordance with the conditions approved in the case of local authorities' schemes ; they must comply with the local by-laws ; and they must be certified by the local authority or, on appeal, by the Minister of Health, to have been completed in a proper and workmanlike manner. Subject to this the builder has a very free hand, and there is no limitation as to the selling price or rent of the houses. The subsidy will be available only for building commenced within twelve months (or at most, in special cases, sixteen months) after the passing of the Act (23rd December 1919). Further information on this subject is given on pages 113 and 114. Grants to private builders.

The Act also provides for revised and improved terms to public utility societies. The annual subsidy of 30 per cent. (based on the loan charges on the borrowed capital) has been increased to 50 per cent. during the Improved terms to public utility societies, &c.

years ending 31st March 1927, after which date it will be 30 per cent. as before. The revised terms are also available for housing trusts and for county councils who wish to provide houses for their employees (section 4).

Luxury building.

One of the chief obstacles to the building of working-class houses by local authorities has been the diversion of the resources of the building trade into other channels. There are large arrears of repair work to be completed, but, apart from that, building works have been put in hand in many parts of the country, which are of less public importance, or of less urgency, than the building of houses. The Act enables a local authority to prohibit what is known as " luxury " building (section 5). This does not mean that useful commercial expansion is to be checked or hampered. The Regulations are printed on pages 684 and 694.

The demolition of dwelling-houses is prohibited in certain circumstances (section 6).

The above provisions are in force for two years from 23rd December 1921 (section 15).

Housing bonds, &c.

The Act also deals on a permanent basis with the issue of Housing Bonds, &c., by local authorities for the purpose of raising the necessary money for their housing schemes (section 7) ; with the acquisition of land for garden cities or town-planning schemes (section 10) ; and certain minor matters.

The Minister's explanation.

On 8th December 1919 Dr. Addison, Minister of Health, in moving the second reading of the Housing (Additional Powers) Bill, which had been introduced four days previously, said that it was still the fact that private persons would not build houses because there was not a reasonable chance of getting an economic return in the shape of a sufficient rent. Further, there was an abundance of remunerative repair work for builders. Therefore, a subsidy was essential to secure the assistance of private individuals and builders to relieve the present great shortage of houses.

Certain other concessions could be made to them in certain circumstances, notably as to the number of houses to the acre. Dr. Addison said: "We have allowed, in some cases, even under the [previous] Bill, in urban areas up to as many as twenty houses per acre, although we have been very reluctant to go above twelve" (*Hansard*, 8th December 1919, col. 559). The Minister said: "The private builder can build more cheaply than the local authority."

The subsidy to public utility societies was to be increased, as under the existing terms they could get very little or no return on their share of the capital.

It was necessary to check luxury building. The Minister had several cases where a person wanting to put up an extravagant building had offered 2*d.* and 3*d.* per hour more for building labour than the rate current in the district, and in one such case the number of bricklayers employed on a housing scheme went down from 162 to 42.

The proposal regarding housing bonds was intended to help local authorities to finance their own housing schemes by issuing bonds. The Minister was opposed to any suggestion that the Chancellor of the Exchequer should raise the money.

Discussing the clause providing for the acquisition of land for the purpose of garden cities and town-planning schemes by the Minister as agent for local authorities or authorised associations, Dr. Addison said that experience had shown that if housing was to be done with proper foresight a good many schemes of this character would have to be undertaken. The London County Council had recently acquired 3,000 acres on the north side of the Thames, to the east of the city; but in many cases the powers in the clause were necessary, as for instance in South Wales, where the proper thing was to have a grouping of authorities and to have residential quarters at the end of valleys with road communications towards the collieries, rather than perched in difficult positions on the hill-sides at great cost.

The subject of the difficulty experienced by some local authorities in raising the necessary money for their housing schemes, had been inquired into by the Treasury Committee on Housing Finance (Mr. W. H. N. Goschen, chairman), which in its interim report (Cmd. 444], dated 27th November 1919, recommended that mortgage loans of local authorities be constituted a trustee security, that they have power to issue local bonds as a trustee security, and that the onus of finding the capital necessary for housing remain on them. It also recommended that the local bonds should be accepted at their face value from people purchasing houses from the local authority, in which connection it may be noted that it was the policy of the Ministry to encourage people to own the houses in which they live.

The Government adopted these recommendations almost entirely, and incorporated the necessary provisions in the new Bill.

A Bill to extend the subsidy period and to strengthen the provisions affecting luxury building, is to be introduced in the first parliamentary session of 1921.

CHAPTER VIII

THE POSITION OF THE PRIVATE BUILDER

THE term " private " builder has latterly and popularly been used by way of distinction from the public body, e.g. the local authority. It means, the " speculative " builder; the " contract " builder; and the building-owner.

During the war, when the subject of the shortage of houses was officially enquired into (see the Report of the Tudor Walters' Committee, Cd. 9191), it was apparent that the local authorities would have to undertake to provide houses on a large scale. But at that early stage it was hoped that the private builder, or private enterprise, would also be made use of. The private builder, principally in mind in this connection, was the speculative builder, who, as principal, and on his own account, built houses with the object (primarily) of selling them at a profit. There was also the private person, who, though not a builder himself, engaged a builder to erect houses for him, usually on contract, such houses being intended either to be sold or to be let.

In the past more than 90 per cent. of working-class houses have been built by private enterprise, mostly by speculative builders. The usual plan has been for a builder to purchase an estate, or several sites according to the scale of his business, and to build a few houses at a time. He obtained temporary financial assistance from a bank, a solicitor, a builder's merchant, or a building society, and sold the houses as soon as possible after completion. It was essential to the continuance of

House-building before the war.

his business that he should have a ready sale, for only in this way could he turn over his capital. He almost always expected to make some profit on the retailing of the land, which he had usually purchased wholesale : in many cases he sold the houses at cost and made his profit by the creation of improved ground rents.

The subsidy question.

For some years before the war, conditions had been hardening against the private builder, and after the war he was not prepared to resume the building of houses for the working classes : apart from anything else, the cost of building had so greatly increased that there was hardly a possibility of getting an economic rent for any new houses, and so no profit would be obtained on such building. That indeed was the general trouble, and the Government had long foreseen, for this and other reasons, that the provision of such houses would have to be at least augmented by the efforts of local authorities, and would have to be subsidised.

Here a further trouble arose. There was at that time a very strong objection to subsidising a private individual, and when the Bill was introduced the grant of a sum of money to a private individual was not then attempted.

The Housing, Town Planning, &c., Act, 1919.

The Housing, Town Planning, &c., Act, 1919, does, however, contain provisions of interest to the private builder. It makes it possible for him to help in the provision of houses.

Section 12 (2) (a) empowers the local authority to acquire land and to "lease or sell it with a view to the erection thereon of houses for the working classes by persons other than the local authority." It can thus acquire, by compulsion if necessary, land which the private builder could not get, at a reasonable price. When, with the consent of the Minister of Health, the local authority so sells or leases the land, it will be under the condition that the private builder will erect and maintain thereon such number of houses suitable for the working classes as may be fixed by the local authority in accordance with plans approved by them (section 15 (1) (*b*)). The conveyance or lease must contain the necessary covenants for the above purposes and, limit the amount of rent which may be charged . . . and the local authority may contribute towards the expenses of the development of the land and the laying out and construction of streets thereon, subject to the condition that the streets are dedicated to the public (section 15 (2)).

But section 12 (3) is probably more attractive. It provides that subject to the conditions of the Minister of Health a local authority may agree to purchase or take on lease working-class houses whether built at the date of the agreement or intended to be built thereafter. *Builder may build houses for sale to the local authorities.*

There are advantages to the builder, to the local authority, and to the public in this provision. After the local authority have approved the site and general outline of the proposals, they can leave it to the contractor to obtain the official approvals necessary at the various stages (site, plans and cost), though they must maintain some supervision. The section also enables the local authority to utilise the services of small builders who will not be in a position to tender for big contracts, or who do not care for contract work under detailed specifications and quantities. In general, builders who know local conditions and requirements, and who prefer the fuller measure of elasticity in the private builder's arrangements—including the substitution of a different material or fitting (equally good and possibly better)— may be fully accommodated. Further, large contractors might run an arrangement of the kind under discussion, concurrently with their other operations.

The local authority may indicate the type of house, taking as instances the plans in the official *Manual on State-Aided Housing Schemes*, or other plans which have *The elasticity and freedom of the system.*

received official approval; or may agree to houses of the type which the builder has already built. The builder will agree to build accordingly at a certain cost per house. The local authority will apply to the Ministry for approval of the agreement, which should include a time limit for the completion of the houses, and on this being obtained the builder will proceed. Some further particulars are given in Circular 39 and Enclosure B therewith.

It may be said that this section 12 (3) is not of great value in view of the offer in the Housing (Additional Powers) Act, 1919, of a direct subsidy to the private builder. To some extent this is true, but whereas the latter subsidy is temporary, section 12 (3) is permanent. Many hundreds of houses have been built under the provisions of the section.

The contract builder pure and simple is also dealt with in Circular 39 and in Enclosure A therewith.

By-laws and other provisions of the 1919 Act. By section 23 of the 1919 Act bricks or building material acquired by a Government department may, until 31st July 1924, be sold, subject to conditions, to any person who undertakes to use them forthwith for the erection or improvement of working-class houses, at a price sufficient to cover the cost of replacement. This provision is perfectly general.

Section 24 provides, briefly, that the private builder is not bound by more restrictive by-laws than operate to affect the new schemes of the local authority. The said new schemes, when approved by the Minister of Health, supersede the local by-laws to any necessary extent.

The subject arises again under the Housing (Additional Powers) Act, 1919 (see the official document on page 119).

Section 25 makes further provision for the relaxation of building by-laws. Regulations have been made on the subject (see page 565).

But notwithstanding these provisions of the Housing, Town Planning, &c., Act, 1919, the speculative builder and the building owner did not come forward to any appreciable extent. The summer and autumn of 1919 passed, and it became clear that the provisions of this Act needed supplementing. Those who had knowledge of the difficulties and the preliminary work required, had not expected a great output of houses by the local authorities during 1919; but the private builder who had his sites already partly developed, and who was otherwise in a better position to make an early start, was apparently not attracted by the terms.

The Government, therefore, took the unusual step of offering a State subsidy to the private builder who built houses for the working classes. The Prime Minister addressed representatives of the Building Trades' Industrial Council on 16th December 1919, and explained the reasons. There was a feeling against subsidising the private man. It was only when they found that they could not get the houses that the Government were in a position to make an offer to the private builder. The delay was inevitable in order to convince the public that it was necessary to take a step never taken in the whole experience of this country. *The Housing (Additional Powers) Act, 1919.*

Legislation was necessary for this purpose, and the Housing (Additional Powers) Bill, 1919, was introduced and rapidly passed by Parliament, receiving the Royal Assent on 23rd December 1919. The Act is given in full on page 368, and a summary of it appears on page 105. The conditions, and a general explanation of the procedure, are given in the official document printed on the next page, and a free explanatory pamphlet—*How to Get a House of Your Own*—can be obtained from any Housing Commissioner, or from the Ministry of Health, Whitehall, S.W.1.

The private builder is affected by section 5 also, which deals with the prohibition of building operations in so far as they interfere with the provision of dwelling-houses ; or, more popularly, the section checks "luxury" building. The regulations made under the section are printed in full on pages 684 and 694.

GRANTS TO PRIVATE PERSONS OR BODIES OF PERSONS CONSTRUCTING HOUSES UNDER THE HOUSING (ADDITIONAL POWERS) ACT, 1919

1. Grants will be made by the Minister of Health under the Housing (Additional Powers) Act, 1919, to persons or bodies of persons who construct houses in accordance with the conditions set out below and who begin the construction of such houses within twelve months of the passing of the Act (viz. within twelve months of the 23rd of December 1919 [1]) and who complete the same within that period or such further period not exceeding four months as the Minister may in any special case allow. No grant can be made in the case of any house the construction of which was begun before the passing of the Act. The total amount of grants to be paid for the United Kingdom will not exceed £15,000,000, and should the number of applications received by the Minister give rise to the expectation that the total sum available for England and Wales will be exceeded, it will of course be necessary to take steps to secure that an undue proportion of the total amount is not distributed to a particular area.

2. The amount of grant payable in the case of houses the construction of which is begun on or after 1st April 1920, and completed within twelve months of the passing of the Act as above will be :—

    (a) In respect of houses containing two living-rooms (i.e. living-room and parlour) and three or four

---

[1] The period is to be extended for a further twelve months.

bedrooms and comprising not less than 920 feet superficial area—£260 per house.

(b) In respect of houses containing one living-room and three bedrooms, and comprising not less than 780 feet superficial area—£240 per house.

(c) In respect of houses containing one living-room and two bedrooms, and comprising not less than 700 feet superficial area—£230 per house.

In the case of one-storey cottages, or bungalows, the minimum superficial areas referred to in paragraphs (a), (b) and (c) above may be reduced by 70 feet super.

No grant will be made in respect of any house with more- than four bedrooms or which has a superficial area in excess of 1,400 feet.

The superficial area will be measured by taking the combined areas of both storeys measured within the external or containing walls of the house. A cellar shall not be taken into account, but any habitable accommodation provided as an attic must be included.

Subject to the express sanction of the Minister, grants will be available for houses built in flats of two or more storeys in height in areas where there is a demand for accommodation of this kind. Each flat which complies with the conditions as to superficial area and accommodation will be treated as one house. In calculating the superficial area, the minimum areas referred to in paragraphs (a), (b) and (c) may be reduced by 70 feet super, but the space occupied by a staircase shall be excluded.

The number of two-bedroom houses in any district in respect of which a grant will be made shall not, without the express sanction of the Minister, exceed 5 per cent. of the total number of houses for which grant will be payable.

If a form of construction is employed for which, in the case of a local authority's scheme, the Ministry of Health would not sanction a loan for a period exceeding forty years, the amount of grant per house will be reduced by one-third.

3.[1] In the case of any house begun within twelve months after the passing of the Act but not certified by the authorised officer of the local authority to have been completed fit for occupation (see Schedule III) within that period, no grant can be made unless the house is completed within sixteen months after the passing of the Act, and then only if the Minister in any special case allows such payment. If in such a case the Minister allows a grant, the grant (unless the Minister is satisfied that the failure to complete the house within twelve months after the passing of the Act is due to circumstances over which the person constructing the house had no control) will be proportionately reduced, i.e. :—

(a) If the house is completed in the thirteenth month after the passing of the Act, a reduction of one-twelfth of the appropriate figure in paragraph 2, above.

(b) If completed in the fourteenth month, a reduction of two-twelfths.

(c) If completed in the fifteenth month, a reduction of three-twelfths.

(d) If completed in the sixteenth month, a reduction of four-twelfths.

4. The planning of the houses must comply with Part I of Schedule I below. The construction of the houses must not fall below the standard prescribed under Parts II and III of Schedule I.

PROCEDURE WHICH MUST BE FOLLOWED BY PERSONS OR BODIES OF PERSONS APPLYING FOR GRANTS

5. Plans shall be submitted to the local authority of the district in which it is proposed to erect the house or houses, in the form required by the by-laws (if any)

[1] The periods mentioned in this paragraph are to be extended by twelve months.

in force with regard to new streets and buildings or by any local Act. In every case, whether by-laws are in force or not, there shall be submitted to the local authority by the person, or persons, proposing to construct the houses :—

   (*a*) a block plan in duplicate drawn to a scale of 1/500 showing the lay-out, roads and sewers ;

   (*b*) complete plans and sections in duplicate of the proposed house or houses drawn to a scale of not less than eight feet to one inch ;

   (*c*) where the houses are to be built of brick or stone, an undertaking in writing that the standard of construction will be in accordance with Part II of Schedule I or equivalent thereto ; and

   (*d*) where some other form of construction approved by the Ministry of Health is proposed, a description of the method to be adopted and an undertaking that the form of construction will be carried out strictly in the form approved by the Ministry and that the standard of construction will comply with the conditions in Part II of Schedule I so far as they are applicable.

6. On receipt of such plans and undertakings and descriptive note, the local authority shall cause them to be examined with all possible speed, and, subject to the compliance of the plans with the conditions set out in Schedule I, below, and with paragraph 2, above, shall issue a certificate (Certificate A) under the hand of their clerk, surveyor, or other duly authorised officer of the local authority, in the form set out in Schedule II, below, accompanied by one set of the plans and sections marked with their approval. If any dispute arises as to the approval of plans, number of houses per acre, or methods of construction, the question shall be referred to the Housing Commissioner of the region in which the houses are proposed to be erected for decision. Upon the application, however, of either party, the Commissioner

shall submit the question for the decision of the Minister.

7. When the houses have been completed the person or body of persons constructing the houses shall apply to the local authority of the district in which the houses have been erected for a certificate that they have been completed in a proper and workmanlike manner and the local authority shall at once cause the houses to be examined and, if satisfied, shall issue a certificate (Certificate B) under the hand of their clerk, surveyor, or other authorised officer in the form set out in Schedule III. If the local authority refuse or neglect to grant such a certificate appeal may be made to the Minister of Health, through the Housing Commissioner, who, if satisfied that the appeal is justified, will himself issue the certificate.

8. The local authority may require the applicant to give an undertaking in writing to pay to them, in respect of any expenses incurred by them in the examination of plans and other works involved, in connection with the applications, a fee not exceeding £3 3s. (three guineas) for each type of house for which separate plans are required, provided that where more than three houses are to be erected to the same plan a fee not exceeding £1 1s. (one guinea) per house may be charged. The fee will be payable after Certificate B has been issued.

9. When any person or body of persons constructing houses has received both the Certificates A and B referred to in paragraphs 6 and 7, above, he shall forward each of the original certificates, together with a written application made on the back of Certificate B for the sum of money to which he claims to be entitled, to the Secretary Ministry of Health, Whitehall, London, S.W.1.

10. The Minister when satisfied as to the correctness of the application will pay the amount due.

11. The local authority shall give a serial number to the Certificates A. and B. The certificates shall be issued in triplicate, one copy being sent to the Housing

Commissioner, and one copy being retained by the local authority.

12. No certificate shall be issued in respect of any house in respect of which any payment out of moneys provided by Parliament may be made under section 7 or section 19 of the Housing, Town Planning, &c., Act, 1919.

13. In the Administrative County of London the existing jurisdiction of the London County Council, the District Surveyors, the Common Council of the City and the Metropolitan Borough Councils with regard to buildings will remain in force in so far as such jurisdiction is not inconsistent with the conditions contained in Schedule I ; and consequently the existing procedure will remain unaltered as regards the submission of plans and other matters. Applications for Certificates A and B, accompanied by the plans and other particulars required under paragraph 5, should be made to the London County Council through the district surveyor of the district in which it is proposed to build, and these applications will be dealt with by the London County Council, who are the local authority for the Administrative County of London (including the City) for this purpose.

MINISTRY OF HEALTH,
   WHITEHALL, S.W.1.
   September 1920.

SCHEDULE I

CONDITIONS PRESCRIBED BY THE MINISTER OF HEALTH
AS TO THE PLANNING AND CONSTRUCTION OF HOUSES
IN RESPECT OF WHICH GRANTS MAY BE MADE UNDER
SECTION 1 OF THE HOUSING (ADDITIONAL POWERS)
ACT, 1919

In so far as the provisions of any building by-laws are inconsistent with the conditions in this Schedule, such provisions shall not apply in respect of houses which comply with these conditions but otherwise such provisions shall apply.

PART I—PLANNING

(a) *Number of houses per acre.* The number of houses per acre should not exceed eight in agricultural areas or twelve in other areas. On land partly developed, however, it will be within the discretion of the local authority to allow a larger number, provided that in no case shall the number of houses per acre exceed twelve in agricultural areas, or twenty in other areas, without the express authority of the Minister. In calculating the number of houses per acre each tenement will count as a house.

(b) The number of houses built in one continuous terrace shall not exceed eight, except with the approval of the local authority.

(c) *Height of rooms.* No house shall be approved which contains a living-room or a bedroom of a less height than 8 feet. In the case of a room partly in the roof, the height of 8 feet shall apply to not less than two-thirds of the area, and no height shall be less than 5 feet. The local authority shall not insist on a greater height than has been determined in the case of any house in their area comprised in an assisted scheme under the Housing, Town Planning, &c., Act, 1919, and approved by the Ministry of Health, and where no relaxation of the height prescribed by the by-laws (if any) in force has been made in the area of the local authority a greater height than 8 feet shall not be required.

(d) *Baths and w.cs.* No house to which a sufficient water supply and drainage is available shall be approved unless a bath and w.c. are provided. Where no drainage is available an earth-closet must be provided.

(e) It shall be open to the local authority, where it appears to them desirable, to approve proposals with regard to the level, width and construction of streets which do not comply in all respects with the building by-laws in force.

(f) It shall be open to the local authority, where it appears to them desirable, to permit the drainage of not more than fourteen houses in any one case by a common drain, without requiring separate intercepting traps and ventilation for each house.

PART II—CONSTRUCTION WHEN HOUSES ARE BUILT IN BRICK, STONE OR CONCRETE

Houses should comply with the standard of construction required by the following specification. It is intended, however, that the normal methods and materials which are customary in each particular district shall be adopted to the extent that such methods and materials do not fall below the standard hereby prescribed.

Specification

Foundations. The foundations are to be of sufficient depths to secure a firm bottom. Where in the opinion of the local authority the nature of the soil requires it, adequate foundations of concrete must be provided not less than 6 inches thick, 12 inches wider than the base of external and party walls, and 9 inches wider than internal walls. The concrete to be composed of one part of good Portland cement to not more than eight parts of good clean aggregate. Other suitable foundations which are approved by the Ministry can be used.

Surface concrete. Where in the opinion of the local authority the nature of the soil requires it, the whole site of the buildings should be covered with a bed of cement or other suitable concrete not less than 4 inches thick.

Drains. The drains, sanitary work, and plumbing are to be laid out and constructed to the approval of the local authority.

Bricks. All bricks are to be good, hard, well-burnt, common bricks ; facing bricks and particularly those below the damp course are to be such as will not scale or perish. Where London stocks can be obtained, approved grizzles or place bricks may be used for party walls and internal walls carrying no weight. Approved old bricks, where available, may also be used.

Mortar. Mortar is to be composed of one part of good lime and not more than three parts of sand, or of one part of Portland cement to four parts of sand.

Brickwork. No main external brick wall is to be less than 9 inches thick if solid, or if hollow than two 4½-inch brick walls with a 2-inch cavity and with galvanised iron ties, two at least for every superficial yard. Cavity walls may also be constructed 9 inches thick with bricks on edge having headers and stretchers alternating in each course. The external face of this wall must be rendered in cement or finished roughcast. In exposed situations, external solid walls must be rendered in cement or hydraulic lime or finished roughcast, or otherwise adequately protected. All division ground floor walls carrying upper floor joists are to be 4½-inch brick. The joints of all brickwork to be filled solid with mortar and well flushed up.

Stone walls. Stone walling may be substituted for brickwork, in which case it must be at least 12 inches in thickness.

Damp courses. Lay adequate damp courses the full thicknesses of all walls.

Other methods of wall construction. (1) Houses framed in hardwood constructed in accordance with the Ministry's specification for cottages of timber construction, and covered with hardwood weather-boarding of the specified scantling, hanging tiles, natural slates, or cement rendering not less than 1 inch thick. If the cement rendering is applied under pressure the framing may be of deal.

(2) Concrete houses must be either built to a special method of construction approved by the Ministry or in accordance with the Ministry's Standard Specification.

(3) In a cavity wall 4½-inch brickwork or 3-inch brick

on edge, built in cement mortar with adequate wall ties can be substituted for one of the concrete faces of cavity walls specified in the Ministry's Standard Concrete Specification.

(4) A solid wall may also be composed of two thicknesses of clinker slabs, with the space between filled in with poured concrete, the total thickness of the unplastered wall being not less than 8 inches. A wall built in this manner must be finished on the outside roughcast or rendered in cement.

(5) Reinforced concrete may be employed, provided it complies with the recognised practice in this type of construction, and is approved by the local authority.

(6) Solid ballast concrete walls 4 inches thick may be used for bungalows of one storey, and 6 inches for two storey cottages, provided that a cavity of at least 2 inches is left between the concrete and an inner or outer lining, and the cavity is ventilated top and bottom, with air spaces through the wall battens to prevent dry rot. In a timber-framed house brick nogging may be used where a 2-inch cavity is provided in accordance with the above.

Inner lining of walls and ceilings. Walls and ceilings of living-rooms and bedrooms should be either plaster or covered with fibrous plaster slabs, compressed sheeting, or framed panelling other than matchboarding.

Timber generally. All timber is to be sound, free from wrack or dead wood, and suitable for its purpose.

The timber for carcassing to be of suitable building quality, reasonably seasoned, and not inferior to good fourth Swedish classification. Equal qualities in Finnish or Russian timber, spruce, red pine, pitch pine, Oregon pine, British Columbia pine, or suitable home-grown timbers may be used.

The timber for joinery to be of suitable joinery quality, well seasoned and dry, and not inferior to good third Swedish or White Sea classification.

Floor joists. Wood floors to be constructed with joists spaced not more than 14 inches apart, and of the following scantlings, or with scantlings of equal strength :—

	Dimensions. Inches. Inches.
Length of bearing not exceeding 5 feet . .	4 × 2
,, ,, ,, 6 ,, . .	4½ × 2
,, 8 ,, . .	5½ × 2
,, 9 ,, . .	6 × 2
,, 10 ,, . .	6½ × 2
,, 11 ,, . .	7 × 2
,, 12 ,, . .	8 × 2

Trimmers and trimming joists are to be ½-inch thicker than the other joists. One row of herringbone strutting to be provided for bearings exceeding 8 feet.

Joists 6-inch by 2-inch can be allowed where the span does not exceed 10 feet, provided a row of 6-inch by 2-inch solid strutting is fixed across the centre of the span, and joists 7-inch by 2-inch can be accepted in lieu of 8-inch by 2-inch where the span does not exceed 12 feet, provided a row of 7-inch by 2-inch solid struttings is fixed across the centre of the span.

Roofs. The roofs to be constructed with rafters spaced not more than 14-inch apart and of the following scantlings or of equal area and suitable depths :—

	Dimensions. Inches. Inches.
Length of bearing not exceeding 5 feet . .	3 × 2
,, ,, ,, 6 ,, . .	3½ × 2
,, ,, ,, 7 ,, . .	4 × 2
,, ,, ,, 8 ,, . .	4½ × 2
,, ,, ,, 9 ,, . .	5 × 2

Where necessary, suitable purlins, hips and valleys to be provided.

These scantlings may be reduced where the minimum sizes specified in the local authority's by-laws allow of such reduction.

Roof coverings. Roofs to be covered with tiles, slates or other suitable fire-resisting material.

Thatch will be accepted subject to compliance with the conditions contained in the Ministry's (Temporary Relaxation of Building By-Laws) Regulations, 1920.

Rendering. The faces of brickwork or walling over smoke flues passing through floors, ceilings, and in roof spaces, to be roughly rendered with cement mortar.

Footings. Footings need not be required at the base of the wall where the building is not more than two storeys high, exclusive of attics, provided that the wall rests upon a layer of cement or other suitable concrete of sufficient thickness and strength laid on the solid ground, or some other solid and sufficient foundation.

Eaves gutters. Eaves gutters are to be cast-iron, the joints made in red lead and bolted, fixed on suitable brackets, or screwed to rafters, or fascias. Compressed asbestos gutters, not less than $\frac{3}{8}$-inch in thickness, painted or coated in pitch on the inside, or properly framed wood gutters not less than 1-inch thick, coated with pitch on the inside, may be used as an alternative.

Fall pipes. All the fall pipes are to be cast-iron or compressed cement asbestos not less than $\frac{3}{8}$-inch thick, or framed up in wood not less than 1 inch in thickness and coated with pitch on the inside.

Soil pipes. All the soil and ventilating pipes to be $3\frac{1}{2}$-inch cast-iron, dipped in Dr. Angus Smith's solution, the joints caulked and run with lead.

PART III—OTHER FORMS OF CONSTRUCTION

(*a*) Grants will also be payable in respect of houses built in accordance with any special form of construction approved by the Ministry of Health and notified as approved in the journal *Housing.*

(*b*) Where a special form of construction including houses built of wood is adopted it must be carried out strictly in the form approved by the Minister and must comply with the conditions in Part II of this Schedule so far as they are applicable.

(c) Houses of timber construction must comply with the Ministry's Standard Specification for Cottages of Timber Construction, so far as the framing and covering are concerned and otherwise with the Specification in Part II of this Schedule.

(Old sound material may be re-used if the scantlings are equal to those described in the above-mentioned specification.)

SCHEDULE II

CERTIFICATE A

To be prepared in triplicate—one copy to be sent at once to the Housing Commissioner

CERTIFICATE OF APPROVAL OF PROPOSALS TO CONSTRUCT HOUSES UNDER SECTION 1 OF THE HOUSING (ADDITIONAL POWERS) ACT, 1919

Note.—This certificate must be carefully preserved by the person or body of persons to whom it is granted, and must be sent to the Ministry of Health (to be retained by them) together with the first Certificate B issued in respect of the houses certified therein.

To.................   Certificate No........

of.........................

This is to certify that the   council have approved the block plans and sections and the method of construction submitted to them on   , 19 , by   of   in respect of the houses described below.

And that the said plans and sections and method of construction comply with the conditions prescribed by the Minister of Health as to the planning and construction of houses, in respect of which grants may be made under section 1 of the Housing (Additional Powers) Act, 1919, and are in material accordance with the conditions as to the number of houses per acre and the standards of structural stability and sanitation approved by the Minister in the case of schemes by local authorities.

And that the method of construction—
is a method which has been approved by the Minister [1]
has been approved by the Housing Commissioner [1]

And that, subject to the conditions set out below,
the person or body of persons named above will be
eligible for the grants which the Minister of Health
may make under section 1 of the Housing (Additional
Powers) Act, 1919.

2 Locality and Description.	Number of Houses.	Accommodation provided (per house).		Floor Space.	3 Method of Construction.	Grant for which eligible (per house).
		Living-rooms.	Bed-rooms.			£ s. d.

The conditions referred to above are as follows :—

(a) The houses when completed must be certified by
the said council or, on appeal, by the Minister
of Health to have been completed in a proper
and workmanlike manner.

(b) If the houses are not completed, fit for occupation,
within twelve months of the 23rd December 1919,
no grant will be payable unless the Minister of
Health in any special case allows a further period
not exceeding four months, and in such case the
amount of the grant may be proportionately reduced in the manner prescribed by the Minister.

[1] Strike out the alternative which is inapplicable. Methods approved
by the Minister include brick and stone, and forms of construction which
have been notified as approved in the official journal *Housing*.

[2] The locality and description must be sufficient for identification.

[3] e.g. brick, concrete, wood, or any approved method of construction.
If available, the trade name of the method should be given.

(c) The houses to which this certificate refers shall be open to inspection at any time before the grant is paid by any duly authorised officer of the local authority or of the Minister of Health.

Given under my hand this   day of   , 1920.

Signed ....

Clerk to the

Surveyor to the   }¹.........council.

Authorised officer of the

SCHEDULE III

CERTIFICATE B

To be prepared in triplicate—one copy being sent at once to the Housing Commissioner

CERTIFICATE THAT HOUSES CONSTRUCTED UNDER SECTION 1 OF THE HOUSING (ADDITIONAL POWERS) ACT, 1919, HAVE BEEN COMPLETED IN A PROPER AND WORKMANLIKE MANNER.

Certificate No........

Note.—This certificate must be carefully preserved by the person or body of persons to whom it is granted, and must be sent to the Ministry of Health in support of any claim for grant that may be made after the issue of this certificate.

To....................

of.............................

This is to certify that the following houses comprised in Certificate A numbered........which was granted on ....1920, by the...............council, have been completed fit for occupation in a proper and workmanlike manner, and in accordance with the particulars given in Certificate A.

And that they were commenced and completed on the dates set opposite to each of them below.

And that the houses as completed comply with the

¹ Strike out inappropriate words.

conditions prescribed by the Minister of Health under the above Act.

1 Locality and Description of Houses.	No.	Particulars of Houses.	Floor Space.	Date of Commencement.	Date of Completion.	Amount of Stock.

Given under my hand this........day of.........\....1920.

Signed......................:........

Clerk to the ⎫

Surveyor to the ⎬ [2].............council.

Authorised officer of the ⎭

If this certificate does not include all the houses comprised in the Certificate A referred to, this should be clearly stated.

CLAIM FOR GRANT

To the Secretary,

Ministry of Health,

Whitehall, London, S.W.1.

$\dfrac{\text{I,}}{\text{We,}}$ being the $\dfrac{\text{person}}{\text{body of persons}}$ to whom the above certificate has been granted, hereby make application for payment of grant(s) amounting to £........claimed by $\dfrac{\text{me}}{\text{us}}$ under the Housing (Additional Powers) Act, 1919, in respect of the houses covered by the above certificate.

Signature.............................

Address ....

Date............

1 The locality and description must be sufficient for identification.

2 Strike out inappropriate words.

9

SCHEDULE IV

Form of notification of Certificates $\frac{A}{B}$ granted by the

.................council relative to the construction of houses under section 1 of the Housing (Additional Powers) Act, 1919.

To the Secretary,   Notification No......

  Ministry of Health,

    Whitehall, London, S.W.1.

I beg to notify that (so many) Certificates $\frac{A}{B}$ particulars of which are given below, have been granted by the above-named council during the $\frac{\text{month}}{\text{week}}$ ended

.....................1920

    Signed....................

     Clerk to................council.

Date...................

Particulars of Certificates issued

(1)	(2)	(3)	(4)	(5)	(6)	(7)	(8)
Class of Certificate. (A or B).	Serial No.	Person or body of persons to whom is sued.	Locality and description of houses.	No. of Houses of type specified in Col. (6).	Type of house, e.g. 2 L.R., 3 B.R.	Grant for which eligible.	Date of completion.
						(Certificate A only.)	(Certificate B only.)	

Note :—

 (a) A separate form must be furnished in respect of each class of certificate.

(b) The information in col. (4) must be sufficient for identification..

(c) Notifications as to certificates A should be furnished monthly, and as to certificates B weekly.

(d) Nil returns need not be furnished, but notifications should be numbered consecutively.

SUPPLY OF GOVERNMENT BUILDING MATERIALS TO PRIVATE PERSONS

Arrangements have been made under which persons building houses for the working classes will be enabled to obtain building materials through the Director of Building Materials Supply who is already supplying materials required for State-aided schemes. The following conditions will apply :—

A certificate must be obtained from the clerk of the local authority or the Housing Commissioner of the Ministry of Health in whose district the houses are to be erected to the effect that :—

(a) The material is required for the purpose of erecting or improving houses for the working classes ;

(b) The development, design and construction are such as, having regard to the standards laid down by the Ministry of Health, the local authority or Commissioner approve :

(c) The houses proposed to be erected are needed and the provision of the same in the manner proposed will, to that extent, relieve the programme of building by the local authority.

It will be a condition of the contract of sale that the purchaser enters into a written undertaking to use the materials forthwith for the sole purpose of erecting or improving houses for the working classes.

Application for the purchase of building materials should be made to the Director of Building Materials Supply, Ministry of Health, Imperial House, Tothill Street, Westminster, S.W.1, who will supply particulars and copies of the certificate and undertaking required.

It is anticipated that the above arrangements will enable builders to effect a saving of 5 per cent. on their materials.

The above sets out the conditions prescribed by the Ministry of Health with the consent of the Treasury under section 23 of the Housing, Town Planning, &c., Act, 1919. The form of certificate should be obtained by the applicant from the Director of Building Materials Supply.

HOUSING OF THE WORKING CLASSES ACT, 1890
[53 & 54 Vict. Ch. 70.]
ARRANGEMENT OF SECTIONS

133

PART III.—WORKING CLASS LODGING HOUSES

PART IV.—SUPPLEMENTAL

Service of notice, &c. on the local authority—88. Prohibition on S. 1 (90).
persons interested voting as members of local authority—89. Penalty
for obstructing the execution of Act—90. Punishment of offences
and recovery of fines—91. Powers of Act to be cumulative
—92. Definition of local authority, districts, local rate—93.
Definitions : " Land."   " Sanitary district."   " Sanitary authority."
" Urban and rural sanitary authority."   " Contributory place."
" Superior court."   " County of London."

Part V.—Application of Act to Scotland

§ 94. Modification as respects reference to Scotch Acts—95. Modifications as regards legal proceedings in Scotland—96. Miscellaneous
modifications—97. Provision as to superior of lands for purpose of
Part II.

Part VI.—Application of Act to Ireland

§ 98. Modification in application of Act to Ireland—99. Adoption
of Part III of Act by town commissioners of small towns in Ireland
—100. Incorporation of sections of 10 & 11 Vict. c. 16. for purposes
of Part III of Act—101. Power of making byelaws for labourers
dwellings in Ireland.

Part VII.—Repeal and Temporary Provisions

§ 102. Repeal of Acts—103. Temporary provisions.
Schedules.

*An Act to consolidate and amend the Acts relating to
Artizans and Labourers Dwellings and the Housing
of the Working Classes.*   [18th August 1890.]

Be it enacted by the Queen's most Excellent Majesty,
by and with the advice and consent of the Lords Spiritual
and Temporal, and Commons, in this present Parliament
assembled, and by the authority of the same, as follows :

1. This Act may be cited as the Housing of the Working   Short title
Classes Act, 1890.   of Act.

This Act has been amended by the other Acts given
in this volume, and throughout the amending Acts it
is referred to as the principal Act (see page 2 for further
notes). It is deemed to include any provisions of the
1909 and 1919 Acts which supersede or amend its provisions (section 47 (1) of the 1909 Act and section 40
of the 1919 Act).

S. 2 (90).

PART I

UNHEALTHY AREAS

Definitions.   2. In this part of this Act—

The expression " this part of this Act " includes any confirming Act, and

The expression " the Acts relating to nuisances " means—

> as respects the county of London and city of London, the Nuisances Removal Acts as defined by the Sanitary Act, 1866, and any Act amending these Acts ; and

29 & 30 Vict.
C, 90. s. 14.

> as respects any urban sanitary district in England, the Public Health Acts ;

and in the case of any of the above-mentioned areas, includes any local Act which contains any provisions with respect to nuisances in that area.

Confirming Act. A confirming Act is not now necessary (see notes to section 8 hereof).

The Nuisances Removal Acts were repealed and consolidated by the Public Health (London) Act, 1891, which with its amending Acts must be regarded as here substituted.

Urban Sanitary District. This part of this Act does not apply to rural districts (see section 3).

Public Health Acts. See the Short Titles Act, 1896, and the Public Health (Ports) Act, 1896, the Public Health Act, 1896, the Public Health Act, 1904, the Public Health Acts Amendment Act, 1907, the Public Health Act, 1908, and the Public Health (Prevention and Treatment of Disease) Act, 1913.

For other definitions see Index, and note the definition of " street " by section 48 of the 1909 Act.

Application of Part I of Act,   3. This part of this Act shall not apply to rural sanitary districts,

Now called "rural districts"—see the Local Govern- S. 3 (90).
ment Act, 1894, section 21 (2).

Scheme by Local Authority

4. Where an official representation as herein-after Local
authority
on being
satisfied by
official repre-
sentation of
the un-
healthiness
of district
to make
scheme for
its improve-
ment. mentioned is made to the local authority that within a certain area in the district of such authority either—

    (a) any houses, courts, or alleys are unfit for human habitation, or

    (b) the narrowness, closeness, and bad arrangement, or the bad condition of the streets and houses or groups of houses within such area, or the want of light, air, ventilation, or proper conveniences, or any other sanitary defects, or one or more of such causes, are dangerous or injurious to the health of the inhabitants either of the buildings in the said area or of the neighbouring buildings ;

and * that the most satisfactory method of dealing with the evils connected with such houses, courts, or alleys, and the sanitary defects in such area is an improvement scheme for the re-arrangement and reconstruction of the streets and houses within such area, or of some of such streets or houses, the local authority shall take such representation into their consideration, and if satisfied of the truth thereof, and of the sufficiency of their re-sources, shall pass a resolution to the effect that such area is an unhealthy area, and that an improvement scheme ought to be made in respect of such area, and after passing such resolution they shall forthwith proceed to make a scheme for the improvement of such area.

Provided always, that any number of such areas may be included in one improvement scheme.

* As altered by the Housing, Town Planning, &c., Act, 1909, section 22,

As herein-after mentioned. See the next section, and section 16.

Local Authority. See page 234. As to joint action by local authorities, see section 38 of the 1909 Act, page 317 ; and as to committees appointed by local authorities for purposes of the Housing Acts—see section 81 hereof, page 225.

Street includes court, alley, street, square or row of houses—see section 29 hereof and section 48 of the 1909 Act.

Improvement Scheme. As to requisites of scheme— see section 6 hereof. As to London—see sections 72 and 73 hereof. Schemes under Part I are improvement schemes, under Part II reconstruction schemes.

Sufficiency of their resources. Until 1922 at the earliest there will be little or no point in these words, inasmuch as if the improvement scheme provides for rehousing, as it usually will do (sections 6 (1) (c) and 11), the local authority will have no further burden in respect of it than a 1d. rate—see section 7 of the 1919 Act—but before incurring any expenditure they must obtain the consent of the Minister of Health if they desire to obtain the State financial assistance.

Generally. There is no statutory form of official representation, but a form suggested by the Ministry, a form of resolution of the local authority, and further useful information prepared by the Ministry, are given on pages 580 to 588, etc.

The official representation must be in writing—section 79 (2) hereof. It should follow the exact words of this (amended) section as far as they apply to the particular case, and the medical officer should furnish the local authority with sufficient facts to enable the members properly to consider the representation.

If satisfied of the truth of the representation the local authority must pass a resolution and forthwith make a scheme. As to default—see section 10 hereof, section 4 (1) of the 1903 Act, section 11 of the 1909 Act, and section 5 of the 1919 Act. The latter which empowers the Ministry to permit the county council to act, or to act itself, at the expense of the local authority will, doubtless, be the most useful. As to county districts— see section 6 of the 1919 Act.

A member of the local authority cannot vote upon

the resolution if it relates to any dwelling house, building S. 4 (90). or land in which he is beneficially interested—section 88 hereof.

As to representation made to the London County Council —see sections 72 and 73 hereof.

It should be noted that schemes under Part I (unhealthy areas) are larger in scope than those under Part II (unhealthy dwelling houses).

It should also be noted that the representation is to certify that an improvement scheme is the most satisfactory method of dealing with the evils—not the only method. An amendment to this effect was made by section 22 of the 1909 Act.

Before preparing a scheme relating to land within half a mile of a royal park or palace, or two miles of Windsor Parks or Castle, the local authority must communicate with the Commissioners of Works—see section 74 of the 1909 Act and notes thereto. See also sections 8, 45 and 73 thereof as to donations of land, ancient monuments, &c., and commons, open spaces and allotments.

Under section 13 of the 1919 Act there is power to acquire in advance lands in areas proposed for inclusion in improvement schemes, after a resolution has been passed under the present section.

The Minister has power to require reports as to the exercise of a local authority's powers—section 37 of the 1909 Act, and section 6 of the 1919 Act.

See section 17 of the 1909 Act as to the duty of a local authority to cause to be made from time to time inspection of their district.

5. (1.) An official representation for the purposes of Official representation, this part of this Act shall mean a representation made by whom to to the local authority by the medical officer of health be made. of that authority, and in London made either by such officer or by any medical officer of health in London.

(2.) A medical officer of health shall make such representation whenever he sees cause to make the same; and if * any justice * of the peace acting within the district for which he acts as medical officer of health, or * six

* As altered by the Housing, Town Planning, &c., Act, 1919, 2nd schedule.

S. 5 (90). or more persons liable to be rated to the local rate complain to him of the unhealthiness of any area within
such district, it shall be the duty of the medical officer
of health forthwith to inspect such area, and to make
an official representation stating the facts of the case,
and whether in his opinion the said area or any part
thereof is an unhealthy area or is not an unhealthy
area.

> *Official Representation.* See general note to section 4
> hereof. It includes also the representation under section
> 16 hereof.
> *Medical Officer.* Including one acting temporarily—
> sections 26 and 79 (1) hereof. As to his power to enter
> premises—see section 36 of the 1909 Act. In case of
> complaint he must forthwith inspect (and report), even
> though well-acquainted with the area. In case of his
> default or of a representation adverse to the complainants,
> they may appeal to the Ministry, which may send an
> inspector—see section 16 hereof. Before amendment by
> the 1919 Act, the complaint was to be made by *two* or
> more justices or *twelve* or more local ratepayers. Any
> six or more ratepayers may appeal (not necessarily the
> same six as make the original complaint)—section 4 (2)
> 1903 Act.

Requisites
of improve-
ment scheme
of local
authority.

6. (1.) The improvement scheme of a local authority shall
be accompanied by maps, particulars, and estimates, and

(a) may exclude any part of the area in respect of
which an official representation is made, or include
any neighbouring lands, if the local authority are
of opinion that such exclusion is expedient or inclusion is necessary for making their scheme
efficient * ; and

(b) may provide for widening any existing approaches
to the unhealthy area or otherwise for opening out

* As altered by the Housing, Town Planning, &c., Act, 1919, section
23.

the same for the purposes of ventilation or health ; S. 6 (90).
and

(c) shall provide such dwelling accommodation, if any, for the working classes displaced by the scheme as is required to comply with this Act ; and

(d) shall provide for proper sanitary arrangements * ; and

(e) may provide for any other matter (including the closing and diversion of highways) for which it seems expedient to make provision with a view to the improvement of the area or the general efficiency of the scheme.

(2.) The scheme shall distinguish the lands proposed to be taken compulsorily.

(3.) The scheme may also provide for the scheme or any part thereof being carried out and effected by † any person having such interest in any property comprised in the scheme as may be sufficient to enable him to carry out and effect the same, under the superintendence and control of the local authority, and upon such terms and conditions to be embodied in the scheme as may be agreed upon between the local authority and such person.

Scheme . . . Maps, particulars, and estimates. See the suggestions of the Ministry, printed on pages 580 to 588. By section 36 of the 1909 Act, there is power to enter the premises for the purpose of survey and valuation.

Scheme efficient. Following these words in the Act before amendment were the words " for sanitary purposes." It follows that the exclusion or inclusion may be made to secure the efficiency from any point of view.

---

* As altered by the Housing, Town Planning, &c., Act, 1909, section 23.

† As altered by the Housing, Town Planning, &c., Act, 1919, 2nd schedule.

S. 6 (90).

But land which does not carry insanitary houses, does not suffer the liability to a reduced rate of compensation, on compulsory acquisition, set out in section 9 of the 1919 Act. In other words the compensation for neighbouring lands is on a different basis ; and for this reason (amongst others) the scheme should clearly indicate the "neighbouring lands." Formerly there was here a considerable difficulty often leading to much opposition and expense. The Acquisition of Land (Assessment of Compensation) Act, 1919, has lessened this, but it is still necessary to proceed with caution.

Taken Compulsorily. See note to section 8 (5) below.

Working Classes Displaced. See sections 11 (2) and 12 (3) hereof, and section 3 of the 1903 Act.

Generally. With the consent of the owners of any right or easement which would be extinguished under section 22 hereof, clauses may be inserted, in the scheme for modifications, &c., in its application to the right or easement—section 27 of the 1909 Act.

Paragraph (e) was added by section 23 of the 1909 Act. In subsection (3) the words printed after " effected by " were, by the 2nd schedule to the 1919 Act, substituted for the words " the person entitled to the first estate of freehold in any property comprised in the scheme or with the concurrence of such person "—in which connection sections 26 and 28 of the 1919 Act should be read. Section 12 (6) hereof also deals with any person having a sufficient interest in the land, carrying the improvement scheme into effect, but in that subsection there is no mention of the superintendence and control of the local authority, whereas under the present subsection, whether the scheme is effected by that person, or with his concurrence, there is such superintendence and control.

Confirmation of Scheme

Publication of notices.

7. Upon the completion of an improvement scheme the local authority shall* forthwith—

(a) publish,* in a newspaper circulating within the district of the local authority, an advertisement

---

* As altered by the Housing, Town Planning, &c., Act, 1919, 2nd schedule.

stating the fact of a scheme having been made, the S. 7 (90).
limits of the area comprised therein, and naming
a place within such area or in the vicinity thereof
where a copy of the scheme may be seen at all
reasonable hours ; and

(b) *serve a notice on every owner or reputed owner, Services of
lessee or reputed lessee, and occupier, except tenants notices.
for a month or a less period than a month, of any
lands proposed to be taken compulsorily, so far as
such persons can reasonably be ascertained, stating
that such lands are proposed to be taken compulsorily for the purpose of an improvement scheme,
and in the case of any owner or reputed owner,
lessee or reputed lessee, requiring an answer stating
whether the person so served dissents or not in
respect of taking such lands ;

(c) Such notice shall be served—

(i) by delivery of the same personally to the person
required to be served, or if such person is absent
abroad, or cannot be found, to his agent, or if
no agent can be found, then by leaving the
same on the premises ; or,

(ii) by leaving the same at the usual or last known
place of abode of such person as aforesaid ; or,

(iii) by post addressed to the usual or last known
place of abode of such person.

(d) One notice addressed to the occupier or occupiers
without naming him or them, and left at any house,
shall be deemed to be a notice served on the occupier
or on all the occupiers of any such house.

Advertisements . . . Notices. For forms, see pages 586
to 588. The Ministry has power to prescribe them,

* As altered by the Housing, Town Planning, &c., Act, 1919, 2nd schedule.

and to dispense with them—section 41 of the 1909 Act. The notices must be signed by the clerk, &c.—section 86 (2) hereof. The notice does not affect the right of an owner as against adjoining owners who injure his easements—*Dye v. Patman* 62 J.P. 135.

Owner . . . There is no definition in this part of this Act.

Occupier . . . The words "except tenants for a month or a less period than a month" were added by the 1919 Act—see also the added *proviso* to section 12 (1) hereof—the effect being that such tenants will not have to be bought out.

Lands proposed to be taken compulsorily. It is only in respect of such lands that notice has to be served. By section 93 hereof, "land" includes any right over land, but following the principle of *Swainston v. Finn* [1883] 48 L.T. (N.S.) 634, *Badham v. Marris* [1882] 45 L.T. (N.S.) 579, and *Bedford v. Dawson* [1875] L.R. 30 Eq. 353, it would appear that notice need not be served on the owner of any such right. See also section 22 hereof and note thereto.

Requiring an answer. An answer need not be required from an occupier. There is no period fixed by the Act in which the answer should be given, and it does not appear that any detriment follows if no answer is given. The names of those who have dissented must accompany the petition—section 8 (2).

Generally. The amendments in the section have eased and quickened the procedure.

As to improvements made in the premises after publication of the advertisement—see section 21 hereof.

If the local authority changes its mind after advertisement and notice it is apparently not bound to take the land, but, at least, when the scheme has been confirmed—section 12 (1)—it must do so. On this point, however, it should be noted that any particular land might be excluded from the scheme by a modification thereof under section 15, and it does not appear that the owner would have any remedy.

The Ministry require evidence of service of notices, &c.—section 8 (2), and see page 589. Service would appear to be good although the owner is known to have left the place—*re Follick* 97 L.T. 645. Service by post shall be deemed to be effected by properly addressing, prepaying and posting a letter containing the document, and, unless the contrary is proved, to have been effected at the time at which the letter would be delivered in the ordinary course of post—Interpretation Act, 1889, section 26. Prepayment must be proved—*Walthamstow U.D.C. v. Henwood* [1897] 1 Ch. 41.

8. (1.) Upon compliance with the foregoing provisions with respect to the publication of an advertisement and the service of notices, the local authority shall present a petition,* to the Local Government Board, praying that an order may be made confirming such scheme.

Making and confirmation of provisional order.

Foregoing Provisions. See section 7 and notes thereto.
Petition. See page 589, where the general instructions are given.

(2.) The petition shall be accompanied by a copy of the scheme, and shall state the names of the owners or reputed owners, lessees or reputed lessees, who have dissented in respect of the taking their lands, and shall be supported by such evidence as the * Local Government Board * (in this part of this Act referred to as the confirming authority), may from time to time require.

Confirming Authority. Now the Ministry of Health, for England and Wales ; the Scottish Board of Health, for Scotland ; and the Irish Local Government Board, for Ireland.

(3.) If, on consideration of the petition and on proof of the publication of the proper advertisements and the service of the proper notices, the confirming authority think fit to proceed with the case, they shall direct a local inquiry to be held in, or in the vicinity of, the area comprised in the scheme, for the purpose of ascertaining the correctness of the official representation

* Words here omitted were repealed by the Statute Law Revision Act, 1908.

10

made as to the area and the sufficiency of the scheme provided for its improvement, and any local objections to be made to such scheme.

Local Inquiry. See section 85 hereof. Subsection (8) below also deals with costs.

Sufficiency of the Scheme. See page 137. As to persons displaced, see section 11 hereof.

(4.) After receiving the report made upon such inquiry, the confirming authority may make a provisional order declaring the limits of the area comprised in the scheme and authorising such scheme to be carried into execution.

Provisional Order. The order is no longer provisional, except in the rare case where section 73 of the 1909 Act applies. It does not require confirmation by Parliament—see section 24 of the 1909 Act and note thereto. Such an order cannot be renewed by the High Court—*Ex parte Ringer* [1909] 73 J.P. 436.

(5.) Such provisional order may be made either absolutely or with such conditions and modifications of the scheme as the confirming authority may think fit, so that no addition be made to the lands proposed in the scheme to be taken compulsorily, and it shall be the duty of the local authority to serve a notice * of any provisional order so made in the manner and upon the persons in which and upon whom notices in respect of lands proposed to be taken compulsorily are required by this part of this Act to be served.*

Modifications. Section 15 also deals with modifications but those are after the scheme has been confirmed. The modifications here dealt with are those shown to be necessary or desirable as the result of the local inquiry, e.g. the inclusion of certain lands as " neighbouring " rather than as " unhealthy " (section 6).

Taken Compulsorily. See section 6 (2). The order

* As altered by the Housing, Town Planning, &c., Act, 1919, 2nd schedule.

cannot add to the lands proposed to be taken com- S. 8 (90).
pulsorily, so that in framing its scheme the local authority
must be careful in coming to a decision.

Notice. Formerly it was necessary to serve a *copy*
of the order, which is usually of a lengthy character.

Required to be served. See section 7 hereof. The
words " except tenants for a month or a less period than
a month " originally appeared at the end of this subsection—see section 7 (*b*) hereof.

(6.) *Repealed by the Housing, Town Planning, &c.,
Act,* 1909.

This repealed subsection required provisional orders
to be confirmed by Act of Parliament.

(7.) The confirming authority may make such order
as they think fit in favour of any person whose lands
were proposed by the scheme to be taken compulsorily
for the allowance of the reasonable costs, charges, and
expenses properly incurred by him in opposing such
scheme.

Opposing, i.e. in connection with the local inquiry
—subsection (3). The presumption is that the Ministry
will fix the amount, but as to this and as to recovery
see subsection (9) below.

(8.) All costs, charges, and expenses incurred by the
confirming authority in relation to any provisional order
under this part of this Act shall, to such amount as the
confirming authority think proper to direct, and all costs,
charges, and expenses of any person to such amount as
may be allowed to him by the confirming authority in
pursuance of the aforesaid power, shall be deemed to be
an expense incurred by the local authority under this
part of this Act, and shall be paid to the confirming
authority and to such person respectively, in such manner
and at such times and either in one sum or by instalments

as the confirming authority may order, with power for the confirming authority to direct interest to be paid at such rate not exceeding five pounds in the hundred by the year as the confirming authority may determine, upon any sum for the time being due in respect of such costs, charges, and expenses as aforesaid.

See section 85 as to the costs of the local inquiry. See also sections 24 and 25 hereof, and subsection (9) below.

(9.) Any order made by the confirming authority in pursuance of this section may be made a rule of a superior court, and be enforced accordingly.

A Superior Court. In England, the Supreme Court —section 93. A rule of court is enforced as a judgment —1 & 2 Vict. c. 110, section 18, in this case most effectively by *mandamus.* If the Ministry did not fix the amount allowed under subsection (7) above, the costs might be taxed in the usual way, on the order being made a rule of court.

9. ("Costs to be awarded in certain cases.") *Repealed by the Housing, Town Planning, &c., Act,* 1909.

Inquiry on refusal of local authority to make an improvement scheme. **10.** Where an official representation is made to the local authority with a view to their passing a resolution in favour of an improvement scheme, and they fail to pass any resolution in relation to such representation, or pass a resolution to the effect that they will not proceed with such scheme, the local authority shall, as soon as possible, send a copy of the official representation, accompanied by their reasons for not acting upon it, to the confirming authority, and, upon the receipt thereof, the confirming authority may direct a local inquiry to be held, and a report to be made to them with respect to the correctness of the official representation made

to the local authority, and any matters connected there- S. 10 (90).
with on which the confirming authority may desire to be
informed.

See section 4 and notes thereto, and especially, sections
5 and 6 of the 1919 Act. See also section 85 hereof as
to local inquiries.

Provision of Dwelling Accommodation for Working Classes displaced by Scheme

11. (1.) *Repealed by the Housing, Town Planning, &c.,*
Act, 1919, section 33.

(2.) * A scheme shall, if the confirming authority so
require (but it shall not otherwise be obligatory on the
local authority so to frame their scheme), provide for
the accommodation of such number of those persons
of the working classes displaced in the area with respect
to which the scheme is proposed in suitable dwellings
to be erected in such place or places either within or
without the limits of the same area as the said authority
on a report made by the officer conducting the local
inquiry may require.

Requisites of improvement scheme as to accommodation of working classes.

See section 6 (1) (c) hereof. There is, however,
not now a great deal of substance in this section, as
under section 1 (1) of the 1919 Act it is the duty of the
local authority " to consider the needs of their area
with respect to the provision of houses for the working
classes " and to submit schemes, &c. It is not generally
intended that there should be re-housing on cleared
unhealthy areas.

Execution of Scheme by Local Authority

12. (1.) When the confirming Act authorising any
improvement scheme of a local authority under this
part of this Act has been passed by Parliament, it shall

Duty of local authority to carry scheme, when confirmed, into execution.

* As altered by the Housing, Town Planning, &c., Act, 1919, section 33.

S. 12 (90). be the duty of that authority to take steps for purchasing the lands required for the scheme, and otherwise for carrying the scheme into execution as soon as practicable : *Provided that the local authority shall not be required to acquire any leasehold interest in any property comprised in a scheme which can be allowed to expire without unduly delaying the execution of the scheme.*

No confirming Act is now necessary. The order made under section 8 (4) hereof is sufficient (see note thereto). As to purchasing the land—see page 156, section 20 hereof and section 7 (1), 9 and 13 of the 1919 Act. See also the Acquisition of Land (Assessment of Compensation) Act, 1919, page 495.

As to default—see section 13 hereof and section 5 of the 1919 Act. See subsection (6) below for a case where purchase may not be necessary.

(2.) They may sell or let all or any part of the area comprised in the scheme to any purchasers or lessees for the purpose and under the condition that such purchasers or lessees will, as respects the land so purchased by or leased to them, carry the scheme into execution ; and in particular they may insert in any grant or lease of any part of the area provisions binding the grantee or lessee to build thereon as in the grant or lease prescribed, and to maintain and repair the buildings, and prohibiting the division of buildings, and any addition to or alteration of the character of buildings without the consent of the local authority, and for the re-vesting of the land in the local authority, or their re-entry thereon, on breach of any provision in the grant or lease.

See section 82 hereof as to application of the proceeds. The provisions set out in the grant or lease (see also subsection (4) below) may be enforced by action

* Words added by the Housing, Town Planning, &c., Act, 1919, 2nd schedule.

for specific performance—*Wolverhampton Corporation v.* S. 12 (90).
Emmons [1901] 1 Q.B. 515.
The new buildings would include factories, workshops
and the like.

(3.) The local authority may also engage with any
body of trustees, society, or person, to carry the whole
or any part of such scheme into effect upon such terms
as the local authority may think expedient, but the local
authority shall not themselves, without the express
approval of the confirming authority, undertake the
rebuilding of the houses or the execution of any part
of the scheme, except that they may take down any or
all of the buildings upon the area, and clear the whole
or any part thereof, and may lay out, form, pave, sewer,
and complete all such streets upon the land purchased
by them as they may think fit, and all streets so laid
out and completed shall thenceforth be public streets,
repairable by the same authority as other streets in the
district.

Engage.   This would include any reasonable agreement—see section 24 as to expenditure.
It was clearly shown, many times, during the debates
on the 1919 Bill, that it was not the general policy of
the Ministry that re-housing should take place on these
areas.
Apparently the sale mentioned in subsection (2) above
may take place either before or after the area is cleared.
See also section 7 (1) of the 1919 Act.
Compare the local authority's power to build under
section 59 hereof.

(4.) Provided that in any grant or lease of any part of
the area which may be appropriated by the scheme for
the erection of dwellings for the working classes the
local authority shall impose suitable conditions and
restrictions as to the elevation, size, and design of the

S. 12 (90).

houses, and the extent of the accommodation to be afforded thereby, and shall make due provision for the maintenance of proper sanitary arrangements.

See subsections (2) and (3) above, and section 11 (2) hereof.

(5.) *Repealed by the Housing, Town Planning, &c., Act,* 1909, *6th schedule.*

(6.) The local authority may, where they think it expedient so to do, without themselves acquiring the land, or after or subject to their acquiring any part thereof, contract with *any person having such interest in any land comprised in an improvement scheme as may be sufficient to enable him to carry out and effect the same* for the carrying of the scheme into effect by him in respect of such land.

See section 6 (3) hereof.

Completion of scheme on failure by local authority.

13. If within five years after the removal of any buildings on the land set aside by any scheme authorised by a confirming Act as sites for working men's dwellings, the local authority have failed to sell or let such land for the purposes prescribed by the scheme, or have failed to make arrangements for the erection of the said dwellings, the confirming authority may order the said land to be sold by public auction or public tender, with full power to fix a reserve price, subject to the conditions imposed by the scheme, and to any modifications thereof which may be made in pursuance of this part of this Act, and to a special condition on the part of the purchaser to erect upon the said land dwellings for the working classes, in accordance with plans to be approved

* As altered by the Housing, Town Planning, &c., Act, 1919, 2nd schedule.

by the local authority, and subject to such other reser- S. 13 (90).
vations and regulations as the confirming authority
may deem necessary.

See notes to section 12, and—as to modifications—
sections 8 (5) and 15. Section 5 of the 1919 Act is
important on the general subject of default of the local
authority—see also section 11 of the 1909 Act. The
power here is limited to the default in respect of land
set aside for working men's dwellings.

14. (" Notice to occupiers by placards.") *Omitted by
the Housing, Town Planning, &c., Act, 1919, 2nd schedule,
and see 5th schedule hereof.*

15. (1.) The confirming authority, on application Power of
from the local authority, and on its being proved to confirming
authority to
their satisfaction that an improvement can be made modify
authorised
in the details of any scheme authorised by a confirming scheme.
Act, may permit the local authority to modify any
part of their improvement scheme which it may appear
inexpedient to carry into execution, but any part of the
scheme respecting the provision of dwelling accommodation for persons of the working class, when so modified,
shall be such as might have been inserted in the original
scheme.

(2.) *Repealed by the Housing, Town Planning, &c.,
Act,* 1909.

This permits modification by abandonment only, but
section 25 of the 1909 Act permits amendment or addition
" to the scheme in matters of detail in such manner as
appears expedient to the Board." It may be anticipated that the Board (Ministry) will take care even in
these modifications in matters of detail, of the interests
of persons thereby affected. There could be a local
inquiry—section 85 hereof.

Provision of dwelling accommodation. See section 11
hereof.

S. 16 (90).

Inquiry on
default of
medical
officer in
certain
cases.

Inquiries with respect to Unhealthy Areas

16. (1.) Where in any district *complaint has been
made* to a medical officer of health of the unhealthiness
of any area within that district, *by any person or
persons competent under the foregoing provisions of
this part of this Act to make such complaint,* and the
medical officer of health has failed to inspect such area,
or to make an official representation with respect thereto,
or has made an official representation to the effect that
in his opinion the area is not an unhealthy area, such
complainant or complainants as the case may be may
appeal to the confirming authority, and *the confirming
authority may* appoint a legally qualified medical
practitioner to inspect such area, and to make representation to the confirming authority, stating the facts
of the case, and whether, in his opinion, the area or any
part thereof is or is not an unhealthy area. The representation so made shall be transmitted by the confirming
authority to the local authority, and if it states that the
area is an unhealthy area the local authority shall
proceed therein in the same manner as if it were an
official representation made to that authority.

Competent under the foregoing provisions. A justice
of the peace or six ratepayers—see section 5 hereof
and notes thereto. See the next subsection as to costs.
Confirming Authority. The Ministry of Health, which
apart from any appeal may require a report from the
local authority—section 37 of the 1909 Act—or a report
under section 6 of the 1919 Act.
May appoint a legally qualified medical practitioner.
The word "may" was originally "shall." As to this
see section 26 of the 1909 Act, which allows any official

* As altered by the Housing, Town Planning, &c., Act, 1919, 2nd
schedule.

of the Ministry to make the inspection or inquiry, and applies section 85 hereof. S. 16 (90).

In the same manner.   See section 4 hereof.

(2.) The confirming authority shall make such order as to the costs of the inquiry as they think just, with power to require the whole or any part of such costs to be paid by the appellants where the medical practitioner appointed is of opinion that the area is not an unhealthy area, and to declare the whole or any part of such costs to be payable by the local authority where he is of opinion that the area or any part thereof is an unhealthy area.

In view of this the complainant or complainants may be advised not to make a formal appeal, and merely to ask the Ministry to use its large powers under section 5 (or 6 where it applies) of the 1919 Act.

(3.) Any order made by the confirming authority in pursuance of this section may be made a rule of a superior court, and be enforced accordingly.

See note to section 8 (9) hereof.

17. (" Proceedings on local inquiry.")   *Repealed by the Housing, Town Planning, &c., Act, 1909.*

18. (" Notice of inquiry to be publicly given.")   *Repealed by the Housing, Town Planning, &c., Act, 1909.*

19. (" Power to administer oath.")   *Repealed by the Housing, Town Planning, &c., Act, 1909.*

Acquisition of Land

20. The clauses of the Lands Clauses Acts, with respect to the purchase and taking of lands otherwise than by agreement shall not, except to the extent set forth in the Second Schedule to this Act, apply to any lands   Acquisition of land.

S. 20 (90). taken in pursuance of this part of this Act, but save as aforesaid the said Lands Clauses Acts, as amended by the provisions contained in the said schedule, shall regulate and apply to the purchase and taking of lands, and shall for that purpose be deemed to form part of this part of this Act in the same manner as if they were enacted in the body thereof ; subject to the provisions of this part of this Act and to the provisions following ; that is to say,

(i.) This part of this Act shall authorise the taking by agreement of any lands which the local authority may require for the purpose of carrying into effect the scheme authorised by any confirming Act, but it shall authorise the taking by the exercise of any compulsory powers of such lands only as are proposed by the scheme in the confirming Act to be taken compulsorily :

(ii.) In the construction of the Lands Clauses Acts, and the provisions in the Second Schedule to this Act, this part of this Act shall be deemed to be the special Act, and the local authority shall be deemed to be the promoters of the undertaking ; and the period after which the powers for the compulsory purchase or taking of lands shall not be exercised shall be three years after the passing of the confirming Act.

Lands Clauses Acts. The Interpretation Act, 1889, section 23, defines them. For England and Wales they are : the Lands Clauses Consolidation Act, 1845 ; the Lands Clauses Consolidation Acts Amendment Act, 1860 ; the Lands Clauses Consolidation Act, 1869 ; the Lands Clauses (Umpire) Act, 1883 ; and the Lands Clauses (Taxation of Costs) Acts, 1895.

The clauses of the Lands Clauses Act " with respect

to the purchase and taking of lands otherwise than by agreement " are sections 18–68 of the Lands Clauses Consolidation Act, 1845. They do not apply to lands taken under this part of the present Act, for the words in the text "except to the extent set forth in the Second Schedule to this Act " have now no effect, as Article 27 of the Schedule (which formerly did set them forth) is now repealed.

The present section may therefore be taken to read : " sections 18–68 of the Lands Clauses Consolidation Act, 1845, shall not apply," &c. Sections 21 and 22 (Compensation) and the Second Schedule hereof (Assessment) take their place—but see notes thereto.

All the other sections in the Lands Clauses Acts, subject to section 34 of the 1909 Act, to the Second Schedule hereof, " to the provisions of this part of this Act, and to the provisions following " are to apply (see following notes and the Second Schedule). It may be noted that by section 121 of the 1845 Act, compensation is to be paid to tenants whose interest in the land is no greater than as tenants for a year or from year to year, if they are required to give up possession before expiry of their terms—see *Wilkins v. Mayor of Birmingham* [1883] 25 Ch. D. 78, and note a similar provision in section 10 (2) of the 1919 Act.

This part of this Act. See section 2 hereof. It includes a provisional order—section 8.

Provisoes. For "confirming Act " read provisional order—sections 8 (4) and 12 (1). The powers of compulsion will lapse on the expiration of three years after the date of the provisional order.

Generally. "Land " includes any right over land— section 93 hereof. Section 9 of the 1919 Act and the Acquisition of Land (Assessment of Compensation) Act, 1919, apply to the amount of compensation payable for land acquired compulsorily.

21. (1.) Whenever the compensation payable in respect of any lands or of any interests in any lands proposed to be taken compulsorily in pursuance of this part of this Act requires to be assessed— Special provision as to compensation.

S. 21 (90).

(a) the estimate of the value of such lands or interests shall be based upon the fair market value, as estimated at the time of the valuation being made of such lands, and of the several interests in such lands, due regard being had to the nature and then condition of the property, and the probable duration of the buildings in their existing state, and to the state of repair thereof, without any additional allowance in respect of the compulsory purchase of an area or of any part of an area in respect of which an official representation has been made, or of any lands included in a scheme which, in the opinion of the arbitrator, have been so included as falling under the description of property which may be constituted an unhealthy area under this part of this Act ; and

(b) in such estimate any addition to or improvement of the property made after the date of the publication in pursuance of this part of this Act of an advertisement stating the fact of the improvement scheme having been made shall not (unless such addition or improvement was necessary for the maintenance of the property in a proper state of repair) be included, nor in the case of any interest acquired after the said date shall any separate estimate of the value thereof be made so as to increase the amount of compensation to be paid for the lands ; and

Generally. See notes to last section. It should be particularly noted that in so far as these provisions are inconsistent or in conflict with the provisions of section 9 of the 1919 Act they shall cease to apply to " unhealthy areas "—that is, these provisions apply only to neighbouring lands (land included in the scheme only S. 21 (90). for the purpose of making the scheme efficient and not on account of sanitary condition) proposed to be taken compulsorily (section 6). Further, the Acquisition of Land (Assessment of Compensation) Act, 1919, applies to the assessment of compensation ; and the rules therein contained (section 2) apply, except so far as they are inconsistent with the provisions of the present Act—see section 7 (1) thereof. For the most part the rules in the said section 2 are very similar to the present provisions, except that under the present provisions there can be an additional allowance for compulsory purchase of the neighbouring lands—*Lord Mayor of Dublin v. Dowling* [1880] L.R. Ir. 6 Q.B. 502.

Lands. See section 93 hereof, but as to easements —see section 22, below ; and *Great Western Railway Co. v. Swindon, &c. Railway Co.* [1884] 9 App. Cas. 787.

As to land bearing rent charge in lieu of tithes—see the Tithe Act, 1878, section 1.

Publication . . . of Advertisement. See section 7 hereof, and section 41 of the 1909 Act.

Principles of Compensation. See general note above. The *basis* is the fair market value, and everything in connection with or affecting the market value will have to be considered. A covenant making a public-house a " tied-house " is to be taken into account if it adds to the market value—*Chandler's Wiltshire Brewery Co., Ltd. v. London County Council* [1903] 1 K.B. 569. Compensation could probably be given for loss of profits and goodwill—*Lord Mayor of Dublin v. Dowling* [1880] L.R. Ir. 6 Q.B. 502. Probably it could be awarded for loss occasioned to the owner by his being turned out, e.g. cost of removal, loss of profits while removing, and fixtures—*Jubb v. Hull Dock Co.* [1846] 9 Q.B. 443. See also *Dye v. Patman* [1897] 62 J.P. 135, *Higgins v. Lord Mayor of Dublin* [1891] 28 L.R. Ir. 484, *Wilkins v. Mayor of Birmingham* [1884] 25 Ch.D. 78, *Cranwell v. Mayor of London* [1870] L.R. 5 Ex. 284, *Leeds Corporation v. Ryder* [1907] A.C. 420 (an interesting case in connection with licensed premises) ; and *Mills v. East London Union* [1872] L.R. 8 C.P. 79.

The Arbitrator. This will be the official arbitrator appointed under section 1 (1) of the Acquisition of Land (Assessment of Compensation) Act, 1919.

S. 21 (90). 　(2.) On the occasion of assessing the compensation payable under any improvement scheme in respect of any house or premises situate within an unhealthy area evidence shall be receivable by the arbitrator to prove—

　(1st) that the rental of the house or premises was enhanced by reason of the same being used for illegal purposes or being so overcrowded as to be dangerous or injurious to the health of the inmates ; or

　(2ndly) that the house or premises are in such a condition as to be a nuisance within the meaning of the Acts relating to nuisances, or are in a state of defective sanitation, or are not in reasonably good repair ; or

　(3rdly) that the house or premises are unfit, and not reasonably capable of being made fit, for human habitation ;

and, if the arbitrator is satisfied by such evidence, then the compensation—

　(a) shall in the first case so far as it is based on rental be based on the rental which would have been obtainable if the house or premises were occupied for legal purposes and only by the number of persons whom the house or premises were under all the circumstances of the case fitted to accommodate without such overcrowding as is dangerous or injurious to the health of the inmates ; and

　(b) shall in the second case be the amount estimated as the value of the house or premises if the nuisance had been abated, or if they had been put into a sanitary condition, or into reasonably good repair, after deducting the estimated expenses of abating

the nuisance, or putting them into such condition
or repair, as the case may be ; and

(*c*) shall in the third case be the value of the land,
.   and of the materials of the buildings thereon.

See notes to foregoing subsection. In view of
section 9 of the 1919 Act, the present subsection has
a very limited application.
For definition of the Acts relating to nuisances, see
section 2 hereof.

22. Upon the purchase by the local authority of any   Extinction
lands required for the purpose of carrying into effect   of rights of
way and
any scheme, all rights of way, rights of laying down or   other easements.
of continuing any pipes, sewers, or drains on, through,
or under such lands, or part thereof, and all other
rights or easements in or relating to such lands, or
any part thereof, shall be extinguished, and all the
soil of such ways, and the property in the pipes, sewers,
or drains, shall vest in the local authority, subject to
this provision, that compensation shall be paid by the
local authority to any persons or bodies of persons proved
to have sustained loss by this section, and such compensation shall be determined in the manner in which compensation for lands is determinable under this part of
this Act, or as near thereto as circumstances admit.

By section 27 of the 1909 Act, an improvement scheme
may provide, with the consent of the persons interested,
for modifications, &c., of this section ; so that, for
instance, the mains, &c., of gas and other companies
may be protected.
The point of this section is that all rights and easements are extinguished, and that all persons who thereby
sustain loss must be compensated by the local authority.
The compensation will be determinable as under section
21 above (see notes thereto), but in *Re Harvey and the
London County Council* [1909] 1 Ch. 528, it was held
that evidence of injury to goodwill or trade cannot be

11

S. 22 (90).

admitted in a claim under this section. As the rights are *extinguished* by this section, the remedy would appear to be compensation from the local authority and not an injunction to prevent the erection or pulling down of buildings. The compensation can be claimed whenever the loss appears. See *Badham v. Morris*, 45 L.T. 579 ; *Swanston v. Finn, &c.* [1883] 52 L.J. Ch. 235 ; and *Barlow v. Ross* [1890] 24 Q.B.D. 381. If access is interfered with, compensation could probably be recovered, and so, generally, with regard to "injurious affection."

Application of lands for accommodation of working classes.

23. A local authority may, for the purpose of providing accommodation for persons of the working classes displaced *in consequence of any improvement scheme, appropriate any lands for the time being belonging to them which are suitable for the purpose, or may purchase by agreement any such further lands as may be convenient.

Appropriate. See the Municipal Corporations Act, 1882, section 111, and section 57 (3) hereof. Note also the power under section 74 (2) hereof. It has been doubted if the present section authorises the appropriation of lands acquired for some other specific purpose —see *Attorney-General v. Hanwell Urban District Council* [1900] 2 Ch. 377 ; *Attorney-General v. Pontypridd Urban District Council* [1906] 2 Ch. 257 ; but by section 95 of the Public Health Acts Amendment Act, 1907, such land may be appropriated to other purposes with the consent of the Ministry, &c., and similarly land acquired for educational purposes—Education (Administrative Provisions) Act, 1905, section 5.

But the Part III powers would be more generally used, as to which see section 10 (2) of the 1919 Act and notes thereto.

See section 4 of the 1900 Act as to keeping accounts in respect of land appropriated.

Purchase by agreement. As to acquisition in advance— see section 13 of the 1919 Act ; as to sale by a tenant

* As altered by the Housing, Town Planning, &c., Act, 1909, 2nd schedule.

for life—see section 31 of that Act; as to donations S. 23 (90).
of land, &c.—see section 8 of the 1909 Act.

Expenses

24. (1.) The receipts of a local authority under this *Formation of improvement fund for purposes of Act.* part of this Act shall form a fund (in this Act referred to as "the Dwelling-house Improvement Fund"), and their expenditure shall be defrayed out of such fund.

The receipts and expenditure will come under review in connection with the State subsidy under section 7 (1) of the 1919 Act, provided that the scheme includes re-housing.

(2.) The moneys required in the first instance to establish such fund, and any deficiency for the purposes of this part of this Act from time to time appearing in such fund by reason of the excess of expenditure over receipts, shall be supplied out of the local rates or out of moneys borrowed in pursuance of this Act.

No deficiency shall be supplied out of borrowed money unless the deficiency arises in respect of money required for purposes to which borrowed money is, in the opinion of the Local Government Board (Ministry of Health) properly applicable—section 30 of the 1909 Act.

For borrowing power—see section 25 hereof.

For definition of "local rates"—see section 92 hereof and First Schedule.

As to application of purchase money of land sold by the local authority—see section 82 hereof.

(3.) In settling any accounts of the local authority in respect of any transactions under this part of this Act, care shall be taken that as far as may be practicable all expenditure shall ultimately be defrayed out of the property dealt with under this part of this Act; and any balances of profit made by the local authority under this part of this Act shall be applicable to any purposes to which the local rate is for the time being applicable.

Separate accounts shall be kept of receipts and expenditure under each part of this Act—section 80 (1) hereof. Note also the special case under section 4 of the 1900 Act.

(4.) Any limit imposed on or in respect of local rates by any other Act of Parliament shall not apply to any rate required to be levied for the purpose of defraying any expenses under this part of this Act.

(5.) The local authority may carry to the account of the Dwelling-house Improvement Fund any such money or produce of any property, as is legally applicable to purposes similar to the purposes of this part of this Act; and in case of doubt as to whether, in any particular case, the purposes are so similar the confirming authority may decide such doubt, and such decision shall be conclusive.

Power of borrowing money for the purposes of Part I of Act.
25. (1.) A local authority may, in manner in this section mentioned, borrow such money as is required for the purposes of this part of this Act on the security of the local rate.

For definition of "local authority" and "local rate"—see section 92 hereof and First Schedule. The maximum period of the loan is 80 years—section 1 (1) of the 1903 Act. For further powers (issue of bonds, &c.)—see sections 7 and 8 of the Housing (Additional Powers) Act, 1919.

(2.) For the purpose of such borrowing, the London County Council may, with the assent of the Treasury, create consolidated stock under the Metropolitan Board of Works Loans Acts, 1869 to 1871, but all moneys required for the payment of the dividends on and the redemption of the consolidated stock created for the purposes of this part of this Act shall be charged to the S. 25 (90). special county account to which the expenditure for the purposes of this part of this Act is chargeable.

The Acts mentioned were repealed by the London County Council (Finance Consolidation) Act, 1912—see sections 3 and 48 thereof.

The " special county account." " The Dwelling-house Improvement Fund "—section 24 (1).

(3.) For the purpose of such borrowing, the Commissioners of Sewers for the City of London may borrow and take up at interest such money on the credit of the local rates, or any of them, as they may require for the purposes of this part of this Act, and may mortgage any such rate or rates to the persons by or on behalf of whom such money is advanced for securing the repayment to them of the sums borrowed, with interest thereon, and for the purposes of any mortgages so made by the Commissioners of Sewers, the clauses of the Commis- 10 & 11 Vict. sioners Clauses Act, 1847, with respect to the mortgages o. 16. to be executed by the Commissioners shall be incorporated with this part of this Act; and in the construction of that Act " the special Act " shall mean this part of this Act; " the commissioners " shall mean the Commissioners of Sewers; " the clerk of the commissioners " shall include any officer appointed for the purpose by the Commissioners of Sewers by this part of this Act; and the mortgages or assignees of any mortgage made as last aforesaid may enforce payment of the arrears of principal and interest due to them by the appointment of a receiver,

For Commissioners of Sewers now read the Common Council of the City of London—City of London Sewers Act, 1897. The " local rates " are now the general rate. The clauses of the Commissioners Clauses

S. 25 (90). Act, 1847, referred to are sections 75–88 ; and as to a receiver—see sections 86 and 87 thereof.

(4.) For the purpose of such borrowing, the urban sanitary authority shall have the same power as they have under the Public Health Acts for the purpose of defraying any expenses incurred by them in the execution of those Acts.

Urban Sanitary Authority. Now the urban district council or the borough council (or corporation).

Public Health Acts. See sections 233–243 of the Public Health Act, 1875. The consent of the Ministry is required.

As to the period of loan (now 80 years) and as to the money not being reckoned as part of the debt—see section 1 of the 1903 Act.

See also section 7 of the Housing (Additional Powers) Act, 1919.

(5.) The Public Works Loan Commissioners may, on the recommendation of the confirming authority, lend to any local authority any money required by them for purposes of this part of this Act, on the security of the local rate.*

The rates of interest at which loans may be made by the Public Works Loan Commissioners out of the Local Loans Fund may be fixed by the Treasury from time to time—the Public Works Loans Act, 1897. For current rates see the Treasury minute dated 1st November 1920, printed on page 536. See also sections 1 /03, 3 /09, and 7 (4) /19. As to temporary loans see the Public Works Loans Act, 1920 (page 487).

Confirming authority. See section 8 (2) hereof.

Local authority . . . local rates. See section 92 hereof and First Schedule.

General Provisions

Provision in case of absence of medical officer of health.

26. In case of the illness or unavoidable absence of a medical officer of health, the authority, board, or

* Words here were repealed by the Housing, Town Planning, &c., Act, 1909.

vestry who appointed him may (subject to the approval S. 26 (90).
of the confirming authority) appoint a duly qualified
medical practitioner, for the period of six months, or
any less period to be named in the appointment.

Section 191 of the Public Health Act, 1875, and other
Acts give the same power. See section 79 hereof as to
the powers of the deputy.

27. (" Power of confirming authority as to advertisements and notices.") *Repealed by the Housing, Town
Planning, &c., Act,* 1909.

28. (" Power of confirming authority to dispense with
notices in certain cases.") *Repealed by the Housing,
Town Planning, &c., Act,* 1909.

As to the two above repealed sections—see section 41
of the 1909 Act.

Part II.—Unhealthy Dwelling-Houses
Preliminary

29. In this part of this Act, unless the context other- Definitions :
wise requires—

The expression " street " includes any court, alley, " Street."
   street, square, or row of houses :

The expression " dwelling-house " * includes any yard, " Dwelling
   garden, outhouses, and appurtenances belonging   house."
   thereto or usually enjoyed therewith, and includes
   the site of the dwelling-house as so defined :

The expression " owner," in addition to the definition " Owner."
   given by the Lands Clauses Acts, includes all lessees
   or mortgagees of any premises required to be dealt
   with under this part of this Act, except persons
   holding or entitled to the rents and profits of such

   * As altered by the Housing, Town Planning, &c., Act, 1909,
section 49.

S. 29 (90).   premises under a lease the original term whereof
is less than twenty-one years : *

"Closing order."   The expression "closing order" means an order
prohibiting the use of premises for human habitation
made under the enactments set out in the Third
Schedule in this Act.

Part II. Sections 29–52. See Chapter II, page 34.
Sections 14 and 15 of the 1909 Act and sections 28 of
the 1919 Act are deemed to be part of Part II of this,
the 1890, Act.

Street. This definition has been extended to Part I
hereof, by section 48 of the 1909 Act. Compare the
more extended definition in section 4 of the Public
Health Act, 1875· Private streets do not appear to be
excluded. See *Merrick v. Liverpool Corporation* [1910]
74 J.P. 445 as to the meaning of "court."

Dwelling-house. After this word there were originally
the words "means any inhabited building, and "—the
effect of the repeal being to include dwelling-houses
whether inhabited or not. Any dwelling-house, or if
it be let in tenements or flats any tenement therein,
may be closed by a closing order. On this point, however,
see *Kirkpatrick v. Maxwelltown Town Council* [1912]
S.C. 288, and *Johnston's Trustees v. Glasgow Corporation*
[1912] S.C. 300, from which it may be concluded that
the better course is to serve a closing order in respect
of each separate tenement in the building.

Owner. By section 3 of the Lands Clauses Act, 1845,
"the word 'owner' should be understood to mean
any person or corporation who, under the provisions
of this or the special Act, would be enabled to sell and
convey lands to the promoters of the undertaking."
Such persons are, under section 7 thereof, all parties
seised, possessed of, or entitled to any such lands, or any
estate or interest therein, including corporations, tenants
in tail or for life, married women seised in their own
right or entitled to dower, guardians, committees of
lunatics and idiots, trustees or feofees in trust for charitable or other purposes, executors and administrators,

* As altered by the Housing, Town Planning, &c., Act, 1909,
section 49.

nd all parties for the time being entitled to the receipt S. 29 (90).
f the rent and profits of any such lands in possession
r subject to any estate in dower, or to any lease for
ife, or for lives and years, or for years or any less interest.

As to further points *R. v. Vestry of St. Marylebone*
1887] 20 Q.B.D. 415 ; and *Osborne v. Skinners Co.*
1891] 60 L.J. M.C. 156, may be read.   Note also section
47 hereof and section 30 of the 1919 Act.

Closing Order.   In effect this. definition is repealed—
see sections 17, 18, 47, 75 and Schedule VI of the 1909
Act.   The present definition is given in section 17 (2)
thereof.

Buildings unfit for Human Habitation

30. It shall be the duty of the medical officer of health Representation by medical officer of health.
of every district to represent to the local authority of
that district any dwelling-house which appears to him
to be in a state so dangerous or injurious to health as
to be unfit for human habitation.

For definitions—see sections 29 and 92 and Schedule I.
Both rural and urban districts are included.   By section
81 hereof the local authority may appoint committees.

The representation by the medical officer must be in
writing—section 79 (2) hereof.   There is, apparently, no
prescribed or recommended form.   The local authority
must give attention to the representation—section 31 (2).

By section 17 (1) of the 1909 Act it is the duty of the
local authority to cause inspections to be made from time
to time—see the Housing (Inspection of District)
Regulations, 1910 (page 570).   See also sections 45
hereof and 5 and 6 of the 1919 Act.

Dangerous . . . habitation.   There is no definition of
the concluding words of this section ; but section 26 (1)
of the 1919 Act provides a useful standard, and *Walker
v. Hobbs* [1889] 23 Q.B.D. 458 ; *Kirkpatrick v. Maxwelltown Burgh* [1912] S.C. 288 ; *Ryall v. Kidwell* [1914]
30 T.L.R. 503 ; *Hall v. Manchester Corporation* [1914]
78 J.P. 315, affirmed House of Lords [1915] 79 J.P. 385 ;
and *London County Council v. Herring* [1894] 2 Q.B. 522,
may be usefully read.

S. 30 (90).

Dwelling-houses in bad repair are not necessarily included in the phrase, but as to these—see section 75 hereof, section 15 of the 1909 Act, and, particularly, section 28 of the 1919 Act.

Certain cellar. dwellings are included by section 17 (7) of the 1909 Act, and see section 43 thereof as to back-to-back houses.

In London there are special provisions, more particularly with regard to lack of water, but in such cases the more convenient remedy will probably be that given under section 26 of the 1919 Act, or section 28 thereof as regards structurally dangerous houses, either in London or elsewhere.

The phrase has to be read in its ordinary meaning, the standard being that of the ordinary reasonable man : it does not follow that a whole building is unfit for human habitation because certain rooms are ; see *Hall v. Manchester Corporation,* above.

Representation on householders' complaint.

31. (1.) If *any justice of the peace acting for a district or any four or more householders in a district complain in writing to the medical officer of health of that district that any dwelling-house is in a condition so dangerous or injurious to health as to be unfit for human habitation, he shall forthwith inspect the same, and transmit to the local authority the said complaint, together with his opinion thereon, and if he is of opinion that the dwelling-house is in the condition aforesaid, shall represent the same to the local authority, but the absence of any such complaint shall not excuse him from inspecting any dwelling-house and making a representation thereon to the local authority.

By section 6 (2) of the Local Government Act, 1894, a parish council can also make complaint under this section.

The representation must be in writing—section 79 (2) hereof. See section 52 as to representation by a county

* As altered by the Housing, Town Planning, &c., Act, 1919, 2nd schedule.

edical officer. See also sections 5 and 6 of the 1919 S. 31 (90).
Act as to default.

(2.) If within three months after receiving the said
complaint and opinion or representation of the medical
officer, the local authority, not being in the administrative
county of London, or not being a rural sanitary authority
in any other county, declines or neglects to take any
proceedings to put this part of this Act in force, the
justice of the peace or householders who signed such
complaint may petition the Local Government Board
for an inquiry, and the said Board after causing an
inquiry to be held may order the local authority to
proceed under this part of this Act, and such order shall
be binding on the local authority.

Note the restrictions in this subsection as compared
with subsection (1), but see section 45 hereof, section 10
of the 1909 Act and section 5 of the 1919 Act—the
latter being the power which, it may be expected, will
now be more commonly used. As to the inquiry—see
section 85 hereof.

The changes in the text made by the 1919 Act permit
a justice of the peace to make the complaint.

Closing Order and Demolition

32. (" Duty of local authority as to closing of dwelling-
house unfit for human habitation.") *Repealed by the
Housing, Town Planning, &c., Act, 1909—see now section
17 thereof.*

33. (" Order for demolition of house unfit for habitation.") *Repealed by the Housing, Town Planning, &c.,
Act, 1909—see now section 18 thereof.*

Sections 17 and 18 of the 1909 Act substitute a new

* As altered by the Housing, Town Planning, &c., Act, 1919, 2nd
schedule.

S. 34 (90). procedure in regard to closing and demolition orders. If they are read here the provisions of Part II can be better followed.

Execution of an order for demolition, and provision as to site. **34.** (1.) Where an order for the demolition of a building has been made, the owner thereof shall within three months after *the order becomes operative proceed to take down and remove the building, and if the owner fails therein the local authority shall proceed to take down and remove the building and shall sell the materials, and after deducting the expenses incident to such taking down and removal, pay over the balance of money (if any) to the owner.

" Order for demolition " is the subject of section 18 of the 1909 Act which should be read as coming before the present section.

As to the word " building "—see sections 18 (2) and 47 of the 1909 Act.

" Three months " mean three calendar months—Interpretation Act, 1889, section 3.

For definition of owner—see section 29 hereof.

For form of order see page 626.

The order becomes operative. These words displace the original words " service of the order." See section 39 (2) of the 1909 Act as to when the order becomes operative.

The Balance. See section 9 of the 1903 Act as to a deficiency.

(2.) Where a building has been so taken down and removed, no house or other building or erection which will be dangerous or injurious to health shall be erected on all or any part of the site of such building ; and if any house, building, or erection is erected contrary to the provisions of this section, the local authority may at any time order the owner thereof to abate the same,

* As altered by the Housing, Town Planning, &c., Act, 1909, 2nd schedule.

and in the event of non-compliance with the order, S. 34 (90).
may at the expense of the owner abate or alter the
same.

In view of building byelaws there is little, if any,
point left in this subsection.

The owner referred to is the owner of the new building.
The order of the local authority must be under seal, &c.,
—section 86 hereof. See the next section as to appeal.
There is no special provision as to the method of recovery
of the ·expense.

35. (1.) Any person aggrieved by an order of the   Appeal
against order
local authority under this part of this Act, may *if he of local
authority.
is not entitled to appeal to the Local Government Board
against the order, appeal against the same to a court of
quarter sessions, and no work shall be done nor proceedings taken under any order until after the appeal 42 & 43 Vict.
c. 49.
is determined or ceases to be prosecuted ; and section
thirty-one of the Summary Jurisdiction Act, 1879,
respecting appeals from courts of summary jurisdiction
to courts of quarter sessions shall apply with the necessary
modifications as if the order of the local authority were
an order of a court of summary jurisdiction.

(2.) Provided that—'

(a) Notice of appeal may be given within one month
after notice of the order of the local authority has
been served on such person ;

(b) The court shall, at the request of either party,
state the facts specially for the determination of
a superior court, in which case the proceedings may
be removed into that court.

Any person aggrieved. It should be noted that the
expression is not " any owner "—section 29—and so

* As altered by the Housing, Town Planning, &c., Act, 1909, 2nd
schedule.

S. 35 (90). would probably include any lessee who is not an owner. For a lengthy discussion of the term, reference may be made to page 559 of *Lumley's Public Health*, 8th edition.

Owners may appeal to the Board. (Ministry) against repairing, closing and demolition orders—sections 15, 17 and 18 of the 1909 Act. The other orders of the local authority include an order to abate—sections 34 (2) and 38 (10)—and an order granting a charge—section 36 (1).

For a manner of service of notice—see section 49 hereof.

For forms of notice of appeal to the Ministry—see the Housing Acts (Forms of Orders and Notices) Order, 1919, page 610.

Quarter Sessions, in the circumstances covered by sub-section (2) (*b*), will find the facts, leaving the inferences therefrom to be drawn by the Divisional Court, which is the superior court referred to. There is no appeal from the Divisional Court unless it, or the Court of Appeal, gives leave to appeal—sections 1 (5) and 2 of the Judicature Act, 1894. No writ is required for the removal to the Divisional Court—section 40 of the Summary Jurisdiction Act, 1879—and for further points see the Rules of the Supreme Court, Order 34, and *Clarke v. Alderbury Union Assessment Committee* [1881] 29 W.R. 334.

Grant of charges by way of annuity to owner on completion of works.

36. (1.) Where any owner has completed in respect of any dwelling-house any works required to be executed by an order of a local authority under this part of this Act, he may apply to the local authority for a charging order, and shall produce to the local authority the certificate of their surveyor or engineer that the works have been executed to his satisfaction, and also the accounts of and vouchers for the costs, charges, and expenses of the works, and the local authority, when satisfied that the owner has duly executed such works and of the amount of such costs, charges, and expenses, and of the costs of obtaining the charging order which have been properly incurred, shall make and order accordingly,

charging on the dwelling-house an annuity to repay the S. 36 (90). amount.

Owner. For definition—see section 29 hereof. There may be several of such owners. The one who does the work gets the charging order.

Works required. Namely for keeping houses in repair, as per (1) section 15 of the 1909 Act (which is deemed to be part of Part II of this (1890) Act—section 39 (2) of the 1919 Act) and (2) section 28 of the 1919 Act. It is doubtful if there are other works required . . . by an order of the local authority : closing and demolition orders under sections 17 and 18 of the 1909 Act, do not themselves require works to be executed—see also section 34 (1) hereof—but the charging order is on the dwelling-house, and where that is demolished there appears to be no power to charge a subsequent building erected on the site. *Arlidge v. Scrase* [1915] 3 K.B. 325 may be usefully read here.

Charging order. This is made by the local authority, and there is an appeal under section 35 hereof. There are other references to charging orders in these Acts—see sections 26 (6) and (8) and 28 of the 1919 Act, and section 15 (5) of the 1909 Act. The incidence of the charge is dealt with in section 37 hereof. See also note to section 26 (8) of the 1919 Act.

Annuity. See further as to this, the two following subsections and section 37.

(2.) The annuity charged shall be a sum of six pounds for every one hundred pounds of the said amount and so in proportion for any less sum, and shall commence from the date of the order, and be payable for a term of thirty years to the owner named in such order, his executors, administrators, or assigns.

The annuity can be transferred—section 37 (5), and can be redeemed—section 19 of the 1909 Act.

(3.) Every such annuity may be recovered by the person for the time being entitled to it by the same means and in the like manner in all respects as if it were

S. 36 (90).   a rentcharge granted by deed out of the dwelling-house by the owner thereof.

See note to section 28 (8) of the 1919 Act. The holder of the rentcharge can distrain (*Dodds v. Thompson* [1865] L.R. 1 C.P. 133) ; an action will be for arrears (*Thomas v. Sylvester* [1873] L.R. 8 Q.B. 368 ; *Re Herbage Rents, Greenwich* [1896] 2 Ch. 811, &c.), and distress may be statute barred (*Jones v. Withers* [1896] 74 L.T. 572).

(4.) Charging orders made under this section shall be made according to the Form marked A. in the Fifth Schedule to this Act, or as near thereto as the circumstances of the case will admit.

The schedule has been repealed by the 1909 Act, section 75, Schedule VI, and so this subsection is inoperative. Forms may be prescribed under section 41 of the 1909 Act, but none appear to have been prescribed affecting this matter.

Incidence of charge.   **37.** (1.) Every charge created by a charging order under this part of this Act shall be a charge on the dwelling-house specified in the order having priority over all existing and future estates, interests, and incumbrances, with the exception of quitrents and other charges incident to tenure, tithe commutation rentcharge, and any charge created under any Act authorising advances of public money ; and where more charges than one are charged under this part of this Act on any dwelling-house such charges shall, as between themselves, take order according to their respective dates.

(2.) A charging order shall be conclusive evidence that all notices, acts, and proceedings by this part of this Act directed with reference to or consequent on the obtaining of such order, or the making of such charge, have been duly served, done, and taken, and that such charge has been duly created, and that it is a valid S. 37 (90). charge on the dwelling-house declared to be subject thereto.

(3.) Every such charging order, if it relates to a dwelling-house in the area to which the enactments relating to the registration of land in Middlesex apply or to a dwelling-house in Yorkshire, shall be registered in like manner as if the charge were made by deed by the absolute owner of the dwelling-house.

(4.) Copies of the charging order and of the certificate of the surveyor or engineer, and of the accounts as passed by the local authority, certified to be true copies by the clerk of the local authority, shall within six months after the date of the order be deposited with the clerk of the peace of the county in which the dwelling-house is situate, and be by him filed and recorded.

(5.) The benefit of any such charge may be from time to time transferred in like manner as a mortgage or rentcharge may be transferred. Any transfer may be in the Form marked B. in the Fifth Schedule to this Act, or in any other convenient form.

Charging order. See section 36 hereof, section 15 (5) of the 1909 Act, and section 26 (7) of the 1919 Act.

Exception. See the addition made by section 20 of the 1909 Act. Reliefs, heriots and fines also take precedence of the charging order as they are "charges incident to tenure," but ground rents do not as they are not such charges.

Subsection 4 does not apply to charging orders under section 27 of the 1919 Act—see subsection (8) thereof.

Subsection 5. The Fifth Schedule has been repealed— 1909 Act section 95, Schedule VI. Forms may be prescribed under section 41 thereof, but none appear to have been prescribed affecting the charge under section 36.

12

S. 38 (90).   *Obstructive Buildings*

Power to
local
authority to
purchase
houses for
opening
alleys, &c.

38. (1.) If a medical officer of health finds that any building within his district, although not in itself unfit for human habitation, is so situate that by reason of its proximity to or contact with any other buildings it causes one of the following effects, that is to say,—

(*a*) It stops *or impedes* ventilation, or otherwise makes or conduces to make such other buildings to be in a condition unfit for human habitation or dangerous or injurious to health ; or

(*b*) It prevents proper measures from being carried into effect for remedying any nuisance injurious to health or other evils complained of in respect of such other buildings ;

in any such case, the medical officer of health shall represent to the local authority that particulars relating to such first-mentioned building (in this Act referred to as " an obstructive building ") stating that in his opinion it is expedient that the obstructive building should be pulled down.

Any building. Not limited to dwelling-houses— *Jackson v. Knutsford Urban District Council* [1914] W.N. 321. A wall in certain circumstances may be a building—*Ellis v. Plumstead Board of Works* [1893] 68 L.T. 291. As to a house being closed because other houses impede its ventilation—see *Hall v. Manchester Corporation* [1914] 78 J.P. N. 208. See also *Merrick v. Liverpool Corporation* [1910] 2 Ch. 449. As to part of a building—see subsections (7) and (11) below.

Representation. The representation must be in writing —section 79.

District. See section 92. *Generally.* See page 45.

(2.) †Any justice of the peace acting for a district, or†

---

* Words added by the Housing, Town Planning, &c., Act, 1909, 2nd schedule.   † Ibid., 1919 Act, 2nd schedule.

any four or more inhabitant householders of a district S. 38 (90). may make to the local authority of the district a representation as respects any building to the like effect as that of the medical officer under this section.

By section 6 (2) of the Local Government Act, 1894, a parish council may make a representation hereunder.

(3.) The local authority on receiving any such representation as above in this section mentioned shall cause a report to be made to them respecting the circumstances of the building and the cost of pulling down the building and acquiring the land, and on receiving such report shall take into consideration the representation and report, and if they decide to proceed, shall cause a copy of both the representation and report to be given to the owner of the lands on which the obstructive building stands, with notice of the time and place appointed by the local authority for the consideration thereof ; and such owner shall be at liberty to attend and state his objections, and after hearing such objections the local authority shall make an order either allowing the objection or directing that such obstructive building shall be pulled down, and such order shall be subject to appeal in like manner as an order of demolition of the local authority under the foregoing provisions of this part of this Act.

As to default of local authority—see sections 5 and 6 of the 1919 Act, section 45 hereof, and sections 10 and 11 of the 1909 Act.

The report will, presumably, be made by the surveyor of the local authority.

As to the duty in London and rural districts to report to the county council, &c.—see section 45 hereof.

As to report to local authority by county medical officer—see section 52 hereof.

As to interested persons voting—see section 88 hereof.

S. 38 (90). *Owner.* See section 29 hereof. Copies will have to be given to each such owner. As to service—see section 49 hereof.

Appeal. To the Local Government Board (now Ministry of Health)—see sections 18, 39 and 47 of the 1909 Act.

(4.) Where an order of the local authority for pulling down an obstructive building is made under this section and either no appeal is made against the order, or an appeal is made and either fails or is abandoned, the local authority shall be authorised to purchase the lands on which the obstructive building is erected in like manner as if they had been authorised by a special Act to purchase the same ; and for the purpose of such purchase the provisions of the Lands Clauses Acts, with respect to the purchase and taking of lands otherwise than by agreement shall be deemed to be incorporated in this part of this Act (subject nevertheless to the provisions of this part of this Act), and for the purpose of the provisions of the Lands Clauses Acts this part of this Act shall be deemed to be the special Act, and the local authority to be the promoters of the undertaking, and such lands may be purchased at any time within one year after the date of the order, or if it was appealed against after the date of the confirmation.

See notes to sections 20 and 41 hereof.

(5.) The owner of the lands may within one month after notice to purchase the same is served upon him declare that he desires to retain the site of the obstructive building and undertake either to pull down or to permit the local authority to pull down the obstructive building, and in such case the owner shall retain the site and shall

receive compensation from the local authority for the pulling down of the obstructive building.

" Month " means calendar month (Interpretation
Act, 1889). As to service of notice—see section 49 hereof.
In addition to the " owners " specified in section 29
hereof it would seem that in accordance with the Lands
Clauses Acts the notice should be served on lessees the
original term of whose lease was less than twenty-one
years, though such lessees could not claim to retain the
site. There would be no point in purchasing from
persons whose tenancies could be terminated by a short
notice. Persons having easements are not entitled to
notice, but they can claim compensation for destroyed
rights, under the Lands Clauses Consolidation Act, 1845,
section 68.

If any owner, being a lessee, wishes to retain the site
and the reversioner to sell, the local authority would
purchase the reversion ; but on this and on the general
subject of retaining the site note the powers of the local
authority under section 39 and Part III hereof.

In *Jackson v. Knutsford Urban District Council* [1914]
2 Ch. 686, the owner wished to retain the site and under-
took to pull down a portion of the building : held, that
he was estopped from setting up that the building was
not obstructive.

(6.) The amount of such compensation, and also the
amount of any compensation to be paid on the purchase of
any lands under this section, shall in case of difference
be settled by arbitration in manner provided in this
part of this Act.

(7.) Where the local authority is empowered to purchase land compulsorily, it shall not be competent for
the owner of a house *or other building* or manufactory to insist on his entire holding being taken, where
part only is proposed to be taken as obstructive, and
where such part proposed to be taken can, in the opinion
of the arbitrator to whom the question of disputed

* Words added by the Housing, Town Planning, &c., Act, 1909, 2nd
schedule.

S. 38 (90). compensation is submitted, be severed from the remainder of the house * or other building * or manufactory without material detriment thereto, provided that compensation may be awarded in respect of the severance of the part so proposed to be taken in addition to the value of that part.

(8.) Where in the opinion of the arbitrator the demolition of an obstructive building adds to the value of such other buildings as are in that behalf mentioned in this section, the arbitrator shall apportion so much of the compensation to be paid for the demolition of the obstructive building as may be equal to the increase in value of the other buildings amongst such other buildings respectively, and the amount apportioned to each such other building in respect of its increase in value by reason of the demolition of such obstructive building shall be deemed to be private improvement expenses incurred by the local authority in respect of such building, and such local authority may, for the purpose of defraying such expenses, make and levy improvement rates on the occupier of such premises accordingly ; and the provisions of the Public Health Acts relating to private improvement expenses and to private improvement rates, shall so far as circumstances admit, apply accordingly in the same manner as if such provisions were incorporated in this Act.

(9.) If any dispute arises between the owner or occupier of any building (to which any amount may be apportioned in respect of private improvement expenses) and the arbitrator by whom such apportionment is made, such dispute shall be settled by two justices in

* Words added by the Housing, Town Planning, &c., Act, 1909, 2nd schedule.

manner provided by the Lands Clauses Acts, in cases S. 38 (90). where the compensation claimed in respect of lands does not exceed fifty pounds.

See section 41 hereof (as to settlement of compensation) and section 28 of the 1909 Act (as to distribution of compensation money, and as to betterment charges). But the arbitration (not the rules for assessing compensation) is now under the Acquisition of Land (Assessment of Compensation) Act, 1919—see sections 1 (1), 2 and 7 thereof. See also *Jackson v. Knutsford Urban District Council* above.

In subsection (8) " such other buildings " are the obstructed ones—subsection (1).

Private Improvement Expenses. See sections 213, 214, 215, 232 and 257 of the Public Health Act, 1875. As to London—see section 46 (1) hereof.

In manner provided by the Lands Clauses Acts. See sections 22 and 24 of the Lands Clauses Consolidation Act, 1845. See also *R. v. Edwards* [1884] 13 Q.B.D. 586.

(10.) Where the owner retains the site or any part thereof, no house or other building or erection which will be dangerous or injurious to health, or which will be an obstructive building within the meaning of this section, shall be erected upon such site or any part thereof ; and if any house, building, or erection is erected on the site contrary to the provisions of this section the local authority may at any time order the owner to abate or alter the said house, building, or erection ; and in the event of non-compliance with such order may, at the expense of the owner thereof, abate or alter the same.

See subsection (5), and also similar provision in section 34 (2) hereof. There is an appeal against the order of the local authority—section 35.

(11.) Where the lands are purchased by the local authority the local authority shall pull down the

S. 38 (90).   obstructive building, or such part thereof as may be obstructive within the meaning of this section, and keep as an open space the whole site, or such part thereof as may be required to be kept open for the purpose of remedying the nuisance or other evils caused by such obstructive building, and may, with the assent of the Local Government Board, and upon such terms as that Board think expedient, sell such portion of the site as is not required for the purpose of carrying this section into effect.

As to the proceeds—see section 82 hereof. Note also section 7 (1) of the 1919 Act, and section 57 (3) hereof.

(12.) A local authority may, where they so think fit, dedicate any land acquired by them under the authority of this section as a highway or other public place.

See also section 39 hereof.

Scheme for Reconstruction

Scheme for area comprising houses closed by closing order.

39. (1.) In any of the following cases, that is to say—

(a) where an order for the demolition of a building has been made in pursuance of this part of this Act, and it appears to the local authority that it would be beneficial to the health of the inhabitants of the neighbouring dwelling-houses if the area of the dwelling-houses of which such building forms part were used for all or any of the following purposes, that is to say, either—

(i) dedicated as a highway or open space, or

(ii) appropriated, sold, or let for the erection of dwellings for the working classes, or

(iii) exchanged with other neighbouring land which is more suitable for the erection of such dwellings, and on exchange will be appropriated, sold, or let S. 39 (90). for such erection ; or

(b) where it appears to the local authority that the closeness, narrowness and bad arrangement or bad condition of any buildings, or the want of light, air, ventilation, or proper conveniences, or any other sanitary defect in any buildings is dangerous or prejudicial to the health of the inhabitants either of the said buildings or of the neighbouring buildings, and that the demolition or the reconstruction and re-arrangement of the said buildings or of some of them is necessary to remedy the said evils, and that the area comprising those buildings and the yards, outhouses, and appurtenances thereof, and the site thereof, is too small to be dealt with as an unhealthy area under Part I of this Act.

the local authority shall pass a resolution to the above effect and direct a scheme to be prepared for the improvement of the said area.

Order for demolition. See section 38 (1) hereof and section 18 of the 1909 Act.

Of which such building forms part. Under section 38 that part which is obstructive can be demolished and the space dedicated, &c. Under the present section the whole dwelling-house can be taken. But if the whole dwelling-house is obstructive, it may be better to proceed under section 38 as no order of the Ministry is required thereunder.

If it is desired to widen, improve, or lengthen a street or public place in London—see sections 80–86 of Michael Angelo Taylor's Act (57 Geo. 3, c. 29).

Paragraph (b) is independent of section 38 hereof and sections 17 and 18 of the 1909 Act. But the local authority can proceed under this paragraph whether the houses have been closed or not, under a closing order ; and usually it will consider in the initial stages whether it requires what it obtains under the above-quoted sections,

S. 39 (90).

including the repair of a particular house or houses (under the closing order procedure, but see also section 28 of the 1919 Act), or whether it requires a reconstruction scheme made as per this section.

As to the evidence and a standard regarding " dangerous or prejudicial to health "—see note to section 4 hereof.

Under Part I. The procedure under Part I is not so simple as that under Part II. Rural districts will necessarily come under Part II as Part I does not apply to them. Urban district authorities will decide which part they will proceed under, subject to the sanction by the Ministry of the scheme, but as to what may be regarded as a standard see section 72 hereof—which in London contemplates up to ten houses as a Part II scheme.

In the county of London the question of whether the scheme is under Part I or Part II has a special financial significance. In the city this does not apply as the Common Council of the city is the local authority under both Parts I and II. But in the county of London —see section 93 hereof—the London County Council is the local authority under Part I and the Metropolitan borough councils are the local authorities under Part II. If a scheme is carried out under Part I the expense falls on the county council, i.e., on the whole of London. These difficulties have been met by sections 46, 72 and 73 hereof, and section 14 of the 1903 Act. By section 46 (5) and (6) the county council may prepare and carry out a scheme under Part II, and the borough may contribute towards the expenses—section 14, 1909 Act— or the county may get an order from the Ministry that the expenses, or a part, should be met by the Metropolitan borough council. By section 72 the borough council shall proceed where the representation relates to not more than ten houses. By section 73 the question of whether the scheme is of general importance to the county of London is dealt with : if the borough decides that it is, or if the county council decides that it is not, a local inquiry may be held and the arbitrator shall report, to the end that the Ministry shall decide, though if the matter has to be dealt with under Part II it may be decided that the London County Council shall make a contribution towards the expense. (See also section 4 of the 1903 Act.)

Shall pass a resolution. As to default—see section S. 39 (90).
31 (2) hereof, sections 5 and 6 of the 1919 Act, and
section 10 of the 1909 Act. Interested members must
not vote—section 88 hereof.

Forms of Reports by the Medical Officer (to precede
the resolution), a Form of Resolution, information as to
Maps, Particulars and Estimates required, and a Form
of Clauses for the Scheme—all suggested by the Ministry
—are given on pages 591 to 593.

By section 23 (2) of the 1909 Act provision may be
made in a reconstruction scheme under Part II for any
matters for which provision may be made in an improvement scheme under Part I—as to which see section 6
hereof.

By section 7 of the 1903 Act neighbouring lands may
be included, but they will get an additional allowance in
respect of compulsory purchase—section 21 (1) (*a*) hereof.

Sites of ancient monuments, &c., cannot be acquired
—see note to section 20 hereof.

By section 13 of the 1919 Act there is power to acquire
lands in advance.

As to duty to carry out the scheme, &c.—see subsection
(8) below.   Generally on the section, see page 46.

(2.) Notice of the scheme may at any time after the
preparation thereof be served in manner provided in
Part I of this Act with respect to notices of lands proposed
to be taken compulsorily under a scheme made in pursuance of that part of this Act, on every owner or reputed
owner, lessee or reputed lessee, and occupier of any part
of the area comprised in the scheme, so far as those
persons can reasonably be ascertained.

See section 7 hereof as to manner of service, but
notice may be served " at any time."   No advertisement
is required, but, unless the Minister grants a dispensation under section 41 (2) of the 1909 Act, the notice
must be served even on " tenants for a month or a less
period than a month."   See also final note to subsection
(1) above.

For Forms of Notices suggested by the Ministry, see
pages 593 to 595.

S. 39 (90). (3.) The local authority shall, after service of such notice, petition the Local Government Board for an order sanctioning the scheme, and the Board may cause a local inquiry to be held, and, if satisfied on the report of such local inquiry that the carrying into effect of the scheme either absolutely, or subject to conditions or modifications would be beneficial to the health of the inhabitants of the said buildings or of the neighbouring dwelling-houses, may by order sanction the scheme with or without such conditions or modifications.

Petition. For instructions of the Ministry and Form of Petition—see page 596.
Inquiry. See section 85 hereof, which also deals with the Order.

(4.) *Upon such order being made, the local authority may purchase the area comprised in the scheme as so sanctioned.

By section 13 of the 1919 Act it can acquire lands in advance.
The order does not require confirmation by Parliament—section 24 (2), 1909 Act. As to borrowing powers—see section 43 hereof and notes to section 25 hereof.

(5.) *Repealed by the Housing, Town Planning, &c., Act,* 1909, *section* 75.

(6.) *Repealed by the Housing, Town Planning, &c., Act,* 1909, *section* 75.

(7.) The order may incorporate the provisions of the Lands Clauses Acts, and for the purpose of those provisions this Act shall be deemed to be the special Act, and the local authority to be the promoters of the undertaking, and the area shall be acquired within three years after the date of the confirmation of the order : Pro-

* As altered by the Housing, Town Planning, &c., Act, 1909, section 75 and 6th schedule.

vided that the amount of compensation shall, in case of S. 39 (90). difference, be settled by arbitration in manner provided by this part of this Act.

See note to section 20 hereof.   As to arbitration— see section 41 hereof.

(8.) *The provisions of Part I of this Act as amended by any subsequent Act relating to the duty of a local authority to carry a scheme when confirmed into execution, to the power of the Local Government Board to enforce that duty, to the completion of a scheme on failure by a local authority, and to the extinction of rights of way and other easements, shall, with the necessary modifications, apply for the purpose of any scheme under this section in like manner as if it were a scheme under Part I of this Act.

As to duty to carry out—see section 12 hereof; power to enforce—sections 31, 38, 39 (8) and 45 hereof, section 4 (1) of the 1903 Act, sections 5 and 6 of the 1919 Act, and section 10 and 11 of the 1909 Act; completion—section 23 hereof; extinction of rights—section 22 hereof, and section 27 of the 1909 Act.

(9.) The Local Government Board, on being satisfied by the local authority that an improvement can be made in the details of any scheme under this section, may by order permit the local authority to modify any part of the scheme which it may appear inexpedient to carry into execution.*

Further on this subject—see section 25 of the 1909 Act. See also note to section 15 hereof.

40. The Local Government Board shall in any order Provisions sanctioning a scheme under this part of this Act require modation of persons of

for accom-

* As altered by the Housing, Town Planning, &c., Act, 1909, 2nd the working and 6th schedules. classes.

S. 40 (90). the insertion in the scheme of such provisions (if any) for the dwelling accommodation of persons of the working classes displaced *in consequence of the scheme as seem to the Board required by the circumstances.

If there is re-housing there will be a State subsidy in respect of the whole scheme, under section 7 (1) of the 1919 Act—see note to section 4. See also section 11 hereof, and section 3 of the 1903 Act.

Settlement of Compensation

Provisions as to arbitration. **41.** In all cases in which the amount of any compensation is, in pursuance of this part of this Act, to be settled by arbitration, the following provisions shall have effect ; (namely,)

(1.) The amount of compensation shall be settled by an arbitrator to be appointed and removable by the Local Government Board.

Settlement of Compensation. This applies where there is a dispute, and in view of the Acquisition of Land (Assessment of Compensation) Act, 1919 (page 495), it is to be expected that there will be fewer disputes.

The preliminary procedure will be a notice to treat —see section 18 of the Lands Clauses Consolidation Act, 1845.

There is a power of entry for survey or valuation— section 36, 1909 Act. See also notes to section 21 hereof.

In all cases . . . , namely obstructive buildings demolished—section 38 hereof—and land taken for schemes under section 39.

Settled by arbitration. By the Acquisition of Land (Assessment of Compensation) Act, 1919 : " where by or under any statute . . . land is authorised to be acquired compulsorily by any . . . local authority, any question of disputed compensation . . . shall be referred to and determined by the arbitration of such one of a panel of official arbitrators to be appointed under

* As altered by the Housing, Town Planning, &c., Act, 1909, 2nd and 6th schedules.

this section as may be selected in accordance with rules S. 41 (90).
made by the Reference Committee under this section "
(subsection 1).   " Provided that nothing in this Act
relating to the rules for assessing compensation shall affect
any special provisions as to the assessment of the value
of land acquired for the purpose of Part I or Part II of
the Housing of the Working Classes Act, 1890 . . . if
and so far as the provisions in those Acts are inconsistent with the rules under this Act . . ."—section
7 (1) proviso.

By section 9 of the Housing, Town Planning, &c.,
Act, 1919, special provisions are made as to the assessment of compensation for slum lands, and the provisions
of the present section (41) cease to apply thereto.

Thus the special provisions of this section as to the
amount of the compensation apply to obstructive
buildings—section 38 hereof—and land included in the
scheme for the purpose of making the scheme efficient.

(2.) In settling the amount of any compensation—

(a) The estimate of the value of the dwelling-
house shall be based on the fair market value as
estimated at the time of the valuation being made
of such dwelling-house, and of the several interests
in such dwelling-house, due regard being had to
the nature and then condition of the property
and the probable duration of the buildings in
their existing state, and to the state of repair
thereof, and without any additional allowance
in respect of compulsory purchase ; and

(b) The arbitrator shall have regard to and make
an allowance in respect of any increased value
which, in his opinion, will be given to other
dwelling-houses of the same owner by the alteration
or demolition by the local authority of any buildings.

(a) Compare the almost identical section 21 (1) (a)
and see note thereto.   If neighbouring lands are included

there may be an extra allowance for compulsory purchase—section 7, 1903 Act. The word here, however,
is "dwelling-house" (which includes outhouses, appurtenances and the site—section 29) while in section 21
"lands and interests" are dealt with, which causes a
doubt if *buildings*, included in a Part II scheme or
under section 38 hereof, but outside the definition of
dwelling-house, are to have compensation hereunder or
under the Acquisition of Land (Assessment of Compensation) Act, 1919, section 2, which prohibits an allowance
for compulsory acquisition (see *Jackson v. Knutsford
Urban District Council* [1914] 2 Ch. 686).

(*b*) See also section 38 (8) hereof.

(3.) Evidence shall be receivable by the arbitrator to
prove—

(1st) that the rental of the dwelling-house was
enhanced by reason of the same being used for
illegal purposes or being so overcrowded as to be
dangerous or injurious to the health of the inmates ;
or

(2ndly) that the dwelling-house is in a state of
defective sanitation, or is not in reasonably good
repair ; or

(3rdly) that the dwelling-house is unfit, and not
reasonably capable of being made fit, for human
habitation ;

and, if the arbitrator is satisfied by such evidence,
then the compensation—

(*a*) shall in the first case so far as it is based on
rental be based on the rental which would have
been obtainable if the dwelling-house was occupied
for legal purposes and only by the number of
persons whom the dwelling-house was under all
the circumstances of the case fitted to accommodate without such overcrowding as is dan-

gerous or injurious to the health of the inmates ; S. 41 (90).
and

(b) shall in the second case be the amount estimated
as the value of the dwelling-house if it had been
put into a sanitary condition, or into reasonably
good repair, after deducting the estimated expense
of putting it into such condition or repair ; and

(c) shall in the third case be the value of the land,
and of the materials of the buildings thereon.

Compare the similar provisions of section 21 (2)
hereof, and see note to section 41 (2) (a) above. The
local authority may tender evidence notwithstanding
that they have not taken any steps with a view to remedying the defects or evils disclosed by the evidence—section
29, 1909 Act. See also section 9 of the 1919 Act.

(4.) On payment or tender to the person entitled to
receive the same of the amount of compensation
agreed or awarded to be paid in respect of the
dwelling-house, or on payment thereof in manner
prescribed by the Lands Clauses Acts, the owner
shall, when required by the local authority, convey
his interest in such dwelling-house to them, or as
they may direct ; and in default thereof, or if the
owner fails to adduce a good title to such dwelling-
house to the satisfaction of the local authority,
it shall be lawful for the local authority, if they
think fit, to execute a deed poll in such manner
and with such consequences as are mentioned in
the Lands Clauses Acts.

See sections 69–83 of the Lands Clauses Consoli-
lation Act, 1845 : all costs connected with the conveyance are payable by the local authority ; the money is
paid into the bank where the owner is incapacitated or
refuses to convey.

13

(5.) Sections thirty-two, thirty-three, thirty-five, thirty-six, and thirty-seven of the Lands Clauses Consolidation Act, 1845, shall apply, with any necessary modifications, to an arbitration and to an arbitrator appointed under this part of this Act.

But see now the Acquisition of Land (Assessment of Compensation) Act, 1919, page 495. See also section 38 (4) hereof.

(6.) The arbitrator may, by one award, settle the amount or amounts of compensation payable in respect of all or any of the dwelling-houses included in one or more order or orders made by the local authority ; but he may, and, if the local authority request him so to do, shall, from time to time make an award respecting a portion only of the disputed cases brought before him.

(7.) In the event of the death, removal, resignation, or incapacity, refusal, or neglect to act of any arbitrator before he shall have made his award, the Local Government Board may appoint another arbitrator, to whom all documents relating to the matter of the arbitration which were in the possession of the former arbitrator shall be delivered.

(8.) The arbitrator may, where he thinks fit, on the request of any party by whom any claim has been made before him, certify the amount of the costs properly incurred by such party in relation to the arbitration, and the amount of the costs so certified shall be paid by the local authority.

(9.) The arbitrator shall not give such certificate where the arbitrator has awarded the same or a less sum than has been offered by the local authority in respect of such claim before the appointment of the arbitrator, and need not give such certificate S. 41 (90). to any party where he considers that such party neglected, after due notice from the local authority, to deliver to that authority a statement in writing within such time, and containing such particulars respecting the compensation claimed, as would have enabled the local authority to make a proper offer of compensation to such party before the appointment of the arbitrator.

(10.) If within seven days after demand the amount so certified be not paid to the party entitled to receive the same, such amount shall be recoverable as a debt from the local authority with interest at the rate of five per cent. per annum for any time during which the same remains unpaid after such seven days as aforesaid.

(11.) The award of the arbitrator shall be final and binding on all parties.

But see now the Acquisition of Land (Assessment of Compensation) Act, 1919, page 495.

Expenses of Borrowing

42. (1.) All expenses incurred by a local authority Expenses of local authority. in the execution of this part of this Act shall be defrayed by them out of the local rate ; and that authority, notwithstanding any limit contained in any Act of Parliament respecting a local rate, may levy such local rate, or any increase thereof, for the purposes of this part of this Act.

Local rate. See section 92.

(2.) Any expenses incurred by a rural sanitary authority under this part of this Act, other than the expenses

S. 42 (90). incurred in and incidental to proceedings for obtaining a closing order, shall be charged as special expenses on the contributory place in respect of which they are incurred.

By section 17 of the 1909 Act the local authority make the closing order so that there will be no expenses in obtaining the order, but there may be expenses in connection with appeals—see also section 18 thereof— which will be general expenses. As to general and special expenses—see sections 229–232 of the Public Health Act, 1875.

Provision as to borrowing. **43.** (1.) A local authority may borrow for the purpose of raising sums required for purchase money or compensation payable under this part of this Act in like manner, and subject to the like conditions, as for the purpose of defraying the expenses of the execution by such authority of the Public Health Acts.

See notes to section 25 hereof.
For purchase money or compensation. See extension by section 1 of the 1894 Act, page 256.
Public Health Acts. Sections 233–243 of the Public Health Act, 1875. The local rate will be the security. See section 1 of the 1903 Act as to term of loans—eighty years.
This section does not apply to London, as to which see section 46.

(2.) The Public Works Loan Commissioners may, if they think fit, lend to any local authority the sums borrowed in pursuance of this part of this Act. .

See notes to section 25 hereof.

Annual account to be presented by the local authority. **44.** Every local authority shall every year present to the Local Government Board, in such form as they may direct, an account of what has been done, and of all moneys received and paid by them during the pre-

vious year, with a view to carrying into effect the purposes S. 44 (90).
of this part of this Act.

See section 80 hereof, and section 7 of the 1919 Act.

Powers of County Councils

45. (1.) Where the medical officer of health, *in- Powers of
spector of nuisances or other officer of the district county
councils.
authority* or any inhabitant householders make a representation or complaint, or give information to any vestry
or district board in the administrative county of London
or to the local board of Woolwich, or to any rural sanitary
authority elsewhere (which vestry, board, or authority
is in this Act referred to as the district authority) or
to the medical officer of such authority either respecting
any dwelling-house being in a state so dangerous or
injurious to health as to be unfit for human habitation,
or respecting an obstructive building, and also where
a closing order has been made as respects any dwelling-
house, the district authority shall forthwith forward
to the county council of the county in which the dwelling-
house or building is situate, a copy of such representation,
complaint, information, or closing order, and shall from
time to time report to the council such particulars as
the council require respecting any proceedings taken
by the authority with reference to such representation,
complaint, information, or dwelling-house.

Representation, or Complaint, or Give Information.
See sections 30, 31 (1) and 38 (1) and (2) hereof, and
section 17 (2) of the 1909 Act.
See also section 52 hereof as to a representation from
the county medical officer of health.
Vestry or district board . . . Now Metropolitan

* Words added by the Housing, Town Planning, &c., Act, 1919,
2nd schedule.

S. 45 (90). borough councils, of which Woolwich is one (London Government Act, 1899). By section 76 (2) hereof the London County Council medical officer of health, &c., is deemed to be a medical officer of health of a local authority. By the Sanitary Officer (London) Order, dated 8th December 1891, any report of the medical officer of health hereunder is to be deemed a special report and copies must be sent to the Board (Ministry) and to the county council.

District authority. This section does not apply to urban districts.

By section 6 (2) of the Local Government Act, 1894, a parish council may make a complaint, &c., which must be forwarded to the county council hereunder.

Unfit for human habitation. Sections 30 and 31 hereof.

Obstructive building. Section 38 hereof.

Closing Order. Section 17, 1909 Act.

Forward to the county council. And to the medical officer of health of the county—section 69, 1909 Act. In case of default the next subsection will apply—see also section 11 of the 1909 Act, and sections 5 and 6 of the 1919 Act.

(2.) Where the county council—

(a) are of opinion that proceedings for a closing order as respects any dwelling-house ought to be instituted, or that an order ought to be made for the demolition of any buildings forming or forming part of any dwelling-house as to which a closing order has been made, or that an order ought to be made for pulling down an obstructive building specified in any representation under this part of this Act ; and

(b) after reasonable notice, not being less than one month, of such opinion has been given in writing to the district authority, consider that such authority have failed to institute or properly prosecute proceedings, or to make the order for demolition, or to take steps for pulling down an obstructive building;

the council may pass a resolution to that effect, and

thereupon the powers of the district authority as respects S. 45 (90). the said dwelling-house and building under this part of this Act (otherwise than in respect of a scheme), shall be vested in the county council, and if a closing order or an order for demolition or for pulling down an obstructive building is made, and not disallowed on appeal, the expenses of the council incurred as respects the said dwelling-house and building, including any compensation paid, shall be a simple contract debt to the council from the district authority.

(3.) Any debt to the council under this section shall be defrayed by the district authority as part. of their expenses in the execution of this part of this Act.

The county council may now make a scheme also —section 5 of the 1919 Act, which section possibly covers in an alternative way the default here dealt with, though it seems to contemplate schemes rather than closing orders, &c.

As to expenses—see section 42 hereof.

The county councils are not entitled to charge for the time of their whole-time medical officer of health or inspector of nuisances in inspecting, &c.—*Durham County Council v. Easington Rural District Council* [1897] 61 J.P. 121.

As to London—see section 46 (5), (6) and (7).

(4.) The county council and any of their officers shall, for the purposes of this section, have the same right of admission to any premises as any district authority or their officers have for the purpose of the execution of their duties under the enactments relating to public health, and a justice may make the like order for enforcing such admission.

See sections 102 and 305 of the Public Health Act, 1875, and sections 10 and 115 of the Public Health Act (London), 1891. See, however, sections 36 and 68

S. 45 (90).

(4) of the 1909 Act. Section 6 of the 1919 Act also refers to inspection by the county medical officer of health. As to obstruction—see section 51 hereof.

Special Provisions as to London

Application of part of Act to London.

46. This part of this Act shall apply to the administrative county of London with the following modifications :—

(1.) The provisions of the Public Health Acts relating to private improvement expenses and to private improvement rates shall, for the purpose of this part of this Act, extend to the county and to the city of London, and in the construction of the said provisions, as respects the county of London, any local authority in that county, and as respects the city of London the Commissioners of Sewers, shall be deemed to be the urban authority.

Private improvement expenses. See section 38 (8) hereof. *Commissioners of Sewers.* Now the Common Council of the city—see note to section 25 (3) hereof.

(2.) The raising of sums required for purchase money or compensation payable under this part of this Act shall be a purpose for which the London County Council or the Commissioners of Sewers of the city of London, may borrow under Part One of this Act, and a purpose for which a vestry or district board may borrow under the Metropolis Management Act, 1855, and the provisions of Part One of this Act with respect to borrowing, and sections one hundred and eighty-three to one hundred and ninety-one of the Metropolis Management Act, 1855, shall apply and have effect accordingly.

18 & 19 Vict. c. 120.

For the borrowing powers under Part I—see section 25 (2) and (3). See also section 1 of the 1894 Act ; and,

particularly, sections 7 and 11 of the Housing (Additional   S. 46 (90).
Powers) Act, 1919.

Vestry or district board.   Now a Metropolitan borough
council.

Metropolis Management Act, 1855.   The borrowing
powers, which appear in sections 183–192 thereof, are
transferred to the Metropolitan borough councils by the
London Government Act, 1899, sections 1 and 4.

See also sections 1 and 14 of the 1903 Act (page 274),
and section 3 of the 1909 Act.

> (3.) The London County Council may, if they think
> fit, lend to a local authority in the administrative
> county of London the sums borrowed in pursuance
> of this part of this Act.

See the London County Council (Finance) Consolidation Act, 1912, section 7.

> (4.) *Repealed by the Statute Law Revision Act,* 1908.

> (5.) Where it appears to the county council, whether
> in the exercise of the powers of a vestry or district
> board or on the representation of a vestry or district
> board or otherwise, that a scheme under this part
> of this Act ought to be made, the council may take
> proceedings for preparing and obtaining the confirma-
> tion of a scheme, and the provisions of this Act
> respecting the scheme shall apply in like manner
> as if they were the vestry or district board, and all
> expenses of and incidental to the scheme and carry-
> ing the same into effect shall, save as herein-after
> mentioned, be borne by the county fund.

Exercise of the Powers.   Under section 45 (2) hereof.

A Scheme.   Under section 39 hereof.   See note to
subsection (1) thereof, headed "Under Part I"; and
sections 72 and 73 hereof.   See also section 5 of the
1919 Act.

> (6.) Where the council consider that such expenses,

or a contribution in respect of them, ought to be paid or made by a vestry or district board, they may apply to a Secretary of State, and the Secretary of State, if satisfied that, having regard to the size of the area, to the number, position, structure, sanitary condition, and neighbourhood of the buildings to be dealt with, the vestry or district board ought to pay, or make a contribution in respect of, the said expenses, the Secretary of State may order such payment or contribution to be made, and the amount thereof shall be a simple contract debt from the vestry or district board to the council.

Secretary of State. Now the Minister of Health.

This subsection will apply only where there is disagreement between the London County Council and the Metropolitan Borough Council—section 14 of the 1903 Act. See also section 33 of the 1909 Act.

(7.) The county council may, if they think fit, pay or contribute to the payment of the expenses of carrying into effect a scheme under this part of this Act by a vestry or district board, and if a vestry or district board consider that the expenses of carrying into effect any scheme under this part of this Act, or a contribution in respect of those expenses, ought to be paid or made by the county council, and the county council decline or fail to agree to pay or make the same, the vestry or district board may apply to a Secretary of State, and if the Secretary of State is satisfied that, having regard to the size of the area, to the number, position, structure, sanitary condition, and neighbourhood of the buildings to be dealt with, the council ought to pay or make a contribution in respect of the said expenses,

he may order such payment or contribution to be S. 46 (90).
made, and the amount thereof shall be a simple
contract debt from the council to the vestry or district board.

See section 73 hereof.   For vestry or district board
read Metropolitan Borough Council, and for Secretary
of State read Minister of Health.

(8.) In the application of this section to Woolwich,
the local board of health shall be deemed to be a
district board, but the raising of any sums required
for purchase money or compensation payable under
this part of this Act shall be a purpose for which
they may borrow under the Public Health Acts,
and the Public Health Acts shall apply accordingly.

Woolwich is now a Metropolitan borough—London
Government Act, 1899.

Supplemental

47. (1.) Where an owner of any dwelling-house is Provision as
to superior
not the person in receipt of the rents and profits thereof, landlord.
he may give notice of such ownership to the local authority,
and thereupon the local authority shall give such owner
notice of any proceedings taken by them in pursuance
of this part of this Act in relation to such dwelling-house.

(2.) If it appears to a court of summary jurisdiction
on the application of any owner of the dwelling-house
that default is being made in the execution of any works
required to be executed on any dwelling-house in respect
of which a closing order has been made, or in the demolition of any building or any dwelling-house or in claiming
to retain any site, in pursuance of this part of this Act,
and that the interests of the applicant will be prejudiced
by such default, and that it is just to make the order,

S. 47 (90). the court may make an order empowering the applicant forthwith to enter on the dwelling-house, and within the time fixed by the order to execute the said works, or to demolish the building or to claim to retain the site, as the case may be, and where it seems to the court just so to do, the court may make a like order in favour of any other owner.

(3.) A court of summary jurisdiction may in any case by order enlarge * the time within which a claim may be made to retain the site of a building.

(4.) Before an order is made under this section notice of the application shall be given to the local authority.

Owner. For definition—see section 29 hereof, from which it will be seen that there may be several owners, including a lessee. The superior landlord's interests are hereby preserved.

As to the effect of subsection (1)—see *Osborne v. Skinners Co.* [1891] 60 L.J. M.C. 156.

The application under subsection (2) must be made in open court—Summary Jurisdiction Act, 1879, section 20. Note also section 30 of the 1919 Act. Sections 28 and 32 thereof and sections 14 and 15 of the 1909 Act may also be usefully read.

For closing and demolition orders—see sections 17 and 18 of the 1909 Act. For claim to retain the site—see section 38 (5) hereof.

Remedies of owner for breach of covenant, &c. not to be prejudiced. **48.** Nothing in this part of this Act shall prejudice or interfere with the right or remedies of any owner for the breach, non-observance, or non-performance of any covenant or contract entered into by a tenant or lessee in reference to any dwelling-house in respect of which an order is made by a local authority under this part of this Act ; and if any owner is obliged to take possession of any dwelling-house in order to comply with any

* Words here were repealed by the Housing, Town Planning, &c., Act, 1909.

such order, the taking possession shall not affect his S. 48 (90). right to avail himself of any such breach, non-observance, or non-performance that may have occurred prior to his so taking possession.

See section 47 and notes thereto. The object is to preserve to the freeholder or lessor his rights or remedies under the lease, notwithstanding closing or demolition orders or his intervention under section 47 (2).

49. (1.) Where the owner of any dwelling-house and Service of his residence or place of business are known to the local notices. authority, it shall be the duty of the clerk of the local authority, if the residence or place of business is within the district of such local authority, to serve any notice by this part of this Act required to be served on the owner, by giving it to him, or for him, to some inmate of his residence or place of business within the district ; and in any other case it shall be the duty of the clerk of the local authority to serve the notice by post in a registered letter addressed to the owner at his residence or place of business.

(2.) Where the owner of the dwelling-house or his residence or place of business is not known to, and after diligent inquiry cannot be found by the local authority, then the clerk of the local authority may serve the notice by leaving it, addressed to the owner, with some occupier of the dwelling-house, or if there be not an occupier, then by causing it to be put up on some con-spicuous part of the dwelling-house.

(3.) Notice served upon the agent of the owner shall be deemed notice to the owner.

See the amendment made by section 13 (1) of the 1903 Act. As to authentification—see section 86 hereof. As to service by post—see note to section 7 hereof.

S. 50 (90).
Description of owner in proceedings.

50.. Where in any proceedings under this part of this Act it is necessary to refer to the owner of any dwelling-house, it shall be sufficient to designate him as the " owner " thereof without name or further description.

Penalty for preventing execution of Act.

51. (1.) If any person being the occupier of any dwelling-house prevents the owner thereof, or being the owner or occupier of any dwelling-house prevents the medical officer of health, or the officers, agents, servants, or workmen of such owner or officer from carrying into effect with respect to the dwelling-house any of the provisions of this part of this Act, after notice of the intention so to do has been given to such person any court of summary jurisdiction on proof thereof may order such person to permit to be done on such premises all things requisite for carrying into effect, with respect to such dwelling-house, the provisions of this part of this Act.

(2.) If at the expiration of ten days after the service of such order such person fails to comply therewith, he shall for every day during which the failure continues be liable on summary conviction to a fine not exceeding twenty pounds : Provided that if any such failure is by the occupier, the owner, unless assenting thereto, shall not be liable to such fine.

See section 90 hereof as to recovery of fines, and section 89 hereof and note thereto, further as to obstruction.

Report to local authority by county medical officer.

45 & 46 Vict. c. 50.

52. A representation from the medical officer of health of any county submitted to the county council and forwarded by that council to the local authority of any district in the county, not being a borough as defined by the Municipal Corporations Act, 1882, shall, for the purposes of this part of this Act, have the like effect as a representation from the medical officer of health of S. 52 (90). the district.

As to the representations referred to—see sections 30 and 38 hereof and section 17 of the 1909 Act. If the local authority do not act—see section 45 hereof, and section 5 of the 1919 Act.

PART III

WORKING CLASS LODGING HOUSES

Adoption of Part III

53. (1.) The expression "lodging houses for the working classes" when used in this part of this Act shall include separate houses or cottages for the working classes, whether containing one or several tenements, and the purposes of this part of this Act shall include the provision of such houses and cottages.

Definition of purposes of Labouring Classes Lodging Houses Acts.

(2.) The expression "cottage" in this part of this Act may include a garden of not more than one acre.

The definition of "cottage" is given as per section 50 of the 1909 Act.

54. ("Adoption of this part of Act.") *Repealed by the Housing of the Working Classes Act, 1900, and the Housing, Town Planning, &c., Act, 1909.*

55. ("Provisions in case of adoption by rural sanitary authority.") *Repealed by the Housing of the Working Classes Act, 1900, and the Housing, Town Planning, &c., Act, 1909.*

Execution of Part III by Local Authority

56. Where this part of this Act has been adopted in any district, the local authority shall have power to carry it into execution (subject to the provisions of this part of this Act with respect to rural sanitary authorities),

Powers of local authority.

S. 56 (90). and for that purpose may exercise the same powers whether of contract or otherwise as in the execution of their duties in the case of the London County Council 18 & 19 Vict. under the Metropolis Management Act, 1855, and the c. 120. 38 & 39 Vict. Acts amending the same, or in the case of sanitary authori- c. 55. ties under the Public Health Acts, or in the case of the Commissioners of Sewers under the Acts conferring powers on such Commissioners.

Adopted. Adoption is no longer necessary—section 1, 1909 Act, and the words in brackets are practically superfluous.

Local authority. See section 92 and the First Schedule hereto. It is now the duty of the local authority to prepare and carry out housing schemes—sections 1 and 2 of the 1919 Act—and if default is made the Ministry may act—section 5 thereof—or in certain cases, whether there is default or not, the Ministry may authorise the county council to act—sections 4 and 5 thereof. Further as to default—see sections 10–13 of the 1909 Act.

As to joint action by local authorities—see section 38 of the 1909 Act, and section 1 (6) of the 1919 Act.

As to London—see section 41 of the 1919 Act.

As to Commissioners of Sewers—see section 25 (3) hereof.

Metropolis Management Act, 1853. Section 149 thereof, and possibly sections 150–156 thereof, but see section 57 hereof as to acquisition of land, and also section 41 of the 1919 Act.

As to expenses and borrowing power of Metropolitan borough councils—see section 3 of the 1900 Act.

Public Health Act. See sections 173 and 174 thereof for powers of contracting by sanitary authorities.

Acquisition of land. **57.** (1.) Land for the purposes of this part of this Act may be acquired by a local authority in like manner 38 & 39 Vict. as if those purposes were purposes of the Public Health c. 55. Act, 1875, and sections one hundred and seventy-five to one hundred and seventy-eight, both inclusive, of that Act (relating to the purchase of lands), shall apply accordingly, and shall for the purposes of this part of S. 57 (90). this Act extend to London in like manner as if the Commissioners of Sewers and London County Council respectively were a local authority in the said sections mentioned.*

As to the purposes of this part—see section 59 hereof, section 11 of the 1903 Act, section 6 of the 1909 Act; and as to additional powers for the acquisition of land—section 2 (3) of the 1909 Act and section 12 of 1919 Act.

By section 8 of the 1909 Act a local authority may accept gifts of land, and see section 31 of the 1919 Act as to the powers of tenants for life to sell for nominal prices, &c., and section 74 hereof and section 7 of the 1909 Act for, amongst other things, reasonable prices, having regard to the purposes.

The quoted sections of the Public Health Act, 1875, still apply to purchase by agreement (see, however, section 5 of the 1909 Act) but compulsory powers are now obtained under section 2 of the 1909 Act. The procedure is regulated by the First Schedule to the Act, but as to the assessment of compensation—see the Acquisition of Land (Assessment of Compensation) Act, 1919.

As to the purchase money or compensation payable by one local authority to another—see section 5 of the 1909 Act.

An urban authority may acquire land outside their district—section 1, 1900 Act; and land may be acquired in anticipation—section 2 (3), 1909 Act. As to deficiency in rates—see section 34 thereof; ancient monuments, &c.—section 45; commons, open spaces and allotments —section 73; and royal parks—section 74 thereof.

As to acquiring water rights—see section 14 of the 1919 Act.

As to dealing with the land acquired—see section 15 of the 1919 Act and notes thereto.

Section 177 of the Public Health Act, 1875, provides as follows : " Any local authority may, with the consent

* Words which followed here were repealed by the Statute Law Revision Act, 1908.

14.

S. 57 (90).   of the Local Government Board, let for any term any lands which they may possess, as and when they may conveniently spare the same." There is some doubt as to this applying to land acquired for housing, but a statutory body holding land to be ultimately used for a particular purpose may use it or allow it to be used for a temporary purpose provided that this does not interfere with its use for the ultimate purpose—*Attorney-General v. Teddington Urban District Council* [1898] 1 Ch. 66. The consent of the Board (Ministry) is not needed to such temporary letting.

(2.) *Repealed by the Housing, Town Planning, &c., Act, 1919, section 50 and 5th schedule.*

(3.) *The local authority may, with the consent of the Local Government Board, appropriate, for the purposes of this part of this Act, any lodging houses so purchased or taken on lease, and any other land which may be for the time being vested in them, or at their disposal.

The words "any lodging houses so purchased or taken on lease" appear to be meaningless, as subsection (2) which allowed such purchase or lease (of any lodging houses for the working classes already or hereafter to be built and provided) is repealed. But see section 12 (3) of the 1919 Act.

As to appropriation—see also section 23 hereof. By section 111 of the Municipal Corporations Act, 1882, a municipal corporation may convert corporate land into sites for working men's dwellings.

Local authority may purchase existing lodging houses.   **58.** The trustees of any lodging houses for the working classes for the time being provided in any district by private subscriptions or otherwise, may, with the consent of a majority of the committee or other persons by whom they were appointed trustees, sell or lease the

* As altered by the Housing, Town Planning, &c., Act, 1919, 2nd schedule.

lodging houses to the local authority of the district, or S. 58 (90). make over to them the management thereof.

See also sections 8 and 9 of the 1909 Act. As to management—see section 61 hereof.

59. The local authority may, on any land acquired Erection of lodging houses. or appropriated by them, erect any building suitable for lodging houses for the working classes, and convert any buildings into lodging houses for the working classes, and may alter, enlarge, repair, and improve the same respectively, and fit up, furnish, and supply the same respectively with all requisite furniture, fittings, and conveniences.

See also section 12 (1) of the 1919 Act. As to acquisition and appropriation—see section 57 (1) and (3) hereof. As to the local authority itself erecting houses—compare section 12 (3) hereof.

The provision of houses is compulsory under a scheme prepared under section 1 of the 1919 Act, section 2 thereof. See notes thereto, section 11 of the 1903 Act, and section 1 of the 1900 Act.

As to the purchase of buildings to be converted—see section 57 hereof, and sections 12 and 16 of the 1919 Act.

By section 3 of the 1903 Act, where local authorities or others in carrying out other works take dwellings occupied by thirty or more persons belonging to the working classes, they may be required to provide other housing accommodation.

60. (" Sale and exchange of lands.") *Repealed by the Housing, Town Planning, &c., Act, 1919, section 50 and 5th schedule.*

Management of Lodging Houses

61. (1.) The general management, regulation, and Management to be vested in local authority. control of the lodging houses established or acquired by a local authority under this part of this Act shall be vested in and exercised by the local authority.

S. 61 (90).   (2.) The local authority may make such reasonable charges for the tenancy or occupation of the lodging houses provided under this part of this Act as they may determine by regulations.

See section 7 of the 1919 Act as to reasonable charges; and section 17 as to non-disqualification of tenants.

The regulations may be altered from time to time without the consent of any superior authority. See section 188 of the Public Health Act, 1875. They are not byelaws.

As to power to repair, furnish, &c.—see section 59 hereof.

The houses are those for the working classes and should be let to such persons, but the term " working classes " is not defined (deliberately so) and the Minister of Health has stated, repeatedly, that the term should be liberally construed. See *Marron v. Cootehill No. 2 Rural District Council* [1915] A.C. 792, as to undue preference under the Irish Acts.

With the consent of the Ministry the houses may be sold or leased, but not to employers to be " tied-houses " —section 15 (1) (*d*) of the 1919 Act.

See section 35, 1909 Act and note thereto as to exemption from inhabited house duty in certain circumstances.

Byelaws for regulation of lodging houses.   **62.** (1.) The local authority may make byelaws for the management, use, and regulation of the lodging houses, and it shall be obligatory on the local authority, except in the case of a lodging house which is occupied as a separate dwelling, by such byelaws to make sufficient provision for the several purposes expressed in the Sixth Schedule to this Act.

(2.) A printed copy or sufficient abstract of the byelaws relating to the management, use, and regulation of the lodging houses shall be put up and at all times kept in every room therein.

For definition of " lodging houses "—see section 53 hereof.

See further as to byelaws—section 26 of the 1919 S. 62 (90).
Act.

As to separate dwellings—see *Weatheritt v. Cantley*
[1901] 2 K.B. 285, 65 J.P. 644; *Kyffin v. Simmons*
[1903] 67 J.P. 228.

63. ("Disqualification of tenants of lodging houses
on receiving parochial relief.") *Repealed by the Housing,
Town Planning, &c., Act,* 1909.

64. ("When lodging houses are considered too ex-
pensive they may be sold.") *Repealed by the Housing,
Town Planning, &c. Act,* 1919, *section* 50 *and 5th
schedule.*

Expenses and Borrowing of Local Authorities.

65. All expenses incurred by a local authority in the Payment of
execution of this part of this Act shall be defrayed— expenses.

> (i.) in the case of an authority in the administrative
> county of London, out of the Dwelling House
> Improvement Fund under Part I of this Act;
> (ii.) in the case of an urban sanitary authority, as
> part of the general expenses of their execution of
> the Public Health Acts.*

Provided that if on the application of the rural sanitary
authority it is so declared*by the county council*then the
said expenses of the rural sanitary authority shall be
defrayed as general expenses of the said authority in
the execution of the Public Health Acts, and if such
expenses are not to be borne by the whole of the district,
shall be paid out of a common fund to be raised in manner
provided by the Public Health Act, 1875, but as if the
contributory places which are to bear those expenses
constituted the whole of the district.

* Words following here, relating to "the case of a rural sanitary
authority," were repealed by the Housing of the Working Classes
Act, 1900, and the Housing, Town Planning, &c., Act, 1909.

S 65 (90). *Administrative County of London.* See section 93 hereof.

As to Metropolitan boroughs—see section 3 of the 1900 Act.

Dwelling House Improvement Fund. See section 24 hereof.

Public Health Acts. See sections 207 and 208 of the Public Health Act, 1875. The expenses are payable out of the local rate (borough or general district rate)— First Schedule hereto.

As to rural sanitary authorities (rural district councils) —see section 31 (1) of the 1909 Act and notes thereto, and note to the First Schedule hereof.

Borrowing for purposes of Part III.

66. The London County Council and the Commissioners of Sewers may borrow for the purpose of the execution of this part of this Act, in like manner and subject to the like conditions as they may borrow for the purposes of Part I of this Act, and a sanitary authority may borrow for the purpose of the execution of this part of this Act in like manner and subject to the like conditions as for the purpose of defraying the above-mentioned expenses.

See section 25 hereof and notes thereto.

As to Metropolitan boroughs—see section 3 of the 1900 Act. As to rural authorities—see section 31 of the 1909 Act.

See also section 65 hereof and section 3 and the Schedule, paragraph (3), to the 1903 Act.

In the 1919 Act there are several references to borrowing powers—sections 4 (2), 8 (1), 18 (3) and (4), and 22 (3).

And there are special powers in sections 7, 8 and 11 of the Housing (Additional Powers) Act, 1919.

Loans to and Powers of Companies, Societies, and Individuals

Loans by Public Works Commissioners.

67. (1.) In addition to the powers conferred upon them by any other enactment, the Public Works Loan Commissioners may, out of the funds at their disposal,

advance on loan to any such body or proprietor as S. 67 (90).
herein-after mentioned ; namely,—

(a) any railway company or dock or harbour company,
or any other company, society, or association
established for the purpose of constructing or
improving, or of facilitating or encouraging the
construction or improvement of dwellings for the
working classes, or for trading or manufacturing
purposes (in the course of whose business, or in the
discharge of whose duties persons of· the working
classes are employed) ;

(b) any private person entitled to any land for an
estate in fee simple, or for any term of years absolute,
whereof not less than fifty years shall for the time
being remain unexpired ;

and any such body or proprietor may borrow from the
Public Works Loan Commissioners such money as may
be required for the purpose of constructing or improving,
or of facilitating or encouraging the construction or
improvement of dwellings for the working classes.

Any other enactment.   The Public Works Loans
Act, 1879, under sections 5 and 6 whereof the commissioners have power to lend to the Peabody Trustees
in London, and to labourers dwellings companies, &c.,
in London and elsewhere, for housing purposes.

Railway Companies . . . See section 68 hereof—
" Powers to Companies."

Loans to public utility societies.   See section 20 of the
1919 Act, which bears this heading, and section 4 of the
1909 Act for extensions of the present section.

Loans to private persons.   See section 21 of the 1919
Act.   The local authority may lend in certain circumstances—see section 22 of the 1919 Act.

As to the rate of interest to be charged—see the
Treasury Minute of 1st November 1920, page 536.

(2.) Such loans shall be made in manner provided by   38 & 39 Vict.
c. 89.

S. 67 (90). the Public Works Loans Act, 1875, subject to the following provisions :—

 (*a*) Any such advance may be made whether the body or proprietor receiving the same has or has not power to borrow on mortgage or otherwise, independently of this Act ; but nothing in this Act shall repeal or alter any regulation, statutory or otherwise, whereby any company may be restricted from borrowing until a definite portion of capital is subscribed for, taken, or paid up.

 (*b*) The period for the repayment of the sums advanced shall not exceed forty years.

 (*c*) No money shall be advanced on mortgage of any land or dwellings solely, unless the estate therein proposed to be mortgaged shall be either an estate in fee simple, or an estate for a term of years absolute, whereof not less than fifty years shall be unexpired at the date of the advance.

 (*d*) The money advanced on the security of a mortgage of any land or dwellings solely shall not exceed one moiety of the value, to be ascertained to the satisfaction of the Public Works Loan Commissioners, of the estate or interest in such land or dwellings proposed to be mortgaged ; but advances may be made by instalments from time to time as the building of the dwellings on the land mortgaged progresses, so that the total advance do not at any time exceed the amount aforesaid ; and a mortgage may be accordingly made to secure such advances so to be made from time to time.

 Paragraph (*b*). Fifty years where the loan is made to a public utility society—section 20 (2) (*a*) of the 1919 Act.

Paragraph (c). See section 20 (2) (b) of the 1919 S. 67 (90).
Act.

Paragraph (d). Seventy-five per cent. instead of one
moiety, under the special conditions of sections 20 (2) (c)
and 21 of the 1919 Act. See also section 4 (1) of the 1909
Act.

(3.) For the purpose of constructing or improving
or facilitating or encouraging the construction or improvement of dwellings for the working classes, every
such body as aforesaid is hereby authorised to purchase,
take, and hold land, and if not already a body corporate
shall, for the purpose of holding such land under this
part of this Act, and of suing and being sued in respect
thereof, be nevertheless deemed a body corporate with
perpetual succession.

This provision removes the difficulty of con-
veying to trustees for the bodies mentioned, who may be
frequently changed. · It also removes difficulties which
might arise under the Mortmain and Charitable Uses
Act, 1888. See also the Working Classes Dwellings Act,
1890, page 254.

68. Any railway company, or dock or harbour company or any other company, society, or association,
established for trading or manufacturing purposes in
the course of whose business or in the discharge of whose
duties persons of the working class are employed, may and
are hereby (notwithstanding any Act of Parliament, or
charter, or any rule of law or equity to the contrary)
authorised at any time to erect, either on their own land
or on any other land (which they are hereby authorised
to purchase and hold for the purpose, and to pay for out
of any funds at their disposal), dwellings for the accommodation of all or any of the persons of the working
class employed · by them.

Powers to companies.

S. 68 (90). Such dwellings must conform to the byelaws—*Manchester, Sheffield and Lincolnshire Railway Companies v. Barnsley Union* [1892] 56 J.P. 149.

Power to water and gas companies to supply water and gas to lodging houses.

69. Any commissioners of waterworks, trustees of waterworks, water companies, gas companies, and other corporations, bodies, and persons having the management of any waterworks, reservoirs, wells, springs, or streams of water, and gasworks respectively, may, in their discretion, grant and furnish supplies of water or gas for lodging houses provided under this part of this Act, either without charge or on such other favourable terms as they think fit.

Inspection of lodging houses.

70. A lodging house established in any district under this part of this Act, shall be at all times open to the inspection of the local authority of that district or of any officer from time to time authorised by such authority.

As to penalty for obstruction—see section 89 hereof.

Application of penalties.

71. Any fine for the breach of any byelaw under this part of this Act shall be paid to the credit of the funds out of which the expenses of this part of this Act are defrayed.

See section 65 hereof.

PART IV

SUPPLEMENTAL

Limit of area to be dealt with on official representation.

72. Where an official representation made to the London County Council in pursuance of Part I of this Act relates to not more than ten houses, the London County Council shall not take any proceedings on such representation, but shall direct the medical officer of health making the same to represent the case to the local authority under Part II of this Act, and it shall be the duty of the local authority to deal with such case in S. 72 (90). manner provided by that part of this Act.

Official representation . . . Part I. See sections 4, 5 and 16 hereof. But though the Metropolitan Borough Council must then Act, the London County Council may contribute towards the payment of the expenses —section 46 (7) hereof.

73. (1.) In either of the following cases :

(a) Where a medical officer of health has represented to any local authority in the county of London under Part II of this Act that any dwelling-houses are in a condition so dangerous or injurious to health, as to be unfit for human habitation, or that the pulling down of any obstructive buildings would be expedient, and such authority resolve that the case of such dwelling-houses or buildings is of such general importance to the county of London that it should be dealt with by a scheme under Part I of this Act ; or

(b) Where an official representation as mentioned in Part I of this Act has been made to the London County Council in relation to any houses, courts, or alleys within a certain area, and that council resolve that the case of such houses, courts, or alleys is not of general importance to the county of London and should be dealt with under Part II of this Act ;

such local authority or council may submit such resolution to a Secretary of State, and thereupon the Secretary of State may appoint an arbitrator, and direct him to hold a local inquiry, and such arbitrator shall hold such inquiry, and report to the Secretary of State as to whether, having regard to the size of the area, to the number of houses to be dealt with, to the position, structure, and sanitary condition of such houses, and of the neigh-

Provisions as to parts of Act under which reports are to be dealt with in county of London.

S. 73 (90). bourhood thereof, and to the provisions of Part I of this Act, the case is either wholly or partially of any and what importance to the county of London, with power to such arbitrator to report that in the event of the case being dealt with under Part II of this Act, the London County Council ought to make a contribution in respect of the expense of dealing with the case.

(2.) The Secretary of State, after considering the report of the arbitrator, may, according as to him seems just, decide that the case shall be dealt with either under Part II of this Act, or under Part I of this Act, and the medical officer of health or other proper officer shall forthwith make the representation necessary for proceedings in accordance with such decision.

For " Secretary of State " read the Minister of Health.
Paragraph (a). The representation is made under sections 30 and 38 hereof.
Paragraph (b). The representation is evidently made under sections 5 and 16 hereof, though the words there used are not those here used—note also that the words of paragraph (b) of section 4 hereof are not here repeated.
Local inquiry. See section 85 hereof.
Contribution in respect of the expense. See section 46 (7) hereof.
Generally. Normally a Part II scheme will be done at the expense of the Metropolitan borough council concerned, while a Part I scheme will be at the expense of the London County Council. The provisions of section 46 (5), (6) and (7) and section 14 of the 1903 Act help to deal with the difficulties which may thus arise, and may be sufficient without recourse to this section.

Amendment of 45 & 46 Vi t. c. 38 as regards erection of buildings for working classes.

74. (1.) The Settled Land Act, 1882, shall be amended as follows :—

(a) Any sale, exchange, or lease of land in pursuance of the said Act, when made for the purpose of the erection on such land of dwellings for the working classes, may be made at such price, or for such S. 74 (90). consideration, or for such rent, as having regard to the said purpose, and to all the circumstances of the case, is the best that can be reasonably obtained, notwithstanding that a higher price, consideration, or rent might have been obtained if the land were sold, exchanged, or leased for another purpose.

*(b) The improvements on which capital money arising under the Settled Land Act, 1882, may be expended enumerated in section twenty-five of the said Act, and referred to in section thirty of the said Act, shall, in addition to cottages for labourers, farm servants, and artizans whether employed on the settled land or not, include the provision of dwellings available for the working classes, either by means of building new buildings or by means of the reconstruction, enlargement, or improvement of existing buildings, so as to make them available for the purpose, if that provision of dwellings is, in the opinion of the court, not injurious to the estate, or is agreed to by the tenant for life and the trustees of the settlement.

This subsection is discussed in the notes to section 31 of the 1919 Act.

(2.) Any body corporate holding land may sell, exchange, or lease the land for the purpose of the erection of dwellings for the working classes at such price, or for such consideration, or for such rent as having regard to the said purposes and to all the circumstances of the case is the best that can reasonably be obtained, notwithstanding that a higher price, consideration,

* As substituted by section 7 (1) of the 1909 Act.

S. 74 (90). or rent might have been obtained if the land were sold, exchanged, or leased for another purpose.

Without this, municipal corporations, colleges, hospitals and other corporate bodies holding lands upon trust could not sell except at the best market price.

Condition to be implied on letting houses for the working classes. **75.** In any contract made after the fourteenth day of August one thousand eight hundred and eighty-five for letting for habitation by persons of the working classes a house or part of a house, there shall be implied a condition that the house is at the commencement of the holding in all respects reasonably fit for human habitation. In this section the expression " letting for habitation by persons of the working classes " means the letting for habitation of a house or part of a house at a rent not exceeding in England the sum named as the limit for the composition of rates by section three of the

32 &.33 Vict. c. 41. Poor Rate Assessment and Collection Act, 1869, and in Scotland or Ireland four pounds.

This has been extended by section 12 of the 1903 Act, which provides that the present section shall, as respects any contract made after 14th August 1903, take effect notwithstanding any agreement to the contrary, &c. See also sections 14 and 15 of the 1909 Act, by which the rateable values named in the quoted Act (£20 in the Metropolis, £13 in Liverpool, £10 Manchester and Birmingham, and £8 elsewhere) are materially extended. But in practice these provisions are largely ineffective to secure good repair, and the remedy will be rather that (to require repairs) given to local authorities by section 28 of the 1919 Act. Where the text applies the tenant can recover damages for breach of the implied condition and can repudiate the contract—see *Walker v. Hobbs*, 23 Q.B.D. 458.

Weekly tenancies do not expire each week-end without notice—*Bowen v. Anderson* [1894] 1 Q.B. 164.

If part of a house is let at a rent within the limits

fixed, apparently the implied condition will extend to S. 75 (90).
the whole house.

A house for which no rent is paid is not within the
section.

Rent is not defined, and there is nothing to indicate
whether rent which includes rates, &c., is to be taken as
the rent.

Reasonably fit for human habitation. These words are
not defined, but section 26 (1) of the 1919 Act may be
taken as a standard. There are also many decided
cases touching on the subject, the leading ones being
Walker v. Hobbs [1889] 23 Q.B.D. 458, and *Ryall v.
Kidwell* [1913] 3 K.B. 123, affirmed [1914] 30 T.L.R. 503.

76. (1.) The London County Council may, with the Medical
consent of a Secretary of State, at any time appoint one health in
or more legally qualified practitioner or practitioners, county of
with such remuneration as they think fit, for the purpose London.
of carrying into effect any part of this Act.

(2.) Any medical officer of health appointed by the
London County Council, and any officer appointed under
this section by the London County Council, shall be deemed
to be a medical officer of health of a local authority within
the meaning of this Act.

See section 68 of the 1909 Act.

77. (" Power to local authority to enter and value
premises.") *Repealed by the Housing, Town Planning,
&c., Act, 1909.*

78. Where a building or any part of a building pur- Compen-
chased by the local authority in pursuance of a scheme tenants for
under Part I or Part II of this Act is not closed by a expense of
closing order, and is occupied by any tenant whose removal.
contract of tenancy is for less than a year, the local
authority, if they require him to give up possession of
such building or part for the purpose of pulling down

S. 78 (90).

the building, may make to the said tenant a reasonable allowance on account of his expenses in removing.

Closing Order, made under section 17 of the 1909 Act, subsection (5) whereof provides for a reasonable allowance on account of the tenant's expense in removing.

Generally. This section appears to cover the case where the local authority have purchased the building and are terminating the tenancy by notice to quit. They may make the tenant an allowance towards removal expenses. If they require him to quit before the notice expires he will usually be entitled to compensation—see section 121 of the Lands Clauses Consolidation Act, 1845.

Duties of
medical
officer of
health.

79. (1.) Anything which under Part I or Part II of this Act is authorised or required to be done by or to a medical officer of health may be done by or to any person authorised to act temporarily as such medical officer of health.

(2.) Every representation made by a medical officer of health in pursuance of this Act shall be in writing.

Temporarily. See section 26 hereof.
Representation. See sections 5, 30 and 38 hereof.
Writing includes " printing, lithography, photography, and other modes of representing or reproducing words in a visible form "—Interpretation Act, 1889, section 20.

Accounts
and audit.

80. (1.) Separate accounts shall be kept by the local authority and their officers of their receipts and expenditure under each part of this Act.

(2.) Such accounts shall be audited in the like manner and with the like power to the officer auditing the same, and with the like incidents and consequences, as the accounts of the local authority are for the time being required to be audited by law.

See also section 4 of the 1900 Act. For other accountancy matters—see sections 24, 42, 44, and 65 hereof,

and section 31 of the 1909 Act.   There are also references S. 80 (90).
thereto in the 1919 Act, notably section 7.

Audited.   By district auditors—see section 71 of the
Local Government Act, 1888, and, as regards Metropolitan
boroughs, section 14 of the London Government Act,
1899.

81. *For the purposes of this Act, a local authority Power of
acting under this Act may appoint so many persons as local authority to
they may think fit, for any purposes of this Act which appoint committees.
in the opinion of such authority would be better regulated
and managed by means of a committee : Provided that
a committee so appointed shall consist as to a majority
of its members of members of the appointing local
authority and shall in no case be authorised to borrow
any money, or to make any rate, and shall be subject to
any regulations and restrictions which may be imposed
by the authority that formed it.

If the local authority desire that the actions of the
committee be confirmed by them, they should make
that restriction.

Note section 71 of the 1909 Act requiring the establishment of a public health and housing committee.

The present section is not repealed by section 56 of
the Local Government Act, 1894.

82. Where a local authority sell any land acquired by Application
them for any of the purposes of this Act, the proceeds of purchase money.
of the sale shall be applied for any purpose, including
repayment of borrowed money, for which capital money
may be applied, and which is approved by the Local
Government Board.

See a similar provision in section 15 (3) of the 1919
Act.   See also section 24 (5) hereof.

83. ("Rates   of   loans   by   Public   Works   Loan

* As altered by the Housing, Town Planning, &c., Act, 1919, 2nd
schedule.

15

S. 83 (90).

Commissioners.") *Repealed by the Housing, Town Planning, &c., Act, 1909, section 75, and 6th schedule. See now section 3 thereof.*

Application of certain provisions as to byelaws. 18 & 19 Vict. c. 120.

84. With respect to byelaws authorised by this Act to be made—

(*a*) sections two hundred and two and two hundred and three of the Metropolis Management Act, 1855, where such byelaws are made by the London County Council, or any nuisance authority in the administrative county of London ; and

38 & 39 Vict. c. 55.

(*b*) the provisions of the Public Health Act, 1875, relating to byelaws, where such byelaws are made by a sanitary authority,

shall apply to such byelaws, and a fine or penalty under any such byelaws may be recovered on summary conviction.

See further as to byelaws—section 62 hereof, and sections 24 and 26 of the 1919 Act.

Paragraph (*a*). The quoted sections empower any Metropolitan borough council to make byelaws, which must be confirmed at a subsequent meeting and by a Secretary of State, and provide for publication, &c.

Paragraph (*b*). The provisions referred to are contained in sections 182–187 of the quoted Act : the byelaws must be confirmed by the Ministry, printed and published, &c.

See section 90 hereof as to recovery of fine.

Local inquiries.

85. *(1.) For the purposes of the execution of their powers and duties under this Act the Local Government Board may cause such local inquiries to be held as the Board see fit, and the costs incurred in relation to any such local inquiry, *and to the local inquiry which any other confirming authority holds or causes to be held,*

* As altered by the Housing, Town Planning, &c., Act 1909, 2nd and 6th schedules.

including the salary or remuneration of any inspector or S. 85 (90). officer of or person employed by the Board *or confirming authority* engaged in the inquiry, shall be paid by the local authorities and persons concerned in the inquiry, or by such of them and in such proportions as the Board *or confirming authority* may direct, and that Board *or authority* may certify the amount of the costs incurred, and any sum so certified and directed by that Board or authority to be paid by any local authority or person shall be a debt to the Crown from such local authority or person.

(2.) Sections two hundred and ninety-three to two hundred and ninety-six and section two hundred and ninety-eight of the Public Health Act, 1875, shall apply for the purpose of any order to be made by the Local Government Board or any local inquiry which that Board cause to be held in pursuance of any part of this Act.

The words printed in italics, though not repealed, are now spent—section 2, 1903 Act.

Local inquiries may be held under sections 8 (3), 31 (2) and 39 (3) hereof, and sections 2 (1), 10 (1) and the First Schedule, paragraph (6), of the 1909 Act. Usually there is an inquiry under the procedure adopted by the Ministry under section 39 of the 1909 Act. But by section 11 (3) of the 1919 Act an inquiry may be dispensed with within two years of 31st July 1919, where otherwise it would be required under section 2 (1) and the First Schedule, paragraph (6), of the 1909 Act.

The inquiry made under section 16 hereof is also by section 26 of the 1909 Act, one of the local inquiries dealt with in the present section.

Sections 293–296 and 298 of the Public Health Act, 1875, are as follows :—

293. " The Local Government Board may from time to time cause to be made such inquiries as are directed by this Act, and such inquiries as they see fit in relation to any

S. 85 (90).

matters concerning the public health in any place, or any matters with respect to which their sanction, approval or consent, is required by this Act."

294. "The Local Government Board may make orders as to the costs of inquiries or proceedings instituted by, or of appeals to, the said Board under this Act, and as to the parties by whom the rates out of which such costs shall be borne ; and any such order may be made a rule of one of the superior courts of law on the application of the person named."

295. "All orders made by the Local Government Board in pursuance of this Act shall be binding and conclusive in respect of the matters to which they refer, and shall be published in such manner as that Board may direct."

296. "Inspectors of the Local Government Board shall, for the purposes of any inquiry directed by the Board, have in relation to witnesses and their examination, the production of papers and accounts, and the inspection of places and matters required to be inspected, similar powers to those which poor law inspectors have under the Acts relating to the relief of the poor for purposes of those Acts."

298. "The reasonable costs of any local inquiry in respect of provisional orders made in pursuance of this Act and of the inquiry preliminary thereto, as sanctioned by the Local Government Board, whether in promoting or opposing the same, shall be deemed to be expenses properly incurred for purposes of this Act by the local authority interested in or affected by such provisional orders, and such costs shall be paid accordingly, and if thought expedient by the Local Government Board, the local authority may contract a loan for the purpose of defraying such costs.

Orders, notices, &c.

86. (1.) An order in writing made by a local authority under this Act shall be under their seal and authenticated by the signature of their clerk or his lawful deputy.

(2.) A notice, demand, or other written document proceeding from the local authority under this Act shall be signed by their clerk or his lawful deputy.

In writing. See note to section 79 hereof.

A Notice, &c., does not require sealing.

Service of notice, &c., on the local authority.

87. Any notice, summons, writ or other proceeding at law or otherwise required to be served on a local authority in relation to carrying into effect the objects

or purposes of this Act, or any of them, may be served S. 87 (90).
upon that authority by delivering the same to their
clerk, or leaving the same at his office with some person
employed there.

By section 13 (2) of the 1903 Act, it may be sent by
registered post.

For service by the local authority—see sections 7,
39 and 49 hereof and section 13 (1) of the 1903 Act.

88. (1.) A person shall not vote as member of a local   Prohibition
authority or county council or any committee thereof   on persons
interested
upon any resolution or question which is proposed or   voting as
members of
arises in pursuance of Part I or Part II *or Part III of   local
authority.
this Act, if it relates to any dwelling house, building,
or land in which he is beneficially interested.

(2.) If any person votes in contravention of this section
he shall, on summary conviction, be liable for each offence
to a fine not exceeding fifty pounds ; but the fact of
his giving the vote shall not invalidate any resolution or
proceeding of the local authority or county council.

Note also section 17 of the 1919 Act.

See section 90 as to recovery of fine.   The information
may be laid by anyone—*R. v. Stewart* [1896] 1 Q.B. 300
at page 303.

89. *Where any person obstructs the medical officer of   Penalty for
health, or any officer of the local authority, or of the   obstructing
the execution
confirming authority mentioned in Part I of this Act, or   of Act.
any person authorised to enter dwelling-houses, premises,
or buildings in pursuance of this Act, in the performance
of anything which such officer, authority or person is
by this Act required or authorised to do, he shall, on
summary conviction, be liable to a fine not exceeding
twenty pounds.

* As altered by the Housing, Town Planning, &c., Act, 1909, section
46 and 2nd schedule.

S. 89 (90).   This part of the Act being supplemental the present
section applies to all the parts (see the remarks of Lord
Reading in *Arlidge v. Scarse* [1915] 2 K.B. 333), but
there is also a special provision for penalty for preventing
execution of Part II, in section 51 hereof. The present
section and section 51 are thus in some cases alternative,
e.g. where an owner prevents the entrance of a duly
authorised person for survey under section 36 of the
1909 Act, an order may be obtained under section 51
hereof or a penalty under the present section (*Arlidge v.
Scarse*, above, which see also as to the owner's responsibility for the tenant's obstruction). It will be noticed
that under section 51 the first procedure is for an order
and that it is only on failure to comply therewith within
ten days that the fine is imposed.

Sections 15, 17 (4), 68 (4) and 70 of the 1909 Act should
also be noticed.

Authorised to enter. See section 36 of the 1909 Act.

Fine. For recovery—see section 90 hereof.

Punishment   **90.** Offences under this Act punishable on summary
of offences
and recovery   conviction may be prosecuted and fines recovered in
of fines.   manner provided by the Summary Jurisdiction Acts.

Summary Jurisdiction Acts. In England, the Summary
Jurisdiction Acts of 1848 and 1879 and any amending
Acts—see definition in the Interpretation Act, 1889.
The chief amending Act is the Summary Jurisdiction
Act, 1884.

In London the fines will be recovered before a police
magistrate ; elsewhere before a stipendiary magistrate or
two justices.

By section 71 hereof any fine for the breach of byelaws
is paid to the credit therein mentioned. Other fines
are to be paid as directed by the Summary Jurisdiction
Act, 1848, section 31, or the Metropolitan Police Courts
Act, 1839, section 47.

Powers of   **91.** All powers given by this Act shall be deemed to
Act to be
cumulative.   be in addition to and not in derogation of any other
powers conferred by Act of Parliament, law, or custom,
and such other powers may be exercised in the same
manner as if this Act had not passed, and nothing in

this Act shall exempt any person from any penalty to S. 91 (90). which he would have been subject if this Act had not passed.

Provided that a local authority shall not, by reason of any local Act relating to a place within its jurisdiction, be exempted from the performance of any duty or obligation to which such authority are subject under any part of this Act.

But see section 33 of the Interpretation Act, 1889, as to two punishments for one offence.

The chief advantage of the present section is that it permits local authorities to proceed, as some of them prefer to do, under the Public Health Acts or local Acts. See also *Hall v. Manchester Corporation* [1915] 79 J.P. 395.

92. In this Act, unless the context otherwise requires, Definition of "district," "local authority," and "local rate," mean local authority, respectively the areas, bodies of persons, and rates districts, specified in the table contained in the First Schedule to local rate. this Act. *

See also section 3 (1) of the 1900 Act, and notes to the First Schedule hereto.

93. In this Act, unless the context otherwise requires— Definitions :
The expression " land " includes any right over land : " Land."
The expression " sanitary district " means the district " Sanitary of a sanitary authority : district."
The expression " sanitary authority " means an urban " Sanitary sanitary authority or a rural sanitary authority : authority."
The expressions " urban sanitary authority " and " Urban " rural sanitary authority " and " contributory and rural sanitary place " have respectively the same meanings as in authority " ; the Public Health Act, 1875 : " contributory place."

* As altered by the Housing, Town Planning, &c., Act, 1909, 6th schedule.

S. 93 (90).
" Superior
court."

The expression " superior court " means the Supreme Court :

" County of London."

The expression " county of London," except where specified to be the administrative county of London, means the county of London exclusive of the city of London.

Land. Including any buildings on the land.

Sanitary authority. Now, in rural districts, the rural district council ; and in urban districts, either the urban district council or the borough council—Local Government Act, 1894, section 21.

Contributary place. See section 229 of the Public Health Act, 1875.

PART V

Sections 94–97 ("Application of Act to Scotland ") omitted from this volume.

PART VI

Sections 98–101 ("Application of Act to Ireland ") omitted from this volume.

PART VII

REPEAL AND TEMPORARY PROVISIONS

Repeal of
Acts.

102.* (1.) Where the Labouring Classes Lodging Houses Acts, 1851 to 1885, have been adopted in any district, that adoption shall be deemed to be an adoption of Part III of this Act, and this Act shall apply accordingly.

* As altered by the Statute Law Revision Act, 1908,

(2.) Any officer appointed under any enactment hereby S. 102 (90).
repealed shall continue and be deemed to be appointed
under this Act.

(3.) Any dwelling houses acquired by the local authority
under the Artizans Dwellings Acts, 1868 to 1885, and
vested in them at the commencement of this Act, shall
he held by such local authority as if they had been acquired
under the provisions of Part III of this Act, and any
land or premises other than dwelling houses so acquired
and held by them at the commencement of this Act shall
be held as if the same had been acquired as a site of
an obstructive building in pursuance of Part II of this
Act, but may with the consent of the authority authorised
by the said part of this Act to consent to the sale of land
so acquired be appropriated for the purposes of Part III
of this Act.

103. The provisions of this Act relating to compensa- Temporary
tion, to the power of the local authority to enter and provisions.
value premises, to the compensation of tenants for expense of removal, shall be applicable in the case of all
improvement schemes which have been confirmed by
Act of Parliament during the session in which this Act
is passed.

(For Schedules, see next page.)

1st Sch. (90).

Sections
54, 92.

SCHEDULES

FIRST SCHEDULE

ENGLAND AND WALES

District.	Local Authority.	Local Rate.

Throughout Act

Urban sanitary district	The urban sanitary authority.	The rate out of which the general expenses of the execution of the Public Health Acts are defrayed.
The city of London .	The *Common Council.	The General Rate.*

(1.) For the purpose of Parts I and III

The county of London .	The County Council of London.	The county fund and the amount payable shall be deemed to be required for special county purposes.

(2.) For the purposes of Part II

A parish other than the parish of Woolwich mentioned in Schedule A. to the Metropolis Management Act, 1855, as amended by the Metropolis Management (Amendment) Act, 1885, and the Metropolis Management (Battersea and Westminster) Act, 1887.	The Vestry elected under the Metropolis Management Act, 1855.	
A district mentioned in Schedule B. to the Metropolis Management Act, 1855, as amended by the Metropolis Management (Amendment) Act, 1885, and the Metropolis Management (Battersea and Westminster) Act, 1887.	The Board of Works for the district elected under the Metropolis Management Act, 1855.	The general rate leviable by such vestry or board under the Metropolis Management Act, 1855.
Parish of Woolwich .	The local board of health.	The district fund and general district rate.

(3.) For the purposes of Parts II and III

Rural sanitary district .	The rural sanitary authority.	The rate out of which the "general" or "special" expenses, as the case may be, of the execution of the Public Health Acts are defrayed.

* As altered by the Housing, Town Planning, &c., Act, 1919,
᠄2nd schedule.

Note   1st Sch. (90).

In any case in the United Kingdom where an urban sanitary authority does not levy a borough rate or any general district rate, but is empowered by a local Act or Acts to borrow money and to levy a rate or rates throughout the whole of their district for purposes similar to those or to some of those for which a general district rate is leviable, it shall be lawful for such sanitary authority to defray the expenses incurred in the execution of Part III of this Act by means of money to be borrowed, and a rate or rates to be levied, under such Local Act or Acts.

Urban sanitary district. Now urban district. The authority is the borough council or the urban district council—see the Local Government Act, 1894, section 21. The rate will be the general district rate ; or, in boroughs, the borough rate or a rate under a local Act—see sections 27 and 210 of the Public Health Act, 1875. See also footnote to the schedule.

County of London. See also section 41 of the 1919 Act. As to the county fund—see section 78 of the Local Government Act, 1881.

(2.) *For the purposes of Part II.* In effect this now disappears, and the following should be added to (3) :—

| A Metropolitan borough | The borough council | The general rate of the borough |

The vestries, &c., have been displaced by the Metropolitan borough councils and the latter have power concurrently with the London County Council for Part III purposes—London Government Act, 1899. See also section 3 of the 1900 Act, page 272, and, particularly, section 41 of the 1919 Act, page 444.

Rural Sanitary district. Now rural district, and the authority is the rural district council—Local

2nd Sch. (90). Government Act, 1894, section 21. As to the rate mentioned—see sections 229 and 230 of the Public Health Act, 1875, and section 31 of the 1909 Act.

SECOND SCHEDULE

Section 20.   PROVISIONS WITH RESPECT TO THE PURCHASE AND TAKING OF LANDS IN ENGLAND OTHERWISE THAN BY AGREEMENT, AND OTHERWISE AMENDING THE LANDS CLAUSES ACTS.

Note

The Acquisition of Land (Assessment of Compensation) Act, 1919, which is printed on page 495, should be read in connection with the subject dealt with in this schedule. Section 1 (1) of that Act provides that where by or under any statute land is authorised to be acquired compulsorily by any local authority, any question of disputed compensation, &c., shall be referred to and determined by an arbitrator selected in accordance with rules from the panel of official arbitrators. But section 7 (1) proviso enacts that nothing in that Act relating to the rules for assessing compensation shall affect any special provisions as to the assessment of the value of land acquired for the purposes of Part I or Part II of this (the 1890) Act, if and so far as the provisions herein are inconsistent with those rules; and it adds that the provisions of the present schedule, as amended "(except paragraphs (4), (5), (29) and (31) thereof) shall apply to an official arbitrator as they apply to an arbitrator appointed under that schedule, and an official arbitrator may exercise all the powers conferred by those provisions on such arbitrator."

This schedule amends the provisions of the Lands Clauses Acts as incorporated by section 20 hereof.

Deposit of Maps and Plans

1-4, 38 & 39 Vict. c. 36. Sch.   (1.) The local authority shall *before making an application for the appointment of an arbitrator as herein-after mentioned* cause to be made out, and to be

* As altered by the Housing, Town Planning, &c., Act, 1919, 2nd schedule.

signed by their clerk or some other principal officer appointed by them, maps and schedules of all lands proposed to be taken compulsorily (which lands are hereinafter referred to as the scheduled lands), together with the names, so far as the same can be reasonably ascertained, of all persons interested in such lands as owners or reputed owners, lessees or reputed lessees, or occupiers, *except tenants for a month or a less period than a month.*

See sections 6 and 8 hereof and notes thereto. As to interests omitted by error—see paragraph (13) of this schedule. As to application for appointment of arbitrator—see paragraphs (4) and (6) below.

(2.) The maps made by the local authority shall be upon such scale and be framed in such manner as may be prescribed by the confirming authority.

(3.) The local authority shall deposit such maps and schedules at the office of the confirming authority, and shall deposit and keep copies of such maps and schedules at the office of the local authority.

The confirming authority is the Ministry of Health—see section 8 hereof.

Appointment of Arbitrator

(4.) After such deposit at the office of the confirming authority as aforesaid, it shall be lawful for the confirming authority, upon the application of the local authority, to appoint an arbitrator between the local authority, and the persons interested in such of the scheduled lands, or lands injuriously affected by the execution of such scheme, so far as compensation for the same *is not made the subject of agreement.

* As altered by the Housing, Town Planning, &c., Act, 1919, 2nd schedule.

2nd Sch. (90).   But see now the Acquisition of Land (Assessment of Compensation) Act, 1919, or note at head of this schedule, as to the arbitrator.

There is no provision as to undue delay in the application by the local authority, but it is their duty to purchase the land when the order has been made—see section 12 and notes thereto. See also the remarks of Blackburn, J., in *Birch v. St. Marylebone Vestry* [1869] 20 L.T., at page 701. There are other proceedings before application—paragraph (6) below.

As to the " lands injuriously affected "—see section 22 hereof.

The alteration affected in the concluding words of the paragraph, namely, " is not made " for " has not been made," apparently contemplates negotiations for agreement up to a late stage in the proceedings.

Proceedings on Arbitration

45 & 46 Vict.
c. 54. Sch.
(1.) *a–f.*

(5.) Before any arbitrator enters upon any inquiry he shall, in the presence of a justice of the peace, make and subscribe the following declaration ; that is to say,

" I *A.B.* do solemnly and sincerely declare, that I will faithfully and honestly, and to the best of my ability, hear and determine the matters referred to me under the provisions of the Housing of the Working Classes Act, 1890.

A.B.

" Made and subscribed in the presence of   ."
And such declaration shall be annexed to the award when made ; and if any arbitrator, having made such declaration wilfully act contrary thereto, he shall be guilty of a misdemeanor.

But see now the Acquisition of Land (Assessment of Compensation) Act, 1919, section 7 (1) proviso, or note at head of this schedule.

(6.) As soon as an arbitrator has been appointed as aforesaid, the confirming authority shall deliver

to him the maps and schedules deposited at their office. 2nd Sch. (90).
*Before applying to the arbitrator to determine the
compensation in respect of any particular lands or
interest therein, the local authority shall send a notice
by post of their intention to the owners or reputed 42 & 43 Vict.
owners, lessees or reputed lessees, so far as they can be c. 63. Sch.
reasonably ascertained.* Art. 1.

Notice by post. See section 7 hereof and paragraph
(32) below.

(7.) In every case in which compensation is payable
under Part I of this Act, by the local authority to any
claimant, and which compensation has not been made
the subject of agreement (in this Act referred to as " a
disputed case "), the arbitrator * after hearing all· such
parties interested in each disputed case as may appear
before him at a time and place of which notice has been
given as in Part I of this Act mentioned, shall proceed
to decide on the amount of compensation to which he
may consider the claimant to be entitled in each case.

In which compensation is payable. See sections 21
and 22 hereof.
As in Part I. Section 18 hereof, now repealed.
The arbitrator is not entitled to know the amount
offered by the local authority—see paragraph (30)
below.

(8.) *The arbitrator shall give notice to the claimants
in disputed cases of a time and place at which the difference between the claimants and the local authority will
be decided by the arbitrator.

As to such notice—see paragraph (32) below.

(9.) After the arbitrator has arrived at a decision on
all the disputed cases brought before him he shall make

* As altered by the Housing, Town Planning, &c., Act, 1919, 2nd
schedule.

2nd Sch. (90). an award under his hand and seal, and such award shall
be final, and be binding and conclusive * upon all persons
whomsoever, and no such award shall be set aside for
irregularity in matter of form, but the arbitrator may
and, if the local authority request him so to do, shall
from time to time make an award respecting a portion
only of the disputed cases brought before him.

See section 6 of the Acquisition of Land (Assessment of Compensation) Act, 1919, as to stating a special
case for the opinion of the High Court ; and further as
to finality—see *Ex parte Strabane Rural District Council*
[1910] 1 I.R. 135.

As to irregularity—see *Carr v. Metropolitan Board of
Works* [1880] 14 Ch.D. 807.

(10.) Such award as aforesaid shall be deposited at
the office of the confirming authority, and a copy thereof
shall be deposited at the office of the local authority.
*The title in the case of a person claiming a fee simple
interest in any lands included in any such award as
aforesaid shall commence twenty years previous to the
date of the claim, except there has been an absolute
conveyance on sale within twenty years, and more than
ten years previous to the claim when the title shall
commence with such conveyance : Provided that the
local authority shall not be prevented if they think fit
from requiring at their own expense any further abstract
or evidence of title respecting any lands included in any
such award as aforesaid in addition to the title hereinbefore mentioned.*

The proviso at the end, which was added by the
1919 Act, takes the place of paragraph (22).

* As altered by the Housing, Town Planning, &c., Act, 1919, 2nd
schedule.

Special Powers of Arbitration

2nd Sch. (90).

(11.) The arbitrator shall have the same power of apportioning any rent-service rentcharge, chief or other rent, payment, or incumbrance, or any rent payable in respect of lands comprised in a lease, as two justices have under the Lands Clauses Consolidation Act, 1845.

Power of arbitrator as to apportionment. 42 & 43 Vict. c. 63. Sch.(2).

See sections 116 and 119 of that Act.

(12.) Notwithstanding anything in section ninety-two of the Lands Clauses Consolidation Act, 1845, the arbitrator may determine that such part of any house, building, or manufactory as is proposed to be taken by the local authority can be taken without material damage to such house, building, or manufactory, and if he so determine may award compensation in respect of the severance of the part so proposed to be taken, in addition to the value of that part, and thereupon the party interested shall be required to sell and convey to the local authority such part, without the local authority being obliged to purchase the greater part or the whole of such house, building, or manufactory.*

Amendment respecting severance of properties, 8 & 9 Vict. c. 18. 42 & 43 Vict. c. 63. Sch.(3).

(13.) The amount of purchase money or compensation to be paid in pursuance of section one hundred and twenty-four of the Lands Clauses Consolidation Act, 1845, in respect of any estate, right, or interest in or charge affecting any of the scheduled lands which the local authority have through mistake or inadvertence failed or omitted duly to purchase or make compensation for, shall be awarded by the arbitrator and be paid, in like manner, as near as may be, as the same would have been awarded and paid if the claim of such estate, right

Omitted interests. 42 & 43 Vict. c. 63. Sch.(4).

* As altered by the Housing, Town Planning, &c., Act, 1919, 2nd schedule.

16

2nd Sch. (90). interest, or charge had been delivered to the arbitrator before the day fixed for the delivery of statements of claims.

If the arbitrator is satisfied that the failure or omission to purchase the said estate, right, interest, or charge, arose from any default on the part either of the claimant or of the local authority, he may direct the costs to be paid by the party so in default.

The quoted section deals with interests not acquired by the promoters before entering upon the lands.

Payment of Purchase Money

Arts. 14–24. See 38 & 39 Vict. c. 36. Sch.

(14.) Within thirty days from the delivery of *a statement in writing by any person claiming any right to or interest in the lands and an abstract of title on which the same is founded to the local authority, the local authority shall, where it appears to them that any person so claiming is absolutely entitled to the lands, estate, or interest claimed by him, deliver to such person, on demand, a certificate stating the amount of the compensation to which he is entitled under the said award.

See also paragraph (23).

(15.) Every such certificate shall be prepared by and at the cost of the local authority ; and where any agreement has been entered into as to the compensation payable in respect of the interest of any person in any lands, the local authority may, where it appears to them that such person is absolutely entitled, deliver to such person a like certificate.

Any lands. Only those compulsorily acquired (paragraph 1), as others do not come under the arbitration.

* As altered by the Housing, Town Planning, &c., Act, 1919, 2nd schedule. .

(16.) The local authority shall, thirty days after 2nd Sch. (90) demand, pay to the party to whom any such certificate is given, or otherwise as herein provided in the cases herein-after mentioned, the amount of moneys specified to be payable by such certificate to the party to whom or in whose favour such certificate is given, his or her executors, administrators, or assigns.

Herein-after mentioned.   Paragraphs (20) and (21).

(17.) If the local authority wilfully make default in such payment as aforesaid, then the party named in such certificate shall be entitled to enter up judgment against the local authority in the High Court, for the amount of the sums specified in such certificate, in the same manner in all respects as if he had been, by warrant of attorney from the local authority, authorised to enter up judgment for the amount mentioned in the certificate, with costs, as is usual in like cases ; and all moneys payable under such certificates, or to be recovered by such judgments as aforesaid, shall at law and in equity be taken as personal estate as from the time of the local authority entering on any such lands as aforesaid.

(18.) When and so soon as the local authority have paid to the party to whom any such certificate as aforesaid is given, or otherwise, as herein provided, in the cases herein-after mentioned, the amount specified to be payable by such certificate to the party to whom or in whose favour the certificate is given, his executors, administrators, or assigns, it shall be lawful for the local authority, upon obtaining such receipt as herein-after mentioned, from time to time to enter upon any lands in respect of which such certificate is given, and thenceforth to hold the same for the estate or interest

2nd Sch. (90). in respect of which the amount specified in such certificate was payable.

Or otherwise, as herein provided. Paid into the bank—paragraphs (20) and (21). See also in *Re Shaw and the Corporation of Birmingham* [1884] 27 Ch.D., at page 619.

Receipt. See the next paragraph.

(19.) In every case in which any moneys are paid by any local authority under this Act for such compensation as aforesaid, the party receiving such moneys shall give to the local authority a receipt for the same, and such receipt shall have the effect of a grant, release, and conveyance of all the estate and interest of such party, and of all parties claiming under or through him, in the lands in respect of which such moneys are paid, provided such receipt has an *ad valorem* stamp of the same amount impressed thereon in respect of the purchase moneys mentioned in such certificate as would have been necessary if such receipt had been an actual conveyance of such estate or interest, every such receipt to be prepared by and at the cost of the local authority.

In every case. Including, presumably, that where the money is paid into the bank under paragraphs (20) and (21).

Such compensation. Under paragraphs (14) and (15) above.

Receipt. Obviously this should identify the lands, &c., in respect of which it is given. The costs are recovered independently and need not have been paid before this receipt is given—paragraph (29).

(20.) If it appears to the local authority, from any such statement and abstract as aforesaid, or otherwise, that the person making any such claim as aforesaid is not absolutely entitled to the lands, estate, or interest in respect of which his claim is made, or is under any disability, or if the title to such lands, estate, or interest 2nd Sch. (90). be not satisfactorily deduced to the local authority, then and in every such case the amount to be paid by the local authority in respect of such lands, estate, or interest as aforesaid shall be paid and applied as provided by the clauses of the Lands Clauses Consolidation Act, 1845, as amended by the Court of Chancery Funds Act, 1872, "with respect to the purchase money or compensation coming to parties having limited interests, or prevented from treating, or not making title."

Statement and Abstract. See paragraph (14).

The effect of this paragraph is that the money can be paid into Court (see paragraph 21) ; but note the alternative in section 5 of the 1909 Act, where one local authority is acquiring from another local authority.

Lands Clauses Consolidation Act, 1845. See sections 69–80 thereof, and, as to costs, &c., note *Ex parte Jones* [1880] 14 Ch.D. 624.

Chancery Funds Act, 1872. This has been amended by the Supreme Court of Judicature (Funds) Act, 1883, and as to the procedure in the Paymaster-General's office—see the Supreme Court Fund Rules.

(21.) Where any person claiming any right or interest in any lands refuses to produce his title to the same, or where the local authority have under the provisions of Part I of this Act taken possession of any lands in respect of the compensation whereof, or of any estate or interest wherein, no claim has been made within one year from the time of the local authority taking possession, or if any party to whom any such certificate has been given or tendered refuses to receive such certificate, or to accept the amount therein specified as payable to him, then and in any such case the amount payable by the local authority in respect of such lands, estate, or interest, or the amount specified in such certificate, shall be paid into the Bank of

2nd Sch. (90). England, in manner provided by the last-mentioned clauses of the Lands Clauses Consolidation Act, 1845, as amended by the Court of Chancery Funds Act, 1872, and the amount so paid into the said Bank shall be accordingly dealt with as by the said Act provided.

See notes to last paragraph, and also paragraphs (24) and (25).

Paragraph (22) is omitted per the Housing, Town Planning, &c., Act, 1919, 2nd schedule.

(23.) If from any reason whatever the local authority does not deliver the certificate aforesaid to any party claiming to be entitled to any interest in any lands the possession whereof has been taken by the local authority as aforesaid, then the right to have a certificate according to the provisions of this Act may, at the cost and charge of the local authority, be enforced by any party or parties, by application to the High Court, in a summary way by petition, and all other rights and interests of any party or parties arising under the provisions of this Act may be in like manner enforced against the local authority by such application as aforesaid.

As to procedure hereunder—see the Judicature Act, 1884, section 13; and the Court of Chancery Act, 1855, section 16 ; and the Rules of the Supreme Court, Order 52, rules 16–18, and Order 55, rule 2 (7).

On other points arising—see *Cork and Youghal Railway Company v. Harnett* [1871] L.R. 5 H.L. 111 ; and *Re Fishguard and Rosslare Railways, &c.* [1908] 1 Ir. R. 321.

Entry on Lands on making Deposit

(24.) Where the local authority are desirous, for the purposes of their works, of entering upon any lands before they would be entitled to enter thereon under the provisions herein-before contained, it shall be lawful for the local authority, at any time after the arbitrator has framed his award, upon depositing in the Bank of England such sum as the arbitrator may certify to be in his opinion the proper amount to be so deposited in respect of any lands authorised to be purchased or taken by the local authority, and mentioned in such award, to enter upon and use such lands for the purposes of the improvement scheme of the local authority : and the arbitrator shall, upon the request of the local authority at any time after he has framed such award, certify under his hand the sum which, in his opinion, should be so deposited by the local authority in respect of any lands mentioned in such award before they enter upon and use the same as aforesaid, and the sum to be so certified shall be the sum or the amount of the several sums set forth in such award as the sum or sums to be paid by the local authority in respect of such lands, or such greater amount as to the arbitrator, under the cirsumstances of the case, may seem proper ; and, notwithstanding such entry as aforesaid, all proceedings for and in relation to the completion of the award, the delivery of certificates, and other proceedings under Part I of this Act, shall be had, and payments made, as if such entry and deposit had not been made ;

Provided that the local authority shall, where they enter upon any lands by virtue of this present provision, pay interest at the rate of five pounds per centum per annum upon the compensation money payable by them in respect of any lands so entered upon, from the time of their entry until the time of the payment of such money and interest to the party entitled thereto, or where, under the provisions of Part I of this Act, such compensation is required to be paid into the Bank of

2nd Sch. (90). England, then until the same, with such interest, is paid into such Bank accordingly ; and where under this provision interest is payable on any compensation money the certificate to be delivered by the local authority in respect thereof shall specify that interest is so payable, and the same shall be recoverable in like manner as the principal money mentioned in such certificate.

But notwithstanding this the local authority may enter to take down a dangerous building, on a magistrate's order—see *Barnett v. Metropolitan Board of Works* [1882] 46 L.T. 384. There is also a power of entry, for survey valuation, &c., given by section 36 of the 1909 Act. They may also enter with consent and as per the provisions of this paragraph. Entry otherwise will be actionable—see *Birmingham and District Land Company v. London and North Western Railway Co.* [1888] 40 Ch.D. 268.

See section 91 of the Lands Clauses Consolidation Act, 1845, as to obtaining possession, and section 89 hereof as to obstruction of the local authority's officer.

(25.) The money so deposited as last aforesaid shall be paid into the Bank of England to such account as may from time to time be directed by any regulation or Act for the time being in force in relation to moneys deposited in the bank in similar cases, or to such account as may be directed by any order of the High Court, and remain in the bank by way of security to the parties interested in the lands which have been so entered upon for the payment of the money to become payable by the local authority in respect thereof under the award of the arbitrator ; and the money so deposited may, on the application by petition of the local authority, be ordered to be invested in Bank Annuities or Government securities, and accumulated : and upon such payment as aforesaid by the local authority it shall be lawful for the High Court, upon a like application, to order the 2nd Sch. (90). money so deposited, or the funds in which the same shall have been invested, together with the accumulation thereof, to be repaid or transferred to the local authority, or, in default of such payment as aforesaid by the local authority, it shall be lawful for the said court to order the same to be applied in such manner as it thinks fit for the benefit of the parties for whose security the same shall so have been deposited.

As to costs and the payment of money out of Court—see *Ex parte Jones* [1880] 14 Ch.D. 624.

Paragraphs (26) and (27) ("Appeal") are omitted, per the Housing, Town Planning, &c., Act, 1919, 2nd schedule.

Costs of Arbitration

(28.) The salary or remuneration, travelling, and See 45 & 46 other expenses of the arbitrator, and all costs, charges, $\frac{\text{Vict. c. 54.}}{\text{Sch. (H).}}$ and expenses (if any) which may be incurred by the confirming authority in carrying the provisions of Part I of this Act into execution, shall, after the amount thereof shall have been certified under this article, be paid by the local authority ; and the amount of such costs, charges, and expenses shall from time to time be certified by the confirming authority after first hearing any objections that may be made to the reasonableness of any such costs, charges, and expenses by or on behalf of the local authority ; and every certificate of the said confirming authority certifying the amount of such costs, charges, and expenses shall be taken as proof in all proceedings at law or in equity of the amount of such respective costs, charges, and expenses, and the

2nd Sch.(90). amount so certified shall be a debt due from the local authority to the Crown and shall be recoverable accordingly.

Further, any such certificate may be made a rule of a superior court on the application of any party named therein, and may be enforced accordingly.

See also sections 8 (8) and (9), 16 and 85 hereof.

(29.) (1.) It shall be lawful for the arbitrator, where he thinks fit, upon the request of any party by whom any claim has been made before him, to certify the amount of the costs properly incurred by such party in relation to the arbitration, and the amount of the costs so certified shall be paid by the local authority ;

Provided that—

See 45 & 46
Vict. c. 54.
Sch. (I).

(a) The arbitrator shall not be required to certify the amount of costs in any case where he considers such costs are not properly payable by the local authority ;

(b) The arbitrator shall not be required to certify the amount of costs incurred by any party in relation to the arbitration, in any case where he considers that such party neglected, after due notice from the local authority, to deliver to that authority a statement in writing within such time, and containing such particulars respecting the compensation claimed, as would have enabled the local authority to make a proper offer of compensation to such party before the appointment of the arbitrator.

(c) No certificate shall be given where the arbitrator has awarded the same or a less sum than has been offered by the local authority in respect of the claim *not less than fourteen days before the date 2nd Sch. (90). of the arbitration in that particular case.*

(2.) If within seven days after demand the amount certified be not paid to the party entitled to receive the same, such amount shall be recoverable as a debt from the local authority with interest at the rate of five per cent. per annum for any time during which the same remains unpaid after such seven days as aforesaid.

But see sections 5 and 7 (1) proviso of the Acquisition of Land (Assessment of Compensation) Act, 1919.

Miscellaneous

(30.) The arbitrator may call for the production of any documents *other than any formal offer made by the local authority* in the possession or power of the local authority, or of any party making any claim under the provisions of Part I of this Act, which such arbitrator may think necessary for determining any question or matter to be determined by him under Part I of this Act, and may examine any such party and his witnesses, and the witnesses for the local authority, on oath, and administer the oaths necessary for that purpose.

(31.) If any arbitrator appointed in pursuance of Part I of this Act die, or refuse, decline, or become incapable to act, the confirming authority may appoint an arbitrator in his place, who shall have the same powers and authorities as the arbitrator first appointed ; and upon the appointment of any arbitrator in the place of an arbitrator dying, or refusing, declining, or be- coming incapable to act, all the documents relating to

---

* As altered by the Housing, Town Planning, &c., Act, 1919, 2nd chedule

2nd Sch. (90). the matter of the arbitration which were in the possession of such arbitrator shall be delivered to the arbitrator appointed in his place, and the local authority shall publish notice of such appointment in the London Gazette.

But see the Acquisition of Land (Assessment of Compensation) Act, 1919, section 7 (1) proviso.

(32.) All notices required by this schedule to be published shall be published in *a newspaper circulating within the jurisdiction of the local authority, and where no other form of service is prescribed all notices required to be served or given by the local authority under this schedule or otherwise upon any persons interested in or entitled to sell lands, shall be served in manner in which notices of lands proposed to be taken compulsorily for the purpose of an improvement scheme are directed by Part I of this Act to be served upon owners or reputed owners, lessees or reputed lessees, and occupiers.

See section 7 hereof.

Application of Schedule to Scotland and Ireland omitted.

Third, Fourth and Fifth Schedules repealed by the Housing, Town Planning, &c., Act, 1909.

SIXTH SCHEDULE

Section 62.   BYELAWS TO BE MADE IN ALL CASES (EXCEPT WHERE A LODGING HOUSE IS USED AS A SEPARATE DWELLING)

For securing that the lodging-houses shall be under the management and control of the officers, servants, or others appointed or employed in that behalf by the local authority.

* As altered by the Housing, Town Planning, &c., Act, 1919, 2nd schedule.

For securing the due separation at night of men and 6th Sch. (90). boys above eight years old from women and girls.

For preventing damage, disturbance, interruption, and indecent and offensive language and behaviour and nuisances.

For determining the duties of the officers, servants, and others appointed by the local authority.

See further as to byelaws—section 26 of the 1919 Act.

The Seventh Schedule (Enactments Repealed) was repealed by the Statute Law Revision Act, 1908.

WORKING CLASSES DWELLINGS ACT, 1890
[53 & 54 Vict. Ch. 16.]

An Act to facilitate Gifts of Land for Dwellings for the Working Classes in Populous Places.

[25th July 1890.]

BE it enacted by the Queen's most Excellent Majesty, by and with the advice and consent of the Lords Spiritual and Temporal, and Commons, in this present Parliament assembled, and by the authority of the same, as follows :

1. Parts I and II of the Mortmain and Charitable Uses Act, 1888, and section sixteen of the Act of the session held in the seventh and eighth years of Her present Majesty, chapter ninety-seven, intituled "An Act for the more effectual application of charitable donations and bequests in Ireland," shall not apply to any assurance, by deed or will, of land, or of personal estate to be laid out in land, for the purpose of providing dwellings for the working classes in any populous place.

Provided as follows :—

(i.) The quantity of land which may be assured by will under this section shall not exceed five acres ; and

(ii.) The deed or will containing the assurance must, within six months, in the case of a deed after the execution thereof, or in the case of a will after the probate thereof, be enrolled in the books of the Charity Commissioners, if the land is situate in England or Wales, and the deed containing the assurance must,

Side-note: Exemption from 51 & 52 Vict. c. 42. Parts I, II, & 7 & 8 Vict. c. 97. s. 16. of gifts for working classes dwellings.

within six months after the execution thereof, be registered in the office for registering deeds in the city of Dublin, if the land is situate in Ireland.

For the purposes of this Act, the expression " populous place " means the administrative county of London, any municipal borough, any urban sanitary district, and any other place having a dense population of an urban character.

2. This Act shall extend to any assurance by deed made within twelve months before the passing of this Act by a person alive at that passing as if it had been made after the passing, except that the assurance shall be enrolled or registered as aforesaid within six months after the passing of this Act. *Application of Act.*

3. (1.) This Act may be cited as the Working Classes Dwellings Act, 1890. *Short title and construction.*

(2.) Expressions used in this Act shall have the same meaning as in the Mortmain and Charitable Uses Act, 1888. *51 & 52 Vict. c. 42.*

Note

By section 8 of the 1909 Act, it is provided that " a local authority may accept a donation of land or money or other property for any of the purposes of the Housing Acts, and it shall not be necessary to enrol any assurance with respect to any such property under the Mortmain and Charitable Uses Act, 1888."

In *Re Sutton, Lewis v. Sutton* [1901] 2 Ch. 640, Buckley, J., expressed the opinion that the present Act did not apply to a case where money had been left to buy land and erect houses for the purpose of supplying *the poor* with dwelling houses at less than their value. In the same case it was held that the bequest was valid and was not affected by section 7 of the Mortmain and Charitable Uses Act, 1891, which amended the above quoted Act of 1888.

HOUSING OF THE WORKING CLASSES ACT, 1894. [57 & 58 VICT. CH. 55.]

An Act to explain the provisions of Part II of the Housing of the Working Classes Act, 1890, with respect to powers of borrowing. [25th August 1894.]

BE it enacted by the Queen's most Excellent Majesty, by and with the advice and consent of the Lords Spiritual and Temporal, and Commons, in this present Parliament assembled, and by the authority of the same, as follows :

Borrowing powers under a scheme for reconstruction. 53 & 54 Vict. c. 70.

1. For any purpose for which a local authority are, by a scheme for reconstruction duly sanctioned under Part II of the Housing of the Working Classes Act, 1890, or by the order sanctioning the scheme, authorised to borrow, the authority shall have power and shall be deemed always to have had power to borrow in like manner and subject to the like conditions as they may borrow under section forty-three of that Act, for the purpose of raising the sums required for the purchase money or compensation therein mentioned, and sections forty-three and forty-six of that Act shall apply accordingly.

2. This Act may be cited as the Housing of the Working Classes Act, 1894.

The purpose of this Act is to permit the local authority to borrow for any purpose of a Part II reconstruction scheme, authorised by the scheme or the sanctioning order. By the sections mentioned they had power to borrow only for the purpose of raising the purchase money or the compensation.

SMALL DWELLINGS ACQUISITION ACT, 1899
[62 & 63 VICT. CH. 44.]

An Act to empower Local Authorities to advance Money for enabling Persons to acquire the Ownership of Small Houses in which they reside.

[9th August 1899.]

Note

By section 49 of the Housing, Town Planning, &c., Act, 1919 (see page 453), certain amendments are made in this Act, and are noted in the text below. The same section further provides that a receipt under seal in the form set out in Part I of the Fourth Schedule to that Act (see page 463) endorsed on . . . a mortgage for money advanced under this Act . . . shall without any reconveyance, &c., operate as a discharge of the mortgaged property, &c. The receipt shall not be liable to stamp duty, and shall be granted free of cost.

While money is so difficult to raise, it is possible that full advantage will not be taken of this Act, which is a valuable and useful one, but it is to be hoped that eventually it will be generally used.

BE it enacted by the Queen's most Excellent Majesty, by and with the advice and consent of the Lords Spiritual and Temporal, and Commons, in this present Parliament assembled, and by the authority of the same, as follows :

Power of local authority to advance money to residents in houses for the purchase of houses.

1. (1.) A local authority for any area may, subject to the provisions of this Act, advance money to a resident in any house within the area for the purpose of enabling him to acquire the ownership of that house ; provided that any advance shall not exceed—

(a) *eighty-five per cent. of that which in the opinion of the local authority is the market value of the ownership ; nor

(b) *Repealed by the Housing, Town Planning, &c., Act,* 1919, *section* 49.

and an advance shall not be made for the acquisition of the ownership of a house where in the opinion of the local authority the market value of the house exceeds *eight hundred pounds.

(2.) Every such advance shall be repaid with interest within such period not exceeding thirty years from the date of the advance as may be agreed upon.

(3.) The interest shall be at such rate as may be agreed upon, not exceeding ten shillings above the rate at which the local authority can at the time borrow from the Public Works Loan Commissioners the money for the advance.

(4.) The repayment may be made either by equal instalments of principal or by an annuity of principal and interest combined, and all payments on account of principal or interest shall. be made either weekly or at any periods not exceeding a half year, according as may be agreed.

* As altered by the Housing, Town Planning, &c., Act, 1919, section 49.

(5.) The proprietor of a house in respect of which an advance has been made may at any of the usual quarter days, after one month's written notice, and on paying all sums due on account of interest, repay to the local authority the whole of the outstanding principal of the advance, or any part thereof being ten pounds or a multiple of ten pounds, and where the repayment is made by an annuity of principal and interest combined, the amount so outstanding and the amount by which the annuity will be reduced where a part of the advance is paid off, shall be determined by a table annexed to the instrument securing the repayment of the advance.

2. Before making an advance under this Act in respect of a house a local authority shall be satisfied— *Procedure for obtaining advance.*

(a) that the applicant for the advance is resident or intends to reside in the house, and is not already the proprietor within the meaning of this Act of a house to which the statutory conditions apply; and

(b) that the value of the ownership of the house is sufficient; and

(c) that the title to the ownership is one which an ordinary mortgagee would be willing to accept; and

(d) that the house is in good sanitary condition and good repair; and

(e) that the repayment to the local authority of the advance is secured by an instrument vesting the ownership (including any interest already held by the purchaser) in the local authority subject to the right of redemption by the applicant, but such instrument shall not contain anything inconsistent with the provisions of this Act.

Conditions affecting house purchased by means of advance.

3. (1.) Where the ownership of a 'house has been acquired by means of an advance under this Act, the house shall, until such advance with interest has been fully paid, or the local authority have taken possession or ordered a sale under this Act, be held subject to the following conditions (in this Act referred to as the statutory conditions), that is to say :—

(a) Every sum for the time being due in respect of principal or of interest of the advance shall be punctually paid :

(b) The proprietor of the house shall reside in the house :

(c) The house shall be kept insured against fire to the satisfaction of the local authority, and the receipts for the premiums produced when required by them :

(d) The house shall be kept in good sanitary condition and good repair :

(e) The house shall not be used for the sale of intoxicating liquors, or in such a manner as to be a nuisance to adjacent houses :

(f) The local authority shall have power to enter the house by any person, authorised by them in writing for the purpose, at all reasonable times for the purpose of ascertaining whether the statutory conditions are complied with.

(2.) The proprietor of the house may with the permission of the local authority (which shall not be unreasonably withheld) at any time transfer his interest in the house, but any such transfer shall be made subject to the statutory conditions.

(3.) Where default is made in complying with the statutory condition as to residence, the local authority

may take possession of the house, and where default
is made in complying with any of the other statutory
conditions, whether the statutory condition as to residence has or has not been complied with, the local
authority may either take possession of the house, or order
the sale of the house without taking possession.

(4.) In the case of the breach of any condition other
than that of punctual payment of the principal and
interest of the advance, the authority shall, previously
to taking possession or ordering a sale, by notice in writing
delivered at the house and addressed to the proprietor,
call on the proprietor to comply with the condition,
and if the proprietor—

(a) within fourteen days after the delivery of the notice
gives an undertaking in writing to the authority
to comply with the notice ; and

(b) within two months after the delivery of the notice
complies therewith,

shall not take possession or order a sale, as the case may
be.

(5.) In the case of the bankruptcy of the proprietor of
the house, or in the case of a deceased proprietor's estate
being administered in bankruptcy under section one
hundred and twenty-five of the Bankruptcy Act, 1883, 46 & 47 Vict.
the local authority may either take possession of the c. 52.
house or order the sale of the house without taking
possession, and shall do so except in pursuance of some
arrangement to the contrary with the trustee in bankruptcy.

4. (1.) Where the ownership of a house has been Provision as
acquired by means of an advance under this Act, the to personal
liability and
person who is the proprietor shall be personally liable powers of
for the repayment of any sum due in respect of the proprietor.

advance until he ceases to be proprietor, by reason of a transfer made in accordance with this Act.

(2.) The provisions of this Act requiring the permission of the local authority to the transfer of the proprietor's interest in a house under this Act shall not apply to any charge on that interest made by the proprietor, so far as the charge does not affect any rights or powers of the local authority under this Act.

Recovery of possession and disposal of house. 5. (1.) Where a local authority take possession of a house, all the estate, right, interest, and claim of the proprietor in or to the house shall, subject as in this section mentioned, vest in and become the property of the local authority, and that authority may either retain the house under their own management or sell or otherwise dispose of it as they think expedient.

(2.) Where a local authority take possession of a house they shall, save as herein-after mentioned, pay to the proprietor either—

(a) such sum as may be agreed upon ; or

(b) a sum equal to the value of the interest in the house at the disposal of the local authority, after deducting therefrom the amount of the advance then remaining unpaid and any sum due for interest ; and the said value, in the absence of a sale and in default of agreement, shall be settled by a county court judge as arbitrator, or if the Lord Chancellor so authorises, by a single arbitrator appointed by the county court judge, and the Arbitration Act, 1889, shall apply to any such arbitration.

52 & 53 Vict. c. 49.

(3.) The sum so payable to the proprietor if not paid within three months after the date of taking possession shall carry interest at the rate of three per cent. per annum from the date of taking possession.

(4.) All costs of or incidental to the taking possession, sale, or other disposal of the house (including the costs of the arbitration, if any) incurred by the local authority, before the amount payable to the proprietor has been settled either by agreement or arbitration, shall be deducted from the amount otherwise payable to the proprietor.

(5.) Where the local authority are entitled under this Act to take possession of a house, possession may be recovered (whatever may be the value of the house) by or on behalf of the local authority either under sections one hundred and thirty-eight to one hundred and forty-five of the County Courts Act, 1888, or under the Small Tenements Recovery Act, 1838, as in the cases therein provided for, and in either case may be recovered as if the local authority were the landlord and the proprietor of the house were the tenant.

51 & 52 Vict. c. 43.
1 & 2 Vict. c. 74.

6. (1.) Where a local authority order the sale of a house without taking possession, they shall cause it to be put up for sale by auction, and out of the proceeds of sale retain any sum due to them on account of the interest or principal of the advance, and all costs, charges, and expenses properly incurred by them in or about the sale of the house, and pay over the balance (if any) to the proprietor.

Procedure as to ordering sale.

(2.) If the local authority are unable at the auction to sell the house for such a sum as will allow of the payment out of the proceeds of sale of the interest and principal of the advance then due to the authority, and the costs, charges, and expenses aforesaid, they may take possession of the house in manner provided by this Act, but shall not be liable to pay any sum to the proprietor.

Suspension of condition as to residence.

7. (1.) An advance may be made to an applicant who intends to reside in a house, as if he were resident, if he undertakes to begin his residence therein within such period not exceeding six months from the date of the advance, as the local authority may fix, and in that case the statutory condition requiring residence shall be suspended during that period.

(2.) The local authority may allow a proprietor to permit, by letting or otherwise, a house to be occupied as a furnished house by some other person during a period not exceeding four months in the whole in any twelve months, or during absence from the house in the performance of any duty arising from or incidental to any office, service, or employment held or undertaken by him, and the condition requiring residence shall be suspended while the permission continues.

(3.) Where the proprietor of a house subject to statutory conditions dies, the condition requiring residence shall be suspended until the expiration of twelve months from the death, or any earlier date at which the personal representatives transfer the ownership or interest of the proprietor in the course of administration; and where the proprietor of any such house becomes bankrupt, or his estate is administered in bankruptcy under section one hundred and twenty-five of the Bankruptcy Act, 1883, and in either case an arrangement under this Act is made with the trustee in bankruptcy, the condition as to residence shall, if the local authority think fit, be suspended during the continuance of the arrangement.

List of advances.

8. (1.) A local authority shall keep at their offices a book containing a list of any advances made by them under this Act, and shall enter therein with regard to each advance—

(i) a description of the house in respect of which the advance is made ;

(ii) the amount advanced ;

(iii) the amount for the time being repaid ;

(iv) The name of the proprietor for the time being of the house ; and

(v) such other particulars as the local authority think fit to enter.

(2.) The book shall be open to inspection at the office of the local authority during office hours free of charge.

9. (1.) A local authority for the purpose of this Act shall be the council of any county or county borough ; and if the council of any urban district not being a county borough, or of any rural district, pass a resolution undertaking to act under this Act, that council shall, subject in the case of the council of a district containing a population according to the last census for the same being of less than ten thousand to the consent of the county council, be the local authority in that district for the purpose of this Act to the exclusion of any other authority : Provided that, if the council of any district are dissatisfied with any refusal or failure of the county council to give their consent, they may appeal to the Local Government Board, and the Local Government Board may, if they think fit, give their consent, and the consent so given shall have the same effect as the consent of the county council.

(2.) Where the council of an urban or rural district becomes the local authority for the purposes of this Act, all the powers, rights, and liabilities of the county council in respect of advances already made by them under this Act for the purchase of the ownership of any house in the district shall rest in the council of the

Local authorities and rates.

urban or rural district, subject to the payment by that council to the county council of the outstanding principal and interest of any such advance.

(3.) All expenses of a local authority in the execution of this Act shall be paid in the case of a county out of the county rate, and in the case of a county borough, out of the borough fund or borough rate, and in the case of an urban or rural district out of any fund or rate applicable to the general purposes of the Public Health Acts ; but no sum shall be raised in any urban or rural district the council of which becomes a local authority for the purposes of this Act on account of the expenses of a county council under this Act.

(4.) If in any local financial year the expenses payable by a council and not reimbursed by the receipts under this Act exceed in a county a sum equal to one halfpenny, and in a county borough or urban or rural district a sum equal to one penny in the pound upon the rateable value of the county, county borough, or district, deducting in the case of a county the rateable value of any urban or rural district in the county, the council of which have become a local authority under this Act, no further advance under this Act shall be made by that council, until the expiration of five years after the end of that financial year or if those expenses at that date exceed one halfpenny or one penny in the pound, as the case may be, on the rateable value for the time being, until they fall below such sum.

(5.) A local authority may borrow for the purposes of this Act in like manner as they may borrow, in the case of a county council for the purposes of the Local Government Act, 1888, and in the case of the council of a county borough for the purpose of section one hundred and six of the Municipal Corporations Act, 1882, and in the case of an urban or rural district council for the purpose of the Public Health Acts, and those Acts shall apply accordingly with the necessary modifications.

(6.) Money borrowed under this Act shall not, in the case of a county council, be reckoned as part of the total debt of a county for the purposes of section sixty-nine, subsection two, of the Local Government Act, 1888, and shall not, in the case of an urban or rural district council, be reckoned as part of their debt for the purpose of the limitation on borrowing under section two hundred and thirty-four, subsection two, of the Public Health Act, 1875. *51 & 52 Vict. c. 41.* *38 & 39 Vict. c. 55.*

(7.) The Public Works Loan Commissioners may in manner provided by the Public Works Loans Act, 1875, lend any money which may be borrowed by a local authority for the purposes of this Act. *38 & 39 Vict. c. 89.*

(8.) Any capital money received or retained by a local authority in payment or discharge of any advance under this Act, or in respect of the sale or other disposal of any house taken possession of under this Act, shall be applied, with the sanction of the Local Government Board, either in repayment of debt or for any other purpose to which capital money may be applied.

(9.) Separate accounts shall be kept by every local authority of their receipts and expenditure under this Act.

(10.) In the application of this Act to the county of London any sanitary authority—

(a) shall have the same powers as an urban district council, and the expenses of such authority shall be paid out of the general rate or in the case of the city of London out of the consolidated rate ; and

(b) may borrow in like manner as they can borrow for the purposes of the Metropolis Management Acts, 1855 to 1893 ; and those Acts shall apply with the necessary modifications.

Residence and owner-ship.

10. (1.) A person shall not be deemed for the purposes of this Act to be resident in a house unless he is both the occupier of and resident in that house.

(2.) For the purposes of this Act "ownership" shall be such interest or combination of interest in a house as, together with the interest of the purchaser of the owner-ship, will constitute either a fee simple in possession or a leasehold interest in possession of at least sixty years un-expired, at the date of the purchase.

(3.) Where the ownership of a house is acquired by means of an advance under this Act, the purchaser of the ownership, or, in the case of any devolution or transfer, the person in whom the interest of the pur-chaser is for the time being vested, shall be the pro-prietor of the house for the purposes of this Act.

11. ("General modifications as regards Scotland.") *Omitted from this volume.*

12. ("Local authorities and rates in Scotland.") *Omitted from this volume.*

13. ("Preparation of titles, &c., in Scotland.") *Omitted from this volume.*

14. ("Application of Act to Ireland.") *Omitted from this volume.*

15. ("Registration of title in Ireland.") *Omitted from this volume.*

Short title.

16. This Act may be cited as the Small Dwellings Acquisition Act, 1899.

SCHEDULES

SCHEDULE A

Section 11.

I, *A.B.*, clerk of the local authority of   ,
with reference to bond and disposition in security [or
other security] dated [insert date], and recorded in the
General Register of Sasines for the county of
            [or as the case may be], on the
day of   for £   , granted by *C.D.*
[name and designation] over the house [shortly describe
same], do hereby certify that said local authority has
taken possession of said house in respect [here set forth
the grounds on which possession has been so taken], and
I grant this certificate in terms of the Small Dwellings
Acquisition Act, 1899.

Dated at   this   day of
                                   (Signed) *A.B.*

SCHEDULE B

Section 11.

No. 1

I, *A.B.*, clerk of the local authority of   ,
with reference to bond and disposition in security [or
other security] dated [insert date], and recorded in the
General Register of Sasines for the county of
            [or as the case may be], on the   day of
            for £   , granted by *C.D.* [name and
designation] over the house [shortly describe same], do
hereby certify that the principal and interest secured
by said bond and disposition in security (or other security)
have been fully paid, and I grant this certificate in terms
of the Small Dwellings Acquisition Act, 1899.

Dated at   this   day of
                                   (Signed) *A.B.*

No. 2

I, *A.B.*, clerk of the local authority of   ,
with reference to the within (or above) written bond
dated [insert date], and recorded in the General Register
of Sasines for the county of   [or as
the case may be], on the   day of   for
£   , granted by *C.D.* [name and designation], do
hereby certify that the principal and interest secured
by said bond and disposition in security (or other security)
have been fully paid, and I grant this certificate in terms
of the Small Dwellings Acquisition Act, 1899.

Dated at   this   day of

(Signed) *A.B.*

HOUSING OF THE WORKING CLASSES ACT,
1900. [63 & 64 VICT. CH. 59.]

An Act to amend Part III of the Housing of the Working Classes Act, 1890.　　　　[8th August 1900.]

BE it enacted by the Queen's most Excellent Majesty, by and with the advice and consent of the Lords Spiritual and Temporal, and Commons, in this present Parliament assembled, and by the authority of the same, as follows :

1. Where any council, other than a rural district council, have adopted Part Three of the Housing of the Working Classes Act, 1890 (in this Act referred to as "the principal Act "), they may, for supplying the needs of their district, establish or acquire lodging houses for the working classes under that Part outside their district.

Exercise of powers outside district.

Adopted. Adoption is no longer necessary—section 1 of the 1909 Act.

This section was passed to remove a difficulty which had arisen in London. As to London now—see section 41 of the 1919 Act, and as to joint schemes affecting the areas of two or more local authorities—see sections 1 (6) and 3 (3) thereof.

On the general subject of these houses—see section 57 of the 1890 Act and notes thereto, but all the provisions applying to the houses will apply equally whether they are inside or outside the district, even including the making of byelaws under section 62 of the 1890 Act. Similarly land outside the district can be acquired compulsorily.

2. (" Adoption of Part Three of Act by rural district

271

S. 3 (00). council. 53 & 54 Vict. c. 70.") *Repealed by the Housing, Town Planning, &c., Act,* 1909.

Provisions as to metropolitan borough councils.

3. (1.) Any expenses incurred by the council of a metropolitan borough under Part III of the principal Act, whether within or without the borough, shall be defrayed as part of the ordinary expenses of the council, and in that Act the expressions " district," " local authority," and " local rate " shall, for the purposes of Part III of the Act, include a metropolitan borough, the council of the borough, and the general rate of the borough.

(2.) Where the council of a metropolitan borough adopt Part III of the principal Act, the power of the council to borrow for the purposes of that Part shall be exerciseable in the like manner and subject to the like conditions as the power of the council to borrow for the purposes of Part II of that Act.

As to the power of the council to borrow—see section 46 of the 1890 Act, and notes thereto.

Accounts.

4. Where land acquired by a council under Part III of the principal Act is appropriated for the purpose of re-housing persons displaced by the council under the powers of any other Part of that Act or of any other enactment, the receipts and expenditure in respect of that land (including all costs in respect of the acquisition and laying out of the land), and of any buildings erected thereon, may be treated as receipts and expenditure under that Part or enactment, but shall be accounted for under a separate head.

See section 80 of the 1890 Act.

5. (" Leases by local authority for building lodging-

houses.") *Repealed by the Housing, Town Planning, &c.,* s. 5 (00) *Act, 1919, section 50, and 5th schedule.*

6. ("Powers of county council to act on default of rural council.") *Repealed by the Housing, Town Planning, &c., Act, 1909.*

7. ("Arbitration as to acquisition of land.") *Repealed by the Housing, Town Planning, &c., Act, 1909.*

8. (1.) This Act may be cited as the Housing of the Working Classes Act, 1900, and the Housing of the Working Classes Acts, 1890 to 1894, and this Act may be cited together as the Housing of the Working Classes Acts, 1890 to 1900.

Short title and extent.

(2.) This Act shall not extend to *Ireland.

SCHEDULE

REPEAL

Session and Chapter.		Short Title.	Extent of Repeal.
53 & 54 Vict. c. 70	–	The Housing of the Working Classes Act, 1890.	The proviso to section fifty-four. Section fifty-five. In section sixty-five, the words from "and save where" to "bear such expenses," and the words "at the time of the publication of the certificate" and "who publish the same."

(This schedule was repealed by the Statute Law Revision Act, 1908.)

* The words "Scotland or" appearing here were repealed by the Housing, Town Planning, &c., Act, 1909.

18

HOUSING OF THE WORKING CLASSES ACT, 1903. [3 Edw. 7. Ch. 39.]

ARRANGEMENT OF SECTIONS

An Act to amend the Law relating to the Housing of the Working Classes. [14th August 1903.]

BE it enacted by the King's most Excellent Majesty, by and with the advice and consent of the Lords Spiritual and Temporal, and Commons, in this present Parliament assembled, and by the authority of the same, as follows :

General Amendments of Law

Maximum term for repayment of loans. 53 & 54 Vict. c. 70. 38 & 39 Vict c. 55.

1. (1.) The maximum period which may be sanctioned as the period for which money may be borrowed by a local authority for the purposes of the Housing of the Working Classes Act, 1890 (in this Act referred to as "the principal Act"), or any Acts amending it, shall

274

be eighty years, and as respects money so borrowed S. 1 (03).
eighty years shall be substituted for sixty years in section
two hundred and thirty-four of the Public Health Act,
1875.

(2.) Money borrowed under the principal Act or any
Acts (including this Act) amending it (in this Act collec-
tively referred to as the Housing Acts) shall not be
reckoned as part of the debt of the local authority for
the purposes of the limitation on borrowing under subsections two and three of section two hundred and thirty-
four of the Public Health Act, 1875.

For the borrowing powers—see sections 25, 43, 46
and 66 of the 1890 Act, and section 1 of the 1894 Act.
As to London—see section 15 hereof.
The period is subject to the sanction of the Ministry.
By section 3 of the 1909 Act there is a similar extension
affecting the Public Works Loan Commissioners.
Note the power to issue bonds, &c., given by sections
7 and 8 of the Housing (Additional Powers) Act, 1919.

2. (1.) His Majesty may by Order in Council assign Transfer of
to the Local Government Board any powers and duties powers and
duties of
of the Secretary of State under the Housing Acts, or Home Office
under any scheme made in pursuance of those Acts, Government
and the powers of the Secretary of State under any Board.
local Act, so far as they relate to the housing of the
working classes, and any such powers and duties so
assigned shall become powers and duties of the Local
Government Board.

(2.) Section eleven of the Board of Agriculture Act, 52 & 53 Vict.
1889, shall apply with respect to the powers and duties c. 30.
transferred under this section as it applies with respect
to the powers and duties transferred under that Act,
with the substitution of the Local Government Board
for the Board of Agriculture and of the date of the

S. 2 (03).   transfer under this section for the date of the establishment of the Board of Agriculture.

All these powers now go to the Minister of Health,
under the Ministry of Health Act, 1919. The Order in
Council under this section was dated 27th February
1905.

Re-housing
obligations
when land is
taken under
statutory
powers.

3. Where under the powers given after the date of the
passing of the Act by any local Act or Provisional Order,
or Order having the effect of an Act, any land is acquired,
whether compulsorily or by agreement, by any authority,
company, or person, or where after the date of the passing
of this Act any land is so acquired compulsorily under
any general Act (other than the housing Acts), the
provisions set out in the Schedule to this Act shall apply
with respect to the provision of dwelling accommodation
for persons of the working class.

This section was designed to carry out the recommendations of a joint committee of the two Houses of Parliament. The private bill standing orders required that
local bills, or bills to confirm Provisional Orders, of the
nature indicated, should contain provisions similar to
those of this section and the schedule, and the committee
recommended that the provisions should be embodied
in a General Act. But it would appear that the section
applies to land acquired compulsorily under the Housing
Acts, even though that may not have been the intention.
Except under section 38 of the 1890 Act, land compulsorily acquired under the Housing Acts requires a
" provisional order or order having the effect of an Act."
But the point is not now of great importance as regards
the duties of local authorities, in view of section 1 (1)
of the 1919 Act. See also sections 11 and 40 of the 1890
Act.

The terms of the section appear to exclude Michael
Angelo Taylor's Act [1817] 57 Geo. 3, c. 29, under
which houses may be acquired by metropolitan borough
councils.

Amendments as to Schemes

4. (1.) If, on the report made to the confirming authority on an inquiry directed by them under section ten of the principal Act, that authority are satisfied that a scheme ought to have been made for the improvement of the area to which the inquiry relates, or of some part thereof, they may, if they think fit, order the local authority to make such a scheme, either under Part I of the principal Act, or, if the confirming authority so direct, under Part II of that Act, and to do all things necessary under the Housing Acts for carrying into execution the scheme so made, and the local authority shall accordingly make a scheme or direct a scheme to be prepared as if they had passed the resolution required under section four or section thirty-nine of the principal Act, as the case may be, and do all things necessary under the Housing Acts for carrying the scheme into effect.

Provisions on failure of local authority to make a scheme.

Any such order of the confirming authority may be enforced by mandamus.

But see now sections 3, 4, and 5 of the 1919 Act.

(2.) Any *six or more ratepayers of the district shall have the like appeal under section sixteen of the principal Act as is given to the *six or more ratepayers who have made the complaint to the medical officer of health mentioned in that section.

5. *Subsection* (1) *repealed by the Housing, Town Planning, &c., Act,* 1919, *section 50, and 5th schedule.*

Amendment of procedure for confirming improvement scheme.

(2.) The order of a confirming authority under subsection four of section eight of the principal Act shall,

* As altered by the Housing, Town Planning, &c., Act, 1919, 2nd schedule.

S. 5 (03). notwithstanding anything in that section, take effect without confirmation by Parliament.*

(3.) For the purposes of the principal Act, the making of an order by a confirming authority, which takes effect under this section without confirmation by Parliament, shall have the same effect as the confirmation of the order by Act of Parliament, and any reference to a Provisional Order, made under section eight of the principal Act, shall include a reference to an order which so takes effect without confirmation by Parliament.

Thus, the order of the Ministry is all sufficient—except in the case of commons, open spaces or allotments—see section 73 of the 1909 Act.

6. ("Power to modify schemes in certain cases.") *Repealed by the Housing, Town Planning, &c., Act, 1909.*

Amendments as to scheme of reconstruction.

7. Where a scheme for reconstruction under Part II of the principal Act is made, neighbouring lands may be included in the area comprised in the scheme if the local authority under whose direction the scheme is made are of opinion that that inclusion is necessary for making their scheme efficient, but the provision of subsection two of section forty-one, as to the exclusion of any additional allowance in respect of compulsory purchase, shall not apply in the case of any land so included.

In this respect a Part II (reconstruction) scheme is thus in the same position as a Part I (improvement) scheme.

Amendments as to Closing Orders, Demolition, &c.

8. ("Amendment of procedure for closing orders.") *Repealed by the Housing, Town Planning, &c., Act, 1909.*

* As altered by the Housing, Town Planning, &c., Act, 1909, 6th schedule.

9. Where the amount realised by the sale of materials under section thirty-four of the principal Act is not sufficient to cover the expenses incident to the taking down and removal of a building, the local authority may recover the deficiency from the owner of the building as a civil debt in manner provided by the Summary Jurisdiction Acts, or under the provisions of the Public Health Acts relating to private improvement expenses.

S. 9 (03).
Power to recover cost of demolition.

Acts. See section 35 of the Summary Jurisdiction Act, 1879, and sections 213–215, 232 and 257 of the Public Health Act, 1875.

10. Where default is made as respects any dwelling house in obeying a closing order, * possession of the house may be obtained (without prejudice to the enforcement of any penalty under that provision), whatever may be the value or rent of the house, by or on behalf of the owner or local authority, either under sections one hundred and thirty-eight to one hundred and forty-five of the County Courts Act, 1888, or under the Small Tenements Recovery Act, 1838, as in the cases therein provided for, and in either case may be obtained as if the owner or local authority were the landlord.

Recovery of possession from occupying tenants in pursuance of closing orders. 51 & 52 Vict. c. 43. 1 & 2 Vict. c. 74.

Any expenses incurred by a local authority under this section may be recovered from the owner of the dwelling-house as a civil debt in manner provided by the Summary Jurisdiction Acts.

After the words " closing order " there formerly appeared the words "in the manner provided by subsection three of section thirty-two of the principal Act." The said section 32 was repealed by the 1909 Act, and closing orders are now made under section 17 thereof. The words in brackets do not now seem to have any effect. The said section 17 provides for a summary order to

* As altered by the Housing, Town Planning, &c., Act, 1909.

S. 10 (03). quit, and that provision will be the more commonly applied.

Section 68 of the National Insurance Act, 1911, gives protection against ejectment which would endanger the life of a sick insured person, but it is doubtful if it has ever been made use of.

Miscellaneous

Powers in connection with provision of dwelling accommodation or lodging-houses.

11. (1.) Any power of the local authority under the Housing Acts, or under any scheme made in pursuance of any of those Acts, to provide dwelling accommodation or lodging-houses, shall include a power to provide and maintain, with the consent of the Local Government Board, and, if desired, jointly with any other person, in connection with any such dwelling accommodation or lodging-houses, any building adapted for use as a shop, any recreation grounds, or other buildings or land which in the opinion of the Local Government Board will serve a beneficial purpose in connection with the requirements of the persons for whom the dwelling accommodation or lodging-houses are provided, and to raise money for the purpose, if necessary, by borrowing.

(2.) The Local Government Board may, in giving their consent to the provision of any land or building under this section, by order apply, with any necessary modifications, to such land or building any statutory provisions which would have been applicable thereto if the land or building had been provided under any enactment giving any local authority powers for the purpose.

See also sections 6, 11, 12, 39, 40, and 59 of the 1890 Act; section 6 of the 1909 Act, and sections 12 and 15 of the 1919 Act.

Condition in contracts for letting houses for the working classes.

12. Section seventy-five of the principal Act (which relates to the condition to be implied on letting houses for the working classes) shall, as respects any contract made after the passing of this Act, take effect notwith-

standing any agreement to the contrary, and any such S. 12 (03).
agreement made after the passing of this Act shall be
void.

See note to section 75 of the 1890 Act.

13. (1.) Any notice required to be served under Part Service of
II of the principal Act upon an owner shall, notwithstanding anything in section forty-nine of that Act,
be deemed to be sufficiently served if it is sent by post
in a registered letter addressed to the owner or his agent
at his usual or last known residence or place of business.

(2.) Any document referred to in section eighty-
seven of the principal Act shall be deemed to be sufficiently served upon the local authority if addressed to
that authority or their clerk at the office of that authority
and sent by post in a registered letter.

Special Provisions as to London

14. The council of a metropolitan borough may, if Agreements
they think fit, pay or contribute towards the payment between
London
of any expenses of the London County Council under County
Council and
subsection five of section forty-six of the principal Act metropolitan
in connection with a scheme of reconstruction, and councils.
borrow any money required by them for the purpose
under subsection two of the said section ; but an order
under subsection six shall not be necessary except in
cases of disagreement between the county council and
the council of the borough.

See section 46 of the 1890 Act, and notes thereto.

15. For the purpose of carrying into effect the provi- Provisions
sions of this Act as to the maximum period for which consequential on ex-
money may be borrowed, eighty years shall be substituted tension of
period for
for sixty years in section twenty-seven of the Metropolitan repayment
of loans.

S. 15 (03).
32 & 33 Vict. c. 102.
18 & 19 Vict. c. 120.

Board of Works (Loans) Act, 1869, and such sum as will be sufficient, with compound interest, to repay the money borrowed within such period, not exceeding eighty years, as may be sanctioned by the London County Council, shall be substituted for two pounds per cent. in section one hundred and ninety of the Metropolis Management Act, 1855.

16. ("Substitution of Secretary of State for Local Government Board.") *Repealed by the Housing, Town Planning, &c., Act, 1909.*

Supplemental

Short title and extent.

17. (1.) This Act may be cited as the Housing of the Working Classes Act, 1903, and the Housing of the Working Classes Acts, 1890 to 1900, and this Act, may be cited together as the Housing of the Working Classes Acts, 1890 to 1903.

(2.) This Act shall not extend to * Ireland.

SCHEDULE

(See note to section 3 hereof)

Section 3, 16.

(1.) If in the administrative county of London or in any borough or urban district, or in any parish not within a borough or urban district, the undertakers have power to take under the enabling Act working-men's dwellings occupied by thirty or more persons belonging to the working class, the undertakers shall not enter on any such dwellings in that county, borough, urban district, or parish, until the Local Government Board have either approved of a housing scheme under this schedule or have decided that such a scheme is not necessary.

* The words "Scotland or" appearing here were repealed by the Housing, Town Planning, &c., Act, 1909.

For the purposes of this schedule a house shall be Sch. (03). considered a working-man's dwelling if wholly or partially occupied by a person belonging to the working classes, and for the purpose of determining whether a house is a working-man's dwelling or not, and also for determining the number of persons belonging to the working classes by whom any dwelling-houses are occupied, any occupation on or after the fifteenth day of December next before the passing of the enabling Act, or, in the . case of land acquired compulsorily under a general Act without the authority of an order, next before the date of the application to the Local Government Board under this schedule, for their approval of or decision with respect to a housing scheme, shall be taken into consideration.

(2.) The housing scheme shall make provision for the accommodation of such number of persons of the working class as is, in the opinion of the Local Government Board, taking into account all the circumstances, required, but that number shall not exceed the aggregate number of persons of the working class displaced ; and in calculating that number the Local Government Board shall take into consideration not only the persons of the working class who are occupying the working-men's dwellings which the undertakers have power to take, but also any persons of the working class who, in the opinion of the Local Government Board, have been displaced within the previous five years in view of the acquisition of land by the undertakers.

(3.) Provision may be made by the housing scheme for giving undertakers who are a local authority, or who have not sufficient powers for the purpose, power for the purpose of the scheme to appropriate land or to acquire land, either by agreement or compulsorily under the authority of a Provisional Order, and for giving any local authority power to erect dwellings on land so appropriated or acquired by them, and to sell or dispose of any such dwellings, and to raise money for the purpose of the scheme as for the purposes of Part III of the principal Act, and for regulating the application of any money arising from the sale or disposal of the dwellings ; and any provisions so made shall have effect as if they had been enacted in an Act of Parliament.

(4.) The housing scheme shall provide that any lands acquired under that scheme shall, for a period of twenty-five years from the date of the scheme, be appropriated for the purpose of dwellings for persons of the working class, except so far as the Local Government Board dispense with that appropriation ; and every conveyance, demise, or lease of any such land shall be endorsed with notice of this provision, and the Local Government Board may require the insertion in the scheme of any provisions requiring a certain standard of dwelling-house to be erected under the scheme, or any conditions to be complied with as to the mode in which the dwelling-houses are to be erected.

(5.) If the Local Government Board do not hold a local inquiry with reference to a housing scheme, they shall, before approving the scheme, send a copy of the draft scheme to every local authority, and shall consider any representation made within the time fixed by the Board by any such authority.

(6.) The Local Government Board may, as a condition of their approval of a housing scheme, require that the new dwellings under the scheme, or some part of them, shall be completed and fit for occupation before pos-

session is taken of any working-men's dwellings under Sch. (03).
the enabling Act.

(7.) Before approving any scheme the Local Government Board may if they think fit require the undertakers to give such security as the Board consider proper for carrying the scheme into effect.

(8.) The Local Government Board may hold such inquiries as they think fit for the purpose of their duties under this schedule, and subsections one and five of section eighty-seven of the Local Government Act, 1888 (which relate to local inquiries), shall apply for the purpose, and where the undertakers are not a local authority shall be applicable as if they were such an authority.

(9.) If the undertakers enter on any working-men's dwelling in contravention of the provisions of this schedule, or of any conditions of approval of the housing scheme made by the Local Government Board, they shall be liable to a penalty not exceeding five hundred pounds in respect of every such dwelling :

Any such penalty shall be recoverable by the Local Government Board by action in the High Court, and shall be carried to and form part of the Consolidated Fund.

(10.) If the undertakers fail to carry out any provision of the housing scheme, the Local Government Board may make such order as they think necessary or proper for the purpose of compelling them to carry out that provision, and any such order may be enforced by mandamus.

(11.) The Local Government Board may, on the application of the undertakers, modify any housing scheme which has been approved by them under this

Schedule, and any modifications so made shall take effect as part of the scheme.

(12.) For the purposes of this schedule—

(a) The expression "undertakers" means any authority, company, or person who are acquiring land compulsorily or by agreement under any local Act or Provisional Order or order having the effect of an Act, or are acquiring land compulsorily under any general Act:

(b) The expression "enabling Act" means any Act of Parliament or Order under which the land is acquired:

(c) The expression "local authority" means the council of any administrative county and the district council of any county district, or, in London, the council of any metropolitan borough in which in any case any houses in respect of which the re-housing scheme is made are situated, or in the case of the city the common council:

(d) The expression "dwelling" or "house" means any house or part of a house occupied as a separate dwelling:

(e) The expression "working class" includes mechanics, artisans, labourers, and others working for wages; hawkers, costermongers, persons not working for wages, but working at some trade or handicraft without employing others, except members of their own family, and persons other than domestic servants whose income in any case does not exceed an average of thirty shillings a week, and the families of any of such persons who may be residing with them.

HOUSING, TOWN PLANNING, &c., ACT, 1909
[9 Edw. 7. Ch. 44.]

ARRANGEMENT OF SECTIONS

Part I.—Housing of the Working Classes

An Act to amend the Law relating to the Housing of the Working Classes, to provide for the making of Town Planning schemes, and to make further provision with respect to the appointment and duties of County Medical Officers of Health, and to provide for the establishment of Public Health and Housing Committees of County Councils.   [3rd December 1909.]

BE it enacted by the King's most Excellent Majesty, by and with the advice and consent of the Lords Spiritual and Temporal, and Commons, in this present Parliament assembled, and by the authority of the same, as follows :

PART I

HOUSING OF THE WORKING CLASSES

Facilities for Acquisition of Lands and other Purposes of the Housing Acts

1. Part III of the Housing of the Working Classes Act, 1890 (in this Part of this Act referred to as the principal Act), shall, after the commencement of this Act, extend to and take effect in every urban or rural district, or other place for which it has not been adopted, as if it had been so adopted.

Part III of the principal Act to take effect without adoption. 53 & 54 Vict. c. 70.

2. (1.) A local authority may be authorised to purchase land compulsorily for the purposes of Part III of the principal Act, by means of an order submitted to the Local Government Board and confirmed by the Board in accordance with the First Schedule to this Act.

Provisions as to acquisition of land under Part III of the principal Act.

19

S. 2 (09).   (2.) The procedure under this section for the compulsory purchase of land shall be substituted for the procedure for the same purpose under section one hundred 38 & 39 Vict. and seventy-six of the Public Health Act, 1875, as c. 55. applied by subsection (1) of section fifty-seven of the principal Act.

(3.) A local authority may, with the consent of and subject to any conditions imposed by the Local Government Board, acquire land by agreement for the purposes of Part III of the principal Act, notwithstanding that the land is not immediately required for those purposes.

For additional powers—see section 12 of the 1919 Act.

See section 57 of the 1890 Act, and notes thereto, on the question of the acquisition of land.

It will be noticed that subsections (1) and (2) above relate to compulsory acquisition, while subsection (3) relates to acquisition by agreement.

The assessment of compensation for land compulsorily acquired is made under the Acquisition of Land (Assessment of Compensation) Act, 1919 (page 495).

Loans by Public Works Loan Commissioners to local authorities.

3. Where a loan is made by the Public Works Loan Commissioners to a local authority for any purposes of the Housing Acts—

(a) The loan shall be made at the minimum rate allowed for the time being for loans out of the Local Loans Fund ; and

(b) If the Local Government Board make a recommendation to that effect, the period for which the loan is made by the Public Works Loan Commissioners may exceed the period allowed under the principal Act or under any other Act limiting the period for which the loan may be made, but the period shall not exceed the period recommended by the Local Government Board, S. 3 (09). nor in any case eighty years ; and

(c) As between loans for different periods, the longer duration of the loan shall not be taken as a reason for fixing a higher rate of interest.

But see now section 7 (4) of the 1919 Act.

See also section 25 (5) of the 1890 Act, and section 1 of the 1903 Act. By the Public Works Loans Act, 1920, temporary loans can be secured up to 30th September 1921 (see page 487).

4. (1.) Where a loan is made by the Public Works Loan Commissioners under section sixty-seven, subsection (2) (*d*), of the principal Act, to a public utility society, the words " two thirds " shall be substituted for the words " one moiety."

(2.) *Repealed by the Housing, Town Planning, &c., Act, 1919, section 50, and 5th schedule.*

See also section 20 of the 1919 Act.

5. (1.) Any purchase money or compensation payable in pursuance of the Housing Acts by a local authority in respect of any lands, estate, or interest of another local authority which would, but for this section, be paid into cour in manner provided by the Lands Clauses Acts or by paragraph (20) of the Second Schedule to the principal Act may, if the Local Government Board consent, instead of being paid into court, be paid and applied as the Board determine.

(2.) Any such decision of the Board as to the payment and application of any such purchase money or compensation shall be final and conclusive.

The effect of this is that the expense in the payment into and out of court can thus be avoided. It applies

Marginal notes:

Loans by Public Works Loan Commissioners to public utility societies. 56 & 57 Vict. c. 39.

Payment of purchase or compensation money (which would otherwise be paid into court) on direction of Local Government Board.

S. 5 (09).   only where the transaction is between two local authorities.

6. ("Provision of public streets," &c.) *Repealed by
the Housing, Town Planning, &c., Act, 1919, section 50,
and 5th schedule.*

Expenditure
of money for
housing pur-
poses in case
of settled
land.
45 & 46 Vict.
c. 38.

7. (1.) The following paragraph shall be substituted
for paragraph (*b*) of subsection (1) of section seventy-
four of the principal Act :—

(*b*) The improvements on which capital money
arising under the Settled Land Act, 1882, may
be expended, enumerated in section twenty-five
of the said Act and referred to in section thirty
of the said Act, shall, in addition to cottages for
labourers, farm servants, and artisans, whether
employed on the settled land or not, include the
provision of dwellings available for the working
classes, either by means of building new buildings
or by means of the reconstruction, enlargement,
or improvement of existing buildings, so as to
make them available for the purpose, if that
provision of dwellings is, in the opinion of the
court, not injurious to the estate or is agreed
to by the tenant for life and the trustees of the
settlement.

(2.) The provision by a tenant for life, at his own
expense, of dwellings available for the working classes
on any settled land shall not be deemed to be an injury
to any interest in reversion or remainder in that land ;
provided that the powers conferred upon a tenant for
life by this subsection shall not be exercised by him
without the previous approval in writing of the trustees
of the settlement.

See section 74 of the 1890 Act, and, particularly, section 31 of the 1919 Act, and notes thereto.

8. A local authority may accept a donation of land or money or other property for any of the purposes of the Housing Acts, and it shall not be necessary to enrol any assurance with respect to any such property under the Mortmain and Charitable Uses Act, 1888.

Donation. Doubtless by will or otherwise. As to gifts to other persons than local authorities—see the Working Classes Dwellings Act, 1890 (page 254).

9. (1.) If in any case it appears to the Local Government Board that the institution of legal proceedings is requisite or desirable with respect to any property required to be applied under any trusts for the provision of dwellings available for the working classes, or that the expediting of any such legal proceedings is requisite or desirable, the Board may certify the case to the Attorney-General, and the Attorney-General, if he thinks fit, shall institute any legal proceedings or intervene in any legal proceedings already instituted in such manner as he thinks proper under the circumstances.

(2.) Before preparing any scheme with reference to property required to be applied under any trusts for the provision of dwellings available for the working classes, the court or body who are responsible for making the scheme shall communicate with the Local Government Board and receive and consider any recommendations made by the Board with reference to the proposed scheme.

The local authority should bring the circumstances to the notice of the Ministry when they have reason to suppose that any trusts having for their object the provision of working-class dwellings are not being properly

Marginal notes: Donations for housing purposes. / 51 & 52 Vict. c. 42. / Provisions with respect to money applicable under trusts for housing purposes.

S. 9 (09).

carried into effect promptly—Local Government Board Memo., 31st December 1909.

Powers of enforcing Execution of Housing Acts

Power of Local Government Board on complaint to enforce exercise of powers.

10. (1.) Where a complaint is made to the Local Government Board—

(a) as respects any rural district by the council of the county in which the district is situate, or by the parish council or parish meeting of any parish comprised in the district, or by any four inhabitant householders of the district ; or

(b) as respects any county district, not being a rural district, by the council of the county in which the district is situated, or by four inhabitant householders of the district ; or

(c) as respects the area of any other local authority by four inhabitant householders of the area ;

that the local authority have failed to exercise their powers under Part II or Part III of the principal Act in cases where those powers ought to have been exercised, the Board may cause a public local inquiry to be held, and if, after holding such an inquiry, the Board are satisfied that there has been such a failure on the part of the local authority, the Board may declare the authority . to be in default, and may make an order directing that authority, within a time limited by the order, to carry out such works and do such other things as may be mentioned in the order for the purpose of remedying the default.

(2.) Before deciding that a local authority have failed to exercise their powers under Part III of the principal Act, the Board shall take into consideration the necessity for further accommodation for the housing of the working classes in such district, the probability that the required accommodation will not be otherwise provided, and the S. 10 (09). other circumstances of the case, and whether, having regard to the liability which will be incurred by the rates, it is prudent for the local authority to undertake the provision of such accommodation.

(3.) Where an order originally made under this section on the council of a county district is not complied with by that council, the Local Government Board may, if they think fit, with the consent of the county council, instead of enforcing that order against the council of the county district, make an order directing the county council to carry out any works or do any other things which are mentioned in the original order for the purpose of remedying the default of the district council.

(4.) Where the Board make an order under this section directing a county council to carry out any works or do any other thing, the order may, for the purpose of enabling the county council to give effect to the order, apply any of the provisions of the Housing Acts or of section sixty-three of the Local Government Act, 1894, 56 & 57 Vic. with such modifications or adaptations (if any) as appear c. 73. necessary or expedient.

(5.) An order made by the Local Government Board under this section shall be laid before both Houses of Parliament as soon as may be after it is made.

(6.) Any order made by the Local Government Board under this section may be enforced by mandamus.

See section 5 of the 1919 Act, and notes thereto, as to Part II ; and note also section 11 hereof. See sections 3 and 4 of the 1919 Act as to Part III, and note, further, sections 12 and 13 hereof.

As to local inquiries—see section 85 of the 1890 Act.

Section 63 of the Local Government Act, 1894, is printed in full on page 377.

S. 11 (09).

Power of Local Government Board to order schemes, &c. to be carried out within a limited time.

11. (1.) Where it appears to the Local Government Board that a local authority have failed to perform their duty under the Housing Acts of carrying out an improvement scheme under Part I of the principal Act, or have failed to give effect to any order as respects an obstructive building, or to a reconstruction scheme, under Part II of that Act, or have failed to cause to be made the inspection of their district required by this Act, the Board may make an order requiring the local authority to remedy the default and to carry out any works or do any other things which are necessary for the purpose under the Housing Acts within a time fixed by the order.

(2.) Any order made by the Local Government Board under this section may be enforced by mandamus.

See sections 4 and 5 of the 1919 Act, and notes thereto. As to " inspection "—see section 17 hereof.

Powers of county council to act in default of rural district council under Part III of the principal Act.

12. Where a complaint is made to the council of a county by the parish council or parish meeting of any parish comprised in any rural district in the county, or by any four inhabitant householders of that district, the county council may cause a public local inquiry to be held, and if, after holding such an inquiry, the county council are satisfied that the rural district council have failed to exercise their powers under Part III of the principal Act in cases where those powers ought to have been exercised, the county council may resolve that the powers of the district council for the purposes of that Part be transferred to the county council with respect either to the whole district or to any parish in the district, and those powers shall be transferred accordingly, and, subject to the provisions of this Act, section sixty-three of the Local Government Act, 1894, shall S. 12 (09). apply as if the powers had been transferred under that Act.

See section 3 of the 1919 Act which provides a simpler procedure.

13. (1.) Where the council of a county are of opinion Power of that for any reason it is expedient that the council county council to should exercise, as respects any rural district in the county, exercise powers of any of the powers of a local authority under Part III rural district council of the principal Act, the council, after giving notice to under Part III of the council of the district of their intention to do so, the principal may apply to the Local Government Board for an order Act. conferring such powers on them.

(2.) Upon such an application being made, the Board may make an order conferring on the county council as respects the rural district all or any of the powers of a local authority under Part III of the principal Act, and thereupon the provisions of the Housing Acts relating to those powers (including those enabling the Public Works Loan Commissioners to lend, and fixing the terms for which money may be lent and borrowed) shall apply as if the council were a local authority under Part III of the principal Act : Provided that the expenses incurred by the county council under any such order shall be defrayed as expenses for general county purposes.

(3.) Where, under any such order, the county council have executed any works in a rural district they may transfer the works to the council of that district on such terms and subject to such conditions as may be agreed between them.

See also sections 3 and 4 of the 1919 Act.

S. 14 (09).   *Contracts by Landlord*

Extension of
section 75 of
the principal
Act.

14. In any contract made after the passing of this
Act for letting for habitation a house or part of a house
at a rent not exceeding—

> (*a*) in the case of a house situate in the adminis-
> trative county of London, forty pounds ;
>
> (*b*) in the case of a house situate in a borough or
> urban district with a population according to
> the last census for the time being of fifty thousand
> or upwards, twenty-six pounds ;
>
> (*c*) in the case of a house situate elsewhere, sixteen
> pounds ;

there shall be implied a condition that the house is at
the commencement of the holding in all respects reasonably fit for human habitation, but the condition aforesaid shall not be implied when a house or part of a house
is let for a term of not less than three years upon the
terms that it be put by the lessee into a condition reasonably fit for occupation, and the lease is not determinable
at the option of either party before the expiration of
that term.

See section 75 of the 1890 Act, and note thereto.

By section 39 (2) of the 1919 Act " sections 14 and 15
of the Housing, Town Planning, &c., Act, 1909, shall be
deemed to be part of Part II of the principal Act."
With regard to the present section (14) it is not very
clear that this provision has a special significance, though
there is the difficulty that in the present section there
is no express provision against contracting out, as there
is in section 75 of the 1890 Act—as per section 12 of the
1903 Act. Of course sections 14 and 15 stand together,
and it may be that the object of section 39 (2) of the 1919
Act is to give an owner, who does repairs under section
15, the right to a charging order under section 36 of the
1890 Act.

That term. It is not clear that a house let for five S. 14 (09). years with the option of determination at the end of three years, is within the exception.

15. (1.) The last foregoing section shall, as respects Condition as contracts to which that section applies, take effect as to keeping houses let to if the condition implied by that section included an persons of the working undertaking that the house shall, during the holding, classes in repair. be kept by the landlord in all respects reasonably fit for human habitation.

(2.) The landlord or the local authority, or any person authorised by him or them in writing, may at reasonable times of the day, on giving twenty-four hours' notice in writing to the tenant or occupier, enter any house, premises, or building to which this section applies for the purpose of viewing the state and condition thereof.

(3.) If it appears to the local authority within the meaning of Part II of the principal Act that the undertaking implied by virtue of this section is not complied with in the case of any house to which it applies, the authority shall, if a closing order is not made with respect to the house, by written notice require the landlord, within a reasonable time, not being less than twenty-one days, specified in the notice, to execute such works as the authority shall specify in the notice as being necessary to make the house in all respects reasonably fit for human habitation.

(4.) Within twenty-one days after the receipt of such notice the landlord may by written notice to the local authority declare his intention of closing the house for human habitation, and thereupon a closing order shall be deemed to have become operative in respect of such house.

(5.) If the notice given by the local authority is not complied with. and if the landlord has not given the notice mentioned in the immediate preceding subsection, the authority may, at the expiration of the time specified in the notice given by them to the landlord, do the work required to be done and recover the expenses incurred by them in so doing from the landlord as a civil debt in manner provided by the Summary Jurisdiction Acts, or, if they think fit, the authority may by order declare any such expenses to be payable by annual instalments within a period not exceeding that of the interest of the landlord in the house, nor in any case five years, with interest at a rate not exceeding five pounds per cent. per annum, until the whole amount is paid, and any such instalments or interest or any part thereof may be recovered from the landlord as a civil debt in manner provided by the Summary Jurisdiction Acts.

(6.) A landlord may appeal to the Local Government Board against any notice requiring him to execute works under this section, and against any demand for the recovery of expenses from him under this section or order made with respect to those expenses under this section by the authority, by giving notice of appeal to the Board within twenty-one days after the notice is received, or the demand or order is made, as the case may be, and no proceedings shall be taken in respect of such notice requiring works, order, or demand, whilst the appeal is pending.

(7.) In this section the expression " landlord " means any person who lets to a tenant for habitation the house under any contract referred to in this section, and includes his successors in title ; and the expression " house " includes part of a house.

(8.) Sections forty-nine and fifty of the principal Act as amended by section thirteen of the Housing of

the Working Classes Act, 1903 (which relate to the S. 15 (09).
service of notices and the description of owner in pro-3 Edw. 7.
c. 39.
ceedings), shall apply for the purposes of this section,
with the substitution, where required, of the landlord
for the owner of a dwelling-house.

(9.) Any remedy given by this section for non-compliance with the undertaking implied by virtue of this
section shall be in addition to and not in derogation of
any other remedy available to the tenant against the
landlord, either at common law or otherwise.

See notes to foregoing section, and to section 75 of
the 1890 Act.

In the committee-stage proceedings on the 1919 Bill,
it was stated by Dr. Addison, Minister of Health, that
this section had never worked. (Standing Committee
Report, col. 75), and doubtless section 28 of the 1919
Act will be more usually made use of for the Minister's
purpose—but see *Walker v. Hobbs*, 23 Q.B.D. 458., *Smith v.
Marrable*, 12 L.J.Ex. 223, *Campbell v. Lord Wenlock*, 4 F.
and F. 716; and *Stanton v. Southwick, The Times,*
30th April 1920.

As to enforcing power of entry—see section 89 of the
1890 Act.

As to closing order—see section 17 hereof.

For forms prescribed for use under this section—see
pages 601 to 607.

16. ("Extension of power of making byelaws with
respect to lodging-houses for the working classes.")
*Repealed by the Housing, Town Planning, &c., Act, 1919,
section 50 and 5th schedule.*

Amendment of Procedure for Closing Orders and Demolition Orders

17. (1.) It shall be the duty of every local authority Duty of
local
authority
as to closing
of dwelling-
house unfit
for human
habitation.
within the meaning of Part II of the principal Act to
cause to be made from time to time inspection of their
district, with a view to ascertain whether any dwelling-
house therein is in a state so dangerous or injurious to

S. 17 (09). health as to be unfit for human habitation, and for that purpose it shall be the duty of the local authority, and of every officer of the local authority, to comply with such regulations and to keep such records as may be prescribed by the Board.

Duty. As to default—see section 11 hereof and section 31 (2) of the 1890 Act.

By section 35 of the 1919 Act, nothing in the Increase of Rent and Mortgage Interest (War Restrictions) Act, 1915, &c., shall be deemed to affect the provisions of this section.

This section supersedes section 32 of the 1890 Act, and the procedure with regard to unhealthy houses can be better followed if it is read in its stead. It is to be deemed to be part of Part II of the 1890 Act— see section 47 hereof. As to " unfit for human habitation "—see section 30 of the 1890 Act.

As to " local authority "—see page 234 ; as to enforcement of its duty—see sections 10 and 11 hereof, and section 5 of the 1919 Act ; and as to power of county councils—see section 45 of the 1890 Act. The local authority can act by a committee—section 81 of the 1890 Act, and, by section 88 thereof, an interested member must not vote.

For the regulations and records—see page 570.

For power of entry—see section 36 hereof.

(2.) If, on the representation of the medical officer of health, or of any other officer of the authority, or other information given, any dwelling-house appears to them to be in such a state, it shall be their duty to make an order prohibiting the use of the dwelling-house for human habitation (in this Act referred to as a closing order) until in the judgment of the local authority the dwelling-house is rendered fit for that purpose.

The preferable procedure is, usually, that under section 28 of the 1919 Act (repair of houses), but the local authority can proceed hereunder ; or under the Public Health Acts if it prefers—section 91 of the 1890

Act (page 230) ; or under the powers of a local Act— S. 17 (09).
Hall v. Manchester Corporation [1915] 79 J.P. 385.

"The new Act does not in any way prescribe the procedure to be adopted by the local authority before making a closing order. This matter is left to their discretion. They should, however, before making an order give due notice to all persons interested in the house, whether within the definition of owner or not, and afford them an opportunity of being heard on the subject "—Local Government Board Memo., dated 31st December 1909. See also *Hall v. Manchester Corporation*, above, and *Kirkpatrick v. Maxwelltown* [1912] S.C. 288.

For form of closing order—see page 616. It must be under seal—section 86 of the 1890 Act.

Some difficulty may arise in the case of a house let in flats or separate tenements, and if only one such flat is in a bad state it would seem better, particularly in view of section 18, to proceed under section 28 of the 1919 Act as to repairs, or under the Public Health Acts as to nuisances. If a closing order refers to the whole house and one of the separate tenements is in good condition, it will be liable to reversal on appeal—*Johnston's Trustees v. Glasgow Corporation* [1912] S.C. 300. A closing order made under a byelaw under the Public Health Act, 1875, section 157, does not prevent another closing order being made hereunder with a view to having the building demolished—*Slight v. Portsmouth (Mayor of)* [1906] 70 J.P. 359.

Merrick v. Corporation of Liverpool [1910] 2 Ch. 449, raised several interesting points in connection with closing orders. The plaintiffs alleged that the corporation wanted to demolish the houses to admit air to other houses and that it was proceeding by closing order, where no compensation for demolition would be payable, instead of by sections 38 or 39 of the 1890 Act, where compensation would be payable. It was held that if this had been proved it would have been sufficient to justify intervention by the court, but it had not been proved. See also *Hall v. Manchester Corporation*, above.

As to other representations to be made by the medical officer of health—see sections 30 and 79 (2) of the 1890 Act.

(3.) Notice of a closing order shall be forthwith served

S. 17 (09).   on every owner of the dwelling-house in respect of which
it is made, and any owner aggrieved by the order may.
appeal to the Local Government Board by giving notice
of appeal to the Board within fourteen days after the
* notice is served upon him.

The fifth word from the end was, formerly, " order."
For Form of Notice—see page 617. By *Rayner v. Stepney
Corporation* [1911] 75 J.P. 468, it would appear that the
notice will be invalid if it does not contain information
about the owner's right of appeal.

Owner. For definition—see section 29 of the 1890
Act. It will not be easy in all cases to discover every
owner as so defined, and in view of section 39 (2) hereof
this causes a difficulty. Some help is given by sections 49
and 50 of the 1890 Act, which deal with service of notices
and description of owner in proceedings. By section 41
hereof the Ministry may dispense with service of notices.
Owners may give notice of their interests—section 47,
1890 Act.

Appeal. See section 39 hereof. This is the appeal
before the works are done. There is another appeal
thereafter—subsection (6), below. For Form of Notice of
Appeal—see page 619.

(4.) Where a closing order has become operative,
the local authority shall serve notice of the order on
the * occupier of the dwelling-house in respect of which
the order is made, and, within such period as is specified
in the notice, not being less than fourteen days after
the service of the notice, the order shall be obeyed by
him, and he and his family shall cease to inhabit the
dwelling-house, and in default he shall be liable on
summary conviction to be ordered to quit the dwelling-
house within such time as may be specified in the order.

Becomes operative. See section 39 (2) hereof, and

* As altered by the Housing, Town Planning, &c., Act, 1919, 2nd
schedule.

note the special cases of section 15 (4) hereof, and section s. 17 (06,. 28 (1) proviso of the 1919 Act.

The occupier, including an occupying owner. The words were, formerly, " every occupying tenant." For the form of notice to be served—see page 620.

Ordered to quit. If he does not obey the order of the Court of Summary Jurisdiction he will be liable to a penalty of £1 per day, not exceeding £20 in all, or to imprisonment up to two months—Summary Jurisdiction Act, 1879, section 34. Or proceedings may be taken under section 10 of the 1903 Act, in which case the owner will be liable for the expense. .

By section 32 of the 1919 Act, if any owner or any other person lets or attempts to let, or occupies or permits to be occupied as a dwelling-house a house closed by a closing order he is liable on summary conviction to a fine not exceeding £20.

(5.) Unless the dwelling-house has been made unfit for habitation by the wilful act or default of the tenant or of any person for whom as between himself and the owner or landlord he is responsible, the local authority may make to every such tenant such reasonable allowance on account of his expense in removing as may be determined by the local authority with the consent of the owner of the dwelling-house, or, if the owner of the dwelling-house fails to consent to the sum determined by the local authority, as may be fixed by a court of summary jurisdiction, and the amount of the said allowance shall be recoverable by the local authority from the owner of the dwelling-house as a civil debt in manner provided by the Summary Jurisdiction Acts.

Summary Jurisdiction Acts. See the Act of 1879, sections 6, 35 and 51.

(6.) The local authority shall determine any closing order made by them if they are satisfied that the dwelling-house, in respect of which the order has been made, has been rendered fit for human habitation.

20

S. 17 (09).   If, on the application of any owner of a dwelling-house, the local authority refuse to determine a closing order, the owner may appeal to the Local Government Board by giving notice of appeal to the Board within fourteen days after the application is refused.

Appeal.   See section 39 hereof.   For the prescribed forms—see page 623.

By section 47 of the 1890 Act the superior landlord may be authorised to enter and do the necessary works.

(7.) A room habitually used as a sleeping place, the surface of the floor of which is more than three feet below the surface of the part of the street adjoining or nearest to the room, * or more than three feet below the surface of any ground within nine feet of the room,* shall for the purposes of this section be deemed to be a dwelling-house so dangerous or injurious to health as to be unfit for human habitation, if the room either—

    (*a*) is not on an average at least seven feet in height from floor to ceiling ; or

    (*b*) does not comply with such regulations as the local authority with the consent of the Local Government Board may prescribe for securing the proper ventilation and lighting of such rooms, and the protection thereof against dampness, effluvia, or exhalation : Provided that if the local authority, after being required to do so by the Local Government Board, fail to make such regulations, or such regulations as the Board approve, the Board may themselves make them, and the regulations so made shall have effect as if they had been made by the local authority with the consent of the Board :

* Words added by the Housing, Town Planning, &c., Act, 1919, 2nd schedule.

Provided that a closing order made in respect of a S. 17 (09) room to which this subsection applies shall not prevent the room being used for purposes other than those of a sleeping place ; and that, if the occupier of the room after notice of an order has been served upon him fails to comply with the order, an order to comply therewith may, on summary conviction, be made against him.

This subsection shall not come into operation until the first day of July nineteen hundred and ten, and a closing order made in respect of any room to which this subsection applies shall not be treated as a closing order in respect of a dwelling-house for the purposes of the next succeeding section.

For the regulations suggested by the Ministry— see page 597.
See also the summary of sections 71–75 of the Public Health Act, 1875, printed on page 65.

18. (1.) Where a closing order in respect of any dwelling- Order for house has remained operative for a period of three months, demolition. the local authority shall take into consideration the question of the demolition of the dwelling-house, and shall give every owner of the dwelling-house notice of the time (being some time not less than one month after the service of the notice) and place at which the question will be considered, and any owner of the dwelling-house shall be entitled to be heard when the question is so taken into consideration.

By section 47 hereof the present section, which supersedes section 33 of the 1890 Act, is deemed to be part of Part II of that Act. See also the next note.
Closing Order. This is made under section 17 hereof, or one may be deemed to have become operative under section 15 (4) hereof, and section 28 (1) of the 1919 Act. Otherwise the closing order becomes operative as per

S. 18 (09).   section 39 (2) hereof. But, by section 47 (2) hereof, the present section refers only to orders made under the Housing Acts, thus excluding from the operation of the present section closing orders made under Public Health Acts.

As to local authority—see note to section 17 (1).

As to owner—see section 29 of the 1890 Act.

For form of notice—see page 625.

(2.) If upon any such consideration the local authority are of opinion that the dwelling-house has not been rendered fit for human habitation, and that the necessary steps are not being taken with all due diligence to render it so fit, or that the continuance of any building, being or being part of the dwelling-house, is a nuisance or dangerous or injurious to the health of the public or of the inhabitants of the neighbouring dwelling-houses, they shall order the demolition of the building.

This is obligatory. But (per *Lancaster v. Burnley Corporation* [1915] 1 K.B. 259) the Ministry may n appeal quash the order, though it has been validly made. In this way the difficulty may be overcome of the " closed " dwelling-house which is not a nuisance or dangerous to the neighbourhood, and which the owner desires to convert to another purpose. Alternatively the local authority, before making the closing order, could inform the owner that if he desires to use such a house for other than housing purposes he should convert it forthwith. But note particularly section 6 of the Housing (Additional Powers) Act, 1919.

For forms of demolition orders—see pages 626 and 630.

For power to determine closing and demolition orders —see subsection (3) below.

(3.) If any owner undertakes to execute forthwith the works necessary to render the dwelling-house fit for human habitation, and the local authority consider that it can be so rendered fit for human habitation, the

local authority may, if they think fit, postpone the opera- S. 18 (09).
tion of the order for such time, not exceeding six months,
as they think sufficient for the purpose of giving the
owner an opportunity of executing the necessary works,
*and if and when the necessary works are completed
to their satisfaction the local authority shall determine
the closing and demolition orders relating to the dwelling-
house.*

For the prescribed forms—see page 636. See also
note to section 17 (6).

(4.) Notice of an order for the demolition of a building
shall be forthwith served on every owner of the building
in respect of which it is made, and any owner aggrieved
by the order may appeal to the Local Government Board
by giving notice of appeal to the Board within twenty-
one days after the * notice is served upon him, or where
the operation of the order has been postponed for any
period within fourteen days after the expiration of that
period.*

See note to section 17 (3). As to taking down
the building, &c.—see section 34 of the 1890 Act, and
notes thereto.
For the prescribed forms—see pages 629 and 635.

19. Any owner of or other person interested in a Power to
redeem
dwelling-house on which an annuity has been charged annuities
by a charging order made under section thirty-six of charged by
charging
the principal Act (which relates to the grant of charges) order under
section 36 of
shall at any time be at liberty to redeem the annuity on the principal
Act.
payment to the person entitled to the annuity of such
sum as may be agreed upon, or in default of agreement
determined by the Local Government Board.

See also section 26 (8) of the 1919 Act.

* As altered by the Housing, Town Planning, &c., Act, 1919, 2nd
schedule.

S. 20 (09).

Provision as
to priority
of charges
under section
37 of the
principal
Act.

20. The charges excepted in subsection (1) of section thirty-seven of the principal Act (which relates to the incidence of charges) shall include charges on the dwelling-house created or arising under any provision of the Public Health Acts, or under any provision in any local Act authorising a charge for recovery of expenses incurred by a local authority.

Restriction
on power of
court of sum-
mary juris-
diction to
extend time.

21. Subsection (3) of section forty-seven of the principal Act (which gives power to a court of summary jurisdiction to enlarge the time for certain matters) shall cease to have effect as respects the time allowed for the execution of any works or the demolition of a building under a closing order or under an order for the demolition of a building.

Amendments with respect to Improvement and Reconstruction Schemes

Amendment
of section 4
of the prin-
cipal Act as
to official
representa-
tion.

22. In section four of the principal Act (which relates to an official representation), the words " that the most satisfactory method of dealing with the evils connected with such houses, courts, or alleys, and the sanitary defects in such area is an improvement scheme " shall be substituted for the words " that the evils connected with such houses, courts, or alleys, and the sanitary defects in such area cannot be effectually remedied otherwise than by means of an improvement scheme."

Amendment
of the princi-
pal Act as to
contents of
schemes.

23. (1.) Section six of the principal Act (which relates to the contents of an improvement scheme) shall be read as if in subsection (1) the words " for sanitary purposes " were omitted in paragraph (a) ; and as if the following paragraph was inserted at the end of that subsection :—

" and

(e) may provide for any other matter (including

the closing and diversion of highways) for which
it seems expedient to make provision with a
view to the improvement of the area or the general
efficiency of the scheme."

(2.) Provision may be made in a reconstruction
scheme under Part II of the principal Act for any matters
for which provision may be made in an improvement
scheme made under Part I of that Act.

See sections 6 and 39 of the 1890 Act.

24. (1.) Paragraphs (*a*) and (*b*) of subsection (2) of
section five of the Housing of the Working Classes Act,
1903 (which limit the cases under which an order confirming an improvement scheme takes effect without
confirmation by Parliament), shall cease to have effect. *Amendment of 3 Edw. 7. c. 39. s. 5.*

(2.) An order of the Local Government Board sanctioning a reconstruction scheme, and authorising the
compulsory purchase of land for the purpose shall,
notwithstanding anything in section thirty-nine of the
principal Act, take effect without confirmation.

See also sections 8, 39 and 73 (1) of the 1890 Act.

25. The Local Government Board may, in the exercise of their power under section fifteen or subsection (9)
of section thirty-nine of the principal Act, permit the
local authority to modify their scheme, not only by the
abandonment of any part of the scheme which it may
appear inexpedient to carry into execution, but also by
amending or adding to the scheme in matters of detail
in such manner as appears expedient to the Board. *Modification of schemes.*

26. Any inspector or officer of the Local Government Board, or any person employed by the Board,
may be directed to make any inspection or inquiry
which is required for the purposes of section sixteen of
the principal Act (which relates to inquiries made on *Inquiries by Local Government Board inspectors as to unhealthy areas.*

S. 26 (09).

the default of a medical officer), and section eighty-five of that Act (which relates to inquiries by the Local Government Board), as amended by this Act, shall apply as respects any inspection or inquiry so held as it applies to local inquiries held under that section.

Amendment as to the vesting of water pipes, &c.

27. An improvement scheme under Part I of the principal Act may, with the consent of the person or body of persons entitled to any right or easement which would be extinguished by virtue of section twenty-two of the principal Act, provide for any exceptions, restrictions or modifications in the application to that right or easement of that section, and that section shall take effect subject to any such exceptions, restrictions, or modifications.

Amendment of section 38 of the principal Act as to distribution of compensation money and as to betterment charges.

28. (1.) The amount of any compensation payable under section thirty-eight of the principal Act (which relates to obstructive buildings) shall, when settled by arbitration in manner provided by that section, be apportioned by the arbitrator between any persons having an interest in the compensation in such manner as the arbitrator determines.

(2.) The power of the arbitrator to apportion compensation under the foregoing provision and to apportion any part of the compensation to be paid for the demolition of an obstructive building amongst other buildings under subsection (8) of the said section thirty-eight may be exercised in cases where the amount to be paid for compensation has been settled, otherwise than by arbitration under the principal Act, by an arbitrator appointed for the special purpose, on the application of the local authority, by the Local Government Board, and the provisions of that Act shall apply as if the arbitrator so appointed had been appointed as arbitrator to settle the amount to be paid for compensation. S. 28 (09).

See notes to section 38 (9) of the 1890 Act.

29. For removing doubts it is hereby declared that a local authority may tender evidence before an arbitrator to prove the facts under the headings (first) (secondly) (thirdly) mentioned in subsection (2) of section twenty-one and subsection (3) of section forty-one of the principal Act, notwithstanding that the local authority have not taken any steps with a view to remedying the defects or evils disclosed by the evidence.

Explanation of sections 21 (2) and 41 (3) of the principal Act.

Amendments with respect to Financial Matters

30. No deficiency in the Dwelling-house Improvement Fund shall be supplied under subsection (2) of section twenty-four of the principal Act out of borrowed money unless the deficiency arises in respect of money required for purposes to which borrowed money is, in the opinion of the Local Government Board, properly applicable.

Amendment as to application of money borrowed for the purpose of the Dwelling-house Improvement Fund.

31. (1.) The expenses incurred by a rural district council after the passing of this Act in the execution of Part III of the principal Act shall be defrayed as general expenses of the council in the execution of the Public Health Acts, except so far as the Local Government Board on the application of the council declare that any such expenses are to be levied as special expenses charged on specified contributory places, or as general expenses charged on specified contributory places, in the district, in such proportions as the district council may determine, to the exclusion of other parts of the district, and a rural district council may borrow for the purposes of Part III of the principal Act in like

Expenses of rural district council under Part III of the principal Act.

S. 31 (09). manner and subject to the like conditions as for the purpose of defraying the above-mentioned general or special expenses.

(2.) The district council shall give notice to the overseers of any contributory place proposed to be charged of any apportionment made by them under this section, and the overseers, if aggrieved by the apportionment, may appeal to the Local Government Board by giving notice of appeal to the Board within twenty-one days after notice has been so given of the apportionment.

This takes the place of the repealed portion of section 65 of the 1890 Act. See also section 66 thereof as to borrowing, and section 86 (2) thereof as to notices.

32. ("Application of proceeds of land sold under Part III of the principal Act.") *Repealed by the Housing, Town Planning, &c., Act, 1919, section 50, and 5th schedule.*

Mode in which contributions by London borough councils to the county council or vice versâ may be made.

33. Any payment or contribution agreed or ordered to be made under subsection (6) or (7) of section forty-six of the principal Act, as amended by section fourteen of the Housing of the Working Classes Act, 1903 (which relate to payments or contributions by borough councils towards the expenses of the county council or by the county council towards the expenses of borough councils in London), may be made either by means of the payment of a lump sum or by means of an annual payment of such amount and for such number of years as may be agreed upon or ordered.

Exemption from section 133 of 8 & 9 Vict. c. 18.

34. Section one hundred and thirty-three of the Lands Clauses Consolidation Act, 1845 (relating to land tax and poor rate), shall not apply in the case of any

lands of which a local authority becomes possessed by S. 34 (09).
virtue of the Housing Acts.

And the local authority is not required to make good
any deficiency in land tax and poor rate caused by their
taking land for housing purposes—the decision in *Vestry
of St. Leonard's, Shoreditch v. London County Council*
[1895] 2 Q.B. 104, being thus nullified.

35. (1.) The assessment to Inhabited House Duty of
any house occupied for the sole purpose of letting lodgings
to persons of the working classes, at a charge of not
exceeding sixpence a night for each person, shall be
discharged by the Commissioners acting in the execution
of the Acts · relating to the Inhabited House Duties,
upon the production of a certificate to the effect that the
house is solely constructed and used to afford suitable
accommodation for the lodgers, and that due provision
is made for their sanitary requirements.

Exemption
of lodging-
houses for
the working
classes from
Inhabited
House Duty.

(2.) The provision of subsection (2) of section twenty-
six of the Customs and Inland Revenue Act, 1890, in
relation to the certificate mentioned therein, shall, so
far as applicable, apply to the certificate to be produced
under this section.

53 & 54 Vict.
· c. 8.

General Amendments

36. Any person authorised in writing stating the
particular purpose or purposes for which the entry is
authorised, by the local authority or the Local Government Board, may at all reasonable times, on giving
twenty-four hours' notice to the occupier and the owner,
if the owner is known, of his intention, enter any house,
premises, or buildings—

Power of
entry.

(a) for the purpose of survey or valuation, in the
case of houses, premises, or buildings which the

S. 36 (09). local authority are authorised to purchase compulsorily under the Housing Acts ; and

(b) for the purpose of survey and examination, in the case of any dwelling-house in respect of which a closing order or an order for demolition has been made ; or

(c) for the purpose of survey and examination, where it appears to the authority or Board that survey or examination is necessary in order to determine whether any powers under the Housing Acts should be exercised in respect of any house, premises, or building.

Notice may be given to the occupier for the purposes of this section by leaving a notice addressed to the occupier, without name or further description, at the house, buildings, or premises.

Sections 51 and 89 of the 1890 Act apply when entry is obstructed—*Arlidge v. Scarse* [1915] 3 K.B. 325. For other powers of entry—see section 47 (2) of the 1890 Act, section 15 (2) hereof, and section 26 (3) of the 1919 Act.

Housing Acts. See section 51 hereof.

Appears that . . . survey or examination is necessary. The passing of the resolution is sufficient evidence— *Arlidge v. Scarse*, above.

Power of Local Government Board to obtain a report on any crowded area.

37. If it appears to the Local Government Board that owing to density of population, or any other reason, it is expedient to inquire into the circumstances of any area with a view to determining whether any powers under the Housing Acts should be put into force in that area or not, the Local Government Board may require the local authority to make a report to them containing such particulars as to the population of the district and other matters as they direct, and the local

authority shall comply with the requirement of the Local S. 37 (09).
Government Board, and any expenses incurred by them
in so doing shall be paid as expenses incurred in the
execution of such Part of the principal Act as the Local
Government Board determine.

See the wider provisions of sections 1–6 of the 1919
Act.

38. Where, upon an application made by one of the Joint action
by local
local authorities concerned, the Local Government authorities.
Board are satisfied that it is expedient that any local
authorities should act jointly for any purposes of the
Housing Acts, either generally or in any special case,
the Board may by order make provision for the purpose,
and any provisions so made shall have the same effect
as if they were contained in a provisional order made
under section two hundred and seventy-nine of the Public
Health Act, 1875, for the formation of a united district.

See also sections 1 (6) and 3 (3) of the 1919 Act as
to joint schemes under Part III (Housing Schemes).
There is an almost identical provision in section 7 (4)
of the Housing (Additional Powers) Act, 1919—see note
thereto.

39. (1.) The procedure on any appeal under this Part Appeals to
Local
of this Act, including costs, to the Local Government Government
Board shall be such as the Board may by rules determine, Board.
and on any such appeal the Board may make such order
in the matter as they think equitable, and any order so
made shall be binding and conclusive on all parties,
and, where the appeal is against any notice, order, or
apportionment given or made by the local authority,
the notice, order, or apportionment may be confirmed,
varied, or quashed, as the Board think just.

Provided that—

S. 39 (09).

    (*a*) the Local Government Board may at any stage of the proceedings on appeal, and shall, ·if so directed by the High Court, state in the form of a special case for the opinion of the court any question of law arising in the course of the appeal ; and

    (*b*) the rules shall provide that the Local Government Board shall not dismiss any appeal without having first held a public inquiry *unless the appellant fails to prosecute his appeal with due diligence.*

(2.) Any notice, order, or apportionment as respects which an appeal to the Local Government Board is given under this part of this Act shall not become operative, until either the time within which an appeal can be made under this Part of this Act has elapsed without an appeal being made, or, in case an appeal is made, the appeal is determined or abandoned, and no work shall be done or proceedings taken under any such notice, order, or apportionment, until it becomes operative.

(3.) The Local Government Board may, before considering any appeal which may be made to them under this Part of this Act, require the appellant to deposit such sum to cover the costs of the appeal as may be fixed by the rules made by them with reference to appeals.

Appeal. Under sections 15 (6), 17 (3) and (6), 18 (4), and 31 (2) hereof. The Ministry must exercise their discretion judicially—*Lancaster v. Burnley Corporation* [1915] 1 K.B. 259.

Quashed. See note to section 18 (2) hereof.

State . . . a . . . case. There are somewhat similar provisions in the Arbitration Act, 1889, section 19 ;

* Words added by the Housing, Town Planning, &c., Act, 1919, 2nd schedule.

and the National Insurance Act, 1911, section 66 (1). S. 39 (09).
In the latter Act it is expressly provided that there is
no appeal, and though there is no similar provision here,
it would still seem that there is no appeal.   There is an
even greater similarity between the present section and
section 44 of the National Insurance Act, 1918.

It is too late to state a case after the award has been
given—*Johnston's Trustees v. Glasgow Corporation* [1912]
S.C. 300.   As to questions of law—see *White v. St.
Marylebone Borough Council* [1915] 3 K.B. 249.

In *Local Government Board v. Arlidge* [1915] A.C. 120,
it was held that the Board may act upon written evidence,
need not hear the appellant orally, and need not disclose
the reports and documents placed before them, and that
the appellant is not entitled to know the name of the
official whose decision the Board's order represents.

40. Notwithstanding anything contained in the prin- Sale and
cipal Act it shall not be obligatory upon a local authority disposal of dwellings.
to sell and dispose of any lands or dwellings acquired or
constructed by them for any of the purposes of the
Housing Acts.

This referred to section 12 (5) of the 1890 Act, repealed
by the Sixth Schedule hereto, which required a sale
within ten years.

41. (1.) The Local Government Board may by order Power to
prescribe the form of any notice, advertisement, or prescribe forms and to
other document, to be used in connection with the dispense with advertise-
powers and duties of a local authority or of the Board ments and notices.
under the Housing Acts, and the forms so prescribed,
or forms as near thereto as circumstances admit, shall
be used in all cases to which those forms are applicable.

(2.) The Local Government Board may dispense
with the publication of advertisements or the service of
notices required to be published or served by a local
authority under the Housing Acts, if they are satisfied

S. 41 (09). that there is reasonable cause for dispensing with the publication or service.

(3.) Any such dispensation may be given by the Local Government Board either before or after the time at which the advertisement is required to be published or the notice is required to be served, and either unconditionally or upon such conditions as to the publication of other advertisements or the service of other notices or otherwise as the Board think fit, due care being taken by the Board to prevent the interests of any person being prejudiced by the dispensation.

The dispensation is not given unless there are very good reasons and there will be no hardship resulting.

Provision as to publication in London Gazette.
42. Where under the Housing Acts, any scheme or order or any draft scheme or order is to be published in the London Gazette, or notice of any such scheme or order or draft scheme or order is to be given in the London Gazette, it shall be sufficient in lieu of such publication or notice to insert a notice giving short particulars of the scheme, order, or draft, and stating where copies thereof can be inspected or obtained in two local newspapers circulating in the area affected by the scheme, order, or draft, or to give notice thereof in such other manner as the Local Government Board determine.

Prohibition of back-to-back houses.
43. Notwithstanding anything in any local Act or byelaw in force in any borough or district, it shall not be lawful to erect any back-to-back houses intended to be used as dwellings for the working classes, and any such house commenced to be erected after the passing of this Act shall be deemed to be unfit for human habitation for the purposes of the provisions of the Housing Acts.

Provided that nothing in this section—

(a) shall prevent the erection or use of a house containing several tenements in which the tenements are placed back to back, if the medical officer of health for the district certifies that the several tenements are so constructed and arranged as to secure effective ventilation of all habitable rooms in every tenement ; or

(b) shall apply to houses abutting on any streets the plans whereof have been approved by the local authority before the first day of May nineteen hundred and nine, in any borough or district in which, at the passing of this Act, any local Act or byelaws are in force permitting the erection of back-to-back houses.

Back-to-back. This phrase is used in a popular and general sense : there is no definition—*Murrayfield Real Estate Company, Limited v. Edinburgh Magistrates* [1912] S.C. 217. See also *White v. St. Marylebone Borough Council* [1915] 3 K.B. 249. Briefly, there must be an air space before and behind each house—or tenement, but see proviso (a), the medical officer's certificate being conclusive.

44. If the Local Government Board are satisfied, by local inquiry or otherwise, that the erection of dwellings for the working classes within any borough, or urban or rural district, is unreasonably impeded in consequence of any byelaws with respect to new streets or buildings in force therein, the Board may require the local authority to revoke such byelaws or to make such new byelaws as the Board may consider necessary for the removal of the impediment.   If the local authority do not within three months after such requisition comply therewith, the Board may themselves revoke such byelaws, and

Power to Local Government Board to revoke unreasonable byelaws.

21

S. 44 (09).   make such new byelaws as they may consider necessary for the removal of the impediment, and such new byelaws shall have effect as if they had been duly made by the local authority and confirmed by the Board.

For another method of dealing with this matter—see section 24 of the 1919 Act, and notes thereto.

Saving of sites of ancient monuments, &c.

53 & 54 Vict. c. 70.

45. Nothing in the Housing Acts shall authorise the acquisition for the purposes of those Acts of any land which is the site of an ancient monument or other object of archæological interest, or the compulsory acquisition for the purposes of Part III of the Housing of the Working Classes Act, 1890, of any land which is the property of any local authority or has been acquired by any corporation or company for the purposes of a railway, dock, canal, water, or other public undertaking, or which at the date of the order forms part of any park, garden, or pleasure ground, or is otherwise required for the amenity or convenience of any dwelling-house.

Ancient Monuments. See the Ancient Monuments Amendment and Consolidation Act, 1913, under which county and borough councils can acquire or become the guardians of such monuments.   See section 73 hereof as to commons and open spaces, and section 74 as to land in .the neighbourhood of royal palaces or parks.   Note also the proviso to section 1 (3) of the 1919 Act.

Minor amendments of Housing Acts.

46. The amendments specified in the second column of the Second Schedule to this Act, which relate to minor details, shall be made in the provisions of the Housing Acts specified in the first column of that Schedule, and section sixty-three of the principal Act (which relates to the disqualification of tenants of lodging-houses on receiving poor relief) shall be repealed.

Definitions ·

47. (1.) Any provisions of this Act which supersede or amend any provisions of the principal Act shall be deemed to be part of that Part of the principal Act in which the provisions superseded or amended are contained.

Provisions of this Part to be deemed to be part of the appropriate Part of the principal Act.

See also section 76 (1) hereof and section 39 (2) of the 1919 Act. Where a provision in this Act is in conflict with the principal Act, the latter is to be treated as superseded—Reading, Lord Chief Justice, in *Arlidge v. Scarse* [1915] 3 K.B. 333.

(2.) Any reference in the Housing Acts to a closing order or to an order for the demolition of a building shall be construed as a reference to a closing order or an order of demolition under this Act.

See sections 15, 17 and 18 hereof.

48. The expression " street " shall, unless the context otherwise requires, have the same meaning in Part I of the principal Act as it has in Part II of that Act, and shall include any court, alley, street, square, or row of houses.

Amendment of definitions in Part I of the principal Act.

See sections 4 and 29 of the 1890 Act.

49. (1.) The words " means any inhabited building and " shall be omitted from the definition of " dwelling-house " in section twenty-nine of the principal Act.

Amendment of definitions for purpose of Part II of the principal Act.

(2.) For the definition of owner in the same section the following definition shall be substituted :—

" The expression ' owner,' in addition to the definition
    given by the Lands Clauses Acts, includes all
    lessees or mortgagees of any premises required
    to be dealt with under this Part of this Act, except
    persons holding or entitled to the rents and

S. 49 (09).

profits of such premises under a lease the original term whereof is less than twenty-one years."

See section 29 of the 1890 Act.

Definition of cottage.

50. For the definition of cottage in section fifty-three of the principal Act the following definition shall be substituted :—

The expression "cottage" in this Part of this Act may include a garden of not more than one acre.

Definition of Housing Acts.

51. In this Part of this Act the expression "Housing Acts" means the principal Act, and any Act amending that Act, including this Act.

See section 52 (2) of the 1919 Act.

Sections 52 and 53 ("Application of Part I to Scotland") omitted from this volume.

PART II

TOWN PLANNING

Preparation and approval of town planning scheme.

54. (1.) A town planning scheme may be made in accordance with the provisions of this Part of this Act as respects any land which is in course of development or appears likely to be used for building purposes, with the general object of securing proper sanitary conditions, amenity, and convenience in connexion with the laying out and use of the land, and of any neighbouring lands :

Provided that where a piece of land already built upon or a piece of land not likely to be used for building purposes is so situate with respect to any land likely to be used for building purposes that the general object of the scheme would be better secured by its inclusion in any town planning scheme made with respect to the last-mentioned land, the scheme may include such piece of land as aforesaid, and may provide for the demolition S. 54 (09). or alteration of any buildings thereon so far as may be necessary for carrying the scheme into effect.

Town Planning Scheme. The object is to ensure that land shall be developed in such a way as to secure proper sanitary conditions, amenity and convenience.

There are two schemes : (1) that under the present part of this Act, and (2) the modified one under section 46 of the 1919 Act. As to the nature, &c., of the present scheme—see section 55, below, and the Fourth Schedule.

Note the provision as to the acquisition of land for the purpose of garden cities and town planning schemes in section 10 of the Housing (Additional Powers) Act, 1919.

May be made. There is compulsion to prepare, &c., in certain circumstances—see section 61 hereof and notes thereto. Either the local authority or the land-owners may originate it—see the next subsection. It takes effect when approved by the Ministry—subsection (5) below.

Provisions of this part of this Act. Sections 54 to 67. By the Fifth Schedule, it will be seen that there have to be publication of notices, submission of plans and estimates, a hearing of objections, &c. &c.

Any land. . . . These words are strictly limited by those which follow them, and those in the proviso below. Yet the words "likely to be used for building purposes" are very wide ; see the extension by subsection (7) below, and note that thereby the decision of the Ministry "whether land is likely to be used for building purposes or not shall be final." Thus the circumstances would be very rare in which land in, or in the neighbourhood of, any town could not be made subject to a town planning scheme ; and by the making of such a scheme at a suit-able moment it would seem to be possible to prevent the erection of buildings anywhere, except in accordance with a scheme. From section 46 of the 1919 Act it will be seen that between 1st January 1923 and 1st January 1926, all the land which is in course of development or appears likely to be used for building purposes, within all boroughs and urban districts which contain a popula-tion exceeding 20,000, is to be made the subject of town planning schemes. Within these limits, therefore, the

S. 54 (09). areas " planned " can be very large. Similarly there seems to be nothing whatever to prevent very small areas from being " planned "—certainly the contrary in the said boroughs and urban districts, as everything, within the limits, has to be dealt with. Thus a local authority could town-plan a comparatively small plot of land, and so prevent the erection of a building which it objected to, even though the building was within the byelaws. (See, however, section 57 (3) hereof.)

On the other hand it is not clear that the Ministry would approve a scheme the object of which was merely to effect a street improvement.

As to land outside the area of the local authority and joint schemes—see the next subsection.

Crown lands cannot be included in a scheme.

The proviso was added by the Third Schedule to the 1919 Act, but substantially it deals with the same subject as the former subsection (3).

As to the hearing of objections and representations by persons affected—see the Fifth Schedule hereto ; and as to the compensation payable—see sections 58 and 59, below.

(2.) * A local authority within the meaning of this Part of this Act may by resolution decide—

> (*a*) to prepare a town planning scheme with reference to any land within or in the neighbourhood of their area in regard to which a scheme may be made under this Act ; or
>
> (*b*) to adopt, with or without any modifications, any town planning scheme proposed by or any of the owners of any land with respect to which the local authority are themselves by this Act authorised to prepare a scheme :

Provided that—

> (i) if any such resolution of a local authority extends

---

* As altered by the Housing, Town Planning, &c., Act, 1919, section 42.

to land not within the area of that local authority, S. 54 (09).
the resolution shall not have effect until it is
approved by the Local Government Board, and
the Board may, in giving their approval, vary the
extent of the land to be included within the
area of the proposed town planning scheme; and

(ii) where any local authorities are desirous of
acting jointly in the preparation or adoption of
a town planning scheme, they may concur in
appointing out of their respective bodies a joint
committee for the purpose, and in conferring
with or without restrictions on any such committee
any powers which the appointing councils might
exercise for the purpose, and the provisions of
sections fifty-seven and fifty-eight of the Local
Government Act, 1894, in regard to joint committees, shall, with the necessary modifications,
apply to any joint committee so appointed.

Local Authority. See section 65 (1).

Resolution. The date of this is important in its effect
on compensation—see section 58 (2). The resolution has
effect at once, as a resolution, except as per proviso (1).
By section 43 (1) of the 1919 Act, the Ministry may
make regulations as to the procedure consequent on the
passing of a resolution, &c.—see that section, which is
given in the notes to section 56 hereof, wherein the subject
is also dealt with. The point is that when the resolution
has been passed the preparation or adoption of a scheme
must proceed with all reasonable speed. The procedure
is almost wholly governed by regulations, as to which
see page 93.

Prepare . . . adopt. The preparation is of a scheme of
the authority's own ; the adoption is of a scheme already
prepared by the owners. The authority cannot, apparently, pay anything to the owners in respect of the
preparation of the latter's scheme, but any expenses in
connection with the adoption can be met by the authority

S 54 (09). —section 65 (2). When the scheme has been adopted by the authority it will then be their scheme, but they will not necessarily meet the whole of the subsequent expenses : they could enter into agreement with the owners—Fourth Schedule, paragraph 13.

It is intended that the authority and the owners should co-operate, and that the county council shall have notice of scheme—section 56.

Proviso (i). One effect of this is dealt with in section 58 (2) ; but the chief effect is if there is land affected which is outside the area of the local authority, no steps shall be taken after passing the resolution until approval is given by the Ministry. It may be presumed that before giving approval the Ministry will consult the authority in whose area such land is situated ; and, possibly, the Ministry will, in suitable circumstances, consider whether or not a joint scheme might be prepared under the next proviso.

Proviso (ii). The provisions of section 57 of the Local Government Act, 1894, are as here indicated. Further, the joint committee cannot be empowered to borrow money or make a rate ; cannot hold office beyond the expiration of fourteen days after the next annual meeting of any of the councils who appointed it ; its costs shall be defrayed by the councils in such proportions as they may agree upon, &c. Section 58 deals with the audit of accounts.

(3.) *

(4.) A town planning scheme prepared or adopted by a local authority shall not have effect, unless it is approved by order of the Local Government Board, and the Board may refuse to approve any scheme except with such modifications and subject to such conditions as they think fit to impose :

The proviso which followed here was repealed by the Housing, Town Planning, &c., Act, 1919, section 44.

* By the Housing, Town Planning, &c., Act, 1919, 3rd schedule, subsection (3) is omitted, its provisions being included in the proviso to subsection (1) thereby added.

As to the procedure before approval is given—see S. 54 (09).
section 56 hereof and notes thereto. The date of the
approval is important for the purposes of claims for
compensation—section 58 (1).

(5.) A town planning scheme, when approved by the
Local Government Board, shall have effect as if it were
enacted in this Act.

There is a very similar provision in section 65 of
the National Insurance Act, 1911, and in *Glasgow Burgh
Insurance Committee v. Scottish Insurance Commissioners*
[1915] 1 S.L.T. 217 the court of session held that the
regulations in question had the same force as if they
were incorporated in the Act and that the court had
no jurisdiction to consider their validity. See also *Ex
parte Ringer* [1909] 73 J.P. 436. But a scheme may
be revoked, &c.—see the next sub-section.

(6.) A town planning scheme may be varied or revoked
by a subsequent scheme prepared or adopted and approved
in accordance with this Part of this Act, and the Local
Government Board, on the application of the responsible authority, or of any other person appearing to
them to be interested, may by order revoke a town
planning scheme if they think that under the special
circumstances of the case the scheme should be so
revoked.

Responsible authority. For definition—see section 55
(2).

(7.) The expression " land likely to be used for building
purposes " shall include any land likely to be used as,
or for the purpose of providing open spaces, roads,
streets, parks, pleasure or recreation grounds, or for the
purpose of executing any work upon or under the land
incidental to a town planning scheme, whether in the
nature of a building work or not, and the decision of

S. 54 (09).

the Local Government Board, whether land is likely to be used for building purposes or not, shall be final.

See subsection (1) above.

Contents of town planning schemes.

55. (1.) The Local Government Board may prescribe a set of general provisions (or separate sets of general provisions adapted for areas of any special character) for carrying out the general objects of town planning schemes, and in particular for dealing with the matters set out in the Fourth Schedule to this Act and the general provisions, or set of general provisions appropriate to the area for which a town planning scheme is made, shall take effect as part of every scheme, except so far as provision is made by the scheme as approved by the Board for the variation or exclusion of any of those provisions.

No " general provisions " have yet been prescribed.

It will be seen that they will deal with matters in considerable detail (Fourth Schedule) ; and in the compulsory scheme under section 46 it is contemplated that matters shall be dealt with much less elaborately.

There is no compulsion upon the Ministry to prescribe " a set of general provisions," and until they are prescribed it would seem that a town planning scheme need not deal with the matters set out in the Fourth Schedule. Note, however, the words " in addition " in the first line of the next subsection.

(2.) Special provisions shall in addition be inserted in every town planning scheme defining in such manner as may be prescribed by regulations under this Part of this Act the area to which the scheme is to apply, and the authority who are to be responsible for enforcing. the observance of the scheme, and for the execution of any works which under the scheme or this Part of this Act are to be executed by a local authority (in this Part of this Act referred to as the responsible authority), S. 55 (09). and providing for any matters which may be dealt with by general provisions, and otherwise supplementing, excluding, or varying the general provisions and also for dealing with any special circumstances or contingencies for which adequate provision is not made by the general provisions, and for suspending, so far as necessary for the proper carrying out of the scheme, any statutory enactments, byelaws, regulations, or other provisions, under whatever authority made, which are in operation in the area included in the scheme.

The proviso which followed here was repealed by the Housing, Town Planning, &c., Act, 1919, section 44.

There being no "general provisions" (see above) the scheme will deal with the matters mentioned herein (as to the regulations, see page 93). The fact that there are no "general provisions" does not prevent the scheme from including any of the matters mentioned in the Fourth Schedule.

When the scheme is approved by the Ministry it has statutory effect—section 54 (5).

Responsible authority. See also the next subsection.

Suspending. . . . any statutory enactments. These are very wide powers, and, following the repeal of the proviso, it is not now necessary to bring before Parliament a scheme which exercises them.

(3.) Where land included in a town planning scheme is in the area of more than one local authority, or is in the area of a local authority by whom the scheme was not prepared, the responsible authority may be one of those local authorities, or for certain purposes of the scheme one local authority and for certain purposes another local authority, or a joint body constituted specially for the purpose by the scheme, and all necessary provisions may be made by the scheme for constituting

S. 55 (09).

the joint body and giving them the necessary powers and duties :

Provided that, except with the consent of the London County Council, no other local authority shall, as respects any land in the county of London, prepare or be responsible for enforcing the observance of a town planning scheme under this Part of this Act, or for the execution of any works which under the scheme or this Part of this Act are to be executed by a local authority.

On the subject of a joint body compare section 54 (2) (ii) ; the joint committee there mentioned is set up merely to prepare or adopt a scheme, but there seems to be no reason why it should not be empowered to carry it out under the present section, though it must be " specially constituted for the purpose by the scheme."

As to the purchase of land in these circumstances— see section 60 (2) hereof.

As to London—see section 66 hereof.

Procedure regulations of the Local Government Board.

56. (1.) The Local Government Board may make regulations for regulating generally the procedure to be adopted with respect to *the preparation or adoption of a town planning scheme* obtaining the approval of the Board to a scheme so prepared or adopted, *the variation or revocation of a scheme* and any inquiries, reports, notices, or other matters required in connexion with the preparation or adoption or the approval of the scheme or preliminary thereto, or in relation to the carrying out of the scheme or enforcing the observance of the provisions thereof *or the variation or revocation of the scheme.*

(2.) Provision shall be made by those regulations—

(a) for securing co-operation on the part of the local authority with the owners and other persons

* As altered by the Housing, Town Planning, &c., Act, 1919, 3rd schedule.

interested in the land proposed to be included in S. 56 (09). the scheme, by *such means as may be provided by the regulations ;

(b) for securing that notice of the proposal to prepare or adopt the scheme should be given at the earliest stage possible to any council interested in the land ; and

(c) for dealing with the other matters mentioned in the Fifth Schedule to this Act.

The above is extended by section 43 of the 1919 Act, as follows :—

(1.) The power of the Local Government Board of making regulations under section fifty-six of the Act of 1909 shall include power to make regulations as to the procedure consequent on the passing of a resolution by a local authority to prepare or adopt a town planning scheme, and provision shall be made by those regulations for securing that a local authority after passing such a resolution shall proceed with all reasonable speed with the preparation or adoption of the town planning scheme, and shall comply with any regulations as to steps to be taken for that purpose, including provisions enabling the Local Government Board in the case of default or dilatoriness on the part of the local authority to act in the place and at the expense of the local authority. .

(2.) Subsection (2) of section fifty-six of the Act of 1909 shall have effect as if the following paragraph were added thereto :

" For securing that the council of the county in which any land proposed to be included in a town planning scheme is situated (1) shall be furnished with a notice of any proposal to prepare or adopt such a scheme and with a copy of the draft scheme before the scheme is made, and (2) shall be entitled to be heard at any public local

* As altered by the Housing, Town Planning, &c., Act, 1919, 3rd schedule.

S. 56 (09).

inquiry held by the Local Government Board in regard to the scheme."

As to the regulations—see page 93. Several questions arising on this section are dealt with in the regulations, but it will usually be advantageous to consult the Ministry.

Power to enforce scheme.

57. (1.) The responsible authority may at any time, after giving such notice as may be provided by a town planning scheme and in accordance with the provisions of the scheme—

(a) remove, pull down, or alter any building or other work in the area included in the scheme which is such as to contravene the scheme, or in the erection or carrying out of which any provision of the scheme has not been complied with ; or

(b) execute any work which it is the duty of any person to execute under the scheme in any case where it appears to the authority that delay in the execution of the work would prejudice the efficient operation of the scheme.

(2.) Any expenses incurred by a responsible authority under this section may be recovered from the persons in default in such manner and subject to such conditions as may be provided by the scheme.

(3.) If any question arises whether any building or work contravenes a town planning scheme, or whether any provision of a town planning scheme is not complied with in the erection or carrying out of any such building or work, that question shall be referred to the Local Government Board, and shall, unless the parties otherwise agree, be determined by the Board as arbitrators, and the decision of the Board shall be final and conclusive and binding on all persons.

Responsible authority. See section 55 (2) and (3).

At any time. In some circumstances it may be ad- S. 57 (09).
vantageous to wait before removing, &c., a building,
and the time for claims for compensation could be fixed
accordingly—see section 58 (1) below.

Paragraph (*b*) should be carefully noted. There must
be a duty to execute under the scheme.

Subsection (3). The provisions of the Regulation of
Railways Act, 1868, apply to the arbitration. See section
62 hereof and note thereto.

58. (1.) Any person whose property is injuriously
affected by the making of a town planning scheme shall,
if he makes a claim for the purpose within the time (if
any) limited by the scheme, not being less than three
months after the date when notice of the approval of
the scheme is published in the manner prescribed by
regulations made by the Local Government Board, be
entitled to obtain compensation in respect thereof from
the responsible authority.

Compensation in respect of property injuriously affected by scheme, &c.

Within the time . . . limited by the scheme. This
could be fixed by the scheme at, say, within the
period between notice to " remove, pull or alter any
building " (as per section 57 (1), above) and three months
thereafter ; and so compensation would not be payable
immediately the scheme was approved.

As to the amount, &c., of the compensation—see
subsection (4) below.

As to the regulations—see page 93.

(2.) A person shall not be entitled to obtain compensation under this section on account of any building erected
on, or contract made or other thing done with respect
to, land included in a scheme after the *date of the
resolution of the local authority to prepare or adopt the
scheme or after the date when such resolution takes
effect as the case may be,* or after such other time as the
Local Government Board may fix for the purpose :

* As altered by the Housing, Town Planning, &c., Act, 1919, 3rd
schedule.

S. 58 (09).   Provided that this provision shall not apply as respects any.work done before the date of the approval of the scheme for the purpose of finishing a building begun or of carrying out a contract entered into before *such date or other time.as aforesaid.*

This has been extended by section 45 of the 1919 Act, which reads as follows :—

The Local Government Board may by special or general order provide that where a resolution to. prepare or adopt a town planning scheme has been passed, or where before the passing of this Act the preparation or adoption of a town planning scheme has been authorised, the development of estates and building operations may be permitted to proceed pending the preparation or adoption and approval of the town planning scheme, subject to such conditions as may be prescribed by the order, and where such permission has been given the provisions of subsection (2) of section fifty-eight of the Act of 1909 which relates to the rights of compensation shall have effect as if the following proviso were added thereto :

"Provided also that this provision shall not apply as respects any building erected, contract made, or other thing done in accordance with a permission granted in pursuance of an order of the Local Government Board allowing the development of estates and building operations to proceed pending the preparation or adoption and approval of the scheme, and the carrying out of works so permitted shall not prejudice any claim of any person to compensation in respect of property injuriously affected by the making of the scheme."

Date when such resolution takes effect. This refers to the circumstances covered by proviso (i) to section 54 (2) hereof.

Or after such other time as the Local Government Board may fix. An actual example, at present the subject of an inquiry, will illustrate the difficulties which may

* As altered by the Housing, Town Planning, &c., Act, 1919, 3rd schedule.

arise.   A firm bought land for the erection of a chemical S. 58 (09).
factory in a residential neighbourhood.   To prevent the
erection, the local authority passed a resolution for a
town planning scheme.   The firm state they bought the
site in May 1919, after inquiries which brought their
purpose before the notice of officials of the local authority,
and then entered into contracts for the erection of the
works.   On 5th September 1919, they were notified that
their plans were disapproved, and they allege that they
first heard of a town planning scheme on 9th September
1919.   The question is as to whether the first proviso
(above) applies, whether the Ministry should grant permission as per the new proviso, or whether the Ministry
should fix " such other time " as would enable the firm to
get compensation.

As to the " date of the approval of the scheme,"
mentioned in the first proviso above—see section 54 (4)
hereof.

As to when a building is begun—see *White v. Sunderland
(Mayor of)* [1903] 88 L.T. 592 ; and *Harrogate Corporation v. Dickinson* [1904] 1 K.B. 468.

(3.) Where, by the making of any town planning
scheme, any property is increased in value, the responsible authority, if they make a claim for the purpose
within the time (if any) limited by the scheme (not
being less than three months after the date when notice
of the approval of the scheme is first published in the
manner prescribed by regulations made by the Local
Government Board), shall be entitled to recover from
any person whose property is so increased in value one-
half of the amount of that increase.

(4.) Any question as to whether any property is
injuriously affected or increased in value within the
meaning of this section, and as to the amount and manner
of payment (whether by instalments or otherwise) of the
sum which is to be paid as compensation under this
section or which the responsible authority are entitled
to recover from a person whose property is increased in

22

S. 58 (09). value, shall be determined by the arbitration of a single arbitrator appointed by the Local Government Board, unless the parties agree on some other method of determination.

A single arbitrator, who under the Arbitration Act, 1889, may be required to state a special case on a point of law.

(5.) Any amount due under this section as compensation to a person aggrieved from a responsible authority, or to a responsible authority from a person .whose property is increased in value, may be recovered summarily as a civil debt.

(6.) Where a town planning scheme is revoked by an order of the Local Government Board under this Act, any person who has incurred expenditure for the purpose of complying with the scheme shall be entitled to compensation in accordance with this section in so far as any such expenditure is rendered abortive by reason of the revocation of the scheme.

Revoked. Under section 54 (6) hereof.

Exclusion or limitation of compensation in certain cases. **59.** (1.) Where property is alleged to be injuriously affected by reason of any provisions contained in a town planning scheme, no compensation shall be paid in respect thereof if or so far as the provisions are such as would have been enforceable if they had been contained in byelaws made by the local authority.

(2.) Property shall not be deemed to be injuriously affected by reason of the making of any provisions inserted in a town planning scheme, which * prescribe the space about buildings or limit the number of buildings to be erected, or prescribe the height or character of

* Words are here omitted per the Housing, Town Planning, &c., Act, 1919, 3rd schedule.

buildings, and which the Local Government Board, S. 59 (09). having regard to the nature and situation of the land affected by the provisions, consider reasonable for the purpose.

(3.) Where a person is entitled to compensation under this Part of this Act in respect of any matter or thing, and he would be entitled to compensation in respect of the same matter or thing under any other enactment, he shall not be entitled to compensation in respect of that matter or thing both under this Act and under that other enactment, and shall not be entitled to any greater compensation under this Act than he would be entitled to under the other enactment.

60. (1.) The responsible authority may, for the purpose of a town planning scheme, purchase any land comprised in such scheme by agreement, or be authorised to purchase any such land compulsorily in the same manner and subject to the same provisions (including any provision authorising the Local Government Board to give directions as to the payment and application of any purchase money or compensation) as a local authority may purchase or be authorised to purchase land situate in an urban district for the purposes of Part III of the Housing of the Working Classes Act, 1890, as amended by sections two and forty-five of this Act.

Acquisition by local authorities of land comprised in a scheme.

(2.) Where land included within the area of a local authority is comprised in a town planning scheme, and the local authority are not the responsible authority, the local authority may purchase or be authorised to purchase that land in the same manner as the responsible authority.

Part III. The reference is to section 57 of the 1890 Act.

S. 60 (09).   Note also the wide powers in sections 12 and 15 of the 1919 Act, and section 10 of the 1919 (Additional Powers) Act, and see the notes thereto.

As to commons, open spaces, land near royal palaces, &c.—see sections 73 and 74 hereof.

As to the purposes of a town planning scheme for which land may be required—see the Fourth Schedule hereto.

Including any provision. See section 5 hereof.

In an urban district. This had reference to paragraph (7) of the First Schedule hereto, which, however, is now repealed.

Responsible authority. See section 55 (2) and (3) hereof.

Powers of Local Government Board in case of default of local authority to make or execute town planning scheme.
   61. (1.) If the Local Government Board are satisfied on any representation, after holding a public local inquiry, that a local authority—

(*a*) have failed to take the requisite steps for having a satisfactory town planning scheme prepared and approved in a case where a town planning scheme ought to be made ; or

(*b*) have failed to adopt any scheme proposed by owners of any land in a case where the scheme ought to be adopted ; or

(*c*) have unreasonably refused to consent to any modifications or conditions imposed by the Board ;

the Board may, as the case requires, order the local authority to prepare and submit for the approval of the Board such a town planning scheme, or to adopt the scheme, or to consent to the modifications or conditions so inserted :

Provided that, where the representation is that a local authority have failed to adopt a scheme, the Local Government Board, in lieu of making such an order as aforesaid, may approve the proposed scheme, subject to such modifications or conditions, if any, as the Board

think fit, and thereupon the scheme shall have effect as S. 61 (09).
if it had been adopted by the local authority and approved
by the Board.

(2.) If the Local Government Board are satisfied on
any representation, after holding a local inquiry, that
a responsible authority have failed to enforce effectively
the observance of a scheme which has been confirmed,
or any provisions thereof, or to execute any works which
under the scheme or this Part of this Act the authority
is required to execute, the Board may order that authority
to do all things necessary for enforcing the observance
of the scheme or any provisions thereof effectively, or
for executing any works which under the scheme or this
Part of this Act the authority is required to execute.

(3.) Any order under this section may be enforced by
mandamus.

See further as to these powers—sections 46 and 47 of
the 1919 Act, which in practice may largely displace this
section.

Public local inquiry.   See section 63 hereof.

62. Where the Local Government Board are authorised
by this Part of this Act or any scheme made thereunder
to determine any matter, it shall, except as otherwise
expressly provided by this Part of this Act, be at their
option to determine the matter as arbitrators or otherwise, and, if they elect or are required to determine
the matter as arbitrators, the provisions of the Regulation
of Railways Act, 1868, respecting arbitrations by the
Board of Trade, and the enactments amending those
provisions, shall apply as if they were herein re-enacted
and in terms made applicable to the Local Government
Board and the determination of the matters aforesaid.

Determination of matters by Local Government Board.

31 & 32 Vict. c. 119.

Regulation of Railways Act, 1868, *&c.*   The effect is

S. 62 (09). that the Ministry may appoint, and fix the remuneration of, an arbitrator whose award may be that of the Ministry ; the arbitrator may call for documents, administer oaths, use his discretion as to procedure and in the absence of parties, make several awards, may award costs ; and his award cannot be set aside for irregularity, &c.

Inquiries by Local Government Board. **63.** Section eighty-five of the Housing of the Working Classes Act, 1890 (which relates to inquiries by the Local Government Board), as amended by this Act, shall apply for any purposes of this Part of this Act as it applies for the purpose of the execution of the powers and duties of the Local Government Board under that Act.

See page 226.

Laying general provisions before Parliament. 56 & 57 Vict. c. 66. **64.** All general provisions made under this Part of this Act shall be laid as soon as may be before Parliament, and the Rules Publication Act, 1893, shall apply to such provisions as if they were statutory rules within the meaning of section one of that Act.

General provisions. See section 55 (1) hereof, and the Fourth Schedule.

Definition of local authority, and expenses. **65.** (1.) For the purposes of this Part of this Act the expression " local authority " means the council of any borough or urban or rural district.

(2.) Any expenses incurred by a local authority under this Part of this Act, or any scheme made thereunder, shall be defrayed as expenses of the authority under the Public Health Acts, and the authority may borrow, for the purposes of this Part of this Act, or any scheme made thereunder, * including the cost of the preparation or adoption of a scheme,* in the same manner and

* These words are added by the Housing, Town Planning, &c., Act, 1919, 3rd schedule.

subject to the same provisions as they may borrow for S. 65 (09). the purposes of the Public Health Acts.

(3.) Money borrowed for the purposes of this Part of this Act, or any scheme made thereunder, shall not be reckoned as part of the debt of a borough or urban district for the purposes of the limitation on borrowing under subsections (2) and (3) of section two hundred and thirty-four of the Public Health Act, 1875.

66. (1.) This Part of this Act shall apply to the adminis- Application trative county of London, and, as respects that county, to London. the London County Council shall be the local authority.

(2.) Any expenses incurred by the London County Council shall be defrayed out of the general county rate and any money may be borrowed by the Council in the same manner as money may be borrowed for general county purposes.

67. (*"Application of Part II to Scotland."*)   *Omitted.*

PART III

County Medical Officers, County Public Health and Housing Committee, &c.

68. (1.) Every county council shall appoint a medical Appoint- officer of health under section seventeen of the Local ment, duties, Government Act, 1888. office of county

This section, except subsection (4), does not apply to medical London—see section 70 hereof. officers.

Excepting the following words, section 17 of the Local c. 41. Government Act, 1888, is repealed by section 75 hereof: "The council of any county may, if they see fit, appoint and pay a medical officer of health or medical officers of health."

(2.) The duties of a medical officer of health of a county shall be such duties as may be prescribed by general order of the Local Government Board and such other duties as may be assigned to him by the county council.

See the order on page 74, and note subsection (8) below.

(3.) The power of county councils and district councils under the said section to make arrangements with respect to medical officers of health shall cease, without prejudice to any arrangement made previously to the date of the passing of this Act.

(4.) The medical officer of health of a county shall, for the purposes of his duties, have the same powers of entry on premises as are conferred on a medical officer of health of a district by or under any enactment.

See section 36 hereof and note thereto. There are powers of entry under the Public Health Acts. As to London—see section 70, below.

(5.) A medical officer of health of a county shall be removable by the county council with the consent of the Local Government Board and not otherwise.

(6.) A medical officer of health of a county shall not be appointed for a limited period only :

Provided that the county council may, with the sanction of the Local Government Board, make any temporary arrangement for the performance of all or any of the duties of the medical officer of health of the county, and any person appointed by virtue of any such arrangement to perform those duties or any of them shall, subject to the terms of his appointment, have all the powers, duties, and liabilities of the medical officer of health of the county.

(7.) A medical officer of health appointed after the passing of this Act under the said section as amended by this section shall not engage in private practice, and S. 68 (09). shall not hold any other public appointment without the express written consent of the Local Government Board.

(8.) An order under this section prescribing the duties of medical officers of health of a county shall be communicated to the county council and shall be laid before Parliament as soon as may be after it is made, and, if an address is presented to His Majesty by either House of Parliament within the next subsequent twenty-one days on which that House has sat next after the order is laid before it praying that the order may be annulled, His Majesty in Council may annul the order and it shall thenceforward be void, but without prejudice to the validity of anything previously done thereunder.

See subsection (2) above.

69. (1.) The clerk of a rural district council shall forward to the medical officer of health of the county a copy of any representation, complaint, information, * or closing order,* a copy of which it is the duty of the district council to forward to the county council under section forty-five of the Housing of the Working Classes Act, 1890 (which relates to the powers of county councils). *Duty of clerk and medical officer of health of district council to furnish information to medical officer of health of county council.*

This section does not apply to London—see section 70, below.

For penalty—see subsection (4) below.

(2.) The medical officer of health of a district shall give to the medical officer of health of the county any information which it is in his power to give, and which the medical officer of health of the county may reasonably require

* Words added by the Housing, Town Planning, &c., Act, 1919, 2nd schedule.

S. 69 (09).   from him for the purpose of his duties prescribed by the Local Government Board.

See the order on page 74, made under section 68 (2), above, from which it appears that in the opinion of the Ministry the expression "a district" means a county district.

(3.) If any dispute or difference shall arise between the clerk or the medical officer of health of a district council and the medical officer of health of a county council under this section, the same shall be referred to the Local Government Board, whose decision shall be final and binding.

(4.) If the clerk or medical officer of health of a district council fails to comply with the provisions of this section, he shall on information being laid by the county council, but not otherwise, be liable on summary conviction in respect of each offence to a fine not exceeding ten pounds.

Extent of Part III.   **70.** The foregoing provisions of this Part of this Act shall not apply to Scotland or, except subsection (4) of section sixty-eight, to the administrative county of London, and, in the application of the said subsection to London, the reference to a medical officer of health of a district shall be construed as a reference to the medical officer of health of a metropolitan borough.

Public health and housing committee of county councils.   **71.** (1.) Every county council shall establish a public health and housing committee, and all matters relating to the exercise and performance by the council of their powers and duties as respects public health and the housing of the working classes (except the power of raising a rate or borrowing money) shall stand referred to the public health and housing committee, and the council, before exercising any such powers, shall, unless in their S. 71 (09). opinion the matter is urgent, receive and consider the report of the public health and housing committee with respect to the matter in question, and the council may also delegate to the public health and housing committee, with or without restrictions or conditions as they think fit, any of their powers as respects public health and the housing of the working classes, except the power of raising a rate or borrowing money and except any power of resolving that the powers of a district council in default should be transferred to the council.

(2.) This section shall not apply to Scotland or the London County Council.

As to the powers and duties of county councils as respects housing—see sections 45 and 52 of the 1890 Act; sections 10, 12, 13 and the present Part III of this Act; and sections 1 (6), 3, 4, 5, 6, 7, 8, 14, 18, 24 (3) and (4) and 36 of the 1919 Act.

72. (" Formation and extension of building societies.") *Repealed by the Housing, Town Planning, &c., Act, 1919, section 50 and 5th schedule.*

PART IV

Supplemental

73. (1.) Where any scheme or order under the Housing Acts or Part II of this Act authorises the acquisition or appropriation to any other purpose of any land forming part of any common, open space, or allotment, the scheme or order, so far as it relates to the acquisition or appropriation of such land, shall be provisional only, and shall not have effect unless and until it is confirmed by Parliament, except where the scheme or order provides for

Provisions as to commons and open spaces.

giving in exchange for such land other land, not being less in area, certified by the Local Government Board after consultation with the Board of Agriculture and Fisheries to be equally advantageous to the persons, if any, entitled to commonable or other rights and to the public.

(2.) Before giving any such certificate the Board shall give public notice of the proposed exchange, and shall afford opportunities to all persons interested to make representations and objections in relation thereto; and shall, if necessary, hold a local inquiry on the subject.

(3.) Where any such scheme or order authorises such an exchange, the scheme or order shall provide for vesting the land given in exchange in the persons in whom the common or open space was vested, subject to the same rights, trusts, and incidents as attached to the common or open space, and for discharging the part of the common, open space, or allotment acquired or appropriated from all rights, trusts, and incidents to which it was previously subject.

(4.) For the purposes of this Act the expression " common " shall include any land subject to be enclosed under the Inclosure Acts, 1845 to 1882, and any town or village green ; the expression " open space " means any land laid out as a public garden or used for the purposes of public recreation, and any disused burial ground ; and the expression " allotment " means any allotment set out as a fuel allotment or a field garden allotment under an Inclosure Act.

This is the only case under these Acts where a confirming Act is necessary.

Section 85 of the 1890 Act applies to the local inquiries.

Note that the expression " allotment " is limited ;

and as to disused burial grounds—see the Disused Burial S. 73 (09). Grounds Act, 1884.

74. (1.) Where any land proposed to be included in Provisions any scheme or order to be made under the Housing as to land in neighbour- Acts or Part II of this Act, or any land proposed to be hood of royal palaces acquired under the Housing Acts or Part II of this Act, or parks. is situate within the prescribed distance from any of the royal palaces or parks, the local authority shall, before preparing the scheme or order or acquiring the land, communicate with the Commissioners of Works, and the Local Government Board shall, before confirming the scheme or order or authorising the acquisition of the land or the raising of any loan for the purpose, take into consideration any recommendations they may have received from the Commissioners of Works with reference to the proposal.

(2.) For the purposes of this section " prescribed " means prescribed by regulations made by the Local Government Board after consultation with the Commissioners of Works.

For the regulations—see page 645.
As to the New Forest and Crown lands—see sections 37 and 38 of the 1919 Act.
For definition of " Housing Acts "—see section 52 (2) of the 1919 Act.

75. The enactments mentioned in the Sixth Schedule Repeal. to this Act are hereby repealed to the extent specified in the third column of that schedule.

76. (1.) This Act may be cited as the Housing, Town Short title Planning, &c., Act, 1909, and Part I of this Act shall be and extent. construed as one with the Housing of the Working Classes Acts, 1890 to 1903, and that Part of this Act and those

S. 76 (09).   Acts may be cited together as the Housing of the Working Classes Acts, 1890 to 1909.

(2.) This Act shall not extend to Ireland.

SCHEDULES

Section 2.   FIRST SCHEDULE

PROVISIONS AS TO THE COMPULSORY ACQUISITION OF LAND BY A LOCAL AUTHORITY FOR THE PURPOSES OF PART III OF THE HOUSING OF THE WORKING CLASSES ACT, 1890

These provisions relate not only to section 2 hereof, which see, but also to compulsory acquisition for town planning purposes—section 60. But as regards the assessment of compensation, they are subject to the Acquisition of Land (Assessment of Compensation) Act, 1919, which is printed on page 495. Section 11 of the Housing, Town Planning, &c., Act, 1919, is also of importance, and the power of entry under section 10 thereof should be noted.

(1.) Where a local authority propose to purchase land compulsorily under this Act, the local authority may submit to the Board an order putting in force as respects the land specified in the order the provisions of the Lands Clauses Acts with respect to the purchase and taking of land otherwise than by agreement.

For the form of the order—see page 529.
See also section 57 of the 1890 Act, and sections 45, 73 and 74 hereof.

(2.) An order under this schedule shall be of no force unless and until it is confirmed by the Board, and the Board may confirm the order either without modification or subject to such modifications as they think fit, and an order when so confirmed shall, save as otherwise expressly

provided by this schedule, become final and have effect 1st Sch. (09).
as if enacted in this Act; and the confirmation by the
Board shall be conclusive evidence that the requirements
of this Act have been complied with, and that the order
has been duly made and is within the powers of this Act.

See note to section 54 (5) hereof.

(3.) In determining the amount of any disputed
compensation under any such order, no additional
allowance shall be made on account of the purchase being
compulsory.

(4.) The order shall be in the prescribed form, and
shall contain such provisions as the Board may prescribe
for the purpose of carrying the order into effect, and of
protecting the local authority and the persons interested
in the land, and shall incorporate, subject to the necessary
adaptations, the Lands Clauses Acts (except section 8 & 9 Vict.
one hundred and twenty-seven of the Lands Clauses c. 18.
Consolidation Act, 1845) and sections seventy-seven to c. 20.
eighty-five of the Railways Clauses Consolidation Act,
1845, but subject to this modification, that any question
of disputed compensation shall be determined by a single
arbitrator appointed by the Board, who shall be deemed
to be an arbitrator within the meaning of the Lands
Clauses Acts, and the provisions of those Acts with
respect to arbitration shall, subject to the provisions of
this schedule, apply accordingly.

For the form of the order—see page 529.
*Except section 127 of the Lands Clauses Consolidation
Act, 1845,* which requires the sale of superfluous land.
See also section 34 hereof (page 314).
*Sections 77–85 of the Railway Clauses Consolidation
Act, 1845.* Briefly, the local authority do not acquire
the minerals unless expressly purchased, but there are

1st Sch. (09). provisions as to subsidence—see *Carlisle v. Northumberland County Council* [1911] 75 J.P. 539.

(5.) The order shall be published by the local authority in the prescribed manner, and such notice shall be given both in the locality in which the land is proposed to be acquired, and to the owners, lessees, and occupiers of that land as may be prescribed.

See the regulations on page 526.

(6.) If within the prescribed period no objection to the order has been presented to the Board by a person interested in the land, or if every such objection has been withdrawn, the Board shall, without further inquiry, confirm the order, but, if such an objection has been presented and has not been withdrawn, the Board shall forthwith cause a public inquiry to be held in the locality in which the land is proposed to be acquired, and the local authority and all persons interested in the land and such other persons as the person holding the inquiry in his discretion thinks fit to allow shall be permitted to appear and be heard at the inquiry.

But see section 11 (2) and (3) of the 1919 Act, by which the Ministry has discretion to refuse to confirm an order though it is not opposed ; and may confirm an order submitted before 31st July 1921, without a public inquiry.

As to the prescribed period—see the regulations on page 526.

Persons interested in the land. Having a legal or equitable interest, whether corporeal or incorporeal, excluding licensees.

Public inquiry. Under section 85 of the 1890 Act.

(7.) *Repealed by the Housing, Town Planning, &c., Act, 1919, section 50, and 5th schedule.*

(8.) The arbitrator shall, so far as practicable, in assessing compensation act on his own knowledge and experience,

but, subject as aforesaid, at any inquiry or arbitration 1st Sch. (09).
held under this schedule the person holding the inquiry
or arbitration shall hear, by themselves or their agents,
any authorities or parties authorised to appear, and
shall hear witnesses, but shall not, except in such cases
as the Board otherwise direct, hear council or expert
witnesses.

(9.) The Board may, with the concurrence of the Lord
Chancellor, make rules fixing a scale of costs to be applicable on an arbitration under this schedule, and an arbitrator under this schedule may, notwithstanding anything in the Lands Clauses Acts, determine the amount
of costs, and shall have power to disallow as costs in
the arbitration the costs of any witness whom he considers to have been called unnecessarily and any other
costs which he considers to have been caused or incurred
unnecessarily.

(10.) The remuneration of an arbitrator appointed
under this schedule shall be fixed by the Board.

(11.) In construing for the purposes of this schedule
or any order made thereunder, any enactment incorporated with the order, this Act together with the order
shall be deemed to be the special Act, and the local
authority shall be deemed to be the promoters of the
undertaking.

By section 123 of the Lands Clauses Consolidation Act, 1845, the local authority will have to exercise
their compulsory powers within three years of the confirmation of the order.

(12.) Where the land is glebe land or other land belonging to an ecclesiastical benefice, the order shall
provide that sums agreed upon or awarded for the purchase of the land, or to be paid by way of compensation

23

1st Sch. (09). for the damage to be sustained by the owner by reason of severance or other injury affecting the land, shall not be paid as directed by the Lands Clauses Acts, but shall be paid to the Ecclesiastical Commissioners to be applied by them as money paid to them upon a sale, under the provisions of the Ecclesiastical Leasing Acts, of land belonging to a benefice.

(13.) In this schedule the expression " Board " means the Local Government Board, and the expression " prescribed " means prescribed by the Board.

(14.) (" *Application to Scotland.*") *Omitted.*

Section 46.

SECOND SCHEDULE
MINOR AMENDMENTS OF HOUSING ACTS

Enactment to be amended.	Nature of Amendment.
Housing of the Working Classes Act, 1890 (53 & 54 Vict. c. 70).	
Section 23 . . .	After the word " displaced " the words " in consequence of " shall be substituted for the word " by."
Section 34 . . .	The words " the order becomes operative " shall be substituted for the words " service of the order."
Section 35 . . .	The words " if he is not entitled to appeal to the Local Government Board against the order " shall be inserted after the word " may " where it first occurs.
Section 38 (1) (a) .	The words " or impedes " shall be inserted after the word " stops."
Section 38 (7) . .	The words " house or other building or manufactory " shall be substituted for the words " house or manufactory " wherever they occur in that subsection.
Section 39 (8) . .	The words " as amended by any subsequent Act " shall be inserted after the word " Act " where it first occurs, and the words " to the power of the Local Government Board to enforce that duty " shall be inserted after the word " execution."
Section 40 . . .	After the word " displaced " the words " in consequence of " shall be substituted for the word " by."
Section 85 . . .	The words " powers and " shall be inserted before the word " duties."
Section 88 . . .	The words " or Part III " shall be inserted after the words " Part II."
Section 89 . . .	After the word " Act " where it first occurs the words " or any person authorised to enter dwelling-houses, premises, or buildings in pursuance of this Act " shall be inserted ; the words " authority or person " shall be substituted for the words " or authority," and the word " he " shall be substituted for the words " such person."

THIRD SCHEDULE

3rd Sch. (09).

MODIFICATIONS OF THE SCHEDULE TO THE HOUSING OF
THE WORKING CLASSES ACT, 1903, IN ITS APPLICA-
TION TO SCOTLAND.

Section 53.

Omitted from this volume.

FOURTH SCHEDULE

Section 55.

MATTERS TO BE DEALT WITH BY GENERAL PROVISIONS
PRESCRIBED BY THE LOCAL GOVERNMENT BOARD

1. Streets, roads, and other ways, and stopping up, or diversion of existing highways.

2. Buildings, structures, and erections.

3. Open spaces, private and public.

4. The preservation of objects of historical interest or natural beauty.

5. Sewerage, drainage, and sewage disposal.

6. Lighting.

7. Water supply.

8. Ancillary or consequential works.

9. Extinction or variation of private rights of way and other easements.

10. Dealing with or disposal of land acquired by the responsible authority or by a local authority.

11. Power of entry and inspection.

12. Power of the responsible authority to remove, alter or demolish any obstructive work.

13. Power of the responsible authority to make agreements with owners, and of owners to make agreements with one another.

4th Sch. (09).   14. Power of the responsible authority or a local authority to accept any money or property for the furtherance of the objects of any town planning scheme, and provision for regulating the administration of any such money or property and for the exemption of any assurance with respect to money or property so accepted 51 & 52 Vict. c. 42. from enrolment under the Mortmain and Charitable Uses Act, 1888.

15. Application with the necessary modifications and adaptations of statutory enactments.

16. Carrying out and supplementing the provisions of this Act for enforcing schemes.

17. Limitation of time for operation of scheme.

18. Co-operation of the responsible authority with the owners of land included in the scheme or other persons interested.*

19. Charging on the inheritance of any land the value of which is increased by the operation of a town planning scheme the sum required to be paid in respect of that increase, and for that purpose applying, with the necessary adaptations, the provisions of any enactments dealing with charges for improvements of land.

Section 56.   FIFTH SCHEDULE

1. Procedure anterior to * the preparation or adoption of * a scheme :—

(a) * Preparation and deposit of plans.*

(b) Publication of notices.

2. Procedure during, on, and after the preparation or adoption and before the approval of the scheme :—

* As altered by the Housing, Town Planning, &c., Act, 1919, 3rd schedule.

(*a*) Submission to the Local Government Board of the proposed scheme, with plans and estimates.

(*b*) Notice of submission of proposed scheme to the Local Government Board.

(*c*) Hearing of objections and representations by persons affected, including persons representing architectural or archæological societies or otherwise interested in the amenity of the proposed scheme.

(*d*) Publication of notice of intention to approve scheme and the lodging of objections thereto.

3. Procedure after the approval of the scheme :—

(*a*) Notice to be given of approval of scheme.

(*b*) Inquiries and reports as to the beginning and the progress and completion of works, and other action under the scheme.

4. Duty, at any stage, of the local authority to publish or deposit for inspection any scheme or proposed scheme, and the plans relating thereto, and to give information to persons affected with reference to any such scheme or proposed scheme.

5. The details to be specified in plans, including, wherever the circumstances so require, the restrictions on the number of buildings which may be erected on each acre, and the height and character of those buildings.

(See next page for 6th Schedule.)

6th Sch. (09).

Section 75.

SIXTH SCHEDULE

ENACTMENTS REPEALED

Session and Chapter.	Short Title.	Extent of Repeal.
51 & 52 Vict. c. 41.	The Local Government Act, 1888.	Section seventeen, from "who shall not hold" to end of the section.
53 & 54 Vict. c. 70.	The Housing of the Working Classes Act, 1890.	The words "for sanitary purposes" paragraph (a) of subsection (1) of section six. Subsection (6) of section eight, and section nine. Subsection (5) of section twelve. Subsection (2) of section fifteen, including the proviso thereto. Sections seventeen, eighteen, and nineteen. In section twenty-five, the words at the end of the section "such loan shall be repaid within such period, not exceeding fifty years, as may be recommended by the confirming authority." Sections twenty-seven and twenty-eight. In section twenty-nine, the words "means any inhabited building and" in the definition of "dwelling-house." Sections thirty-two and thirty-three. In section thirty-nine, the words "by agreement" in subsection (4) where those words first occur, and all after the word "sanctioned" to the end of that subsection; subsections (5) and (6); the words "to costs to be awarded in certain cases by a Committee of either House of Parliament" in subsection (8); and subsection (9) from "Provided that" to the end. In subsection (3) of section forty-seven, the words "the time allowed under any order for the execution of any works or the demolition of a building, or". In section fifty-three, subsection (2). Section fifty-four, so far as unrepealed. Section fifty-five, so far as it applies to Scotland. Section sixty-three. Section sixty-five, from "and (iii)" to the end of the section. In section sixty-six, the words "or special." Section seventy-seven. Section eighty-three. In section eighty-five, the words "not exceeding three guineas a day." Section ninety-two, from "but in" to the end of the section. Subsection (3) except paragraph (c), and subsection (4) of section ninety-four.

Session and Chapter.	Short Title.	Extent of Repeal:
53 & 54 Vict. c. 70.	The Housing of the Working Classes Act, 1890.	Subsections (1), (2), (7), (8) and (14) of section ninety-six. In subsection (3) of section ninety-seven the words "the time allowed under any order for the execution of any works or the demolition of a building or." The First Schedule, so far as it applies to Scotland. The Third, Fourth, and Fifth Schedules.
59 & 60 Vict. c. 31.	The Housing of the Working Classes Act, 1890, Amendment (Scotland) Act, 1896.	Section three.
63 & 64 Vict. c. 59.	The Housing of the Working Classes Act, 1900.	Sections two, six, and seven. In section eight the words "Scotland or".
3 Edw. 7. c. 39	The Housing of the Working Classes Act, 1903.	Paragraphs (a) and (b) of sub-section (2) of section five, sections six and eight, in section ten the words "in the manner provided by subsection three of section thirty-two of the principal Act," and section sixteen. In section seventeen the words "Scotland or".

HOUSING ACT, 1914 [4 & 5 Geo. 5. Ch. 31.]

An Act to make provision with respect to the Housing of Persons employed by or on behalf of Government Departments where sufficient dwelling accommodation is not available. [10th August 1914.]

BE it enacted by the King's most Excellent Majesty, by and with the advice and consent of the Lords Spiritual and Temporal, and Commons, in this present Parliament assembled, and by the authority of the same, as follows :

Powers of the Local Government Board and Commissioners of Works for the purpose of housing persons employed by Government departments.

1. (1.) The Local Government Board shall have power, with the approval of the Treasury, to make arrangements with any authorised society within the meaning of this Act for the purpose of the provision, maintenance, and management of dwellings and gardens and other works or buildings for or for the convenience of persons employed by or on behalf of Government departments on Government works where sufficient dwelling accommodation is not available for those persons, and the Commissioners of Works shall have power for the same purpose, with the consent of the Treasury, given after consultation with the Local Government Board, to acquire and dispose of land and buildings, and to build dwellings, and do all other things which appear to them necessary or desirable for effecting that purpose.

(2.) The Local Government Board may, with the approval of the Treasury, assist any authorised society with whom arrangements are made under this Act on such conditions as they think fit by becoming holders of the share or loan capital thereof or making loans thereto or otherwise as they think fit.

Where the Local Government Board make arrangements under this Act with any authorised society in connexion with the provision or maintenance of dwellings within any borough, the council of the borough shall have the like power, with the approval of the Local Government Board, of assisting the society as the Local Government Board have under this Act with the approval of the Treasury.

Any expenses incurred by the council under this provision shall be defrayed in the same manner as expenses of the council under Part III of the Housing of the Working Classes Act, 1890; and the council shall have the like power to borrow for the purposes of this provision as they have for the purposes of that Part of that Act. *53 & 54 Vict. c. 70.*

2. (1.) The Treasury shall, as and when they think fit, issue out of the Consolidated Fund or the growing produce thereof such sums as may be required for the purpose of meeting any expenditure which is, in the opinion of the Treasury, of a capital nature and which is incurred with the consent or approval of the Treasury by or on behalf of the Local Government Board, or the Commissioners of Works for the purposes of this Act, not exceeding in the aggregate two million pounds; and any expenses incurred for those purposes by the Local Government Board, or the Commissioners of Works, not being, in the opinion of the Treasury, of the nature of capital expenditure, shall be defrayed out of moneys provided by Parliament, and any receipts arising in connexion therewith shall be paid into the Exchequer. *Payment of expenses incurred under Act.*

(2.) The Treasury may, if they think fit, for the purpose of providing money for sums so authorised to be issued out of the Consolidated Fund, or for repaying to that Fund any part of the sums so issued, borrow by means of terminable annuities for a term not exceeding thirty years; and all sums so borrowed shall be paid into the Exchequer.

(3.) The said annuities shall be paid out of moneys provided by Parliament, and, if those moneys are insufficient, shall be charged on and paid out of the Consolidated Fund of the United Kingdom or the growing produce thereof.

(4.) The Treasury may also, if they think fit, for the same purpose borrow money by means of the issue of Exchequer bonds and the Capital Expenditure (Money) Act, 1904, shall have effect as if this Act had been in force at the time of the passing of that Act.

4 Edw. 7. c. 21.

(5.) The Treasury shall, within six months after the end of every financial year, cause to be made out and laid before the House of Commons accounts showing the amount of any expenditure of a capital nature incurred by the Local Government Board and the Commissioners of Works, respectively, under this Act, and of the money borrowed and the securities created under this Act; and any such accounts of expenditure shall be audited and reported upon by the Comptroller and Auditor-General as appropriation accounts in manner provided by the Exchequer and Audit Departments Act, 1866.

29 & 30 Vict. c. 39.

Interpretation, application, and short title.

3. (1.) In this Act the expression " authorised society " means any society, company, or body of persons approved by the Treasury whose objects include the erection, improvement, or management of dwellings for working

classes, which does not trade for profit, or whose constitution forbids the payment of any interest or dividend at a rate exceeding five per cent. per annum.

(2.) In the application of this Act to Scotland the Local Government Board for Scotland shall be substituted for the Local Government Board, and " burgh " shall be substituted for " borough."

(3.) This Act shall not apply to Ireland.

(4.) This Act may be cited as the Housing Act, 1914.

This is a war-time measure, and is not now of great importance. The £2,000,000 referred to is shown by House of Commons Paper, number 8 (ordered to be printed on 11th February 1919), to have been expended to the extent of £1,422,942 2s. 11d.; namely, £601,600 by the Local Government Board Scotland (through the Scottish National Housing Company, Limited—mainly for housing in connection with the Rosyth dockyard), and £821,342 3s. 11d. by H.M. Office of Works (for the Woolwich Arsenal housing scheme).

HOUSING (No. 2) ACT, 1914
[4 & 5 Geo. 5. Ch. 52.]

An Act to give the Board of Agriculture and Fisheries in Agricultural districts and the Local Government Board elsewhere powers with respect to Housing and to make similar provision for Scotland. [10th August 1914.]

BE it enacted by the King's most Excellent Majesty, by and with the advice and consent of the Lords Spiritual and Temporal, and Commons, in this present Parliament assembled, and by the authority of the same, as follows :

Powers as to acquisition of land and buildings for housing purposes.

1. (1.) The Board of Agriculture and Fisheries in agricultural districts and the Local Government Board elsewhere shall have power during the period of one year from the passing of this Act to acquire, with the consent of the Treasury and with the concurrence of the Development Commissioners, land and buildings for housing purposes, and, with the consent of the Treasury, shall have power to dispose of any land or buildings so acquired.

(2.) The Board of Agriculture and Fisheries and the Local Government Board respectively shall have power to do all other things which may appear to them necessary or desirable for housing purposes in connection with any land or buildings so acquired, and to make any arrangements for housing purposes with any local authority or authorised society within the meaning of this Act :

Provided that neither the Board of Agriculture and Fisheries nor the Local Government Board shall, in the

exercise of their powers under this Act, in any case
themselves build any dwellings unless they are satisfied
after holding a public local inquiry that in that case
there is an insufficiency of dwelling accommodation for
the working classes, or that the existing accommodation
is unsuitable and that dwelling accommodation cannot
be otherwise satisfactorily provided.

2. (1.) The Treasury shall, as and when they think
fit, issue out of the Consolidated Fund or the growing
produce thereof such sums as may be required for the
purpose of meeting any expenditure which is, in the
opinion of the Treasury, of a capital nature, and which
is incurred with the consent or approval of the Treasury,
not exceeding in the aggregate four million pounds,
and any expenses incurred for those purposes by the
Board of Agriculture and Fisheries or the Local Government Board not being, in the opinion of the Treasury,
of the nature of capital expenditure, shall be defrayed
out of moneys provided by Parliament, and any receipts
arising in connection therewith shall be paid into the
Exchequer.

Payment of expenses incurred under the Act.

(2.) The Treasury may, if they think fit, for the purpose
of providing money for sums so authorised to be issued
out of the Consolidated Fund, or for repaying to that
fund any part of the sums so issued, borrow by means of
terminable annuities for a term not exceeding thirty
years ; and all sums so borrowed shall be paid into the
Exchequer.

(3.) The said annuities shall be paid out of moneys
provided by Parliament, and if those moneys are insufficient, shall be charged on and paid out of the Consolidated Fund of the United Kingdom or the growing
produce thereof.

(4.) The Treasury may also, if they think fit, for the same purpose, borrow money by means of the issue of Exchequer Bonds; and the Capital Expenditure (Money) Act, 1904, shall have effect as if this Act had been in force at the time of the passing of that Act.

4 Edw. 7. c. 21.

(5.) The Treasury shall, within six months after the end of every financial year, cause to be made out and laid before the House of Commons accounts showing the amount of any expenditure of a capital nature incurred by the Board of Agriculture and Fisheries and the Local Government Board respectively, under this Act, and of the money borrowed and the securities created under this Act; and any such accounts of expenditure shall be audited and reported upon by the Comptroller and Auditor-General as appropriation accounts in manner provided by the Exchequer and Audit Departments Act, 1866.

29 & 30 Vict. c. 39.

3. (1.) In this Act, unless the context otherwise requires,—

Interpretation, application, and short title.

The expression "housing purposes" means the provision, maintenance, improvement, and management of dwellings and gardens and other works or buildings for or for the convenience of persons belonging to the working classes; and

The expression "local authority" means the local authority for the purposes of Part III of the Housing of the Working Classes Act, 1890; and

53 & 54 Vict. c. 70.

The expression "authorised society" means any society, company, or body of persons approved by the Treasury, whose objects include the erection, improvement, or management of dwellings for working classes, which does not trade for profit, or whose constitution forbids the payment of any interest or dividend at a rate exceeding five per cent. per annum.

(2.) In the application of this Act to Scotland the Local Government Board for Scotland shall be substituted for the Local Government Board, and the Board of Agriculture for Scotland shall be substituted for the Board of Agriculture and Fisheries.

(3.) This Act shall not apply to Ireland.

(4.) This Act may be cited as the Housing (No. 2) Act, 1914.

This is also a war-time measure. It was intended to meet possible unemployment in the building trade ; but this did not arise, and the powers in section 1 (1) expired without having been exercised. The Act was subsequently extended to Ireland.

HOUSING, TOWN PLANNING, &c., ACT, 1919

[9 & 10 Geo. 5. Ch. 35.]

ARRANGEMENT OF SECTIONS

PART I.—HOUSING OF THE WORKING CLASSES

Board and other Departments—35. Provisions of Housing Acts not to be affected by the Increase of Rent and Mortgage Interest (War Restrictions) Act, 1915—36. Compensation in cases of subsidence—37. Application of Act to New Forest—38. Extension of powers of Commissioners of Woods—39. Procedure and minor amendments of Housing Acts—40. Construction—41. Application to London of certain provisions of the Housing Acts.

Part II.—Town Planning

§ 42. Removal of necessity to obtain previous authorisation of Local Government Board to preparation or adoption of town planning scheme—43. Extension of power to make regulations as to procedure—44. Repeal of provisos to ss. 54 (4) and 55 (2) of 9 Edw. 7. c. 44—45. Power to permit development of estates pending preparation and approval of town planning schemes—46. Preparation of town planning schemes—47. Power of Local Government Board to require town planning scheme—48. Consequential and minor amendments.

Part III.—Acquisition of Small Dwellings

§ 49. Amendment of 62 & 63 Vict. c. 44.

Part IV.—General

§ 50. Repeals—51. Extent—52. Short title.
Schedules.

An Act to amend the enactments relating to the Housing of the Working Classes, Town Planning, and the acquisition of small dwellings.   [31st July 1919.]

BE it enacted by the King's most Excellent Majesty, by and with the advice and consent of the Lords Spiritual and Temporal, and Commons, in this present Parliament assembled, and by the authority of the same as follows :

PART I

HOUSING OF THE WORKING CLASSES

Schemes under Part III of Act of 1890

1. (1.) It shall be the duty of every local authority within the meaning of Part III of the Housing of the Working Classes Act, 1890 (hereinafter referred to as the principal Act), to consider the needs of their area with respect to the provision of houses for the working

Duty of local authority to prepare housing schemes. 53 & 54 Vict. c. 70.

24

classes, and within three months after the passing of this Act, and thereafter as often as occasion arises, or within three months after notice has been given to them by the Local Government Board, to prepare and submit to the Local Government Board a scheme for the exercise of their powers under the said Part III.

Duty. This is the point of this Act; previously the local authorities had power to build if they thought fit. For enforcement—see sections 3 and 4. The duty is "to consider the needs . . . and . . . to prepare and submit" a scheme; for duty to carry out the scheme—see section 2.

Local authority. For definition see page 11.

Part III deals with "Working-Class Lodging Houses" the erection of lodging-houses, dwelling-houses and cottages, &c. (see page 207).

To consider the needs. For discussion (see page 17). See also section 26 (5) hereof.

Houses for the Working Classes. For definition—see section 40 (page 441).

Occasion arises. See subsection (5) below.

Within three months after notice. Subsection (5) does not fix any time limit within which action must be taken after an "occasion arises," but these words here would enable the Local Government Board (Ministry of Health) to require action within three months.

Scheme. This is not defined except as by the next subsection, and no scheme is required by, or referred to in, Part III of the 1890 Act. See also page 18.

Their powers, i.e. to erect dwelling-houses, &c. (see pages 11, 13, 211 and 394).

(2.) A scheme under this section shall specify—

(a) the approximate number and the nature of the houses to be provided by the local authority;

(b) the approximate quantity of land to be acquired and the localities in which land is to be acquired;

(c) the average number of houses per acre:

(d) the time within which the scheme or any part S. 1 (19).
  thereof is to be carried into effect ;
and the scheme may contain such incidental, consequential and supplemental provisions (including provisions
as to the subsequent variation of the scheme) as may
appear necessary or proper for the purpose of the scheme.

Nature. It will be seen from D.89 (page 18) that the
Ministry interprets this to mean that the scheme shall
show how many houses with two, three or four bedrooms,
&c., are proposed, how many are block dwellings, and so
on.
Average number of houses per acre. In the official
Manual on the Preparation of State-Aided Housing Schemes,
this matter is discussed fully (see page 23), but the local
authorities are nowhere bound by the eight to twelve
houses per acre therein mentioned, though the
Ministry have powers (under the next subsection, (3),
and section 7) to check any unreasonable variations
from these figures. It is only an approved scheme
which secures the financial assistance under section 7.

(3.) The Local Government Board may approve any
such scheme or any part thereof without modification
or subject to such modifications as they may think fit,
and the scheme or part thereof when so approved shall
be binding on the local authority ; but if the Board
consider the scheme inadequate they may refuse to
approve the scheme and require the authority to prepare
and submit to them an adequate scheme within such
time as they may fix, or they may approve the scheme
or part thereof subject to the condition that the authority
prepare and submit to them a further scheme within
such time as they may fix :
  Provided that local authorities in preparing, and
the Local Government Board in approving, any scheme
shall take into account, and so far as possible preserve,

existing erections of architectural, historic, or artistic interest, and shall have regard to the natural amenities of the locality, and, in order to secure that the houses proposed to be built under the scheme shall be of a suitable architecture and that the natural amenities of the locality shall not be unnecessarily injured, the Local Government Board may, in any case where it appears to them that the character of the locality renders such a course expedient, require as a condition of their approval the employment by the local authority of an architect to be selected from a panel of architects nominated for the purpose by the Royal Institute of British Architects.

May approve. Subsection (4), below, speaks of final approval; hence the approval here would appear to mean " subject to subsection (4)," and in practice it is " provisional." Probably where an unexpected change in circumstances compelled a change in the scheme, the Ministry could withdraw its approval so as to approve and make binding the changed scheme, if desired by the local authority; but short of that the scheme when approved (subject to subsection (4)) would appear to be binding on the Ministry also—a matter of importance in view of section 7. It would appear also that the Ministry can refuse to approve the scheme only if it considers it inadequate. In any case it must exercise its discretion reasonably.

Proviso. Those interested in the genesis of the proviso may read the speech of the Marquis of Salisbury in the House of Lords on 8th July 1919 (Parliamentary Debates, column 290). See also section 45 of the 1909 Act, " Saving of Sites of Ancient Monuments, &c."

(4.) Before the Local Government Board finally approve a scheme, the local authority shall furnish to them estimates of the cost of the scheme and of the rents expected to be derived from the houses provided under the scheme.

Finally approve. See subsection (3) above.

Cost . . . rents. See section 7 (2), proviso (i). It does S. 1 (19). not appear expressly that these estimates are part of the scheme, and so binding on the local authority when approved. See the form on page 560.

(5.) If the Local Government Board consider as respects any local authority that an occasion for the preparation of a new scheme has arisen, they shall give notice to that effect to the local authority, and thereupon such an occasion shall be deemed to have arisen.

See subsection (1) above. When the occasion has arisen a new scheme must be prepared and submitted, but no time limit is fixed, though the Ministry may give three months notice. It is possible that this subsection is redundant, inasmuch as the whole ground is covered by subsection (1), unless its purpose is to define the words " occasion arises."

(6.) Where the local authorities concerned or the Local Government Board are of opinion that a scheme should be made affecting the areas of two or more local authorities, such a scheme shall be prepared by the local authorities jointly and the local authority of each area to which any part of any such joint scheme applies may, or, if the Local Government Board after giving the local authority an opportunity of being heard so direct, shall carry out that part of the joint scheme, and for the purposes of this subsection " local authority " shall, in any case where the Local Government Board consent, and subject to any conditions which the Board may prescribe, include a county council.

As to joint action—see section 38 of the 1909 Act. Apart from this county councils are not local authorities under the housing schemes here dealt with ; but they may act in place of local authorities under sections 3 and 5 (see also sections 4, 6 and 7), and under section 8 they may provide houses for their employees. They may also act under sections 10, 12 and 13 of the 1909 Act. The London County Council is in a special position —see section 41.

By section 1 of the 1900 Act any local authority, other than a rural district council, "may, for supplying the needs of their district, establish or acquire lodging houses for the working classes" under Part III of the principal Act, outside their district.

Shall be prepared. For enforcement—see sections 3 (3) and 4 hereof.

Prescribe. By regulations, but none have yet been made.

(7.) Local authorities in preparing, and the Local Government Board in approving, schemes shall make inquiry respecting and take into account any proposals by other bodies and persons to provide housing accommodation.

Other bodies, e.g. public utility societies, housing trusts, private persons, and, presumably, county councils acting under section 8.

Proposals. These would appear to be definite proposals, rather than contingent projects or matters merely talked of. In this case, as the proposals would be made to the Ministry or the local housing commissioners, the inquiry would not be troublesome ; and further, the plans would have to be submitted to the local authority.

(8.) Where any proposals as to the provision of houses for the working classes have before the passing of this Act been submitted to the Local Government Board by a local authority and those proposals have been approved by the Board, either before or after the passing of this Act, the proposals may, if the Board so direct, be treated, for any of the purposes of this Act, as if they were a scheme submitted and approved under this section.

2. It shall be the duty of a local authority on which obligations are imposed by any such scheme to carry that scheme into effect within such time as may be specified in the scheme or within such further time as may be allowed by the Local Government Board.

See section 1 (2) and (3) ; and, for enforcement, sections 3 and 4.

See section 7 (1) as to the period in which the scheme is to be carried out to receive the financial assistance thereunder.

Power of County Councils and Local Government Board to act in place of Local Authorities

3. (1.) Where the Local Government Board are satisfied that a local authority have failed or are not prepared to fulfil their obligations as to the preparation of schemes under this Act, or their obligations under any such scheme, or that for any other reason it is desirable that any such obligation should be performed by the county council instead of by the local authority, the Board, after considering the circumstances of the case and giving the local authority and the county council an opportunity of being heard, may, if they think fit, by order, transfer to the council of the county, in which the district of the local authority is comprised, the obligation to prepare and carry out a scheme, or to carry out in whole or in part the provisions of a scheme prepared by the local authority.

Failed or are not prepared. " Not prepared " appears to mean both " not equipped " and " not willing."

See also sections 10, 12 and 13 of the 1890 Act.

Obligations. See sections 1 and 2. Apparently, one of the obligations can be transferred so that the county council can be required to carry out the first scheme or

S 3 (19).

part of it, and the local authority the remainder or any subsequent one.

For any other reason. As, for instance, where it would result in a saving of time or money, or where it would be more convenient and effective, or where the county council has the land or machinery.

See also subsection (3) below, and section 1 (6) as to joint schemes.

An opportunity of being heard. The Ministry has to be " satisfied," then to consider the circumstances of the case, and to give the authority an opportunity of being heard. There is no requirement of a public inquiry or of a hearing by counsel. The essence of the present Act is quick action. But reasonable notice will have to be given by the Ministry. And doubtless if the county council objected to doing the work, the Ministry would proceed under the next section.

(2.) Where the Board make an order under this section, the order may, for the purpose of enabling the county council to give effect to the order, apply any of the provisions of the Housing Acts or section sixty-three of the Local Government Act, 1894, with such modifications and adaptations as appear necessary or expedient :

56 & 57 Vict. c. 73.

Provided that the local authority shall be entitled to appeal to the Local Government Board if, in their opinion, the amount of the expenses, which the county council require them to defray or propose to charge against their district, is excessive or unreasonable, or against any refusal by a county council to make an order under the said section sixty-three vesting in the local authority all or any of the powers, duties, property, debts, and liabilities of the county council in relation to the powers transferred to them, and upon any such appeal the Board may make such order as they may deem just, and an order so made shall be binding on the county council and the local authority.

Housing Acts.   See section 52 (2) hereof.
Section 63 of the Local Government Act, 1894, reads as follows :—

(1.) Where the powers of a district council are by virtue of a resolution under this Act transferred to a county council, the following provisions shall have effect :—

(a) Notice of the resolution of the county council by virtue of which the transfer is made shall be forthwith sent to the district council and to the Local Government Board :

(b) The expenses incurred by the county council shall be a debt from the district council to the county council, and shall be defrayed as part of the expenses of the district council in the execution of the Public Health Acts, and the district council shall have the like power of raising the money as for the defraying of those expenses :

(c) The county council for the purpose of the powers transferred may on behalf of the district council borrow subject to the like condition, in the like manner, and on the security of the like fund or rate, as the district council might have borrowed for the purpose of those powers :

(d) The county council may charge the said fund or rate with the payment of the principal and interest of the loan ; and the loan with the interest thereon shall be paid by the district council in like manner, and the charge shall have the like effect, as if the loan were lawfully raised and charged on that fund or rate by the district council :

(e) The county council shall keep separate accounts of all receipts and expenditure in respect of the said powers :

(f) The county council may by order vest in the district council all or any of the powers, duties, property, debts, and liabilities of the county council in relation to any of the said powers, and the property, debts, and liabilities so vested shall be deemed to have been acquired or incurred by the district council for the purpose of those powers.

(2.) Where a rural district is situate in two or more counties a parish council complaining under this Act may complain to the county council of the county in which the parish is situate, and if the subject matter of

S. 3 (19).

the complaint affects any other county the complaint shall be referred to a joint committee of the councils of the counties concerned, and any question arising as to the constitution of such joint committee shall be determined by the Local Government Board, and if members of the joint committee are not appointed, the members who are actually appointed shall act as the joint committee.

(3.) This section shall apply in cases where a joint scheme has been, or in the opinion of the Board ought to be, prepared with the substitution of references to the local authorities concerned and their districts for references to the local authority and the district of the local authority.

Joint scheme. See section 1 (6) hereof.

Power of Local Government Board to act in place of the local authority.

4. (1.) Where the Local Government Board are satisfied that a local authority, or, in cases where any powers or duties of a local authority have been transferred to a county council, such council, or, in cases where a joint scheme has been or in the opinion of the Board should be prepared, the local authorities concerned, have failed to fulfil their obligations as to the preparation of schemes under this Act or their obligations under any such schemes, the Board may, after considering the circumstances of the case, and after giving the local authority, authorities, or county council an opportunity of being heard, themselves prepare and carry out a scheme or take such steps as may be necessary to carry out any scheme prepared by the local authority or council, or by two or more local authorities jointly, and shall for that purpose have all the powers of a local authority under the Housing Acts, and those Acts shall, with the necessary modifications and adaptations, apply accordingly.

Transferred to a county council. See section 3 hereof.

Joint scheme.   See section 1 (6) hereof.   S. 4 (19).
Obligations.   See sections 1 and 2 hereof.
An opportunity of being heard.   See note to section 3 (1)
hereof.
Housing Acts.   See section 52 (2) hereof.

(2.) Any expenses incurred by the Board in the exercise of such powers as aforesaid shall in the first instance
be paid out of moneys provided by Parliament, but
the amount certified by the Board to have been so
expended, and to be properly payable by a local authority
shall on demand be paid to the Board by the local authority
and shall be recoverable as a debt due to the Crown,
and the payment of the sum so payable to the Board
shall be a purpose for which the local authority may
borrow under Part III of the principal Act.

May borrow under Part III.   See section 66 of the
Act of 1890 and note thereto.

5. Without prejudice to any other powers for enforcing
the provisions of the Housing Acts, where the Local
Government Board are satisfied that any area within
the district of a local authority is an area in respect of
which the local authority ought to exercise their powers
under Part I or Part II of the principal Act, the Board
may by order require the local authority to make a
scheme for the improvement of such area either under
Part I or under Part II of that Act and to do all things
necessary under the Housing Acts for carrying into
execution the scheme so made, and, if the local authority
fail within such time as may be prescribed by the order
to make a scheme to the satisfaction of the Local Government Board and to carry the scheme into execution,
the Board may either by order empower the county
council to make and carry out a scheme, or themselves

*Power to act
in default
of local
authority
under
Parts I
and II of
principal
Act.*

S. 5 (19). make and take such steps as may be necessary to carry out a scheme, and the provisions of the last two foregoing sections of this Act in regard to the powers of county councils and the Board, as the case may be, shall apply.

Other powers for enforcing. See sections 10, 13, 16, 31, 38, 39 (8) and 45 of the 1890 Act, section 4 (1) of the 1903 Act, and sections 10 and 11 of the 1909 Act, and notes thereto.

Satisfied. See section 6, below, for one means.

Powers under Part I or Part II. Including those to make improvement or reconstruction schemes for unhealthy areas (Part I) and unhealthy dwelling houses (Part II). If the local authority fail to effect these schemes the Ministry may do so, or may empower the county council, at the expense of the local authority—having thus the same power as in the case of (Part III) housing schemes (see sections 3 and 4 hereof). Under section 4 of the 1890 Act the local authority are not required to act unless satisfied of the sufficiency of their resources, but see note to that section.

No " scheme " is necessary in the case of closing or demolition orders under sections 17 and 18 of the 1909 Act, and unless the evils which such orders are directed against come under section 39 of the 1890 Act, and so become the subjects of a " scheme " the present section apparently does not apply. But section 10 of the 1909 Act applies and gives a remedy. The same is true of obstructive buildings—section 38 of the 1890 Act—but in that case the remedy is given by section 11 of the 1909 Act.

Inspection by county medical officer of health. **6.** Where a representation is made to the Local Government Board as respects any county district that the local authority have failed to exercise their powers under Part I or Part II of the principal Act, the Board may direct the county council to instruct the medical officer of health of the county to inspect such district and to make a report to the Board as to the exercise of the powers aforesaid by the local authority.

See notes to section 5, above.
County district excludes county boroughs.
The representation may be made by any person or
body.
This section provides one means of setting in motion
the powers of section 5, above.

Financial Provisions

7. (1.) If it appears to the Local Government Board **Power to**
that the carrying out by a local authority, or by a county **recoup losses.**
council to whom the powers of a local authority have
been transferred under this Act, of any scheme approved
under section one of this Act, or the carrying out of a
re-housing scheme in connection with a scheme made
under Part I or Part II of the principal Act, including
the acquisition, clearance, and development of land
included in the last-mentioned scheme, and whether the
re-housing will be effected on the area included in that
scheme or elsewhere, or the carrying out of any scheme
approved by the Board for the provision of houses for
persons in the employment of or paid by a county council
or a statutory committee thereof, has resulted or is
likely to result in a loss, the Board shall, if the scheme
is carried out within such period after the passing of
this Act as may be specified by the Board with the
consent of the Treasury, pay or undertake to pay to the
local authority or county council out of moneys provided by Parliament such part of the loss as may be
determined to be so payable under regulations made by
the Board with the approval of the Treasury, subject to
such conditions as may be prescribed by those regulations.

Carrying out. Including preparation. Anything which
is part of the approved scheme will get the State subsidy,
subject to the regulations.

S. 7 (19). *Transferred under this Act.* By sections 3 and 5, above.

Scheme approved. It is only to an approved scheme that the State subsidy is given. The re-housing scheme under Parts I or II of the 1890 Act must be confirmed or sanctioned by the Ministry—see sections 8, 11, 39 and 40 of that Act. There is no subsidy for a slum clearance scheme unless it is accompanied by re-housing.

Note section 2 (2) of the Housing (Additional Powers) Act, 1919.

Provision of houses . . . by a county council. See section 8 hereof.

Within such period. See article 111 of the below-mentioned regulations.

Regulations. See pages 537 (Local Authorities) and 76 (County Councils). Further as to these regulations—see subsections (2), (3) and (4) below.

(2.) Such regulations shall provide that the amount of any annual payment to be made under this section shall—

(a) in the case of a scheme carried out by a local authority, be determined on the basis of the estimated annual loss resulting from the carrying out of any scheme or schemes to which this section applies, subject to the deduction therefrom of a sum not exceeding the estimated annual produce of a rate of one penny in the pound levied in the area charge-able with the expenses of such scheme or schemes ; and

(b) in the case of a scheme for the provision of houses for persons in the employment of or paid by a county council, or a statutory committee thereof, be an amount equivalent *during the period ending on the thirty-first day of March nineteen hundred and twenty-seven to fifty per centum and thereafter* to thirty per centum of the annual loan charges as calculated in accordance with the regulations

on the total capital expenditure incurred by the S. 7 (19).
county council for the purposes of the scheme :
Provided that the regulations shall include provisions—

(i) for the reduction of the amount of the annual
payment in the event of a failure on the part of
the local authority or county council to secure
due economy in the carrying out and administration of a scheme to charge sufficient rents or otherwise to comply with the conditions prescribed by
the regulations ;

(ii) for the determination of the manner in which
the produce of a rate of one penny in the pound
shall be estimated ; and

(iii) for any adjustment which may be necessary
in consequence of any difference between the
estimated annual produce and the actual produce
of the said rate of one penny in the pound.

The financial basis of the State subsidy to local
authorities is given in the regulations printed on page 537 ;
and to county councils in the regulations printed on
page 76.

As to rents and the general management of the houses
—see section 61 of the 1890 Act.

The words printed in italics were added by section 4
of the Housing (Additional Powers) Act, 1919, their
effect being to render additional assistance to county
councils for the purposes and the period named.

(3.) Every regulation so made shall be laid before
both Houses of Parliament as soon as may be after it
is made, and, if an address is presented by either House
within twenty-one days on which that House has sat
next after any such regulation is laid before it praying
that the regulation may be annulled, His Majesty in
Council may annul the regulation, but without prejudice
to the validity of anything previously done thereunder.

This is taken, substantially, from the National Insurance Act, 1911, section 65, but there is no provision that the regulations made under the present section " shall have effect as if enacted in this Act "—an omission of possible importance in view of expressions used in *Glasgow Insurance Committee v. Scottish Insurance Commissioners*. See also hereon *R. v. Baggallay, Hurlock v. Shinn* [1913] I. K.B. 290, and *O'Neill v. Middlesex Insurance Committee* [1916] I. K.B. 331.

Section 19 (3) hereof is in identical terms.

(4.) Where a loan is made by the Public Works Loan Commissioners for the purposes of a scheme towards the losses on which the Local Government Board are liable to contribute under this section the loan shall, notwithstanding anything in section three of the Housing, Town Planning, &c., Act, 1909, be made on such terms and conditions as the Treasury may prescribe.

This subsection shall be deemed to have had effect as from the first day of April, nineteen hundred and nineteen, as respects any proposals made by a local authority and approved by the Local Government Board before the passing of this Act as respects which the Board may have signified their intention to direct that they shall be treated as a scheme for the purposes of this section.

A Treasury Minute, dated 1st November 1920 (see page 536), fixes the present rate of interest on loans from the Local Loans Fund.

See also note to section 3 of the 1909 Act (page 291), and note to section 25 (5) of the 1890 Act (page 166).

(5.) The provisions of this section relating to the carrying out of a scheme for the provision of houses for persons in the employment of or paid by county councils shall apply to the Lancashire Asylums Board, the West Riding of Yorkshire Asylums Board or other body

constituted for the purpose of the administration of the S. 7 (19).
Lunacy Acts, on behalf of any combination of county
councils and county borough councils.

See the foregoing subsections hereof and the next
section. In most counties the county council is the
asylum authority, but not in the cases of Lancashire
and the West Riding of Yorkshire. Where the asylum
authority provides houses for its servants, it will get
the State subsidy like the county councils.

8. (1.) Where money is borrowed by a county council
for the purpose of the provision of houses for persons
in the employment of or paid by the council or a statutory
committee thereof, or of acquiring land for such houses,
the maximum period for repayment shall be eighty
years, and as respects money so borrowed eighty years
shall be substituted for thirty years in subsection (5)
of section sixty-nine of the Local Government Act, 1888.

Powers of county councils in connection with the housing of their employees.

51 & 52 Vict. c. 41.

See subsection (3) below, and also section 18 (4) hereof.
The said section 69 (5) reads, " a loan under this section
shall be repaid within such period, not exceeding thirty
years, as the county council, with the consent of the
Local Government Board, determine in each case."

(2.) Where a loan is made by the Public Works Loan
Commissioners to a county council for any such purposes
as aforesaid, it shall be made on the same terms and
conditions as a loan to a local authority for the purposes
of the Housing Acts.

See section 7 (4) hereof; sections 25, 43, 46 and 66
of the 1890 Act and section 1 of the 1903 Act, and notes
thereto.

(3.) A county council shall have power and shall be
deemed always to have had power to provide houses
for persons in the employment of or paid by the council
or a statutory committee thereof, and for that purpose

25

a county council may be authorised to acquire land in like manner as a local authority may be authorised to acquire land for the purposes of Part III of the principal Act.

This section shall apply to any such board or body as is mentioned in subsection (5) of section seven of this Act in like manner as it applies to a county council, with the substitution of a reference to the provisions fixing the period within which such board or body is required to repay loans for the reference to subsection (5) of section sixty-nine of the Local Government Act, 1888.

Deemed always. . . . Certain county councils have provided houses for persons in their employment. This subsection sets at rest any doubt as to their powers in that regard.

To acquire land in like manner. See sections 10, 11 and 12 hereof and notes thereto. Note the power to acquire for garden cities, &c.—section 10 of the Housing (Additional Powers) Act, 1919. For power to acquire water rights—see section 14 hereof. Section 57 of the 1890 Act is the original section dealing with acquisition for Part III purposes.

With the substitution of. The asylums boards mentioned in section 7 (5) hereof will not borrow under the provisions of the Local Government Act, 1888, but under their own special Acts—namely, the Lancashire County Lunatic Asylums Act and the West Riding of Yorkshire Lunatic Asylums Act.

Provisions as to the Acquisition and Disposal of Land, &c.

Provisions as to assessment of compensation. **9.** (1.) Where land included in any scheme made or to be made under Part I or Part II of the principal Act (other than land included in such a scheme only for the purpose of making the scheme efficient and not on account of the sanitary condition of the premises thereon or of those premises being dangerous or prejudicial to health) is acquired compulsorily, the compensation to be paid for the land, including any buildings thereon, _{S. 9 (19).} shall be the value at the time the valuation is made of the land as a site cleared of buildings and available for development in accordance with the requirements of the building byelaws for the time being in force in the district:

Provided that, if in the opinion of the Local Government Board it is necessary that provision should be made by the scheme for the re-housing of persons of the working classes on the land or part thereof when cleared, or that the land or a part thereof when cleared should be laid out as an open space, the compensation payable to all persons interested in any land included in the scheme (other than as aforesaid) for their respective interests therein shall be reduced by an amount ascertained in accordance with the rules set forth in the First Schedule to this Act.

Schemes under Part I or Part II. These are improvement and reconstruction schemes affecting unhealthy areas and unhealthy dwelling-houses. Under section 6 of the 1890 Act (page 140) the improvement scheme made by the local authority may include any neighbouring lands for making their improvement scheme efficient; and under section 38 thereof (page 178) an order may be made for the demolition of an obstructive building and the land on which it is erected may be acquired. In either case these lands—namely, those referred to in the parenthesis—are not subject to the provisions of the present section, but are to be dealt with under sections 21 and 41 of the 1890 Act; subject, however, to the Acquisition of Land (Assessment of Compensation) Act, 1919, section 7 (1) proviso.

The compensation to be paid. The First Schedule reads as follows :—

RULES FOR DETERMINING THE AMOUNT OF REDUCTION OF COMPENSATION

(a) The value of the whole of the land included in the scheme shall first be ascertained on the basis of its value as a cleared site available for development in accordance with the requirements of the building byelaws in force in the district.

(*b*) The value of the whole of the said land shall next be ascertained on the basis of its value as a cleared site subject to the requirements of the scheme as to the provision to be made for the re-housing of persons of the working classes or the laying out of open spaces on the land or any part thereof.

(*c*) The difference between the amounts ascertained under paragraph (*a*) and paragraph (*b*) shall then be computed.

(*d*) The amount by which the compensation payable for the respective interests in the land to which section nine of this Act applies, as ascertained in accordance with the principle laid down in that section, is to be reduced shall be a fraction thereof equal to the amount arrived at under paragraph (*c*) when divided by the amount arrived at under paragraph (*a*).

It should first be noted that " building byelaws " are defined by section 40 hereof ; and that the lands included in the scheme for the purpose of making it efficient are not subject to these deductions (see above). The remainder of the words in the subsection and the schedule can be explained by an illustration :—

Let the whole of the land in the area (including that for making the scheme efficient) be valued per rule (*a*) in the schedule at £100,000.

Let the whole of the land (as aforesaid) be valued per rule (*b*) in the schedule at £60,000.

Then the constant factor, per rules (*c*) and (*d*), by which the value of the " insanitary " land will be reduced is—

$$\frac{100,000-60,000}{100,000}=\frac{2}{5}$$

Such reduction applies, of course, only where the proviso applies.

As a site cleared of buildings. It would appear that no compensation is to be paid for the buildings. In that case it will be to the advantage of all interested in the buildings to preserve them from becoming condemned. In this connection reference should be made to section 30 hereof, which gives the court power to authorise the superior landlord to enter and execute works. Section 12 (1) (b) hereof gives another power of dealing with this bad property. See also section 28 as to the repair of houses.

. In some cases, however, it may be to the advantage of the ground landlord if the property is made the subject of a scheme. It is not the policy of the Ministry that re-housing should take place in slum areas, but rather that the re-housing should be on the outskirts of cities. Except in special cases, the Ministry may not be of opinion that " it is necessary that provision should be made by the scheme for the re-housing of persons of the working classes on the land or a part thereof when cleared, or that an open space be provided." In that case the commercial value would be paid, to the considerable advantage of the ground landlord who has let the land on a long lease, and has seen the area steadily degenerating into a slum.

Generally. The subject of unhealthy areas and houses is dealt with in Chapter III.

(2.) The provisions of sections twenty-one and forty-one of the principal Act shall cease to apply as respects lands to which the provisions of this section apply, in so far as such first-mentioned provisions are inconsistent or in conflict with the provisions of this section.

The effect of this subsection is that the insanitary property does not get the advantages of the quoted sections, but only those advantages subject to subsection (1) above. See the notes to the quoted sections.

10. (1.) Where an order authorising a local authority to purchase land compulsorily for the purposes of Part III of the principal Act has been made and confirmed under the provisions of Part I of the Housing, Town Planning, &c., Act, 1909, then, at any time after notice to treat has been served, the local authority may, after giving

S. 10 (19).

8 & 9 Vict.
c. 18.

not less than fourteen days' notice to the owner and occupier of the land, enter on and take possession of the land or such part thereof as is specified in the notice without previous consent or compliance with sections eighty-four to ninety of the Lands Clauses (Consolidation) Act, 1845, but subject to the payment of the like compensation for the land of which possession is taken and interest on the compensation awarded as would have been payable if those provisions had been complied with.

This subsection covers the case of compulsory purchase ; subsection (2) covers purchase by agreement.

Section 2 of the Act of 1909 authorises a local authority to purchase land compulsorily for the provision of lodging houses for the working classes (Part III of the 1890 Act) by means of an order submitted to the Local Government Board, and confirmed by the Board in accordance with the First Schedule to the 1909 Act—see pages 289 and 350. See also sections 5 and 28 of that Act.

The procedure for compulsory purchase is outlined in the Housing Acts (Compulsory Purchase) Regulations, 1919, printed on page 526.

As to the compensation to be paid—see the Acquisition of Land (Assessment of Compensation) Act, 1919, page 495.

This section is very similar to section 2 of the Land Settlement (Facilities) Act, 1919, 9 and 10 Geo. 5. c. 59.

The present subsection, section 11 (3) below, and the regulations above referred to, expedite progress with housing schemes. The order will be more quickly made and confirmed. On confirmation notice to treat may be given, and then, after fourteen days' notice to the owner and occupier of the land, the local authority may take possession, subject to the payment of compensation subsequently awarded. See also the Unemployment (Relief Works) Act, 1920, page 488.

Owner and Occupier. By sections 18 and 121 of the Lands Clauses Consolidation Act, 1845, the promoters are required to serve a notice to treat on all parties S. 10 (19). interested in the lands to be taken, and the claim of each party is to be separately assessed ; but a tenant whose interest in the land is for less than a year is not entitled to a notice to treat, though if possession of the lands occupied by him is required before the expiration of his term or interest, he is entitled to compensation.

(2.) Where a local authority have agreed to purchase land for the purposes of Part III of the principal Act, or have determined to appropriate land for those purposes, subject to the interest of the person in possession thereof, and that interest is not greater than that of a tenant for a year or from year to year, then, at any time after such agreement has been made, or such appropriation has been approved by the Local Government Board, the local authority may, after giving not less than four-teen days' notice to the person so in possession, enter on and take possession of the land or such part thereof as is specified in the notice without previous consent but subject to the payment to the person so in possession of the like compensation with such interest thereon as aforesaid as if the local authority had been authorised to purchase the land compulsorily and such person had in pursuance of such power been required to quit possession before the expiration of his term or interest in the land, but without the necessity of compliance with sections eighty-four to ninety of the Lands Clauses (Consolidation) Act, 1845.

Agreed to purchase. See section 57 of the Act of 1890.
Purposes of Part III. The provision of working-class lodging houses.
Determined to appropriate. See sections 23 and 57 (3) of the Act of 1890.
Person in possession. The object of this subsection is to cover the case where the local authority have

S. 10 (19). reached the position of landlords, and so are able to give the tenant (of the nature mentioned) notice to quit: they do not need to await the expiration to the notice to quit, but can enter after fourteen days' notice, subject to the payment of the compensation which is due under section 121 of Lands Clauses Consolidation Act, 1845. In the case of the occupier having a greater interest than that of a tenant from year to year, the local authority could not proceed under this subsection, but, if they required early possession, would have to proceed by purchase, compulsory or otherwise—see subsection (1) above, and, particularly, the note headed " Owner and Occupier." If the local authority, being landlords, like to give notice to quit and to await its expiration, they do not need to pay anything to the tenant.

As aforesaid. See the above subsection (1) and notes thereto.

Amendment of procedure for compulsory acquisition of land.

11. (1.) Paragraph (7) of the First Schedule to the Housing, Town Planning, &c., Act, 1909 (which provides for special procedure in the case of the acquisition of land, for the purposes of Part III of the principal Act, situate in London or in a borough or urban district), shall cease to have effect.

Paragraph 7, required a special inquiry (by an impartial person, &c.) where the land proposed to be acquired was situate in London or in a borough or urban district, even if no objection had been made. But, subject to subsection (3) below, a public inquiry has still to be held where an objection is made. See also subsection (2) below.

As to the compensation to be paid for land acquired compulsorily—see the Acquisition of Land (Assessment of Compensation) Act, 1919 (page 495).

(2.) Where the confirming of an order made under that schedule is opposed, the Local Government Board shall, before confirming the order, duly consider the report of the person by whom, under paragraph (6)

of the said schedule, a public inquiry is held, and the S. 11 (19).
Local Government Board shall not confirm any order
for the compulsory acquisition of land under that schedule,
even when the order is unopposed, if they are of opinion
that the land is unsuited for the purpose for which it is
proposed to be acquired.

Paragraph (6). See page 352. By paragraph 2 of
the same schedule, the order submitted to the Board
by the local authority is of no force until it is confirmed
by the Board. But the Board had not the option,
previously, to refuse to confirm an unopposed order,
though it could modify it.
    There is no appeal from the Board (Ministry), but if
it acts improperly or does not act judiciously, the local
authority might get redress by *certiorari* and *mandamus.*

(3.) Notwithstanding the provisions of paragraph (6)
of the First Schedule to the Housing, Town Planning,
&c., Act, 1909, any order for the compulsory acquisition
of land which is duly submitted after the date of the
passing of this Act, and before the expiration of two
years from that date, by a local authority under the
provisions of Part I of the Housing, Town Planning, &c.,
Act, 1909, may be confirmed by the Local Government
Board without a public inquiry.

Paragraph 6. See note to subsection (2) above. It
requires a public inquiry when an objection is made.
    Passing of this Act. 31st July 1919.
    Part I of the Act of 1909 relates to housing of
the working classes.
    Generally. This subsection is of importance, particu-
larly as it applies also to the acquisition of water rights
(section 14, below) ; but, doubtless, the Ministry will be
careful before confirming, especially where water rights
are in question.   ₒ
    See the Housing Acts (Compulsory Purchase) Regula-
tions and the Housing Acts (Compulsory Purchase)

S. 11 (19).

Amendment Regulations, 1919, printed on pages 526 and 531.

(4.) The amendments to the said schedule effected by this Act shall apply to that schedule as originally enacted but not as applied by any other enactment.

Amendments effected. See preceding subsection. Section 50 hereof repeals the seventh paragraph of the said schedule.

Said schedule. First Schedule to the Act of 1909—see page 350.

As applied by any other enactment. By the Education Act, 1918, the procedure to be followed by education authorities when acquiring land for the erection of schools was laid down by reference to the First Schedule to the Act of 1909. Education authorities have, therefore, to proceed in accordance with that schedule as originally enacted.

Additional powers as to acquisition of land and houses.

12. (1.) The powers of a local authority to acquire land for the purposes of Part III of the principal Act shall be deemed to include power—

(a) to acquire any houses or other buildings on the land proposed to be acquired as a site for the erection of houses for the working classes ; and

(b) to acquire any estate or interest in any houses which might be made suitable as houses for the working classes, together with any lands occupied with such houses ;

and the local authority shall have power to alter, enlarge, repair and improve any such houses or buildings so as to render them in all respects fit for habitation as houses for the working classes.

Powers . . . to acquire land for the purposes of Part III. The purposes of Part III are the provision of houses or cottages for the working classes, &c.—see section 53 of the 1890 Act. By section 57 of that Act they may acquire land for those purposes (by agreement or compulsory purchase), or they may appropriate for those S. 12 (19). purposes any land vested in them or at their disposal. See also sections 58 and 59 thereof, section 1 of the 1900 Act, section 11 of the 1903 Act, and sections 2 (3), 8, 40, 45, 73 and 74 of the 1909 Act. Note also the power of acquisition for garden city purposes, &c., conferred by section 10 (1) of the Housing (Additional Powers) Act, 1919.

The compulsory acquisition procedure is laid down in the 1909 Act, section 2 and the First Schedule, but the assessment of compensation is now governed by the Acquisition of Land (Assessment of Compensation) Act, 1919 (page 495).

As to acquisition by agreement, sections 175–178 of the Public Health Act, 1875, apparently still apply, though several of their provisions have been modified— see sections 13, 14 and 15 hereof, and section 40 of the 1909 Act. The general effect of sections 175–178 of the Public Health Act, 1875, is that a local authority may for the purposes of the Act purchase, take on lease, sell or exchange any lands, in or out of their district ; buy up any water-mill, dam or weir which interferes with their drainage or water supply ; let for any term any of their lands which they can conveniently spare ; and purchase from the Duchy of Lancaster. The Lands Clauses Consolidation Acts, 1845, 1860, and 1869, &c., are also applied, and may be useful when dealing with limited interests and the payment of money into Court, &c.

As to the disposal of the land or buildings—see section 15 hereof.

To qualify for the State assistance under section 7 hereof, the acquisition must first be approved by the Minister.

Which might be made suitable. These words cover many possibilities, including houses subject or liable to a closing order, and houses which though not yet slums are below the modern standard, perhaps primitive as regards sanitary arrangements or otherwise unsuitable. The local authority can acquire such houses and alter, enlarge, repair and improve them. As regards the latter houses—section 28 hereof should be read : in a sense it gives an alternative,and permits the local authority to require the owner to effect repairs. Both these powers are important, as for some years, until the housing shortage is overtaken, many people will have to live in adapted or repaired houses. It should be noticed, however, that the presumption under the present subsection is that the houses are not suitable, while under section 28 the contrary is the case ; though the proviso to section 28 (1) refers to the house which " is not capable without reconstruction of being rendered fit for human habitation." Probably such a house could be purchased by the local authority under the present subsection— of course at a reduced price. The matter is of some importance as, owing to the restriction of rents and high costs, it is at present difficult to induce some landlords to spend money in repairing or improving their property.

The words cover the work of turning large houses into flats, on which subject reference may also be made to section 27 hereof. See also the Ministry's *Manual on the Conversion of Houses into Flats for the Working Classes*, price 1s.

(2.) The purposes for which land may be acquired under Part III of the principal Act shall be deemed to include—

(a) the lease or sale of the land, under the powers conferred by this Act, with a view to the erection thereon of houses for the working classes by persons other than the local authority ; and

(b) the lease or sale under the powers conferred by this Act of any part of the land acquired with a view to the use thereof for purposes which in the opinion of the local authority are necessary or desirable for or incidental to the development of the land as a building estate, including the provision, maintenance, and improvement of houses and gardens, factories, workshops, places of worship, places of recreation, and other works or buildings for or for the convenience of persons belonging to the working classes and other persons.

Purposes . . . under Part III. See note to last S. 12 (19).
subsection.

Powers conferred by this Act. See section 15 hereof.
The powers of sale or lease are to be exercised subject
to the consent of the Minister of Health.

Persons other, including public utility societies, housing
trusts, and private individuals, who have no power to
acquire land compulsorily. See section 18 (1) hereof.

Paragraph (b). Note that the wide terms hereof are restricted by the words "development of the land as a
building estate."

Under section 11 of the 1903 Act, there is power to
provide and maintain shops, recreation grounds, &c.,
with the consent of the Ministry.

(3.) Subject to the consent of the Local Government
Board and to such conditions as the Board may prescribe,
a local authority may, for the purposes of Part III of
the principal Act, contract for the purchase by or lease
to them of houses suitable for the working classes, whether
built at the date of the contract or intended to be built
thereafter.

Prescribe by regulations. No regulations appear to
have been made by the Ministry, but they have issued
a circular (No. 39).

Part III. This subsection re-enacts in somewhat
more careful terms section 57 (3) of the 1890 Act, which
is repealed, by section 50 and the Fifth Schedule hereof.
Some doubts had arisen as to the interpretation of that
subsection.

Some private builders have availed themselves of
these powers, but for the most part they are at present
proceeding under section 1 of the Housing (Additional
Powers) Act, 1919, whereby they secure a State subsidy.

Purchase. But if the house purchased has received
a grant under the Housing (Additional Powers) Act, 1919,
the local authority will not get additional assistance
under section 7 hereof—see section 2 (2) of that
Act.

S. 13 (19)

Power to acquire in advance lands in areas proposed for inclusion in improvement schemes under Parts I and II of principal Act.

13. Where a local authority have under section four of the principal Act passed a resolution that an area is an unhealthy area and that an improvement scheme ought to be made in respect of such area, or have under section thirty-nine of the principal Act passed a resolution directing a scheme to be prepared for the improvement of an area, the local authority may, with the consent of and subject to any conditions imposed by the Local Government Board, acquire by agreement any lands included within the area notwithstanding that the scheme may not at the time of acquisition have been made by the local authority or confirmed or sanctioned by the Local Government Board ; and the acquisition of such lands shall be deemed to be a purpose for which the local authority may borrow money under and subject to the provisions of Part I or, as the case may be, Part II of the principal Act.

Section 4 of the principal Act provides that a local authority, on being satisfied of the unhealthiness of an area, shall, under certain conditions, make an improvement scheme.

Section 39 of the principal Act deals substantially with the same subject, but technically for unhealthy houses rather than for areas.

A resolution is preliminary to the making of a scheme, and confirmation or sanction is necessary before it can be carried out.

Provisions of Part I or . . . Part II. Section 25 of the 1890 Act deals with the power of borrowing money for the purposes of Part I, and sections 43 and 46 for the purposes of Part II ; but as regards the latter there is an extension by section 1 of the Act of 1894.

Object of the section. The object of the section is to enable the local authority to acquire by agreement land to be included in the improvement scheme, before the scheme is made or is approved by the Ministry. The negotiations in connection with the approval of the scheme sometimes occupy about seven months, and during that period the local authority may have an opportunity to purchase the land by agreement.   Under the old Acts they could not avail themselves of such an opportunity. The subsection has nothing to do with the prior acquisition of land under Part III, as to which—see section 2 (3) of the 1909 Act.

14. A local authority or a county council may, not- withstanding anything in section three hundred and twenty-seven or section three hundred and thirty-two of the Public Health Act, 1875, but subject to the pro- visions of section fifty-two of that Act, be authorised to abstract water from any river, stream, or lake, or the feeders thereof, whether within or without the district of the local authority or the county, for the purpose of affording a water supply for houses provided or to be provided under a scheme made under the Housing Acts, and to do all such acts as may be necessary for affording a water supply to such houses, subject to a prior obligation of affording a sufficient supply of water to any houses or agricultural holdings or other premises that may be de- prived thereof by reason of such abstraction, in like manner and subject to the like restrictions as they may be autho- rised to acquire land for the purposes of the scheme :

Provided that no local authority or county council shall be authorised under this section to abstract any water which any local authority, corporation, company, or person are empowered by Act of Parliament to impound, take or use for the purpose of supply within any area, or any water the abstraction of which would, in the opinion of the Local Government Board, injuriously affect the working or management of any canal or inland navigation.

Or a county council.   Even though the county council may have nothing to do with the housing scheme.

S. 14 (19).

Sections 327 *and* 332 *of the Public Health Act*, 1875, provide that nothing in that Act shall authorise any local authority to interfere with or injuriously affect certain navigation and water rights, &c.

Section 52 *of that Act* is as follows :—

Restriction
on construc-
tion of
waterworks
by local
authority.

"52. Before commencing to construct waterworks within the limits of supply of any water company empowered by Act of Parliament or any order confirmed by Parliament to supply water, the local authority shall give written notice to every water company within whose limits of supply the local authority are desirous of supplying water, stating the purposes for which and (as far as may be practicable) the extent to which water is required by the local authority.

" It shall not be lawful for the local authority to construct any waterworks within such limits if and so long as any such company are able and willing to supply water proper and sufficient for all reasonable purposes for which it is required by the local authority ; and any difference as to whether the water which any such company are able and willing to lay on is proper and sufficient for the purposes for which it is required or whether the purposes for which it is required are reasonable, or (if and so far as the charges of the company are not regulated by Parliament) as to the terms of supply, shall be settled by arbitration in manner provided by this Act."

Note that by section 45 of the 1909 Act, the Housing Acts give no authority to compulsorily acquire for housing purposes, land which has been acquired by a water company.

The general subject of water rights, apart from the present section (14), is a big and difficult one. See particularly sections 51 to 70 of the Public Health Act, 1875, which are fully discussed on pages 117 to 146 of *Lumley's Public Health*, 8th edition. Section 62 of that Act is summarised on page 61 hereof, and there are summaries of provisions in other Acts on pages 60 to 65.

May be authorised, presumably by the Ministry of Health, which doubtless would have to be satisfied on the points raised in the proviso. If the authority were incorrectly given, it would be null and void.

Housing Acts. See section 52 (2) hereof. Apparently
the power here applies also to houses erected by public
utility societies and housing trusts, inasmuch as they
present " schemes " (see section 19), but it is question-
able if it applies to houses erected by private persons ;
nor does it allow a local authority which is building no
new houses to start a water scheme.

Prior obligation of affording a sufficient supply. The
premises deprived have the first claim, but only to a
sufficient supply and not necessarily to as large a supply
as they previously enjoyed. " Other premises " would
include an industrial undertaking or workshop, &c.

In like manner. . . .   See notes to sections 11 (3) and
12 (1) hereof. During the committee stage of the 1919
Act, Major (now Lord) Astor on behalf of the Ministry,
in discussing the acquisition of water rights, said : " No
authority can . . . go outside its area and invade
another area without the express sanction of the Local
Government Board, and we give the undertaking that
we will notify any authority that appears [to be], or
might be, affected by the proposal " (*Debates*, cols.
138–9).

The object of this section is to enable local authorities
and county councils to secure a water supply for houses
built under a housing scheme, without the necessity
of promoting a private Bill in Parliament.

15. (1.) Where a local authority have acquired or Powers of
appropriated any land for the purposes of Part III of dealing with
the principal Act, then, without prejudice to any of acquired.
their other powers under that Act, the authority may—

    (*a*) lay out and construct public streets or roads and
        open spaces on the land ;

    (*b*) with the consent of the Local Government Board
        sell or lease the land or part thereof to any person
        for the purpose and under the condition that that
        person will erect and maintain thereon such number
        of houses suitable for the working classes as may be
        fixed by the local authority in accordance with
        plans approved by them, and when necessary will

26

lay out and construct public streets or roads and open spaces on the land, or will use the land for purposes which, in the opinion of the local authority, are necessary or desirable for or incidental to the development of the land as a building estate in accordance with plans approved by the local authority, including the provision, maintenance, and improvement of houses and gardens, factories, workshops, places of worship, places of recreation and other works or buildings for, or for the convenience of, persons belonging to the working classes and other persons ;

(c) with the consent of the Local Government Board sell the land or exchange it for land better adapted for those purposes, either with or without paying or receiving any money for equality of exchange ;

(d) with the consent of the Local Government Board sell or lease any houses on the land or erected by them on the land, subject to such covenants and conditions as they may think fit to impose either in regard to the maintenance of the houses as houses for the working classes or otherwise in regard to the use of the houses, and upon any such sale they may, if they think fit, agree to the price being paid by instalments or to payment of part thereof being secured by a mortgage of the premises :

Provided that it shall be a condition of such sale or lease that the houses shall not be used by any person for the time being having any interest therein for the purpose of housing persons in his employment.

Acquired or appropriated. . . . See note to section 10 (2) hereof.

Any land. This is not only the land acquired under S. 15 (19). section 12 (2).

Other powers. Note the powers in section 11 of the 1903 Act.

With the consent of the Local Government Board. It will be noticed that this consent is necessary under each paragraph except (*a*). There is no appeal, but see note to section 11 (2) hereof.

Paragraph (*b*). The major portion of this paragraph is a repetition of section 12 (2) hereof, which permits the acquisition. The Ministry would doubtless be entitled to full particulars of the sale or lease, including the " plans approved."

It would seem that, with the consent of the Ministry, the local authority could lease or sell the land for the erection of better class houses, as well as factories, &c., in accordance with plans approved by the local authority.

The sale could be to public utility societies, &c., in which connection see section 18 (1) hereof.

If the person to whom the land is so sold or let fails to erect, &c., in accordance with the condition, the local authority will have the remedy of " specific performance " —see *Wolverhampton Corporation v. Emmons* [1901] 1 K.B. 515, and *Molyneux v. Richard* [1906] 1 Ch. 34. at page 40.

Paragraph (*c*). This re-enacts, substantially, section 60 of the 1890 Act, which is repealed by this Act. Section 175 of the Public Health Act, 1875 (which applies to the acquisition of land under section 57 of the 1890 Act), also contains a power of sale or exchange.

" Better adapted " is restrictive. Once the land is acquired (see section 12) it cannot be exchanged, even for land equally adapted for housing (or incidental) purposes. But it can be sold—in each case with the consent of the Board (Ministry)—even to a purchaser who does not intend to apply it to housing purposes. See also subsections (2) and (3) below.

Paragraph (*d*). The Ministry would doubtless be entitled to full particulars of the covenants, conditions, &c. With regard to the sale subject to mortgage, reference should be made to the Acquisition of Small Dwellings Act, page 257.

The proviso is to prevent these houses from being " tied," but it is submitted that it prevents the purchaser from letting to tenants who may happen to be in his employment, even though they be the only persons wanting the houses. The proviso as passed in committee read : " Provided that it should be a condition of such sale or lease that the houses should not be sold or leased to an employer for the purpose of housing persons in his employment." In moving the present form of words, the Minister in charge on the report stage said : " It may be that a person would purchase houses and sell them to somebody else for the purpose of using them as tied houses, and those words [e.g. the present form] are introduced to prevent that being done. They would cover the first or second stage of these sales " (Dr. Addison, *Hansard*, 27th May 1919, col. 657).

(2.) Where a local authority under this section sell or lease land subject to any condition as to the erection thereon of houses, or the laying out and construction of streets or the development of the land, there shall be included in the conveyance or lease all such covenants and conditions as may be necessary to secure compliance with the condition aforesaid within a reasonable period, and to limit the amount of the rent which may be charged in respect of the land or any part thereof or in respect of the houses erected thereon ; and the local authority may contribute or agree to contribute towards the expenses of the development of the land and the laying out and construction of streets thereon, subject to the condition that the streets are dedicated to the public.

Under this section. See subsection 1 (*b*) above.
The present subsection takes the place of section 6 of the 1909 Act, repealed by the Fifth Schedule hereto.

(3.) Land and houses sold or leased under the provisions of this section shall be sold or leased at the best price or for the best rent that can reasonably be obtained, having regard to any condition imposed, and any capital money received in respect of any transaction under this section shall be applied in or towards the purchase of S. 15 (19). other land for the purposes of Part III of the principal Act, or with the consent of the Local Government Board to any purpose, including the repayment of borrowed money, to which capital money may be properly applied.

Best price. . . . Any loss would come under the provisions of section 7 hereof—see Articles VII (5) and VIII (3) of the Local Authorities (Assisted Housing Schemes) Regulations, 1919, pages 546 and 547.

Having regard to any condition imposed. One condition is presumably that of subsection (1) (*d*) above—namely, as the maintenance of the houses as houses for the working classes. This would allow a price or rent less than the best one, in cases where the best could be obtained from a person wanting a house as, for instance, a week-end cottage.

Generally. The latter part of this subsection substantially re-enacts section 32 of the 1909 Act, which is repealed by this Act. There is an almost identical provision in section 82 of the 1890 Act.

16. For the purpose of assisting in the preparation Power of and carrying out of schemes under this Act, or for the Local Government purpose of securing the immediate provision of dwelling Board to assist in accommodation in the area of any local authority pending preparation the preparation of a scheme by such authority, the of schemes. Local Government Board may, with the consent of the Treasury, acquire and hold lands and buildings, erect buildings, alter, enlarge, repair, and improve buildings and dispose of any lands or buildings so acquired or erected, and for such purposes the Board may exercise any of the powers of a local authority under the Housing Acts in regard to the acquisition and disposal of land and buildings.

Any of the powers. See sections 12 to 15 hereof and notes thereto. See also the Regulations on page 531.

It is not expected that this section will be put to

S. 16 (19). frequent use as regards its wider powers, though those powers ·have been valuable in some instances, notably in the conversion of houses into flats. For the rest the section will probably be used to enable the Ministry to erect buildings for exhibition or experimental purposes— as for instance model huts, houses of a new type, buildings in concrete or other slabs, &c., &c. In an emergency, especially if the local authority showed a disposition to avail itself of the three months allowed under section 1 (see, however, section 1 (5)), the wider powers would enable the Ministry to act at once.

As to the body to ultimately bear the cost of converting houses into flats—see section 3 of the Housing (Additional Powers) Act, 1919.

Occupation of house at a rental from local authority not to disqualify for election to local authority. **17.** For removing doubts it is hereby enacted that a person shall not, by reason only of the fact that he occupies a house at a rental from a local authority within the meaning of Part III of the principal Act, be disqualified from being elected or being a member thereof or any committee thereof.

Provisions for the assistance of public utility societies, housing trusts, and other persons

Powers of promoting and assisting public utility societies. **18.** (1.) A local authority within the meaning of Part III of the principal Act, or a county council, may promote the formation or extension of or, subject to the provisions of this section, assist a public utility society whose objects include the erection, improvement or management of houses for the working classes, and where such a society is desirous of erecting houses for the working classes which, in the opinion of the Local Government Board, are required, and the local authority of the area in which the houses are proposed to be built are unwilling to acquire land with a view to selling or leasing the same to the society, the county council, on the application of the society, may for this purpose S. 18 (19). acquire land and exercise all the powers of a local authority under the Housing Acts in regard to the acquisition and disposal of land, and the provisions of those Acts as to the acquisition of land by local authorities within the meaning of Part III of the principal Act shall apply accordingly.

Local Authority within the meaning of Part III. See page 11.
Public Utility Society. These societies are discussed fully in Chapter VI, page 94.   For definition—see section 40 hereof.
Powers of a local authority. . . . See sections 10, 11, 12, 14 and 15 hereof and notes thereto.

(2.) Any such local authority or county council with the consent of, and subject to any regulations or conditions which may be made or imposed by, the Local Government Board may, for the assistance of such a society—

(*a*) make grants or loans to the society ;

(*b*) subscribe for any share or loan capital of the society ;

(*c*) guarantee or join in guaranteeing the payment of interest on money borrowed by the society or of any share or loan capital issued by the society ;

on such terms and conditions as to rate of interest and repayment or otherwise and on such security as the local authority or council think fit, and, notwithstanding the provisions of section four of the Industrial and Provident 56 & 57 Vict. Societies Act, 1893, where a local authority or county c. 39. council assist such a society under this subsection, the local authority or council shall not be prevented from having or claiming an interest in the shares of the society exceeding two hundred pounds.

S. 18 (19). *Regulations.* No regulations or conditions appear to have been made or imposed as yet.

Section 4 of the Industrial and Provident Societies Act, 1893. This, and the general subject of public utility societies, is discussed in Chapter VI.

(3.) Any expenses incurred by a local authority (other than the London County Council) under the provisions of this section shall be defrayed in the same manner as the expenses of the local authority under Part III of the principal Act, and the raising of money for the purpose of making grants or loans to or subscribing for the capital of a society under this section shall be a purpose for which the authority may borrow under that Part of that Act.

Other than the London County Council. The London County Council is a local authority as per section 41 hereof. It is excluded under this subsection but comes under the next subsection, which applies to county councils.

Expenses. See section 65 of the 1890 Act, and section 31 of the 1909 Act, and notes thereto.

Borrow. See section 66 of the 1890 Act, section 3 (2) of the 1900 Act, section 1 of the 1903 Act, and section 3 of the 1909 Act, and notes thereto.

(4.) Any expenses incurred by a county council under this section shall be defrayed as expenses for general county purposes, and the raising of money for the purpose of making grants or loans to or subscribing for the capital of a society under this section shall be a purpose for which the council may borrow; provided that, where money is borrowed by the county council for that purpose, the maximum period for repayment shall be fifty years, and as respects money so borrowed fifty years shall be substituted for thirty years in subsection (5) of section sixty-nine of the Local Government Act, 1888.

The same period is mentioned in section 20 (2) (a) S. 18 (19).
below.

The concluding words of this subsection are identical
with those of section 8 (1) hereof, which see.

19. (1.) Where a public utility society or a housing Power of
trust as defined by this Act has submitted to the Local contributing
to costs in-
Government Board a scheme for the provision of houses curred by
public utility
for the working classes and the scheme is approved by societies and
housing
the Board, then, if the scheme is carried out within such trusts.
period after the passing of this Act as may be specified
by the Board with the consent of the Treasury, the
Board may pay or undertake to pay out of moneys
provided by Parliament such contributions towards the
cost of carrying out the scheme as may be determined
to be payable under regulations made by the Board
with the approval of the Treasury subject to such
conditions (including conditions as to audit of accounts
by district auditors) as may be prescribed by those
regulations.

Public utility society . . . housing trust. See page 94,
and, for definitions, section 40.

Provision of houses. The scheme could include the
conversion of houses not at present suitable as houses
for the working classes—see also section 20 (1).

Scheme is approved. The plans will also have to be
submitted to the local authority in the usual way.

Carried out within such period. See Article III of the
below-mentioned regulations—reasonable progress before
31st July 1920, carried into effect by 31st July 1922,
or such later date as the Minister may allow.

Such contributions. See subsection (2) below, and
note section 2 (2) of the Housing (Additional Powers)
Act, 1919.

Regulations. See the Public Utility Societies (Financial
Assistance) Regulations, 1919, and the Housing Trusts
(Financial Assistance) Regulations, 1919, printed on pages
651, 661, 669 and 673. Further regulations—namely, The

S. 19 (19). Public Utility Societies (Sale of Houses) Regulations 1920—deal with the conditions of sale, including price, of houses by public utility societies, and are printed on page 663.

(2.) Such regulations shall provide that the amount of any annual payment to be made under this section shall be equivalent *during the period ending on the thirty-first day of March nineteen hundred and twenty-seven to fifty per centum and thereafter* to thirty per centum of the annual loan charges which would have been payable in accordance with the regulations on the total capital expenditure incurred by the public utility society or housing trust for the purposes of the scheme if the amount of that expenditure had been borrowed from the Public Works Loan Commissioners :

Provided that the regulations shall include provision for the reduction of the amount of the annual payment in the event of the Local Government Board being satisfied that the capital expenditure incurred by the public utility society or housing trust has been excessive.

See subsection (1) above.

The words in italics were added by section 4 of the Housing (Additional Powers) Act, 1919, their effect being to provide additional financial assistance to public utility societies and housing trusts.

As to the proviso, compare section 7 (2) hereof.

(3.) Every regulation so made shall be laid before both Houses of Parliament as soon as may be after it is made, and, if an address is presented by either House within twenty-one days on which that House has sat next after any such regulation is laid before it praying that the regulation may be annulled, His Majesty in Council may annul the regulation, but without prejudice to the validity of anything previously done thereunder.

This is identical with section 7 (3) hereof. See note S. 19 (19).
thereto.

20. (1.) The purposes referred to in subsection (1) Loans to
of section sixty-seven of the principal Act for which public utility
the Public Works Loan Commissioners may advance societies.
money on loan shall extend to the purchase of houses
which may be made suitable as houses for the working
classes and to the purchase and development of land
by a public utility society.

Section 67 (1) of the Act of 1890 (see page 214) enables
the Public Works Loan Commissioners to advance on
loan to public utility societies such money. as may be
required for the purpose of constructing or improving,
&c., dwellings for the working classes.
See also Chapter VI.
For rate of interest—see page 536.

(2.) Notwithstanding anything contained in the Public 38 & 39 Vict.
Works Loans Act, 1875, or any Act amending that Act, c. 89.
where a loan is made by the Public Works Loan Commissioners under section sixty-seven of the principal
Act to a public utility society for the purpose of carrying
out a scheme for the provision of houses for the working
classes approved by the Local Government Board :—

(*a*) The maximum period for the repayment of the loan
shall be fifty instead of forty years ;

(*b*) Money may be lent on the mortgage of an estate
for a term of years absolute whereof a period not
less than ten years in excess of the period fixed for
the repayment of the sums advanced remains
unexpired at the date of the loan ;

(*c*) In the case of loans made during such period after
the passing of this Act as may be specified by the
Board with the consent of the Treasury, the money
advanced on the security of a mortgage of any land

S. 20 (19). or dwellings solely shall not exceed seventy-five per cent. of the purchase price of the land and of the cost of its development and of the houses proposed to be mortgaged as certified by the Local Government Board ; but advances may be made by instalments in respect of the purchase money of the land to be acquired, and of the cost of its development, and in respect of the building of any house or houses on the land mortgaged as such building progresses, so that the total of the advances do not at any time exceed the amount aforesaid ; and a mortgage may accordingly be made to secure advances so to be made from time to time.

This extends the maximum periods, &c., and otherwise eases the conditions specified in section 67 (2) of the 1890 Act.

Period . . . specified by the Board. No period has been specified as yet.

Loans to private persons. **21.** During a period of two years from the passing of this Act, the money which may be advanced by the Public Works Loan Commissioners to any private person for the purpose of constructing houses for the working classes on the security of a mortgage of any land or dwellings solely may, if the Commissioners think fit and if the houses are constructed in accordance with plans approved by the Local Government Board, exceed the amount specified in subsection (2) of section sixty-seven of the principal Act, but shall not exceed seventy-five per centum of the value of the estate or interest in such land or dwellings proposed to be mortgaged, and advances may be made by instalments from time to time as the building of the houses on the land mortgaged progresses, so that the total of the advances does not at

any time exceed the amount last mentioned, and a S. 21 (19).
mortgage may accordingly be made to secure advances
so to be made from time to time.

Two years. . . . This Act was passed on 31st July 1919.
It has been continued by the Expiring Laws Continuance
Act 1920.

Private person. Section 67 of the 1890 Act (page 214)
is extended by this section, which it will be noticed is
similar to section 20 (2) (*c*) above. By the said section 67
the Public Works Loan Commissioners may, out of the
funds at their disposal, advance on loan to any private
person entitled to any land for an estate in fee simple
(i.e. freehold), or for any term of years absolute (i.e.
leasehold), whereof not less than fifty years shall for
the time being remain unexpired, such money as may be
required for the purpose of constructing or improving,
&c., dwellings for the working classes. In the present
section the word " improving " is omitted, and so it is
only where houses are being constructed that the extension of the said section 67 applies. It will be noticed
further that the extension is made only if the Commissioners think fit and if the houses are constructed in
accordance with plans approved by the Board (Ministry).
It will be understood that the private person gets no
State subsidy, under section 7 hereof ; but he can borrow
in this way even if he has no power to borrow independently of the 1890 Act—section 67 (2) (*a*) thereof. For
the rate of interest on the loan see the Treasury Minute
of 1st November 1920 (page 536), whereby the rate is
fixed at 7 per cent. for loans up to thirty years, and 7¼
per cent. for loans up to forty years.

See the next section for loans for the *improvement* of
housing accommodation.

Under section 2 (7) of this Act the local authority
must take into account any proposals under this section.

22. (1.) Where the owner of a house or building Loans by
local
applies to the local authority, within the meaning of authorities
for the im-
Part III of the principal Act, of the district in which provement
of housing
the house is situated for assistance for the purpose of accommodation.
carrying out works for the reconstruction, enlargement,

or improvement thereof, and the local authority are of opinion that after the works are carried out the house or building would be in all respects fit for habitation as a house or as houses for the working classes, and that the circumstances of the district in regard to housing accommodation are such as to make it desirable that the works should be carried out, the local authority may lend to the owner the whole or any part of such sum as may be necessary to defray the cost of the works, and any costs, charges, or expenses incidental thereto.

Provided that the loan shall not exceed one half of the estimated value of the property mortgaged, unless some additional or collateral security is given sufficient to secure the excess.

(2.) Before the works are commenced, full particulars of the works and, where required by the local authority, plans and specifications thereof shall be submitted to the local authority for their approval, and before any loan is made the authority shall satisfy themselves that the works in respect of which the loan is to be made have been carried out in a satisfactory and efficient manner.

(3.) The raising of money for the purpose of making a loan under this section shall be a purpose for which the local authority may borrow for the purposes of Part III of the principal Act.

(4.) For the purpose of this section " owner " means any person whose interest, or any number of persons whose combined interests constitute either an estate of fee simple in possession or, in the case of copyhold land, a similar estate, or a leasehold interest in possession for a term of years absolute whereof a period of not less than ten years in excess of the period fixed for the repayment of the loan remains unexpired at the date of the loan.

See the previous section for loans for the construction S. 22 (19).
of houses ; the present section deals with reconstruction,
enlargement or improvement of existing premises.   For
the Form of Application, &c., see page 579.

Local authority. . . .   See page 11.   The local
authority have unrestricted power under this section,
e.g. nothing has to be approved by the Ministry.   They
must take into account (see section 2 (7) hereof) any
proposals under this section.

Subsection (1) appears to contemplate a loan or advance
before the works are completed, indeed to help the works
to be commenced.   But subsection (2) prohibits the loan
until the works are done.   There thus appears to be
nothing to induce the owner to apply to the local authority
unless he cannot borrow elsewhere, or unless he can
borrow more cheaply from the local authority—on which
latter point it may be noted that the rate of interest to
be charged by the local authority is not specified.   However, the section is by no means useless, as the property
is, by hypothesis, unfit for habitation—in which case,
even after renovation, a private lender might be difficult
to find.   Further, the local authority might agree to
lend, subject to subsection (2), thus encouraging the
owner to make the improvements.

As to subsection (3)—see note (" Borrow ") to section
18 (3) hereof.

The final portion of subsection (4) is similar to section
20 (2) (*b*).

23. Subject to any conditions prescribed by the Local
Government Board with the consent of the Treasury,
any bricks or other building materials which have been
acquired by a Government Department for the purpose
of the erection or improvement of houses for the working
classes, may during a period of five years from the passing
of this Act be sold to any person who undertakes to use
the same forthwith for the purpose of erecting or improving houses for the working classes and to comply with the
said conditions at a price sufficient to cover the cost of
replacement at the time of sale of the materials so sold.

*Provisions
as to sale of
building
materials.*

S. 23 (19). *Five years* from 31st July 1919.

Object of the section. The section is designed to meet the case, primarily, of the private owner who has duties imposed upon him to effect repairs under section 28 hereof (see also section 26), yet at the time the Act was passed had difficulty in getting bricks or other building materials. It also helps private persons to build (see section 21) and, generally, gives a better opportunity to private enterprise. Section 12 (3) also deals with houses built by private enterprise. At the date of the passing of this Act a large proportion of the stocks of bricks and timber in the country had been taken over by the Government. In the House of Commons on 3rd November 1919, the President of the Board of Trade (Sir A. Geddes) said that Government timber, for the purpose of building cottages under approved schemes big enough to take large supplies, should be disposed of through the Ministry of Munitions at the lowest possible figure not involving an actual loss.

Relaxation of Byelaws

Relaxation of byelaws.

24. (1.) Where in pursuance of a housing scheme to which this section applies new buildings are constructed, or public streets and roads are laid out and constructed, in accordance with plans and specifications approved by the Local Government Board, the provisions of any building byelaws shall not apply to the new buildings and new streets constructed and laid out in pursuance of the scheme so far as those provisions are inconsistent with the plans and specifications approved by the Local Government Board, and, notwithstanding the provisions of any other Act, any street laid out and constructed in accordance with such plans and specifications may be taken over and thereafter maintained by the local authority :

Provided that, as regards the administrative county of

London, the Board shall not approve any plans and S. 24 (19). specifications inconsistent with the provisions of any building byelaws in force in the county except after consultation with the London County Council on the general question of the relaxation of such provisions in connection with housing schemes.

To which this section applies. See subsection (3) below. It includes the schemes of public utility societies, housing trusts, &c.

New buildings. " The question whether a building is a new building or not has been decided over and over again to be a question of fact "—Coleridge, Chief Justice, in *James v. Wyvil* [1884] 48 J.P. 725. There are special definitions in the Public Health Act, 1875 (section 159) and the Public Health Acts Amendment Act, 1907.

Building Byelaws. See section 40 (page 441). It may be noted that under section 44 of the 1909 Act, the Ministry can revoke unreasonable byelaws, but that section is so worded as to make it almost useless.

Any other Act. Principally the Public Health Act, 1875, and subsequent Acts. See pages 316, 325 and 438 of *Lumley's Public Health* (8th edition). Though a street is less than twenty feet in width it can be taken over.

London County Council. The position of the London County Council is special (see the arguments in *Hansard,* 27th May 1919, cols. 682–4), but the consultation is only on the general question, i.e. there is not a consultation in respect of every separate scheme, and there is no appeal from the decision of the Ministry.

(2.) Where the Local Government Board have approved plans and specifications which in certain respects are inconsistent with the provisions of any building byelaws in force in the district in which the works are to be executed, any proposals for the erection therein of houses and the laying out and construction of new streets which do not form part of a housing scheme to which this section applies may, notwithstanding those provisions,

27

S 24 (19).

be carried out if the local authority or, on appeal, the Local Government Board are satisfied that they will involve departures from such provisions only to the like extent as in the case of the plans and specifications so approved, and that, where such plans and specifications have been approved subject to any conditions, the like conditions will be complied with in the case of proposals to which this subsection applies :

Provided that, in the application of this subsection to the administrative county of London, the expression "local authority" means the London County Council with respect to the matters within their jurisdiction and the Common Council of the City of London or the council of a metropolitan borough (as the case may be) with respect to other matters.

This subsection extends any relaxation of byelaws made in any district, under the previous subsection, to building proposals (in the same district) which are not housing schemes to which this section applies—see the next subsection. The proposals go first to the local authority, but there is an appeal to the Ministry. It is important that the limitations of this subsection be appreciated. To take an instance, the Ministry might approve plans for semi-detached houses with back gardens where there was no back road ; this would not mean that back roads could be dispensed with in all building schemes within the district.

(3.) The housing schemes to which this section applies are schemes made by a local authority or county council under the Housing Acts, or by a public utility society or housing trust, and approved by the Local Government Board.

Housing Acts. See section 52 (2) hereof.
Public utility society or housing trust. See sections 19 and 40 hereof.

(4.) Subject to any conditions which may be prescribed S. 24 (19). by the Local Government Board, the provisions of any building byelaws shall not apply to any new buildings and new streets constructed and laid out by a county council or local authority in accordance with plans and 8 Edw. 7. specifications approved by the Board of Agriculture 10 Edw. 7. and Fisheries under the Small Holdings and Allotments & 1 Geo. 5. Acts, 1908 and 1910, or any Act amending the same.

Prescribed. No conditions appear to have been prescribed as yet.

Generally. County councils and other local authorities, under the Small Holdings and Allotments Acts, 1908 and 1910, and the Land Settlement (Facilities) Act, 1919, will provide a number of houses suitable for the working classes, and in regard to such houses, which form part of the small holding scheme and are not, therefore, part of a housing scheme under this Act, there may be a relaxation of byelaws, subject to conditions specified by the Ministry.

25. (1.) Notwithstanding the provisions of any building byelaws, a local authority may, during a period of three years from the passing of this Act, consent to the erection and use for human habitation of any buildings erected or proposed to be erected in accordance with any regulations made by the Local Government Board. Consent of local authority to erection and use of buildings.

(2.) The local authority may attach to their consent any conditions which they may deem proper with regard to the situation, sanitary arrangements, and protection against fire of such buildings, and may fix and from time to time extend the period during which such buildings shall be allowed to be used for human habitation.

(3.) If any person feels aggrieved by the neglect or refusal of the local authority to give such consent or by the conditions on which such consent is given, or as to the period allowed for the use of such buildings for

S. 25 (19). human habitation, he may appeal to the Local Government Board, whose decision shall be final, and shall have effect as if it were the decision of the local authority, provided that the Board may, before considering any such appeal, require the appellant to deposit such sum, not exceeding ten pounds, to cover the costs of appeal as may be fixed by rules to be made by them.

This Act was passed on 31st July 1919. The regulations referred to are given on page 565.

As to building byelaws—see section 40 hereof (page 441).

7 Edw. 7. c. 53. (4.) Section twenty-seven of the Public Health Act, Amendment Act, 1907, shall not apply to any buildings to which this section applies.

The said section deals with temporary buildings, and contemplates different circumstances from those existing and expected during the three years to 31st July 1922.

(5.) In the application of this section to the administrative county of London, the expression "local authority" means the London County Council with respect to matters within their jurisdiction, and the Common Council of the City of London or the council of a metropolitan borough (as the case may be) with respect to other matters.

Miscellaneous

Byelaws respecting houses divided into separate tenements. 54 & 55 Vict c. 76. **26.** (1.) The power of making and enforcing byelaws under section ninety of the Public Health Act, 1875, and section ninety-four of the Public Health (London) Act, 1891, shall in the case of houses intended or used for occupation by the working classes be deemed to include the making and enforcing of byelaws—

This section practically re-enacts, in much wider S. 26 (19).
terms, section 16 of the 1909 Act, hereby repealed
(section 50) and the above-quoted sections.

By section 90 of the Public Health Act, 1875, as
amended by section 8 of the Housing of the Working
Classes Act, 1885, a local authority is empowered to make
byelaws for the following matters :—

(1.) For fixing and from time to time varying the
number of persons who may occupy a house or part
of a house which is let in lodgings or occupied by
members of more than one family, and for the separation of the sexes in a house so let or occupied ;

(2.) For the registration of houses so let or occupied ;

(3.) For the inspection of such houses ;

(4.) For enforcing drainage and the provision of privy
accommodation for such houses, and for promoting
cleanliness and ventilation in such houses ;

(5.) For the cleansing and lime-washing at stated
times of the premises, and for the paving of the
courts and courtyards thereof ;

(6.) For giving of notices and the taking of precautions
in case of any infectious disease.

Section 94 of the Public Health (London) Act, 1891,
is in practically identical terms.

The said section 90 does not apply to common lodging-
houses within the provisions of that Act.

Those wishing to pursue this subject in fuller detail
are recommended to *Lumley's Public Health* (8th
edition), pages 158 to 162.

For the Ministry's new model byelaws—see page 637.
As to the case where no byelaws or insufficient byelaws
are made—see subsection (5) below.

As to the administrative county of London—see
subsection (10) below.

As to repairs—see section 28 hereof.

(a) for fixing and from time to time varying the
number of persons who may occupy a house or part
of a house which is let in lodgings or occupied by
members of more than one family, and for separation of the sexes therein ;

(b) for the registration and inspection of such houses ;

(c) for enforcing drainage and promoting cleanliness and ventilation of such houses :

(d) for requiring provision adequate for the use of and readily accessible to each family of—

> (i) closet accommodation ;
>
> (ii) water supply and washing accommodation ;
>
> (iii) accommodation for the storage, preparation, and cooking of food ;

and, where necessary, for securing separate accommodation as aforesaid for every part of such house which is occupied as a separate dwelling ;

(e) for the keeping in repair and adequate lighting of any common staircase in such houses ;

(f) for securing stability, and the prevention of and safety from fire ;

(g) for the cleansing and redecoration of the premises at stated times, and for the paving of the courts and courtyards ;

(h) for the provision of handrails, where necessary, for all staircases of such houses ;

(i) for securing the adequate lighting of every room in such houses ;

and any such byelaws, in addition to any other penalty, may prohibit the letting for occupation by members of more than one family of any such house unless the same are complied with, subject in the case of houses so let or occupied at the time when such byelaws come into force to the allowance of a reasonable time for the execution of any works necessary to comply therewith.

By comparison with section 90 of the Public Health Act, 1875 (quoted above), it will be seen that most of paragraph (d), paragraphs (e) and (f), and from the beginning of paragraph (*h*) to the end of the subsection, S. 26 (19). are new.

Paragraph (a).   In *Weatheritt v. Cantlay* [1901] 2 K.B. 285, it was held that a block of artizans' dwellings (landlord non-resident) which was divided into tenements, occupied by different families, was not a " house let in lodgings or occupied by members of more than one family." In *Kyffin v. Simmons* [1903] 67 J.P. 227, it was held that the following was such a house : an ordinary six-roomed house, not specially constructed to be let in separate tenements, which had a common staircase and one common front door which was always kept open ; on each floor were two rooms let to and occupied by a separate family and the landlord was non-resident, &c.

As to building byelaws (new buildings)—see section 40 hereof, page 441.

Washing accommodation.   This is not laundry washing, but washing of the person, so that a mere tap without a sink would be insufficient.

" *Enforcing* " *and* " *Penalty.*"   Under section 183 of the Public Health Act, 1875, the local authority may impose penalties by the byelaws, not exceeding five pounds for each offence, and in the case of a continuing offence a further penalty not exceeding forty shillings for each day after written notice of the offence.

(2.) Such byelaws may impose the duty of executing any work required to comply therewith upon the owner within the meaning of the Public Health Acts of any such house, or upon any other person having an interest in the premises, and may prescribe the circumstances and conditions in and subject to which any such duty is to be discharged.

Owner.   Section 4 of the Public Health Act, 1875, contains the following definition : " Owner " means the person for the time being receiving the rack-rent of the lands or premises in connection with which the word is used, whether on his own account or as agent or trustee for any other person, or who would so receive the same if such lands or premises were let at a rack-rent.   " Rack-rent " means rent which is not less than two-thirds of the full net annual value of the property out of which the rent arises, and the full net annual value shall be taken to be the rent at which the property might reasonably be expected to let from year to year, free from all usual tenant's rates and taxes, and tithe commutation rent-charge (if any), and deducting therefrom the probable average annual cost of the repairs, insurance, and other expenses (if any) necessary to maintain the same in a state to command such rent.

(3.) For the purpose of discharging any duty so imposed, the owner or other person may at all reasonable times enter upon any part of the premises, and section fifty-one of the principal Act shall apply as if for the reference to the provisions of Part II of that Act there were substituted a reference to the provisions of such byelaws, and as if the persons on whom such duty is imposed were the owner and any inmate of the premises were the occupier of a dwelling-house.

This re-enacts section 16 (2) of the 1909 Act, repealed by section 50 hereof. In *Arlidge v. Islington Borough Council* [1909] 2 K.B. 127, it was held that a byelaw made under section 94 of the Public Health (London) Act, 1891 (see subsection (1) hereof), was bad because it required work to be done by a landlord who might have no right of entry. This subsection gives this right, and, in the latter part, enables it to be enforced under the said section 51 (see page 206).

(4.) Where an owner or other person has failed to execute any work which he has been required to execute under the byelaws, the local authority by whom such byelaws are enforced may, after giving to him not less than twenty-one days' notice in writing, themselves execute the works and recover the costs and expenses, and for that purpose the provisions of subsection (5) of section fifteen of the Housing, Town Planning, &c., Act, 1909, with respect to the execution of works and the recovery of expenses by local authorities, shall apply as S. 26 (19). if the owner or other person were the landlord, and with such other adaptations as may be necessary.

The costs and expenses may be recovered as a civil debt, or in annual instalments—see the said section 15 (5) (page 299).

This subsection re-enacts section 16 (3) of the 1909 Act, repealed by section 50 hereof.

(5.) If in the opinion of the Local Government Board premises are being occupied by members of more than one family or are intended to be converted for such occupation in the district of any local authority, and either no byelaws have been made by the local authority for the purposes specified in subsection (1) of this section, or the byelaws made are not sufficient properly to regulate such occupation or conversion, the Local Government Board may themselves make byelaws for such purposes which shall have effect and shall be enforced as if they had been made by the local authority.

The object of this subsection was explained by Dr. Addison as follows : " I have seen two people with two families, and sometimes even with three families, living in one room. . . . I am going to make provision that local authorities should not have byelaws allowing this kind of thing ; and it would mean that they would require housing accommodation so as to obviate that kind of overcrowding. It is to lay down a standard in drawing up a scheme as to the housing needs of the district that we want this provision " (Parliamentary Debates, Standing Committee A, 14th May 1919, col. 231).

The Minister has issued model byelaws (see page 637).

(6.) Where the person on whom obligations are imposed by any byelaws made for the purposes specified in subsection (1) of this section with respect to houses so occupied as aforesaid holds the premises under a lease

or agreement and satisfies the local authority that compliance with such byelaws is contrary to the provisions of
the lease or agreement, or that the whole or any part of
the expenses of carrying out the obligations ought to
be borne by his lessor or other superior landlord, the
local authority may make application to the county
court, and the county court may, after giving the lessor
or any such superior landlord an opportunity of being
heard,—

> (a) in the first case, order that the provisions of the
> lease or agreement be relaxed so far as they are
> inconsistent with the requirements of the byelaws ;
> (b) in the second case, grant to the person who carries
> out the works necessary for compliance with the
> byelaws, on proof to the satisfaction of the local
> authority that the works have been properly carried
> out, a charging order charging on the premises an
> annuity to repay the expenses properly incurred in
> carrying out the works or such part of those expenses
> as the county court consider ought to be so charged.

(7.) the annuity shall be of such amount and extend
over such number of years as the county court may
determine.

(8.) Subsection (3) of section thirty-six and section
thirty-seven except subsection (4) of the principal Act,
and section nineteen of the Housing, Town Planning,
&c., Act, 1909, shall apply to charging orders and annuities
under this section in like manner as to charging orders
and annuities under the said section thirty-six.

In the first case, i.e. where he satisfies the local authority
that compliance with the said byelaws is contrary to the
provisions of his lease, &c.

In the second case, i.e. where he satisfies the local

authority that the whole or any part of the expenses S. 26 (19). ought to be borne by his lessor or other superior landlord. Note that the charge is on the premises and not on any particular interest therein.

The principal Act. Section 36 (3) of the 1890 Act provides that the annuity "may be recovered by the person for the time being entitled to it by the same means and in like manner in all respects as if it were a rent-charge granted by deed out of the dwelling-house by the owner thereof." A rent-charge may be recovered by (1) distress after twenty-one days from the time appointed for payment ; (2) entry and receipt of the rents and profits if unpaid for forty days ; (3) if unpaid for forty days, by demise by deed to a trustee for a term of years on trust by mortgage, sale, or demise, &c. ; or by all or any of these means, &c. (Conveyance Act, 1881, section 44). It may also be recovered by an action—see *Hyde v. Berners* [1889] 53 J.P. 453, which deals with this and other questions arising.

Section 37 of the 1890 Act (see page 176) relates to the incidence of the charge—giving it certain priority, and allowing it to be transferred like a mortgage or rent-charge, &c. Note that subsection (4) of the said section 37 is omitted in respect of the charge granted under the present section.

Section 19 of the Act of 1909 (see page 309) gives power to the owner or other person interested to redeem the charge.

(9.) Where a local authority have themselves acquired a leasehold interest in any house under the powers conferred upon them by this Act, the Local Government Board, on the application of the local authority, may make a similar order with regard to the relaxation of the provisions of the lease and to charging an annuity on the premises as might, had the lessee not been the local authority, have been made on the application of the local authority by the county court, and in that case the decision of the Local Government Board as to the

S. 26 (19). amount and duration of any such annuity shall be final.

Powers conferred . . . by this Act. See section 12 hereof.

Similar order. See subsection (6) above.

(10.) This section shall apply to the administrative county of London with the following modifications :—

(a) As respects the county of London, the byelaws for the purposes specified in subsection (1) of this section shall be made by the London County Council, and any byelaws so made shall supersede any byelaws made for those purposes by the council of any metropolitan borough, and shall be observed and enforced by the council of each metropolitan borough except as regards byelaws for the purposes specified in paragraph (f) of subsection (1) which shall be enforced by the London County Council ;

(b) As respects the City of London, such byelaws shall be made and enforced by the common council except as regards byelaws for the purposes specified in paragraph (f) of subsection (1), which shall be made and enforced by the London County Council.

Administrative County of London. The County of London and the City of London. See section 93 of the 1890 Act.

As regards the water supply of tenement houses in London—see section 78 of the London County Council (General Powers) Act, 1907, which is summarised on page 64.

Power to authorise conversion of a house into several tenements.

27.. Where it is proved to the satisfaction of the county court on an application by the local authority or any person interested in a house that, owing to changes in the character of the neighbourhood in which such house is situate, the house cannot readily be let as a single tenement but could readily be let for occupation if converted into two or more tenements, and that, by reason of the S. 27 (19). provisions of the lease or of any restrictive covenant affecting the house or otherwise, such conversion is prohibited or restricted, the court, after giving any person interested an opportunity of being heard, may vary the terms of the lease or other instrument imposing the prohibition or restriction so as to enable the house to be so converted subject to such conditions and upon such terms as the court may think just.

This section is not restricted by any such term as " working classes "—*Johnston v. Maconochie*, Court of Appeal, 22nd October 1920.   But the person making the application has to prove the various facts specified, and it will not always be easy to do that, inasmuch as changes in the character of a neighbourhood are often of a very gradual character.   The fact that a house is difficult to let will not be sufficient in itself.

The point of turning houses into flats is also touched on in section 12 (1) hereof.   See also *Burton v. London and Counties House Property, &c., Co., Ltd. (The Times*, 18th May 1920).

The opportunity of being heard, given to " any person interested," would doubtless cover the owner or occupier of an adjoining house who might object to a neighbouring house being turned into a flat.

28. (1.) If the owner of any house suitable for occu- Repair of pation by persons of the working classes fails to make houses. and keep such house in all respects reasonably fit for human habitation then, without prejudice to any other powers, the local authority may serve a notice upon the owner of such house requiring him within a reasonable time, not being less than twenty-one days, specified in the notice, to execute such works as may be necessary to make the house in all respects reasonably fit for human habitation :

Provided that, if such house is not capable without

reconstruction of being rendered fit for human habitation, the owner may, within twenty-one days after the receipt of such notice, by written notice to the local authority declare his intention of closing the house for human habitation, and thereupon a closing order shall be deemed to have become operative in respect of such house. Any question arising under this proviso shall, in case of difference between the owner and the local authority, be determined by the Local Government Board.

(2.) If the notice of the local authority is not complied with, the local authority may—

(a) at the expiration of the time specified in that notice if no such notice as aforesaid has been given by the owner; and

(b) at the expiration of twenty-one days from the determination by the Local Government Board if such notice has been given by the owner, and the Local Government Board have determined that the house is capable without reconstruction of being made fit for human habitation;

do the work required to be done.

(3.) Any expenses incurred by the local authority under this section may be recovered in a court of summary jurisdiction, together with interest at a rate not exceeding five pounds per centum per annum from the date of service of a demand for the same till payment thereof from the owner, and until recovery of such expenses and interest the same shall be a charge on the premises. In all summary proceedings by the local authority for the recovery of any such expenses, the time within which such proceedings may be taken shall be reckoned from the date of the service of notice of demand.

(4.) The local authority may by order declare any

such expenses to be payable by monthly or annual S. 28 (19). instalments within a period not exceeding thirty years with interest at a rate not exceeding five pounds per centum per annum from the date of the service of notice of demand until the whole amount is paid, and any such instalments and interest or any part thereof may be recovered in a summary manner from the owner or occupier, and, if recovered from the occupier, may be deducted by him from the rent of such premises.

(5.) In this section "owner" shall have the same meaning as in the Public Health Act, 1875.

(6.) This section shall be deemed to be part of Part II. of the principal Act.

Owner. See note to section 26 (2).

Suitable for occupation. See note to section 29, below; and also the final note to section 12 (1).

Make and keep. The owner could be called upon to make an addition to the existing structure, i.e. something beyond a repair—see general note, below.

Any other powers. See, particularly, sections 15 and 17 of the 1909 Act and notes thereto; and also Chapter III, page 34, where the general question of unfit houses is discussed. The question of cost should be considered, as any irrecoverable loss under this section does not rank for financial assistance under section 7.

Serve a notice. See section 49 of the 1890 Act and note thereto.

For the forms of notices prescribed for use under this section—see the Housing Acts (Form of Orders and Notices) Order, 1919 (page 610).

Local authority. As this section is deemed to be part of Part II of the 1890 Act, the local authority is, in the case of a rural district, the rural district council; in the case of an urban district, the urban district council, or the corporation or council of a borough; in the case of a metropolitan borough, the borough council; and in the case of the City of London, the common council (see page 34). As to power of entry, see section 89 of the 1890 Act.

Closing Order. See section 17 (2) of the 1909 Act.

Determined by the Local Government Board. There is no appeal.

Charge on the premises. See page 177 ; and *Birmingham Corporation v. Baker*, L.R., 17 Ch., D. 782, 46 J.P. 42. The local authority does not appear to have power to borrow money for expenses under subsection (3).

Subsection (6). This enables the powers of Part II to be exercised in connection with the repair of houses, and also applies the remedy of section 5 hereof where the local authority fails to exercise its powers.

Generally. The house in question is one " suitable for occupation by persons of the working classes." This phrase is, doubtless, meant to exclude mansions and the like. The section applies to empty as well as occupied houses. Note that there is nothing in the section to compel the local authority to take action, and compare on this point section 26 (5).

The section is based largely on section 15 of the 1909 Act, which in practice it will, doubtless, almost entirely supersede.

Section 26 (1) hereof may be usefully read as an indication of the standard implied in the words " in all respects reasonably fit for human habitation," and, in particular, it would seem that each house ought to have a separate water supply, a separate closet, proper drainage and ventilation, and accommodation for the storage, preparation and cooking of food. *Proudfoot v. Hart* [1890] 25 Q.B.D. 42, is also helpful, though there does not appear to be any decided case upon the words, which are frequently used throughout the Acts. In case of dispute the Ministry does not decide.

Information to tenants of houses for the working classes.

29. In the case of houses intended or used for occupation by the working classes, the name and address of the medical officer of health for the district and of the landlord or other person who is directly responsible for keeping the house in all respects reasonably fit for human habitation shall be inscribed in every rent book or, where a rent book is not used, shall be delivered in writing to the tenant at the commencement of the tenancy and before any rent is demanded or collected ; and, if S. 29 (19). any person demands or collects any rent in contravention of the provisions of this section, he shall in respect of each offence be liable on summary conviction to a fine not exceeding forty shillings.

See section 28 above, and section 15 of the 1909 Act. By section 28 the owner is responsible ; section 15 of the 1909 Act makes the landlord responsible in respect of certain small dwellings. The landlord is not necessarily the owner. But the expression in section 28 is "any house suitable for occupation," while the words here are "intended or used for occupation." A house may be used for occupation in an emergency though it is not suitable. However, the chief difficulty is that there is no definition of "working classes" for the purposes of these provisions, and in many cases it will be puzzling to know whether or not the information named has to be given. Some general hints as to the meaning of the term are given in *London County Council v. Davis* [1897] 62 J.P. 68 ; *Crow v. Davis* [1903] 67 J.P. 319 ; and *White v. St. Marylebone Council* [1915] 3 K.B. 249.

By the Statement of Rates Act, 1919, every demand or receipt for rent, which includes rates paid by the owner, shall state the amount of such rates, but only one statement is required per period.

30. (1.) Where it is proved to the satisfaction of the court, on an application in accordance with rules of court of any person entitled to any interest in any land used in whole or in part as a site for houses for the working classes, that the premises on the land are or are likely to become dangerous or injurious to health or unfit for human habitation, and that the interests of the applicant are thereby prejudiced, or that the applicant should be entrusted with the carrying out of a scheme of reconstruction or improvement approved by the local authority

Power to authorise superior landlord to enter and execute works.

28

of the district in which the land is situate, the court may make an order empowering the applicant forthwith to enter on the land and within the time fixed by the order to execute such works as may be necessary, and may order that any lease or agreement for a lease held from the applicant and any derivative underlease shall be determined, subject to such conditions and to the payment of such compensation as the court may think just.

(2.) The court shall include in its order provisions to secure that the proposed works are carried out and may authorise the local authority in whose area the land is situated or which has approved a scheme of reconstruction or improvement under this section to exercise such supervision or take such action as may be necessary for the purpose.

(3.) For the purposes of this section, " court " means the High Court of Justice, and the Court of Chancery of the county palatine of Lancaster or Durham or the county court, where those courts respectively have jurisdiction.

The general object of this section is to enable the superior landlord to take steps to prevent the property degenerating into a slum. If it did so degenerate and was acquired under section 9 hereof, there would be a serious loss to the superior landlord. The order of the court will be conditional on the proposed works being carried out.

Extension of powers under Settled Land Acts. **31.** The powers conferred upon a tenant for life by the Settled Land Acts, 1882 to 1890, shall include the following further powers :—

    (a) A power to make a grant in fee simple or absolutely, or a lease for any term of years, for a nominal price or rent or for less than the best price or rent which

could be obtained for the purpose of the erection S. 31 (19).
thereon of dwellings for the working classes or the
provision of gardens to be held in connection therewith.   Provided that no more than two acres in the
case of land situate in an urban district or ten acres
in the case of land situate in a rural district shall be
granted as a site for such dwellings or gardens in
any one parish without payment of the full price
or rent for the excess, except under an order of the
court ;

(b) A power, where money is required for the provision
of dwellings available for the working classes, to raise
the money on mortgage of the settled land or of any
part thereof by conveyance of the fee simple or other
the estate subject to the settlement or by creation of
a term of years in the settled land or any part thereof
or otherwise, and the money so raised shall be
capital money for that purpose and may be paid or
applied accordingly.

It may be convenient to note here the other changes
in the Settled Land Acts effected by the Housing Acts.
Section 74 (1) of the Act of 1890 reads as follows :—
    " The Settled Land Act, 1882, should be amended as
    follows :—
        " (a) Any sale, exchange, or lease of land in pur-
        suance of the said Act, when made for the
        purpose of the erection on such land of
        dwellings for the working classes, may be
        made at such price, or for such consideration,
        or for such rent, as having regard to the said
        purpose, and to all the circumstances of the
        case, is the best that can be reasonably
        obtained, notwithstanding that a higher price,
        consideration, or ' rent might have been
        obtained if the land were sold, exchanged, or
        leased for another purpose ;
        " (b) The improvements on which capital money

arising under the Settled Land Act, 1882, may be expended, enumerated in section twenty-five of the said Act, and referred to in section thirty of the said Act, shall, in addition to cottages for labourers, farm servants, and artizans, include the provision of dwellings available for the working classes, either by means of building new buildings or by means of the reconstruction, enlargement, or improvement of existing buildings so as to make them available for the purpose, if that provision of dwellings is in the opinion of the court not injurious to the estate or is agreed to by the tenant for life and the trustees of the settlement."

The above paragraph (*b*) is printed as per section 7 (1) of the 1909 Act, and subsection (2) thereof reads :—

" The provision by a tenant for life, at his own expense, of dwellings available for the working classes on any settled land shall not be deemed to be an injury to any interest in reversion or remainder in that land ; provided that the powers conferred upon a tenant for life by this subsection should not be exercised by him without the previous approval in writing of the trustees of the settlement."

It is to be noted that the expression " working classes " in the above-quoted paragraphs (*a*) and (*b*) of the 1890 Act has effect as if it " included all classes of persons who earn their livelihood by wages or salaries ; provided that this section shall apply only to buildings of a rateable value not exceeding £100 per annum " (Settled Land Act, 1890, section 18). But apparently this definition does not apply to section 7 (2) of the 1909 Act (above-quoted), nor to the present section of the 1919 Act (i.e. section 31).

Briefly, paragraph (*a*) relaxes the provisions of the Settled Land Act, 1882 : the tenant for life is not required to secure the best price which could be secured in any event, but only the best price having regard to the object stated (i.e. erection of working class dwellings).

Paragraph (*b*) as amended provides that capital money may be expended in providing dwellings *available for the working classes*, without recourse to the courts if the tenant for life and the trustees agree. In *Re Caverley's*

Settled Estates [1904] 1 Ch. 150, it was held that dwellings S. 31 (19).
suitable for the working classes but actually occupied
by tenants of a different class were not *available* for the
working classes.   The improvements referred to include
those under Part I of the Act of 1890 (unhealthy areas)—
see sections 6 (3) and 12 (6) of that Act.

The effect of the 1919 Act, section 31, is to enable the
tenant for life to (*a*) practically give land, within limits,
to local authorities or any other body or person for the
erection thereon of working class dwellings, or for gardens
(e.g. allotments), and (*b*) to raise money by mortgage of
the settled land for the provision of such dwellings.

32. If any owner of a house in respect of which a   Penalty on
re-letting
closing order is in force, or any other person, lets or   house
ordered to
attempts to let or occupies or permits to be occupied   be closed.
that house or any part thereof as a dwelling-house, he
shall on summary conviction be liable to a fine not
exceeding twenty pounds.

Closing order.   See section 17 of the 1909 Act.
Permits to be occupied.   By section 17 (4) of the 1909
Act if the tenant fails to quit the closed house, the local
authority may obtain an order to quit from the courts.
Suppose the local authority fails to exercise this power
and the owner takes no steps to turn the tenant out, is
he permitting the house to be occupied within this section ?
The word used in the marginal note is " re-letting," and
it would seem that this is the offence aimed at, viz.
re-letting *as a dwelling-house.*
Not exceeding £20, however long the offence continues.

33. The enactments regulating the provision to be   Amendment
of s. 11 of
made under Part I of the principal Act for the accom-   principal
Act.
modation of persons of the working classes displaced by
the operation of a scheme under that Part shall be the
same in cases where the area comprised in the scheme
is situate in the county or city of London as in other
cases, and accordingly subsection (1) of section eleven
of that Act, and in subsection (2) the words " where "

S. 33 (19). and "comprises an area situate elsewhere than in the county or city of London, it" shall be repealed.

Arrangements between the Local Government Board and other Departments. **34.** The Local Government Board may make arrangements with any other Government Department for the exercise or performance by that Department of any of their powers and duties under the Housing Acts which in their opinion could be more conveniently so exercised and performed, and in such case the Department and officers of the Department shall have the same powers and duties as are by the Housing Acts conferred on the Local Government Board and their officers.

As, for instance, the Board of Agriculture in connection with small holdings.

Provisions of Housing Acts not to be affected by the Increase of Rent and Mortgage Interest (War Restrictions) Act, 1915. 5 & 6 Geo. 5. c. 97. **35.** Nothing in the Increase of Rent and Mortgage Interest (War Restrictions) Act, 1915, or in the enactments amending that Act, shall be deemed to affect the provisions of section seventeen of the Housing, Town Planning, &c., Act, 1909, or to prevent a local authority from obtaining possession of any house the possession of which is required by them for the purpose of exercising their powers under the Housing Acts or under any scheme made under those Acts.

Section 5 (1) of the Increase of Rent and Mortgage Interest (Restrictions) Act, 1920, provides that no order for the recovery of a dwelling-house to which that Act applies, or for the ejectment of a tenant therefrom, shall be made so long as the tenant fulfils the conditions of his tenancy, &c. (see p. 715). The present section provides that an order to quit under section 17 (4) of the Act of 1909 is not an order within the above section 5 (1).

Compensation in cases of subsidence. 54 & 55 Vict. c. 40. **36.** Notwithstanding anything in section fifty of the Brine Pumping (Compensation for Subsidence) Act, 1891, a local authority or county council shall be entitled to

compensation in accordance with the provisions of that S. 36 (19).
Act in respect of any injury or damage to any houses
belonging to such local authority or council, and provided
under a housing scheme towards the losses on which the
Local Government Board is liable to contribute under this
Act.

While the Act quoted makes provision for compensation to the owners of property suffering for subsidence of
ground caused by the pumping of brine, section 50
specifically excludes local authorities, amongst others,
from the right to compensation under the Act. The
present section removes that disability as, obviously, is
necessary, since it prevents or discourages local authorities
from building.

37. The provision of houses under the Housing Acts Application
of Act to
shall be deemed to be a local sanitary requirement for New Forest.
the purpose of the New Forest (Sale of Lands for Public 1 Edw. 7.
c. cxcviii.
Purposes) Act, 1902. Provided that the total area of Local and
Private.
land being part of the New Forest which may be sold
or let for the provision of houses shall not exceed 30
acres.

In many parts of the New Forest no land is available
for building houses for the working classes except Crown
lands, and the Act quoted empowers the Commissioners
of Woods to sell such land for sanitary purposes only.

38. The Commissioners of Woods may under and in Extension of
powers of
accordance with the provisions of the Crown Lands Commissioners of
Acts, 1829 to 1906, sell or let to a local authority for the Woods.
purposes of Part III of the principal Act any part of the
land described on the duplicate plans which have been
deposited with the Clerk of Parliaments and the Clerk of
the House of Commons notwithstanding that such land
may be part or parcel of a royal park, if the Local Government Board, after holding a local inquiry, are satisfied

S. 38 (19). that the acquisition of the land by the local authority for such purposes as aforesaid is desirable in the national interest.

The land referred to is situated at the extreme eastern boundary of Bushey Park, near Hampton Court. It has been used for grazing His Majesty's horses, and, latterly, for allotments. The Commissioners could not otherwise sell land which is part of a royal park (see also section 74 of the 1909 Act), and though it is open to question whether this piece of land ever was part of the royal park, it was thought best by this section to meet all the circumstances.

Procedure and minor amendments of Housing Acts.

39. (1.) The amendments specified in the second column of the Second Schedule to this Act (which relate to procedure under Part I and Part II of the principal Act and to minor details) shall be made in the provisions

3 Edw. 7, c. 39.

of the principal Act the Housing of the Working Classes Act, 1903, and the Housing, Town Planning, &c., Act, 1909, specified in the first column of that schedule.

(2.) Sections fourteen and fifteen of the Housing, Town Planning, &c., Act, 1909, shall be deemed to be part of Part II of the principal Act.

Second Schedule. See page 556. The amendments have been noted in the text of the Acts to which they refer. For the most part they considerably simplify the procedure.

Sections 14 *and* 15. As to the point of subsection (2)—see section 36 (1) of the 1890 Act and note thereto, headed "Works required." The landlord doing the repairs required under the said section 15 cán get a charging order.

Construction.

40. This Part of this Act shall be construed as one with the principal Act, and any provisions of this Part of this Act which supersede or amend any provisions of the principal Act shall be deemed to be part of that Part of the principal Act in which the provisions super-

seded or amended are contained, and references in this S. 40 (19).
Part of this Act to the principal Act or to any provision
of the principal Act shall be construed as references to
that Act or provision as amended by any subsequent
enactment, including this Part of this Act ;

In this Part of this Act—

The expression "houses for the working classes"
has the same meaning as the expression "lodging-
houses for the working classes" has in the principal
Act.

See section 53 of the 1890 Act, page 207.

The expression "sale" includes sale in consideration
of an annual rent-charge, and the expression
"sell" has a corresponding meaning ;

The expression "public utility society" means a
society registered under the Industrial and Provident Societies Acts, 1893 to 1913, the rules
whereof prohibit the payment of any interest or
dividend at a rate exceeding six per cent. per
annum ;

The expression "housing trust" means a corporation or body of persons which, by the terms of
its constituent instrument, is required to devote
the whole of its funds, including any surplus
which may arise from its operations, to the provision of houses for persons the majority of whom
are in fact members of the working classes, and
to other purposes incidental thereto ;

The expression "building byelaws" includes byelaws made by any local authority under section
one hundred and fifty-seven of the Public Health
Act, 1875, as amended by any subsequent enact-

S. 40 (19).

ment, with respect to new buildings including the drainage thereof and new streets, and any enactments in any local Acts dealing with the construction and drainage of new buildings and the laying out and construction of new streets, and any byelaws made with respect to such matters under any such local Act.

"Building Byelaws"—see sections 24 and 25 hereof. Section 157 of the Public Health Act, 1875, reads as follows :—

Power to make byelaws respecting new buildings, &c.

"Every urban authority may make byelaws with respect to the following matters ; that is to say :

" (1.) With respect to the level width and construction of new streets, and the provisions for the sewerage thereof ;

" (2.) With respect to the structure of walls, foundations, roofs and chimneys of new buildings, for securing stability and the prevention of fires, and for purposes of health ;

" (3.) With respect to the sufficiency of the space about buildings to secure a free circulation of air, and with respect to the ventilation of buildings ;

" (4.) With respect to the drainage of buildings, to water-closets, earth-closets, privies, ashpits and cesspools in connection with buildings, and for the closing of buildings or parts of buildings unfit for human habitation, and to prohibition of their use for such habitation ;

"And they may further provide for the observance of such byelaws by enacting therein such provisions as they think necessary as to the giving of notices, as to the deposit of plans and sections by persons intending to lay out streets or to construct buildings, as to inspection by the urban authority, and as to the power of such authority (subject to the provisions of this Act) to remove, alter, or pull down any work begun or done in contravention of such byelaws : Provided that no byelaws made under this section shall affect any building erected in any place (which at the time of the passing of this Act is included in an urban sanitary district) before the Local Government Acts came into force in S. 40 (19). such place, or any building erected in any place (which at the time of the passing of this Act is not included in an urban sanitary district) before such place becomes constituted or included in an urban district, or by virtue of any order of the Local Government Board subject to this enactment.

"The provisions of this section and of the two last preceding sections shall not apply to buildings belonging to any railway company and used for the purposes of such railway under any Act of Parliament."

This section was extended and amended by the Public Health Act, 1890, section 23, in places where Part III of that Act has been adopted. The section provides as follows :

" (1.) Section one hundred and fifty-seven of the Public Health Act, 1875, shall be extended so as to empower every urban authority to make byelaws with respect to the following matters; that is to say :

"The keeping water-closets supplied with sufficient water for flushing ;

"The structure of floors, hearths, and staircases, and the height of rooms intended to be used for human habitation ;

"The paving of yards and open spaces in connection with dwelling-houses ; and

"The provision in connection with the laying out of new streets of secondary means of access where necessary for the purpose of the removal of house refuse and other matters.

" (2.) Any byelaws under that section as above extended with regard to the drainage of buildings, and to water-closets, earth-closets, privies, ashpits, and cesspools, in connection with buildings, and the keeping water-closets supplied with sufficient water for flushing, may be made so as to affect buildings erected before the times mentioned in the said section.

" (3.) The provisions of the said section (as amended by this Act), so far as they relate to byelaws with respect to the structure of walls and foundations of new buildings for purposes of health, and with respect to the matters mentioned in subsections (3) and (4) of the said section, and with respect to the structure of floors, the height of rooms to be used for human habitation, and to the

S. 40 (19). keeping of water-closets supplied with sufficient water for flushing, shall be extended so as to empower rural authorities to make byelaws in respect to the said matters, and to provide for the observance of such byelaws, and to enforce the same as if such powers were conferred on the rural authorities by virtue of an order of the Local Government Board made on the day when this part of this Act is adopted ; and section one hundred and fifty-eight of the Public Health Act, 1875, shall also apply to any such authority, and shall be in force in every rural district where this part of this Act is adopted.

" (4.) Every local authority may make byelaws to prevent buildings which have been erected in accordance with byelaws made under the Public Health Acts from being altered in such a way that if at first so constructed they would have contravened the byelaws."

See also sections 15, 16, 17, 22, 23, 24, 25, 26, 27 and 33 of the Public Health Act, 1907.

The subject of building byelaws is discussed at great length in *Lumley's Public Health*, at page 325 *et seq.* (8th edition).

In many local Acts there are provisions dealing with the construction and drainage of new buildings, &c.

As to other byelaws—see section 26 hereof.

Application to London of certain provisions of the Housing Acts.

41. (1.) For the purposes of the application of Part III of the principal Act to the county of London—

(a) the London County Council shall be the local authority for the county, to the exclusion of any other authority, so far as regards the provision of any houses outside the administrative county of London ;

(b) the council of a metropolitan borough shall be the local authority for the metropolitan borough, to the exclusion of any other authority, so far as regards the provision of houses within the metropolitan borough ;

Provided—

(i) that nothing in this section shall prejudice or affect the rights, powers and privileges of the

London County Council in regard to any lands, S. 41 (19). buildings or works acquired, provided or carried out by the County Council before the date of the passing of this Act; and

(ii) that where the London County Council are satisfied that there is situate within the area of a metropolitan borough land suitable for development for housing, the county council may submit a scheme for the approval of the Local Government Board for the development of such land to meet the needs of districts situate outside the area of such borough, and the county council may carry into effect any scheme which is so approved, and such approval shall have the like effect as if it had been given under section one of this Act;

(c) the Local Government Board may by order direct that any of the powers or duties of the council of a metropolitan borough under Part III of the principal Act shall be transferred to the London County Council, or that any of the powers or duties of the London County Council under Part III of the principal Act shall be transferred to the council of a metropolitan borough.

(2.) Any loss which may be incurred by the council of a metropolitan borough in carrying out a scheme to which section seven of this Act applies shall be repaid to them by the London County Council, and any payments so made by the London County Council shall be deemed to have been made as part of the expenses incurred by them in carrying out a scheme to which that section applies.

(3.) The London County Council and the Common Council of the City of London may at any time enter

S. 41 (19). into an agreement for carrying out any scheme for the purposes of Part I or Part III of the principal Act, and for the apportionment of the expenses incurred in carrying out such scheme, and, if the scheme is a scheme to which section seven of this Act applies, any payments made under such apportionment by the county council and the common council shall be deemed to have been made as part of the expenses incurred in carrying out a scheme to which that section applies.

Part III relates to the provision of houses for the working classes, which is also the chief purpose of the present Act.

County of London. The administrative county of London is defined in section 93 of the 1890 Act. It has an area of 116·9 square miles. Its population in 1911 was 4,521,685, and its assessable value on 6th April 1917 was £45,341,004. It was formed out of the parishes and places sending representatives to the Metropolitan Board of Works.

Local Authority. See page 11. The local authorities exercising jurisdiction in the administrative County of London (excluding the City) are the London County Council and twenty-eight metropolitan borough councils.

Common Council of the City of London. This is the local authority for the city. Part II of the Act of 1890 is not included, as it relates to unhealthy houses as distinct from unhealthy areas, and the London County Council has no authority under it.

Object of the section. The object of this section is to meet the special problem of London with its overlapping authorities, and the solution offered has been generally accepted. There appears to be one point, however, calling for notice. If the London County Council under proviso (ii) submits a scheme within the area of a metropolitan borough there is nothing to compel it to notify the borough thereof, and as the scheme may affect the projects of the borough it will be readily seen that it would like to have such notice. To meet this Dr. Addison, during the committee stage of the Bill, gave a pledge on behalf of the Ministry as follows : " Where it is a

material scheme, or where there is any reason to consult S. 41 (19).
borough councils, we will do so, and give them a fair
opportunity of being heard. I will go further and say
that we will send to the borough council information
when schemes are submitted to us" (Parliamentary
Debates, Standing Committee A, 15th May 1919, col.
295).

On the words "outside the administrative county of
London"—see section 1 of the 1900 Act.

Proviso (i) makes it clear that the London County
Council can manage and develop properties which it has
already in the areas of some of the metropolitan boroughs.

Proviso (ii) is above referred to. The concluding
words make it clear that the scheme will qualify for the
State subsidy under section 7 hereof.

Paragraph (c) covers emergencies, and also defaults
by either the London County Council or a borough
council in preparing and carrying out housing schemes.
It is in addition to sections 3 and 4 hereof.

PART II

TOWN PLANNING

42. It shall not be necessary for a local authority to
obtain the authority of the Local Government Board
to prepare or adopt a town planning scheme, and accordingly for subsection (2) of section fifty-four of the Housing,
Town Planning, &c., Act, 1909 (hereinafter referred to
as the Act of 1909), the following provision shall be
substituted :— *Removal of necessity to obtain previous authorisation of Local Government Board to preparation or adoption of town planning scheme*

"(2.) A local authority within the meaning of this
Part of this Act may by resolution decide—

"(a) to prepare a town planning scheme with
reference to any land within or in the neighbourhood of their area in regard to which a
scheme may be made under this Act ; or

"(b) to adopt, with or without any modifica-

S. 42 (19).

tions, any town planning scheme proposed by all or any of the owners of any land with respect to which the local authority are themselves by this Act authorised to prepare a scheme :

" Provided that—

" (i) if any such resolution of a local authority extends to land not within the area of that local authority, the resolution shall not have effect until it is approved by the Local Government Board, and the Board may, in giving their approval, vary the extent of the land to be included within the area of the proposed town planning scheme ; and

" (ii) where any local authorities are desirous of acting jointly in the preparation or adoption of a town planning scheme, they may concur in appointing out of their respective bodies a joint committee for the purpose, and in conferring with or without restrictions on any such committee any powers which the appointing councils might exercise for the purpose, and the provisions of sections fifty-seven and fifty-eight of the Local Government Act, 1894, in regard to joint committees, shall, with the necessary modifications, apply to any joint committee so appointed."

This is discussed on page 327.

Extension of power to make regulations as to procedure.

43. (1.) The power of the Local Government Board of making regulations under section fifty-six of the Act of 1909 shall include power to make regulations as to the procedure consequent on the passing of a resolution by a local authority to prepare or adopt a town planning scheme, and provision shall be made by those regulations

for securing that a local authority after passing such S. 43 (19)
a resolution shall proceed with all reasonable speed with
the preparation or adoption of the town planning scheme,
and shall comply with any regulations as to steps to be
taken for that purpose, including provisions enabling the
Local Government Board in the case of default or dilatoriness on the part of the local authority to act in the place
and at the expense of the local authority.

(2.) Subsection (2) of section fifty-six of the Act of 1909
shall have effect as if the following paragraph were added
thereto :

> " For securing that the council of the county in
> which any land proposed to be included in a town
> planning scheme is situated (1) shall be furnished
> with a notice of any proposal to prepare or adopt
> such a scheme and with a copy of the draft scheme
> before the scheme is made, and (2) shall be entitled
> to be heard at any public local inquiry by the Local
> Government Board in regard to the scheme."

See page 33.

44. The proviso to subsection (4) of section fifty-four Repeal of
and the proviso to subsection (2) of section fifty-five of provisos to
ss. 54 (4) &
the Act of 1909 (which provisos relate to the publication 55 (2) of
9 Edw. 7.
and laying before Parliament of town planning schemes) c. 44.
are hereby repealed.

45. The Local Government Board may by special or Power to
general order provide that where a resolution to prepare permit development of
or adopt a town planning scheme has been passed, or estates
pending
where before the passing of this Act the preparation or preparation
and approval
adoption of a town planning scheme has been authorised, of town
planning
the development of estates and building operations may schemes.
be permitted to proceed pending the preparation or

29

S. 45 (19).   adoption and approval of the town planning scheme, subject to such conditions as may be prescribed by the order, and where such permission has been given the provisions of subsection (2) of section fifty-eight of the Act of 1909 which relates to the rights of compensation shall have effect as if the following proviso were added thereto :

> " Provided also that this provision shall not apply as respects any building erected, contract made, or other thing done in accordance with a permission granted in pursuance of an order of the Local Government Board allowing the development of estates and building operations to proceed pending the preparation or adoption and approval of the scheme, and the carrying out of works so permitted shall not prejudice any claim of any person to compensation in respect of property injuriously affected by the making of the scheme."

This is discussed on page 336.

Resolution. See section 42, above.

Authorised. Previously to the passing of this Act authorisation was necessary—see section 42, above.

Preparation of town planning schemes.   **46.** (1.) The council of every borough or other urban district containing on the first day of January nineteen hundred and twenty-three a population according to the last census for the time being of more than twenty thousand shall, within three years after that date, prepare and submit to the Local Government Board a town planning scheme in respect of all land within the borough or urban district in respect of which a town planning scheme may be made under the Act of 1909.

(2.) Without prejudice to the powers of the council under the Act of 1909, every scheme to which this section

applies shall deal with such matters as may be deter- S. 46 (19).
mined by regulations to be made by the Local Government Board.

(3.) Every regulation so made shall be laid before
both Houses of Parliament as soon as may be after it
is made, and, if an address is presented by either House
within twenty-one days on which that House has sat
next after any such regulation is laid before it praying
that the regulation may be annulled, His Majesty in
Council may annul the regulation, but without prejudice
to the validity of anything previously done thereunder.

Within three years, i.e. before 1st January 1926. If
default is made—see the next section, particularly subsection (3) thereof.

May be made. . . . See section 54 of the Act of 1909.

Powers of the council. See sections 54–66 of the Act
of 1909.

Regulations. None have yet been made.

Subsection (3). See section 7 (3) and note thereto.

47. (1.) Where the Local Government Board are Power of
Local
Government
Board to
require town
planning
scheme.
satisfied after holding a public local inquiry that a town
planning scheme ought to be made by a local authority
as respects any land in regard to which a town planning
scheme may be made under the Act of 1909, the Board
may by order require the local authority to prepare and
submit for their approval such a scheme, and, if the
scheme is approved by the Board, to do all things necessary for enforcing the observance of the scheme or any
provisions thereof effectively, and for executing any
works which, under the scheme or under Part II of the
Act of 1909, the authority are required to execute.

(2.) Any order made by the Local Government Board
under this section shall have the same effect as a resolution of the local authority deciding to prepare a town

S. 47 (19).   planning scheme in respect of the area in regard to which the order is made.

(3.) If the local authority fail to prepare a scheme to the satisfaction of the Board within such time as may be prescribed by the order, or to enforce the observance of the scheme or any provisions thereof effectively, or to execute any such works as aforesaid, the Board may themselves act, or in the case of a borough or other urban district the population of which is less than 20,000, or of a rural district, may, if the Board think fit, by order, empower the county council to act in the place and at the expense of the local authority.

Public local inquiry. See section 85 of the Act of 1890, and notes thereto.

Under the Act of 1909. See sections 54 to 67 (page 324, *et seq.*).

Resolution of the local authority. See section 42 hereof.

Subsection (3). This section is like section 61 of the Act of 1909 with the difference that in case of the local authority's default " the Board may themselves act," &c. It is not quite clear that the Board (Ministry) may act at the expense of the local authority—compare section 4 (2) hereof ; and as to the recovery of the county council's expenses—compare section 3 (2) hereof.

Consequential and minor amendments.   **48.** The amendments specified in the second column of the Third Schedule to this Act (which relate to consequential and minor matters) shall be made in the provisions of Part II of the Act of 1909 mentioned in the first column of that schedule.

PART III

ACQUISITION OF SMALL DWELLINGS

49. The following amendments shall be made in the Small Dwellings Acquisition Act, 1899 :—

(a) In subsection (1) of section one " eight hundred pounds " shall be substituted for " four hundred pounds " as the limit on the market value of houses in respect of which advances may be made :

(b) In paragraph (a) subsection (1) of section one " eighty-five per cent." shall be substituted for " four-fifths " with respect to the limitation on the amount which may be advanced :

(c) Paragraph (b) of subsection (1) of section one shall be repealed :

(d) A receipt under seal in the form set out in Part I of the Fourth Schedule to this Act (with such variations and additions (if any) as may be thought expedient) endorsed on, or written at the foot of, or annexed to, a mortgage for money advanced under the Act which states the name of the person who pays the money and is executed by a local authority shall, without any re-conveyance, re-assignment or release, operate as a discharge of the mortgaged property from all principal money and interest secured by, and from all claims under the mortgage, and shall have such further operation as is specified in Part II of that schedule :

Provided that—

(a) nothing in this provision shall affect the right of any person to require the re-conveyance, re-assignment, surrender, release, or transfer to be executed in lieu of a receipt ; and

S. 49 (19).

(*b*) the receipt shall not be liable to stamp duty and shall be granted free of cost to the person who pays the money.

The Act with these amendments noted therein is printed on page 257.

Note paragraph (*d*) and that the deed discharging the mortgage is not liable to stamp duty. For the Fourth Schedule—see page 463.

PART IV

GENERAL

Repeals.

50. The enactments specified in the Fifth Schedule to this Act are hereby repealed to the extent specified in the third column of that schedule.

Extent.

51. This Act shall not extend to Scotland or Ireland.

There are separate Acts for Scotland and Ireland.

Short title

52. (1.) This Act may be cited as the Housing, Town Planning, &c., Act, 1919.

(2.) The Housing of the Working Classes Acts, 1890 to 1909, and this Act so far as it amends those Acts may be cited together as the Housing Acts, 1890 to 1919, and are in this Act referred to as the " Housing Acts."

(3.) Part II of the Housing, Town Planning, &c., Act, 1909, and Part II of this Act may be cited together as the Town Planning Acts, 1909 and 1919.

(4.) The Small Dwellings Acquisition Act, 1899, and Part III of this Act may be cited together as the Small Dwellings Acquisition Acts, 1899 and 1919.

The Housing of the Working Classes Acts, 1890 to 1909, are defined in section 76 of the 1909 Act. The definition of " Housing Acts " now given removes some

confusion caused by the definition given in section 51 S. 52 (19).
of the 1909 Act.   But even yet Parts III and IV of the
1909 Act are excluded, although in Part IV there is
section 76 which contains the definition of " the Housing
of the Working Classes Acts, 1890 to 1909."

For construction of Part I of this Act—see section 40.

SCHEDULES

FIRST SCHEDULE

Section 9
(see p. 387).

RULES FOR DETERMINING THE AMOUNT OF REDUCTION OF COMPENSATION

(a) The value of the whole of the land included in
the scheme shall first be ascertained on the basis of its
value as a cleared site available for development in
accordance with the requirements of the building byelaws
in force in the district.

(b) The value of the whole of the said land shall next
be ascertained on the basis of its value as a cleared site
subject to the requirements of the scheme as to the
provision to be made for the re-housing of persons of the
working classes or the laying out of open spaces on the
land or any part thereof.

(c) The difference between the amounts ascertained
under paragraph (a) and paragraph (b) shall then be
computed.

(d) The amount by which the compensation payable
for the respective interests in the land to which section
nine of this Act applies, as ascertained in accordance
with the principle laid down in that section, is to be
reduced shall be a fraction thereof equal to the amount
arrived at under paragraph (c) when divided by the
amount arrived at under paragraph (a).

2nd Sch. (19).

SECOND SCHEDULE

Section 39 (see p. 440).

AMENDMENTS AS TO PROCEDURE UNDER PART I AND PART II OF THE PRINCIPAL ACT AND MINOR AMENDMENTS OF THE HOUSING ACTS

Enactment to be amended.	Nature of Amendment.
Housing of the Working Classes Act, 1890 (53 & 54 Vict. c. 70) : s. 5 (2)	For the words " two or more justices " there shall be substituted the words " any justice," and for the word " twelve " there shall be substituted the word " six."
s. 6 (3)	For the words " the person entitled to the first estate of freehold in any property comprised in the scheme, or with the concurrence of such person " there shall be substituted the words " any person having such interest in any property comprised in the scheme as may be sufficient to enable him to carry out and effect the same."
s. 12 (6)	For the words " the person entitled to the first estate of freehold in any land comprised in an improvement scheme " there shall be substituted the words " any person having such interest in any land comprised in an improvement scheme as may be sufficient to enable him to carry out and effect the same."
s. 7	After the words " the local authority shall " there shall be inserted the word " forthwith."
s. 7 (a)	The words " during three consecutive weeks in the month of September or October or November " shall be omitted. Substitute " a " for " some one and the same."
s. 7 (b)	The words " during the month next following the month in which such advertisement is published " shall be omitted. After " occupier " there shall be inserted " (except tenants for a month or a less period than a month)."

Enactment to be amended.	Nature of Amendment.	2nd Sch. (19).
Housing of the Working Classes Act, 1890 (53 & 54 Vict. c. 70) (*contd.*) :		
s. 8 (5)	For the word ' copy " ' there shall be substituted the word " notice." The words " except tenants for a month or a less period than a month " shall be omitted.	
s. 12 (1)	At end there shall be inserted the words " provided that the Local Authority shall not be required to acquire any leasehold interest in any property comprised in a scheme which can be allowed to expire without unduly delaying the execution of the scheme."	
s. 14	The whole section shall be omitted.	
s. 16 (1)	For the words ' twelve or more ratepayers have complained " there shall be substituted the words " complaint has been made," and after the word " district " there shall be inserted the words " by any person or persons competent under the foregoing provisions of this part of this Act to make such complaint," and for the word " ratepayers " there shall be substituted the words " complainant or complainants, as the case may be." For the words from " and upon " to " the confirming authority shall " there shall be substituted the words " and the confirming authority may."	
s. 31 (1)	For the words ' in any district any four or more householders living in or near to any street" there shall be substituted the words " any justice of the peace acting for a district, or any four or more householders in a district," and the words " in or near that street " shall be omitted.	
s. 31 (2)	Before the word " householders " there shall be inserted the words " justice of the peace or ".	
s. 38 (2)	Before the words " any four or more inhabitant householders of " there shall be inserted the words " any justice of the peace acting for a district, or ".	

2nd Sch. (19).	Enactment to be amended.	Nature of Amendment.
	Housing of the Working Classes Act, 1890 (53 & 54 Vict. c. 70) (*contd.*):	
	s. 45 (1)	After the words "where the medical officer of health" there shall be inserted the words "inspector of nuisances or other officer of the district authority."
	s. 57 (3)	The words "if not a rural sanitary authority" and the words "and if a rural sanitary authority with the consent of the county council of the county in which the land is situate" shall be omitted.
	s. 81	The word "or" shall be inserted before the words "to make any rate." The words "out of their own number," and the words "or to enter into any contract" shall be omitted. After the words "provided that a committee so appointed shall" there shall be inserted the words "consist as to a majority of its members of members of the appointing local authority, and shall".
	First Schedule . .	For the words "The Commissioners of Sewers" there shall be substituted "The Common Council," and for the words "The sewer rate and the consolidated rate levied by such Commissioners, or either of such rates," there shall be substituted the words "The General Rate."
	Second Schedule— Paragraph (1) .	For the words "as soon as practicable after the passing of the confirming Act" there shall be substituted the words "before making an application for the appointment of an arbitrator as hereinafter mentioned." After the word "occupiers" there shall be inserted the words "except tenants for a month or a less period than a month."
	Paragraph (4) .	For the words "has not been" there shall be substituted the words "is not."

Enactment to be amended.	Nature of Amendment.
Housing of the Working Classes Act, 1890 (53 & 54 Vict. c. 70) : Second Schedule (*contd.*)—	
Paragraph (6) .	For the words beginning " and the local authority shall publish " to the end of the paragraph there shall be substituted the words " Before applying to the arbitrator to determine the compensation in respect of any particular lands or interest therein, the local authority shall send a notice by post of their intention to the owners or reputed owners, lessees or reputed lessees, so far as they can be reasonably ascertained."
Paragraph (7) .	The words from " shall ascertain " to " willing to pay; and " shall be omitted, and for the words " he shall proceed " there shall be substituted the words " shall proceed."
Paragraph (8) .	The words " by causing such notice to be published or otherwise in such manner as he thinks advisable " and the words " in disputed cases as to the amount of compensation to be paid " shall be omitted.
Paragraph (9) .	The words " (subject to the provisions concerning an appeal hereinafter contained) " shall be omitted.
Paragraph (10) .	For the words from " and the local authority shall thereupon " to the end of the paragraph there shall be inserted the words " The title in the case of a person claiming a fee simple interest in any lands included in any such award as aforesaid shall commence twenty years previous to the date of the claim except there has been an absolute conveyance on sale within twenty years and more than ten years previous to the claim when the title shall commence with such conveyance. Provided that the local authority shall not be prevented if they think fit from requiring at their own expense any further abstract or evidence of title respecting any lands included in any such award as aforesaid in addition to the title hereinbefore mentioned."
Paragraph (12) .	The words from " The local authority, or any person interested " to the end of the paragraph shall be omitted

2nd Sch. (19).

Enactment to be amended.	Nature of Amendment.
Housing of the Working Classes Act, 1890 (53 & 54 Vict. c. 70) : Second Schedule (*contd.*)— Paragraph (14)	For the words " such statement and abstract as aforesaid " there shall be substituted the words " a statement in writing by any person claiming any right to, or interest in, the lands and an abstract of title on which the same is founded."
Paragraphs (22), (26) and (27).	These paragraphs shall be omitted.
Paragraph (29) (1) (c).	For the words " before the appointment of the arbitrator " there shall be substituted the words " not less than 14 days before the date of the arbitration in that particular case."
Paragraph (30)	After the word " documents " there shall be inserted the words " other than any formal offer made by the local authority."
Paragraph (32)	Substitute " a " for " someone and the same."
Housing of the Working Classes Act, 1903 (3 Edw. 7. c. 39) : s. 4 (2)	For the word " twelve " : in both places where the word " twelve " occurs there shall be substituted the word " six."
Housing, Town Planning, &c., Act, 1909 (9 Edw. 7. c. 44) : s. 17 (3)	For the word " order," where it last occurs, shall be substituted the word " notice."
s. 17 (4)	For the words " every occupying tenant " shall be substituted the words " the occupier."
s. 17 (7)	After the words " nearest to the room " insert the words " or more than three feet below the surface of any ground within nine feet of the room."
s. 18 (3)	At the end the following words shall be inserted : " and if and when the necessary works are completed to their satisfaction, the local authority shall determine the closing and demolition orders relating to the dwelling-house."

Enactment to be amended.	Nature of Amendment.
Housing, Town Planning, &c., Act, 1909 (9 Edw. 7. c. 44) (*contd.*): s. 18 (4)	For the word "order," where it last occurs, shall be substituted the word "notice"; and at the end of the subsection the following words shall be inserted: "or where the operation of the order has been postponed for any period within fourteen days after the expiration of that period."
s. 39 (1)	At the end of the proviso (*b*) the following words shall be inserted: "unless the appellant fails to prosecute his appeal with due diligence."
s. 69 (1)	For the words "or information" shall be substituted the words "information or closing order."

THIRD SCHEDULE

Section 48 (see p. 452).

MINOR AND CONSEQUENTIAL AMENDMENTS OF THE PROVISIONS AS TO TOWN PLANNING

Enactment to be amended.	Nature of Amendment.
Housing, Town Planning, &c., Act, 1909 (9 Edw. 7. c. 44): Section 54 . . .	At the end of subsection (1) the following proviso shall be inserted:— "Provided that where a piece of land already built upon or a piece of land not likely to be used for building purposes is so situate with respect to any land likely to be used for building purposes that the general object of the scheme would be better secured by its inclusion in any town planning scheme made with respect to the last-mentioned land, the scheme may include such piece of land as aforesaid, and may provide for the demolition or alteration of any buildings thereon so far as may be necessary for carrying the scheme into effect." Subsection (3) shall be omitted.

3rd Sch (19).

Enactment to be amended.	Nature of Amendment.
Housing, Town Planning, &c., Act, 1909 (9 Edw. 7. c. 44) (*contd.*):	
Section 56 . . .	In subsection (1) for the words " application for authority to prepare or adopt a town planning scheme, the preparation of the scheme " there shall be substituted the words " the preparation or adoption of a town planning scheme," and after the word " adopted " there shall be inserted the words " the variation or revocation of a scheme," and after the words " the provisions thereof " there shall be inserted the words ' or the 'variation or revocation of the scheme.' In paragraph (*a*) of subsection (2) for the words " at every stage of the proceedings, by means of conferences and such other means·'" there shall be substituted the words " by such means."
Section 58 . . .	In subsection (2) for the words " time at which the application for authority to prepare the scheme was made " there shall be substituted the words " date of the resolution of the local authority to prepare or adopt the scheme or after the date when such resolution takes effect as the case may be " and for the words " the application was made " there shall be substituted the words " such date or other time as aforesaid."
Section 59 . . .	In subsection (2) the words " with a view to securing the amenity of the area included in the scheme or any part thereof " shall be omitted.
Section 65 . . .	In subsection (2) after the words " made thereunder " where they secondly occur there shall be inserted the words "including the cost of the preparation or adoption of a scheme."
Fourth Schedule . .	In paragraph (18) the words ' by means of conferences, &c." shall be omitted.
Fifth Schedule . .	In paragraph (1) for the words " and for the purpose of an application for authority to prepare or adopt " there shall be substituted the words " the preparation or adoption of," and for the words " Submission of plans and estimates " there shall be substituted the words " Preparation and deposit of plans."

FOURTH SCHEDULE

4th Sch. (19).

PART I

Section 49
(see p. 453).

FORM OF ENDORSED RECEIPT

The local authority of   hereby acknowledge
that they have this   day of   19 ,
received the sum of £   representing the [aggre-
gate] [balance remaining owing in respect of the] principal
money secured by the within [above] written [annexed]
mortgage [and by an indenture of further charge dated,
&c., *or otherwise as required*] together with all interest
and costs, the payment having been made by
of [&c.] and   of [&c.] out of money in their
hands properly applicable for the discharge of the mortgage [*or otherwise as required*].

In witness, &c.

PART II

EFFECT OF ENDORSED RECEIPT

(1.) Any such receipt shall operate—

(a) In the case of land in fee simple comprised in
the mortgage, as a conveyance or re-conveyance
(as the case may be) of the land to the person (if
any) who immediately before the execution of the
receipt was entitled in fee simple to the equity of
redemption, or otherwise to the mortgagor in fee
simple to the uses (if any) upon the trusts subject
to the powers and provisions which at that time
are subsisting or capable of taking effect with
respect to the equity of redemption or to uses
(if any) which correspond as nearly as may be

with the limitations then affecting the equity of redemption ;

(b) In the case of other property, as an assignment or re-assignment (as the case may be) thereof to the extent of the interest which is the subject-matter of the mortgage, to the person who immediately before the execution of the receipt was entitled to the equity of redemption :

Provided that (except as hereinafter mentioned) where, by the receipt, the money appears to have been paid by a person who is not entitled to the immediate equity of redemption, then, unless it is otherwise expressly provided, the receipt shall operate as if the mortgage had been a statutory mortgage and the benefit thereof had, by deed expressed to be made by way of statutory transfer or mortgage, been transferred to him ; but this provision shall not apply where the mortgage is paid off out of capital money, or other money in the hands of a personal representative or trustee properly applicable for the discharge of the mortgage, unless it is expressly provided that the receipt is to operate as a transfer.

(2.) Nothing in this schedule shall confer on a mortgagor a right to keep alive a mortgage, paid off by him, so as to affect prejudicially any subsequent incumbrancer ; and where there is no right to keep the mortgage alive, the receipt shall not operate as a transfer.

(3.) In any such receipt the same covenants shall be implied as if the person who executes the receipt had by deed been expressed to convey the property as mortgagee.

(4.) Where a mortgage consists of a mortgage and a further charge or of more than one deed, it shall be sufficient if the receipt refers either to all the deeds whereby the mortgage money is secured or to the aggregate amount of the mortgage money thereby secured and is endorsed on, written at the foot of, or annexed to, one of the mortgage deeds.

(5.) In this schedule the expression " mortgage " " mortgage money " " mortgagor " and " mortgagee " have the same meanings as in the Conveyancing Act, 1881.

4th Sch. (19)

44 & 45 Vict. c. 41.

FIFTH SCHEDULE

ENACTMENTS REPEALED

Section 50 (see p. 454).

Session and Chapter.	Short Title.	Extent of Repeal.
53 & 54 Vict. c. 70.	The Housing of the Working Classes Act, 1890.	Sections fourteen, sixty and sixty-four and sub-section (2) of section fifty-seven.
63 & 64 Vict. c. 59.	The Housing of the Working Classes Act, 1900.	Section five.
3 Edw. 7. c. 39.	The Housing of the Working Classes Act, 1903.	Subsection (1) of section five.
9 Edw. 7. c. 44.	The Housing, Town Planning, &c., Act, 1909.	Subsection (2) of section four, sections six, sixteen, thirty-two and seventy-two and in the First Schedule the paragraph numbered (7).

30

HOUSING (ADDITIONAL POWERS) ACT, 1919
[9 & 10 Geo. 5. Ch. 99.]

ARRANGEMENT OF SECTIONS

*An Act to make further provision for the better housing
of the people, to authorise the acquisition of land for
the development of garden cities or for the purposes
of town planning schemes, and to make further provision with respect to the borrowing powers of public
authorities and bodies and with respect to the securities
issued by them.* [23rd December 1919.]

BE it enacted by the King's most Excellent Majesty,
by and with the advice and consent of the Lords
Spiritual and Temporal, and Commons, in this present
Parliament assembled, and by the authority of the same, .
as follows :

Provision
for payment
of money to
persons con-
structing
houses.

1. (1.) Subject to the provisions of this Act, the
Minister of Health (in this Act referred to as "the
Minister") may, in accordance with schemes made by
him with the approval of the Treasury, make grants out

of moneys provided by Parliament to any persons or S. 1 (A.P.).
bodies of persons constructing houses.

Subject.   See the present section, and section 2.

Any persons.   The chief purpose of the Act is to provide a subsidy or grant to private persons, firms, or bodies
building houses within the conditions (see page 119).
The total of the grant is £15,000,000, and for points
arising—see notes to section 2 (1) and (2) below.   Persons
enlarging or repairing existing houses do not get a
grant.

(2.) Grants under this section shall be made only in
respect of houses—

(a) which comply with the conditions prescribed by
    the Minister and are in material accordance with the
    conditions as to the number of houses per acre and
    the standards of structural stability and sanitation
    approved by the Minister in the case of any scheme
    submitted by a local authority under section one of
    the Housing, Town Planning, &c., Act, 1919 ;   9 & 10 Geo. 5.
c. 35.

Conditions prescribed.   These are given in full on page
119.   See also the note next below, and, particularly,
subsection (3) below.

Material accordance.   The conditions as to the number
of houses per acre and the standards of structural stability
and sanitation, are not prescribed as regards the schemes
of the local authorities, but such schemes are approved
by the Minister when submitted, and they are in general
accordance with the Manual issued by the Ministry (see
page 23) and the Ministry's standard specification for
cottages.

The local byelaws in so far as they are not abrogated or
relaxed (see above) would also have to be observed, but
only so far as they are consistent with the aforesaid
prescribed conditions—see subsection (3) below.

The words following " conditions prescribed by the
Minister " are in the nature of an instruction to the
Minister as to what the conditions should be which
he prescribes, and it would appear from the official

document, printed on page 114, that the Minister has adopted this procedure.

By the prescribed conditions the houses to receive the grant are strictly limited as to size, &c. (pages 114 and 119).

(b) which are certified by the local authority of the area in which the houses are situate, or on appeal by the Minister, to have been completed in a proper and workmanlike manner ;

The certificates to be used are shown on page 126 *et seq.* The appeal is referred to in paragraph 7 on page 118, and in the paragraph which completes this subsection.

(c) the construction of which is begun within twelve months after the passing of this Act and which are completed within that period or such further period not exceeding four months as the Minister may in any special case allow :

Provided that a proportionate reduction of the grant shall be made in respect of any house which is not completed within the said period of twelve months unless the Minister is satisfied that the failure to complete the house within that period was due to circumstances over which the person constructing the house had no control.

In any special case. For instance, where the houses are not completed before 23rd December 1920 because of bad weather, or a strike, or transport or similar difficulties beyond the control of the builder ; but the Minister's power is not limited to these instances.

Proportionate reduction. See paragraph 3 on page 116, for the amount thereof, the official figures (a reduction of one-twelfth of the grant for each extra month) being those indicated by the word " proportionate." It would seem clear that in the instances given in the immediately preceding note, there might be no reduction, but the builder will not be entitled to even a reduced grant unless the Minister expressly allows in each particular

case a further period, and this period is not fixed at S. 1 (A.P.).
four months but at "not exceeding four months," e.g.
the Minister may allow, in a particular case, only one
month extra. The Government has undertaken to extend
the periods of these grants by twelve months, so that the
words "twelve months" in the section will then read
"twenty-four months."

Any person aggrieved by the refusal or neglect of a
local authority to grant a certificate under this subsection
in respect of any house may appeal to the Minister,
and, if the Minister is satisfied that the house has been
completed in a proper and workmanlike manner, he
shall certify accordingly.

(3.) In so far as the provisions of any building byelaws
are inconsistent with the conditions prescribed by the
Minister under this section, those provisions shall not
apply in respect of any houses which comply with those
conditions :

Provided that, as regards the administrative county
of London, the Minister shall not prescribe any conditions inconsistent with the provisions of any building
byelaws in force in the county except after consultation
with the London County Council on the general question
of the relaxation of such provisions in connexion with the
construction of houses under this Act.

In this Act the expression "building byelaws" has
the same meaning as in Part I of the Housing, Town
Planning, &c., Act, 1919.

Prescribed by the Minister. See page 119.
"*Building byelaws.*" See section 40 of the said Act
(page 441).

2. (1.) The aggregate amount of the grants to be Aggregate
made for the purposes of the preceding section of this amount of
Act shall not exceed fifteen million pounds. grants.

S. 2 (A.P.).

Thus there would be a maximum of 600,000 houses provided under the preceding section, on the basis of an average grant of £250 per house. If private builders propose to build more than this maximum, the Ministry will have to adopt restrictive measures.

(2.) A grant shall not be made under the preceding section of this Act in respect of any house in respect of which any payment out of moneys provided by Parliament may be made under section seven or section nineteen of the Housing, Town Planning, &c., Act, 1919, and a payment shall not be made under those sections in respect of any house in respect of which a grant has been made under the preceding section of this Act.

Briefly, there will not be two State payments in respect of the one house—a point for local authorities and public utility societies to observe if they buy a house erected by a private person.

Provision as to expenses under s. 16 of 9 & 10 Geo. 5. c. 35.

*3. (1.) Any expenses incurred by the Minister under section sixteen of the Housing, Town Planning, &c., Act, 1919, in connexion with the conversion of buildings into separate tenements shall, subject as hereinafter provided, be paid out of moneys provided by Parliament :

Provided that such part of any such expenses as would have been borne by the local authority if they had been expenses incurred in carrying out a scheme to which section seven of the said Act applies shall be payable by that authority and shall be recoverable from that authority as a debt due to the Crown, and the certificate of the Minister as to the part of the expenses to be borne by the local authority shall be conclusive.

(2.) The provision of money for the payment of any

* See section 15 (p. 485) as to expiry.

amounts payable by a local authority under this section S. 3 (A.P.).
shall be a purpose for which the authority may borrow
under Part III of the Housing of the Working Classes 53 & 54 Vict.
Act, 1890. c. 70.

(3.) The Minister may make orders containing such
provisions with regard to the vesting in the local authority
of any buildings converted into separate tenements
under the provisions of the said section sixteen and such
consequential and supplemental provisions as the Minister
may think necessary, and any order so made shall be
binding on the local authority.

This supplies an omission in section 16 of the Housing,
Town Planning, &c., Act, 1919, by which the Minister
has power to acquire and alter, &c., buildings, and
has exercised it to acquire houses to be turned into flats.
The said power was " to assist in the preparation of
schemes " in the emergency, pending the preparation
of a scheme by the local authority.   In effect the section
enables the Minister to treat himself as being the representative or agent of the appropriate local authority in
respect of such conversions.   The local authority can
more conveniently collect the rents and manage the
flats.   He has power to vest the flats in the local authority
though the local authority object, and his certificate as
to the part of the expenses to be borne by the local
authority is conclusive.

As to borrowing powers—see section 66 of the 1890
Act.

4. Section seven of the Housing, Town Planning, &c., Amendment
Act, 1919 (which provides for the recoupment out of of s. 7 and
s. 19 of
moneys provided by Parliament of losses incurred in 9 & 10 Geo. 5.
c. 35. with
connexion with certain schemes), and section nineteen respect to
amount of
of that Act (which provides for the contributions out of annual
moneys provided by Parliament towards costs incurred payments.
by public utility societies and housing trusts) shall respectively have effect as though for the words " equivalent

S. 4 (A.P.). to thirty per centum of the annual loan charges,"
where they occur in each of those sections, there were
substituted the words " equivalent during the period
ending on the thirty-first day of March nineteen hundred
and twenty-seven, to fifty per centum and thereafter to
thirty per centum of the annual loan charges."

Prohibition of building operations which interfere with provision of dwelling-houses.   ***5.** (1.) Where it appears to a local authority that
the provision of dwelling accommodation for their area
is or is likely to be delayed by a deficiency of labour or
materials arising out of the employment of labour or
material in the construction within their area of any
works or buildings (other than works or buildings authorised or required by, under, or in pursuance of any Act
of Parliament), and that the construction of those works
or buildings is in the circumstances of the case of less
public importance for the time being than the provision
of dwelling accommodation, the authority may by order
prohibit for such time and on such terms and subject
to such conditions as the Minister may from time to
time prescribe, and either in whole or in part, the construction of those works or buildings.

Local authority. See section 11 hereof.

Dwelling accommodation. Not only in new houses,
but by the enlargement or repair of existing houses,
residential hotels, and the like.

Likely to be delayed. There is an appeal from the local
authority's decision—see the next subsection. But
this is only one of the conditions : the other is, briefly,
that the other works are less urgent, and where the other
works are the erection of a factory giving employment
to a large number of people, it is obviously a matter

---

* Expires on 22nd December 1921.

for careful adjustment. "Luxury building" is what is S. 5 (A.P.). chiefly aimed at.

Construction . . . of any works or buildings. See the definition in subsection (6) below.

Authorised or required by . . . Act of Parliament, e.g. buildings by railway companies and the like. The building of a post office could not be prohibited under this subsection.

Conditions as the Minister may . . . prescribe. See page 684.

(2.) Any person aggrieved by an order made by a local authority under this section may, subject to rules of procedure to be made by the Minister, appeal to the Minister, and on any such appeal the Minister shall refer all such cases to a standing tribunal of appeal, consisting of five persons, to be appointed by the Minister, which shall have power either to annul the order or to make such order in the matter as the local authority could have made, and the decision of the tribunal of appeal in the matter shall be final and not subject to appeal to or review by any court.

Rules of procedure. See page 694. There must be a hearing—*Rex v. Tribunal of Appeal—Ex parte Alhambra Picture House (Huddersfield), Ltd. (The Times,* 12th June 1920).

(3.) Where any appeal against an order made under this section is not finally determined within fourteen days after the date on which notice of appeal against the order was given, the operation of the order shall be suspended as from the expiration of the said fourteen days until the appeal has been finally determined.

So that the building can proceed, if in fourteen days after notice of appeal has been given the appeal has not been determined.

(4.) If any person acts in contravention of or fails to

S. 5 (A.P.).   comply with any of the provisions of an order made under this section, he shall be liable on summary conviction to a fine not exceeding one hundred pounds, and, if the offence is a continuing offence, to a fine not exceeding fifty pounds for each day during which the offence continues, and, where the person guilty of an offence under this section is a company, every director and officer of the company shall be guilty of the like offence unless he proves that the act constituting the offence took place without his consent or connivance.

(5.) In any action or proceedings for breach of a contract to construct any works or buildings, it shall be a good defence to the action or proceedings to prove that the non-fulfilment of the contract was due to compliance with an order made under this section.

(6.) In this section the expression " construction of any works or buildings " includes the making of alterations or additions to existing works or buildings.

Large houses, residential hotels and the like are not interfered with by this section.

(7.) Any rules of procedure made by the Minister under this section shall be laid before both Houses of Parliament as soon as may be after they are made.

Prohibition on demolition of dwelling-houses.   *6. (1.) If any person at any time after the third day of December, nineteen hundred and nineteen, without the permission in writing of the local authority within whose area the house is situate, demolishes, in whole or in part, or uses otherwise than as a dwelling-house any house which was at that date in the opinion of the local authority reasonably fit or reasonably capable without reconstruction of being rendered fit for human

* Expires on 22nd December 1921.

habitation, he shall be liable on summary conviction S. 6 (A.P.). in respect of each house demolished or so used to a fine not exceeding one hundred pounds or to imprisonment for a term not exceeding three months or to both such imprisonment and fine, and, where the person guilty of an offence under this section is a company, every director and officer of the company shall be guilty of the like offence unless he proves that the act constituting the offence took place without his consent or connivance.

3rd December 1919. The day prior to the introduction of the Bill.

Reasonably fit. Even though not actually in occupation as a dwelling house, but see subsection (3) below.

This section is supplemental to section 28 of the Housing, Town Planning, &c., Act, 1919, which see. By sections 14 and 15 of the 1909 Act the landlord of dwelling-houses not exceeding a specified rental must keep them in repair, and if he does not, the local authority can do the work and recover the cost. But there was nothing to prevent him from closing the houses. The said section 28, which applies to all houses suitable for occupation by the working classes, allows the landlord to close the houses only if they are not capable without reconstruction of being rendered fit for human habitation. The present section applies to all houses, including residential hotels, &c.—see subsection (3) below (whether for the working classes or not), but relates to demolition and the use otherwise than as dwelling-houses. The said section 28 would prevent the owner from demolishing a house after notice to repair had been given. The present section prohibits anyone from demolishing at any time (before 23rd December 1921) without the written permission of the local authority—or from the use otherwise than as a dwelling-house. It does not prevent him from keeping a house empty.

(2.) Any person to whom permission to demolish a house has been refused by a local authority under this section, may appeal to the Minister on the ground that the house is not capable without reconstruction of being rendered fit for human habitation, and any such appeal shall be dealt with in the same manner as an appeal under subsection (2) of the preceding section of this Act.

The appeal procedure is not the same as that under section 28 (1) of the Housing, Town Planning, &c., Act, 1919, though the point at issue is the same—namely, as the capability of the house for being rendered fit for occupation. For the Rules, see page 706.

(3.) Notwithstanding anything in this section, the permission of the local authority shall not be required in the case of any house the demolition of which is required or authorised by, under, or in pursuance of any Act of Parliament, or which is used otherwise than as a dwelling-house for any statutory purposes or which was occupied and used otherwise than as a dwelling-house before the third day of December, nineteen hundred and nineteen.

In this section the expression "dwelling-house" means a building constructed or adapted to be used wholly or principally for human habitation.

The first part of this subsection permits the demolition without permission of houses which, for instance, a railway company may have statutory power to demolish. Demolition for post office purposes could not be prohibited under this section.

Occupied and used otherwise. This is quite general. If a dwelling-house (see the definition) was occupied and used otherwise than as a dwelling-house *before* 3rd December 1919, it can be demolished without permission.

The definition of dwelling-house would include large houses and residential hotels, and would prevent them from being let or sold for business purposes; but as to shop premises containing rooms for habitation, see

Davison v. Birmingham Industrial Co-operative Society,   S. 6 (A.P.).
Ltd., Court of Appeal, 22nd October 1920.

7. (1.) A local authority (including a county council)   Powers of
may, with the consent of the Minister, borrow any sums   borrowing
for purpose
which they have power to borrow for the purposes of   of Housing
Acts.
the Housing Acts, 1890 to 1919, by the issue of bonds
(in this Act referred to as "local bonds") in accordance
with the provisions of this Act.

Including a county council. County councils have
housing powers under the 1919 Act, notably section 8
thereof. See also note to section 1 (6) thereof.

Have power to borrow. For power to borrow under
Part I (improvement schemes)—see section 25 of the 1890
Act; under Part II (reconstruction schemes)—see
section 43 thereof; and under Part III (housing schemes)
—see section 66 thereof. See also section 1 of the 1903
Act; sections 8, 13, 18 (3) and (4), and 22 (3) of the 1919
Act; and sections 3 (2) and 10 (3) of the present Act.

Local bonds . . . provisions of this Act. See subsection
(3) below, and the schedule for the provisions. In connection with the present housing effort, one of the greatest
difficulties of many local authorities has been that of
raising the necessary capital moneys. On 31st October
1919, the Treasury appointed a committee to report on the
subject and its Interim Report [Cmd. 444] recommended
these Local Bonds. Previously the smaller local authorities, under £200,000 rateable value, had been helped with
loans from the Local Loans Fund (see sections 25 and 66
of the 1890 Act), but the said committee recommended
(paragraph 20) that, whenever conditions admitted,
they should endeavour to finance themselves. The said
committee referred to the capital required to provide
535,000 houses in England and Wales and Scotland
within three years, being £429,750,000; but it does not
follow that this sum will be required to be raised by these
local bonds.

(2.) A county council may lend to any local authority
within their area any money which that authority have
power to borrow for the purposes of the Housing Acts,

S. 7 (A.P.). 1890 to 1919, and may, with the sanction of the Minister and irrespective of any limit of borrowing, raise the money required for the purpose either by the issue of local bonds under this section or by a loan subject to the like conditions and in the like manner as any other loan raised for the purpose of their powers and duties, and subject in either case to any conditions which the Minister may by general or special order impose.

Order. See the Housing (Loans by County Councils) Order, 1920—S.R. & O. 1465, page 80.

(3.) The provisions set out in the Schedule to this Act shall have effect with respect to local bonds.

See page 486.

(4.) Where on an application made by two or more local authorities the Minister is satisfied that it is expedient that those authorities should have power to make a joint issue of local bonds, the Minister may by order make such provision as appears to him necessary for the purpose, and any such order shall provide for the securing of the bonds issued upon the joint rates, property and revenues of the authorities.

The provisions of any such order shall have effect as if they were contained in a Provisional Order made 38 & 39 Vict. under section two hundred and seventy-nine of the Public c. 55. Health Act, 1875.

The effect of the concluding paragraph, which is practically identical with that of section 38 of the 1909 Act, is not very clear, more particularly as to whether or not the Provisional Order has to be confirmed by Parliament —see section 297 of the 1875 Act. Section 280 of that Act deals with the "governing body of united district" —section 281 with "contents of Provisional Order forming united district," and subsequent sections with

meetings, expenses, &c., of the joint board. These S. 7 (A.P.).
sections are fully discussed on page 612 *et seq.* of *Lumley's*
Public Health (8th edition). No confirmation by Parliament is necessary in the Scottish case, see section 13
(1) (f) hereof.

(5.) Any local authority by whom any local bonds
have been issued may, without the consent of the Minister,
borrow for the purpose of redeeming those bonds.

8. Subsection (2) of section one of the Public Authori- Subsection
ties and Bodies (Loans) Act, 1916 (which gives power $\frac{(2) \text{ of s. 1 of}}{6 \text{ & 7 Geo. 5.}}$
temporarily to certain local authorities to borrow money $\frac{\text{c. 69. to be}}{\text{perpetual.}}$
by means of the issue of securities to bearer and whether
within or without the United Kingdom), shall be a
permanent enactment, and accordingly the words " during
the continuation of the present war and a period of six
months thereafter " in that subsection shall be repealed.

This is in accordance with the recommendation of the
Treasury Committee on housing finance : " We have considered the possibility of local authorities borrowing abroad
and we understand that some authorities have already
been approached by representatives of American financial
institutions. We think that this method of borrowing
presents far-reaching advantages, and, provided money
can be obtained on reasonable terms, should be encouraged "—paragraph 15 [Cmd. 444].

9. Section one of the Trustee Act, 1893 (which specifies Power of
the securities in which trust funds may be invested), $\frac{\text{trustees to}}{\text{invest in}}$
shall have effect as though there were included therein $\frac{\text{certain}}{\text{securities}}$
local bonds issued under this Act and mortgages of any $\frac{\text{issued by}}{\text{local}}$
fund or rate granted after the passing of this Act under authorities.
the authority of any Act or Provisional Order by a local $\frac{56 \text{ & 57 Vict.}}{\text{c. 53.}}$
authority (including a county council) which is authorised
to issue local bonds under this Act.

This follows the recommendations of paragraphs 13
and 24 of Cmd. 444.

S. 10 (A.P.).

Acquisition of land for purpose of garden cities or town planning schemes.

10. (1.) Where the Minister is satisfied that any local authority (including a county council) or two or more local authorities jointly, or any authorised association, are prepared to purchase and develop any land as a garden city (including a garden suburb or a garden village), or any land in regard to which a town-planning scheme may be made for the purpose of such a scheme for the area in which the land is situate, in accordance with a scheme approved by the Minister, and have funds available for the purpose, he may, with the consent of the Treasury and after consultation with the Board of Trade, the Board of Agriculture and Fisheries, and the Minister of Transport, acquire that land on behalf of the authority or association either by compulsion or by agreement in any case in which it appears to him necessary or expedient so to do for the purpose of securing the development of the land as aforesaid, and may do all such things as may be necessary to vest the land so acquired in the local authority or association.

Local authority. For definition—see section 11 hereof.
Authorised association. For definition—see subsection (4) below.
In regard to which a town planning scheme may be made. See section 54 of the 1909 Act. This is in addition to " any land as a garden city."
Acquire that land. Subject to the provisions of subsection (2) below.

(2.) The provisions of the Housing Acts, 1890 to 1919, relating to the powers of a local authority to acquire land for the purposes of Part III of the Housing of the Working Classes Act, 1890, shall apply for the purpose of the acquisition of land by the Minister under this section, and the Minister in exercising his powers of acquiring land under this section shall be subject to the same conditions as are applicable to the acquisition of S. 10 (A.P.). land under the Housing Acts, 1890 to 1919, by a local authority :

Provided that, in the case of an order for the compulsory acquisition of land on behalf of an authorised association, the order shall be laid before each House of Parliament and shall not be confirmed by the Minister unless and until both Houses by resolution have approved the order, nor, if any modifications are agreed to by both Houses, otherwise than as so modified.

See section 57 of the 1890 Act ; sections 2, 45, 60 and 73 of the 1909 Act ; and sections 12 and 15 of the 1919 Act.

(3.) A local authority shall have power to acquire land for the purposes of a scheme approved by the Minister under this section, and to develop any land so acquired in accordance with the scheme, and shall have power to borrow, as for the purposes of the Housing Acts, 1890 to 1919, any money required for the purpose of so acquiring or developing any land.

See note to section 7 (1) hereof as to borrowing. The power to acquire and develop for the purposes here mentioned is new, but see Part II of the 1909 Act.

(4.) In this section " authorised association " means any society, company or body of persons approved by the Minister whose objects include the promotion, formation, or management of garden cities (including garden suburbs and garden villages), and the erection, improvement or management of buildings for the working classes and others, which does not trade for profit or whose constitution forbids payment of any interest or dividend at a higher rate than six per centum per annum.

31

S. 11 (A.P.).

Meaning of local authority. 53 & 54 Vict. c. 70.

11. In this Act the expression "local authority" means the local authority within the meaning of Part III of the Housing of the Working Classes Act, 1890 :

Provided that for the purpose of the application of the provisions of this Act (other than those relating to expenses under section sixteen of the Housing, Town Planning, &c., Act, 1919) to the county of London the London County Council shall be the local authority to the exclusion of any other authority, and that in the city of London the London County Council shall be the local authority for the purpose of the certificate as to the completion of houses to be given under the provisions of this Act relating to the payment of money to persons constructing houses.

Local authority. See page 234.
Other than those. . . . See section 3 (1) hereof ; the effect being that the metropolitan borough councils are the authority in London in respect of such expenses.

Execution of Act in county of London. 57 & 58 Vict. c. ccxiii.

12. For the purpose of securing the proper execution of this Act in the administrative county of London, the London County Council shall have the power to require a district surveyor under the London Building Act, 1894, to perform within his district such duties as the Council think necessary for that purpose, and the Council may pay to a district surveyor such remuneration as they may determine in respect of any duties performed by him in pursuance of this section.

The said surveyor will make the inspection, &c., for the purposes of the certificates under section 1 hereof.

Application to Scotland.

13. (1.) This Act shall apply to Scotland subject to the following modifications :—

(a) References to the Minister of Health shall be construed as references to the Scottish Board of Health ;

(*b*) A reference to the Board of Agriculture and Fisheries shall be construed as a reference to the Board of Agriculture for Scotland ;

(*c*) References to section one, section seven and section nineteen of the Housing, Town Planning, &c., Act, 1919, shall be construed as references to section one, section five and section sixteen, respectively, of the Housing, Town Planning, &c. (Scotland), Act, 1919 ;

(*d*) References to the Housing Acts, 1890 to 1919, shall be construed as references to the Housing (Scotland) Acts, 1890 to 1919 ;

(*e*) A reference to building byelaws shall be construed as a reference to building regulations as defined by section thirty-one of the Housing, Town Planning, &c. (Scotland), Act, 1919 ;

(*f*) A reference to a Provisional Order made under section two hundred and seventy-nine of the Public Health Act, 1875, shall be construed as a reference to an Order made under subsection (3) of section sixty-four of the National Insurance Act, 1911.

(2.) Section sixteen of the Housing, Town Planning, &c., Act, 1919, shall apply to Scotland as if it had been enacted in Part I of the Housing, Town Planning, &c. (Scotland), Act, 1919, with the substitution of the Scottish Board of Health for the Local Government Board, and references in this Act to the said section sixteen shall be construed as references to that section as so applied.

(3.) Section eighteen of the Improvement of Land Act, 1864, shall not have effect in the case of landowners in Scotland making applications for loans under that Act for the construction or reconstruction of houses for the working classes.

(4.) The section of this Act relating to power of trustees

S. 13 (A.P.). to invest in certain securities issued by local authorities shall not apply, and in lieu thereof—

Local bonds issued under this Act shall be bonds within the meaning of paragraph (*b*) of section three of the Trusts (Scotland) Act, 1898.

61 & 62 Vict. c. 42.

Application to Ireland.

14. This Act, in its application to Ireland, shall have effect with the following modifications, namely :—

(1.) References to the Minister of Health or to the Minister shall be construed as references to the Local Government Board for Ireland :

(2.) References to the Housing Acts, 1890 to 1919, shall be construed as references to the Housing of the Working Classes (Ireland) Acts, 1890 to 1919, references to the Housing, Town Planning, &c., Act, 1919, shall be construed as references to the Housing (Ireland) Act, 1919, and references to section seven and to section nineteen of the first-mentioned Act shall respectively be construed as references to section five and to section fifteen of the last-mentioned Act :

9 & 10 Geo. 5. c. 45.

41 & 42 Vict. c. 52.

(3.) References to the Public Health Act, 1875, shall be construed as references to the Public Health (Ireland) Act, 1878, and references to section two hundred and seventy-nine of the first-mentioned Act shall be construed as references to section twelve of the last-mentioned Act :

(4) The reference to the Board of Agriculture and Fisheries shall not apply :

(5.) Section sixteen of the Housing, Town Planning, &c., Act, 1919, shall apply to Ireland as if it had been enacted in Part I of the Housing (Ireland) Act, 1919, with the substitution of " the Local Govern-

ment Board for Ireland " for " the Local Government S. 14 (A.P.).
Board " and references in this Act to the said section
sixteen shall be construed as references to that
section as so applied.

15. (1.) This Act may be cited as the Housing (Addi- Short title
tional Powers) Act, 1919. and
duration.

(2.) The provisions of this Act, other than the provisions thereof relating to powers of borrowing for the
purpose of the Housing Acts, 1890 to 1919, the Public
Authorities and Bodies (Loans) Act, 1916, trustee securities, and the acquisition of land for the purpose of garden
cities and town-planning schemes, shall continue in force
for two years only from the commencement thereof, and no
longer :

Provided that section thirty-eight of the Interpretation 52 & 53 Vict.
Act, 1889 (which relates to the effect of repeals), shall, c. 63.
in relation to the provisions of this Act which cease to be
in force on the expiration of the period aforesaid, apply
as if these provisions had been repealed by another Act
passed on the date of the expiration of the said period.

Provisions relating to powers of borrowing. . . .   Section
7 hereof.
   The Public Authorities and Bodies (Loans) Act, 1916.
Section 8 hereof.
   Trustee securities.   Section 9 hereof.
   Acquisition of land. . . .   Section 10 hereof.

Section 7
(p. 478).

SCHEDULE

Provisions as to Local Bonds

1. Local bonds shall—

    (a) be secured upon all the rates, property and revenues of the local authority :

    (b) bear interest at such rate of interest as the Treasury may from time to time fix :

    (c) be issued in denominations of five, ten, twenty, fifty, and one hundred pounds and multiples of hundred pounds :

    (d) be issued for periods of not less than five years.

54 & 55 Vict. c. 39.

2. Local bonds shall be exempt from stamp duty under the Stamp Act, 1891, and no duty shall be chargeable under section eight of the Finance Act, 1899, as amended by section ten of the Finance Act, 1907, in respect of the issue of any such bonds.

62 & 63 Vict. c. 9.
7 Edw. 7. c. 13.

3. The provisions of section one hundred and fifteen of the Stamp Act, 1891 (which relates to composition for stamp duty), shall, with the necessary adaptations, apply in the case of any local authority by whom local bonds are issued as if those bonds were stock or funded debt of the authority within the meaning of that section.

4. A local authority shall, in the case of any person who is the registered holder of local bonds issued by that authority of a nominal amount not exceeding in the aggregate one hundred pounds, pay the interest on the bonds held by that person without deduction of income tax, but any such interest shall be accounted for and charged to income tax under the third case of Schedule D. in the First Schedule to the Income Tax Act, 1918, subject, however, to any provision of that Act with respect to exemption or abatement.

8 & 9 Geo. 5. c. 40.

5. Local bonds issued by a local authority shall be accepted by that authority at their nominal value in

payment of the purchase price of any house erected by
or on behalf of any local authority in pursuance of any
scheme under the Housing Acts, 1890 to 1919.

6. The Minister may, with the approval of the Treasury,
make regulations with respect to the issue (including terms
of issue), transfer and redemption of local bonds and the
security therefor, and any such regulations may apply,
with or without modifications, any provisions of the
Local Loans Act, 1875, and the Acts amending that Act,
and of any Act relating to securities issued by the London
County Council or by any other local or public body.

For the Regulations, see page 698.

PUBLIC WORKS LOANS ACT, 1920

[10 & 11 Geo. 5.   Ch. 61.] [23rd December 1920]

5.—(1) Subject to the provisions of this section, the
Public Works Loan Commissioners may advance out of
the Local Loans Fund to local authorities within the
meaning of the Housing Acts, 1890 to 1919, and on the
like security as sums borrowed for the purposes of those
Acts, any sums which those authorities have power to
borrow for those purposes :

Power to make temporary advances from Local Loans Fund to local authorities for housing purposes.

Provided that—

    (a) the amount of an advance to any local authority
shall not exceed such sum as may be approved by
the Treasury and the Minister of Health in that
behalf ; and

    (b) the amount advanced shall be repaid by the local
authority to the Local Loans Fund within a period
of twelve months from the date of the advance.

(2) Interest on advances under this section shall be
payable at such a rate as the Treasury may from time to
time fix or, if at any time and so long as the rate originally
fixed by the Treasury in the case of any advance is less than
the bank rate for the time being in force, at the bank rate.

(3) A local authority to whom an advance has been
made under this section may, without the consent of the
Minister of Health, borrow any money required for the
purpose of repaying the advance.

(4) The power to make advances under this section shall
not be exercised after the thirtieth day of September,
nineteen hundred and twenty-one.

UNEMPLOYMENT (RELIEF WORKS) ACT, 1920

[10 & 11 Geo. 5. Ch. 57.]

*An Act to make better provision for the employment of un-
employed persons by facilitating the acquisition of, and
entry on, land required for works of public utility, and
for purposes connected therewith.* [3rd December 1920.]

Be it enacted by the King's most Excellent Majesty, by
and with the advice and consent of the Lords Spiritual
and Temporal, and Commons, in this present Parliament
assembled, and by the authority of the same, as follows :

Provision
for facili-
tating the
compulsory
acquisition
of, and entry
on, land
required for
works of
public
utility.

9 Edw. 7.
c. 44.
9 & 10 Geo. 5.
c. 35.
53 & 54 Vict.
c. 70.

1. Subject as hereinafter provided, the provisions of
the Housing, Town Planning, &c., Act, 1909, and of the
Housing, Town Planning, &c., Act, 1919, which relate
to the procedure for the compulsory acquisition of land for
the purposes of Part III of the Housing of the Working
Classes Act, 1890, by the Minister of Health and local
authorities, and to entry on land acquired for those purposes, shall apply to the compulsory acquisition of land
for the purpose of works of public utility and of land
which may be acquired in connection with any such works,
and to the entry on land acquired for that purpose, as if
those enactments were herein re-enacted with the necessary adaptations and modifications and with the substitution of the appropriate Government department for the
Minister of Health and of the local authority having power
to execute a work of public utility for the local authority
within the meaning of the said Part III :

Provided that—

(a) the powers conferred by this section shall not be exercised except where it is certified by the Minister of Labour that, having regard to the amount of unemployment existing in any area, it is desirable that the provisions of this section should be put into operation with a view to the speedy provision of employment for unemployed persons from that area, and the Minister of Labour shall take into consideration any representations which may be made to him by any local authority to the effect that he should issue a certificate under this section ; and

(b) no order authorising the compulsory acquisition of any land for any purpose shall be made under any enactment as applied by this section, unless an order authorising the compulsory acquisition of that land for that purpose could have been made under some enactment in force at the commencement of this Act ; and

(c) where an enactment in force at the commencement of this Act, which authorises the compulsory acquisition of land for any purpose for which land has been authorised to be acquired compulsorily by an order made under this Act, contains a provision that the arbitrator in determining the amount of any disputed compensation shall have regard to the extent to which the remaining and contiguous lands and hereditaments belonging to the same proprietor may be benefited by the proposed work for which the land is authorised to be acquired, that provision shall have effect as respects land authorised to be acquired compulsorily by the said order.

Power to
enter on and
acquire land
for construc-
tion and
improvement
of roads.

2. (1.) If it appears to the Minister of Labour that immediate action is necessary for the purpose of dealing with unemployment, and that land cannot be acquired under the foregoing provisions of this Act with such expedition as the case requires, he may certify accordingly, and thereupon the Minister of Transport (in this section referred to as " the Minister ") or, with the approval of the Minister, any local authority, shall, subject to the provisions of this section, have power forthwith to enter upon and take possession of any such land as may be required for or in connection with the construction of any arterial road, being a road which the Minister or the local authority, as the case may be, has or have power to construct or required by the local authority for the improvement of any road, with a view to the employment of unemployed persons in the construction or improvement of the road :

Provided that nothing in the foregoing provision shall authorise the Minister or any local authority to enter on any permanent building or structure, or to enter upon or take possession of any land unless that land could, under some enactment in force at the commencement of this Act, have been authorised to be acquired compulsorily for, or in connection with, the construction or improvement of a road.

(2.) Before entering on any land under this Act, the Minister or local authority shall give seven days' notice in writing of the intention so to do to the owner and occupier of the land.

A notice for the purposes of this provision may be served either—

(a) by delivering it to or leaving it at the usual or last known place of abode of the person on whom it is to be served ; or

(b) by sending it by post in a prepaid letter addressed to that person at his usual or last known place of abode ; or

(c) by delivering it to some person on the premises or, if there is no person on the premises who can be so served, by affixing it on some conspicuous part of the premises ;

and any such notice may be addressed by the description of the " owner " or the " occupier " of the premises (naming them) without further name or description.

(3.) Where the Minister or a local authority enter upon any land in pursuance of this section, he or they shall, by virtue of this section, have power to acquire the land compulsorily, and for the purpose of the acquisition of any such land the provisions of the Lands Clauses Acts shall, subject to the provisions of this section, be deemed to be incorporated in this Act.

(4.) The Minister or local authority shall, as soon as may be after entering on any land under this section, serve notice under section eighteen of the Lands Clauses Consolidation Act, 1845, of the intention to take the land, and shall add to the notice a statement that the entry on the land is made in pursuance of this Act, and shall in all respects be liable as if such notice had been given on the date of entering on the land. _8 & 9 Vict. c. 18._

(5.) The power conferred by this section to enter on land may, save as hereinbefore in this section provided, be exercised without notice to or the consent of any person and without compliance with the provisions of sections eighty-four to ninety of the Lands Clauses Consolidation

Act, 1845, but such entry shall be without prejudice to the liability to pay compensation for the land and interest thereon as from the date on which entry is made, such compensation and interest to be ascertained in accord-
9 & 10 Geo. 5 c. 57. ance with the provisions of the Acquisition of Land (Assessment of Compensation) Act, 1919.

Contribution by local authorities to works outside their area. **3.** (1.) With a view to the provision of employment for the unemployed persons in their area, a local authority may, subject to the approval of the Minister of Health, enter into agreements with any Government department or local authority by whom any work of public utility is being, or is about to be, constructed for the payment of a contribution by that authority towards the expenses which may be incurred in carrying out that work, and any two or more local authorities may, subject to the like approval, make schemes with a view to providing for the employment of the unemployed persons in their areas on works of public utility and may by any such schemes make arrangements as to the manner in which the expenses incurred in connection with the works are to be defrayed.

(2.) A local authority shall have power, with the approval of the Minister of Health, to borrow money for the purposes of any agreement entered into or any scheme made by the authority under this section, in the case of the council of a county in the same manner as for the purposes specified in section sixty-nine of the Local
51 & 52 Vict. c. 41. Government Act, 1888, in the case of the council of a metropolitan borough under the Metropolis Management Acts, 1855 to 1893, in the case of the Common Council of the City of London under the City of London Sewers Acts, 1848 to 1897, and in the case of any other council

in the same manner as for the purposes of the Public Health Acts, 1875 to 1908.

(3.) In this section the expression " local authority " means the council of a county or a county borough, or of an urban or rural district :

Provided that, for the purposes of the application of the provisions of this section to the administrative county of London, the local authorities shall be the London County Council, the councils of metropolitan boroughs, and the Common Council of the City of London.

4. The provisions of subsection (2) of section nine of the Development and Road Improvement Funds Act, 1909, shall not apply with respect to the construction of any new road where the Minister of Labour certifies that, having regard to the exceptional amount of unemployment in any area, it is desirable that the construction of the new road should be proceeded with forthwith with a view to the speedy provision of employment for unemployed persons from that area.

Section 9 (2) of 7 Edw. 7. c. 47, not to apply in certain cases.

5. (1.) In this Act the expression " work of public utility " means the construction or improvement of roads (including bridges, viaducts, and subways) or other means of transit, the widening or other improvement of waterways, the construction or improvement of harbours, the construction of sewers or waterworks, afforestation, the reclamation or drainage of land, and any other work, being a work which a local authority has power to execute, which is approved for the purposes of this Act by the appropriate Government department as a work of public utility.

Interpretation and saving.

(2.) If any question arises in any case as to what department is the appropriate Government department within the meaning of this Act, the question shall be referred to and determined by the Treasury.

(3.) The provisions of this Act shall be in addition to and not in substitution for any power of any Government department or local authority to enter upon or acquire any land for the purposes of any work of public utility.

6. (" Application to Scotland and Ireland.") *Omitted from this volume.*

Short title.　**7.** (1.) This Act may be cited as the Unemployment (Relief Works) Act, 1920.

(2.) This Act shall continue in force for twelve months and no longer unless Parliament otherwise determines :

Provided that the expiry of this Act shall not—

   (*a*) affect the previous operation thereof or of anything duly done or suffered thereunder ;　or

   (*b*) affect any right, privilege, obligation or liability
acquired, accrued or incurred thereunder ;　or

   (*c*) affect any legal proceeding, arbitration, remedy or
investigation in respect of such right, privilege,
obligation or liability as aforesaid ;

and any such legal proceeding, arbitration, remedy or investigation may be instituted, enforced or continued as if this Act had not expired.

ACQUISITION OF LAND

ACQUISITION OF LAND (ASSESSMENT OF COMPENSATION) ACT, 1919

[9 & 10 Geo. 5. Ch. 57.]

ARRANGEMENT OF SECTIONS

An Act to amend the law as to the Assessment of Compensation in respect of Land acquired compulsorily for public purposes and the costs in proceedings thereon.

[19th August 1919.]

BE it enacted by the King's most Excellent Majesty, by and with the advice and consent of the Lords Spiritual and Temporal, and Commons, in this present Parliament assembled, and by the authority of the same, as follows :

1. (1.) Where by or under any statute (whether passed before or after the passing of this Act) land is authorised to be acquired compulsorily by any Government Department or any local or public authority, any question of disputed compensation, and, where any part of the land to be acquired is subject to a lease which comprises

Tribunal for assessing compensation in respect of land compulsorily acquired for public purposes.

S. 1.

land not acquired, any question as to the apportionment of the rent payable under the lease, shall be referred to and determined by the arbitration of such one of a panel of official arbitrators to be appointed under this section as may be selected in accordance with rules made by the Reference Committee under this section.

(2.) Such number of persons, being persons with special knowledge in the valuation of land, as may be appointed for England and Wales, Scotland and Ireland by the Reference Committee, shall form a panel of persons to act as official arbitrators for the purposes of this Act in England and Wales, Scotland and Ireland respectively : Provided that of the members of the said panel for England and Wales one at least shall be a person having special knowledge of the valuation of land in Wales and acquainted with the Welsh language.

(3.) A person appointed to be a member of the panel of official arbitrators shall hold office for such term certain as may be determined by the Treasury before his appointment, and whilst holding office shall not himself engage, or be a partner of any other person who engages, in private practice or business.

(4.) There shall be paid out of moneys provided by Parliament to official arbitrators such salaries or remuneration as the Treasury may determine.

(5.) The Reference Committee—

    (a) for England and Wales shall consist of the Lord Chief Justice of England, the Master of the Rolls and the President of the Surveyors' Institution ;

    (b) for Scotland shall consist of the Lord President of the Court of Session, the Lord Justice Clerk and the Chairman of the Scottish Committee of the Surveyors'. Institution ;

    (c) for Ireland shall consist of the Lord Chief Justice of Ireland, the Master of the Rolls in Ireland and the President of the Surveyors' Institution, or (if the President of the Surveyors' Institution thinks

fit) a person, being a member of the council of s. 1.
that institution and having special knowledge of
valuation of land in Ireland appointed by him to
act in his place.

2. In assessing compensation, an official arbitrator shall
act in accordance with the following rules :— Rules for
the assess-
ment of
compensa-
tion.

(1.) No allowance shall be made on account of the
acquisition being compulsory :

(2.) The value of land shall, subject as hereinafter
provided, be taken to be the amount which the land
if sold in the open market by a willing seller might
be expected to realise : Provided always that the
arbitrator shall be entitled to consider all returns
and assessments of capital value for taxation made
or acquiesced in by the claimant :

(3.) The special suitability or adaptability of the land
for any purpose shall not be taken into account if
that purpose is a purpose to which it could be applied
only in pursuance of statutory powers, or for which
there is no market apart from the special needs of
a particular purchaser or the requirements of any
Government Department or any local or public
authority : Provided that any *bonâ fide* offer [1] for
the purchase of the land made before the passing of
this Act which may be brought to the notice of the
arbitrator shall be taken into consideration :

(4.) Where the value of the land is increased by reason
of the use thereof or of any premises thereon in a
manner which could be restrained by any court, or
is contrary to law, or is detrimental to the health of
the inmates of the premises or to the public health,
the amount of that increase shall not be taken into
account :

(5.) Where land is, and but for the compulsory

---

[1] Even though an agreement based thereon becomes void—*Percival
v. Peterborough Corporation* (King's Bench Divisional Court, 13th
October 1920).

32

acquisition would continue to be, devoted to a purpose of such a nature that there is no general demand or market for land for that purpose, the compensation may, if the official arbitrator is satisfied that reinstatement in some other place is *bonâ fide* intended, be assessed on the basis of the reasonable cost of equivalent reinstatement :

(6.) The provisions of Rule (2) shall not affect the assessment of compensation for disturbance or any other matter not directly based on the value of land.

For the purposes of this section, an official arbitrator shall be entitled to be furnished with such returns and assessments as he may require.

Provision as to procedure before official arbitrators.

3. (1.) In any proceedings before an official arbitrator, not more than one expert witness on either side shall be heard unless the official arbitrator otherwise directs :

Provided that, where the claim includes a claim for compensation in respect of minerals, or disturbance of business, as well as in respect of land, one additional expert witness on either side on the value of the minerals, or, as the case may be, on the damage suffered by reason of the disturbance may be allowed.

(2.) It shall not be necessary for an official arbitrator to make any declaration before entering into the consideration of any matter referred to him.

(3.) The official arbitrator shall, on the application of either party, specify the amount awarded in respect of any particular matter the subject of the award.

(4.) The official arbitrator shall be entitled to enter on and inspect any land which is the subject of proceedings before him.

(5.) Proceedings under this Act shall be heard by an official arbitrator sitting in public.

(6.) The fees to be charged in respect of proceedings before official arbitrators shall be such as the Treasury may prescribe.

(7.) Subject as aforesaid, the Reference Committee S. 3.
may make rules regulating the procedure before official
arbitrators.

4. Where notices to treat have been served for the Consolida
acquisition of the several interests in the land to be tion of
proceedings
acquired, the claims of the persons entitled to such on claims for
interests shall, so far as practicable, and so far as not compensation in
agreed and if the acquiring authority so desire, be heard respect of
various
and determined by the same official arbitrator, and the interests in
Reference Committee may make rules providing that the same
land.
such claims shall be heard together, but the value of
the several interests in the land having a market value
shall be separately assessed.

5. (1.) Where the acquiring authority has made an Provisions as
unconditional offer in writing of any sum as compensation to costs.
to any claimant and the sum awarded by an official
arbitrator to that claimant does not exceed the sum
offered, the official arbitrator shall, unless for special
reasons he thinks proper not to do so, order the claimant
to bear his own costs and to pay the costs of the acquiring
authority so far as such costs were incurred after the
offer was made.

(2.) If the official arbitrator is satisfied that a claimant
has failed to deliver to the acquiring authority a notice
in writing of the amount claimed by him giving sufficient
particulars and in sufficient time to enable the acquiring
authority to make a proper offer, the foregoing provisions
of this section shall apply as if an unconditional offer
had been made by the acquiring authority at the time
when in the opinion of the official arbitrator sufficient
particulars should have been furnished and the claimant
had been awarded a sum not exceeding the amount of
such offer.

The notice of claim shall state the exact nature of the
interest in respect of which compensation is claimed, and
give details of the compensation claimed, distinguishing

the amounts under separate heads and showing how the amount claimed under each head is calculated, and when such a notice of claim has been delivered the acquiring authority may, at any time within six weeks after the delivery thereof, withdraw any notice to treat which has been served on the claimant or on any other person interested in the land authorised to be acquired, but shall be liable to pay compensation to any such claimant or other person for any loss or expenses occasioned by the notice to treat having been given to him and withdrawn, and the amount of such compensation shall, in default of agreement, be determined by an official arbitrator.

(3.) Where a claimant has made an unconditional offer in writing to accept any sum as compensation and has complied with the provisions of the last preceding subsection, and the sum awarded is equal to or exceeds that sum, the official arbitrator shall, unless for special reasons he thinks proper not to do so, order the acquiring authority to bear their own costs and to pay the costs of the claimant so far as such costs were incurred after the offer was made.

(4.) Subject as aforesaid, the costs of an arbitration under this Act shall be in the discretion of the official arbitrator who may direct to and by whom and in what manner those costs or any part thereof shall be paid, and the official arbitrator may in any case disallow the cost of counsel.

(5.) An official arbitrator may himself tax the amount of costs ordered to be paid, or may direct in what manner they are to be taxed.

(6.) Where an official arbitrator orders the claimant to pay the costs, or any part of the costs, of the acquiring authority, the acquiring authority may deduct the amount so payable by the claimant from the amount of compensation payable to him.

(7.) Without prejudice to any other method of recovery,

the amount of costs ordered to be paid by a claimant, or such part thereof as is not covered by such deduction as aforesaid shall be recoverable from him by the acquiring authority summarily as a civil debt.

(8.) For the purpose of this section, costs include any fees, charges, and expenses of the arbitration or award.

6. (1.) The decision of an official arbitrator upon any question of fact, shall be final and binding on the parties, and the persons claiming under them respectively, but the official arbitrator may, and shall, if the High Court so directs, state at any stage of the proceedings, in the form of a special case for the opinion of the High Court, any question of law arising in the course of the proceedings, and may state his award as to the whole or part thereof in the form of a special case for the opinion of the High Court.

(2.) The decision of the High Court upon any case so stated shall be final and conclusive, and shall not be subject to appeal to any other court.

7. (1.) The provisions of the Act or order by which the land is authorised to be acquired, or of any Act incorporated therewith, shall, in relation to the matters dealt with in this Act, have effect subject to this Act, and so far as inconsistent with this Act those provisions shall cease to have or shall not have effect :

Provided that nothing in this Act relating to the rules for assessing compensation shall affect any special provisions as to the assessment of the value of land acquired for the purposes of Part I or Part II of the Housing of the Working Classes Act, 1890, or under the Defence of the Realm (Acquisition of Land) Act, 1916, and contained in those Acts respectively, or any Act amending those Acts, if and so far as the provisions in those Acts are inconsistent with the rules under this Act and the provisions of the Second Schedule to the Housing of the Working Classes Act, 1890 as amended

S. 7.

by any subsequent enactment (except paragraphs (4), (5), (29), and (31) thereof) shall apply to an official arbitrator as they apply to an arbitrator appointed under that schedule, and an official arbitrator may exercise all the powers conferred by those provisions on such arbitrator.

(2.) The provisions of this Act shall apply to the determination of the amount of rent or compensation payable in respect of land authorised to be hired com-

8 Edw. 7.
c. 36.

pulsorily under the Small Holdings and Allotments Act, 1908, or any Act amending that Act, and any matter required thereby to be determined by a valuer appointed by the Board of Agriculture and Fisheries shall be determined by an official arbitrator in accordance with this Act.

Power to refer to Commissioners of Inland Revenue or to agreed arbitrator.

8. (1.) Nothing in this Act shall prevent, if the parties so agree, the reference of any question as to disputed compensation or apportionment of rent to the Commissioners of Inland Revenue or to an arbitrator agreed on between the parties.

(2.) Where a question is so referred to the Commissioners of Inland Revenue, the Commissioners shall not proceed by arbitration, but shall cause an assessment to be made in accordance with the rules for the assessment of compensation under this Act, and the following provisions shall have effect :—

(a) The parties shall comply with any direction or requirements as to the furnishing of information (whether orally or in writing) and the production of documents and otherwise ;

(b) Any officer of the Commissioners appointed for the purpose shall be entitled to enter on and inspect any land which is subject to the reference to them ;

(c) The Commissioners, if either party so desires within such time as the Commissioners may allow, shall give the parties an opportunity of being heard before such officer of the valuation office of the Commissioners as the Commissioners may appoint for the purpose ;

(d) The assessment when made shall be published to the parties and take effect as if it were an award of an official arbitrator under this Act ;

(e) if either party refuses or neglects to comply with any direction or requirement of the Commissioners, the Commissioners may decline to proceed with the matter, and in that case the question shall be referred to an official arbitrator as if there had been no reference to the Commissioners, and the official arbitrator when awarding costs shall take into consideration any report of the Commissioners as to the refusal or neglect which rendered such a reference to him necessary.

(3.) Where a question is referred to an arbitrator under subsection (1) of this section, the provisions of this Act, except sections one and four and so much of section three as requires proceedings to be in public and as provides for the fixing of fees, shall apply as if the arbitrator was an official arbitrator.

(4.) Either party to a claim for compensation may require the Commissioners for Inland Revenue to assess the value of the land in respect of which the claim arises, and a copy of any such assessment shall be sent forthwith by the Commissioners to the other party, and a certified copy of such assessment shall be admissible in evidence of that value in proceedings before the official arbitrator, and the officer who made the assessment shall attend, if the official arbitrator so require, to answer such questions as the official arbitrator may think fit to put to him thereon.

9. An official arbitrator may on the application of any person certify the value of land being sold by him to a Government department or public or local authority,

S. 9.

and the sale of the land to the department or authority at the price so certified shall be deemed to be a sale at the best price that can reasonably be obtained.

Saving for statutory purchases of statutory undertakings.

10. (1.) The provisions of this Act shall not apply to any purchase of the whole or any part of any statutory undertaking under any statutory provisions in that behalf prescribing the terms on which the purchase is to be effected.

(2.) For the purposes of this section, the expression "statutory undertaking" means an undertaking established by Act of Parliament or order having the force of an Act, and the expression "statutory provisions" includes the provisions of an order having the force of an Act.

Application to Scotland and Ireland.

11. (1.) This Act shall apply to Scotland subject to the following modifications:—

(a) The provisions of this Act other than the provisions of the section thereof relating to rules for the assessment of compensation shall apply to the determination of any question which, under subsection (11) of section seven or section seventeen of the

1 & 2 Geo. 5. c. 49.

Small Landholders (Scotland) Act, 1911, is referred to arbitration, as if the Board of Agriculture for Scotland were the acquiring authority, and as if in the said subsection (11) there were substituted for the Lord Ordinary on the Bills and the Lord Ordinary, except where the Lord Ordinary is therein last referred to, such person as may be prescribed by rules made by the Reference Committee for Scotland ; and the provisions of that Act, including

8 Edw. 7. c. 64.

the Second Schedule to the Agricultural Holdings (Scotland) Act, 1908, as thereby applied, shall in relation to such determination have effect subject to the aforesaid provisions of this Act :

(b) "High Court" means either division of the Court

of Session; "arbitrator" means arbiter, and S. 11.
" easement " means servitude.

(2.) This Act shall apply to Ireland subject to the
following modifications :—

Nothing in this Act shall affect the determination of
the price or compensation to be paid on the compulsory acquisition of land by the Irish Land Commission or Congested Districts Board for Ireland
under any statute or the special provisions contained
in the Labourers (Ireland) Act, 1885, and the enact- 48 & 49 Vict.
ments amending the same, with respect to the c. 77.
jurisdiction of the Irish Land Commission in cases
where land is taken compulsorily under those provisions for a term of years.

12. (1.) This Act may be cited as the Acquisition of Short title,
Land (Assessment of Compensation) Act, 1919, and shall commence-
come into operation on the first day of September nine- ment and
teen hundred and nineteen, but shall not apply to the interpretation.
determination of any question where before that date
the appointment of an arbitration, valuation, or other
tribunal to determine the question has been completed,
or a jury has been empanelled for the purpose.

(2.) For the purposes of this Act, the expression
" land " includes water and any interests in land or
water and any easement or right in, to, or over land or
water, and " public authority " means any body of
persons, not trading for profit, authorised by or under
any Act to carry on a railway, canal, dock, water or other
public undertaking.

STATUTORY RULES AND ORDERS, 1919. No. 1,836 ── L. 30

LAND, ACQUISITION OF, ENGLAND

ASSESSMENT OF COMPENSATION

The Acquisition of Land (Assessment of Compensation) Rules, 1919, dated 2nd December 1919, made by the Reference Committee for England and Wales under the Acquisition of Land (Assessment of Compensation) Act, 1919 (9 & 10 Geo. 5. c. 57).

In pursuance of the Acquisition of Land (Assessment of Compensation) Act, 1919, the Reference Committee for England and Wales constituted under that Act hereby make the following rules :—

Short title.

1. These rules may be cited as the Acquisition of Land (Assessment of Compensation) Rules, 1919.

Interpretation.

2. (1.) In these rules, unless the context otherwise requires :—

The expression " the Act " means the Acquisition of Land (Assessment of Compensation) Act, 1919 ;

The expression " arbitrator " means an official arbitrator ;

The expression " question " means any question of disputed compensation, or any question of the apportionment of a rent, which is to be referred to and determined by arbitration in manner provided by the Act.

(2.) The Interpretation Act, 1889, applies for the purpose of the interpretation of these rules as it applies for the purpose of the interpretation of an Act of Parliament.

Application for selection of official arbitrator.

3. (1.) Where any question has arisen either the acquiring authority or the claimant may at any time after the expiration of fourteen days from the date on which the notice to treat was served send to the Reference Committee an application for the selection of an arbitrator.

(2.) The acquiring authority or the claimant, as the case may be, shall, immediately after sending the application to the Reference Committee, send notice of the fact to the claimant or the acquiring authority, as the case may be, together with a copy of the application.

(3.) An application for the selection of an arbitrator Rules.
shall be in the form set out in the schedule to these
rules or in a form to the like effect.

4. (1.) The Reference Committee, on receiving a valid Selection of
application for the selection of an arbitrator, shall, as official
soon as may be, proceed to select from the panel an arbitrator.
arbitrator to deal with the case.

(2.) The Reference Committee shall, as soon as they
have selected the arbitrator, inform the acquiring authority
and the claimant of the name and address of the person
so selected.

5. (1.) The arbitrator selected shall, as soon as may be, Considera-
proceed with the determination of the question in dispute, tion of
and shall arrange with the acquiring authority and the by official
claimant the time and place of the hearing. arbitrator.

(2.) The Reference Committee shall send to the arbitrator selected a copy of the application for the appointment of an arbitrator, and the acquiring authority and
the claimant shall furnish to the arbitrator on his request
any document or other information which it is in their
or his power to furnish and which the arbitrator may
require for the purpose of considering and determining
the case.

(3.) Subject to the provisions of the Act and of these
rules the proceedings before an arbitrator shall be such
as the arbitrator, subject to any special directions of the
Reference Committee, may in his discretion think fit.

6. The Reference Committee may, in the case of the Power to
death or the incapacity of the arbitrator originally select
selected, or if it is shown to the committee that it is official
expedient so to do, in any other case, at any time before arbitrator.
the arbitrator has made his award, revoke the reference
of the question to the selected arbitrator and select
another arbitrator for the purpose of determining the
question.

7. (1.) Where notices to treat have been served for Consolida-
the acquisition of the several interests in the land to be tion of
acquired and questions as to the amount of compensation relating to
have arisen in the case of any two or more of those several
interests the acquiring authority may, subject as herein- the same
after provided, either on making the application for the land.
selection of an arbitrator to hear the claims or at any
time thereafter make an application to the Reference
Committee to have the same person selected as the

arbitrator to hear and determine all the claims to which the application relates :

Provided that no such application shall be made as respects a claim if an arbitrator has already entered on the consideration of the claim.

(2.) On receiving an application under this rule the Reference Committee shall select the same person to act as arbitrator in respect of all the claims to which the application relates, and so far as necessary for that purpose may revoke any selection previously made.

(3.) An application under this rule shall be in the form set out in the schedule to these rules or in a form to the like effect.

(4.) Where the same person has been selected under this rule to act as arbitrator in respect of two or more claims the acquiring authority may at any time after he has been so selected apply to him for an order that all the claims shall be heard together.

(5.) Notice of intention to apply to the arbitrator for such an order as aforesaid shall be sent to each claimant and the notice shall specify the date on which and the place at which the arbitrator will hear any objection which may be made to the application.

(6.) If any claimant objects to have his claim heard together with the other claims he shall within seven days after the receipt of the notice aforesaid send notice of his objection to the acquiring authority and the arbitrator.

(7.) Where the acquiring authority apply for an order under this rule the arbitrator after taking into consideration any objection made to the application shall make such order in the matter as he thinks proper having regard to all the circumstances of the case.

(8.) On an application for an order under this rule an order for consolidation may be made if the arbitrator thinks fit with respect to some only of the claims, and the order may in any case be made subject to such special directions as to costs, witnesses, method of procedure, and otherwise as the arbitrator thinks proper.

Provision as to payment of fees prescribed by Treasury. 8. (1.) If the fees prescribed by the Treasury in pursuance of the powers conferred on them by subsection (6) of section 3 of the Act include a fee in respect of an application under these rules or a fee in respect of the hearing before an official arbitrator, the prescribed

fee shall be collected by means of adhesive stamps affixed Rules.
to or stamps impressed on the application and the award
of the arbitrator respectively.

(2.) Any application under these rules which is not
properly stamped in accordance with the foregoing
provision shall be treated as invalid, and the award of
an official arbitrator shall not be delivered out by him
unless and until it has been properly stamped in accordance with the said provision.

9. Any notice or other document required or authorised Provision as
to be sent to any person for the purpose of these rules to sending
shall be deemed to be duly sent by post addressed notice.
to that person at his ordinary address, and the address
of the Reference Committee shall for this purpose be—
J. Johnston, Esq., Secretary to the Reference Committee,
Room 174, Royal Courts of Justice, Strand, London,
W.C.2.

10. Save as herein otherwise expressly provided, any Informali-
failure on the part of any authority or any person to ties not
comply with the provisions of these rules shall not render to invalidate
the proceedings, or anything done in pursuance thereof, proceedings.
invalid, unless the arbitrator so directs.

SCHEDULE

A

FORM OF APPLICATION FOR SELECTION OF OFFICIAL
ARBITRATOR

Acquisition of Land (Assessment of Compensation)
Act, 1919

Application for Selection of Official Arbitrator.

To the Reference Committee.

I, being the claimant [*or*, We being the acquiring
authority] specified in the annexed particulars, hereby
apply for the selection, pursuant to the above Act, of
an official arbitrator to hear and determine the question
of which particulars are annexed.

[1] Signed....................

Date....................

[1] If the application is signed by an agent, add " by
....................his [*or* their] agent."

Particulars

Name and address of acquiring authority :

....

....

....

Name and address of acquiring authority's solicitor or agent :

....

....

....

Name and address of claimant :

....

....

....

Name and address of claimant's solicitor or agent :

....

....

....

Description of land to be acquired :

....

Situation of land to be acquired :

County....................

Parish ....

Nature of question (whether as to amount of compensation or apportionment of rent) :

....

Interest in respect of which compensation is claimed :

....

B

FORM OF APPLICATION TO HAVE SAME PERSON APPOINTED AS ARBITRATOR ON CLAIMS IN RESPECT OF VARIOUS INTERESTS IN SAME LAND.

Acquisition of Land (Assessment of Compensation) Act, 1919

Application to have same person appointed as arbitrator on claims in respect of various interests in same land. To the Reference Committee.

We, being the acquiring authority in the case of the land specified in the annexed particulars, apply, pursuant to the rules made under the above Act, to have the same person selected as the official arbitrator to hear and determine all the claims for compensation made in respect of the several interests in the said land.

No official arbitrator has been selected in the case of any of the said claims [*or* an official arbitrator has already been selected in the case of the claims of the persons numbered................in the annex of particulars, namely Mr..............................in the case of No. 1...................*state the facts*].

[1] Signed....................

Date...............

[1] If the application is signed by an agent of the applicants, add " by...................their agent."

Particulars

Name and address of acquiring authority :

....

....

....

Name and address of acquiring authority's solicitor or agent :

....

....

....

Description of land to be acquired :

....

Situation of land to be acquired :

County....................

Parish ....

Names and addresses of (i) persons entitled to the several interests in the land, and (ii) their respective solicitors or agents :	Nature of interest.
1. (i)	1.
(ii)	
2. (i)	2.
(ii)	
3. (i)	3.
(ii)	

We, the Reference Committee for England and Wales under the Acquisition of Land (Assessment of

Rules.   Compensation) Act, 1919, have made the above rules in
pursuance of the powers conferred on us by the said Act.

READING, *C.J.*
STERNDALE, *M.R.*
ANDREW YOUNG, *P.S.I.*

2nd December 1919.

STATUTORY RULES AND ORDERS, 1920, No. 285.

ACQUISITION OF LAND (ASSESSMENT OF COMPENSATION) FEES RULES, 1920.

In pursuance of subsection (6) of section 3 of the
Acquisition of Land (Assessment of Compensation) Act,
1919, the Lords Commissioners of His Majesty's Treasury
hereby make the following rules :—

1. (1) These rules may be cited as the Acquisition of
Land (Assessment of Compensation) Fees Rules, 1920.

(2) In these rules the expression " the Act " means
the Acquisition of Land (Assessment of Compensation)
Act, 1919.

2. On every application for the selection of an arbitrator
made in accordance with the rules made under the Act
by the Reference Committee there shall be paid the fee
of £1.

3. (1) On an award by an official arbitrator under the
Act there shall be paid a fee calculated by reference to
the amount awarded to the claimant in accordance with
the following scale :—

SCALE OF FEES ON AWARDS   .

Amount awarded	Amount of fee.
Not exceeding £200	£5 5s.
Exceeding £200 but not exceeding £500	£5 5s. with an addition of £1 1s. in respect of every £50 or part of £50 by which the amount awarded exceeds £200.
Exceeding £500 but not exceeding £1,000	£11 11s. with an addition of £1 1s. in respect of every £100 or part of £100 by which the amount awarded exceeds £500.
Exceeding £1,000	£16 16s. with an addition of £1 1s. in respect of every £200 or part of £200 by which the amount awarded exceeds £1,000, but not exceeding in any case £105.

(2) In addition to the fee payable under the scale
aforesaid, there shall, where the hearing before the

arbitrator in respect of any claim or matter referred to Fees. him occupies more than one day, be paid for each day or part of a day after the first day a further fee on the following scale :—

Amount awarded.	Amount of fee.	
	£	s.
Not exceeding £500	5	5
Exceeding £500 and not exceeding £5,000 . .	10	10
Exceeding £5,000 and not exceeding £20,000 .	21	0
Exceeding £20,000	42	0

For the purpose of the foregoing provision any time spent by the arbitrator in viewing any land which is the subject matter of the proceedings before him shall be treated as part of the hearing :

A day shall be taken to be a working period of five hours.

Dated 24th February 1920.

JAMES PARKER,

J. TOWYN JONES,

Two of the Lords Commissioners of His Majesty's Treasury.

NOTE.—The fees prescribed in the above scale are in addition to the stamp duty charged on awards by the Stamp Act, 1821.

STATUTORY RULES AND ORDERS, 1920, No. 690

THE ACQUISITION OF LAND (ASSESSMENT OF COMPENSATION) FEES (NO. 2) RULES, 1920, DATED 5TH MAY 1920, MADE BY THE TREASURY UNDER SECTION 3 (6) OF THE ACQUISITION OF LAND (ASSESSMENT OF COMPENSATION) ACT, 1919.

In pursuance of subsection (6) of section 3 of the Acquisition of Land (Assessment of Compensation) Act, 1919, the Lords Commissioners of His Majesty's Treasury hereby make the following rule :—

1. (i) These rules may be cited as the Acquisition of Land (Assessment of Compensation) Fees (No. 2) Rules, 1920.

33

(ii) In these rules, the expression " original rules " means the Acquisition of Land (Assessment of Compensation) Fees Rules, 1920.

(iii) In these rules, the expression " the Act " means the Acquisition of Land (Assessment of Compensation) Act, 1919.

2. Where the award of an official arbitrator under the Act is an award in terms of rent or other annual payment, the following scales of fees marked A and B shall be substituted for the scales set forth in rule 3 (1) and rule 3 (2) respectively of the original rules :—

Amount awarded.	Amount of fee.
	A
Not exceeding £10 per annum	£5 5s.
Exceeding £10 per annum but not exceeding £25 per annum	£5 5s. with an addition of £1 1s. in respect of every £2 10s. or part of £2 10s. by which the rent, &c., awarded exceeds £10 per annum.
Exceeding £25 per annum but not exceeding £50 per annum	£11 11s. with an addition of £1 1s. in respect of every £5 or part of £5 by which the rent, &c., awarded exceeds £25 per annum.
Exceeding £50 per annum	£16 16s. with an addition of £1 1s. in respect of every £10 or part of £10 by which the rent, &c., awarded exceeds £50, but not exceeding in any case £105.
	B
Not exceeding £25 per annum	£5 5s.
Exceeding £25 per annum and not exceeding £250 per annum	£10 10s.
Exceeding £250 per annum and not exceeding £1,000 per annum	£21.
Exceeding £1,000 per annum	£42.

Dated 5th May 1920.

JAMES PARKER,
J. TOWYN JONES,

Two of the Lords Commissioners of His Majesty's Treasury.

GENERAL HOUSING MEMORANDUM No. 6

COMPULSORY ACQUISITION OF LAND FOR HOUSING

AMENDMENTS INTRODUCED BY THE HOUSING, TOWN PLANNING, &c., ACT, 1919

Extended powers in regard to the compulsory acquisition of land for housing have been conferred by the Housing, Town Planning, &c., Act, 1919.

(1) Section 12 of the Act authorises a local authority to acquire houses, together with the lands occupied with such houses.

(2) Section 10 gives them power to enter on land compulsorily acquired at any time after notice to treat has been served, after giving fourteen days' notice to the owner and occupier.

(3) Section 11 (1) withdraws the special procedure previously required in connection with the compulsory acquisition of land situate in London or in a borough or urban district, where objection is raised to the acquisition.

(4) Section 11 (2) prescribes that the Minstry shall not confirm an order, even if it is unopposed, if they are of opinion that the land is unsuited for the purpose for which it is proposed to be acquired.

(5) Section 11 (3) gives the Ministry power to confirm without a public inquiry any order, even if opposed, which is submitted after the date of the passing of the Act (31st July 1919) and within two years from that date.

AMENDMENTS IN PROCEDURE

Compulsory Purchase Orders

In order to expedite progress with housing schemes, the Ministry of Health have decided to amend the Form of Compulsory Purchase Order, 1911, so as to shorten the procedure which local authorities have hitherto been required to adopt under that Order in submitting proposals for the compulsory acquisition of land for housing.

G.H.M. 6.

The changes which have been made are as follows :—

Former Procedure	*Procedure now to be Adopted*
(1) *Advertisement* The first of the two advertisements prescribed by the Order must be published not later than the *tenth* day after the making of the compulsory purchase order.	(1) The first of the two advertisements prescribed by the Order must be published not later than the *seventh* day after the making of the compulsory purchase order.
(2) *Deposit of Plan* The plan must be deposited not later than the *tenth* day from the making of the order and must be kept deposited not less than *one month* from the date of the publication of the *second and last* advertisement.	(2) The plan must be deposited not later than the *seventh* day from the making of the order and must be kept deposited not less than *fourteen days* from the date of the publication of the *first advertisement*.
(3) *Service of Notice* Notice of the order must be served on the owners, lessees and occupiers not later than the *tenth* day after the making of the order.	Notice of the order must be served on the owners, lessees and occupiers not later than the *seventh* day after the making of the order.
(4) *Objections* Objections must be presented within *one month* from the date of the publication of the *second and last* advertisement.	Objections must be presented within *fourteen days* from the date of the publication of the *first advertisement*.

AMENDMENTS AS TO ASSESSMENT OF COMPENSATION

The Acquisition of Land Act, which has now received the Royal Assent, provides that any question of disputed compensation in respect of land compulsorily acquired for public purposes, shall be determined by an official arbitrator. The Act prescribes the method of appointment of arbitrators, the basis on which the arbitrator is to proceed in assessing compensation and the procedure to be adopted.

Section 12 provides that the Act shall come into operation on the 1st of September 1919, but shall not apply to the determination of any question where the appointment of an arbitrator has been completed before that date.

STEPS TO BE TAKEN BY THE LOCAL AUTHORITY IN CONNECTION WITH COMPULSORY ACQUISITION OF LAND OR HOUSES

1. *Making of the Order.* An order should be prepared in the form prescribed in the regulations and, on the

authority of the council or the housing committee, the order should be sealed with the council's seal.

- 2. *Service of Notice.* Notice of the order must be served on the owners, lessees and occupiers, as described in the regulations, not later than the *seventh* day after the making of the order. The notice must include a copy of the order, to which must be appended a notice that any objections must be made to the Ministry of Health within *fourteen days* from the date of the *first* advertisement, and a statement of the period, time and place during and at which the deposited plan may be inspected.

3. *Deposit of Plan.* The plan referred to in the schedule to the order must be deposited not later than the *seventh* day from the making of the order, and must be kept deposited not less than *fourteen* days from the date of the publication of the *first* advertisement. The plan must be deposited at a convenient place, must be open for inspection by persons interested or affected at all reasonable hours, without fee, and the local authority must arrange to provide any necessary explanation.

4. *Advertisement.* The order must be advertised twice, in two successive weeks, in one or more of the local newspapers. The advertisements must be headed " First Advertisement " and " Second and Last Advertisement," respectively. The first advertisement must be published not later than the seventh day after the making of the order. The advertisement must contain, in addition to a copy of the order, a notice stating that any objections must be sent to the Ministry of Health within *fourteen days* after the publication of the *first* advertisement, and a statement of the period, time and places during and at which the deposited plan may be inspected.

5. *Objections.* Before submitting the order to the Ministry for confirmation, the local authority must allow a period of *fourteen days* from the date of the first advertisement to elapse, during which objections may be made to the Ministry by persons interested.

6. *Submission for Confirmation.* After making and advertising the order, depositing the plan, giving notice to the owners, lessees and occupiers, and allowing the period for the submission of objections to elapse, the

G.H.M. 6.   local authority should forthwith submit the order to the Ministry for confirmation. The Ministry should be furnished with the following documents and particulars :—

(a) The original order sealed by the council, and a copy thereof.

(b) A copy of each of the newspapers in which the advertisements were inserted.

(c) A definite statement that the plan was deposited for the period prescribed.

(d) A copy of the plan deposited.

(e) A definite statement that notice was given to the owners, lessees and occupiers.

(f) A copy of the notice and a statement showing the names of all owners, lessees and occupiers, and the manner and date of service in each case.

(g) A formal application by resolution of the council or of the housing committee for the Ministry's confirmation of the order.

7. *Confirmation.* For a period of two years from the 31st July 1919, it will be within the discretion of the Ministry to determine whether a public inquiry shall be held into the proposals of the local authority for the compulsory acquisition. If it is held, it will be held by a representative of the Ministry. The Ministry will not confirm an order, if they are of opinion that the land is unsuited for the purpose for which it is sought to be acquired.

8. *Notice after Confirmation.* Upon receipt of information that the Ministry have confirmed the order, the local authority must serve a copy of the compulsory order as confirmed on every owner, lessee and occupier as soon as practicable, and they should give notice to treat and inform the Ministry that this has been done.

9. *Provision of Copies.* The local authority must furnish a copy of the order free of charge to any person interested in the land who applies for one, and must furnish a copy of the plan to any such person for the reasonable cost of preparing the same.

10. *Powers of entry after notice of treat has been given.* The local authority may enter on the land when an order has been made and confirmed, after giving *fourteen*

days' notice to the owner and occupier, without awaiting G.H.M. 6. the result of the assessment of compensation.

A further memorandum will be issued shortly explaining the procedure under the Acquisition of Land Act.

MINISTRY OF HEALTH,
WHITEHALL, S.W. 1.
September 1919.

GENERAL HOUSING MEMORANDUM No. 11

COMPULSORY ACQUISITION OF LAND FOR HOUSING

INTRODUCTION

1. In view of the time occupied and the costs incurred in purchasing land by compulsory powers, an order should not be made until careful consideration has been given to the possibility of obtaining an alternative site. This is particularly the case in rural areas where the cost incurred in acquiring the land compulsorily may be disproportionate to the value of the land.

2. Where an alternative site is not available and negotiations for the purchase have proved abortive, a compulsory order may be made subject to the provisions of paragraph 3, but it should be borne in mind that the service of the order does not preclude the possibility of coming to an agreement. (See paragraph 2 of Notice to Treat.)

3. Before confirming an order, the Minister is required (a) to satisfy himself that the site to which the proposed order relates is not unsuited for the purpose for which it is proposed to be acquired ; (b) to consider any objections which may be made to the order, and, when necessary, to cause a public enquiry to be held ; (c) to satisfy himself that the land can be acquired at a reasonable price ; and he desires, therefore, to be informed at the earliest practicable date of the intention of a local authority to make a compulsory purchase order. Cases in which local authorities will find such orders necessary will, no doubt, fall into one of two classes :—

G.H.M. 11.

 (i) Where the owner is unwilling to sell the land at any price.

 (ii) Where the owner is willing to sell, but no agreement can be reached as to price. In such cases, the local authority will, no doubt, in accordance with the usual procedure, have placed negotiations in the hands of the Inland Revenue Valuer, and the compulsory purchase order will be proposed because his negotiations have failed.

Where the local authority is in a position to begin building at an early date, negotiations should not be unduly prolonged. After any such case has been in the hands of the District Valuer for, say, one month, the council should request him to report the position of the negotiations, and if there is no reasonable possibility of an immediate agreement the question of adopting compulsory powers should be considered. The District Valuer should be informed, however, immediately it is decided to make an order.

4. It is suggested that at the earliest stage practicable a letter should be sent to the Commissioner notifying him of the intention of the council to make a compulsory purchase order, and that a copy of this letter should be sent to the Ministry for information. The letter should state the name and area of the site, and should be accompanied by a report from the District Valuer as to the conduct of the negotiations, and stating the price asked by the owner and any offer made by the valuer with a view to settlement; if practicable, a copy of the draft order and of the plan of the site should also be enclosed.

PROCEDURE IN CONNECTION WITH MAKING OF ORDER AND APPLICATION FOR CONFIRMATION

5. (a) Information as to the steps to be taken at this stage is contained in General Housing Memorandum No. 6, to which reference should be made.

(b) The Minister desires that the cost of making the compulsory order should be kept to the lowest possible figure.

(c) It will be desirable in suitable cases to intimate (by a letter sent to the owner when the compulsory

order is forwarded) that the service of the order is made G.H.M. 11.
primarily to ensure early entry upon the land, and does
not preclude negotiations with a view to settlement,
and that if the owner desires to proceed with this end
in view he should communicate with the District
Valuer.

PROCEDURE SUBSEQUENT TO THE CONFIRMATION OF THE
ORDER

6. The following procedure should be adopted
after the Compulsory Purchase Order has been confirmed :—

(i) Copies of the confirmed order will be sent by the
Ministry to the local authority, and, under the
Housing Acts (Compulsory Purchase) Regulations, 1919, the local authority are required to
serve a copy on every owner, lessee and occupier
of the land to which the compulsory order
relates. This should be done forthwith. The
local authority should at the same time serve
notice to treat, and also (*see* section 10 (1) of
the Housing, Town Planning, &c., Act, 1919)
notice of their intention to enter on, and take
possession of the land after the expiration of
not less than fourteen days after the notice
to treat has been served. It is suggested that
the copy of the confirmed order, the notice to
treat and the notice of intention to enter
should be served at the same time. Copies of
a draft notice to treat, and notice of intention
to enter, which might be used in this connection,
are appended to this memorandum.

If immediate entry is desired, care should be
taken to give the tenant notice under Section
10 (2) of the Housing, and Town Planning
Act, 1919, at the proper time. In cases where
agreement has been or can be come to with the
tenant he need not be served with a notice to
treat.

(ii) The local authority should wait a reasonable
period (twenty-one days is suggested) for the
receipt of a claim. If this is received, a copy

G.H.M. 11.

should be forwarded to the Ministry, and if no claim is received this fact should be reported after the expiration of the stated period.

(iii) The Ministry will in due course inform the local authority if they consider it desirable that an unconditional offer should now be made, and, if so, will inform them of the amount they are prepared to endorse, and in such case such an offer should immediately be made. It will be seen that under Section 5 of the Acquisition of Land (Assessment of Compensation) Act, 1919, the making of an unconditional offer, in writing, by the acquiring authority has a material bearing on the question of costs.

(iv) If· the unconditional offer is refused, the local authority should take steps to have an arbitrator appointed under the provisions of the Acquisition of Land (Assessment of Compensation) Act, 1919. The arbitrator will be selected in accordance with the rules made by the reference committee under the Act, which, it is anticipated, will be issued very shortly.

(v) The arbitration will be conducted under rules to be made by the reference committee, but in all cases the Ministry will expect that the District Valuer should give evidence before the referee.

7. In normal circumstances the matter should be referred to the official Arbitrator defined by Section 1 of the Acquisition of Land (Assessment of Compensation) Act, 1919, but no objection will be taken by the Ministry to the case being heard by an agreed arbitrator under section 8 (1).

8. In cases where the Inland Revenue Valuer has not already valued or conducted negotiations on behalf of the local authority, the latter, if they so desire, may, when serving notice to treat, and without waiting for a claim, ask the owner whether he is prepared to accept an assessment by the Commissioner of Inland Revenue under section 8 (1). If he agrees, a joint submission should be agreed and sent to the Secretary, Land Values, Commissioners of Inland Revenue, Somerset House, W.C.2,

·If the owner refuses the procedure will be as laid down G.H.M. 11.
in 6 above

THE HOUSING ACTS, 1890 TO 1919
NOTICE TO TREAT

WHEREAS by an Order made on the   day of
      19 , by the   Council, and confirmed
on the   day of   19   by the Minister
of Health the provisions of the Lands Clauses Acts with
respect to the purchase and taking of land otherwise
than by agreement were, subject as therein mentioned,
put in force as respects the purchase by the council
of the hereditaments described in the schedule
hereto :—

Now the council hereby give you notice

1. That they require to purchase and take for the purposes and under the provisions of the Housing Acts 1890
to 1919 and of the Acts incorporated therewith the
hereditaments mentioned and described in the schedule
hereunder written and delineated on the plan attached
hereto and therein coloured   and which said
hereditaments the council are by the said Acts authorised
to purchase and take.

2. That they are willing to treat with you and every
of you for the purchase of the hereditaments so required
as aforesaid, and as to the compensation to be made to
you and every of you for the damage that may be sustained by you and every of you by reason of the execution
of the works authorised by the said Acts.

3. And the council hereby demand from you and each
and every of you the particulars of your respective
estates and interests in the hereditaments so required as
aforesaid together with all charges and interests to which
the same are subject and of the claims made by you
and each of you in respect thereof which several particulars
should be stated in the accompanying form of claim and
delivered to the   at   .

4. And the council hereby further give you notice
that if for 21 days after the service hereof you shall fail
to state the particulars of your respective claims in
respect of the said hereditaments so required or to treat
with the council in respect thereof, or if you or any of

G.H.M. 11.   you respectively and the council shall not agree as to the amount of compensation to be paid by the council for or in respect of your respective interests in the said hereditaments so required or the interests therein which you respectively are by the said Acts, or the Acts incorporated therewith, enabled to sell, or for any damage that may be sustained by you respectively as aforesaid the council will forthwith proceed to require the amount of such compensation to be settled in manner directed by the Acquisition of Land (Assessment of Compensation) Act, 1919, for settling cases of disputed compensation.

5. And the council in case you, having a greater interest therein than as tenant at will, claim compensation in respect of any unexpired term or interest under any lease or grant of the hereditaments so required as aforesaid, hereby requires you to produce the lease or grant in respect of which such claim is made or the best evidence thereof in your power.

     Dated this   day of   19

               On behalf of the

                          Town Clerk.

                     Clerk to the Council.

(Address of the offices of the Council).

To

    of

    and to all persons having or claiming

    any estate or interest in the said here-

    ditaments.

            THE SCHEDULE above referred to.

CLAIM BY OWNER FOR COMPENSATION FROM THE COUNCIL

THE HOUSING ACTS, 1890 TO 1919

FORM OF CLAIM

To be sent in within 21 days from receipt of Notice to Treat to the

Schedule of claim to be filled in and signed by Owners and Lessees of Property, or their Solicitors, required by the   under powers contained in the above Acts and the Acts of Parliament therewith incorporated.

G.H.M. 11.

Name, address and description of claimant.	Description of Property (whether land, house, or other property, and by what name known and short description from Notice to Treat).	Nature of Interest. If Freehold state whether Tenant in Fee, in tail or for life. If Copyhold, state name of Manor, names and addresses of Lord and Steward, and full particulars as to rents, services, etc. If Leasehold, then for what term or number of years, of whom held, at what rent, and whether as Sub-Lessee or direct from the owner, and generally state all charges and incumbrances affecting such respective estates, whether as Owner, Lessee or Sub-Lessee.	Particulars of claim, and in such particulars distinguish the amount claimed for the value of the land from the amount claimed for damage and the numbers on the plan in respect of which the claim is made.	Date and other short particulars of Documents of Title.	Names of persons having custody of documents and place or places where same may be inspected.

Mr.

of   is the agent appointed by me to treat
for the sale of the property to which this claim relates
and Messrs.   of   will act as my
Solicitors.

Dated this   day of   19 .

(Signature of Claimant).

THE HOUSING ACTS, 1890 TO 1919

NOTICE OF ENTRY

To

of

WHEREAS by an Order made on the   day of
19 , by the   Council, and
confirmed on the   day of   19 , by
the Minister of Health the provisions of the Lands Clauses
Acts with respect to the purchase and taking of land
otherwise than by agreement were, subject as therein
mentioned, put in force as respects the purchase by the
Council of the property described in the Schedule hereto :

AND WHEREAS Notice to Treat for the said property
has been served upon you :

NOW THEREFORE The Council in exercise of the power
conferred upon them by sub-section (1) of Section 10
of the Housing, Town Planning, &c., Act, 1919, HEREBY
GIVE YOU NOTICE that they will upon the expiration

G.H.M. 11.   of fourteen days from the service of this Notice upon
you, enter on and take possession of the said property.
THE SCHEDULE above referred to.
Dated this   day of   19
On behalf of the
Town Clerk.
Clerk to the Council.

STATUTORY RULES AND ORDERS, 1919, No. 1175

HOUSING OF THE WORKING CLASSES, ENGLAND

ACQUISITION OF LANDS

The Housing Acts (Compulsory Purchase) Regulations,
1919. Dated 29th August 1919.[1]

65,408

The Minister of Health, in pursuance of the powers
conferred on Him by the First Schedule to the Housing,
Town Planning, &c., Act, 1909, and of all other powers
enabling Him in that behalf, hereby makes the following
Regulations :—

ARTICLE I—These Regulations may be cited as " the
Housing Acts (Compulsory Purchase) Regulations, 1919."

ARTICLE II—The Housing, &c. (Form of Compulsory
Purchase Order, &c.) Order, 1911, made by the Local
Government Board on the 14th day of June 1911, is
hereby revoked, except so far as it relates to any Com-
pulsory Order made thereunder before the date of these
Regulations.

ARTICLE III—An Order made by a Local Authority
under the First Schedule to the Housing, Town Planning,
&c., Act, 1909 (herein-after referred to as " the Compulsory Order "), shall be in the Form set forth in the
Schedule hereto, or in a Form substantially to the like
effect.

ARTICLE IV—(1) Before submitting the Compulsory
Order to the Minister of Health for confirmation, the
Local Authority shall cause the same to be published
by advertisement in two successive weeks in one or more
of the local newspapers circulating in the District of the

[1] See the additions by the two documents next following.

Local Authority and in the Parish or Parishes in which the land to which the Compulsory Order relates is situated.

(2) The advertisements shall be headed respectively "First Advertisement" and "Second and Last Advertisement," and the first of the said advertisements shall be published not later than the seventh day after the making of the Compulsory Order.

(3) Each of the said advertisements shall contain in addition to a copy of the Compulsory Order a notice setting out the following particulars :—

    (a) a statement that any objection to the Compulsory Order must be presented to the Minister of Health within the period of fourteen days from and after the date of the publication of the first advertisement ; and

    (b) a statement of the period, times, and place or places during and at which the deposited plan referred to in the Schedule to the Compulsory Order may be inspected by or on behalf of any person interested in the land to which the Compulsory Order relates.

(4) The plan referred to in the Schedule to the Compulsory Order shall be deposited by the Local Authority not later than the seventh day after the making of the Compulsory Order at a place convenient for the purposes of inspection, and shall be kept deposited thereat for a period not being less than fourteen days from the date of the publication of the first advertisement ; and the said plan shall be open for inspection by any person interested or affected, without payment of any fee, at all reasonable hours on any weekday during the said period. The Local Authority shall also make suitable provision for affording to any such person inspecting the said plan any necessary explanation or information in regard thereto.

ARTICLE V—(1) The Local Authority shall, not later than the seventh day after the making of the Compulsory Order, cause notice thereof to be given to every owner, lessee, and occupier of the land to which the Compulsory Order relates, and every such notice shall include a copy of the Compulsory Order, to which shall be appended a notice containing the particulars mentioned in paragraph (3) of Article IV of these Regulations.

(2) The Local Authority shall furnish a copy of the

Compulsory Order, free of charge, to any person interested in the land to which the Compulsory Order relates, upon his applying for the same.

ARTICLE VI—The period within which an objection to a Compulsory Order may be presented to the Minister of Health by a person interested in the land to which the Compulsory Order relates shall be the period of fourteen days from and after the date of the publication of the first advertisement of the Compulsory Order.

ARTICLE VII—(1) The Local Authority shall as soon as practicable after the confirmation of the Compulsory Order cause a copy of the Compulsory Order as confirmed to be served on every owner, lessee, and occupier of the land to which the Compulsory Order relates.

(2) A copy of the Compulsory Order as confirmed shall be furnished free of charge by the Local Authority to any person interested in the land authorised to be purchased upon his applying for the same, and a copy of any plan to which reference is made in the Compulsory Order as confirmed shall also be furnished by the Local Authority to any such person upon his applying for such copy and paying the reasonable cost of preparing the same.

ARTICLE VIII—Every notice or other document which in pursuance of paragraph (1) of Article V or of paragraph (1) of Article VII of these Regulations is required to be given or served by the Local Authority to or on an owner, lessee, or occupier, shall be served :—

(a) by delivery of the same personally to the person required to be served, or, if such person is absent abroad or cannot be found, to his agent ; or

(b) by leaving the same at the usual or last known place of abode of such person as aforesaid ; or

(c) by post as a registered letter addressed to the usual or last known place of abode of such person ; or

(d) in any case to which the three preceding paragraphs are inapplicable, by affixing the notice or other document upon some conspicuous part of the land to which the notice or document relates ; or

(e) in the case of a notice required to be served on a local authority or corporate body or company, by delivering the same to their clerk or secretary or leaving the same at his office with some person employed there, or by post as a registered letter addressed to such clerk or secretary at his office.

ARTICLE IX—Articles III to VIII of these Regulations shall not apply to any Compulsory Order made before the date hereof.

Schedule

THE HOUSING ACTS, 1890-1919

ORDER FOR THE PURPOSE OF THE COMPULSORY ACQUISITION OF LANDS

The*   hereby make the following Order :—

1. The provisions of the Lands Clauses Acts with respect to the purchase and taking of land otherwise than by agreement are, subject as herein-after provided, hereby put in force as respects the purchase by the* of the lands described in the Schedule hereto for the†

2. The Lands Clauses Acts (except Section 127 of the Lands Clauses Consolidation Act, 1845), as modified, varied or amended by the First Schedule to the Housing, Town Planning, &c., Act, 1909, the Housing, Town Planning, &c., Act, 1919, and the Acquisition of Land (Assessment of Compensation) Act, 1919, and Sections 77 to 85 of the Railways Clauses Consolidation Act, 1845, are, subject to the necessary adaptations, incorporated with this Order, and the provisions of those Acts shall apply accordingly.

‡3. The sums agreed upon or awarded for the purchase of the lands described in the Schedule to this Order, being glebe land or other land belonging to an ecclesiastical benefice, or to be paid by way of compensation for the damage to be sustained by the owner by reason

* Here insert title of the Authority making the Order.
† Here insert " purposes of Part III of the Housing of the Working Classes Act, 1890," or " purpose of [a town planning scheme] under the Town Planning Acts, 1909 and 1919," as the circumstances require. In the case of a town-planning scheme, the name of the Authority who made the scheme and the date or short title of the scheme should be stated.
‡ Insert this Article where the lands described in the Schedule to the Order include glebe land or other land belonging to an ecclesiastical benefice.

34

of severance or other injury affecting any such land,
shall not be paid as directed by the Lands Clauses Acts,
but shall be paid to the Ecclesiastical Commissioners to
be applied by them as money paid to them upon a sale,
under the provisions of the Ecclesiastical Leasing Acts,
of land belonging to a benefice.

[3.] This Order shall come into operation as from 'the
date of its confirmation by the Minister of Health.

THE SCHEDULE above referred to.

Numbers on Plan deposited at the Offices of the*	Quantity, Description and Situation of the Lands.	Owners or reputed Owners.	Lessees or reputed Lessees.	Occupiers.

Given under the Seal of the*
    this   day of   19
         (L.S.)

Given under the Official Seal of the Minister of Health,
    this Twenty-ninth day of August, in the year One
    thousand nine hundred and nineteen.

(L.S.)   *Charles Knight,*
Assistant Secretary, Ministry of Health.

* Here insert title of the Authority making the Order.

STATUTORY RULES AND ORDERS, 1919, No. 1556

HOUSING OF THE WORKING CLASSES AND TOWN PLANNING, ENGLAND

ACQUISITION OF LANDS

The Housing Acts (Compulsory Purchase) Amendment Regulations, 1919. Dated 23rd October 1919 [1]

65,605

The Minister of Health, in pursuance of the powers conferred on him by the First Schedule to the Housing, Town Planning, &c., Act, 1909, and of all other powers enabling him in that behalf, hereby makes the following Regulations :—

1. These Regulations may be cited as " The Housing Acts (Compulsory Purchase) Amendment Regulations, 1919," and shall be read as one with the Housing Acts (Compulsory Purchase) Regulations, 1919, herein-after called the principal Regulations.

2. Where the Minister of Health makes an Order for the compulsory acquisition of land under the powers conferred on him by Section 16 of the Housing, Town Planning, &c., Act, 1919, for the purpose of securing the immediate provision of dwelling accommodation in the area of any Local Authority, the principal Regulations shall be read and have effect subject to the following modifications :—

(*a*) The following Articles shall be substituted for Articles IV, V, and VI of the principal Regulations :—

" Article IV—(1) The Minister shall cause the Compulsory Order to be published by advertisement in one or more newspapers circulating in the district of the Local Authority and in the parish or parishes in which the land to which the Compulsory Order relates is situated.

" (2) The said advertisement shall be published

---

[1] These regulations relate only to the special case of Section 16 of the 1919 Act, page 405.

not later than the second day after the making of the Compulsory Order.

" (3) The said advertisement shall contain in addition to a copy of the Compulsory Order a notice setting out the following particulars :—

" (a) a statement that any objection to the Compulsory Order must be presented to the Minister of Health within the period of seven days from and after the date of the publication of the advertisement ; and

" (b) a statement of the period, times, and place or places during and at which the deposited plan referred to in the Schedule to the Compulsory Order may be inspected by or on behalf of any person interested in the land tó which the Compulsory Order relates.

" (4) The plan referred to in the Schedule to the Compulsory Order shall be deposited by the Minister not later than the second day after the making of the Compulsory Order at a place convenient for the purposes of inspection, and shall be kept deposited thereat for a period not being less than seven days from the date of the publication of the first advertisement ; and the said plan shall be open for inspection by any person interested or affected, without payment of any fee, at all reasonable hours on any week-day during the said period. The Minister shall also make suitable provision for affording to any such person inspecting the said plan any necessary explanation or information in regard thereto.

" Article V—(1) The Minister shall, not later than the second day after the making of the Compulsory Order, cause notice thereof to be given to every owner, lessee, and occupier of the land to which the Compulsory Order relates, and every such notice shall include a copy of the Compulsory Order, to which shall be appended a notice containing the particulars mentioned in paragraph (3) of Article IV of these Regulations.

" (2) The Minister shall furnish a copy of the

Compulsory Order, free of charge, to any person interested in the land to which the Compulsory Order relates, upon his applying for the same.

"Article VI—The period within which an objection to a Compulsory Order may be presented to the Minister by a person interested in the land to which the Compulsory Order relates shall be the period of seven days from and after the date of the application of the advertisement of the Compulsory Order."

(b) "The Minister" shall be substituted for "the Local Authority" in Articles III and VII of the principal Regulations.

3. Notwithstanding anything in these Regulations, the Minister may in any case to which these Regulations apply direct that the period during which objections may be presented to a Compulsory Order shall be fourteen days in lieu of seven days.

4. These Regulations shall apply in the case of any Compulsory Order made by the Minister after the twenty-third day of October, One thousand nine hundred and nineteen, for the purpose of securing the immediate provision of dwelling accommodation, but without prejudice to any Compulsory Order made by the Minister under the principal Regulations before that date or to any proceedings consequent thereon in the exercise by him in pursuance of Section 16 of the Housing, Town Planning, &c., Act, 1919, of any powers of a Local Authority.

Given under the Official Seal of the Minister of Health this Twenty-third day of October, One thousand nine hundred and nineteen.

(L.S.) E. R. FORBER,
Assistant Secretary, Ministry of Health.

STATUTORY RULES AND ORDERS, 1920, No. 167

HOUSING, ENGLAND

ACQUISITION OF LANDS

The Housing Acts (Compulsory Purchase) Amendment Regulations, 1920. Dated 6th February 1920.

65,856

The Minister of Health, in pursuance of the powers conferred on him by the First Schedule to the Housing, Town Planning, &c., Act, 1909,[1] and of all other powers enabling him in that behalf, hereby makes the following Regulations :—

1. These Regulations may be cited as " The Housing Acts (Compulsory Purchase) Amendment Regulations, 1920," and shall be read as one with the Housing Acts (Compulsory Purchase) Regulations, 1919[2] (hereinafter called " the principal Regulations ").

2. Article IV of the principal Regulations shall be read and have effect as if the following paragraph was inserted at the end thereof :—

" (5) Notwithstanding anything contained in this Article, where the land to which the Compulsory Order relates is situated within a rural district and does not exceed five acres in extent, the said Order shall be deemed to have been sufficiently published if not later than the seventh day after the making of the said Order one copy thereof has been affixed to the land in some conspicuous position and a further copy to a Notice Board outside the offices of the Local Authority, each of the said copies having appended to it a notice setting out the particulars specified in paragraph (3) of this Article, and for this purpose the date on which the said notices are so affixed shall be treated as the date of the publication of the first advertisement."

3. Nothing in these Regulations shall affect any Order made by the Minister of Health under the powers

[1] 9 E. 7 c. 44.   [2] S.R. & O., 1919, No. 1175.

conferred on him by Section 16 of the Housing, Town Planning,.&c., Act, 1919.

Given under the Official Seal of the Minister of Health this Sixth day of February, in the year One thousand nine hundred and twenty.

(L.S.)   E. R. FORBER,
Assistant Secretary, Ministry of Health.

APPENDIX II

PROVISION OF HOUSES

RATES OF INTEREST ON LOCAL LOANS

(From "The London Gazette," 2nd November 1920)

The Lords Commissioners of His Majesty's Treasury hereby give notice, that in pursuance of the powers conferred on them by the Public Works Loan Act, 1897 (60 & 61 Vict., c. 51), the Public Works Loans Act, 1918 (8 & 9 Geo. 5, c. 27), the Housing, Town Planning, &c., Act, 1919 (9 & 10 Geo. 5, c. 35), the Housing, Town Planning, &c. (Scotland), Act, 1919 (9 & 10 Geo. 5, c. 60), and the Housing (Ireland) Act, 1919 (9 & 10 Geo. 5, c. 45), their Lordships have been pleased to direct by their Minute of the 1st instant that on loans granted out of the Local Loans Fund on and after 1st November 1920 there shall be chargeable in lieu of the rates fixed by the Treasury Minutes of the 30th August 1919 and the 21st November 1919, the following rates of interest, viz :—

I—HOUSING LOANS — Rate of Interest, Per Cent.

(A) Loans in respect of *subsidised* Housing Schemes :—
   (1) Loans to local authorities secured on local rates :
      Any period 6½
   (2) Loans to public utility societies as defined by the Housing Acts, 1919 :
      Not exceeding 50 years . . . 6½

In the case of loans under these heads granted since 1st April 1919, at provisional rates of interest, the loans shall be revised where necessary, so as to bear interest at the above rates as from the commencement of the loan, such rate to be the permanent rate of the loans.

(B) Loans in respect of schemes *not receiving subsidy* under the Housing Acts :—
   (1) To companies and private persons limiting their profits to 6¾ per cent. per annum (subject to Income Tax) :
      Not exceeding 30 years . . . 6½
      Not exceeding 40 years . . . 6¾
   (2) To companies and private persons not so limiting their profits to 6¾ per cent. (subject to Income Tax) :
      Not exceeding 30 years . . . 7
      Not exceeding 40 years . . . 7¼

II—OTHER LOANS   Rate of Interest.
                                    Per Cent.

(*I*) Loans to local authorities for any purposes of the Small
     Holdings Acts :—
         Any period . .   .   .   . $6\frac{1}{2}$

(*II*) Other loans secured on local rates :—
         Not exceeding 30 years   . .   . $6\frac{1}{2}$
         Not exceeding 50 years   . .   . $6\frac{3}{4}$

(*III*) Loans not secured on local rates :—
     (*a*) Loans under the Harbour and Passing Tolls Act, 1861 :
         (i) With collateral security :
             Not exceeding 30 years   . .   . $6\frac{1}{2}$
             Not exceeding 50 years   . .   . $6\frac{3}{4}$
         (ii) Without collateral security :
             Not exceeding 30 years   . .   .   7
             Not exceeding 50 years   . .   . $7\frac{1}{4}$
     (*b*) Other loans not secured on local rates (except loans to
         Territorial Associations, which, under section 6
         of the Public Works Loans Act, 1908, bear
         interest at the rate prescribed for loans on the
         security of local rates) :
             Not exceeding 30 years   . .   .   7
             Not exceeding 50 years   . .   . $7\frac{1}{4}$

STATUTORY RULES AND ORDERS, 1919. No. 2,047

HOUSING OF THE WORKING CLASSES, ENGLAND

The Local Authorities (Assisted Housing Schemes) Regulations, 1919. Dated 31st December 1919

65,736

Whereas by subsection (1) of section 7 of the Housing, Town Planning, &c., Act, 1919, it is enacted that if it appears to the Local Government Board that the carrying out by a local authority, or by a county council to whom the powers of a local authority have been transferred under that Act, of any scheme approved under section 1 of that Act or the carrying out of a re-housing scheme in connection with a scheme made under Part I or Part II of the Housing of the Working Classes Act, 1890, including the acquisition, clearance and development of land included in the last-mentioned scheme, and whether the re-housing will be effected on the area included in that scheme or elsewhere, has resulted or is likely to result in a loss, the Board shall, if the scheme is carried out within such period after the passing of that Act as may be

specified by the Board with the consent of the Treasury,
pay or undertake to pay to the local authority or county
council, out of moneys provided by Parliament, such
part of the loss as may be determined to be so payable
under regulations made by the Board with the approval
of the Treasury, subject to such conditions as may be
prescribed by those regulations;

And whereas by subsection (2) of the said section 7
it is enacted that such regulations shall provide that the
amount of any annual payment to be made under the
section shall, in the case of a scheme carried out by a
local authority, be determined on the basis of the estimated annual loss resulting from the carrying out of
any scheme or schemes to which the section applies,
subject to the deduction therefrom of a sum not exceeding
the estimated annual produce of a rate of one penny
in the pound levied in the area chargeable with the
expenses of such scheme or schemes.

Now, therefore, the Minister of Health, in pursuance
of his powers under the recited enactments and under
any other statutes in that behalf, hereby makes the
following regulations :—

ARTICLE I—(1.) These regulations may be cited as
" The Local Authorities (Assisted Housing Schemes)
Regulations, 1919."

(2.) The Housing (Assisted Scheme) Regulations, 1919,
so far as they are in force at the date of this order, are
hereby revoked.

ARTICLE II—(1.) In these regulations unless the contrary intention appears :—

    (a) The expression " the Minister " means the Minister
        of Health ;

    (b) The expression " Local Authority " means any
        local authority referred to in section 7 of the
        Housing, Town Planning, &c., Act, 1919, and
        includes a county council to whom the powers
        of a local authority have been transferred under
        that Act ;

    (c) The expression " the Housing Acts " means the
        Housing Acts, 1890 to 1919 ;

    (d) The expression " the Act of 1890 " means the
        Housing of the Working Classes Act, 1890 ;

    (e) The expression " the Act of 1919 " means the
        Housing, Town Planning, &c., Act, 1919 ;

(*f*) The expression " rate " means the rate out of which
the expenses of the execution of Part III of
the Act of 1890 are defrayed ; Assisted Housing Schemes Regulations.

(*g*) The expression "the produce of a rate of one
penny in the pound " means the amount certified
as such in accordance with the rules set out in
Schedule A to these regulations.

(2.) The Interpretation Act, 1889, applies to the interpretation of these regulations as it applies to the
interpretation of an Act of Parliament.

ARTICLE III—For the purposes of these regulations—

(1.) The schemes towards the losses on which the
Minister is liable to contribute under section 7 of the
Act of 1919, out of moneys provided by Parliament,
shall include :—

(*a*) Any scheme under Part III of the Act of 1890,
including any proposals to which subsection (8)
of section 1 of the Act of 1919 applies ; and

(*b*) Any re-housing scheme in connection with a scheme
under Part I or Part II of the Act of 1890,
including the acquisition, clearance and development of land included in the last-mentioned
scheme, and whether the re-housing will be
effected on the area included in that scheme or
elsewhere ;

in so far (in each case) as the scheme is approved by the
Minister ; and all such schemes, in so far as they are
carried out at the expense of any one local authority,
shall be regarded together as one scheme, and, if a payment may be made as herein provided in respect thereof,
are hereinafter together referred to as an "assisted
scheme."

(2.) No such payment shall continue to be made :—

(i) In the case of a scheme under Part III of the Act
of 1890 unless the Minister is satisfied that
reasonable progress has been made with the
carrying into effect of the scheme within twelve
months from the passing of the Act of 1919,
or such further period as the Minister may
allow ;

(ii) In the case of a scheme under Part I or Part II
of the Act of 1890, unless the Minister is satisfied
that reasonable progress has been made with
the carrying into effect of the scheme within

four years from the passing of the Act of 1919, or such further period as the Minister may allow ;

(iii) In the case of any scheme or part of a scheme under Part III of the Act of 1890, unless such scheme or part of a scheme is carried into effect within three years from the passing of the Act of 1919, or such further period as the Minister may allow ; or

(iv) In the case of any scheme or part of a scheme under Part I or Part II of the Act of 1890, unless such scheme or part of a scheme is carried into effect within six years from the passing of the Act of 1919, or such further period as the Minister may allow.

(3.) No such payment shall be made :—

(i) In respect of the cost of acquiring or clearing a site under Part I or Part II of the Act of 1890 where the site was acquired or cleared (as the case may be) before the 6th day of February 1919 ; or

(ii) In respect of any scheme made or carried into effect by the Minister or the county council in default of the local authority, unless the Minister otherwise directs.

(4.) In determining whether a further period may be allowed as hereinbefore provided the Minister shall have regard to the supplies of labour and material available from time to time and all other local or general circumstances affecting the carrying into effect of the scheme, and if part only of a scheme has been carried into effect within the periods allowed under paragraphs (iii) and (iv) of sub-division (2) of this Article, that part of the scheme may, with the approval of the Minister, and subject to the provisions of these regulations, be regarded as the assisted scheme.

(5.) A scheme or part of a scheme shall be deemed to have been carried into effect when all the houses to be provided or acquired thereunder are let or available for letting, and also, in the case of a scheme under Part I or Part II of the Act of 1890, when the site or area affected has been cleared to the satisfaction of the Minister.

ARTICLE IV—(1.) The local authority shall for the purposes of an assisted scheme, or a scheme which, in the opinion of the Minister, is likely to become an assisted

scheme, keep separate accounts, to be called "The
Housing (Assisted Scheme) Accounts," including a separate
revenue account, to be called "The Housing (Assisted
Scheme) Revenue Account." Assisted
Housing
Schemes
Regulations

· (2.) They shall cause to be credited to the Housing
(Assisted Scheme) Revenue Account in each financial
year :—

   (a) the produce of a rate of one penny in the pound
      levied in the area chargeable with the expenses
      of the assisted scheme, or such less amount as
      may be necessary to meet the deficit for the
      financial year ;

   (b) the rents (inclusive of rates where rates are payable
      by the owner) in respect of any houses provided
      or acquired by them under the assisted scheme ;
      and

   (c) any other income which in the opinion of the
      Minister may properly be credited to the said
      account.

(3.) They shall cause to be debited to the Housing
(Assisted Scheme) Revenue Account in each financial
year :—

   (a) the sums required for interest and repayment of
      principal in respect of all moneys borrowed by
      them for the purposes of the assisted scheme
      (including moneys borrowed for the purchase of
      land which is approved by the Minister as part
      of the assisted scheme) which in the opinion of
      the Minister may properly be debited to the
      said account ;

   (b) the rates, taxes, rents or other charges payable
      by them in respect of any land or houses acquired,
      leased or provided by them under the assisted
      scheme, including any sums payable by way of
      rent, with the approval of the Minister, to any
      other account of the local authority, in respect
      of land acquired by them for some other purpose
      and appropriated for purposes of the assisted
      scheme ;

   (c) the annual premium payable by them in respect of
      the insurance against fire of any houses acquired
      or provided by them for the purposes of the
      assisted scheme ;

   (d) the expenditure incurred in respect of supervision

and management of the houses acquired or provided by them under the assisted scheme ;

(e) the expenditure incurred by them in and about the repair or maintenance of any property acquired or provided by them for the purposes of the assisted scheme, whether such expenditure is incurred by way of a fixed annual contribution to a repairs fund or otherwise ; and

(f) any other expenses which in the opinion of the Minister may properly be debited to the said account.

(4.) (a) In the case of the council of a borough whose accounts under the Housing Acts are not otherwise subject to audit by the district auditor, the Housing (Assisted Scheme) Accounts shall be made up and shall be audited by the district auditor in like manner, and subject to the same provisions, as the accounts of an urban district council, and for this purpose enactments relating to the audit .by district auditors of those accounts, and to all matters incidental thereto and consequential thereon, shall apply, so far as necessary, in lieu of the provisions of the Municipal Corporations Act, 1892, relating to accounts and audit.

(b) In every case as soon as practicable after the conclusion of each financial year the local authority shall forward to the Minister a copy of the Housing (Assisted Scheme) Revenue Account, certified by the district auditor.

ARTICLE V—Except with the approval of the Minister, the local authority shall not borrow moneys for the purposes of an assisted scheme, or a scheme which, in the opinion of the Minister, is likely to become an assisted scheme, at a higher rate of interest than that fixed for the time being in the case of loans by the Public Works Loan Commissioners to local authorities for the purposes of assisted schemes.

ARTICLE VI—Subject to the provisions of these regulations and provided that these regulations are complied with the annual payment to be made by the Minister to the local authority out of moneys provided by Parliament (hereinafter referred to as " the Exchequer subsidy ") shall be determined by the Minister as follows :—

(a) During the period before any part of the assisted scheme has been carried into effect the

Exchequer subsidy shall be an amount equivalent to the deficit in the Housing (Assisted Scheme) Revenue Account made up at the conclusion of each financial year, in accordance with the provisions of Article IV of these regulations ;

(b) during the period after any part of the assisted scheme has been carried into effect, and before the whole of the assisted scheme has been carried into effect the Exchequer subsidy, in respect of that part of the assisted scheme which has been carried into effect, shall be calculated upon the basis of an estimate submitted to the Minister by the local authority and approved by the Minister, and, in respect of that part of the assisted scheme which has not been carried into effect, shall be an amount equivalent to the deficit under the last-mentioned part of the assisted scheme as shown by the entries relating thereto in the Housing (Assisted Scheme) Revenue Account at the conclusion of the financial year ;

(c) during the remainder of the period or periods allowed for the repayment of the loans raised by the local authority for the purposes of the assisted scheme the Exchequer subsidy shall be calculated upon the basis of estimates submitted to the Minister by the local authority and approved by the Minister ;

(d) The first of the estimates referred to in the preceding paragraph shall be submitted to the Minister by the local authority as soon as possible after the whole of the assisted scheme has been carried into effect, and a revised estimate shall be submitted as soon as possible after the 31st day of March 1927, and further revised estimates after the conclusion of each tenth financial year during the remainder of the period or periods last-mentioned ;

(e) Each of the estimates referred to in paragraphs (b) and (c) of this Article shall be in a form approved by the Minister and shall be an estimate of the average annual income and expenditure of the local authority under the assisted scheme, or under that part of the assisted scheme which has been carried into effect (as the case may be),

Assisted Housing Schemes Regulations.

in respect of the period ending at the conclusion
of the financial year after which the next estimate
is to be submitted under these regulations ;

(*f*) The estimate shall in each case be accompanied
by an estimate of the annual produce of a rate
of one penny in the pound hereinbefore referred
to, and in the framing of such estimate regard
shall be had to the produce of a rate of one penny
in the pound during the last financial year before
the date of such estimate, and to any probable
increase or decrease of the assessable value of
the district of the local authority during the
period to which the estimate relates ;

(*g*) The Exchequer subsidy, in so far as it is calculated
upon an estimate, shall be determined on the
basis of the average annual deficit to be incurred
by the local authority under the assisted scheme
(or under that part of the assisted scheme which
has been carried into effect, as the case may be),
as shown by the estimate last made by the local
authority under this Article, and shall be the
equivalent of the amount of the said average
annual deficit subject to the deduction from the
said average annual deficit of the estimated
produce of a rate of one penny in the pound
hereinbefore referred to ;

Provided that in the determination of the
amount of the Exchequer subsidy during the
period to which paragraph (*b*) of this Article
applies, there shall be added to the amount of
the said average annual deficit an amount
equivalent to the deficit referred to in the said
paragraph (*b*).

(*h*) In this Article the expression " part of the assisted
scheme " means so much of the assisted scheme
as will be carried out under Parts I and II of
the Act of 1890, or under Part III of the Act of
1890, as the case may be.

ARTICLE VII—(1.) In any determination of the amount
of the Exchequer subsidy, whether based on an estimate
or otherwise, such deductions may be made from the
amount of the deficit upon which the Exchequer subsidy
is calculated as will in the opinion of the Minister
represent—

(a) an item of expenditure or estimated expenditure which is excessive or not properly chargeable to the debit of the assisted scheme ; or Assisted Housing Schemes Regulations.

(b) the omission from the account or estimate of any item of income which should be included therein ; or

(c) any deficiency of income or estimated income which is due to the insufficiency of the rents charged or proposed to be charged by the local authority ; or

(d) any deficiency of income or estimated income which is due to the failure of the local authority to secure due economy in the carrying out or administration of the scheme.

(2.) For the purposes of sub-division (1) (a) of this Article the following items of expenditure, or estimated expenditure, in respect of any one financial year, shall not be regarded as excessive :—

(a) A charge, in respect of unoccupied houses and uncollected rents, not exceeding five per centum of the gross estimated rent ;

(b) a contribution to a repairs fund not exceeding fifteen per centum of the gross estimated rent ;

(c) a charge in respect of the cost of supervision and management not exceeding five per centum of the gross estimated rent ; and

(d) any item of expenditure referred to in this sub-division of this Article which exceeds the percentages thereby prescribed, but which the Minister, having regard to the special circumstances of the case, considers to be reasonable.

(3.) The Minister shall, not later than the 31st day of March 1927, after consultation with local authorities or with any associations of local authorities, and after such inquiry as he may consider necessary for the purpose, make such revision, if any, of the percentages mentioned in sub-division (2) of this Article as appears to him to be just and equitable.

(4.) (a) In the event of any difference of opinion arising between the Minister and the local authority with regard to any of the matters referred to in paragraphs (c) or (d) of sub-division (1) of this Article the question at issue shall be referred for decision to a tribunal appointed as hereinafter provided, and the decision of such tribunal

35

shall be final and conclusive, and the amount of the Exchequer subsidy shall (if necessary) be altered accordingly.

(b) Such tribunal shall consist of four members, of whom two shall be nominated by the Minister, one shall be nominated by the Association of Municipal Corporations, and one shall be nominated by the Urban District Councils Association and the Rural District Councils Association jointly, and of a chairman to be appointed by the four members so nominated.

(5.) In any determination of the sufficiency of the rents charged or to be charged by the local authority, regard shall be had to the rules set out in Schedule B to these regulations.

(6.) For the purposes of sub-division (2) of this Article the gross estimated rent shall be deemed to be the total amount of the rents, rates and water charges payable in respect of the houses included in the assisted scheme less the total amount of the rates and water charges payable in respect of the said houses during the financial year.

(7.) Where the local authority apply any capital moneys, including any accumulated funds, belonging to them for defraying any expenditure incurred by them for purposes of an assisted scheme for which the local authority are authorised to borrow moneys, the rate of interest on the capital moneys or funds so applied shall be calculated as follows :—

(a) where moneys have been borrowed by the local authority for the purposes of the assisted scheme from sources other than moneys or funds belonging to the local authority, the rate of interest shall be the same as that payable on the moneys last previously so borrowed :

(b) where no moneys have been borrowed by the local authority as aforesaid the rate of interest shall be the same as that in force for the time being for loans for assisted schemes advanced by the Public Works Loan Commissioners.

ARTICLE VIII—(1.) The amount of the Exchequer subsidy, when determined under these regulations, shall not be varied by the Minister during the period for which the Exchequer subsidy was fixed except as hereinafter provided or except with the concurrence of the

Lords Commissioners of His Majesty's Treasury and of the local authority. Assisted Housing Schemes Régulations.

(2.) The Exchequer subsidy in respect of any financial year shall be varied so far as may be necessary in consequence of any difference between the produce of a rate of one penny in the pound in that year and the estimate of the produce of the said rate submitted under Article VI of these regulations.

(3.) When any land or buildings included in an assisted scheme are leased or sold by the local authority, the Minister may make such adjustment of the amount of the Exchequer subsidy as may be necessary in consequence of the lease or sale and of the appropriation of the rents or proceeds of the sale:

Provided that the adjustment shall in no case be such as to increase the contribution to be made by the local authority from the rates towards the annual cost of the assisted scheme, and that if, as the result of the appropriation of the rents or proceeds of the sale, the annual deficit to be incurred by the local authority under the assisted scheme is reduced, a proportion of the amount by which the deficit is reduced shall, subject to such conditions as the Minister may determine, be applied under any such adjustment in reduction of the said contribution, as well as of the Exchequer subsidy.

(4.) When the period allowed for the repayment of any of the loans raised by the local authority for the purposes of the assisted scheme has expired, the amount of the Exchequer subsidy shall be reduced by the Minister, so far as may be necessary, in consequence of such repayment.

ARTICLE IX—The Exchequer subsidy shall be payable in such instalments as the Minister may think fit (including payments on account, during the periods mentioned in paragraphs (a) and (b) of Article VI of these regulations, based on the probable deficit for the year as certified by the local authority), but the Minister may, if he thinks fit, withhold payment of the final instalment of the Exchequer subsidy until the provisions of sub-division (4) (b) of Article IV of these regulations have been complied with.

ARTICLE X—In any case where one area is affected by two or more assisted schemes the Minister may make such adjustments as may be necessary for securing that in the calculation of the total amount of the Exchequer subsidies, in any one financial year, under both or all the assisted schemes affecting the said area, there shall not be taken into account, in respect of that area, the produce, or estimated annual produce, of a rate of more than one penny in the pound.

SCHEDULE A

RULES TO BE OBSERVED IN THE DETERMINATION OF THE AMOUNT PRODUCED BY A RATE OF ONE PENNY IN THE POUND

1. The produce of a rate during any financial year shall be the amount actually realised during that year by the collection of that rate, in accordance with a return made by the duly authorised financial officer of the local authority and certified by the district auditor.

2. For the purposes of the foregoing rule, the amount of the rate or rates collected during the financial year shall be regarded as having been collected in respect of the rate or rates made for that year.

3. The produce of a rate of one penny in the pound shall be that proportion of the produce of a rate which one penny bears to the total amount in the pound of the said rate.

4. Where it is desired to ascertain the amount of the produce of a rate of one penny in the pound levied in any area comprising two or more parts which are differentially rated, the said amount shall be separately ascertained in respect of each of these parts in accordance with the foregoing rules, and the sum of the amounts so ascertained shall be the produce of a rate of one penny in the pound levied in the said area.

SCHEDULE B

RULES WITH REGARD TO THE DETERMINATION OF RENTS

1. The local authority in first fixing the rents under an assisted scheme shall have regard to :—

    (a) the rents obtaining in the locality for houses for the working classes ;

    (b) any increase in the rent of houses for the working classes authorised under the Increase of Rent and Mortgage Interest (War Restrictions) Act,

1915, and any Acts amending or extending that Act ; *Assisted Housing Schemes Regulations.*

(c) any superiority in the condition or amenity of the houses to be let by them under the assisted scheme or in the accommodation provided therein ; and

(d) the classes of tenant in the district for whom the houses are provided.

2. The rent to be charged after the 31st day of March 1927, shall, if reasonably possible, having regard to the conditions then prevailing and to the classes of tenant in the district for whom the houses were provided, be sufficient to cover (in addition to the expenses of maintenance and management of the houses and a suitable allowance for depreciation) the interest which would have been payable on the capital cost of building the houses if they had been built after that date.

3. If it is not found reasonably possible after the 31st day of March 1927, to obtain the rent prescribed by rule 2, the rent shall be the best rent which can reasonably be obtained from the classes of tenant in the district for whom the houses were provided, regard being had to any superiority of such houses in accommodation, construction or amenities as compared with houses previously built in the district.

Given under the official seal of the Minister of Health this Thirty-first day of December, in the year One thousand nine hundred and nineteen.

(L.S.) CHRISTOPHER ADDISON,
Minister of Health.

We approve these regulations—

JAMES PARKER, } *Lords Commissioners*
J. TOWYN JONES, } *of His Majesty's Treasury.*

STATUTORY RULES AND ORDERS, 1920, No. 487

HOUSING, ENGLAND

The Housing Accounts Order (Local Authorities), 1920, dated 31st March 1920.

66,165.

To the councils of the several administrative counties in England and Wales ;—

To the councils of the several metropolitan boroughs, municipal boroughs and other urban districts, in England and Wales ;—

To the councils of the several rural districts in England and Wales ;—

And to all others whom it may concern.

Whereas by the Local Authorities (Assisted Housing Schemes) Regulations, 1919,[1] the Minister of Health, with the approval of the Treasury, made regulations in pursuance of section 7 of the Housing, Town Planning, &c., Act, 1919,[2] with regard to the payments to be made by the Minister to local authorities in respect of assisted schemes (as defined in the said regulations) towards the losses on which the Minister is liable to contribute under the said section 7 out of moneys provided by Parliament ;

And whereas by Article IV of the said regulations it is provided that the local authority shall, for the purposes of an assisted scheme, or a scheme which in the opinion of the Minister is likely to become an assisted scheme, keep separate accounts to be called the Housing (Assisted Scheme) Accounts, and it is further provided that in the case of the council of a borough whose accounts under the Housing Acts, 1890 to 1919, are not otherwise subject to audit by the district auditor, the Housing (Assisted Scheme) Accounts shall be made up and shall be audited by the district auditor in the manner and subject to the provisions therein mentioned :

Now, therefore, the Minister of Health, in pursuance

---

[1] S.R. & O., 1919, No. 2047.   [2] 9–10 Geo. 5. c. 35.

of his powers under section 5 of the District Auditors Housing
Accounts
Order. Act, 1879,[1] and all other enactments in that behalf, hereby orders and prescribes, subject to any departure to which he may from time to time assent, as follows :—

ARTICLE I—This order may be cited as " The Housing Accounts Order (Local Authorities), 1920."

ARTICLE II—In this order, unless the contrary intention appears :—

(a) The expression " the Minister " means the Minister of Health ;

(b) The expression " the regulations " means the Local Authorities (Assisted Housing Schemes) Regulations, 1919 ;

(c) The expressions " local authority " and " assisted schemes " have the same meaning as the like expressions respectively have in the Local Authorities (Assisted Housing Schemes) Regulations, 1919 ;

(d) The expression " financial period " means, in the case of a local authority other than a rural district council, the year ending on the 31st day of March, and, in the case of a local authority being a rural district council, the half-year ending on the 31st day of March or the 30th day of September, as the case may require.

ARTICLE III—The officer charged with the duty of keeping the Housing (Assisted Scheme) Accounts of the local authority (hereinafter referred to as " the Accounting Officer ") shall punctually and accurately enter up the several accounts, books and statements relating to the assisted scheme which are prescribed by this Article, together with such other accounts or books of account as the Minister may direct or the local authority may decide to be necessary, that is to say :—

LEDGER ACCOUNTS

(1) Ledger Accounts on the double-entry system according to Form A in the schedule to this order.

(a) These accounts shall include—

---

[1] 42-3 Vict. c. 6.

PERSONAL ACCOUNTS

ACCOUNTS OF OFFICERS

In all cases

Treasurer's Account (the Cash Book),
Rent Collectors' Accounts,
   and where circumstances require
Other Cash Officers' Accounts,
Storekeepers' Accounts.

ACCOUNTS OF DEBTORS

In all cases

Tenants' (Rent) Account,
Council (Rate Contribution) Account,
Minister of Health (Exchequer Subsidy) Account,
   and where circumstances require
Mortgagors' Accounts,
Investment Accounts,
Other Debtors' Accounts.

ACCOUNTS OF CREDITORS

In all cases

Mortgagees' (or other Lenders) Accounts,
Inland Revenue (Income Tax) Account,
Other Creditors' Account or Accounts,
   and where circumstances require
Purchaser's (Instalment) Account,
Tenants' (Deposits) Accounts.

IMPERSONAL ACCOUNTS

INCOME CLASSIFICATION ACCOUNTS

In all cases

Rent Income Account,
Rate Contribution Account,
Exchequer Subsidy Account,
   and where circumstances require
Other Income Accounts.

EXPENDITURE CLASSIFICATION ACCOUNTS

In all cases

Repayment of Loans Account,
Loan Interest Account,
Rates, Rents, Insurance and other charges Account,
Management Expenses Account,
   and where circumstances require
Other Expenditure Accounts.

FUND OR FINAL ACCOUNTS

In all cases

Housing (Assisted Scheme) Revenue Account,
Maintenance and Repairs Reserve Fund Account.

(b) An amount equal to the estimated annual provision
required to cover the cost of maintenance and repair
shall be transferred each year from the Housing (Assisted
Scheme) Revenue Account to the Maintenance and
Repairs Reserve Fund Account, to which shall be charged
the actual expenditure upon maintenance and repair,
and any deficiency which may arise in this account shall
be made good forthwith by transfer from the Housing
(Assisted Scheme) Revenue Account.

(c) In connection with the capital outlay the following
ledger accounts shall also be kept :—

Capital Asset Accounts ;
Discharged Capital Outlay Account ;

and these accounts shall maintain a record of the original
cost of the capital assets acquired and *per contra* of the
portions thereof which have been defrayed out of revenue
(1) by loan repayment ; (2) by the setting aside of sinking
funds ; or (3) by direct charge.

(d) Where expenditures which do not create capital
assets are spread over a period of years by the help of
loans, there shall also be kept :—

Deferred Charges Accounts ;

including, as far as they may be required, accounts of
Discount on Stock Issues and Expenses of Stock and
Bond Issues. The balances of these accounts shall be
reduced as and when the expenditures are defrayed
out of revenue by loan repayment or otherwise.

(e) Where Sinking or Redemption Funds have to be
compiled for the discharge of loan debt the following
accounts shall also be kept :—

Sinking Fund Contributions Account.
Treasurer's Sinking (or Redemption) Fund
Account.
Sinking (or Redemption) Fund Investment
Accounts.
Sinking (or Redemption) Fund Expenses Account.

(f) Where houses or other property are sold or

instalments of purchase money are received a separate Treasurer's Account shall be kept in the ledger entitled the

Treasurer's (Proceeds of Sale) Account.

Such items of loan repayment or sinking fund contribution as the Minister may from time to time direct shall be paid out of this account, and the sums remaining therein shall be invested in loans which the local authority is authorised to borrow, including loans for the purchase of other land for the purposes of ,Part III of the principal Act, or in any securities in which trustees are for the time being authorised to invest. The income derived from these investments shall be carried to the Housing (Assisted Scheme) Revenue Account.

(g) There shall be entered in the ledger a

Housing (Assisted Scheme) Balance Sheet ;

the entries in which shall be arranged under the headings appearing in Form B in the schedule hereto or such of them as may be needed and in accordance with the directions set out at the foot of that form.

TERRIER OF HOUSING ESTATES

(2) A Terrier, in Form C in the schedule hereto, of all real property acquired by the local authority, giving the particulars set out in the form and in the instructions appended thereto.

REGISTER OF TENANCIES

(3) A Register in which one page or more is allotted to each house or other property available for letting. In this register there shall be entered from time to time the name of each tenant, the date when his occupation begins, the date when it ends, the agreed rent, any orders in regard to the writing-off of rents, and any other matters connected with the tenancies.

RENT ACCOUNT BOOK

(4) A Rent Account Book in Form D in the schedule hereto, or in such amplified form as may be better adapted to the requirements of the case, setting out in the same order and with the same reference numbers as appears

in the Register of Tenancies and in columns provided for the purpose each house available for letting, the name of each tenant in occupation during the period of account, and the other particulars set forth in the form.

This book shall be totalled up and balanced at the close of each quarter or of such `other period as the local authority may direct.

Housing Accounts Order.

SINKING (OR REDEMPTION) FUND RECORD

(5) A book shewing in respect of each sinking or redemption fund which has to be compiled for the discharge of loan debt, (a) the amount to which such fund should amount at the close of each financial year in the loan period ; (b) the total amount of debt discharged by the fund up to the end of each financial year, and (c) the amount (if any) remaining on hand invested or uninvested.

ARTICLE IV—(1) The accounts relating to the assisted scheme shall include, and shall be confined to, the items of income and expenditure falling due within, or at the close of, the financial period.

(2) The accounts, books and statements hereinbefore prescribed shall be duly made up and balanced immediately after the close of each financial period, and thereupon the Accounting Officer shall submit the Ledger Accounts and Balance Sheet to the local authority or appropriate committee.

(3) When the accounts have been approved by the local authority, their acceptance as accounts of the local authority shall be attested by the signature of the presiding chairman upon the Housing (Assisted Scheme) Balance Sheet.

(4) It shall be the duty of the Accounting Officer to present at audit the Housing (Assisted Scheme) Accounts of the local authority, together with all vouchers, documents and evidence which are required for the purposes of audit.

ARTICLE V—The treasurer and every officer or other person who receives or disburses money or materials on behalf of the local authority shall keep a personal book of account containing a prompt and accurate record of all such receipts and disbursements, shall balance

such book of account at the close of each financial period
and at such other dates as the local authority may direct,
and shall submit the same at the audit together with
such vouchers, documents and evidence as may be required for the purposes of audit.

ARTICLE VI—(1) The rent collector shall deposit all
sums which he has collected with the treasurer at the
close of each week, or more frequently if the local authority
so direct.

(2) He shall use such receipt check books as the local
authority may direct, and shall preserve therein an
accurate record of the amounts and dates of his collec-
tions.

(3) If, instead of or in addition to directing the use
by the rent collector of receipt check books, the local
authority elect to supply each tenant with a tenant's
rent book, the collector shall mark and initial each
rent payment in the rent book of the tenant.

(4) He shall make out and submit promptly after the
close of each financial period, and at such other dates
as the local authority may direct, a full statement of
such of the rents which it was his duty to collect as may
not in fact have been collected, and of the reason for such
non-collection.

SCHEDULE

FORM A

Ledger Account

Dr.   Cr.

Date.	Folio of corresponding Credit.	Account of corresponding Credit.	Description of Item.	Amount.	Total.	Date.	Folio of corresponding Debit.	Account of corresponding Debit.	Description of Item.	Amount.	Total.
				£ s. d.	£ s. d.					£ s. d.	£ s. d.

FORM B

Housing (Assisted Scheme) Balance Sheet

Housing
Accounts
Order.

CAPITAL LIABILITIES	CAPITAL ASSETS.
Stock or loans outstanding. Prospective purchasers' advances. Other special liabilities. Overspent loan balances.	Houses and other property.[1] Loans owing to the Council. Sinking Funds (investments and cash). Proceeds of sale (investments and cash). Loan moneys in hand. Sundry Debtors.
CAPITAL OUTLAY DISCHARGED	DEFERRED CHARGES.
By Loan Repayment. By Sinking Fund provisions. By direct charge on revenue.	Expenses of Stock or Bond issues. Discounts on Stock issues.
REVENUE LIABILITIES.	REVENUE ASSETS
Tradesmen and others. Income Tax unpaid. Unclaimed dividends. Other special liabilities. Overspent cash balances.	Rents uncollected. Exchequer subsidy receivable. Rate contribution receivable. Other uncollected income. Repairs fund investments. Cash balances in hand. Materials in hand.
FUND BALANCES	FUND DEFICIENCIES
Repairs fund. Revenue Account.	Revenue account.

[1] The asset is to be shown at original cost. Only those properties which remain in the possession of the authority are to be included on the balance sheet.

Either on the balance sheet, or in connection therewith, the balances connected with each authorised borrowing are to be separately entered in such manner as to show their due correspondence.

using
ounts
er.

Form C

Terrier of Housing Estates

Reference No.	Address of House or other property.	Description.	Apportionment of original cost.			Date when ready for occupation.	Terms and particulars of Sale (if any). Signature of Clerk to the Council and date of entry.
			Items.	Amounts.	Loan period.		
				£ s. d.			

This Terrier should include all real property held by the council in connection with the assisted scheme.

The apportionment of original cost entered in the Terrier should be brought to a total therein, and the agreement of this total with the capital outlay shewn upon the Balance Sheet of the Housing (Assisted Scheme) Accounts should be established.

If loans are granted to purchasers on mortgage of the houses concerned, the amounts of such loans, together with the terms in regard to interest and repayment, should be entered.

If agreements are entered into for instalment payments by prospective purchasers, the numbers and amount of such instalments, the dates when they fall due, and any other terms of the agreement, together with the date of the agreement, should be entered.

Form D

Rent Account Book

Rent Account Book

Quarter ending..............

Reference No.	Situation of House.	Name of Tenant.	Unoccupied period (if any). From	To	Amount of Rent per week. £ s. d.	Total Rent for Quarter. £ s. d.	Proportion charged in respect of rates. £ s. d.	Arrears of Rent brought forward. £ s. d.	Total to be collected. £ s. d.	Weekly Rent Collections. 1st Week. £ s. d.	2nd Week. £ s. d.	3rd Week. £ s. d.	4th Week. £ s. d.	5th Week. £ s. d.	6th Week. £ s. d.	7th Week. £ s. d.	8th Week. £ s. d.	9th Week. £ s. d.	10th Week. £ s. d.	11th Week. £ s. d.	12th Week. £ s. d.	13th Week. £ s. d.	Totals. £ s. d.	Written off as irrecoverable in respect of unoccupied periods. £ s. d.	Other amounts written off as irrecoverable. Amount. £ s. d.	Cause.	Arrears of Rent carried forward. £ s. d.
Totals																											

A column to record the deposit to the credit of each tenant at the end of the quarter may be added when it is desirable.

(L.S.)   Given under the official seal of the Minister of Health, this Thirty-first day of March, in the year One thousand nine hundred and twenty.

F. L. Turner, Assistant Secretary, Ministry of Health.

MINISTRY OF HEALTH

HOUSING ACTS, 1890–1919

ASSISTED SCHEME (LOCAL AUTHORITY)

STATEMENT OF ESTIMATED ANNUAL INCOME AND
EXPENDITURE

This statement must be filled up and submitted, in
duplicate, to the Housing Commissioners, for transmission to the Ministry of Health, immediately tenders
for the erection of houses forming a section or part of a
scheme have been provisionally accepted.   For detailed
instructions as to the filling up of this form see page .

Name of Local Authority .... { Borough Council / Urban District Council / Rural District Council

Site of Scheme...

Scheme Number....................Section of Scheme.............
(1st, 2nd, 3rd, &c.)

Estimated Income.	£ s. d.	*Estimated Expenditure.*	£ s. d.
From rents, including rates and water charges where these are paid by Local Authority (*see* Table D) . .		Loan charges : (1) Table A . . (2) Table B . . (3) Table C . .	
Less allowance for un-occupied houses and uncollected rents .		Rates, if paid by Local Authority (Table D) .	
		Taxes (give particulars)..	
Estimated net receipts from rents . .		Insurance . . .	
From other sources (if any) specifying them .		Water charges, if paid by Local Authority (Table D) . . .	
		Repairs and Maintenance	
		Supervision and collec-tion of rents . .	
		Other expenditure (if any). Give particulars	
Balance (excess of ex-penditure over income)		Balance (excess of income over expenditure) .	

Signed.................................
Clerk [or Financial Officer] to the Local Authority
Date.....................19....

A—LAND

Estimated income and expenditure.

	Acres or decimal of an acre.	Apportioned cost or rent. £
Area in present section of scheme . .		
Area in previous sections of scheme (if any) .		
Area in further sections of scheme (if any) .		
Total for scheme purposes . .		
Purpose.		
Area reserved for other purposes (e.g. schools, allotments, &c.), specifying them . . .		
Value of any existing buildings on land .		
Total area and cost		

If land bought for housing purposes.

Date of Loan sanctioned.	Period sanctioned.	Amount. £	Rate of Interest per cent.	Loan Charges (including interest). £	When first payments due.
Total .		Total .			

Where it is proposed to charge rent for land which has been acquired by a Local Authority for other purposes and appropriated for housing purposes, such rent must be based on a valuation by the Inland Revenue District Valuer. Loans will not be sanctioned in respect of such land.

36

Estimated
income and
expenditure.

B—DEVELOPMENT

1. Particulars of loans sanctioned or required for street works, sewers, &c.

Date of sanction.	Amount. £	Purpose.	Period sanctioned.	Rate of Interest per cent.	Loan Charges (including interest). £	First payment due.
Total			Total			

2. Amount charged to present section of scheme £........Annual loan charges thereon £........

3. Amount charged to previous sections (if any) £........Annual loan charges thereon £........

4. Amount to be charged to future sections (if any) £........Annual loan charges thereon £........

C—BUILDINGS

1. Particulars of loans sanctioned or required for buildings, fencing, &c.

Date of sanction.	Amount. £	Purpose.	Period sanctioned.	Rate of Interest per cent.	Loan Charges (including interest). £	First payment due.
Total			Total			

2. Amount charged to present section of scheme £........Annual loan charges thereon £........

3. Amount charged to previous sections (if any) £........Annual loan charges thereon £........

4. Amount to be charged to future sections (if any) £........Annual loan charges thereon £........

D—RENT, RATES AND WATER CHARGES

(PRESENT SECTION OF SCHEME ONLY)

		Type A.*	Type B.*	Type C.*	Type D.*	Type E.*	Type F.*	Type G.*	Type H.*	Type K.*	Total.
1. Number of houses of each type											
2. Estimated cost per house of each type	(a) Land										—
	(b) Development										—
	(c) Buildings										—
Total											—
3. Estimated economic rent per house based on two-thirds of above total cost, excluding	(a) Per week										—
	(b) Per annum										—
4. Weekly rent per house proposed, *excluding rates*											—
5. Estimated annual Rateable Value per house											—
6. Annual rent receivable (Gross Estimated Rent—*see* page 4)	(a) Per house										—
	(b) For all houses in 1 above										
7. Annual rates (at....in the £)	(a) Per house										
	(b) For all houses in 1 above										—
8. Annual charge for water supply	(a) Per house										
	(b) For all houses in 1 above										
9. Total annual rent so receivable	(a) Per house (agreeing with totals of 6 (a), 7 (a) and 8 (a) above)										—
	(b) For all houses in 1 above (agreeing with totals of 6 (b), 7 (b) and 8 (b) above)										
10. If inclusive rent is to be charged, state proposed rent	(a) Per week for each house										—
	(b) Per annum for each house										—
	(c) Total per ann. for all houses in 1 above										

* Type A. Living room, scullery, 2 bedrooms.
  ,,   B.   ,,   ,,   ,,   3   ,,
  ,,   C.   Parlour, living room, scullery, 2 bedrooms.
  ,,   D.   ,,   ,,   ,,   ,,   3   ,,
  ,,   E.   ,,   ,,   ,,   ,,   4   ,,
  ,,   F.   Tenements in block dwellings.
If there are other types, insert figures in columns G, H, and K, and insert particulars below.

Type G. ....
  ,,   H. ....
  ,,   K. ....

Estimated income and expenditure.

INSTRUCTIONS

1. *Loan Charges.*—Under this head should be entered the *annual* sums (including principal and interest without deduction of Income Tax) required to repay the estimated capital cost in question on the annuity system. The loan periods on which the calculations should be made are 80 years for land, 60 years for buildings, 30 years for sewers and water supply, 20 years for streets. The cost of land should include legal expenses, if any, and the cost of the other works, a proportion for architect's fees, &c. The rate of interest on borrowed money should, of course, be that actually paid where the money has already been raised under a loan sanction of the Ministry, but should otherwise be taken at the rate at which the local authority anticipate that they will be able to borrow.

For the convenience of local authorities a table is appended showing the equal *half-yearly* payments needed to repay a loan of £100 in a given number of years at various percentages.

Number of years	5 per cent.	5¼ per cent.	5½ per cent.	5¾ per cent.	6 per cent.
20 .	3 19 8	4 1 4¼	4 3 0¾	4 4 9½	4 6 6¼
30 .	3 4 8½	3 6 6¾	3 8 5¼	3 10 4	3 12 3¼
60 .	2 12 8¾	2 14 11½	2 17 2½	2 19 6	3 1 9½
80 .	2 10 11¾	2 13 4¼	2 15 8¾	2 18 1½	3 0 6½

2. *Rent.*—In fixing the rents inserted in the return the local authority should bear in mind the considerations set out in paragraphs 16 to 22 of General Housing Memorandum No. 8.

3. In completing the main statement, the following rules should be observed :—

(*a*) The annual deduction in respect of unoccupied houses and uncollected rents must not exceed 5 per cent. of the gross estimated rent.

(*b*) The annual deduction for cost of repairs and maintenance must not exceed 15 per cent. of the gross estimated rent.

(*c*) The annual deduction for cost of supervision and management must not exceed 5 per cent. of the gross estimated rent.

The gross estimated rent, where rent is inclusive of rates and water charges, is the estimated inclusive rent, less rates and water charges.

Estimated income and expenditure.

4. The figures to be inserted in 3 (*b*) of Table D will be arrived at by calculating the interest on two-thirds of the totals shown in 2 of that table at the rate at which the loans have been raised, and adding thereto the annual amounts required to provide for (1) allowance for unoccupied houses ; (2) repairs and maintenance ; (3) supervision and collection of rents ; (4) insurance and (5) such allowance in respect of depreciation beyond the allowance for repairs and maintenance as may be necessary. The method by which (5) has been arrived at should be indicated below.

STATUTORY RULES AND ORDERS, 1920, No. 2128

THE MINISTRY OF HEALTH (TEMPORARY RELAXATION OF BUILDING BYELAWS) REGULATIONS, 1920, DATED 12TH NOVEMBER 1920

MADE BY THE MINISTER OF HEALTH UNDER SECTION 25 OF THE HOUSING, TOWN PLANNING, &c., ACT, 1919

The Minister of Health, in pursuance of the powers conferred on him by subsection (1) of section 25 of the Housing, Town Planning, &c., Act, 1919, and of all other powers enabling him in that behalf, hereby makes the following regulations :—

1. (1.) These regulations may be cited as "The Ministry of Health (Temporary Relaxation of Building Byelaws) Regulations, 1920."

   (2.) The Ministry of Health (Temporary Relaxation of Building Byelaws) Regulations, 1919,[1] are hereby revoked without prejudice to any consent given or other thing done under those Regulations.

2. A local authority, notwithstanding the provisions of any building byelaws,[2] may, during a period

---

[1] S.R. & O., 1919, No. 1477.
[2] Section 40 of the Housing, Town Planning, &c., Act, 1919, enacts that, for the purposes of Part I of the Act, the expression " building byelaws " includes byelaws made by any local authority under section one hundred and fifty-seven of the Public Health Act, 1875, as amended

of three years from the 31st July 1919, consent to the erection and use for human habitation, of any building erected or proposed to be erected, which complies with the conditions set out in the schedule hereto.

3. The deposit to be received from a person appealing to the Minister of Health against the neglect or refusal of a local authority to give such consent as aforesaid, or against the conditions on which such consent is given or against the decision of the local authority as to the period for which the building may be allowed to be used for human habitation, shall be the sum of ten pounds: provided that the Minister of Health may in any case, if he thinks fit, require a deposit of less than ten pounds or may dispense with a deposit.

4. The Interpretation Act, 1889,[1] applies to the interpretation of these Regulations as it applies to the interpretation of an Act of Parliament.

SCHEDULE

1. The whole ground or site of the building within the external walls shall, wherever the dampness of the site or the nature of the soil renders this precaution necessary, be covered with a layer of good cement concrete at least 4 inches thick finished shovel face.

2. (1.) Each external wall of the building shall either:

(a) to a height of not less than 6 inches above the surface of the ground adjoining the wall, be constructed of good cement concrete not less than 6 inches thick, or of brickwork composed of good whole bricks or stonework, all brickwork or stonework in the wall to be properly bonded and solidly put together with good lime or cement mortar, and to be not less than $4\frac{1}{2}$ inches thick ; or

(b) be carried at a height not less than 6 inches above the surface of the adjoining ground upon sufficient piers constructed of good bricks, stone,

by any subsequent enactment, with respect to new buildings including the drainage thereof and new streets, and any enactments in any local Acts dealing with the construction and drainage of new buildings and the laying-out and construction of new streets, and any byelaws made with respect to such matters under any such local Act.

[1] 52–3 V., c. 63.

or other hard and suitable materials similarly bonded and put together, or of good cement concrete, or in the case of a building erected before the 13th October 1919, and not subsequently re-erected, upon wooden piles or other supports of sufficient strength and in good condition.

(2.) Each external wall or pier of the building shall rest on concrete or on some other solid and sufficient foundation.

(3.) Every wall or pier of the building shall be provided with a proper damp-proof course of asphalt, or slates laid in cement, or of some other durable material impervious to moisture, beneath the level of the lowest floor and of the lowest timbers, and at a height of not less than 6 inches above the surface of the ground adjoining the wall:

Provided that where application is made to a local authority for their consent to the use for human habitation of a building of a permanent nature existing at the time when the application is made and there are no signs of dampness in the walls and the soil is dry, the provision of a damp-proof course shall not be required if the following conditions are satisfied, namely—

An impervious paving shall be provided outside the house at the ground level and adjoining all the external walls. This paving shall extend for a distance of at least 3 feet from the walls, and shall be continuous with a skirting of impervious material carried up on the exterior walls for a distance of at least 6 inches, and shall be sloped so as effectually to carry away all rain and waste water that may fall thereon from the walls of the house.

3. Every external wall of the building shall be constructed of good and suitable material and so as to be of sufficient stability and weather-proof.

4. The roof of the building shall be so constructed and supported as to be of sufficient stability and shall be covered externally with suitable fire-resisting and weather-proofing material;

Provided that it shall not be necessary to cover the roof with fire-resisting material if the following conditions are observed, namely—

(a) The building shall not be of more than two storeys in height and shall not comprise or form part of a block of more than 4 separate dwellings under one roof.

(b) (1) The building shall be distant

(i) at least 10 feet from the boundary of its curtilage except at any point where its curtilage adjoins that of a dwelling-house forming part of the same block ;

(ii) at least 20 feet from the nearest building, other than an out-building standing in the same curtilage or a dwelling-house forming part of the same block ;

(iii) at least 30 feet from the nearest public carriageway used or likely to be used for through traffic ;

(iv) at least 60 feet from the nearest boundary of any railway on which steam engines are used.

(2) Every block of 4 dwelling-houses having a roof not covered with fire-resisting material shall be isolated by a distance of 60 feet from any other dwelling-house having a roof not covered with fire-resisting material.

(3) Every group of 4 dwelling-houses having roofs not covered with fire-resisting material shall be isolated by a distance of at least 60 feet, every group of 24 such dwelling-houses by a distance of at least 180 feet, and every group of 96 such dwelling-houses by a distance of at least 540 feet, from any other such dwelling-house.

In this rule—

A " group of 4 dwelling-houses " means any 4 dwelling-houses the buildings comprising which are so situated that there can be drawn, passing through all the buildings, a line on which the distance between one building and the next in succession is in every case less than 60 feet.

A " group of 24 dwelling-houses " means any 24 . dwelling-houses the buildings comprising which are so situated that there can be drawn, passing through all the buildings, a line on which the distance between one building and the next in succession is in every case less than 180 feet.

A " group of 96 dwelling-houses " means any 96 dwelling-houses the buildings comprising which are so situated that there can be drawn, passing through all the buildings, a line on which the distance between one building and the next in succession is in every case less than 540 feet.

(4) For the purposes of this proviso all distances shall be measured horizontally to the nearest part of the building, other than the eaves or verge of the roof.

(c) Every chimney of the building shall be carried up to a height of not less than 5 feet above the ridge of the roof in brickwork or other solid incombustible material, which, where the chimney passes through the material forming the roof, shall be not less than 9 inches thick and rendered externally.

5. Where the building is intended to form two or more dwellings, the dwellings shall be separated by solid partitions of incombustible material not less than 3 inches thick, carried up to the under side of the roof-covering and resting throughout their entire length on solid continuous walls which as regards construction and damp-proof course shall comply with the provisions of paragraph 3 of this Schedule :

Provided that where any such partition is over an open passage between two dwellings it may rest on a sufficient arch or bressummer of fire-resisting material.

APPENDIX III

DOCUMENTS MAINLY RELATING TO IMPROVEMENT (PART I) AND RECONSTRUCTION (PART II) SCHEMES FOR UNHEALTHY AREAS

STATUTORY RULES AND ORDERS, 1910, No. 919

HOUSING OF THE WORKING CLASSES, ENGLAND

. UNHEALTHY HOUSES

The Housing (Inspection of District) Regulations, 1910, *dated* 2nd *September* 1910

55,578

To the several local authorities in England and Wales for the purposes of Part II of the Housing of the Working Classes Act, 1890 ;—
And to all others whom it may concern.

Whereas by subsection (1) of section 17 of the Housing, Town Planning, &c., Act, 1909, it is enacted that it shall be the duty of every local authority within the meaning of Part II of the Housing of the Working Classes Act, 1890 (hereinafter referred to as " the local authority ") to cause to be made from time to time inspection of their district, with a view to ascertain whether any dwelling-house therein is in a state so dangerous or injurious to health as to be unfit for human habitation, and that for that purpose it shall be the duty of the local authority, and of every officer of the local authority, to comply with such regulations and to keep such records as may be prescribed by the Local Government Board.

Now therefore, we, the Local Government Board, in pursuance of the powers given to us in that behalf, by this order, prescribe the following regulations ; that is to say—

ARTICLE I—(1.) The local authority shall as early as practicable after the date of this order take into consideration the provisions of subsection (1) of section 17 of the Act of 1909, and shall determine the procedure to be adopted under these regulations, to give effect to the requirements of that subsection in regard to the inspection of their district from time to time.

(2.) The local authority shall as part of their procedure make provision for a thorough inspection to be carried out from time to time according to the varying needs or circumstances of the dwelling-houses or localities in the district of the local authority.

(3.) The local authority shall cause to be prepared from time to time by the medical officer of health, or by an officer designated by them but acting under his direction and supervision, a list or lists of dwelling-houses the early inspection of which is, in the opinion of the medical officer of health, desirable. The list or lists may, if thought fit, relate to the dwelling-houses within a defined area of the district without specifying each house separately therein.

ARTICLE II— The inspection under and for the purposes of subsection (1) of section 17 of the Act of 1909 shall be made by the medical officer of health, or by an officer designated by the local authority but acting under his direction and supervision, and the officer making inspection of any dwelling-house shall examine the state of the dwelling-house in relation to the following matters, namely :—

(1) The arrangements for preventing the contamination of the water supply.

(2) Closet accommodation.

(3) Drainage.

(4) The condition of the dwelling-house in regard to light, the free circulation of air, dampness, and cleanliness.

(5) The paving, drainage, and sanitary condition of any yard or out-houses belonging to or occupied with the dwelling-house.

(6) The arrangements for the deposit of refuse and ashes.

(7) The existence of any room which would in pursuance of subsection (7) of section 17 of the Act of 1909 be a dwelling-house so dangerous or injurious to health as to be unfit for human habitation.

(8) Any defects in other matters which may tend to render the dwelling-house dangerous or injurious to the health of an inhabitant.

ARTICLE III—Records of the inspection of dwelling-houses made under and for the purposes of subsection (1) of section 17 of the Act of 1909 shall be prepared under the direction and supervision of the medical officer of health, and shall be kept by the officer of the local authority making the inspection or by some other officer appointed or employed for the purpose by the local authority.

The records may be kept in a book or books or on separate sheets or cards, and shall contain information, under appropriate headings, as to :—

(1) The situation of the dwelling-house, and its name or number.

(2) The name of the officer who made the inspection.

(3) The date when the dwelling-house was inspected.

(4) The date of the last previous inspection and a reference to the record thereof.

(5) The state of the dwelling-house in regard to each of the matters referred to in Article II of these regulations.

(6) Any action taken by the medical officer of health, or other officer of the local authority, either independently or on the directions of the local authority.

(7) The result of any action so taken.

(8) Any further action which should be taken in respect of the dwelling-house.

ARTICLE IV—The local authority shall, as far as may be necessary, take into consideration at each of their ordinary meetings the records kept in pursuance of Article III of these regulations, and shall give all such directions and take all such action within their powers as may be necessary or desirable in regard to any dwelling-house to which the records relate, and a note of any directions so given and the result of any action taken shall be added to the records.

ARTICLE V—The medical officer of health shall include in his annual report information and particulars in tabular form in regard to the number of dwelling-houses inspected under and for the purposes of section 17 of the Act of 1909, the number of dwelling-houses which on inspection were considered to be in a state so dangerous or injurious to health as to be unfit for human habitation, the number of representations made to the local authority with a view to the making of closing orders, the number of closing orders made, the number of dwelling-houses the defects in which were remedied without the making of closing orders, the number of dwelling-houses which after the making of closing orders were put into a fit state for human habitation, and the general character of the defects found to exist. He shall also include any other information and particulars which he may consider desirable in regard to the work of inspection under the said section. Inspection of District Regulations.

ARTICLE VI—The medical officer of health and any other officer of the local authority shall observe and execute all lawful orders and directions of the local authority in regard to or incidental to the inspection of the district of the local authority under and for the purposes of section 17 of the Act of 1909, and the execution of these regulations.

ARTICLE VII—In these regulations " the Act of 1909 " means the Housing, Town Planning, &c., Act, 1909.

ARTICLE VIII—These regulations may be cited as the Housing (Inspection of District) Regulations, 1910.

Given under the seal of office of the Local Government Board, this Second day of September, in the year One thousand nine hundred and ten.

(L.S.) JOHN BURNS,
President.

H. C. MONRO,
Secretary.

55,916   (19*th* November 1910.)

HOUSING ACTS

Forms of Advertisement and Notices : Improvement
                    Scheme

To the several local authorities in England and Wales
    for the purposes of Part I of the Housing of the
    Working Classes Act, 1890, as amended by the
    Housing of the Working Classes Act, 1903, and
    the Housing, Town Planning, &c., Act, 1909 ;—
And to all others whom it may concern.

Whereas by section 27 of the Housing of the Working
Classes Act, 1890 (hereinafter referred to as " the Act
of 1890 "), which section is included in Part I of the Act
of 1890, it was enacted as follows :—

" The confirming authority may by order prescribe
the forms of advertisements and notices under this Part
of this Act ; it shall not be obligatory on any persons
to adopt such forms, but the same, when adopted, shall
be deemed sufficient for all the purposes of this Part of
this Act."

And whereas, in pursuance of the said enactment,
the Secretary of State and the Local Government Board,
as the confirming authorities within the meaning of Part I
of the Act of 1890, by the orders described in the First
Schedule to this order (which orders are hereinafter
referred to as " the Orders "), prescribed certain Forms of
Advertisement and Notices under Part I of the Act of
1890 ;

And whereas by an order of the Privy Council issued
in pursuance of section 2 of the Housing of the Working
Classes Act, 1903, and dated the 27th day of February
1905, all the powers and duties of the Secretary of State
under the Housing Acts were transferred to the Local
Government Board ;

And whereas the said section 27 of the Act of 1890
was repealed by section 75 of the Housing, Town Planning, &c., Act, 1909 (hereinafter referred to as " the
Act of 1909 "), and by section 41 of the Act of 1909,
which section is included in Part I of the Act of 1909,
it is enacted as follows :—

"The Local Government Board may by order prescribe the form of any notice, advertisement, or other document to be used in connection with the powers and duties of a local authority or of the Board under the Housing Acts, and the forms so prescribed, or forms as near thereto as circumstances admit, shall be used in all cases to which those forms are applicable." *Forms prescribed, Part I scheme.*

And whereas, by virtue of section 51 of the Act of 1909, in Part I of that Act the expression "Housing Acts" means the Act of 1890, and any Act amending that Act, including the Act of 1909 ;

And whereas it is expedient that, in pursuance of the said section 41 of the Act of 1909, forms should be prescribed which shall be used in substitution for the forms prescribed by the orders :

Now therefore, we, the Local Government Board, in pursuance of the powers given to us by the Statutes in that behalf, by this order do prescribe the several forms set forth in the Second Schedule to this order to be used in connection with the powers and duties of a local authority under Part I of the Act of 1890 ; and we hereby declare that the said forms shall be in substitution for the forms prescribed by the orders described in the First Schedule to this order.

FIRST SCHEDULE

Order of the Secretary of State dated the 5th day of November 1890, and addressed to the London County Council and to the Commissioners of Sewers of the City of London.

Order of the Local Government Board dated the 2nd day of October 1890, and addressed to the several Urban Sanitary Authorities for the time being in England and Wales.

SECOND SCHEDULE

I—FORM OF ADVERTISEMENT (see also page 586).

HOUSING OF THE WORKING CLASSES ACTS, 1890 TO 1909

Advertisement of an Improvement Scheme

Notice is hereby given that the [1]
have in pursuance of the powers vested in them for that purpose by Part I of the Housing of the Working Classes

Act, 1890, as amended by the Housing of the Working Classes Act, 1903, and the Housing, Town Planning, &c., Act, 1909, made a scheme for the improvement of the area [or areas] the limits of which are stated in the Schedule hereunder, and which contains [or contain] approximately [2]

A copy of the said scheme, accompanied by maps distinguishing the lands proposed to be taken compulsorily and by particulars and estimates, has been deposited at †   and may be seen at all reasonable hours.

SCHEDULE [3]

The area to which the scheme relates is bounded as follows :—

> On the north by
> On the south by
> On the east by
> On the west by

or

The area to which the scheme relates is bounded by a line commencing (*set out the entire linear boundary*) :

or

The area to which the scheme relates consists of the following streets and other places or parts thereof :

Dated this   day of   , 19 .

Signature of clerk of local authority..................

Directions for filling up this form

Insert—
   [1] Description of the local authority.
   [2] The aggregate superficial extent of the area or areas.
   [3] One of the three alternative forms should be used as may be convenient.   If the scheme includes more than one area, the particulars indicated should be given as regards each area.

† *The place of deposit must be within the area or in the vicinity thereof. See section 7 (a) of the Act of 1890.*

II—FORM OF NOTICE TO OWNERS AND LESSEES

HOUSING OF THE WORKING CLASSES ACTS, 1890 TO 1909

Notice to owner or reputed owner, lessee or reputed lessee, of intention to take lands compulsorily under an Improvement Scheme (see also page 587).

To [1]

TAKE NOTICE that a petition is about to be presented

by the [2]   to the
Local Government Board in pursuance of Part I of the
Housing of the Working Classes Act, 1890, as amended
by the Housing of the Working Classes Act, 1903, and
the Housing, Town Planning, &c., Act, 1909, praying
that an order may be made confirming an Improvement
Scheme, whereby it is proposed to take compulsorily
the lands described in the Schedule hereunder, in which
lands you are believed to be interested, as owner or reputed
owner, or lessee or reputed lessee.

You are therefore hereby required to return to me on
or before the   day of   next an
answer in writing stating whether you dissent or not in
respect of the taking of the lands described in the said
Schedule.

A copy of the said scheme, accompanied by maps
distinguishing the lands proposed to be taken compulsorily and by particulars and estimates, has been
deposited at †   and may be seen at
all reasonable hours.

SCHEDULE referred to in the foregoing Notice

Name of Street, Court, Alley, or other Place.	Description of Lands‡ proposed to be taken.	Owner or reputed Owner.	Lessee or reputed Lessee.	Occupier.

Dated this   day of   , 19 .
Signature of clerk of local authority.................

Directions for filling up this form

Insert—

[1] Name, residence, or place of business, and description, where
known, of owner or reputed owner, lessee or reputed lessee,
as the case may require.

[2] Description of local authority.

† *The place of deposit must be within the area or in the vicinity thereof.
See section 7 (a) of the Act of 1890.*

‡ *" Lands " includes messuages, tenements, hereditaments, houses,
and buildings of any tenure, and any right over land.*

37

III—FORM OF NOTICE TO OCCUPIERS (see also p. 588)

HOUSING OF THE WORKING CLASSES ACTS, 1890 TO 1909

*Notice to occupier or occupiers (not being owners or reputed
owners or lessees or reputed lessees) of intention to
take lands compulsorily under an Improvement Scheme*

To ¹   the occupier of
the land †

or

[To the occupier or occupiers of the house] ‡

which in the Schedule hereunder is described as the lands
proposed to be taken.

TAKE NOTICE that a petition is about to be presented
by the ²   to the Local Government Board
in pursuance of Part I of the Housing of the Working
Classes Act, 1890, as amended by the Housing of the
Working Classes Act, 1903, and the Housing, Town
Planning, &c., Act, 1909, praying that an order may be
made confirming an Improvement Scheme, whereby it is
proposed to take compulsorily the lands described in
the Schedule hereunder.

A copy of the said scheme, accompanied by maps
distinguishing the lands proposed to be taken compulsorily and by particulars and estimates, has been
deposited at §   and may
be seen at all reasonable hours.

SCHEDULE referred to in the foregoing Notice

Name of Street, Court, Alley, or other Place.	Description of Lands† proposed to be taken.

Dated this   day of   , 19 .

Signature of clerk of local authority..................

Directions for filling up this form

Insert—

    ¹ The name of the occupier.

    ² Description of local authority.

    † " *Lands* " *includes messuages, tenements, hereditaments, houses, and
buildings of any tenure, and any right over land.*

    ‡ *The alternative address within these brackets is available only where
the property to be taken is a house.*

    § *The place of deposit must be within the area or in the vicinity thereof.
See section 7 (a) of the Act of* 1890.

Given under the seal of office of the Local Government Forms.
Board, this Nineteenth day of November, in the
year One thousand nine hundred and ten.

(L.S.) JOHN BURNS,
H. C. MONRO, *President.*
Secretary.

*Author's note on the above Order (Forms of Advertisement
and Notices [55,916; 19th November, 1910], and on the
forms appearing on pages 580 to 597.*

It does not appear that the above Order has been
revoked, but in the *Manual on Unfit Houses and Unhealthy
Areas,* issued by the Ministry of Health, certain slightly
different forms are suggested. On this point it will be
noticed that Section 41 of the 1909 Act provides that the
forms prescribed " or forms as near thereto as circumstances permit, shall be used."

The slight differences referred to mainly relate to the
changed circumstances arising out of the legislation
subsequent to the issue of the above Order, e.g. the heading of the suggested Form of Advertisement is now
" Housing Acts, 1890 to 1919," and the words " the
Minister of Health " now displace " the Local Government Board."

Therefore the modern forms (namely those suggested
on pages 580 to 597), may be taken to be but an up-to-
date edition of the forms prescribed in the above Order.
They do not state (as do the prescribed forms) either that
the lands proposed to be taken compulsorily are distinguished on the maps, or the contents of the area or
areas. The scheme, however, must distinguish the lands
proposed to be taken compulsorily, it must be accompanied by particulars—Section 6 of the 1890 Act—and in
each case information is to be given in the notice, showing
where a copy of the scheme can be seen.

In the prescribed Notice to Occupiers, there is no
reference to the fact that notice is not given to tenants
for a month or a less period than a month : the suggested
form makes it clear that, following an alteration in Section
7 of the 1890 Act made by Section 39 of the 1919 Act,
notice to such tenants is not now necessary.

It will be understood that the prescribed forms relate

to a Part I (Improvement) Scheme. There do not appear
to be any prescribed forms relating to a Part II (Reconstruction) Scheme, but forms suggested by the Ministry
of Health for a Part II Scheme are given on pages 591
to 597. The Ministry has power to prescribe forms—
Section 41 of the 1909 Act—and, with regard to the
" Instructions " on page 589, it is provided in Section 8
(2) of the 1890 Act that the petition for confirmation of
the scheme " shall be supported by such evidence as the
Local Government Board . . . may from time to time.
require."
   In connection with the forms it will be useful to read
the summary of the law given in Chapter III, page 34.

FORMS AND INSTRUCTIONS WITH REFERENCE TO PART I AND PART II SCHEMES

*(The following forms are suggested, subject to any necessary
adaptations—see the Official Manual on Unfit Houses
and Unhealthy Areas)*

Part I Schemes

1—FORM OF OFFICIAL REPRESENTATION OF THE MEDICAL OFFICER OF HEALTH

(Sections 4 and 5, 1890 Act.)

Name of Local Authority....................

HOUSING ACTS, 1890 TO 1919

Designation of Area.........................

OFFICIAL REPRESENTATION OF THE MEDICAL OFFICER
OF HEALTH

To the Council of

of

I,   , medical officer of health for the
        do hereby represent [1] that in my opinion,
within a certain area, described in the schedule hereto
   (a) there are certain houses, courts and alleys which
        are unfit for human habitation,
   or (b) the narrowness, closeness and bad arrangement,

[1] The medical officer of health when making his representation
should bear in mind the alternatives admissible under section 4 /90.

or the bad condition of the streets and houses
or groups of houses within such area, or the
want of light, air, ventilation or proper conveniences, or other sanitary defects, or one or
more of such causes, are dangerous or injurious
to the health of the inhabitants of the buildings
in the said area or of the neighbouring buildings,
and that the most satisfactory method of dealing with
the evils connected with such houses, courts or alleys,
and the sanitary defects in such area, is an improvement
scheme for the re-arrangement and re-construction of
the streets and houses within such area, or of some of
such streets and houses.

Forms suggested, Part I. scheme.

Dated this   day of   19 . .

(Signature)

Medical Officer of Health.

SCHEDULE

The area to which the above official representation
relates is coloured red on the map annexed hereto and
is bounded by a line commencing (set out the entire
boundary line).

2—RESOLUTION OF LOCAL AUTHORITY DECIDING THAT
IMPROVEMENT SCHEME SHOULD BE MADE, AND
GIVING NECESSARY INSTRUCTIONS FOR ITS PRE-
PARATION.

(Section 4, 1890 Act.)

The official representation of the medical officer of
health under the Housing Acts, 1890 to 1919, was submitted.

RESOLVED—

1. That the council, having taken into consideration
the official representation of the medical officer of health,
dated   19   , and being satisfied of the truth
thereof and of the sufficiency of their resources, declare
that the area described in such representation is an
unhealthy area, and that an improvement scheme ought
to be made in respect of the area.[1]

[1] If the local authority decide to exclude any part of the area or
to include any neighbouring lands under section 6 (1) (a) of the Act
of 1890, the resolution should be extended so as to indicate this.

2. That the clerk be instructed to prepare a draft scheme, in accordance with the provisions of Part I of the Housing of the Working Classes Act, 1890, as amended by subsequent Acts, and that the surveyor prepare the necessary plans, particulars and estimates.

3—MAPS, PARTICULARS, ESTIMATES, &c.
(*Section* 6, 1890 *Act*.)

Maps.

The following maps [1] should be prepared in connection with the scheme :—

Map No. 1 on the scale of $\frac{1}{500}$, or on a scale approximating to this, showing the lands included in the improvement scheme, the unhealthy area being coloured pink, and any "neighbouring lands" which have been included in the scheme in order to make it efficient being coloured blue.

The several properties should be numbered consecutively on this map. Each parcel of land, notwithstanding that several may belong to one owner, should be separately numbered, the outside boundaries of each parcel being defined by hard lines, and the buildings (if any) on each parcel being linked into it, so that it may be seen to what properties each number applies.

Map No. 2 on the scale of $\frac{1}{500}$, or on a scale approximating to this, showing the proposals for dealing with the cleared area, indicating any proposed new dwelling accommodation, street planning, open spaces or playgrounds or other intended developments. On this map any lands proposed to be used for re-housing should be coloured yellow and any lands proposed to be appropriated as open spaces green.

Map No. 3 on the scale of six inches to the mile, showing any site or sites where re-housing accommodation is to be provided which is not within the area comprised in the scheme, and the position of each site in relation to the area included in the scheme.

[1] The maps should be carefully checked. It is important that all buildings and boundaries should be correctly shown. All buildings should be hatched, and buildings other than dwelling houses and their appurtenances should have their character lettered upon them. A certificate by the competent official as to the correctness of the map must be given on the map itself.

(*Note.*—The Minister of Health will require two copies, mounted on linen, of each of the above maps. If in any case the lands included in the scheme as " the unhealthy area " do not comprise all the lands to which the official representation extended, a copy of the map prepared in connection with the official representation should be supplied to the Ministry.) <sub/>

Forms suggested, Part I. scheme.

Particulars of the Scheme

The scheme should be accompanied by a statement giving the following particulars :—

    (i) The acreage of the area comprised in the scheme ;

    (ii) The number of persons of the working classes who will be displaced by the scheme ;

    (iii) The number of persons for whom dwelling accommodation is to be provided ;

    (iv) Where the accommodation is to be provided ;

    (v) Any other necessary information or explanations.

Estimates

The estimates should distinguish the cost of the acquisition of the lands comprised in the scheme and the cost of the laying out and construction of new streets and the erection of new buildings, and should also specify the estimated value of any surplus lands and recoupments.

The Book of Reference

The book of reference should be in the following form and should be prepared on the ground at the same time as, and in conjunction with, the Map No. 1, each parcel of land being numbered to correspond with that map, and being described so as to show clearly what properties are covered by each number.

NAME OF LOCAL AUTHORITY..................

HOUSING ACTS, 1890 TO 1919

Designation of Improvement Scheme............

BOOK OF REFERENCE

Book of reference to the Map No. 1 of the area included in the above-mentioned scheme,

Forms
suggested,
Part I.
scheme.

Number on Map No. 1.	Description of Lands.	Situation.	Names and addresses of		Occupiers.
			Owners or reputed Owners.	Lessees or reputed Lessees.	

4—FORMS OF CLAUSES FOR IMPROVEMENT SCHEMES
(*Section* 6, 1890 *Act.*)

The purposes for which Part I or Part II schemes may be made are substantially the same, and it is suggested that the following clauses should be used as the basis for any scheme so far as they are applicable, and with any necessary adaptations or additions.

SHORT TITLE

This scheme may be cited as the   Improvement Scheme 19 .

INTERPRETATION

In this scheme the council means the

LIMITS OF SCHEME AND UNHEALTHY AREA

All the lands coloured pink on the map marked Map No. 1, annexed to this scheme, are included in the scheme as an unhealthy area.

Alternative Form for use when " Neighbouring Lands "
are included to make the scheme efficient

LIMIT OF SCHEME

All the lands coloured pink and blue on the map marked Map No. 1, annexed to this scheme, are included in this scheme.

LIMITS OF UNHEALTHY AREA

The lands coloured pink on the said Map No. 1 are included in the scheme as an unhealthy area.

The lands coloured blue on the said map are not part of the unhealthy area, but are included in order to make the scheme efficient.

ACQUISITION OF LANDS

All the lands included in the scheme are intended to be acquired compulsorily in default of agreement.

CLEARANCE OF AREA

After obtaining possession of the lands included in the scheme the council shall cause all the buildings (*or* the following buildings *or* except the following buildings) within the limits of the scheme to be demolished and the sites to be cleared.

LAY-OUT OF THE CLEARED AREA

The council shall lay out the cleared area in the manner shown on Map No. 2 annexed to this scheme.

All the existing highways in the area may be closed, appropriated, widened, or diverted by the council so far as may be necessary for the purposes of the scheme.

RE-HOUSING UPON AREA

On the lands coloured yellow on Map No. 2 the council shall erect in accordance with plans to be approved by the Minister of Health, suitable dwellings for the accommodation of   persons of the working classes.

OPEN SPACES

The lands coloured green on Map No. 2 shall be appropriated for the purposes of an open space.

DISPOSAL OF SURPLUS LANDS

Such of the lands in the scheme as shall not be required for the purpose of providing accommodation for persons of the working class or for the laying out of new streets or the improvement of streets or for the purposes of open spaces may, with the approval of the Minister of Health, be sold, leased, or otherwise disposed of as the council may think fit.

5—Resolution of Local Authority making Improvement Scheme

(*Section* 6, 1890 *Act.*)

RESOLVED—

That the Improvement Scheme under Part I of the Housing of the Working Classes Act, 1890, as amended by subsequent Acts, now submitted, for the
unhealthy area, together with the plans, particulars and estimates relating to the scheme, be, and the same are hereby made and adopted, and that all necessary steps be taken to obtain confirmation thereof.

6—Form of Advertisement

(*Section* 7, 1890 *Act.*)

HOUSING ACTS, 1890 TO 1919

Advertisement of an Improvement Scheme

Notice is hereby given that the   Council of   have, in pursuance of the powers vested in them for that purpose by Part I of the Housing of the Working Classes Act, 1890, as amended by subsequent Acts, made a scheme for the improvement of the area [*or areas*] the limits of which are stated in the schedule hereunder.

A copy of the scheme, accompanied by maps, particulars and estimates, has been deposited at the (*specify the place of deposit, which must be within the area, or in the vicinity thereof*) and may be seen at all reasonable hours.

SCHEDULE

(One of the alternative forms should be used as may be convenient. If the scheme includes more than one area, the particulars indicated should be given as regards each area.)

The area to which the scheme relates is bounded as follows :—

On the north by
On the south by
On the east by
On the west by

or

The area to which the scheme relates is bounded by

a line commencing (*set out the entire linear boundary*) :
Dated this day of , 19 .
Signature of Clerk of Local Authority..........

FORM OF NOTICE TO OWNERS AND LESSEES
(*Section 7, 1890 Act.*)

HOUSING ACTS, 1890 TO 1919

Notice to owner or reputed owner, lessee or reputed lessee, of intention to take lands compulsorily under an Improvement Scheme.

To (*insert name, residence, or place of business, and description, where known, of owner or reputed owner, lessee or reputed lessee, as the case may require*).

TAKE NOTICE that a petition is about to be presented by the Council of to the Minister of Health, in pursuance of Part I of the Housing of the Working Classes Act, 1890, as amended by subsequent Acts, praying that an order may be made confirming an improvement scheme whereby it is proposed to take compulsorily the lands described in the schedule hereunder, in which lands you are believed to be interested, as owner or reputed owner, or lessee or reputed lessee.

You are therefore hereby required to return to me on or before the day of next an answer in writing stating whether you dissent or not in respect of the taking of the lands described in the said schedule.

A copy of the said scheme, accompanied by maps, particulars and estimates, has been deposited at and may be seen at all reasonable hours.

SCHEDULE referred to in the foregoing Notice

Name of Street, Court, Alley, or other Place.	Descripton of Lands[1] proposed to be taken.	Owner or reputed Owner.	Lessee or reputed Lessee.	Occupier.

Dated this day of , 19 .
Signature of Clerk of Local Authority..........

[1] " Lands " includes messuages, tenements, hereditaments, houses, and buildings of any tenure, and any right over land.

FORM OF NOTICE TO OCCUPIERS

(*Section* 7, 1890 *Act*.)

HOUSING ACTS, 1890 TO 1919

*Notice to occupier or occupiers (not being owners or reputed
owners, or lessees, or reputed lessees, or tenants for
a month or a less period than a month) of intention
to take lands compulsorily under an Improvement
Scheme.*

To (*insert name of occupier*) the occupier of
the land [1]

or

[To the occupier or occupiers of the house] [2]
which in the schedule hereunder is described as the
lands proposed to be taken.

TAKE NOTICE that a petition is about to be presented
by the Council of to the Minister
of Health in pursuance of Part I of the Housing of the
Working Classes Act, 1890, as amended by subsequent
Acts, praying that an order may be made confirming
an improvement scheme whereby it is proposed to take
compulsorily the lands described in the schedule hereunder.

A copy of the said scheme, accompanied by maps,
particulars and estimates, has been deposited at [3]
and may be seen at all reasonable hours.

SCHEDULE referred to in the foregoing Notice

Name of Street, Court, Alley or other Place.	Description of Lands1 proposed to be taken.

Dated this day of , 19 .
Signature of Clerk of Local Authority. . . . .

[1] " Lands " includes messuages, tenements, hereditaments, houses,
and buildings of any tenure, and any right over land.

[2] The alternative address within these brackets is available only
where the property to be taken is a house.

[3] The place of deposit must be within the area or in the vicinity
thereof, see Section 7 (*a*) of the Act of 1890.

7—INSTRUCTIONS AS TO APPLICATION FOR CONFIRMATION
OF PART I SCHEME

(Section 8, 1890 Act.)

The application must be made by a petition which
should be accompanied by :—

(1) A copy of the official representation.

(2) Two copies of the improvement scheme.

(3) Particulars and estimates as specified on page   .

(4) Two copies, mounted on linen, of the maps specified
on pages   and   .

(5) The book of reference.

(6) Information as to the rates of mortality in the
area comprised in the scheme, as compared with
the rates for the whole of the district.

(7) A detailed statement showing as regards each
house in the area comprised in the scheme which
is occupied by persons of the working classes—

    (*a*) the number of such occupants ;

    (*b*) the weekly rent paid ;

    (*c*) the occupations and places of employment
of the tenants.

(8) A detailed statement showing the number of empty
houses fit for habitation and suitable for persons
of the working classes, within a distance of half
a mile from the area comprised in the scheme,
together with information as to the rentals of
such houses.

(9) A certificate signed by the clerk to the local
authority, or other person competent to give
such certificate, of the publication of an advertisement in accordance with the requirements
of section 7 (*a*) of the Act of 1890 as amended
by section 5 of the Act of 1903, and section 39
of the Act of 1919.

(10) A certificate signed by the clerk to the local
authority, or other person competent to give
such certificate, of compliance with the requirements of section 7 of the Act of 1890, as
amended by section 5 of the Act of 1903 and
section 39 of the Act of 1919, as to the service
of notices.

8—FORM OF PETITION

(Section 8, 1890 *Act.)*

HOUSING ACTS, 1890 TO 1919

Improvement Scheme, 19 .

To the Minister of Health :—

Petition of the   *(name of Local Authority).*

(hereinafter called " the Council.")

Sheweth as follows :—

·1. AN official representation, of which a copy is annexed, has been made to the Council by their medical officer of health pursuant to the provisions of Part I of the Housing of the Working Classes Act, 1890.

2. THE official representation was taken into consideration by the Council at a meeting held on the day of   19 , and the Council, being satisfied of the truth thereof and of the sufficiency of their resources, passed a resolution to the effect that an improvement scheme ought to be made in respect of the area referred to in the resolution.

3. A copy of the scheme made by the Council, with maps, particulars and estimates (in duplicate) is annexed.

4. THE names of the owners, or reputed owners, lessees or reputed lessees, who have dissented in respect of the taking of their lands for the purposes of the scheme are set out in the schedule hereto.

The Council pray that an order may be made confirming the scheme.

THE SCHEDULE REFERRED TO

Owners or reputed Owners.	Lessees or reputed Lessees.	Number of property in book of reference.

(Signed)....................

(L.S.)   Chairman of Council.

(Date)...........   ....

Clerk.

Part II Schemes

1 (a)—FORM OF REPORT OF THE MEDICAL OFFICER OF HEALTH

(Section 39, 1890 *Act.)*

Name of Local Authority...................

HOUSING ACTS, 1890 TO 1919

Designation of Area........................

Report of the medical officer of health with a view to proceedings under section 39 [1] of the Housing of the Working Classes Act, 1890.

To the....................

(Name of Local Authority) of.................

I, medical officer of health for , do hereby report that orders have been made for the demolition of the buildings described in the schedule hereto, and, in my opinion, it would be beneficial to the health of the inhabitants of the neighbouring dwelling houses if the area of the dwelling houses of which such buildings form or formed part were used for all or any of the following purposes, that is to say—*(delete what is not relevant)*—(1) dedicated as a highway or open space, or (2) appropriated, sold or let, for the erection of dwellings for the working classes, or (3) exchanged with other neighbouring land which is more suitable for the erection of such dwellings, and on exchange will be appropriated, sold or let for such erection.

The reasons for my opinion are :—

SCHEDULE REFERRED TO

(Here specify buildings in respect of which Demolition Orders have been made).

....

....

(Signature of Medical Officer of Health).........

(Date)................

[1] This form is included for the purpose of any case arising under sub-section (1) (a), but the majority of cases will no doubt fall under sub-section (1) (b), for the purposes of which the following form is suggested.

1 (b)—FORM OF REPORT OF THE MEDICAL OFFICER OF
HEALTH

(*Section* 39, 1890 *Act.*)

Name of Local Authority....................

HOUSING ACTS, 1890 TO 1919

Designation of Area.......................

Report of the medical officer of health with a view to
proceedings under section 39 of the Housing of the
Working Classes Act, 1890.

To the....................

(*Name of Local Authority*)....................

I,   medical officer of health for   ,
do hereby report that in my opinion the closeness, narrowness, and bad arrangement or bad condition of the
buildings comprised in the area described in the schedule
hereto, or the want of light, air, ventilation or proper
conveniences, or other sanitary defects in such buildings
are dangerous or prejudicial to the health of the inhabitants, of the said buildings or of the neighbouring
buildings, and that the demolition or the reconstruction
and re-arrangement of the said buildings or of some of
them is necessary to remedy the said evils.

(Signature of Medical Officer of Health)............

(Date)..........19....

SCHEDULE REFERRED TO

(*Here define area of improvement scheme. The area may
also be coloured on an accompanying map.*)

....
....

2—RESOLUTION OF LOCAL AUTHORITY DIRECTING A
SCHEME TO BE PREPARED FOR AN IMPROVEMENT
SCHEME UNDER SECTION 39 (1) (b) IN PART II OF
THE HOUSING OF THE WORKING CLASSES ACT, 1890

Resolved—

(1) That the Council, having taken into consideration
the report of the medical officer of health, dated the
        day of   19 , with reference to the
area (*insert description of area*)   , and being of
opinion that the area is one to which the provisions of
section 39 (1) (b) of the Housing of the Working Classes

Act, 1890, apply, hereby direct a scheme to be prepared for the improvement of the area.[1]

Resolved—

(2) That the clerk be instructed to prepare a draft scheme in accordance with the provisions of Part II of the Housing of the Working Classes Act, 1890, as amended by subsequent Acts, and that the surveyor prepare the necessary plans, particulars and estimates.

Forms suggested, Part II. scheme.

3—MAPS, PARTICULARS, ESTIMATES, &C.
(Section 39, 1890 Act.)
As in Part I Scheme, see page 582.

4—FORM OF CLAUSES FOR PART II SCHEMES
(Section 39, 1890 Act.)
As in Part I Scheme, see page 584.

5—RESOLUTION OF LOCAL AUTHORITY MAKING AN IMPROVEMENT SCHEME UNDER SECTION 39 (1) (*b*) IN PART II OF THE HOUSING OF THE WORKING CLASSES ACT, 1890

Resolved—

That the scheme under section 39 (1) (*b*) in Part II of the Housing of the Working Classes Act, 1890, as amended by subsequent Acts, now submitted, for the improvement of the area (*insert description of area*), together with the plans, particulars, and estimates relating to the said scheme be, and the same are hereby made and adopted, and that all necessary steps be taken for obtaining sanction thereto.

I
6—FORM OF NOTICE TO OWNERS AND LESSEES
(Section 39 (2), 1890 Act.)
HOUSING ACTS, 1890 TO 1919

Notice to owner or reputed owner, lessee or reputed lessee, of Improvement Scheme under Section 39 of the Housing of the Working Classes Act, 1890

[1] If neighbouring lands are added to make the scheme efficient the resolution should be extended.

38

To (*name, residence, or place of business, and description,
where known, of owner or reputed owner, lessee or reputed
lessee, as the case may require*).

TAKE NOTICE that a petition is about to be presented
by the (*description of Local Authority*) to the Minister of
Health in pursuance of Part II of the Housing of the
Working Classes Act, 1890, as amended by subsequent
Acts, praying that an order may be made sanctioning
an improvement scheme, whereby it is proposed to
take by agreement or compulsorily the lands described
in the schedule hereunder, in which lands you are believed
to be interested, as owner or reputed owner, or lessee or
reputed lessee.

You are therefore hereby required to return to me on
or before the   day of   next an
answer in writing stating whether you dissent or not in
respect of the taking of the lands described in the said
schedule.

A copy of the said scheme, accompanied by maps,
particulars and estimates, has been deposited at [1]
     and may be seen at all reasonable hours.

SCHEDULE referred to in the foregoing Notice

Name of Street, Court, Alley, or other Place.	Description of Lands[2] proposed to be taken.	Owner or reputed Owner.	Lessee or reputed Lessee.	Occupier.

Dated this   day of   19

Signature of Clerk of Local Authority...........

[1] The place of deposit should be within the area or in the vicinity
thereof.

[2] " Lands " includes messuages, tenements, hereditaments, houses,
and buildings of any tenure, and any rights over land.

II

FORM OF NOTICE TO OCCUPIERS [1]

(Section 39 (2), 1890 *Act.)*

HOUSING ACTS, 1890 TO 1919

*Notice to occupier or occupiers (not being owners or reputed
owners or lessees or reputed lessees of an Improvement
Scheme under Section 39 of the Housing of the Working
Classes Act,* 1890)

To *(insert name of occupier)* the occupier of the land

or

[To the occupier or occupiers of the house] [2]
which in the schedule hereunder is described as the lands
proposed to be taken.

TAKE NOTICE that a petition is about to be presented by
the *(insert designation of Local Authority)* to the Minister
of Health in pursuance of Part II of the Housing of the
Working Classes Act, 1890, as amended by subsequent
Acts, praying that an order may be made sanctioning
an improvement scheme, whereby it is proposed to take
by agreement or compulsorily the lands described in
the schedule hereunder.

A copy of the said scheme, accompanied by maps,
particulars and estimates, has been deposited at [3]
and may be seen at all reasonable hours.

SCHEDULE referred to in the foregoing Notice

Name of Street, Court, Alley or other Place.	Description of Lands [4] proposed to be taken.

Dated this day of , 19 .

Signature of Clerk of Local Authority...........

[1] Application may be made to the Minister of Health to dispense
under section 41 (2) of the Act of 1909 with the service of this Notice
in the case, for instance, of a tenant for a month or a less period than
a month.

[2] The alternative address within these brackets is available only
where the property to be taken is a house.

[3] The place of deposit should be within the area or in the vicinity
thereof.

[4] " Lands " includes messuages, tenements, hereditaments, houses,
buildings and of any tenure, and any right over land.

7—INSTRUCTIONS AS TO APPLICATION FOR SANCTION TO PART II SCHEME

(Section 39 (3), 1890 *Act.)*

Application must be by a petition, which should be accompanied by :—

(1) A copy of any relevant report of the medical officer of health or of a committee in regard to the area to which the scheme relates.

(2) A copy of the resolution of the local authority under section 39 (1) of the Act of 1890.

(3) The documents and particulars specified under headings (2) to (8), on page 589.

(4) A certificate signed by the clerk to the local authority, or other person competent to give such certificate, of compliance with the requirements of sections 39 (2) and 7 (*b*), (*c*) and (*d*) of the Act of 1890 as amended by section 5 of the Act of 1903 and section 39 of the Act of 1919, as to the service of notices.

(5) A statement of the names of all the owners or reputed owners, lessees or reputed lessees, who have dissented in respect of the taking of their lands.

8—FORM OF PETITION

(Section 39 (3), 1890 *Act.)*

Name of Local Authority...................

HOUSING ACTS, 1890 TO 1919

......................Improvement Scheme, 19

To the Minister of Health.

Petition of the ....*(name of Local Authority).*

(hereinafter called " the Council ")

Sheweth as follows :—

1. A report, a copy of which is annexed, has been made to the Council by their medical officer of health, relating to an area specified in the report.

2. The report was taken into consideration by the Council at a meeting held on the   day of   19 , and as it appeared to them that the area was one to which the provisions of section 39 (1)

(*b*) of the Housing of the Working Classes Act, 1890, as amended by subsequent Acts, apply, they passed a resolution to that effect and directed a scheme to be prepared for the improvement of the area referred to in the resolution.

3. A copy of the scheme made by the Council, with maps, particulars and estimates (in duplicate) is annexed.

4. The names of the owners or reputed owners, lessees or reputed lessees, who have dissented in respect of the taking of their lands for the purposes of the scheme, are set out in the schedule hereto.

The Council pray that an order may be made sanctioning the scheme.

THE SCHEDULE REFERRED TO

Owners or reputed Owners.	Lessees or reputed Lessees.	Number of Property in Book of Reference.

(Signed).....................

(L.S.)   Chairman of Council.

Date..........19 .   ...

                                           Clerk.

REGULATIONS OF LOCAL AUTHORITY IN REGARD TO UNDERGROUND ROOMS USED AS SLEEPING PLACES

Underground Rooms, Draft Regulations.

(*Draft Clauses suggested by the Local Government Board in Circular dated 17th April* 1914)

REGULATIONS PRESCRIBED BY THE
    UNDER SECTION 17 (7) OF THE HOUSING, TOWN PLANNING, &c., ACT, 1909

Every room habitually used as a sleeping place the surface of the floor of which is more than *three feet* below

the surface of the part of the street adjoining or nearest
to the room shall comply with the following regulations,
namely :—

1. The subsoil of the site of the room shall be effectually
drained by means of a properly trapped and ventilated
subsoil drain wherever the dampness of the site renders
such a precaution necessary.

2. Every drain passing under the room, other than a
drain for the drainage of the subsoil of the site of the
room, shall be gas-tight and water-tight.

3. The room shall be effectually protected against
the rising of any effluvium or exhalation by being properly
asphalted, or by being covered with a layer of good
cement concrete at least *six inches* thick, or *four inches*
thick if properly grouted, laid upon the ground of the
site of the entire room, or in some equally effectual
manner.

4. The space if any beneath the floor of the room
shall be provided with adequate means of ventilation.

5. (i) Every wall of the room shall be provided with
an efficient horizontal damp-proof course, which shall
be composed of materials impervious to moisture, and
shall if the floor of the room be formed of woodwork
be beneath the level of the lowest timbers or wordwork
of such floor, and shall in every other case be not less
than *one inch* below the level of the upper surface of such
floor.

(ii) No part of any wall of the room shall, where it is
practicable to avoid it, be in contact with the ground
or earth.

Provided that where any wall of the room is in contrast
with the ground or earth, such wall or such part thereof
as is so in contact shall, unless constructed as a hollow
wall, have an efficient vertical damp-proof course extending from the lowest horizontal damp-proof course
therein to a height of at least *six inches* above the surface
of the contiguous ground or earth.

6. Unless the room is provided with a fireplace and a
flue properly constructed and properly connected with
such fireplace, it shall be provided with special and adequate means of ventilation by one or more suitably
placed apertures or air shafts.

7. An area or open space properly paved with impervious material and effectually drained by means of a

properly trapped gulley, shall adjoin the room and shall
extend either—

  (a) throughout the entire length of one side thereof ;
  or

  (b) at least throughout the entire width of any window
      or windows required by these regulations and
      (except where the area of such window or windows
      shall be not less than *one-seventh* of the floor
      area of the room) for *three feet* on each side of
      such window or windows.

Any such area shall be not less than *two feet* wide
in every part thereof, and shall be open upwards from a
level *three inches* below the level of the damp-proof
course in the adjoining wall of the room.

Provided (a) that where a bay window in the room
having side lights overlooks such an area the width
thereof in front of such window may be *one foot* at the
least ; and

  (b) that any steps necessary for access to any part of
the building comprising the room may be placed in or
over such an area or open space if they are so placed as
not to be over or across any window of the room required
by the regulation in that behalf.

8. (i) The room shall be effectually lighted by means
of one or more windows opening directly into the
external air.

(ii) Every such window shall be so constructed that
one-half at the least may be opened, and that the opening
may extend to the top of the window.

(iii) The total area of such window or windows clear
of the sash frames shall be equal at the least to *one-eighth*
of the floor area of the room, and a portion of such total
area equal in extent to at least *one-tenth* of such floor
area shall be so situated that a line making an angle
of *thirty degrees* with a horizontal plane can be drawn
upwards from any point thereon in a vertical plane at
right angles to the plane of the window, so as not to
intersect within a distance of *ten feet* measured horizontally from the window any wall of any area adjoining
the room, or any other wall or any kerb or other obstruction except an open fence.

For the purposes of this paragraph a bay window
having side lights shall be assumed to be equivalent to
a flat window of the same area and of the same height in

Under-
ground
Rooms,
Draft
Regulations

relation to the room, and situated at a distance from the outside area wall equal to the mean width of the area.

(iv) In estimating the area of a window or windows for the purpose of this regulation no account shall be taken of any part of any such window which is above the mean level of the ceiling of the room.

(v) Any such window or windows shall overlook the area or open space provided in pursuance of the regulation in that behalf.

APPENDIX IV

OTHER PARTS I AND II DOCUMENTS, MAINLY RELATING TO A HOUSE OR HOUSES OUT OF REPAIR OR OTHERWISE UNFIT

STATUTORY RULES AND ORDERS, 1910, No. 2

HOUSING OF THE WORKING CLASSES, ENGLAND

FORMS

Order of the Local Government, dated 11th January 1910, under section 41 of the Housing, Town Planning, &c., Act, 1909 (9 Edw. 7. c. 44), prescribing Forms of certain Notices and other Documents

Forms. (Keeping houses in repair.)

54,930

To the several local authorities in England and Wales for the purposes of Part I of the Housing, Town Planning, &c., Act, 1909 ;—
And to all others whom it may concern.

Whereas by section 41 of the Housing, Town Planning, &c., Act, 1909, it is enacted as follows :—

The Local Government Board may by order prescribe the form of any notice, advertisement, or other document, to be used in connection with the powers and duties of a local authority or of the Board under the Housing Acts, and the forms so prescribed, or forms as near thereto as circumstances admit, shall be used in all cases to which those forms are applicable :

And whereas, by virtue of section 51 of the Housing, Town Planning, &c., Act, 1909, in Part I of that Act the expression "Housing Acts" means the Housing of the Working Classes Act, 1890, and any Act amending that Act, including the Housing, Town Planning, &c., Act, 1909 :

Forms.
(Keeping
houses in
repair.)

Now therefore, we, the Local Government Board, by this order, do prescribe the several forms hereinafter set forth as the forms of certain notices and other documents to be used in connection with the powers and duties of a local authority under the Housing Acts.

(*As to partial repeal, see page* 610.)

HOUSING, TOWN PLANNING, &c., ACT, 1909

PART I

Section 15 (2)

FORM No. 1

Form of Notice by person authorised by the local authority before entry for the purpose of viewing the state and condition of a house to which section 15 *of the Housing, Town Planning, &c., Act,* 1909, *applies.*

To [1]   the [2]
of the house [3]

Take Notice that in pursuance of subsection (2) of section 15 of the Housing, Town Planning, &c., Act, 1909, I, [4]
being a person duly authorised in writing by the [5]
       intend, on the †   day of
19 , at any time between the hours of §
in the forenoon and   in the afternoon, to enter the above-mentioned house for the purpose of viewing the state and condition thereof.

Dated this   day of   , 19 .

Signature.............................⎱ of person
Description............................. ⎰authorised
Residence or Place of Business.............⎰ to enter.

Directions for filling up this form

Insert—
[1] The name and description, where known, of tenant *or* occupier.
[2] "Tenant" *or* "occupier."
[3] Such a description of the house as may be sufficient identification.
[4] Name and description of person authorised by the local authority to enter.
[5] Description of the local authority.

† *Twenty-four hours' notice must be given.*
§ *Entry must be at reasonable times of the day.*

HOUSING, TOWN PLANNING, &c., ACT, 1909

PART I

Section 15 (3)

FORM No. 2

Form of Notice requiring landlord to execute works in the case of a house to which section 15 of the Housing, Town Planning, &c., Act, 1909, applies.

To [1]   , the landlord of the house [2]

TAKE NOTICE—

That it appears to the [3]

that the undertaking implied by virtue of section 15 of the Housing, Town Planning, &c., Act, 1909, to the effect that the above-mentioned house to which that section applies shall be kept by you in all respects reasonably fit for human habitation, has not been complied with ;

And that, in pursuance of subsection (3) of the said section, the said [3]

do hereby require you within a period of †

days, ending on the   day of   , One thousand nine hundred and   , to execute the works herein specified as being necessary to make the said house in all respects reasonably fit for human habitation, that is to say, the several works hereinafter set forth, namely [4]—

Dated this   day of   , 19

Signature of clerk of local authority..................

Directions for filling up this form

Insert—

    [1] Name, residence or place of business, and description, where known, of landlord.

    [2] Such a description of the house as may be sufficient for its identification.

    [3] Description of the local authority.

    [4] Description of works to be executed.

† *A reasonable time, not being less than twenty-one days, must be specified.*

Note.—By subsection (4) of section 15 of the Housing, Town Planning, &c., Act, 1909, it is provided that—

    Within twenty-one days after the receipt of such notice [i.e.

Forms.
(Keeping
houses in
repair.)

a written notice by the local authority to the landlord pursuant to section 15 (3)] the landlord may by written notice to the local authority declare his intention of closing the house for human habitation, and thereupon a closing order shall be deemed to have become operative in respect of such house.

Subsection (5) of that section is in these terms :—

If the notice given by the local authority is not complied with, and if the landlord has not given the notice mentioned in the immediately preceding subsection, the authority may, at the expiration of the time specified in the notice given by them to the landlord, do the work required to be done and recover the expenses incurred by them in so doing from the landlord as a civil debt in manner provided by the Summary Jurisdiction Acts, or, if they think fit, the authority may by order declare any such expenses to be payable by annual instalments within a period not exceeding that of the interest of the landlord in the house, nor in any case five years, with interest at a rate not exceeding five pounds per cent. per annum, until the whole amount is paid, and any such instalments or interest or any part thereof may be recovered from the landlord as a civil debt in manner provided by the Summary Jurisdiction Acts.

With respect to appeals, subsection (6) of the same section enacts as follows :—

A landlord may appeal to the Local Government Board against any notice requiring him to execute works under this section, and against any demand for the recovery of expenses from him under this section or order made with respect to those expenses under this section by the authority, by giving notice of appeal to the Board within twenty-one days after the notice is received, or the demand or order is made, as the case may be, and no proceedings shall be taken in respect of such notice requiring works, order, or demand, whilst the appeal is pending.

And section 39 contains the following provisions :—

(1.) The procedure on any appeal under this Part [i.e. Part I] of this Act, including costs, to the Local Government Board shall be such as the Board may by rules determine, and on any such appeal the Board may make such order in the matter as they think equitable, and any order so made shall be binding and conclusive on all parties, and, where the appeal is against any notice, order, or apportionment given or made by the local authority, the notice, order, or apportionment may be confirmed, varied, or quashed, as the Board think just.

Provided that—

(a) the Local Government Board may at any stage of the proceedings on appeal, and shall, if so directed by the High Court, state in the form of a special case for the opinion of the court any question of law arising in the course of the appeal ; and

(b) the rules shall provide that the Local Government Board shall not dismiss any appeal without having first held a public local inquiry.

(2.) Any notice, order, or apportionment as respects which an appeal to the Local Government Board is given under this Part of this Act shall not become operative, until either the time within which an appeal can be made under this Part of this Act has elapsed without an appeal being made, or in case an appeal is made, the appeal is determined or abandoned, and no work shall be done or proceedings taken under any such notice, order, or apportionment, until it becomes operative.

(3.) The Local Government Board may, before considering any

appeal which may be made to them under this Part of this Act, Forms. require the appellant to deposit such sum to cover the costs of (Keeping the appeal as may be fixed by the rules made by them with refer-　houses in ence to appeals.　　repair.)

For Rules determining the procedure on any such appeal, see page 608.

HOUSING, TOWN PLANNING, &c., ACT, 1909

PART I

Section 15 (4)

FORM No. 3

Form of Notice declaring intention of landlord to close for human habitation a house to which section 15 *of the Housing, Town Planning, &c., Act,* 1919, *applies.*

To the [1]
WHEREAS by a notice dated the　　　　day of　　　, 19 , the local authority in pursuance of subsection (3) of section 15 of the Housing, Town Planning, &c., Act, 1909, have required the landlord of the house [2]　　　　to execute, within the time specified in that notice, such works as are specified in the said notice as being necessary to make the said house in all respects reasonably fit for human habitation :

Now therefore, I, the landlord, do by this notice declare my intention of closing the said house for human habitation.

As witness my hand this　　　　day of　　　, 19 .

Signature............................⎫
Residence or Place of Business..........⎬ of Landlord.
Description.......... ....⎭

Directions for filling up this form

Insert—
　[1] Description of the local authority.
　[2] Such a description of the house as may be sufficient for its identification.

Note.—By subsection (4) of section 15 of the Housing, Town Planning, &c., Act, 1909, it is provided that within twenty-one days after the receipt of the notice of the local authority in pursuance of subsection (3) of that section, the landlord may by written notice to the local authority declare his intention of closing the house for human habitation, and thereupon a closing order shall be deemed to have become operative in respect of such house.

HOUSING, TOWN PLANNING, &c., ACT, 1909

PART I

Section 15 (5)

FORM No. 4

*Form of Order declaring Expenses incurred by the local
authority in the case of a house to which section 15 of the
Housing, Town Planning, &c., Act, 1909, applies to be
payable by Annual Instalments.*

To [1]   , the landlord of the
house [2]

WHEREAS by a notice dated the   day of   ,
19   , we, the [3]
in pursuance of subsection (3) of section 15 of the Housing,
Town Planning, &c., Act, 1909, have required the landlord of the above-mentioned house to execute, within
the time specified in that notice, the works specified in
the said notice as being necessary to make the said
house in all respects reasonably fit for human habitation ;

And whereas the said notice has not been complied
with and the landlord has not given in pursuance of subsection (4) of the said section a notice declaring his
intention of closing the said house for human habitation ;

And whereas we, the said [3]
in pursuance of subsection (5) of the same section have
done the work required to be done, and have incurred in
so doing expenses amounting to the sum of £   :   :

Now therefore, we, the said [3]
do, by this our order, declare that the said expenses
amounting to the sum of £   :   :   shall
be payable by annual instalments within a period not
exceeding †   years, with interest at the rate of §
     pounds per cent. per annum, until the whole
amount is paid.

Dated this   day of   , 19   .

(To be sealed with the common seal of the local authority)

Signature of clerk of local authority.................

Directions for filling up this form

Insert—
   [1] Name, residence or place of business, and description, where
      known, of landlord.
   [2] Such a description of the house as may be sufficient for its
      identification.

³ Description of the local authority.

† *The period to be specified must not exceed that of the interest of the landlord in the house, nor in any case five years.*

§ *The rate of interest must not exceed five pounds per cent. per annum.*

Forms.
(Keeping
houses in
repair.)

Note.—By subsection (5) of section 15 of the Housing, Town Planning, &c., Act, 1909, it is provided that any instalments or interest or any part of any instalment or interest under an order of the local authority declaring their expenses to be payable by annual instalments may be recovered from the landlord as a civil debt in manner provided by the Summary Jurisdiction Acts.

With respect to appeals, subsection (6) of the same section enacts as follows :—

> A landlord may appeal to the Local Government Board against any notice requiring him to execute works under this section, and against any demand for the recovery of expenses from him under this section or order made with respect to those expenses under this section by the authority, by giving notice of appeal to the Board within twenty-one days after the notice is received, or the demand or order is made, as the case may be, and no proceedings shall be taken in respect of such notice requiring works, order, or demand whilst the appeal is pending.

And section 39 contains the following provisions :—

> (1.) The procedure on any appeal under this Part [i.e. Part I] of this Act, including costs, to the Local Government Board shall be such as the Board may by rules determine, and on any such appeal the Board may make such order in the matter as they think equitable, and any order so made shall be binding and conclusive on all parties, and, where the appeal is against any notice, order, or apportionment given or made by the local authority, the notice, order, or apportionment may be confirmed, varied or quashed, as the Board think just.

Provided that—

> (a) the Local Government Board may at any stage of the proceedings on appeal, and shall, if so directed by the High Court, state in the form of a special case for the opinion of the court any question of law arising in the course of the appeal ; and

> (b) the rules shall provide that the Local Government Board shall not dismiss any appeal without having first held a public local inquiry.

> (2.) Any notice, order, or apportionment as respects which an appeal to the Local Government Board is given under this Part of this Act shall not become operative, until either the time within which an appeal can be made under this Part of this Act has elapsed without an appeal being made, or, in case an appeal is made, the appeal is determined or abandoned, and no work shall be done or proceedings taken under any such notice, order, or apportionment, until it becomes operative.

> (3.) The Local Government Board may, before considering any appeal which may be made to them under this Part of this Act, require the appellant to deposit such sum to cover the costs of the appeal as may be fixed by the rules made by them with reference to appeals.

For Rules determining the procedure on any such appeal, see page 608.
[*Note.*—The remainder of this order is repealed by S.R. & O., 1919, No. 1424, see page 610.]

65,473   (10*th October* 1919.)

STATUTORY RULES AND ORDERS, 1919, No. 1423

Appeal
Procedure
Rules.

THE HOUSING ACTS (APPEAL PROCEDURE)
RULES, 1919

MADE BY THE MINISTER OF HEALTH WITH REFERENCE
TO PROCEDURE ON APPEALS UNDER SECTION 39 OF
THE HOUSING, TOWN PLANNING, &C., ACT, 1909

THE Minister of Health, under the powers conferred on
him by section 39 of the Housing, Town Planning, &c.,
Act, 1909, and all other powers enabling him in that
behalf, hereby revokes the rules with reference to appeals
made by the Local Government Board on the 11th day
of January 1910, and makes the following rules :—

ARTICLE I—These rules may be cited as " The Housing
Acts (Appeal Procedure) Rules, 1919."

ARTICLE II—(1) An appeal to the Minister of Health
under Part I of the Housing, Town Planning, &c., Act,
1909, shall be made by sending to the Minister a notice
of appeal in the form prescribed by the Housing Acts
(Form of Orders and Notices) Order, 1919, signed by the
appellant or by his duly authorised agent, together
with the original notice, order, or demand appealed
against or a true copy thereof.

(2) The appellant shall notify the local authority
forthwith of any appeal to the Minister of Health.

(3.) The appellant shall send to the Minister either
with his notice of appeal, or within fourteen days thereafter, a concise statement in writing of the facts and
contentions on which he relies.

(4) The appellant shall deposit with the Minister
within fourteen days from the date of his notice of appeal
the sum of ten pounds, provided that the Minister may,
if he thinks fit, require the deposit of a less sum than
ten pounds or may dispense with the deposit.

ARTICLE III—The Minister shall, as soon as may be
after receipt of the statement aforesaid, send to the local
authority a copy of the notice of appeal and of the said
statement.

ARTICLE IV—The local authority shall, within ten

days after the receipt by them of the said notification, inform the Minister whether and to what extent they admit the facts stated in the appellant's documents, and shall send to the Minister a concise statement of the facts and contentions on which they rely.

ARTICLE V—(1) The Minister may at any stage of the proceedings allow the amendment of any notice, statement, or particulars on such terms as he may think fit.

(2) The Minister may at any time require the appellant or the local authority to furnish in writing such further particulars as he may think necessary.

ARTICLE VI—The Minister shall not dismiss any appeal without having first held a public local inquiry, unless the appellant has failed to prosecute his appeal, with due diligence, in which event the Minister may determine the appeal summarily.

ARTICLE VII—The costs of any appeal, including the costs of any public local inquiry held in connection therewith, shall be in the discretion of the Minister, who may direct to and by whom and in what manner those costs or any part thereof shall be paid and may tax or settle the amount of costs to be so paid or any part thereof.

ARTICLE VIII—The Minister may, if he thinks fit, and subject to such conditions as he may impose, proceed with the consideration of any appeal notwithstanding any failure or omission by any person to comply with any of the requirements of these rules.

Given under the official seal of the Minister of Health, this Tenth day of October, in the year One thousand nine hundred and nineteen.

(L.S.)

I. G. GIBBON,

Assistant Secretary, Ministry of Health.

65,480   (10th October 1919.)

STATUTORY RULES AND ORDERS, No. 1424

THE HOUSING ACTS (FORM OF ORDERS AND NOTICES) ORDER, 1919, DATED THE 10TH DAY OF OCTOBER, 1919

MADE BY THE MINISTER OF HEALTH UNDER SECTION 41 OF THE HOUSING, TOWN PLANNING, &c., ACT, 1909, PRESCRIBING FORMS OR CERTAIN NOTICES AND OTHER DOCUMENTS

THE Minister of Health, under the powers conferred on him by section 41 of the Housing, Town Planning, &c., Act, 1909, and by all other powers enabling him in that behalf hereby makes the following order :—

ARTICLE I—This order may be cited as " the Housing Acts (Form of Orders and Notices) Order, 1919."

ARTICLE II—The forms set out in the schedule hereto, or forms substantially to the like effect, shall be the forms to be used in connection with the powers and duties of a local authority under the Housing Acts, 1890 to 1919, in all cases to which those forms are applicable.

ARTICLE III—The order of the Local Government Board dated the 11th day of January 1910 (S. R. & O. No. 2, 1910), is hereby revoked except in so far as it prescribed a form or forms for use under section 15 of the Housing, Town Planning, &c., Act, 1909.

SCHEDULE

FORM No. 1—Form of notice by person authorised by the local authority or Minister of Health before entry for the purpose of survey and examination, or valuation, under section 36 of the Housing, Town Planning, &c., Act, 1909.

FORM No. 2—Form of notice requiring owner to execute works in the case of a house to which section 28 of the Housing, Town Planning, &c., Act, 1919, applies.

FORM No. 3—Form of notice declaring intention of owner to close for human habitation a house, to which section 28 of the Housing, Town Planning, &c., Act, 1919, applies.

FORM No. 4—Form of order declaring expenses incurred by the local authority in the case of a house to which section 28 of the Housing, Town Planning, &c., Act, 1919, applies, to be payable by monthly or annual instalments.

FORM No. 5—Form of Closing Order.

FORM No. 6—Form of Notice of Closing Order.

FORM No. 7—Form of Notice of Appeal against a Closing Order.

FORM No. 8—Form of Notice of Closing Order which has become Operative.

FORM No. 1

FORM OF NOTICE BY PERSONS AUTHORISED BY THE LOCAL AUTHORITY OR MINISTER OF HEALTH BEFORE ENTRY FOR THE PURPOSE OF SURVEY AND EXAMINATION FOR VALUATION UNDER SECTION 36 OF THE HOUSING, TOWN PLANNING, &C., ACT, 1909

HOUSING ACTS, 1890 TO 1919

To [1] *   the [2]
of the house [3] buildings [3] premises [3]

TAKE NOTICE that in pursuance of section 36 of the Housing, Town Planning, &c., Act, 1909, I, [4]
being a person duly authorised in writing by the [5]
          intend, on the †   day of   19 ,
at any time between the hours of ‡   in the
forenoon and   in the afternoon, to enter the
above-mentioned house for the purpose of survey and
examination *or* survey or valuation.

Dated this   day of   , 19 .

Signature...........................⎫ of person
Description ....⎬ authorised
Residence or Place of Business..........⎭ to enter.

Forms.

Directions for filling up this form

Insert—

¹ The name and description, where known, of occupier *or* owner.

² " Occupier " *or* " owner."

³ Such a description of the house, buildings or premises as may be sufficient for identification.   Strike out the words not required.

⁴ Name and description of person authorised by the local authority to enter.

⁵ Description of the local authority.

* *Notice must be given to the occupier and also to the owner if the owner is known.   Notice may be given to the occupier by leaving a notice addressed to the occupier, without name or further description, at the house, buildings or premises.*

† *Twenty-four hours' notice must be given.*

‡ *Entry must be at reasonable times of the day.*

Form No. 2

Form of Notice requiring Owner to execute works in the case of a house to which section 28 of the Housing, Town Planning, &c., Act, 1919, applies

Housing Acts, 1890 to 1919

To ¹   , the owner of the house ²

Take Notice :—

That it appears to the ³

that the above-mentioned house is a house suitable for occupation by persons of the working classes, and that you have failed to make and keep it in all respects reasonably fit for human habitation ;

And that, in pursuance of subsection (1) of section 28 of the Housing, Town Planning, &c., Act, 1919, the said ⁵

do hereby require you within a period of *   days, ending on the   day of   , 19 , to execute the following works as being necessary to make the said house in all respects reasonably fit for human habitation, namely ⁴—

Dated this   day of   , 19

Signature of clerk of local authority................

Note.—Under section 28 of the Housing, Town Planning, &c., Act, 1919, if the owner of any house suitable for occupation by persons of the working classes fails to make and keep such house in all respects reasonably fit for human habitation, the local authority may serve a notice on the owner requiring him within a reasonable time, not being less than twenty-one days, specified in the notice, to execute such works as may be necessary to make the house in all respects reasonably fit for human habitation. Provided that if the house is not capable without reconstruction of being rendered fit for human habitation, the owner may within twenty-one days after the receipt of the notice requiring the execution of such works, by written notice to the local authority declare his intention of closing the house for human habitation, and thereupon a closing order shall be deemed to have become operative in respect of such house. Any such declaration by the owner must be in the prescribed form.

Any question arising under this proviso is in case of difference between the owner and the local authority, to be determined by the Minister of Health.

If the notice of the local authority is not complied with, the local authority may—

(a) At the expiration of the time specified in that notice, if no notice to close the house has been given by the owner ; and

(b) At the expiration of twenty-one days from the determination by the Minister of Health if such notice has been given by the owner and the Minister of Health has determined that the house is capable without reconstruction of being, made fit for human habitation ;

do the work required to be done.

Any expenses incurred by the local authority under this section may be recovered in a court of summary jurisdiction, together with interest at a rate not exceeding five pounds per centum per annum from the date of service of a demand for the same till payment thereof from the owner, and such expenses and interest are to be a charge on the premises until recovered. In all summary proceedings by the local authority for the recovery of any such expenses, the time within which such proceedings may be taken is to be reckoned from the date of the service of notice of demand.

The local authority may by order declare any such expenses to be payable by monthly or annual instalments within a period not exceeding thirty years with interest at a rate not exceeding five pounds per centum per annum from the date of the service of notice of demand until the whole amount is paid, and any such instalments and interest or any part thereof may be recovered in a summary manner from the owner or occupier, and if recovered from the occupier may be deducted by him from the rent of such premises.

Directions for filling up this form

Insert—

  [1] Name, residence or place of business, and description, where known, of owner.

  [2] Such a description of the house as may be sufficient for its identification.

  [3] Description of the local authority.

  Description of works to be executed.

* *A reasonable time, not being less than twenty-one days, must be specified.*

FORM No. 3

FORM OF NOTICE DECLARING INTENTION OF OWNER TO
  CLOSE FOR HUMAN HABITATION A HOUSE TO WHICH
  SECTION 28 OF THE HOUSING, TOWN PLANNING, &C.,
  ACT, 1919, APPLIES

HOUSING ACTS, 1890 TO 1919

To the ¹

WHEREAS by a notice dated the   day
of   , 19 , the local authority in pursuance
of subsection (1) of section 28 of the Housing, Town
Planning, &c., Act, 1919, have required the owner of the
house ²   to
execute, within the time specified in that notice, the
works which are specified in the said notice as being
necessary to make the said house in all respects reasonably fit for human habitation ;

And whereas it appears to me, the owner of the house,
that the house it not capable, without reconstruction, of
being rendered fit for human habitation.

Now, therefore, I do by this notice declare my intention
of closing the said house for human habitation.

As witness my hand this   day of
        , 19 .

Signature.............................⎫
Residence or Place of Business ....⎬ of owner.
Description ....⎭

Note.—By subsection (1) of section 28 of the Housing, Town Planning, &c., Act, 1919, it is provided that within twenty-one days after
the receipt of the notice of the local authority in pursuance of that
subsection, the owner may, if the house is not capable without reconstruction of being rendered fit for human habitation, by written
notice to the local authority declare his intention of closing the house
for human habitation, and thereupon a closing order shall be deemed
to have become operative in respect of such house.

Directions for filling up this form

Insert—
    ¹ Description of the local authority.
    ² Such a description of the house as may be sufficient for its
    identification.

FORM No. 4

FORM OF ORDER DECLARING EXPENSES INCURRED BY
THE LOCAL AUTHORITY IN THE CASE OF A HOUSE
TO WHICH SECTION 28 OF THE HOUSING, TOWN
PLANNING, &C., ACT, 1919, APPLIES TO BE PAYABLE
BY MONTHLY OR ANNUAL INSTALMENTS

HOUSING ACTS, 1890 TO 1919

To [1]
 the $\begin{Bmatrix} \text{owner [2]} \\ \text{occupier} \end{Bmatrix}$ of the
house [3]

WHEREAS by a notice dated the   day of
       , 19   , we, the [4]
in pursuance of subsection (1) of section 28 of the Housing,
Town Planning, &c., Act, 1919, have required of the
owner of the above-mentioned house to execute, within
the time specified in that notice, the works specified in
the said notice as being necessary to make the said house
in all respects reasonably fit for human habitation :

(a) [5] And whereas the said notice has not been complied
       with and the owner has not given in pursuance
       of the said subsection a notice declaring his
       intention of closing the said house for human
       habitation ;

(b) [6] And whereas · notice having been given by the
       owner in pursuance of the said subsection declar-
       ing his intention of closing the said house for
       human habitation, the Minister of Health has
       determined that the house is capable without
       reconstruction of being made fit for human
       habitation and twenty-one days have elapsed
       since the date of such determination by the
       . Minister of Health ;

And whereas we, the said [4]
in pursuance of subsection (2) of the same section have
done the work required to be done, and have incurred in
so doing expenses amounting to the sum of £   :   :

Now, therefore, we, the said [4]
do, by this our order, declare that the said expenses
amounting to the sum of £   :   :   shall be

payable by $\begin{Bmatrix} \text{monthly [6]} \\ \text{annual} \end{Bmatrix}$ instalments of £   :   ::

Forms.

within a period not exceeding * years, with interest at the rate of † pounds per cent. **per** annum, until the whole amount is paid.

Dated this day of , 19 .

(To be sealed with the common seal of the local authority)

Signature of clerk of local authority.................

Note.—By subsection (4) of section 28 of the Housing, Town Planning, &c., Act, 1919, it is provided that any instalment or interest or any part of any instalments or interest under an order of the local authority declaring their expenses to be payable by monthly or annual instalments may be recovered in a summary manner from the owner or occupier, and if recovered from the occupier may be deducted by him from the rent of the premises.

Directions for filling up this form

Insert—

¹ Name, residence or place of business, and description, where known, of owner or occupier.

² Strike out the word not required.

³ Such a description of the house as may be sufficient for its identification.

⁴ Description of the local authority.

⁵ Strike out paragraph (*a*) or (*b*) as the case may be.

⁶ Strike out either " monthly " or " annual."

* *The period to be specified must not exceed thirty years.*

† *The rate of interest must not exceed five pounds per cent. per annum.*

FORM No. 5

FORM OF CLOSING ORDER

HOUSING ACTS, 1890 TO 1919

WHEREAS under subsection (2) of section 17 of the Housing, Town Planning, &c., Act, 1909, it is the duty of the local authority if, on the representation of the medical officer of health, or of any other officer of the local authority, or other information given, any dwelling-house appears to the local authority to be in a state so dangerous or injurious to health as to be unfit for human habitation, to make a closing order, that is to say, an order prohibiting the use of the dwelling-house for human habitation until in the judgment of the local authority the dwelling-house is rendered fit for that purpose ;

And whereas it appears to the ¹

on ²

that the dwelling-house ³ is in a state so dangerous or injurious to health as to be unfit for human habitation :

Now, therefore, we, the said [1] in pursuance of subsection (2) of section 17 of the Housing, Town Planning, &c., Act, 1909, do, by this our order, prohibit the use of the said dwelling-house for human habitation, until, in our judgment, it is rendered fit for that purpose.

Dated this   day of   , 19 .

(*To be sealed with the common seal of the local authority*)

Signature of clerk of local authority.................

Directions for filling up and adapting this form

Insert—
  [1] Description of the local authority.
  [2] " The representation of the medical officer of health " *or* " the representation of the (*specify the officer*) " *or* " information given."
  [3] Such a description of the dwelling-house as may be sufficient for its identification.

FORM No. 6

FORM OF NOTICE OF CLOSING ORDER

HOUSING ACTS, 1890 TO 1919

To [1]   owner of the dwelling-house [2]

TAKE NOTICE :—

That the [3]

have in pursuance of the Housing, Town Planning, &c., Act, 1909, made a closing order prohibiting the use for human habitation of the above-mentioned dwelling-house until in the judgment of the local authority the dwelling-house is rendered fit for that purpose ;

A copy [4] of the said closing order is annexed.

Dated this   day of   , 19

Signature of clerk of local authority.................

Note.—The owner of the dwelling-house can appeal to the Minister of Health against the closing order within fourteen days after notice thereof is served on him by giving notice of appeal in the form annexed. On such an appeal the substantial question to be considered is whether the house in its present state is so dangerous or injurious to health as to be unfit for human habitation. If the owner does not appeal against the closing order, the order becomes operative at the expiration of fourteen days after it was served, and it is then the duty of the local authority to serve notice on the occupier requiring him and his family to quit the house within a specified period not being less than fourteen days. It is open to the owner to take steps to render the house fit for habitation, and when he has done so, to apply to the local authority to determine the closing order. If the local authority

Forms. refuse his application he may then, within fourteen days after such refusal, give notice of appeal against it to the Minister of Health.

The procedure on appeal is governed by rules made by the Minister of Health.

The Acts provide—

    (a) That the Minister of Health shall not dismiss any appeal without having first held a public local inquiry, unless the appellant fails to prosecute his appeal with due diligence ;

    (b) That the Minister of Health may, before considering any appeal, require the appellant to deposit such sum to cover the costs of the appeal, as may be fixed by the rules. The sum at present fixed is a sum not exceeding £10.

Any person who lets or attempts to let or occupies or permits to be occupied any house in respect of which a closing order is in force is liable to a fine of £20.

Directions for filling up this form

Insert—

    [1] Name, residence or place of business, and description, where known, of owner.

    [2] Such a description of the dwelling-house as may be sufficient for its identification.

    [3] Description of the local authority.

    [4] The form annexed must be filled up so as to agree with the closing order sealed by the local authority.

Rules determining the procedure on any such appeal have been made by the Minister of Health, and have been placed on sale (S. R. and O., 1919, No. 1423, price 1d., or by post 1½d.), so that copies may be purchased, either directly or through any bookseller, from His Majesty's Stationery Office at the following addresses : Imperial House, Kingsway, London, W.C.1 ; 28 Abingdon Street, London, S.W.1 ; 37 Peter Street, Manchester ; and 1 St. Andrew's Crescent, Cardiff. (See p. 608.)

* COPY OF BEFORE-MENTIONED CLOSING ORDER

CLOSING ORDER

HOUSING ACTS, 1890 TO 1919

WHEREAS under subsection (2) of section 17 of the Housing, Town Planning, &c., Act, 1909, it is the duty of the local authority if, on the representation of the medical officer of health, or of any other officer of the local authority, or other information given, any dwelling-house appears to the local authority to be in a state so dangerous or injurious to health as to be unfit for human habitation, to make a closing order, that is to say, an order prohibiting the use of the dwelling-house for human habitation until in the judgment of the local authority the dwelling-house is rendered fit for that purpose ;

And whereas it appears to the

on

that the dwelling-house   is in a state so

    * *An exact copy of the closing order should be given here.*

dangerous or injurious to health as to be unfit for human Forms.
habitation :

Now, therefore, we, the said
in pursuance of subsection (2) of section 17 of the Housing,
Town Planning, &c., Act, 1909, do, by this our order,
prohibit the use of the said dwelling-house for human
habitation, until, in our judgment, it is rendered fit for
that purpose.

Dated this   day of   , 19
      (L.S.)
Signature of clerk of local authority..................

FORM OF NOTICE OF APPEAL AGAINST A CLOSING ORDER

HOUSING ACTS, 1890 TO 1919

(Notice of appeal may be given by filling up and sending to the
Minister of Health either this print or a copy of it, within fourteen
days after the day on which notice of the closing order was served.)

Full name of appellant..........................
Full address of appellant...................
Full address of the dwelling-house, in respect of which the
    appeal is made...............................
I, the undersigned, being an owner of the above-mentioned dwelling-house, hereby appeal against a closing
order in respect of the dwelling-house made by the
(*state name of local authority*).......................
notice of which was served on me on (*state date*)....:...
    , 19...
My interest in the dwelling-house is (*state whether
freeholder, or lessee under a lease the original term whereof
was not less than twenty-one years, or mortgagee, or what
other interest the appellant has in the house*) :—

The grounds on which I appeal are (*if the appeal is on
the ground that the house is not in a state so dangerous or
injurious to health as to be unfit for human habitation, the
exact reason for this contention should be stated. If the
appeal is on technical grounds, full particulars should be
given*).

Signature of appellant............................
    Date...................

Note.—The closing order appealed against or a copy of it must be
forwarded to the Minister of Health with this appeal.
The appellant must notify the local authority forthwith of any
appeal to the Minister of Health.

FORM NO. 7

FORM OF NOTICE OF APPEAL AGAINST A CLOSING ORDER

HOUSING ACTS, 1890 TO 1919

(Notice of appeal may be given by filling up and sending to the Minister of Health either this print or a copy of it, within fourteen days after the day on which notice of the closing order was served.)

Full name of appellant.............................

Full address of appellant..........................

Full address of the dwelling-house, in respect of which the appeal is made..................................

I, the undersigned, being an owner of the above-mentioned dwelling-house, hereby appeal against a closing order in respect of the dwelling-house made by the (*state name of local authority*)........................ notice of which was served on me on (*state date*)........ ......, 19...

My interest in the dwelling-house is (*state whether freeholder, or lessee under a lease the original term whereof was not less than twenty-one years, or mortgagee, or what other interest the appellant has in the house*) :—

The grounds on which I appeal are (*if the appeal is on the ground that the house is not in a state so dangerous or injurious to health as to be unfit for human habitation, the exact reason for this contention should be stated. If the appeal is on technical grounds, full particulars should be given*).

Signature of appellant..............................

Date...................

Note.—The closing order appealed against or a copy of it must be forwarded to the Minister of Health with this appeal.

The appellant must notify the local authority forthwith of any appeal to the Minister of Health.

FORM NO. 8

FORM OF NOTICE OF CLOSING ORDER WHICH HAS BECOME OPERATIVE

HOUSING ACTS, 1890 TO 1919

To [1]   , the occupier of the dwelling-house [2]

TAKE NOTICE :—

That on the   day of   , 19 ,
                    [3] in pursuance of the Housing,

Town Planning, &c., Act, 1909, made a closing order Forms. prohibiting the use for human habitation of the above-mentioned dwelling-house until in the judgment of the local authority the dwelling-house is rendered fit for that purpose ;

And that the closing order has now become operative ;

And also that in pursuance of subsection (4) of section 17 of the Housing, Town Planning, &c., Act, 1909, within* days after the service of this notice the said closing order must be obeyed by you, and you and your family must cease to inhabit the said dwelling-house.

Dated this day of , 19

Signature of clerk of local authority..................

Note.—By subsection (4) of section 17 of the Housing, Town Planning, &c., Act, 1909, as amended by section 39 of the Housing, Town Planning, &c., Act, 1919, it is enacted as follows :—

Where a closing order has become operative, the local authority shall serve notice of the order on the occupier of the dwelling-house in respect of which the order is made, and, within such period as is specified in the notice, not being less than fourteen days after the service of the notice, the order shall be obeyed by him, and he and his family shall cease to inhabit the dwelling-house, and in default he shall be liable on summary conviction to be ordered to quit the dwelling-house within such time as may be specified in the order.

Subsection (5) of the first-mentioned section is in these terms :—

Unless the dwelling-house has been made unfit for habitation by the wilful act or default of the tenant or of any person for whom as between himself and the owner or landlord he is responsible, the local authority may make to every such tenant such reasonable allowance on account of his expenses in removing as may be determined by the local authority with the consent of the owner of the dwelling-house, or, if the owner of the dwelling-house fails to consent to the sum determined by the local authority, as may be fixed by a court of summary jurisdiction, and the amount of the said allowance shall be recoverable by the local authority from the owner of the dwelling-house as a civil debt in manner provided by the Summary Jurisdiction Acts.

Any person who lets or attempts to let or occupies or permits to be occupied any house in respect of which a closing order is in force is liable to a fine of £20.

Directions for filling up this form

Insert—
    1 Name of occupier.
    2 Such a description of the dwelling-house as may be sufficient for its identification.
    3 Description of the local authority.

* *The period must be not less than fourteen days after the service of the notice.*

Forms.

FORM No. 9

FORM OF ORDER DETERMINING CLOSING ORDER

HOUSING ACTS, 1890 TO 1919

To [1]   , owner of the dwelling-house [2]

WHEREAS on the   day of   , 19 . , in pursuance of the Housing Acts, 1890 to 1919, a closing order was made by us, the [3]   , in respect of the above-mentioned dwelling-house, and by the said closing order, we, the said [3] prohibited the use of the said dwelling-house for human habitation until, in our judgment, the dwelling-house should be rendered fit for that purpose ;

And whereas we, the said [3] are satisfied that the said dwelling-house has been rendered fit for human habitation :

Now therefore, we, the said [3] do hereby determine the closing order aforesaid.

Dated this   day of   , 19 .

(To be sealed with the common seal of the local authority)

Signature of clerk of local authority.................

Directions for filling up this form

Insert—
  [1] Name, residence or place of business, and description, where known, of owner.
  [2] Such a description of the dwelling-house as may be sufficient for its identification.
  [3] Description of the local authority.

FORM No. 10

FORM OF NOTICE OF REFUSAL OF LOCAL AUTHORITY TO DETERMINE A CLOSING ORDER

HOUSING ACTS, 1890 TO 1919

To [1]   , the owner of the dwelling-house [2]

TAKE NOTICE that the [3]   , having considered your application to them to determine the closing order made by them in pursuance of the Housing Acts, 1890 to 1919, on the   day of   , 19 , in respect of the above-mentioned dwelling-house, have this day refused to determine the said closing order.

Dated this   day of   , 19 .

Signature of clerk of local authority..................

Note.—Under the provisions of subsection (6) of section 17 of the Housing, Town Planning, &c., Act, 1909 :

The local authority are required to determine any closing order made by them if they are satisfied that the dwelling-house, in respect of which the order has been made, has been rendered fit for human habitation.

If, on the application of any owner of a dwelling-house, the local authority refuse to determine a closing order, the owner may appeal to the Minister of Health by giving notice of appeal to him within fourteen days after the application is refused. Notice of any such appeal must be in the form annexed.

Procedure on Appeal

The procedure on any such appeal is governed by rules made by the Minister of Health.

The Acts provide :—

(a) That the Minister of Health shall not dismiss any appeal without having first held a public local inquiry unless the appellant fails to prosecute his appeal with due diligence.

(b) That the Minister of Health may before considering any appeal, require the appellant to deposit such sum to cover the costs of the appeal, as may be fixed by the rules. The sum at present fixed is a sum not exceeding £10.

Direction for filling up this form

Insert—

¹ Name, residence or place of business, and description, where known, of owner.

² Such a description of the dwelling-house as may be sufficient for its identification.

³ Description of the local authority.

Rules determining the procedure on any such appeal have been made by the Minister of Health, and have been placed on sale (S. R. and O., 1919, No. 1423, price 1d., or by post 1½d.), so that copies may be purchased, either directly or through any bookseller from His Majesty's Stationery Office at the following addresses : Imperial House, Kingsway, London, W.C.1 ;   28 Abingdon Street, London, S.W.1 ;   37 Peter Street, Manchester ; and 1 St. Andrew's Crescent, Cardiff. (See p. 608.)

FORM OF NOTICE OF APPEAL AGAINST REFUSAL OF LOCAL AUTHORITY TO DETERMINE A CLOSING ORDER

(Notice of appeal may be given by filling up and sending to the Minister of Health either this print or a copy of it within fourteen days after the day on which the notice of refusal of the local authority to determine the closing order was served on the appellant.)

Full name of appellant.............................

Full address of appellant...........................

Full address of the dwelling-house, in respect of which the appeal is made...............................

I, the undersigned, being an owner of the above-mentioned dwelling-house, hereby appeal against the refusal of (*state name of local authority*) to determine a closing order made by them in respect of the dwelling-house. Notice of the refusal of the council to determine the closing order was received by me on the (*state date*) , 19 .

My interest in the dwelling-house is (*state whether a freeholder or lessee under a lease the original term whereof was not less than twenty-one years, or mortgagee, or what other interest the appellant has in the house*).

The grounds on which I appeal are (*if the appeal is on the ground that the dwelling-house has been rendered fit for human habitation, the repairs or improvements carried out should be specified. If the appeal is on technical grounds, full particulars should be given*) :—

Signature of appellant........................

Date....................

Note.—The closing order and the formal refusal of the local authority to determine it, or a copy of them, must be forwarded to the Minister of Health with this appeal.

The appellant must notify the local authority forthwith of any appeal to the Minister of Health.

FORM No. 11

FORM OF NOTICE OF APPEAL AGAINST REFUSAL OF LOCAL AUTHORITY TO DETERMINE A CLOSING ORDER

HOUSING ACTS, 1890 TO 1919

(Notice of appeal may be given by filling up and sending to the Minister of Health either this print or a copy of it within fourteen days after the day on which the notice of refusal of the local authority to determine the closing order was served on the appellant.)

Full name of appellant............................

Full address of appellant............................

Full address of the dwelling-house, in respect of which the appeal is made............................

I, the undersigned, being an owner of the above-mentioned dwelling-house, hereby appeal against the refusal of (*state name of local authority*) to determine a closing order made by them in respect of the dwelling-house. Notice of the refusal of the council to determine the closing order was received by me on the (*state date*) , 19 .

My interest in the dwelling-house is (*state whether a*

freeholder or lessee under a lease the original term whereof Forms. *was not less than twenty-one years, or mortgagee, or what other interest the appellant has in the house*).

The grounds on which I appeal are (*if the appeal is on the ground that the dwelling-house has been rendered fit for human habitation, the repairs or improvements carried out should be specified. If the appeal is on technical grounds, full particulars should be given*) :—

Signature of appellant..............................

Date...................

Note.—The closing order and the formal refusal of the local authority to determine it, or a copy of them, must be forwarded to the Minister of Health with this appeal.

The appellant must notify the local authority forthwith of any appeal to the Minister of Health.

Form No. 12

Form of Notice of Time and Place at which the Question of the Demolition of a Dwelling-house will be Considered

HOUSING ACTS, 1890 TO 1919

To [1]   , owner of the dwelling-house [2]

Whereas on the   day of   , 19 , in pursuance of the Housing Acts, 1890 to 1919, a closing order was made by the [3] in respect of the above-mentioned dwelling-house, and the said closing order has remained operative for a period of three months ;

Take Notice, that the question of the demolition of the said dwelling-house will be considered by the said [3]
at   on
the *   day of   , 19 , at
o'clock in the   noon, when any owner of the said dwelling-house will be entitled to be heard.

Dated this   day of   , 19 .

Signature of clerk of local authority...................

Direction for filling up this form

Insert—
   [1] Name, residence or place of business, and description, where known, of owner.
   [2] Such a description of the dwelling-house as may be sufficient for its identification.
   [3] Description of the local authority.
   * *The time must be not less than one month after the service of this notice.*

40

FORM No. 13

FORM OF ORDER FOR DEMOLITION OF DWELLING-HOUSE

HOUSING ACTS, 1890 TO 1919

WHEREAS on the   day of   , 19   , in
pursuance of the Housing Acts, 1890 to 1919, a closing
order was made by us, the [1]   in
respect of the dwelling-house [2]   and
the said closing order has remained operative for a
period of three months ;

And whereas after complying with the requirements
of subsection (1) of section 18 of the Housing, Town
Planning, &c., Act, 1909, and upon consideration of the
question of the demolition of the said dwelling-house, we,
the said [1]   are of
opinion that the dwelling-house has not been rendered
fit for human habitation, and that the necessary steps
are not being taken with all due diligence to render it
so fit ;

Now therefore, we, the said [1]   ,
in pursuance of subsection (2) of section 18 of the Housing,
Town Planning, &c., Act, 1909, do order the demolition
of the dwelling-house aforesaid.

Dated this   day of   , 19   .

(To be sealed with the common seal of the local authority)
Signature of clerk of local authority.................

Direction for filling up this form
Insert—
[1] Description of the local authority.
[2] Such a description of the dwelling-house as may be sufficient
for its identification.

FORM No. 14

FORM OF NOTICE OF ORDER FOR DEMOLITION OF A DWELLING-HOUSE

HOUSING ACTS, 1890 TO 1919

To [1]   , owner of the dwelling-
house [2]

TAKE NOTICE :—

That the [3]   have in pursuance of
the Housing, Town Planning, &c., Act, 1909, made an

order for the demolition of the above-mentioned dwelling-house.

A copy ⁴ of the demolition order is annexed.

Dated this   day of   , 19

Signature of clerk of local authority..................

Note.—Section 18 of the Housing, Town Planning, &c., Act, 1909, as amended by subsequent Acts is to the following effect :—

Where a closing order in respect of any dwelling-house has remained operative for a period of three months, the local authority are to take into consideration the question of the demolition of the dwelling-house, and are to give every owner of the dwelling-house notice of the time (being some time not less than one month after the service of the notice) and place at which the question will be considered, and any owner of the dwelling-house is to be entitled to be heard when the question is so taken into consideration.

If upon any such consideration the local authority are of opinion that the dwelling-house has not been rendered fit for human habitation, and that the necessary steps are not being taken with all due diligence to render it so fit, or that the continuance of any building, being or being part of the dwelling-house, is a nuisance or dangerous or injurious to the health of the public or of the inhabitants of the neighbouring dwelling-houses, they are to order the demolition of the building.

If any owner undertakes to execute forthwith the works necessary to render the dwelling-house fit for human habitation, and the local authority consider that it can be so rendered fit for human habitation, the local authority may, if they think fit, postpone the operation of the order for such time, not exceeding six months, as they think sufficient for the purpose of giving the owner an opportunity of executing the necessary works, and if and when the necessary works are completed to their satisfaction, the local authority shall determine the closing and demolition orders relating to the dwelling-house.

Notice of an order for the demolition of a building is to be forthwith served on every owner of the building in respect of which it is made, and any owner aggrieved by the order may appeal to the Minister of Health by giving notice of appeal to the Minister within twenty-one days after the notice is served upon him, or where the operation of the order has been postponed for any period within fourteen days after the expiration of that period.

Notice of any such appeal must be in the form annexed.

Procedure on Appeal

The procedure on any such appeal is governed by rules made by the Minister of Health.

The Acts provide :—

    (a) That the Minister of Health shall not dismiss any appeal without having first held a public local inquiry unless the appellant fails to prosecute his appeal with due diligence.

    (b) That the Minister of Health may before considering any appeal, require the appellant to deposit such sum to cover the costs of the appeal, as may be fixed by the rules. The sum at present fixed is a sum not exceeding £10.

A demolition order does not become operative until either the time within which an appeal can be made has elapsed, without an appeal being made, or in case an appeal is made, the appeal is determined or abandoned.

Forms.

Directions for filling up this form
Insert—
¹ Name, residence or place of business, and description, where known, of owner.
² Such a description of the dwelling-house as may be sufficient for its identification.
³ Description of the local authority.
⁴ The form annexed must be filled up so as to agree with the demolition order sealed by the local authority.

Rules determining the procedure on any such appeal have been made by the Minister of Health, and have been placed on sale (S. R. and O., 1919, No. 1423, price 1d., or by post 1½d.), so that copies may be purchased, either directly or through any bookseller, from His Majesty's Stationery Office, at the following addresses : Imperial House, Kingsway, London, W.C.1 ; 28 Abingdon Street, London, S.W.1 ; 37 Peter Street, Manchester ; and 1 St. Andrew's Crescent, Cardiff. (See p. 608.)

* COPY OF THE ABOVE-MENTIONED DEMOLITION ORDER

ORDER FOR DEMOLITION OF A DWELLING-HOUSE

HOUSING ACTS, 1890 TO 1919

WHEREAS. on the   day of   , 19 , in pursuance of the Housing Acts, 1890 to 1919, a closing order was made by us, the   in respect of the dwelling-house   , and the said closing order has remained operative for a period of three months ;

And whereas after complying with the requirements of subsection (1) of section 18 of the Housing, Town Planning, &c., Act, 1909, and upon consideration of the question of the demolition of the said dwelling-house, we, the said   are of opinion that the dwelling-house has not been rendered fit for human habitation, and that the necessary steps are not being taken with all due diligence to render it so fit ;

Now therefore, we, the said
in pursuance of subsection (2) of section 18 of the Housing, Town Planning, &c., Act, 1909, do order the demolition of the dwelling-house aforesaid.

Dated this   day of   , 19

(L.S.)

Signature of clerk of local authority.................

* *An exact copy of the demolition order should be given here.*

FORM OF NOTICE OF APPEAL AGAINST A DEMOLITION ORDER

(Notice of appeal may be given by filling up and sending to the Minister of Health, either this print, or a copy of it, within twenty-one days after the day on which the notice of the demolition order was served, or, if the operation of the demolition order has been postponed for a period not exceeding six months, within fourteen days after the expiration of that period.)

Full name of appellant...............................

Full address of appellant...........................

Full address of the dwelling-house, in respect of which the appeal is made ....

I, the undersigned, being an owner of the above-mentioned dwelling-house, hereby appeal against a demolition order in respect of the dwelling-house made by the (*state name of local authority*)

which was served on me on (*state date, and, if the operation of the demolition order was postponed for any period, state the date on which that period expired*)

, 19 .

My interest in the dwelling-house is (*state whether a freeholder, or lessee under a lease the original term whereof was not less than twenty-one years, or mortgagee, or what other interest the appellant has in the house*)..............

....

The grounds on which I appeal are (*if the appeal is on the ground that the dwelling-house has been rendered fit for human habitation, the repairs or improvements which have been carried out should be specified*).

Signature of appellant.............................

Date...................

Note.—The demolition order appealed against and also if possible the closing order, or a copy of them, must be forwarded to the Minister of Health with this appeal.

The appellant must notify the local authority forthwith of any appeal to the Minister of Health.

FORM No. 15

FORM OF NOTICE OF APPEAL AGAINST A DEMOLITION ORDER

HOUSING ACTS, 1890 TO 1919

(Notice of appeal may be given by filling up and sending to the Minister of Health, either this print, or a copy of it, within twenty-one days after the day on which the notice of demolition order was served, or, if the operation of the demolition order has been postponed for a period not exceeding six months, within fourteen days after the expiration of that period.)

Full name of appellant...............................

Full address of appellant...........................

Full address of the dwelling-house, in respect of which the appeal is made..............................

I, the undersigned, being an owner of the above-mentioned dwelling-house, hereby appeal against a demolition order in respect of the dwelling-house made by the (*state name of local authority*) which was served on me on (*state date, and, if the operation of the demolition order was postponed for any period, state the date on which that period expired*)

, 19 .

My interest in the dwelling-house is (*state whether a freeholder, or lessee under a lease the original term whereof was not less than twenty-one years, or mortgagee, or what other interest the appellant has in the house*)...........

....

The grounds on which I appeal are (*if the appeal is on the ground that the dwelling-house has been rendered fit for human habitation, the repairs or improvements which have been carried out should be specified*).

Signature of appellant...............................

Date...................

Note.—The demolition order appealed against, and also, if possible, the closing order, or a copy of them, must be forwarded to the Minister of Health with this appeal.

The appellant must notify the local authority forthwith of any appeal to the Minister of Health.

Form No. 16

Form of Order for Demolition of Building being or being part of a Dwelling-house the Continuance of which is a Nuisance or Dangerous or Injurious to the Health of the Public or of the Inhabitants of the Neighbouring Dwelling-houses

HOUSING ACTS, 1890 to 1919

Whereas on the   day of   , 19 , in pursuance of the Housing Acts, 1890 to 1919, a closing

order was made by us, the [1]
in respect of the dwelling-house [2]   and
the said closing order has remained operative for a period
of three months ;

And whereas after compliance with the requirements
of subsection (1) of section 18 of the Housing, Town
Planning, &c., Act, 1909, and upon consideration of the
question of the demolition of the said dwelling-house, we,
the said [1]   are of
opinion that the continuance of the [3]   is
[4] a nuisance and [4] dangerous or injurious to the health
of the public and [4] dangerous or injurious to the health
of the inhabitants of the neighbouring dwelling-houses ;

Now therefore, we, the said [1]
in pursuance of subsection (2) of section 18 of the Housing,
Town Planning, &c., Act, 1909, do order the demolition
of the [5]   :

Dated this   day of   , 19 .

(To be sealed with the common seal of the local authority)

Signature of clerk of local authority..................

Directions for filling up and adapting this form
Insert—
   [1] Description of the local authority.
   [2] Such a description of the dwelling-house as may be sufficient
       for its identification.
   [3] " Said dwelling-house " *or* " part of the said dwelling-house,"
       as the case may be, followed in the latter case by such a de-
       scription of the part as may be sufficient for its identification.
   [4] Strike out any words that are inapplicable.
   [5] " Said dwelling-house " *or* " said part of the said dwelling-house,"
       as the case may be.

FORM No. 17

FORM OF NOTICE OF ORDER FOR DEMOLITION OF BUILDING
BEING OR BEING PART OF A DWELLING-HOUSE THE
CONTINUANCE OF WHICH IS A NUISANCE OR DANGEROUS
OR INJURIOUS TO THE HEALTH OF THE PUBLIC
OR OF THE INHABITANTS OF THE NEIGHBOURING
DWELLING-HOUSES

HOUSING ACTS, 1890 TO 1919

To [1]   , owner of the dwelling-
house [2]

TAKE NOTICE :—

That the [3]   have in pursuance

Forms.

of the Housing, Town Planning, &c., Act, 1909, made an order for the demolition of the building therein described, being or being part of the above-mentioned dwelling-house.

A copy ' of the demolition order is annexed.

Dated this   day of   , 19   .

Signature of clerk of local authority..................

Note.—Section 18 of the Housing, Town Planning, &c., Act, 1909, as amended by subsequent Acts is to the following effect :—

Where a closing order in respect of any dwelling-house has remained operative for a period of three months, the local authority are to take into consideration the question of the demolition of the dwelling-house, and are to give every owner of the dwelling-house notice of the time (being some time not less than one month after the service of the notice) and place at which the question will be considered, and any owner of the dwelling-house is to be entitled to be heard when the question is so taken into consideration.

If upon any such consideration the local authority are of opinion that the dwelling-house has not been rendered fit for human habitation, and that the necessary steps are not being taken with all due diligence to render it so fit, or that the continuance of any building, being or being part of the dwelling-house, is a nuisance or dangerous or injurious to the health of the public or of the inhabitants of the neighbouring dwelling-houses, they are to order the demolition of the building.

If any owner undertakes to execute forthwith the works necessary to render the dwelling-house fit for human habitation, and the local authority consider that it can be so rendered fit for human habitation, the local authority may, if they think fit, postpone the operation of the order for such time, not exceeding six months, as they think sufficient for the purpose of giving the owner an opportunity of executing the necessary works, and if and when the necessary works are completed to their satisfaction, the local authority shall determine the closing and demolition orders relating to the dwelling house.

Notice of an order for the demolition of a building is to be forthwith served on every owner of the building in respect of which it is made, and any owner aggrieved by the order may appeal to the Minister of Health by giving notice of appeal to the Minister within twenty-one days after the notice is served upon him, or where the operation of the order has been postponed for any period within fourteen days after the expiration of that period.

Notice of such appeal must be in the form annexed.

Procedure on Appeal

The procedure on any such appeal is governed by rules made by the Minister of Health.

The Acts provide :—

    (a) That the Minister of Health shall not dismiss any appeal without having first held a public local inquiry unless the appellant fails to prosecute his appeal with due diligence.

    (b) That the Minister of Health may before considering any appeal, require the appellant to deposit such sum to cover the costs of the appeal, as may be fixed by the rules. The sum at present fixed is a sum not exceeding £10.

A demolition order does not become operative until either the time

within which an appeal can be made has elapsed, without an appeal Forms.
being made, or in case an appeal is made, the appeal is determined or
abandoned.

Directions for filling up this form

Insert—

 ¹ Name, residence or place of business, and description, where
   known, of owner.
 ² Such a description of the dwelling-house as may be sufficient
   for its identification.
 ³ Description of the local authority.
 ⁴ The form annexed must be filled up so as to agree with the
   demolition order sealed by the local authority.

*Rules determining the procedure on any such appeal have been made
by the Minister of Health, and have been placed on sale (S. R. and O.,
1919, No. 1423, price 1d., or by post 1½d.), so that copies may be purchased, either directly or through any bookseller, from His Majesty's
Stationery Office, at the following addresses : Imperial House, Kingsway,
London, W.C.1 ; 28 Abingdon Street, London, S.W.1 ; 37 Peter Street,
Manchester ; and 1 St. Andrew's Crescent, Cardiff. (See p. 608).*

* COPY OF ABOVE-MENTIONED DEMOLITION ORDER

ORDER FOR DEMOLITION OF BUILDING BEING OR BEING
    PART OF A DWELLING-HOUSE THE CONTINUANCE OF
    WHICH IS A NUISANCE OR DANGEROUS OR INJURIOUS
    TO THE HEALTH OF THE PUBLIC OR OF THE INHABI-
    TANTS OF THE NEIGHBOURING DWELLING-HOUSES

HOUSING ACTS, 1890 TO 1919

WHEREAS on the   day of   , 19 , in
pursuance of the Housing Acts, 1890 to 1919, a closing
order was made by us, the
in respect of the dwelling-house   and the
said closing order has remained operative for a period of
three months ;

And whereas after compliance with the requirements
of subsection (1) of section 18 of the Housing, Town
Planning, &c., Act, 1909, and upon consideration of the
question of the demolition of the said dwelling-house,
we, the said   are of
opinion that the continuance of the   is

Now therefore, we, the said   ,
in pursuance of subsection (2) of section 18 of the Housing,
Town Planning, &c., Act, 1909, do order the demolition
of the

Dated this   day of   , 19
(L.S.)

Signature of clerk of local authority..................

   * *An exact copy of the demolition order should be given here*

FORM OF NOTICE OF APPEAL AGAINST AN ORDER FOR DEMOLITION OF A BUILDING BEING OR BEING PART OF A DWELLING-HOUSE THE CONTINUANCE OF WHICH IS A NUISANCE OR DANGEROUS OR INJURIOUS TO THE HEALTH OF THE PUBLIC OR OF THE INHABITANTS OF THE NEIGHBOURING DWELLING-HOUSES

HOUSING ACTS, 1890 TO 1919

(Notice of appeal may be given by filling up and sending to the Minister of Health, either this print, or a copy of it, within twenty-one days after the day on which the notice of demolition order was served, or, if the operation of the demolition order has been postponed for a period not exceeding six months, within fourteen days after the expiration of that period.)

Full name of appellant..............................

Full address of appellant..........................

Full address of dwelling-house affected by the appeal, together with (where the appeal relates to a building being part only of a dwelling-house) such a description of the building as may be sufficient for its identification...

I, the undersigned, being an owner of the above-mentioned dwelling-house, hereby appeal against an order for demolition of ¹ the said dwelling-house *or* ¹ the above-mentioned building being part of the said dwelling-house, made by (*state name of local authority*)
which was served on me on (*state date, and, if the operation of the demolition order was postponed for any period, state the date on which that period expired*)
, 19 .

My interest in the building is (*state whether a freeholder, or lessee under a lease the original term whereof was not less than twenty-one years, or mortgagee, or what other interest the appellant has in the building*)

The grounds on which I appeal are

Signature of appellant............................
        Date...................

Note.—The demolition order appealed against, and also, if possible, the closing order, or a copy of them, must be forwarded to the Minister of Health with this appeal.

The appellant must notify the local authority forthwith of any appeal to the Minister of Health.

¹ Strike out the words which are inapplicable.

FORM No. 18

FORM OF NOTICE OF APPEAL AGAINST AN ORDER FOR DEMOLITION OF A BUILDING BEING OR BEING PART OF A DWELLING-HOUSE THE CONTINUANCE OF WHICH IS A NUISANCE OR DANGEROUS OR INJURIOUS TO THE HEALTH OF THE PUBLIC OR OF THE INHABITANTS OF THE NEIGHBOURING DWELLING-HOUSES

HOUSING ACTS, 1890 TO 1919

(Notice of appeal may be given by filling up and sending to the Minister of Health, either this print, or a copy of it, within twenty-one days after the day on which the notice of demolition order was served, or, if the operation of the demolition order has been postponed for a period not exceeding six months, within fourteen days after the expiration of that period.)

Full name of appellant.............................

Full address of appellant..........................

Full address of dwelling-house affected by the appeal, together with (where the appeal relates to a building being part only of a dwelling-house) such a description of the building as may be sufficient for its identification...

I, the undersigned, being an owner of the above-mentioned dwelling-house, hereby appeal against an order for demolition of [1] the said dwelling-house *or* [1] the above-mentioned building being part of the said dwelling-house, made by (*state name of local authority*)

which was served on me on (*state date, and, if the operation of the demolition order was postponed for any period, state the date on which that period expired*)

, 19 .

My interest in the building is (*state whether a freeholder, or lessee under a lease the original term whereof was not less than twenty-one years, or mortgagee, or what other interest the appellant has in the building*).

The grounds on which I appeal are

Signature of appellant.............................

Date.....................

Note.—The demolition order appealed against and also if possible the closing order, or a copy of them, must be forwarded to the Minister of Health with this appeal.

The Appellant must notify the local authority forthwith of any appeal to the Minister of Health.

[1] Strike out the words which are inapplicable.

FORM No. 19

FORM OF ORDER POSTPONING OPERATION OF ORDER OR DEMOLITION OF A DWELLING-HOUSE

HOUSING ACTS, 1890 TO 1919

To [1]   , owner of the dwelling-
house [2]

WHEREAS on the   day of   , 19 , we
the [3]   made an order
for the demolition of the above-mentioned dwelling-
house ;

And whereas [4]
an owner of the said dwelling-house, has now undertaken
to execute forthwith the works necessary to render the
said dwelling-house fit for human habitation, we, the
said [5]
in pursuance of subsection (3) of section 18 of the Housing,
Town Planning, &c., Act, 1909, do hereby postpone the
operation of the said order for a period of *
from the date of the said order.

Dated this   day of   , 19 .

(To be sealed with the common seal of the local authority)

Signature of clerk of local authority.................

Directions for filling up this form

Insert—
  [1] Name, residence or place of business, and description, where
    known, of owner.
  [2] Such a description of the dwelling-house as may be sufficient
    for its identification.
  [3] Description of the local authority.
  [4] Name, residence or place of business, and description, where
    known, of the owner who undertakes to execute the necessary
    works.

* *The time must be such time, not exceeding six months, as the local
authority think sufficient for the purpose of giving the owner an opportunity of executing the necessary works.*

FORM No. 20

FORM OF ORDER DETERMINING CLOSING AND DEMOLITION ORDERS

HOUSING ACTS, 1890 TO 1919

To [1]   , owner of the dwelling-
house [2]

WHEREAS on the   day of   , 19 , in

pursuance of the Housing Acts, 1890 to 1919, a demolition Forms.
order was made by us the [3] in respect
of the above-mentioned dwelling-house ;

And whereas the works necessary to render the said
dwelling-house fit for human habitation have been
completed to our satisfaction ;

Now therefore, we, the [3] do hereby
determine the closing and demolition orders relating to
the dwelling-house.

Dated this day of , 19 .

(To be sealed with the common seal of the local authority)

Signature of clerk of local authority.................

Directions for filling up this form

Insert—
  [1] Name, residence or place of business, and description, where
    known, of owner.
  [2] Such a description of the dwelling-house as may be sufficient
    for its identification.
  [3] Description of the local authority.

Given under the official seal of the Minister of Health,
  this Tenth day of October, in the year One thousand
  nine hundred and nineteen.

(L.S.) I. G. GIBBON,
Assistant Secretary, Ministry of Health.

Draft Model By-laws, Series xiii b (section 26, Housing Lodgings'
by-laws.
  Town Planning, &c., Act, 1919).

BY-LAWS

made by the [1]
with respect to houses intended or used for occupation
by the working classes and let in lodgings or occupied by
members of more than one family in [2]

INTERPRETATION OF TERMS

1. In these by-laws, unless the context otherwise
requires :—

" Council " means the [1]

" District " means the [2]

" Lodging-house " means a house or part of a house
    intended or used for occupation by the working
    classes and let in lodgings or occupied by members
    of more than one family :

" Occupier " [3] means the person by whom or on whose behalf a lodging-house is let in lodgings or for occupation by members of more than one family, or who for the time being receives, or is entitled to receive, whether on his own account or as agent or trustee for any other person, the profits arising from such letting :

" Lodger " means a person to whom any room or rooms in a lodging-house may have been let as a lodging or for his use and occupation :

" Owner " [4] means the person for the time being receiving, whether on his own account or as agent or trustee for any other person, a rack-rent within the meaning of the Public Health Act, 1875, from an occupier, or who would so receive that rack-rent if the lodging-house were let to an occupier.

General

2. No proceedings shall be taken against any person for an offence against any of the by-laws numbered [5] 6, 10, 14, 15, 16, 19 and 20, unless and until a notice in writing has been served upon him by the council requiring him within a period specified in the notice to comply with the by-laws and he has failed to do so.

[1] " Mayor, aldermen, and burgesses of the borough of
, acting by the council"; *or* "Urban [*or* rural] district council of ," as the case may be.
[2] Insert name of borough or urban or rural district.
[3] This word has been inserted as probably describing most precisely the person indicated. But where a local authority have in force by-laws using some other word, such as " tenant," in this place, there is no objection to their continuing to use it if to do so will make for administrative convenience.
[4] Section 26 of the Housing, Town Planning, &c., Act, 1919, provides that the by-laws may impose the duty of executing any work upon the owner within the meaning of the Public Health Acts, or any other person having an interest in the premises, and that where a lessee carries out work under the by-laws and it is reasonable that the whole or any part of the expenses should be borne by the lessor, the county court may, on the application of the local authority, grant an order charging the expenses on the premises. The county court may also on the application of the local authority relax any provisions in a lease which are inconsistent with the requirements of the by-laws.
Local circumstances should be taken into consideration in determining on what person any particular obligation should be imposed by the by-laws.
[5] The printed numbers, or such numbers as correspond to them, should be inserted.

3. A person shall not let for occupation by members of more than one family any lodging-house which does not comply with these by-laws.

Provided that in the case of a house so let or occupied at the date of the confirmation of these by-laws, any by-law which renders necessary the execution of any works shall not apply until the expiration of three months from the date of confirmation.

4. Nothing in the following by-laws shall be deemed to dispense with any requirements in by-laws or statutory provisions regulating the erection of new buildings or the alteration of existing buildings.

5. Any notices required or authorised by these by-laws to be given to any person may be served personally or by registered letter addressed to his usual or last known residence or place of business.

For fixing the number of persons who may occupy a house or part of a house which is let in lodgings or occupied by members of more than one family

6. A person shall not knowingly permit any room in a lodging-house wholly or partly used as a sleeping apartment to be occupied at any one time by a greater number of persons than will allow *three hundred and sixty* cubic feet of free air space for each person of an age exceeding ten years, and *two hundred and fifty* cubic feet of free air space for each person of an age not exceeding ten years.

For the registration and inspection of such houses

7. Where the council by a notice in writing signed by the   require for the purposes of registration the particulars hereinafter specified the occupier shall within the period, if any, specified in the notice furnish such particulars, namely—

(a) The total number of rooms in the house ;

(b) The total number of rooms let in lodgings or occupied by members of more than one family ;

(c) The dimensions and manner of use of each room ;

(d) The number, age, and sex of the occupants of each room used for sleeping ;

(e) The full name of the person to whom each room is let ;

(f) The name and address of the owner of the house.

8. Every person residing in a lodging-house shall, at all reasonable times when required by the medical officer of health, the inspector of nuisances, or the surveyor of the council, afford such officer free access to the interior of the premises and to the interior of any room or rooms let to him.

9. A person shall not wilfully delay or obstruct any officer of the council who has lawfully entered any lodging-house for the purpose of inspecting the premises, or, without reasonable excuse, neglect or refuse to render him such assistance as he may reasonably require for the purpose of inspection.

For enforcing drainage and promoting cleanliness and ventilation of such houses

For securing the adequate lighting of every room in such houses

10. Every owner of a lodging-house shall at all times
(a) Keep in good order and condition all drains and means of drainage, and every closet, sink and bath ;
(b) Provide and maintain in connection with every tap from which water may be drawn efficient means for carrying off any waste water from the tap ;
(c) Provide every habitable room of the house with a window or windows opening directly into the external air and having where practicable a total area, exclusive of the sash frames, equal at the least to one-tenth of the floor area of the room, and capable of being opened at the top and to at least one-third of the extent of the window ;
(d) Provide every closet in the house with efficient means of ventilation directly into the external air, and with a window of an area of not less than two square feet exclusive of the sash frame, opening where practicable directly into the external air ;
(e) Provide and maintain adequate means of ventilation for every room, passage or staircase.
11. Every occupier of a lodging-house shall
(a) Keep thoroughly clean and wholesome every common staircase, landing and passage, and every

cistern or other receptacle for the storage of water supplied to the premises ;

(b) Keep thoroughly clean and wholesome all beds, bedclothes, and bedding furnished by him ;

(c) After the termination of the letting of any room therein to any lodger and before the room is occupied by any other lodger, thoroughly cleanse the floor of the room and so far as may be necessary every part of the premises and the fittings or appliances which have been exclusively used by the first-mentioned lodger and will be exclusively used by the succeeding lodger.

12. Every lodger in a lodging-house shall

(a) Every day before the hour of *two o'clock* in the afternoon remove all filth and refuse from every room which has been let to him and thoroughly cleanse every receptacle which has been used for filth or refuse ;

(b) Keep thoroughly clean and wholesome every staircase, landing and passage to the exclusive use of which he is entitled ;

(c) Keep thoroughly clean every window, fixture or fitting, and all paint, in every room let to him ;

(d) Keep thoroughly clean and wholesome all beds, bedclothes and bedding belonging to and used by him or any member of his family ;

(e) Keep open for at least *one hour* in the day every window of every room let to him and used as a sleeping apartment, unless reasonably prevented by the state of the weather or any other sufficient cause ;

(f) Keep thoroughly clean and wholesome the floor of every room let to him.

13. A lodger in a lodging-house shall not keep or permit to be kept any animal in any room let to him or elsewhere upon the premises in such manner as to render the room or premises filthy or unwholesome.

For requiring provision adequate for the use of and readily accessible to each family of—

      (i) closet accommodation ;

      (ii) water supply and washing accommodation ;

      (iii) accommodation for the storage, preparation and cooking of food ;

41

*and, where necessary, for securing separate accommoda-
tion as aforesaid for every part of such house which is
occupied as a separate dwelling*

14. Every owner of a lodging-house shall provide
adequate for the use of and readily accessible to each
family by whom any part of the house is occupied

(a) *Water*-closet accommodation ;

(b) A supply of water for domestic use ;

(c) Accommodation for washing clothes ;

(d) Accommodation for the storage of food in a reasonably cool position with proper ventilation from the
external air wherever practicable and with protection from dust and flies ;

⸰(e) Accommodation for the preparation and cooking of
food ;

and, where necessary, separate accommodation as aforesaid for every part of the house which is occupied as a
separate dwelling.

*For the keeping in repair and adequate lighting of any
common staircase in such houses*

15. Every owner of a lodging-house shall

(a) Keep every common staircase in the lodging-house
in a state of good repair ;

(b) Wherever practicable provide every common staircase with adequate means of lighting by natural
light, including, in the case of a new building
constructed for use as a lodging-house, a window
or windows on the staircase at each storey opening
directly into the external air ;

(c) Provide and keep efficient adequate means for the
artificial lighting of every common staircase.

*For securing stability and the prevention of and safety from
fires*

16. Every owner of a lodging-house shall carry out such
works as may from time to time be necessary for securing
that the house shall be throughout of adequate stability.

17. A person erecting a new building intended to be
used as a lodging-house shall construct of incombustible
material every wall, the floor of every room above the
ground floor, and, if the building comprises more than
two storeys above the ground level, every landing and
the floor of every corridor or passage.

Provided that any such floor or landing may be constructed of timber if all the spaces between the joists are filled in with good concrete, pugging, or other solid and incombustible material at least three inches thick, and the underside of the floor or landing is completely covered with a sufficient thickness of good plaster or other suitable incombustible material properly fixed.

18. Every occupier of a lodging-house shall cause every flight of stairs, passage and other means of escape in the house to be kept free from obstruction, and every door in connection with such means of escape to be so fitted that it can be readily opened.

For the cleansing and redecoration of the premises at stated times, and for the paving of the courts and courtyards

19. Every owner of a lodging-house shall
(a) In the month of   in each year thoroughly cleanse every part of the premises and renew all unclean or unwholesome paint and wall paper or other wall covering ;
(b) Pave every court and courtyard with impervious pavement sloped to a properly constructed channel leading to a trapped gully grating so arranged as effectively to carry off all rain or waste water ; and
(c) At all times keep in good order and proper repair the pavement, channel and grating.

For the provision of handrails, where necessary, for all staircases of such houses

20. Every owner of a lodging-house shall cause every flight of stairs in every staircase in the lodging-house to be furnished, where necessary, with a sufficient handrail or handrails securely fixed.

Penalties

21. Every person who shall offend against any of these by-laws shall be liable for every offence to a penalty not exceeding five pounds and in the case of a continuing offence to a further penalty of forty shillings for each day during which the offence continues after written notice of the offence has been served on him by the council.

Lodgings'
by-laws.

Repeal of By-laws [1]

22. From and after the date of the confirmation of these by-laws, the by-laws relating to houses let in lodgings or occupied by members of more than one family which were made on the   day of
            in the year One thousand
hundred and   by the
and were confirmed on the   day of
in the year One thousand   hundred and
                    , by [the Local Government Board] [the Minister of Health] [one of the Principal Secretaries of State of Her late Majesty, Queen Victoria] shall be repealed.

----

[1] If this clause is not included in the series submitted to the Minister of Health for approval, it should be stated whether or not there are any by-laws in force upon the subject.

APPENDIX V

SUNDRY DOCUMENTS

55,763   (*2nd September* 1910.)

HOUSING, TOWN PLANNING, &c., ACT, 1909

Regulations under section 74 (*the prescribed distance from Royal Palaces or Parks*)

To the several local authorities in England and Wales for the purposes of the Housing, Town Planning, &c., Act, 1909 ;—

And to all others whom it may concern.

Whereas by section 74 of the Housing, Town Planning, &c., Act, 1909 (hereinafter referred to as "the Act") it is enacted as follows :—

"74. (1.) Where any land proposed to be included in any scheme or order to be made under the Housing Acts or Part II of this Act, or any land proposed to be acquired under the Housing Acts or Part II of this Act, is situate within the prescribed distance from any of the royal palaces or parks, the local authority shall, before preparing the scheme or order or acquiring the land, communicate with the Commissioners of Works, and the Local Government Board shall, before confirming the scheme or order or authorising the acquisition of the land or the raising of any loan for the purpose, take into consideration any recommendations they may have received from the Commissioners of Works with reference to the proposal.

"(2.) For the purposes of this section 'prescribed' means prescribed by regulations made by the Local Government Board after consultation with the Commissioners of Works."

Now therefore, we, the Local Government Board,

after consultation with the Commissioners of Works, do hereby make the following regulations under and for the purposes of the above-cited section 74, that is to say—

The prescribed distance for the purposes of subsection (1) of section 74 of the Act shall, in the case of Windsor Castle, Windsor Great Park, and Windsor Home Park, be two miles, and, in the case of any other Royal Palace or Park, be half a mile.

Given under the seal of office of the Local Government Board, this Second day of September, in the year One thousand nine hundred and ten.

(L.S.)   JOHN BURNS,
                                                 President.

H. C. MONRO,
          Secretary. ,

LOCAL OR PRIVATE BILLS

EXTRACTS FROM STANDING ORDERS OF THE HOUSE OF COMMONS

Deposit of statement relating to working-class houses (see Sect. 3, 1903 Act, page 276).

38. " Where any Bill contains or revives or extends power to take compulsorily or by agreement any land in any local area as defined for the purposes of this Order and such taking involves, or may involve, the taking in that area of any house or houses occupied either wholly or partially by thirty or more persons of the working class, whether as tenants or lodgers, the promoters shall deposit in the Private Bill Office and at the office of the central authority on or before the 21st day of December, a statement giving the description and postal address of each of such houses, its number on the deposited plans, the parish in which it is situate, and the number (so far as can be ascertained) of persons of the working class residing in it, and also a copy of so much of the deposited plans (if any) as relates thereto.

" This Order shall not apply where a statement in pursuance of this Order was deposited in respect of the Act, the powers of which are proposed to be revived or extended.

" For the purposes of this Order the expression ' local area' means, (1) as respects London, the Administrative County of London; (2) as respects England and Wales (outside London) any borough, or other urban district, and any elsewhere than in a borough or other urban district, parish ; and (3) as respects Ireland, any urban district.

" The expression ' house ' means any house or part of a house occupied as a separate dwelling.

" The expression ' working class ' means mechanics, artisans, labourers, and others working for wages, hawkers, costermongers, persons not working for wages but working at some trade or handicraft without employing others except members of their own family, and persons, other than domestic servants, whose income in any case does not exceed an average of thirty shillings a week, and the families of any of such persons who may be residing with them.

" The expression ' Central Authority' means, as regards England and Wales, the Local Government Board; and as regards Ireland, the Local Government Board for Ireland.

" The expression ' Bill' includes a Bill confirming a Provisional Order."

ACCOMMODATION FOR WORKMEN

184A. In the case of every Bill authorising the construction of works outside the county of London or any municipal borough the committee to which the Bill is referred shall take this order into their consideration, and if they are of opinion that such a number of workmen will probably be simultaneously employed upon the works as having regard to the nature and situation of the works to make such an inquiry desirable, they shall inquire into the question of the sufficiency of the accommodation and service available or proposed by the promoters to be provided under the Bill— *Provision of accommodation for workmen on works.*

(1) for the proper housing and sanitary requirements of persons employed in constructing the works authorised by the Bill ;

(2) for the treatment of cases of sickness or accident, including accommodation for dealing with infectious disease ;

and if they think that further accommodation or service

for those purposes ought to be provided they shall insert in the Bill such clauses as in their opinion are necessary to secure the provision of satisfactory accommodation or service for those purposes by the local authority, company, or person authorised to execute the works.

LOANS UNDER SECTION 22 OF THE HOUSING, TOWN PLANNING, &c., ACT, 1919

1. Form of application by owner for loan for the purpose of carrying out works for reconstruction, enlargement or improvement of a house.

This form should be completed in duplicate and sent by the owner to the clerk to the local authority for the district in which the house is situated.

(1) Name of owner . . . . .
(2) Address . . . . .
(3) Address of house in respect of which application is made . . . .
(4) Rateable value . . . . .
(5) Nature of owner's interest, *i.e.* whether freehold, copyhold or leasehold. If leasehold, the date on which the lease expires should be stated . . . . .
(6) Is the house occupied at present ? If so—
  (a) Name of occupier . . .
  (b) his occupation or business . . .
  (c) by whom is the rent received .
(7) Are there any charges on the property ?
  (If so, give particulars) . . .
(8) Particulars of the works of reconstruction, enlargement or improvement for which the loan is sought. (If full particulars of these works are given in the estimate (see next question) they need not be given here) . . . .
(9) Estimated cost of works. (Two copies of estimate should be attached) . .
(10) Do you undertake to let the houses solely to persons of the working classes ? .
(11) What rent is it proposed to charge for the house when reconstructed, enlarged or improved ? . . . .
(12) Amount of loan for which application is made . . . . .
(13) What security is offered for repayment of loan ? . . . . .

Signed.......................
Address.....................
....
Date........................

2. Documents to be forwarded by the local authority to the Housing Commissioner in connection with any application for sanction to a loan for the purposes of section 22 of the Act of 1919.

(1) Copy of resolution of the local authority applying to the Minister of Health for sanction to a loan.

(2) Copy of form or forms of application received from owner (or owners) and of documents forwarded by him.

(3) Copy of valuation of the owner's interest in the house (or houses) by the Inland Revenue Valuer.

(4) It should be stated whether any closing order or other order or notice has been served in respect of the house. Particulars should be given of any order or notice which has been served.

APPENDIX VI

PUBLIC UTILITY SOCIETIES

STATUTORY RULES AND ORDERS, 1919. No. 1428

HOUSING OF THE WORKING CLASSES, ENGLAND

The Public Utility Societies (Financial Assistance) Regulations, 1919. Dated 6th October 1919.

65,242

To the councils of the several administrative counties in England and Wales ;—

To the mayor, aldermen, and commons of the city of London, in common council assembled ;—

To the councils of the several metropolitan boroughs, municipal boroughs, and other urban districts in England and Wales ;—

To the councils of the several rural districts in England and Wales ;—

To all public utility societies registered under the Industrial and Provident Societies Acts, 1893 to 1913 ;—

And to all others whom it may concern.

Whereas by subsection (1) of section 19 of the Housing, Town Planning, &c., Act, 1919, it is enacted that where a public utility society as defined by that Act has submitted to the Local Government Board a scheme for the provision of houses for the working classes and the scheme is approved by the Board, then, if the scheme is carried out within such period after the passing of that Act as may be specified by the Board with the consent of the Treasury, the Board may pay or undertake to pay out of moneys provided by Parliament such contributions towards the cost of carrying out the scheme as may be determined to be payable under regulations made by the Board, with the approval of the Treasury, subject Financial
Assistance
Regulations. to such conditions (including conditions as to audit of accounts by district auditors) as may be prescribed by those regulations ;

And whereas by subsection (2) of the said section it is enacted that the regulations shall provide that the amount of any annual payment to be made under the section shall be equivalent to 30 per centum of the annual loan charges which would have been payable in accordance with the regulations on the total capital expenditure incurred by the public utility society for the purposes of the scheme if the amount of that expenditure has been borrowed from the Public Works Loan Commissioners ;

And whereas by section 40 of that Act the expression " public utility society " is defined as follows :—

> " The expression ' public utility society ' means a society registered under the Industrial and Provident Societies Acts, 1893 to 1913, the rules whereof prohibit the payment of any interest or dividend at a rate exceeding 6 per cent. per annum."

Now therefore, the Minister of Health, in pursuance of his powers under the recited enactments and under any other Statutes in that behalf, hereby makes the following regulations :—

ARTICLE I—In these regulations, unless the contrary intention appears :—

(a) The expression " the Minister " means the Minister of Health ;

(b) The expression " the Act of 1919 " means the Housing, Town Planning, &c., Act, 1919 ;

(c) The expression " public utility society " has the same meaning as in the Act of 1919 ;

(d) The expression " local authority " means the local authority within the meaning of Part III of the Housing of the Working Classes Act, 1890, for the district in which the houses are provided or to be provided by the public utility society.

ARTICLE II—Subject to the provisions of these regulations, and provided that these regulations are complied with :—

(1.) An annual contribution out of moneys provided by Parliament (hereinafter referred to as " the Exchequer subsidy ") may be made by the

Minister towards the cost of carrying out a
scheme submitted by a public utility society
(hereinafter referred to as " the society ") and
approved by the Minister ;

(2.) The Exchequer subsidy shall be an amount [1] *the
equivalent during the period ending on the 31st
day of March 1927, of 50 per cent., and thereafter
of* 30 per cent. of the annual charges, in respect
of interest and repayment of principal, on the
capital raised by the society under the approved
scheme :

Provided that in the case of the annual charges
incurred by the society before the houses are
completed, if the balance of those charges, after
deducting the Exchequer subsidy, is defrayed,
out of borrowed moneys, such moneys shall not
for the purposes of this Article, be included as
part of the capital raised by the society under
the approved scheme :

Provided also that the Minister may reduce the
amount of the Exchequer subsidy in any case
in which he is satisfied that the capital expenditure incurred by the society has been excessive.

(3.) The Exchequer subsidy shall be payable in two
half-yearly instalments, or in such other manner
as the Minister may think fit, during the periods
allowed for the repayment of the loans raised
from the Public Works Loan Commissioners
for the purposes of the approved scheme, or,
where no loans have been so raised, during the
period of fifty years from the date on which the
scheme was approved by the Minister, and shall
be reduced by the Minister so far as may be
necessary when the period allowed for the repayment of any one of the said loans has expired :

(4.) For the purposes of this Article the annual charges
on the capital raised by the society shall be
deemed to be the annual charges which would
have been payable, by way of equal annual
instalments of principal with interest combined,
on the like amount of capital if it had been

[1] See Article 2 (1) of the Public Utility Societies (Financial Assistance)
Regulations, 1920 (page 662).

borrowed from the Public Works Loan Commis- Financial
sioners on the terms granted for the time being Assistance
to public utility societies whether the capital has Regulations.
in fact been borrowed from the Public Works
Loan Commissioners or otherwise provided.

ARTICLE III—(1.) The Exchequer subsidy shall cease
to be payable—

(a) in any case in which the Minister is not satisfied
that reasonable progress has been made with the
carrying into effect of the scheme within twelve
months from the passing of the Act of 1919,
[1] *or such later date as the Minister may allow, regard
being had to the supplies of labour and material
available from time to time and all other local
or general circumstances affecting the carrying into
effect of the scheme ;* and

(b) in respect of any scheme or part of a scheme not
carried into effect before the expiry of a period
of three years from the passing of the Act of 1919,
or such later date as the Minister may allow,
regard being had to the supplies of labour and
material available from time to time and all
other local or general circumstances affecting the
carrying into effect of the scheme.

(2.) For the purposes of these regulations a scheme or
part of a scheme shall be deemed to have been carried
into effect when all the houses to be provided thereunder
are let or available for letting.

ARTICLE IV—(1.) The scheme as submitted for approval
shall be accompanied by detailed plans, specifications,
and estimates of the cost of the works, by a balance sheet [2]
showing the estimated annual income and expenditure
under the scheme and by a copy of the rules or proposed
rules of the society.

(2.) The carrying out of the works shall be subject
to the supervision of the Minister, exercised either through
his own officers or through the local authority.

ARTICLE V—For the purposes of Article II (2) of these
regulations the sum to be included in the capital raised
by the society under the approved scheme in respect of

---

[1] Words added by Article 2 (2) of the Public Utility Societies (Financial Assistance) Regulations, 1920 (page 662).

[2] See page 657.

Financial
Assistance
Regulations.

the professional charges paid or to be paid by the society, in connection with the building of the houses and the lay-out of the estate under the scheme, shall not exceed 5 per cent. of the gross capital expenditure approved by the Minister.

ARTICLE VI—The rents to be charged for houses included in the scheme shall be subject to the approval of the Minister, and shall not be altered without the consent of the Minister.

ARTICLE VII—The society shall not sell any land or houses included in the approved scheme, except with the consent of the Minister, and subject to regulations [1] to be made by the Minister, with the concurrence of the Public Works Loan Commissioners.

ARTICLE VIII—(1.) The society shall keep separate accounts relating to the approved scheme, and those accounts shall be made up and shall be audited by a district auditor in like manner, and subject to the same provisions, as the accounts of an urban district council, and for this purpose the enactments relating to the audit by district auditors of the last-named accounts and to all matters incidental thereto and consequential thereon, shall apply to the said accounts of the society.[2]

(2.) So far as may be necessary for the purpose of his duties under sub-division (1) of this Article the district auditor shall have access to all the books, deeds, documents and accounts of the society.

(3.) A balance sheet and summary of the accounts relating to the approved scheme for each financial year shall, during the ensuing financial year, be open to inspection by any person at the office of the society on payment of a fee of one shilling, and a copy of the balance sheet and summary shall be sent to the local authority at the conclusion of the financial year to which it relates.

ARTICLE IX—The society, in consideration of the payment of the Exchequer subsidy, shall give an undertaking, in a form approved by the Minister, that in the event of the dissolution of the society before the Exchequer subsidy has ceased to be payable, they will, if required by the Minister, after paying the outstanding charges (if any) in respect of the moneys borrowed by them, and after paying off all shares at par, devote the

[1] See page 663.   [2] See page 675.

remainder of the proceeds of the sale of the property, or such part thereof as the Minister may determine, towards the repayment of the Exchequer subsidies. Financial Assistance Regulations.

ARTICLE X—(1.) The rules of the society and any amendment thereof shall be subject to the approval of the Minister.

(2.) The rules of the society shall, unless the Minister otherwise allows, be so framed as to give effect to the following provisions ·—

(i) The objects of the society shall include the provision, improvement and management of houses for the working classes.

(ii) Every member of the society shall hold at least one share (of the value at the least of £1) in the society, and the board of management of the society shall not refuse to admit to membership of the society any person who has been for three months a tenant of the society.

(iii) Tenants [or if the society so determine tenant members] may elect annually from among themselves a tenants' [or tenant members'] committee, and such committee shall have such rights, powers and duties (in addition to those which are expressly conferred on or vested in them by the rules of the society), as the board of management of the society, with the concurrence of such committee, may determine. Each tenant [or tenant member] shall be entitled to one vote at the election of the members of the said committee.

(iv) The management of the business of the society shall be vested in a board of management, of whose members (as from the date of the first annual general meeting of the society after the approval of the scheme) at least one quarter shall be tenant members appointed by the tenants' [or tenant members'] committee.

(v) At all general meetings of the society each fully paid-up share against which there is no set-off in the books of the society shall carry one vote, and not less than five times that amount of loan stock held by a member shall carry one vote :

Provided that the possession of loan stock apart from membership shall not entitle its holder either to a vote or to attendance at meetings of the society :

Provided also that a limitation may be imposed on the number of votes which may be recorded at any meeting by any one member.

(vi) Each tenant shall have undisturbed occupancy of his house and garden so long as—

(a) he fulfils the tenancy regulations made by the board of management ; and

(b) he pays any rent or debts due from him to the society ; and

(c) he and the occupants of his house avoid any conduct detrimental to good neighbourship :

Provided that the tenant shall not be given notice to quit by the board of management on the ground of conduct detrimental to good neighbourship except with the concurrence of the tenants' [or tenant members'] committee.

(vii) Any profits remaining to the society after providing for—

(a) the annual charges, in respect of interest and repayment of principal, on the loans and loan stock raised by the society ;

(b) the taxes, rates, rents, insurance premiums, or other charges payable by the society in respect of any land or houses belonging to them ;

(c) the costs of administration and management and of repairs of property ;

(d) such allocations to a reserve fund as may be determined by the board of management ;

(e) any other necessary expenses incurred by the board of management ; and

(f) a dividend not exceeding the rate authorised by the statutes in force, on the capital of the share society ;

shall be applied in such manner as may be determined by the board of management, for the benefit of the tenants generally.

ARTICLE XI—These regulations may be cited as "The Public Utility Societies (Financial Assistance) Regulations, 1919," and shall, unless and until revoked or altered by the Minister, with the approval of the Lords Commissioners of His Majesty's Treasury, apply and have effect with respect to any scheme made by a public utility society and approved by the Minister in accordance with these regulations :

Provided that, in any case where a difficulty arises with regard to the application of these regulations, the Minister may, by order, make such minor modification of these regulations as may be necessary, in regard to any particular scheme, for the purpose of giving effect to the intention of these regulations. *Financial Assistance Regulations.*

Given under the official seal of the Minister of Health, this Sixth day of October, in the year One thousand nine hundred and nineteen.

(L.S.) CHRISTOPHER ADDISON,
Minister of Health.

We approve these regulations—

J. TOWYN JONES,
R. A. SANDERS,
*Lords Commissioners of
His Majesty's Treasury.*

MINISTRY OF HEALTH

HOUSING ACTS, 1890–1919

ASSISTED SCHEME (PUBLIC UTILITY SOCIETY)

STATEMENT OF ESTIMATED ANNUAL INCOME AND EXPEN-
DITURE TO BE SUBMITTED BY A PUBLC UTILITY SOCIETY
IN RESPECT OF EACH SCHEME FOR WHICH FINANCIAL
ASSISTANCE IS CLAIMED UNDER THE TERMS OF THE
HOUSING, TOWN PLANNING, &C., ACT, 1919 (SEE
ARTICLE IV OF THE ABOVE REGULATIONS).

INSTRUCTIONS

1. This form should be completed in duplicate and the two copies should be submitted to the Housing Commissioner dealing with the scheme in question at the same time as the provisionally accepted tender for the erection of the houses is submitted.

2. In completing the main statement the following rules should be observed :—

(a) The annual deduction in respect of unoccupied houses and uncollected rents should not exceed 5 per cent. of the gross estimated rent ;

(b) The annual deduction for cost of repairs and maintenance should not exceed 15 per cent. of the gross estimated rent ;

(c) The annual deduction for cost of supervision and

42

Financial
assistance.

management should not exceed 5 per cent. of the gross estimated rent.

The gross estimated rent, where rent is inclusive of rates and water charges, is the estimated inclusive rent, less rates and water charges.

3. The supplementary tables must be completed in all cases in which they are applicable.

4. *Loan charges.* Under this head should be entered the *annual* sums (including principal and interest without deduction of income tax) required to repay the estimated amount of the loans on the annuity system. In the case of money to be advanced by the Public Works Loan Commissioners, the period for repayment on which these loan charges should be calculated is fifty years, and the rate of interest should be taken at $5\frac{3}{4}$ per cent.[1] The loan charges for any sum can be obtained from the half-yearly charge for £100, which on the basis of fifty years and $5\frac{3}{4}$ per cent. is £3 1*s.* 1*d.*

5. Where a scheme is being proceeded with in sections, only the charges properly attributable to the section in question must be entered.

MAIN STATEMENT

Scheme No. . . . .   P.U.S. . . . .

Section of scheme (1st, 2nd, &c.

. . . .)   Local Authority . . . .

Estimated Annual Income	Estimated Annual Expenditure
£ s. d.	£ s. d.
From inclusive rents .	Loan charges on Govern-
Less allowance for	ment loans . .
unoccupied houses	Charges on privately sub-
and uncollected	scribed capital . .
rents . .	Rates . . .
	Taxes . . .
Estimated net receipts	Insurance . .
from rents . .	Water supply . .
From other sources (if	Repairs and maintenance
any) specifying	Management and collec-
them :—	tion of rents . .
	Balance to reserve .
. . . .	
. . . .	
Estimated State Sub-	
sidy . . .	

Date. . . . .   Signed. . . . . *Secretary to P.U.S.*

[1] See, however, p. 536.

SUPPLEMENTARY TABLES
A—LAND

Total area of site...acres.
Total cost of rent of site (as approved by Ministry) £................
Area in present section of scheme................................
Apportioned cost (or rent) of present section, £................

B—DEVELOPMENT

Total cost of development (i.e. street works, sewers, &c.) as approved
by Ministry, £.................
Apportioned cost to present section of scheme, £................

C—BUILDINGS

Total cost of houses in present section, £................

D—CAPITAL AND LOAN CHARGES

	Amount.	Annual Charges
[1] Advances required from Public Works Loan Commissioners	....	....
[2] Privately subscribed capital	....	....
Total cost of present section of scheme	....	....

[1] This must not exceed 75 per cent. of the total cost of the section.
[2] Give below particulars as to this capital, i.e. amount of share, capital, loans and loan stock, and also particulars as to annual charges including rate of interest (which must not exceed 6 per cent.), and as to security for loans.

E—AUTHORISED CAPITAL OF SOCIETY

Total amount authorised by rules . . £................

Amount already borrowed in respect of previous
schemes . . . . . . £................

Financial
assistance.

F—RENTS AND RATES (PRESENT SECTION OF SCHEME
ONLY)

Type of House.	Number of each.	Proposed weekly rent per house excluding rates.	Total annual rent from each type.	Cost per house.	Estimated R.V. per house.	Rates in £	Total annual rates per type.
Living-room, scullery, 2 bedrooms . .	....	....	....	....	....	....	......
Living-room, scullery, 3 bedrooms . .	....	....	....	....	....	....	......
Parlour, living-room, scullery, 2 bedrooms	....	....	....	....	....	....	......
Parlour, living-room, scullery, 3 bedrooms	....	....	....	....	....	....	......
Parlour, living-room, scullery, 4 bedrooms	....	....	....	....	....	....	......
Tenements in block dwellings . . (Give particulars of accommodation).	....	....	....	....	....	....	......
....	....	....	....	....	....	....	......
....	....	....	....	....	....	....	......
Other types (specify)	....	....	....	....	....	....	......
....	....	....	....	....	....	....	......
....	....	....	....	....	....	....	......

Total rent . ... Total rates . ...

G—WATER SUPPLY (IF NOT INCLUDED IN F)   Financial
assistance.

Class of house.	Estimated Ass. value for water rate.	Water rate in pound.	Water charge per house.	Number of each.	Total annual charge for water supply per type.
Living-room, scullery, 2 bedrooms . . .	....	......	......	....	....
Living-room, scullery, 3 bedrooms . . .	....	......	......	....	....
Parlour, living-room, scullery, 2 bedrooms. .	....	......	......	....	....
Parlour, living-room, scullery, 3 bedrooms . .	....	......	......	....	....
Parlour, living-room, scullery, 4 bedrooms . .	....	......	......	....	....
Tenements in block dwellings . . .	....	......	......	....	....
....	....	......	......	....	....
....	....	......	......	....	....
Other types (specify) .	....	......	......	....	....
....	....	......	......	....	....
....	....	......	......	....	....

Total water charge   .   . ..

H—ESTIMATED STATE SUBSIDY

Total cost of present section of scheme, £................
Loan charges on three-fourths of this amount, calculated as if borrowed
    on the annuity system of repayment for a period of 50 years at
    [1] 5¾ per cent., £................
40 per cent. of these loan charges, £................

STATUTORY RULES AND ORDERS, 1920, No. 134

HOUSING, ENGLAND

The Public Utility Societies (Financial Assistance) Regulations, 1920. Dated 30th January 1920

65,798

Whereas by section 4 of the Housing (Additional
Powers) Act, 1919,[2] the provisions of section 19 of the
Housing, Town Planning, &c., Act, 1919,[3] with respect

[1] See, however, page 536.   [2] 9–10 Geo 5. c. 99.   [3] 9–10 Geo. 5. c. 35.

Financial assistance.

to the amount of the annual payment to be made to a public utility society are varied, and it is expedient that certain consequential amendments should be made in the Public Utility Societies (Financial Assistance) Regulations, 1919 [1] :

Now therefore, the Minister of Health, in pursuance of the powers conferred on him by section 19 of the Housing, Town Planning, &c., Act, 1919, and of all other powers enabling him in that behalf, hereby makes the following regulations :—

1. These regulations may be cited as the Public Utility Societies (Financial Assistance) Regulations, 1920, and shall be construed as one with the Public Utility Societies (Financial Assistance) Regulations, 1919, hereinafter called the principal regulations.

2. (1.) Paragraph (2) of Article II of the principal regulations shall have effect as though for the words " the equivalent of 30 per cent. of the annual charges " there were substituted·the words " the equivalent during the period ending on the 31st day of March 1927, of 50 per cent., and thereafter of 30 per cent. of the annual charges."

(2.) Sub-paragraph (a) of paragraph (1) of Article III of the principal regulations shall have effect as though after the words " within twelve months from the passing of the Act of 1919 " there were added the words " or such later date as the Minister may allow, regard being had to the supplies of labour and material available from time to time and all other local or general circumstances affecting the carrying into effect of the scheme."

3. Where a house included in a scheme submitted to and approved by the Minister is sold by the society, the Minister may, at the request of the society, pay to any mortgagee a sum equal to the capitalised value as at the date of the sale of the Exchequer subsidy apportioned in respect of that house towards the discharge of the liability of the society to the mortgagee.

Given under the official seal of the Minister of Health, this Thirtieth day of January, in the year One thousand nine hundred and twenty.

(L.S.)   CHRISTOPHER ADDISON,
Minister of Health.

[1] S.R. & O., 1919, No. 1428 (page 650).

We approve these regulations—

JAMES PARKER,

J. TOWYN JONES,

Two of the Lords Commissioners
of His Majesty's Treasury.

STATUTORY RULES AND ORDERS, 1920. No. 107

HOUSING, ENGLAND

Sale of
houses.

The Public Utility Societies (Sale of Houses) Regulations,
1920, dated 28th January 1920, made by the Minister
of Health under section 19 (1) of the Housing, Town
Planning, &c., Act, 1919 (9 & 10 Geo. 5. c. 35)

65,704

Whereas by subsection (1) of section 19 of the Housing, Town Planning, &c., Act, 1919, it is enacted that where a public utility society as defined by that Act has submitted to the Local Government Board a scheme for the provision of houses for the working classes and the scheme is approved by the Board, then, if the scheme is carried out within such period after the passing of that Act as may be specified by the Board, with the consent of the Treasury, the Board may pay or undertake to pay out of moneys provided by Parliament such contributions towards the cost of carrying out the scheme as may be determined to be payable under regulations made by the Board, with the approval of the Treasury, subject to such conditions (including conditions as to audit of accounts by district auditors) as may be prescribed by those regulations :

And whereas by regulations made by the Minister of Health under that subsection and intituled the Public Utility Societies (Financial Assistance) Regulations, 1919,[1] it is provided that a public utility society shall not sell any land or houses included in any approved scheme except with the consent of the said Minister and subject to regulations to be made by him with the concurrence of the Public Works Loan Commissioners :

Now therefore, the Minister of Health, in pursuance of

[1] S.R. & O., 1919, No. 1428 (page 650).

Sale of
houses.

his powers under the recited enactments and of all other powers thereunto enabling him, with the concurrence of the Public Works Loan Commissioners, hereby makes the following regulations :—

1. These regulations may be cited as the Public Utility Societies (Sale of Houses) Regulations, 1920, and shall be read as one with the Public Utility Societies (Financial Assistance) Regulations, 1919 (hereinafter called "the principal regulations ").

2. In these regulations, unless the context otherwise requires :—

(a) The expression "the Act of 1919" means the Housing, Town Planning, &c., Act, 1919 ;

(b) the expression "society" means a public utility society ;

(c) The expression "scheme" means a scheme for the provision of houses for the working classes prepared by a society and approved by the Minister under subsection (1) of section 19 of the Act of 1919 ;

(d) The expression "house" means a house comprised in a scheme, and includes any yard, garden, outhouses and appurtenances belonging thereto ;

(e) The expression "Exchequer subsidy" means an annual contribution out of moneys provided by Parliament, made by the Minister, towards the cost of carrying out a scheme ;

(f) The expression "the Commissioners" means the Public Works Loan Commissioners ;

(g) The expression "local authority" means the local authority within the meaning of Part III of the Housing of the Working Classes Act, 1890,[1] for the district in which the houses are provided or to be provided by the society ;

(h) The expression "sale" includes the grant of a lease or, if the property is leasehold, of an under-lease for a term of not less than ninety years where the yearly rent reserved by such lease or underlease does not exceed five shillings ; and the expressions "sell" and "purchaser" have a corresponding meaning.

3. Before selling any house the society shall be satisfied

[1] 53–4 Vict. c. 70.

that the proposed purchaser is the occupier or, if the Sale of houses. house is unoccupied, the intending occupier of the house.

4. The conveyance or other instrument transferring the house to the purchaser shall contain covenants on the part of the purchaser in the terms set out in the First Schedule to these regulations with such modifications as may be required in the case of a lease or underlease and such other modifications, if any, as the Minister may approve.

5. The society shall not, without the consent of the Minister, and subject to such conditions, if any, as he may impose, grant any licence with regard to the user of any house which they may be empowered to grant by any of the covenants referred to in the last preceding article.

6. (i) Before selling or contracting to sell any house, the society shall prepare and submit for the approval of the Minister a schedule apportioning among the several houses included in the scheme the total approved cost of the scheme, such apportionment being based on—

(a) the value of the interest of the society in the site of the house ;

(b) the amount expended by the society in the erection of the house ; and

(c) a fair proportion of the general expenditure of the society in connection with the scheme :

Provided that in calculating the expenditure under the foregoing heads no account shall be taken of any expenditure by the society towards which no Exchequer subsidy is being made, and any such expenditure shall be shown separately in the schedule.

(ii) The cost of a house so calculated and approved by the Minister, less any loan or part of a loan in respect of the said cost which has from time to time been repaid, is referred to in these regulations as the "approved value " and, in the case of a society which provides for the repayment of loans by the creation of a sinking fund, the sums standing to the credit of such sinking fund shall, for the purpose of ascertaining the approved value of a house, be treated as though they had been applied in or towards repayment of loans.

7. No house shall be sold at a price which is less than the percentage of the approved value of the house shown in the Second Schedule to these regulations.

8. So much of the purchase money as is equivalent

Sale of
houses.

to the minimum price at which the house may be sold, as shown by the said Second Schedule, shall, unless the Minister otherwise directs, be applied by the society as follows :—

(a) First, to the repayment of so much of any outstanding loans borrowed from the Commissioners in respect of the house as will reduce the yearly payment to the Commissioners on account of principal and interest on the loan to an amount not exceeding an Exchequer subsidy equivalent, during the period before the 31st day of March 1927 to 50 per cent., and, thereafter, to 30 per cent. of the annual charges, as defined in Article II (4) of the principal regulations, on the capital raised by the society and approved by the Minister in respect of that house ; and

(b) Secondly, to the repayment of loans borrowed for the purpose of the scheme otherwise than from the Commissioners, or to the repayment or extinction of any shares or loan stock issued for the purpose of the scheme.

9. Every sale made by a society under these regulations shall be made in accordance with rules to be made by the society and approved by the Minister.

10. Nothing in these regulations shall extend to the sale of a house by the Commissioners in the exercise of a power of sale as mortgagees of the property, or to the sale of a house by the society to any local authority.

FIRST SCHEDULE

Form of Covenants to be inserted in Conveyance

1. The Purchaser hereby for himself and his assigns covenants with the society and their assigns, the owner or owners for the time being of any land comprised in the scheme under section 19 (1) of the Housing, Town Planning, &c., Act, 1919, of which the premises hereby conveyed form part—

(a) that except with the licence in writing of the society, or, if the society has dissolved, of the local authority, the premises hereby conveyed shall not at any time hereafter be used for any other Sale of houses. purpose than that of a private dwelling-house ; and

(b) that the said premises shall not be used for any purpose which shall be or become in any way a nuisance or annoyance to the society or their assigns or their tenants, or to the owners or tenants of any adjoining property.

2. The purchaser hereby covenants with the society—

(a) that upon his ceasing for a period of more than four calendar months to reside in the premises hereby conveyed, or upon his death, the society shall have the option (to be exercised within three calendar months after notice of that event has been given to them) of re-purchasing the premises for a sum equal to the purchase price paid under these presents, less such amount as may be agreed between the parties hereto as representing depreciation, or, in default of agreement, as may be determined in the manner hereinafter mentioned, and that for this purpose the purchaser, or his personal representative, as the case may be, shall as soon as may be, give notice to the society of that event ; and

(b) that if at any time he desires to sell or otherwise dispose of the premises hereby conveyed, he will give notice thereof to the society and the society shall have, within three calendar months from the date of such notice, an option to re-purchase the premises upon the terms mentioned in paragraph (a).

3. Any question arising under the last clause as to the amount to be allowed for depreciation shall be determined by a valuer to be nominated jointly by the parties, or, if they fail to agree, by the Minister of Health, and the cost of the valuation shall be borne by the society, unless the amount allowed by the valuer for depreciation is less by more than 10 per cent. of the amount claimed in that respect by the purchaser, in which case the cost of the valuation shall be borne by the purchaser.

4. The purchaser further covenants with the society that if at any time he desires to mortgage or charge the premises hereby conveyed or any part thereof, the instrument creating such mortgage or charge shall contain such

Sale of
houses.

covenants on the part of the mortgagee as will secure
to the satisfaction of the society that upon any exercise
by the mortgagee of his right of sale or foreclosure the
society shall have a right of pre-emption in the same
manner and upon the same terms as are specified in the
last two preceding clauses, and that for this purpose the
purchaser will submit for the approval of the society a
draft of the said instrument.

5. The expression " local authority " means the local
authority within the meaning of Part III of the Housing
of the Working Classes Act, 1890, for the area in which
the premises hereby conveyed are situated.

SECOND SCHEDULE

Date of Sale.		Percentage of Approved Value.
Before 1st April	1921	63
,, ,,	1922	64
,, ,,	1923	65
,, ,,	1924	66
,, ,,	1925	67
,, ,,	1926	68
,, ,,	1927	69
After 31st March	1927	70

Given under the official seal of the Minister of Health,
    this Twenty-eighth day of January, in the year One
    thousand nine hundred and twenty.

(L.S.)   CHRISTOPHER ADDISON,
                                    Minister of Health.

We approve these regulations—

JAMES PARKER,
J. TOWYN JONES,
    Lords Commissioners of
    His Majesty's Treasury.

STATUTORY RULES AND ORDERS, 1919. No. 1429

HOUSING OF THE WORKING CLASSES, ENGLAND

The Housing Trusts (Financial Assistance) Regulations, 1919. Dated 6th October 1919

65,243

To the councils of the several administrative counties in England and Wales ;—

To the mayor, aldermen, and commons of the city of London, in common council assembled ;—

To the councils of the several metropolitan boroughs, municipal boroughs, and other urban districts in England and Wales ;—

To the councils of the several rural districts in England and Wales ;—

To the trustees of all housing trusts as herein defined ;—

And to all others whom it may concern.

Whereas by subsection (1) of section 19 of the Housing, Town Planning, &c., Act, 1919, it is enacted that where a housing trust as defined by that Act has submitted to the Local Government Board a scheme for the provision of houses for the working classes and the scheme is approved by the Board, then, if the scheme is carried out within such period after the passing of that Act as may be specified by the Board, with the consent of the Treasury, the Board may pay or undertake to pay out of moneys provided by Parliament such contributions towards the cost of carrying out the scheme as may be determined to be payable under regulations made by the Board, with the approval of the Treasury, subject to such conditions (including conditions as to audit of accounts by district auditors) as may be prescribed by those regulations ;

And whereas by subsection (2) of the said section it is enacted that the regulations shall provide that the amount of any annual payment to be made under the section shall be equivalent to 30 per centum of the annual loan charges which would have been payable in accordance

Financial assistance.

with the regulations on the total capital expenditure incurred by the housing trust for the purposes of the scheme if the amount of that expenditure had been borrowed from the Public Works Loan Commissioners ;

And whereas by section 40 of that Act the expression " housing trust " is defined as follows :—

> " The expression ' housing trust ' means a corporation or body of persons which, by the terms of its constituent instrument, is required to devote the whole of its funds, including any surplus which may arise from its operations, to the provision of houses for persons the majority of whom are in fact members of the working classes, and to other purposes incidental thereto " :

Now therefore, the Minister of Health, in pursuance of his powers under the recited enactments and under any other statutes in that behalf, hereby makes the following regulations :—

ARTICLE I—In these regulations, unless the contrary intention appears :—

(a) The expression " the Minister " means the Minister of Health ;

(b) The expression " the Act of 1919 " means the Housing, Town Planning, &c., Act, 1919 ;

(c) The expressions " housing trust " and " public utility society " have the same meaning as in the Act of 1919 ;

(d) The expression " local authority " means the local authority within the meaning of Part III of the Housing of the Working Classes Act, 1890, for the district in which the houses are built or to be built by the housing trusts.

ARTICLE II—Subject to the provisions of these regulations and provided that these regulations are complied with :—

(1.) An annual contribution out of moneys provided by Parliament (hereinafter referred to as " the Exchequer subsidy ") may be made by the Minister towards the cost of carrying out a scheme submitted by a housing trust and approved by the Minister, and the amount of the Exchequer subsidy shall be calculated as hereinafter provided.

(2.) The amount of the Exchequer subsidy shall be the

equivalent of 30 per centum of the annual Financial
assistance. charges which would have been payable, in respect of interest and repayment of principal, on the capital expended by the trustees for the purposes of the approved scheme if that capital had been raised by way of a loan advanced by the Public Works Loan Commissioners, on the same terms as those granted for the time being to a public utility society for the like purposes :

Provided that the Minister may reduce the amount of the Exchequer subsidy in any case in which he is satisfied that the capital expenditure incurred by the trustees has been excessive.

(3.) The Exchequer subsidy shall be payable in two half-yearly instalments or in such other manner as the Minister may think fit during the period of fifty years from the date on which the scheme is approved by the Minister, and for the purposes of sub-division (2) of this Article that date shall be the date from which the annual charges therein referred to shall be deemed to become payable.

ARTICLE III—(1.) The Exchequer subsidy shall cease to be payable—

(a) in any case in which the Minister is not satisfied that reasonable progress has been made with the carrying into effect of the scheme within twelve months from the passing of the Act of 1919 ; and

(b) in respect of any scheme or part of a scheme not carried into effect before the expiry of a period of three years from the passing of the Act of 1919, or such later date as the Minister may allow, regard being had to the supplies of labour and material available from time to time and all other local or general circumstances affecting the carrying into effect of the scheme.

(2.) For the purposes of these regulations a scheme or part of a scheme shall be deemed to have been carried into effect when all the houses to be provided thereunder are let or available for letting.

ARTICLE IV—(1.) The scheme, as submitted for approval, shall be accompanied by detailed plans, specifications, and estimates of the cost of the works.

Financial
assistance.

(2.) The carrying out of the works shall be subject to the supervision of the Minister, exercised either through his own officers or through the local authority.

ARTICLE V—The capital expenditure in respect of which the annual charges referred to in Article II (2) of these regulations shall be deemed to be payable shall not include any sum in respect of the professional charges to be paid by the trustees in excess of 5 per centum of the gross capital expenditure approved by the Ministry.

ARTICLE VI—The rents to be charged for houses included in the scheme shall be subject to the approval of the Minister, and shall not be altered without the consent of the Minister.

ARTICLE VII—The trustees shall not sell any land or houses included in the scheme, except with the consent of, and subject to conditions laid down by, the Minister.

ARTICLE VIII—(1.) The trustees shall keep separate accounts relating to the approved scheme, and those accounts shall be made up and shall be audited by a district auditor [1] in like manner, and subject to the same provisions, as the accounts of an urban district council, and for this purpose the enactments relating to the audit by district auditors of the last-named accounts and to all matters incidental thereto and consequential thereon, shall apply to the said accounts of the trustees.

(2.) So far as may be necessary for the purpose of his duties under sub-division (1) of this Article the district auditor shall have access to all the books, deeds, documents and accounts of the trustees.

ARTICLE IX—These regulations may be cited as " The Housing Trusts (Financial Assistance) Regulations, 1919," and shall, unless and until revoked or altered by the Minister, with the approval of the Lords Commissioners of His Majesty's Treasury, apply and have effect with respect to any scheme made by a housing trust and approved by the Minister in accordance with these regulations :

Provided that, in any case where a difficulty arises, with regard to the application of these regulations, the Minister may, by order, make such minor modification of these regulations as may be necessary, in

[1] See page 675.

regard to any particular scheme, for the purpose of giving effect to the intention of these regulations. Financial
assistance.

Given under the official seal of the Minister of Health, this Sixth day of October, in the year One thousand nine hundred and nineteen.

(L.S.)   CHRISTOPHER ADDISON,
Minister of Health.

We approve these regulations—

J. TOWYN JONES,
R. A. SANDERS,

Lords Commissioners of
His Majesty's Treasury.

STATUTORY RULES AND ORDERS, 1920, No. 135

HOUSING, ENGLAND

The Housing Trusts (Financial Assistance) Regulations,
1920. Dated 30th January 1920

65,796

Whereas by section 4 of the Housing (Additional Powers) Act, 1919,[1] the provisions of section 19 of the Housing, Town Planning, &c., Act, 1919,[2] with respect to the amount of the annual payment to be made to a housing trust are varied, and it is expedient that certain consequential amendments should be made in the Housing Trusts (Financial Assistance) Regulations, 1919 [3]:

Now therefore, the Minister of Health, in pursuance of the powers conferred on him by section 19 of the Housing, Town Planning, &c., Act, 1919, and of all others powers enabling him in that behalf, hereby makes the following regulations :—

1. These regulations may be cited as the Housing Trusts (Financial Assistance) Regulations, 1920, and shall be construed as one with the Housing Trusts (Financial Assistance) Regulations, 1919, hereinafter called the principal regulations.

2. (1) Paragraph (2) of Article II of the principal regulations shall have effect as though for the words " the equivalent of 30 per cent. of the annual charges "

---

[1] 9–10 Geo. 5. c. 99.   [2] 9–10 Geo. 5. c. 35.   [3] S.R. & O., 1919, No. 1429.

43

Financial assistance. there were substituted the words " the equivalent during the period ending on the 31st day of March 1927, of 50 per cent., and thereafter of 30 per cent. of the annual charges."

(2) Sub-paragraph (*a*) of paragraph (1) of Article III of the principal regulations shall have effect as though after the words " within twelve months from the passing of the Act of 1919 " there were added the words " or such later date as the Minister may allow, regard being had to the supplies of labour and material available from time to time and all other local or general circumstances affecting the carrying into effect of the scheme."

3. A tenant of a house included in a scheme submitted by a housing trust and approved by the Minister shall have undisturbed occupancy of his house and garden so long as—

(*a*) he fulfils the tenancy regulations made by the trustees ; and

(*b*) he pays any rent or debts due from him to the trustees ; and

(*c*) he and the occupants of his house avoid any conduct detrimental to good neighbourship.

Given under the official seal of the Minister of Health, this Thirtieth day of January, in the year One thousand nine hundred and twenty.

(L.S.)   CHRISTOPHER ADDISON.
                              Minister of Health.

We approve these regulations—

JAMES PARKER,
J. TOWYN JONES,
             *Two of the Lords Commissioners
             of His Majesty's Treasury.*

STATUTORY RULES AND ORDERS, 1920, No. 683

HOUSING, ENGLAND

*The Housing Accounts Order (Societies and Trusts), 1920,
dated 4th May 1920, made by the Minister of Health,
under section 5 of the District Auditors Act, 1879
(42 & 43 Vict. c. 6).*

66,089.

To all Public Utility Societies registered under the Industrial and Provident Societies Acts, 1893 to 1913 ;—

To the Trustees of all Housing Trusts as defined in the Housing, Town Planning, &c., Act, 1919 [1] ;—

And to all others whom it may concern.

Whereas by the Public Utility Societies (Financial Assistance) Regulations, 1919 and 1920,[2] and the Housing Trusts (Financial Assistance) Regulations, 1919 and 1920,[3] the Minister of Health, with the approval of the Treasury, made Regulations in pursurance of subsection 1 of section 19 of the Housing, Town Planning, &c., Act, 1919, with regard to the contributions to be made by the Minister out of moneys provided by Parliament, to public utility societies and housing trusts towards the cost of carrying out any approved scheme for the provision of houses for the working classes ;

And whereas by Article VIII of each of the said Regulations it is provided that the societies and the trustees shall keep separate accounts relating to the approved scheme, and it is further provided that the accounts shall be audited by a district auditor in the manner and subject to the provisions therein mentioned.

Now therefore, the Minister of Health, in pursuance of his powers under section 5 of the District Auditors Act, 1879, and all other enactments in that behalf, hereby Orders and Prescribes, subject to any departure to which he may from time to time assent, as follows :—

ARTICLE I—This Order may be cited as " The Housing Accounts Order (Societies and Trusts), 1920."

[1] 9-10 G. 5. c. 35.
[2] S.R. & O., 1919, No. 1428 and S.R. & O., 1920, No. 134.
[3] S.R. & O., 1919, No. 1429 and S.R. & O., 1920, No. 135.

ARTICLE II—In this Order, the expressions " society " and " trust " have the same meaning as the expressions " public utility society " and " housing trust " in the Housing, Town Planning, &c., Act, 1919.

ARTICLE III—(1) The officer charged with the duty of keeping the accounts of the society or trust (hereinafter referred to as the " accounting officer ") shall duly make up and balance a separate set of double-entry ledger accounts for the approved housing scheme of the society or trust comprising,—

    (a) Personal accounts of the creditors, debtors, and cash officers.

    (b) Revenue and net revenue accounts.

    (c) Capital account or accounts.

(2) There shall be entered in the ledger a Housing (Approved Scheme) Balance Sheet in the form prescribed in the First Schedule to this Order.

ARTICLE IV—Such primary books, as are necessary for keeping account with the several tenants and otherwise for the purposes of recording the transactions which have to be entered in the several ledger accounts, shall be kept by the officer or officers to whom the duties in connection therewith are allotted by the society or trust.

Each officer or other person who receives money or material pertaining to the approved housing scheme shall promptly enter up and duly balance a debit and credit account of his transactions.

ARTICLE V—(1) The accounts of the approved scheme of the society or trust shall be made up and balanced to the 31st March in each year and submitted to the society or to the trust as soon as may be after that date.

(2) It shall be the duty of the accounting officer to submit these accounts to the district auditor at the time and place appointed by him for the audit.

(3) The officers or others who have personal accounts to render under this Order shall submit such accounts balanced to the 31st March in each case at the time and place appointed for the audit.

ARTICLE VI—The accounting officer shall prepare and submit to the district auditor at every audit a financial statement in duplicate in the form prescribed in the Second Schedule to this Order, and shall affix to one of the said statements an Audit Stamp of the value prescribed in the First Schedule to the District Auditors Act, 1879.

THE FIRST SCHEDULE

HOUSING (APPROVED SCHEME) BALANCE SHEET

CAPITAL LIABILITIES.	CAPITAL ASSETS.
Loans outstanding. Public Works Loans Commissioners, Do. Other lenders. Share Capital subscribed. Loan Stock subscribed.	Houses and other property (at original cost). Other Capital Assets (if any). Sinking Fund Assets (if any). Capital money in hand.
DISCHARGED CAPITAL OUTLAY (including Sinking Fund provision).	
REVENUE LIABILITIES.	REVENUE ASSETS.
Inland Revenue. Other creditors.	Tenants' rents uncollected. Other debtors. Cash in hands of treasurer. Do. other officers.
FUND BALANCES.	
Repairs Reserve Fund. Net Revenue Balance.	

THE SECOND SCHEDULE

............................(Insert name of Public
.   Utility Society or Housing Trust.)

FINANCIAL STATEMENT

The District Auditors Act, 1879 (*42 Vict. c.* 6).

STATEMENT OF THE INCOME AND EXPENDITURE OF THE ABOVE-NAMED SOCIETY (*or* TRUST) FOR THE YEAR ENDED THE 31ST DAY OF MARCH, 19 .

Name of Accounting
Officer   or   other
person keeping the ....
Accounts.

Office Address.....................

INCOME AND EXPENDITURE OF THE————— —

FOR THE YEAR ENDED THE

INCOME.

	£ s. d.	£ s. d.
Exchequer subsidy	— —	
Rents	— —	
Contributions from local authorities :—		
Other income :— [1]		
Total income	£	
Balance at beginning of the year .	£	
Total income and balance . .	£	

[1] Small items may be classed as " Miscellaneous."

PART II

RECEIPTS.

	£ s. d.	£ s. d.
Loans received	— —	
Other receipts :—		
Total receipts	£	
Balance at beginning of the year .	£	
Total receipts and balance . .	£	

NOTE.—If Sinking Funds or Maintenance Reserve Funds are set up,
Financial

PUBLIC UTILITY SOCIETY (*OR* HOUSING TRUST) Accounts Order.

31ST DAY OF MARCH, 19——

REVENUE.

EXPENDITURE.

	£ s. d.	£ s. d.
Administrative expenses	— —	
Maintenance and repairs to property . .	— —	
Taxes, rates and insurance . . .	— —	
Interest on loans (including Income Tax) .	— —	
Amount of debt repaid	— —	
Other expenditure :— [1]		
Total expenditure	£	
Balance at end of the year . .	£	
Total expenditure and balance . .	£	

[1] Small items may be classed as "Miscellaneous."

CAPITAL.

EXPENDITURE.

	£ s. d.	£ s. d.
Loan expenditure	— —	
Other expenditure :—		
Total expenditure	£	
Balance at end of the year . .	£	
Total expenditure and balance . .	∴	

the necessary entries should be made in the Revenue portion of the Statement.

Accounts
Order.

PART III—SUMMARY OF INCOME AND EXPENDITURE.

Income.

	£	s.	d.
On Revenue Account			
On Capital Account			
Total income . . . . . £			

Expenditure.

	£	s.	d.
On Revenue Account			
On Capital Account			
Total expenditure . . . . £			

Less amount, if any, disallowed at Audit .

Amount allowed at Audit .   .   .   £

Signed ....Accounting Officer.

....................day of................19........

I hereby certify that I have compared the entries in this Financial
Statement with the accounts of the Society (*or* Trust) relating thereto,
that I have ascertained by Audit the correctness of this Statement, and
that the expenditure of the Society (*or* Trust) during the year ended
the 31st day of March, 19.., included in this Statement and allowed
by me at the Audit is [1]..

....

As witness my hand this.............day of.............19...

..............| Stamp. |... ....District Auditor.

[1] The amount to be inserted in words at length.

Given under the Official Seal of the Minister of Health
this Fourth day of May, in the year One thousand
nine hundred and twenty.

(L.S.)   F. L. TURNER,
                    Assistant Secretary, Ministry of Health.

MODEL RULES FOR PUBLIC UTILITY SOCIETIES

ACCEPTED BY THE MINISTRY AS AFFORDING SUFFICIENT
COMPLIANCE WITH THE SPECIFIC POINTS DEALT
WITH IN THE ARTICLE X OF THE PUBLIC
UTILITY SOCIETIES (FINANCIAL ASSISTANCE)
REGULATIONS, 1919

1. *Membership.* The members of the society shall be those persons whose names are appended to these rules, and any other persons whom the board of management may admit. Every member shall hold at least one share in the society. The board of management shall not refuse to admit to membership of the society any person who has been a tenant of the society for not less than three months.

2. *Management of Business of Society.* The management of the business of the society shall be vested in the board of management for the time being, who may either directly or by delegation exercise all such powers as may be exercised by the society, except those expressly required by these rules or by statute to be exercised by the society in general meeting.

3. *Appointment of Board of Management.* The board of management, from the date of registration of the society to the first annual general meeting of the society, shall consist of those persons whose names are appended to these rules, with power to add to their number. In all subsequent periods the board shall consist of not less than five or more than twelve members. Two of such members, or, if the total number of members exceeds eight, three of such members shall be tenant members appointed by the tenant members' committee. The remaining members shall be elected at the annual general meeting of the society.[1]

4. *Tenant Members' Committee.* Tenant members shall elect annually from among themselves a tenant members'

[1] The rules may, if desired, provide for the representation of local authorities on the board of management.

committee [1] consisting of   members and each
tenant member shall be entitled to one vote for the
election of such committee. The committee, in addition
to the rights, powers and duties which are conferred on
or vested in them by these rules, shall have such rights,
powers and duties as may be delegated to them, with
their concurrence, by the board of management.

5. *Votes of Members.* At all general meetings of the
society each fully paid-up share against which there is
no set-off in the books of the society shall carry one vote,
and five times that amount of loan stock held by a
member or tenant member shall carry one vote, but the
possession of loan stock apart from membership shall
not entitle its holder either to a vote or to attendance at
meetings. Votes may be given personally or by proxy.[2]

6. *Security of Tenure.* Each tenant shall have undisturbed occupancy of his house and garden so long as—

(*a*) He fulfils the tenancy regulations made by the
board of management ;

(*b*) He pays any rent or debts due from him to the
Society ; and

(*c*) He and the occupants of his house avoid any conduct detrimental to good neighbourship :.

Provided that a tenant shall not be given notice to
quit by the board of management on the ground of
conduct detrimental to good neighbourship except with
the concurrence of the tenant members' committee.

7. *Application of Profits.* Any profits remaining to the
society after providing for—

(*a*) The annual charges in respect of interest and
repayments of principal, on the loans and loan
stock raised by the society ;

(*b*) The taxes, rates, rents, insurance premiums, or
other charges payable by the society in respect
of any land or houses belonging to them ;

(*c*) The costs of administration and management and
of repairs of property ;

(*d*) Such allocations to a reserve fund as may be
determined by the board of management ;

[1] The committee may, if desired, be a tenants' committee, appointed
by all the tenants of the society. But in that case the rules must
provide that the members of the board of management appointed
by the committee must be tenant members of the society. See rule 4.

[2] The regulations admit of further limitation being imposed on the
number of votes which may be recorded by any one member.

(*e*) Any other necessary expenses incurred by the board of management ; and

(*f*) A dividend not exceeding the rate authorised by rule ¹, on the share capital of the society ; shall be applied, in such manner as the board of management may determine, for the benefit of the tenants generally.

8. *Regulations by the Minister of Health.* In order that financial assistance may be obtained from the Exchequer under the Housing, Town Planning, &c., Act, 1919, towards the loan charges in respect of any houses provided by the society under a scheme approved by the Minister of Health under that Act, the regulations made by the Minister [which are set out in the appendix to these rules]² shall in all respects be complied with, and these rules, so far as they apply to any subject-matter of those regulations, shall have effect subject to those regulations.

¹ Under the Housing, Town Planning, &c., Act, 1919, the rate may be 6 per cent.
² The words in square brackets may be omitted.

APPENDIX VII

ADDITIONAL POWERS ACT DOCUMENTS

STATUTORY RULES AND ORDERS, 1920, No. 56

HOUSING, ENGLAND

The Housing (Regulation of Building) Order, 1920, dated 22nd January 1920, made by the Minister of Health under section 5 (1) of Housing (Additional Powers) Act, 1919 (9 & 10 Geo. 5. c. 99).

65,788.

The Minister of Health, under the powers conferred on him by section 5 (1) of the Housing (Additional Powers) Act, 1919,[1] and all other powers enabling him in that behalf, hereby makes the following order :—

1. This order may be cited as the Housing (Regulation of Building) Order, 1920.

2. (1) In this order unless the context otherwise requires :—

"The Act" means the Housing (Additional Powers) Act, 1919 ;

"The Minister" means the Minister of Health ;

"Building Owner" means the person for whom or on whose behalf any works or buildings are being or are proposed to be constructed [2] ;

"Builder" means the person who is directly employed by the building owner to construct any works or buildings, or, where no person is so employed, means the building owner ;

"Order" means an order made by a local authority under subsection (1) of section 5 of the Act.

[1] The operation of section 5 of the Act is limited by section 15 to two years from the 23rd December 1919.

[2] By section 5 (6) of the Act the expression "construction of any works or buildings" is defined as including the making of alterations or additions to existing works or buildings.

(2) The Interpretation Act, 1889,[1] shall apply to the interpretation of this order as it applies to the interpretation of an Act of Parliament.

3. (1) Before making an order in respect of any works or buildings the local authority shall give to the building owner and builder of those works or buildings not less than seven days' notice of their intention to make such order, and shall take into consideration any representations or objections in writing which may be made by the building owner or builder or by any other person who satisfies the local authority that he is a person who would be aggrieved by the proposed order, if made.

(2) The local authority may, in any case in which they think fit, afford to any person who is entitled to make and has made such representations or objections as aforesaid an opportunity of appearing before and being heard by the local authority or by any committee appointed or authorised for that purpose by the local authority.

4. (1) Any order made by the local authority after considering any representations or objections so made shall come into force on the date specified in the order, not being later than twenty-one days after the date thereof.

(2) The order may contain provisions authorising any work which may be specified therein for the purpose of the preservation or protection of the works or buildings under construction, and may exempt from the operation of the order any part of the works or buildings if the local authority is satisfied that the employment of labour or materials on that part of the works or buildings will not interfere with the provision of dwelling accommodation for the area of the local authority.

5. An order shall remain in force for such period not exceeding six months as may be specified therein :

Provided that it shall be lawful for the local authority, if they think fit, at any time to vary or rescind the order or from time to time to extend the order for a further period not exceeding six months ; but in the case of any proposed variation (except by way of relaxing the terms of the order) or of any proposed extension of the order the provisions of article 3 of this order shall apply in all respects as they apply to the making of the original order.

---

[1] 52–3 Vict. c. 63.

Regulation of Building Order.

6. A duly certified copy of any order made by a local authority or of any order varying, rescinding, or extending an existing order shall forthwith be served upon the building owner and builder and upon the persons, if any, who have made representations or objections with regard thereto.

7. (1) Any notice, order, or other document which in pursuance of the provisions of this order is required to be given or served by the local authority to or upon any building owner or builder or other person may be served :—

> (a) by sending the same by post as a registered letter to, or leaving it at, the usual or last known address or place of business of the person required to be served or by delivery of the same personally to him ; or
>
> (b) in the case of the building owner or the builder, if his name or address is not known to the local authority, by addressing the same to the building owner or the builder, as the case may be, and delivering it to the person in charge of the works or buildings under construction or affixing it in some conspicuous manner to the site of the works or buildings or proposed works or buildings.

(2) In the case of a company or other corporate body delivery of any notice, order, or other document to their clerk or secretary or other person employed at their office shall be deemed to be delivery thereof personally to the person required to be served.

8. The forms set out in the schedule to this order or forms substantially to the like effect shall be used by the local authority for the purpose of this order.

9. The Minister may upon the application of a local authority dispense with the service of any notices required by this order or with any other requirement of this order if he is satisfied that there is reasonable cause for such dispensation, and any such dispensation may be given either before or after the time at which the notice is required to be served or other act or thing required to be done.

SCHEDULE

FORM 1

NOTICE OF PROPOSAL TO PROHIBIT CONSTRUCTION OF WORKS OR BUILDINGS

HOUSING (ADDITIONAL POWERS) ACT, 1919

To [1]   of

the $\left\{\begin{matrix}\text{building owner [2]}\\\text{builder}\end{matrix}\right\}$ of the works and buildings in
course of construction [*or* proposed to be constructed]
at [3]   ,

being a place within the area of the council.

TAKE NOTICE that on the   day of
, 19   , the [4]
(hereinafter called " the council ") proposed to make an
order under section 5 (1) of the Housing (Additional
Powers) Act, 1919, prohibiting the construction of the
above-mentioned works or buildings on the ground that
the provision of dwelling accommodation for the area of
the council is or is likely to be delayed by a deficiency
of labour or materials arising out of the employment of
labour or materials in the construction of those works
or buildings, and that the construction of the said works
or buildings is of less public importance for the time being
than the provision of dwelling accommodation.

AND TAKE NOTICE that the council will consider any
representations or objections in writing addressed to the
clerk to the council at their office at [5]
which reach the said office not later than the
day of   , 19   .

[AND TAKE NOTICE that you may appear before the
council [*or* before the   committee of
the council] at their office at   on the
day of   , 19   , and will be
heard in support of your representations or objections.]

Dated this   day of   , 19   .

Signature of clerk of local authority

. . . .

[1] Insert name, residence or place of business, and description, if
known, of building owner or builder. If the name of the building

owner or builder is not known, the notice may be addressed to "the
building owner" or "the builder," as the case may be. If the address
of either is not known, the notice may be served by being delivered
to the person in charge of the works or building, or by being affixed
in a conspicuous manner to the site.

² Strike out the word not required.

³ Insert such a description of the site as will suffice for its identification.

⁴ Insert name of local authority.

⁵ Insert address of local authority's office.

FORM 2

FORM OF ORDER UNDER SECTION 5 (1) OF THE HOUSING (ADDITIONAL POWERS) ACT, 1919, PROHIBITING CONSTRUCTION OF WORKS OR BUILDINGS

WHEREAS it has appeared to the ¹
(hereinafter called "the council") that the provision
of dwelling accommodation for their area is or is likely
to be delayed by a deficiency of labour or materials
arising out of the employment of labour and materials
in the construction ² of the works or buildings upon a
site within the area of the council hereinafter described
and that the construction of those works or buildings
is of less public importance for the time being than the
provision of dwelling accommodation :

AND WHEREAS the notices required by the Housing
(Regulation of Building) Order, 1920, to be served on the
building owner and builder of the said works or buildings
have been duly served and the council have taken into
consideration all representations and objections made
to them in accordance with the terms of the said order :

NOW, THEREFORE, the council in exercise of the powers
conferred on them by subsection (1) of section 5 of the
Housing (Additional Powers) Act, 1919, hereby make
the following order :—

1. [Save as hereinafter provided] the construction of
the works and buildings now under construction or
proposed to be constructed at ³
                              is hereby prohibited.

2. This order shall come into operation on the
         day of   , 19 , and shall con-
tinue in operation until the   day of
              , 19 .

3. Notwithstanding anything in this order, the following

work may be carried out for the purpose of the preservation or protection of the said works and buildings :— Regulation of Building Order.

[*Specify in detail the nature of the work authorised*]

4. The following portions of the works and buildings are exempted from this order :—

[*Specify in detail the exempted portions*]

Dated this   day of   , 19 .

(*To be sealed with the common seal of the local authority*)
Signature of clerk of local authority,

....

Note.—Any person who is served by the local authority with a copy of this order is entitled to appeal to the Minister of Health within seven days after the copy of the order is served on him by giving notice of appeal in the form annexed. Any other person who is aggrieved by the order may appeal to the Minister of Health within fourteen days after the date of the order by giving similar notice of appeal.

Rules determining the procedure on any such appeal are contained in the Regulation of Building (Appeal Procedure) Rules, 1920, which have been placed on sale, so that copies may be purchased, either directly or through any bookseller, from His Majesty's Stationery Office at the following addresses : Imperial House, Kingsway, London, W.C.1 ; 28 Abingdon Street, London, S.W.1 ; 37 Peter Street, Manchester ; and 1 St. Andrew's Crescent, Cardiff.

Under section 5 (4) of the Housing (Additional Powers) Act, 1919, any person who acts in contravention of or fails to comply with any of the provisions of this order is liable on summary conviction to a fine not exceeding £100, and if the offence is a continuing offence, to a fine not exceeding £50 for each day during which the offence continues.

[1] Insert name of local authority.

[2] By section 5 (6) of the Housing (Additional Powers) Act, 1919, the expression " construction of any works or buildings " is defined as including the making of alterations or additions to existing works or buildings.

[3] Insert such a description of the site as will suffice for its identification.

FORM OF NOTICE OF APPEAL AGAINST ORDER OF LOCAL AUTHORITY

HOUSING (ADDITIONAL POWERS) ACT, 1919

(Notice of appeal may be given by filling up and sending either this print or a copy of it to the Clerk to the Appeal Tribunal, Housing Department, Ministry of Health, Whitehall, London, S.W.1. Such notice must be given, in the case of a building owner, builder, or other person who has been served by the local authority with a copy of the order against which the appeal is made, within seven days after the date on which the copy is served on him. In the case of any other person aggrieved by the order notice of appeal must be given within fourteen days after the date of the order.)

Regulation
of Building
Order.

Full name of appellant.............................

Full address of appellant..........................

Address or description of the works or buildings in respect
of which the appeal is made...................

....

I, the undersigned, being the $\frac{\text{builder}^1}{\text{building owner}}$ within
the meaning of the Housing (Regulation of Building)
Order, 1920, of the above-mentioned works or buildings,
hereby appeal to the Minister of Health against the order
dated the   , 19   , and made
by the ³   prohibiting
the construction of the said works or buildings.

[*Or* ³

I, the undersigned, being a person aggrieved by an
order dated the   , 19   , and made by
the ³
prohibiting the construction of the said works or buildings,
hereby appeal to the Minister of Health against the said
Order.]

[⁴ A certified copy of the said order was received by
me on the   , 19   , and [a copy thereof] is
enclosed herewith.]

The grounds on which I appeal are as follows :—

(*Here insert a concise statement of the facts and grounds on
which the appeal is based*)

Signature of appellant...............

Date............

¹ Strike out whichever is inapplicable.
² Strike out if inapplicable.
³ State name of local authority.
⁴ Strike out if the appellant has not been served with a certified
copy of the order.

FORM 3

FORM OF ORDER RESCINDING ORDER UNDER SECTION 5 (1) OF THE HOUSING (ADDITIONAL POWERS) ACT, 1919, PROHIBITING CONSTRUCTION OF WORKS OR BUILDINGS

WHEREAS by an order dated the   day of
19   , the ¹
(hereinafter called "the council") prohibited the

construction of the works or buildings under construction Regulation
of Building
Order. or proposed to be constructed at ²
and the said order expires on the   day of   .

AND WHEREAS it has appeared to the council that the grounds on which the said order was based no longer hold good and that the operation of the said order should accordingly be rescinded :

NOW THEREFORE the council in exercise of the powers conferred on them by subsection (1) of section 5 of the Housing (Additional Powers) Act, 1919, hereby rescind the said order.

Dated this   day of   , 19 .

(To be sealed with the common seal of the local authority)
Signature of clerk of local authority

. . . .

¹ Insert name of local authority.
² Insert such a description of the site as will suffice for its identification.

FORM 4

FORM OF ORDER VARYING ORDER UNDER SECTION 5 (1) OF THE HOUSING (ADDITIONAL POWERS) ACT, 1919, PROHIBITING CONSTRUCTION OF WORKS OR BUILDINGS

WHEREAS by an order dated the   day of   ,
19 , the ¹
(hereinafter called " the council ") prohibited the construction of the works or buildings under construction or proposed to be constructed at ²
and the said order expires on the   day of   .

AND WHEREAS it has appeared to the council that it is expedient that the terms of the said order should be varied in the manner hereinafter appearing :

³AND WHEREAS the notices required by the Housing (Regulation of Building) Order, 1920, to be served upon the building owner and builder of the said works or buildings have been duly served by the council and the council have taken into consideration all representations and objections made to them in accordance with the terms of the said order :

NOW THEREFORE the council in exercise of the powers conferred on them by subsection (1) of section 5 of the Housing (Additional Powers) Act, 1919, hereby order

Regulation
of Building
Order.

that the terms of the said order dated the   day
of   , 19 , and relating to the works and
buildings above referred to shall be varied as follows :

[*Specify in detail the variations of the original order*]

Dated this   day of   , 19 .

(*To be sealed with the common seal of the local authority*)

Signature of clerk of local authority

. . . .

Note.—[³ Any person who is served by the local authority with a copy
of this order is entitled to appeal to the Minister of Health within seven
days after the copy of the order is served on him by giving notice
of appeal in the form annexed. Any other person who is aggrieved
by the order may appeal to the Minister of Health within fourteen
days after the date of the order by giving similar notice of appeal.]

See page 694. Rules determining the procedure on any such appeal are contained
in the Regulation of Building (Appeal Procedure) Rules, 1920, which
have been placed on sale, so that copies may be purchased, either
directly or through any bookseller, from His Majesty's Stationery
Office, at the following addresses : Imperial House, Kingsway, London,
W.C.1 ; 28 Abingdon Street, London S.W.1 ; 37 Peter Street, Manchester ; and 1 St. Andrew's Crescent, Cardiff.

Under section 5 (4) of the Housing (Additional Powers) Act, 1919
any person who acts in contravention of or fails to comply with any
of the provisions of this order is liable on summary conviction to a fine
not exceeding £100, and if the offence is a continuing offence, to a fine
not exceeding £50 for each day during which the offence continues.

¹ Insert name of local authority.
² Insert such a description of the site as will suffice for its identification.
³ This should be struck out in cases where the variation is by way
of a relaxation of the terms of the original order.

FORM 5

FORM OF ORDER EXTENDING ORDER UNDER SECTION 5 (1)
OF THE HOUSING (ADDITIONAL POWERS) ACT, 1919,
PROHIBITING CONSTRUCTION OF WORKS OR BUILDINGS

WHEREAS by an order dated the   day of

19 , the ¹
(hereinafter called "the council") prohibited the construction of the works or buildings under construction
or proposed to be constructed at ²
and the said order expires on the   day of   .

AND WHEREAS it has appeared to the council that the
grounds on which the said order was based still hold

good and that the operation of the said order should Regulation of Building Order. be extended accordingly :

AND WHEREAS the notices required by the Housing (Regulation of Building) Order, 1920, to be served upon the building owner and builder of the said works or buildings have been duly served by the council and the council have taken into consideration all representations and objections made to them in accordance with the terms of the said order :

Now THEREFORE the council in exercise of the powers conferred on them by subsection (1) of section 5 of the Housing (Additional Powers) Act, 1919, hereby order that the said order dated the   day of   , 19 , and relating to the works and buildings above referred to shall continue in operation until the   day of   , 19 .

Dated this   day of   , 19 .

(To be sealed with the common seal of the local authority)

Signature of clerk of local authority

. . . .

Note.—Any person who is served by the local authority with a copy of this order is entitled to appeal to the Minister of Health within seven days after the copy of the order is served on him by giving notice of appeal in the form annexed. Any other person who is aggrieved by the order may appeal to the Minister of Health within fourteen days after the date of the order by giving similar notice of appeal.

Rules determining the procedure of any such appeal are contained See page 694. in the Regulation of Building (Appeal Procedure) Rules, 1920, which have been placed on sale, so that copies may be purchased, either directly or through any bookseller, from His Majesty's Stationery Office, at the following addresses : Imperial House, Kingsway, London, W.C.1 ; 28 Abingdon Street, London, S.W.1 ; 37 Peter Street, Manchester ; and 1 St. Andrew's Crescent, Cardiff.

Under section 5 (4) of the Housing (Additional Powers) Act, 1919, any person who acts in contravention of or fails to comply with any of the provisions of this order is liable on summary conviction to a fine not exceeding £100, and if the offence is a continuing offence, to a fine not exceeding £50 for each day during which the offence continues.

¹ Insert name of local authority.
² Insert such a description of the site as will suffice for its identification.

Given under the official seal of the Minister of Health, this Twenty-second day of January, in the year One thousand nine hundred and twenty.

(L.S.)   CHRISTOPHER ADDISON.

STATUTORY RULES AND ORDERS, 1920, No. 57

HOUSING, ENGLAND

*The Regulation of Building (Appeal Procedure) Rules,
1920, dated 22nd January 1920, made by the Minister
of Health under section 5 (2) of the Housing (Additional
Powers) Act, 1919 (9 & 10 Geo. 5. c. 99).*

65,789.

The Minister of Health, under the powers conferred on
him by section 5 (2) of the Housing (Additional Powers)
Act, 1919, and all other powers enabling him in that
behalf, hereby makes the following rules :—

1. These rules may be cited as the Regulation of
Building (Appeal Procedure) Rules, 1920.

2. (1) In these rules, unless the context otherwise
requires—

"The Act" means the Housing (Additional
Powers) Act, 1919 ;

"The Minister" means the Minister of Health ;

"Order" means an order made by a local
authority under section 5 (1) of the Act ;

"Appeal tribunal" means the standing tribunal
of appeal to be appointed by the Minister under
Section 5 (2) of the Act ;

"Clerk to the appeal tribunal" means such person
as the Minister may from time to time appoint to
act as clerk to the appeal tribunal ;

"Building owner" and "builder" have the same
meaning as in the Housing (Regulation of Building)
Order, 1920.[1]

(2) The Interpretation Act, 1889,[2] shall apply to the
interpretation of these rules as it applies to the interpretation of an Act of Parliament.

3. (1) An appeal to the Minister from an order made
by a local authority by any person aggrieved thereby
shall be made by sending to the clerk to the appeal
tribunal a notice of appeal signed by the appellant or
by his duly authorised agent.

(2) Such notice of appeal must be sent in the case of
a building owner or builder or other person who has been

---

[1] S.R. & O., 1920, No. 56.   [2] 52-3 Vict. c. 63.

served by the local authority with a certified copy of the order within seven days after the date on which the said copy is served on him, or in the case of any other person aggrieved by the order within fourteen days after the date of the order.

(3) In the case of a building owner or builder or other person who has been served with a certified copy of the order, such certified copy or a copy thereof shall be sent with the notice of appeal.

4. The clerk to the appeal tribunal shall, as soon as may be after receipt of the notice aforesaid, send to the local authority a copy of the notice of appeal.

5. The local authority shall, within seven days after the receipt by them of the said notification, send a notice to the clerk to the appeal tribunal and to the appellant stating whether and to what extent they admit the facts stated in the appellant's notice of appeal and including a concise statement of the grounds on which the order is based.

6. The appeal tribunal may at any stage of the proceedings allow the amendment of any notice, statement, or particulars on such terms as they think fit, and may require the appellant or the local authority within a specified time to furnish in writing such further particulars as they think necessary.

7. (1) If, after considering the notice of appeal and the statement of the local authority in reply and any further particulars which may have been furnished by either party, the appeal tribunal are of opinion that the case is of such a nature that it can properly be determined without a hearing, they may dispense with a hearing, and may determine the appeal summarily.

(2) Subject as aforesaid, the appeal tribunal shall fix a date for the hearing of the appeal, and shall give not less than seven days' notice to the appellant and the local authority of the time and place of the hearing.

8. Before the consideration of an appeal made by any person other than the building owner or builder or other person who has been served by the local authority with a certified copy of the order against which the appeal is made, the appeal tribunal shall decide whether the appellant is a person aggrieved by the order, and their decision shall be final and conclusive.

9. The procedure of the appeal tribunal at the hearing

of an appeal shall be such as they may from time to time determine.

10. The appeal tribunal may, if they think fit, and subject to such conditions as they may impose, proceed with the consideration of any appeal, notwithstanding any failure or omission by any person to comply with the requirements of these rules.

11. The decision of the appeal tribunal shall be in writing signed by the chairman and clerk, and a copy of the decision shall forthwith be sent to the appellant and to the local authority.

12. The forms set out in the schedule to these rules or forms substantially to the like effect shall be used for the purpose of these rules.

13. (1) Any notice or other document required or authorised by these rules to be sent to the clerk to the appeal tribunal shall be sufficiently sent if sent by post in a registered letter addressed to the Clerk of the Appeal Tribunal, Ministry of Health, Whitehall, London, S.W.1.

(2) Any notice or other document required or authorised by these rules to be sent by the clerk to the appeal tribunal or by the local authority to any appellant shall be sufficiently sent if sent by post to the address stated in the notice of appeal.

(3) Unless the contrary is proved any notice or document sent as aforesaid shall be deemed to be served at the time at which a letter would be delivered in the ordinary course of post.

SCHEDULE

Form I

Form of Notice of Appeal against Order of Local Authority

HOUSING (ADDITIONAL POWERS) ACT, 1919

(Notice of appeal may be given by filling up and sending either this print or a copy of it to the Clerk to the Appeal Tribunal, Housing Department, Ministry of Health, Whitehall, London, S.W.1. Such notice must be given, in the case of a building owner, builder, or other person who has been served by the local authority with a copy of the order against which the appeal is made, within seven days after the date on which the copy is served on him. In the case of any other person aggrieved by the order notice of appeal must be given within fourteen days after the date of the order.)

Full name of appellant..............................
Full address of appellant..........................

Address or description of the works or buildings in re- spect of which the appeal is made................

Appeal
Procedure
Rules.

....

I, the undersigned, being the $\dfrac{\text{builder}^1}{\text{building owner}}$ within the meaning of the Housing (Regulation of Building Order, 1920, of the above-mentioned works or buildings, hereby appeal to the Minister of Health against the order dated the , 19 , and made by the [2] prohibiting the construction of the said works or buildings,

[*Or* [3]

I, the undersigned, being a person aggrieved by an order dated the , 19 , and made by the [2] prohibiting the construction of the said works or buildings, hereby appeal to the Minister of Health against the said order.]

[[4] A certified copy of the said order was received by me on the , 19 , and [a copy thereof] is enclosed herewith.]

The grounds on which I appeal are as follows :—

[*Here insert a concise statement of the facts and grounds on which the appeal is based*]

Signature of appellant...................

Date..............

[1] Strike out whichever is inapplicable.
[2] State name of local authority.
[3] Strike out if inapplicable.
[4] Strike out if the appellant has not been served with a certified copy of the order.

Form II

Form of Statement of Reply by Local Authority

HOUSING (ADDITIONAL POWERS) ACT, 1919

In the matter of an appeal made by [1]
of · against an order
dated the , 19 , prohibiting the
construction of works or buildings at [5]

Appeal Procedure Rules.

The grounds on which the above-mentioned order was based are as follows :—

[*Here insert concise statement of grounds*]

The following facts stated in the appellant's notice of appeal are admitted :—

[*Here insert statement of facts admitted*]

Dated the   day of   , 19

Signature of clerk of local authority,

....

[1] State name and address of appellant.
[2] Insert description of site.

Given under the official seal of the Minister of Health, this Twenty-second day of January, in the year One thousand nine hundred and twenty.

(L.S.)   CHRISTOPHER ADDISON.

STATUTORY RULES AND ORDERS, 1920, No. 197

HOUSING, ENGLAND

The Housing (Local Bonds) Regulations, 1920, dated 25th February 1920, made by the Minister of Health under paragraph (6) of the Schedule to the Housing (Additional Powers) Act, 1919 (9 & 10 Geo. 5. c. 99).

65,811.

Local Bonds Regulations.

The Minister of Health in pursuance of the powers conferred upon him by paragraph (6) of the schedule to the Housing (Additional Powers) Act, 1919, hereby makes the following regulations :—

Title and Interpretation

1. These regulations may be cited as the Housing (Local Bonds) Regulations, 1920.

2. (1) In these regulations, unless the context otherwise requires—

" the Act " means the Housing (Additional Powers) Act, 1919 ;

" holder " means registered holder.

(2) The Interpretation Act, 1889 (52 & 53 Vict. c. 63) applies to the interpretation of these regulations as it applies to the interpretation of an Act of Parliament.

Issue of Local Bonds

3. (1) Local bonds shall be issued at par and interest thereon shall be payable half-yearly on the thirty-first day of March and the thirtieth day of September in each year : Provided that in the case of any person who holds on the thirtieth day of September bonds to a nominal value not exceeding £50, the local authority may pay interest yearly on the thirty-first day of March, paying in addition interest at the rate applicable to the bonds on any interest which has accrued in respect of the period up to the thirtieth day of September.

(2) Applications for local bonds shall be for amounts of five, ten, twenty, fifty or one hundred pounds or multiples of one hundred pounds.

(3) Local bonds shall, subject to the provisions of this Article, be repayable at par at the office of the local authority not less than five years after the date of issue according to the terms of issue, and no interest shall be payable thereon in respect of any period after the date upon which the bond is repayable.

(4) Where a local authority accepts a local bond issued by another local authority in payment or part payment of the purchase price of a house erected in pursuance of any scheme under the Housing Acts, 1890 to 1919, the local authority by whom the bond was issued shall, if so requested by the other local authority, redeem the bond by paying the nominal amount thereof to that local authority.

(5) The first payment of interest on any local bond shall be adjusted in accordance with the date of issue of the bond and any sum paid by way of repayment or redemption shall include interest accrued to the date of repayment or redemption.

(6) Nothing in this Article shall be construed as prohibiting a local authority from redeeming a local bond at any time by agreement with the holder of the bond, if they shall think fit to do so.

(7) A local bond repaid or redeemed by a local authority shall be cancelled.

Registration and Certificates

4. A local authority issuing local bonds shall appoint a registrar for the purposes of these regulations, and may direct him to act on their behalf for the purposes of all or any of the things which they are authorised to do under these regulations.

5. (1) The local authority shall keep a register (hereinafter called the " local bonds register ") of all persons who are holders for the time being of local bonds.

(2) The local bonds register shall contain the following particulars :—

(a) the name, address and description of each holder, a statement of the denomination of the bonds held by him and the periods for which they are issued and the numbers and dates of the certificates issued to him as hereinafter provided ;

(b) the date of registration of each holder and the date on which he ceased to be so registered.

(3) The local bonds register shall be *prima facie* evidence of any matter entered therein in accordance with these regulations and of the title of the persons entered therein as holders of local bonds.

6. (1) The local authority shall issue to each holder of a local bond a certificate in respect thereof, duly numbered and dated, and specifying the denomination of the bond and the period for which it is issued.

(2) The certificate shall be *prima facie* evidence of the title of the person therein named, his executors, administrators or assigns, to the bond therein specified, but the want of a certificate, if accounted for to the satisfaction of the local authority, shall not prevent the holder of a bond from disposing of and transferring the bond.

(3) If a certificate is worn out or damaged, the local authority, on the production thereof, may cancel it and issue a new certificate in lieu thereof.

(4) If a certificate is lost or destroyed, the local authority on proof thereof to their satisfaction, and, if they so

require, on receiving an indemnity against any claims Local
Bonds
Regulations. in respect thereof, may give a new certificate in lieu of the certificate lost or destroyed.

(5) An entry of the issue of a substituted certificate shall be made in the local bonds register.

(6) A certificate shall be in the form set out in the schedule hereto or in a form substantially to the like effect.

Transfer of Local Bonds

7. (1) The transfer of a local bond shall be by deed, in the form set out in the schedule hereto or in a form substantially to the like effect.

(2) A local bond may be transferred in whole or in part, so however that any part transferred shall not be for an amount other than an amount for which a local bond may be issued by a local authority.

(3) Unless the local authority have compounded for stamp duty, every deed of transfer shall be duly stamped and the consideration shall be truly stated therein.

(4) The deed of transfer shall be delivered to and retained by the local authority and the local authority shall enter a note thereof in a book to be called the "register of transfers of local bonds," and shall endorse on the deed of transfer a notice of that entry.

(5) The local authority shall, upon receipt of the deed of transfer duly executed together with the certificate issued in respect of the bond, enter the name of the transferee in the local bonds register and shall issue a new certificate or certificates to the transferee, or to the transferor and transferee, as the case may require.

(6) Until the deed of transfer and the certificate have been delivered to the local authority as aforesaid, the local authority shall not be affected by the transfer, and the transferee shall not be entitled to receive any payment of interest on the bond.

(7) The local authority before registering a transfer of a local bond may, if they think fit, require evidence by statutory declaration or otherwise of the title of any person claiming to make the transfer.

Closing of Local Bonds Register

8. The local authority may close the local bonds register for a period not exceeding thirty days immediately

Local
Bonds
Regulations.

before the thirty-first day of March and the thirtieth day of September in any year respectively, and notwithstanding the receipt by the local authority during those periods of any deed of transfer, the half-yearly payment of interest next falling due may be made to the persons registered as holders of local bonds on the date of the closing of the register.

Transmission of Local Bonds

9. (1) Any person becoming entitled to a local bond by reason of the death or bankruptcy of a holder or by any lawful means other than a transfer may, by the production of such evidence of title as the local authority may require, either be registered as holder of the bond, or, instead of being himself registered, may make such transfer of the bond as the holder could have made, and the local authority shall issue a certificate accordingly.

(2) Until such evidence as aforesaid has been furnished to the local authority, the local authority shall not be affected by the transmission of the bond and no person claiming by virtue thereof shall be entitled to receive any payment of interest thereon.

(3) Where two or more persons are registered as holders of a local bond they shall be deemed to be joint holders with right of survivorship between them.

Interest on Local Bonds

10. (1) Unless the holder of a local bond otherwise requests, the local authority may pay the interest thereon by posting a warrant to the holder at his address as shown in the local bonds register.

(2) The posting by the local authority of a letter containing an interest warrant addressed to a holder as aforesaid shall, as respects the liability of the local authority, be equivalent to the delivery of the warrant to the holder himself.

11. The local authority shall not be required to pay any executors or administrators any interest on local bonds held by their testator or intestate until the probate of the will or the letters of administration has or have been left with the local authority for registration.

12. The local authority before paying any interest

on any local bonds may, if they think fit, require evidence by statutory declaration or otherwise of the title of any person claiming a right to receive the interest. Local Bonds Regulations.

13. Where more persons than one are registered as joint holders of a local bond, any one of them may give an effectual receipt for any interest thereon, unless notice to the contrary has been given to the local authority by any other of them.

General

14. No notice of any trust shall be entered in the local bonds register or in any other book kept by the local authority or be receivable by the local authority.

15. (1) If at any time any interest due on any local bonds remains unpaid for two months after demand in writing, the persons entitled thereto may apply to the High Court for a receiver and the court may, if it thinks fit, appoint a receiver on such terms as it thinks fit.

(2) The receiver shall have the like power of collecting, receiving, recovering and applying moneys, and of assessing, making and recovering all rates for the purpose of obtaining the same, as the local authority or any officer thereof would or might have, and such other powers and duties as the court thinks fit, and shall apply all moneys so collected and received, after paying all such costs as the court may direct, for the purposes of these regulations.

16. A person taking or holding local bonds shall not be concerned to enquire or to take notice whether the issue thereof was or was not in accordance with these regulations, or whether or not the local authority or any meeting thereof was properly constituted or convened, or whether or not the proceedings at a meeting of the local authority were legal or regular, or to see to the application of any money raised by the issue of local bonds or be answerable for any loss or misapplication thereof.

17. If at any time any interest on any local bonds is unclaimed at the time for payment thereof, the amount shall, nevertheless, on demand at any subsequent time, be paid to the person showing his right thereto, but without interest in the meantime.

18. Where the local authority sell, lease or otherwise

Local
Bonds
Regulations.

dispose of any land or property charged as security for any local bonds, the land or property shall in the hands of the purchaser or lessee be absolutely free from any charge for that purpose and he shall not be bound to enquire into the application of the money arising from such sale, lease or disposal, or be in any way responsible for the misapplication or non-application thereof.

19. A local authority may pay such expenses in connection with the issue of local bonds (including commission) as the Minister may approve.

SCHEDULE

FORM OF CERTIFICATE OF REGISTRATION

Certificate of Registration of a Local Bond

No. . .

. . . . . . % local bond for £. . . . . . . .issued by. . . . .
REPAYABLE. . . . . .19 , ...
. . . .
at the office of the local authority (*see* back).

THIS is to certify that. . . . . .of. . . . .
. . . . .is the registered holder of a local bond for
. . . . .pounds (£   ) issued by the above-named local authority under the Housing (Additional Powers) Act, 1919, and the Housing (Local Bonds) Regulations, 1920.

Signed. . . . .
Registrar.

Date. . . . .

No deed transferring the whole or any part of the registered bonds represented by this certificate will be registered until the certificate has been delivered to the registrar of the authority.

Change of address must be notified to the registrar.

Issue of Local Bonds

1. Local bonds are issued at par and interest will be payable half-yearly on the thirty-first day of March and the thirtieth day of September. The bonds will bear interest from the date of purchase. [1] When the total holding does not exceed £50 interest will be paid yearly on the thirty-first day of March.

[1] To be omitted if the local authority does not adopt this provision.

2. Local bonds are issued for amounts of five, ten, Local twenty, fifty or one hundred pounds or multiples of one Bonds Regulations. hundred pounds.

3. Local bonds are issued for periods of five or more years and are repayable at par at the office of the local authority at the end of the period of issue. No interest will be payable thereon in respect of any period after the date on which the bond is repayable.

4. Local bonds are secured upon all the rates, revenues and property of the local authority, including the grant to be paid by the Government in aid of the housing scheme.

5. Trustees may invest in local bonds unless expressly forbidden by the instrument creating the trust.

6. Local bonds may be transferred (free of expense [1]) from one person to another by the execution of a transfer deed to be lodged with the bond certificate at the office of the local authority.

7. If at any time the holder of a local bond purchases a house erected by a local authority under the Housing Acts, the bond will be accepted at face value, together with accrued interest, in part payment of the purchase price.

8. No income tax will be deducted at the source from the interest on the bonds when the total holding does not exceed £100, but the holders will be assessable to income tax in the ordinary way to the extent of their liability.

FORM OF DEED OF TRANSFER

Registered Local Bonds

I,

in consideration of the sum of
paid by
hereinafter called the transferee do hereby assign and transfer to the said transferee :—

To hold unto the transferee,   executors, administrators, and assigns subject to the several con- ditions on which
held the same immediately before the execution hereof ;

[1] To be omitted if the local authority have not compounded for stamp duty.

45

Local
Bonds
Regulations.

and   the said transferee do
hereby agree to accept and take the said
subject to the conditions aforesaid.

As witness our hands and seals, this   day
of   in the year of our Lord One thousand
nine hundred and   .
Given under the official seal of the Minister of Health,
   this Twenty-fifth day of February, in the year One
   thousand nine hundred and twenty.
(L.S.)   CHRISTOPHER ADDISON,
                              Minister of Health.

We approve these regulations,
         JAMES PARKER,
         J. TOWYN JONES,
                    Two of the Lords Commissioners
                    of His Majesty's Treasury.

STATUTORY RULES AND ORDERS, 1920.   No. 560.

HOUSING, ENGLAND

The Prohibition of Demolition (Appeal Procedure) Rules,
   1920, dated 12th April 1920, made by the Minister
   of Health under section 5 (2) of the Housing (Additional
   Powers) Act, 1919 (9 & 10 Geo. 5. c. 99).

66,017.

The Minister of Health, under the powers conferred
on him by section 5 (2) of the Housing (Additional
Powers) Act, 1919, and all other powers enabling him in
that behalf, hereby makes the following rules :—

1. These rules may be cited as the Prohibition of
Demolition (Appeal Procedure) Rules, 1920.

2. (1) In these rules, unless the context otherwise
requires—

   " The Act " means the Housing (Additional
   Powers) Act, 1919 ;

   " The Minister " means the Minister of Health ;

   " Appeal tribunal " means the standing tribunal
   of appeal to be appointed by the Minister under
   section 5 (2) of the Act ;

   " Clerk to the appeal tribunal " means such

person as the Minister may from time to time appoint to act as clerk to the appeal tribunal.

(2) The Interpretation Act, 1889,[1] shall apply to the interpretation of these rules as it applies to the interpretation of an Act of Parliament.

3. An appeal under section 6 (2) of the Act to the Minister from a refusal by a local authority to give permission to demolish a house, in whole or in part, shall be made by sending to the clerk to the appeal tribunal a notice of appeal signed by the appellant or by his duly authorised agent.

4. The clerk to the appeal tribunal shall, as soon as may be after receipt of the notice aforesaid, send to the local authority a copy of the notice of appeal.

5. The local authority shall, within seven days after the receipt by them of the said notification, send a notice to the clerk to the appeal tribunal and to the appellant stating whether and to what extent they admit the facts stated in the appellant's notice of appeal and including a concise statement of the grounds on which permission was refused.

6. The appeal tribunal may at any stage of the proceedings allow the amendment of any notice, statement, or particulars on such terms as they think fit, and may require the appellant or the local authority within a specified time to furnish in writing such further particulars as they think necessary.

7. (1) If, after considering the notice of appeal and the statement of the local authority in reply and any further particulars which may have been furnished by either party, the appeal tribunal are of opinion that the case is of such a nature that it can properly be determined without a hearing, they may dispense with a hearing, and may determine the appeal summarily.

(2) Subject as aforesaid, the appeal tribunal shall fix a date for the hearing of the appeal, and shall give not less than seven days' notice to the appellant and the local authority of the time and place of the hearing.

8. The procedure of the appeal tribunal at the hearing of an appeal shall be such as they may from time to time determine.

9. The appeal tribunal may, if they think fit, and

Demolition Appeal Rules.

---
[1] 52-3 Vict. c. 63.

Demolition
Appeal
Rules.

subject to such conditions as they may impose, proceed with the consideration of any appeal, notwithstanding any failure or omission by any person to comply with the requirements of these rules.

10. The decision of the appeal tribunal shall be in writing signed by the chairman and clerk, and a copy, of the decision shall forthwith be sent to the appellant and to the local authority.

11. The forms set out in the schedule to these rules or forms substantially to the like effect shall be used for the purpose of these rules.

12. (1) Any notice or other document required or authorised by these rules to be sent to the clerk to the appeal tribunal shall be sufficiently sent if sent by post in a registered letter addressed to the Clerk of the Appeal Tribunal, Ministry of Health, Whitehall, London, S.W.1.

(2) Any notice or other document required or authorised by these rules to be sent by the clerk to the appeal tribunal or by the local authority to any appellant shall be sufficiently sent if sent by post to the address stated in the notice of appeal.

(3) Unless the contrary is proved any notice or document sent as aforesaid shall be deemed to be served at the time at which a letter would be delivered in the ordinary course of post.

SCHEDULE

FORM 1

Form of Notice of Appeal against a refusal of permission to demolish a house

HOUSING (ADDITIONAL POWERS) ACT, 1919

(Notice of appeal may be given by filling up and sending a copy of . this form to the Clerk to the Appeal Tribunal, Ministry of Health, Whitehall, London, S.W.1.)

Full name of appellant............................
Full address of appellant.........................
....
Address of house in respect of which the appeal is made
....
I, the undersigned, being the ¹...........of the above-mentioned house hereby appeal to the Minister of

Health against the refusal of [2]......................
to grant permission to me to demolish [part of [3]] the said
house.   Such permission was refused by the said local
authority on the ....day of ....192 .

My appeal is based on the ground that the said house
is not capable without reconstruction of being rendered
fit for human habitation. [4]

> [*Here insert a concise statement of the facts and grounds
> of the appeal, including the estimated present value
> of the house and detailed particulars of the work
> required for rendering the house fit for human habita-
> tion and of the estimated cost of the work.*]

Signature of Appellant.....................
Date...............................

[1] State appellant's interest in the house.
[2] State name of the local authority.
[3] Strike out these words, if inappropriate.
[4] This is the only ground of appeal which the Act permits.

FORM 2

Form of Statement of Reply by Local Authority

HOUSING (ADDITIONAL POWERS) ACT, 1919

In the matter of an appeal made by [1]...............
of.....................................against the
refusal of [2]...................to grant permission to
him to demolish the house [3].........................
The following facts stated in the appellant's notice of
appeal are admitted :—

[*Here insert statement of facts admitted*]

The grounds on which permission was refused are as
follows :—

[*Here insert statement of grounds*]

Dated this............day of............192 .
....

Signature of clerk of local authority.

[1] Insert name and address of appellant.
[2] Insert name of local authority.
[3] Insert address of house.

Given under the official seal of the Minister of Health,
this Twelfth day of April, in the year One thousand
nine hundred and twenty.

(L.S.)   CHRISTOPHER ADDISON,
                              Minister of Health.

APPENDIX VIII

INCREASE OF RENT AND MORTGAGE INTEREST (RESTRICTIONS) ACT, 1920

[10 & 11 Geo. 5. Ch. 17.]

*An Act to consolidate and amend the Law with respect to
the increase of rent and recovery of possession of
premises in certain cases, and the increase of the rate
of interest on, and the calling in of securities on such
premises, and for purposes in connection therewith.*

[2nd July 1920.]

BE it enacted by the King's most Excellent Majesty,
by and with the advice and consent of the Lords Spiritual
and Temporal, and Commons, in this present Parliament
assembled, and by the authority of the same, as follows :

Restrictions on Increase of Rent and Mortgage Interest

Restriction on increasing rent and mortgage interest.

1. Subject to the provisions of this Act, where the rent
of any dwelling-house to which this Act applies, or the
rate of interest on a mortgage to which this Act applies,
has been, since the twenty-fifth day of March nineteen
hundred and twenty, or is hereafter, increased, then,
if the increased rent or the increased rate of interest
exceeds by more than the amount permitted under this
Act the standard rent or standard rate of interest, the
amount of such excess shall, notwithstanding any agreement to the contrary, be irrecoverable from the tenant
or the mortgagor, as the case may be :

Provided that, where a landlord or mortgagee has

increased the rent of any such dwelling-house or the S. 1.
rate of interest on any such mortgage since the said date,
but before the passing of this Act, he may cancel such
increase and repay any amount paid by virtue thereof,
and in that case the rent or rate shall not be deemed
to have been increased since that date.

2. (1) The amount by which the increased rent of a Permitted
dwelling-house to which this Act applies may exceed the increases in
standard rent shall, subject to the provisions of this rent.
Act, be as follows, that is to say :

(a) Where the landlord has since the fourth day of
August nineteen hundred and fourteen incurred,
or hereafter incurs, expenditure on the improvement or structural alteration of the dwelling-house
(not including expenditure on decoration or repairs), an amount calculated at a rate per annum
not exceeding six, or, in the case of such expenditure
incurred after the passing of this Act, eight per
cent. of the amount so expended :

Provided that the tenant may apply to the
county court for an order suspending or reducing
such increase on the ground that such expenditure
is or was unnecessary in whole or in part, and the
court may make an order accordingly :

(b) An amount not exceeding any increase in the
amount for the time being payable by the landlord
in respect of rates over the corresponding amount
paid in respect of the yearly, half-yearly or other
period which included the third day of August
nineteen hundred and fourteen, or in the case of
a dwelling-house for which no rates were payable
in respect of any period which included the said
date, the period which included the date on which
the rates first became payable thereafter :

(c) In addition to any such amounts as aforesaid,
an amount not exceeding fifteen per cent. of
the net rent :

Provided that, except in the case of a dwelling-house to which this Act applies but the enactments repealed by this Act did not apply, the amount of such addition shall not, during a period of one year after the passing of this Act, exceed five per cent. :

(d) In further addition to any such amounts as aforesaid—

(i) where the landlord is responsible for the whole of the repairs, an amount not exceeding twenty-five per cent. of the net rent ; or

(ii) where the landlord is responsible for part and not the whole of the repairs, such lesser amount as may be agreed, or as may, on the application of the landlord or the tenant, be determined by the county court to be fair and reasonable having regard to such liability :

(e) In the case of dwelling-houses let by a railway company to persons in the employment of the company, such additional amount, if any, as is required in order to give effect to the agreement dated the first day of March nineteen hundred and twenty, relating to the rates of pay and conditions of employment of certain persons in the employment of railway companies, or any agreement, whether made before or after the passing of this Act, extending or modifying that agreement.

(2) At any time or times, not being less than three months after the date of any increase permitted by paragraph (d) of the foregoing subsection, the tenant or the sanitary authority may apply to the county court for an order suspending such increase, and also any increase under paragraph (c) of that subsection, on the ground that the house is not in all respects reasonably fit for human habitation, or is otherwise not in a reasonable state of repair.

The court on being satisfied by the production of a

certificate of the sanitary authority or otherwise that S. 2.
any such ground as aforesaid is established, and on being
further satisfied that the condition of the house is not
due to the tenant's neglect or default or breach of express
agreement, shall order that the increase be suspended
until the court is satisfied, on the report of the sanitary
authority or otherwise, that the necessary repairs (other
than the repairs, if any, for which the tenant is liable)
have been executed, and on the making of such order
the increase shall cease to have effect until the court is
so satisfied.

(3) Any transfer to a tenant of any burden or liability
previously borne by the landlord shall, for the purposes
of this Act, be treated as an alteration of rent, and
where, as the result of such a transfer, the terms on
which a dwelling-house is held are on the whole less
favourable to the tenant than the previous terms, the
rent shall be deemed to be increased, whether or not the
sum periodically payable by way of rent is increased,
and any increase of rent in respect of any transfer to a
landlord of any burden or liability previously borne by
the tenant where, as the result of such transfer, the
terms on which any dwelling-house is held are on the
whole not less favourable to the tenant than the previous
terms, shall be deemed not to be an increase of rent for
the purposes of this Act : Provided that, for the purposes
of this section, the rent shall not be deemed to be increased
where the liability for rates is transferred from the landlord to the tenant, if a corresponding reduction is made
in the rent.

(4) On any application to a sanitary authority for a
certificate or report under this section a fee of one shilling
shall be payable, but, if the authority as the result of
such application issues such a certificate as aforesaid,
the tenant shall be entitled to deduct the fee from any
subsequent payment of rent.

(5) For the purposes of this section, the expression

" repairs " means any repairs required for the purpose of keeping premises in good and tenantable repair, and any premises in such a state shall be deemed to be in a reasonable state of repair, and the landlord shall be deemed to be responsible for any repairs for which the tenant is under no express liability.

(6) Any question arising under subsection (1), (2) or (3) of this section shall be determined on the application either of the landlord or the tenant by the county court, and the decision of the court shall be final and conclusive.

Limitation as to permitted increases in rent.

3. (1) Nothing in this Act shall be taken to authorise any increase of rent except in respect of a period during which but for this Act the landlord would be entitled to obtain possession, or any increase in the rate of interest on a mortgage except in respect of a period during which, but for this Act, the security could be enforced.

(2) Notwithstanding any agreement to the contrary, where the rent of any dwelling-house to which this Act applies is increased, no such increase shall be due or recoverable until or in respect of any period prior to the expiry of four clear weeks, or, where such increase is on account of an increase in rates, one clear week, after the landlord has served upon the tenant a valid notice in writing of his intention to increase the rent, which notice shall be in the form contained in the First Schedule to this Act, or in a form substantially to the same effect. If a notice served as aforesaid contains any statement or representation which is false or misleading in any material respect, the landlord shall be liable on summary conviction to a fine not exceeding ten pounds unless he proves that the statement was made innocently and without intent to deceive. Where a notice of an increase ʼof rent which at the time was valid has been served on any tenant, the increase may be continued without service of any fresh notice on any subsequent tenant.

(3) A notice served before the passing of this Act of an intention to make any increase of rent which is

permissible only by virtue of this Act shall not be deemed S. 3.
to be a valid notice for the purpose of this section.

4. The amount by which the increased rate of interest Permitted
payable in respect of a mortgage to which this Act applies increase in rate of
may exceed the standard rate, shall be an amount not mortgage
exceeding one per cent. per annum : interest.

Provided that—

   (a) the rate shall not be increased so as to exceed
       six and a half per cent. per annum ; and
   (b) except in the case of a dwelling-house to which
       this Act applies but the enactments repealed by
       this Act did not apply, the increase during a period
       of one year after the passing of this Act shall not
       exceed one-half per cent. per annum.

Further Restrictions and Obligations on Landlords and
Mortgagees

5. (1) No order or judgment for the recovery of Restriction
possession of any dwelling-house to which this Act applies, on right to possession.
or for the ejectment of a tenant therefrom, shall be
made or given unless—

   (a) any rent lawfully due from the tenant has not
       been paid, or any other obligation of the tenancy
       (whether under the contract of tenancy or under
       this Act) so far as the same is consistent with the
       provisions of this Act has been broken or not
       performed ; or
   (b) the tenant or any person residing with him has
       been guilty of conduct which is a nuisance or
       annoyance to adjoining occupiers, or has been
       convicted of using the premises or allowing the
       premises to be used for an immoral or illegal
       purpose, or the condition of the dwelling-house
       has, in the opinion of the court, deteriorated owing
       to acts of waste by or the neglect or default of the
       tenant or any such person ; or
   (c) the tenant has given notice to quit, and in

. 5.

consequence of that notice the landlord has contracted to sell or let the dwelling-house or has taken any other steps as a result of which he would, in the opinion of the court, be seriously prejudiced if he could not obtain possession ; or

(d) the dwelling-house is reasonably required by the landlord for occupation as a residence for himself, or for any person bonâ fide residing or to reside with him, or for some person in his whole time employment or in the whole time employment of some tenant from him, and (except as otherwise provided by this subsection) the court is satisfied that alternative accommodation. reasonably equivalent as regards rent and suitability in all respects, is available ; or

(e) the landlord is a local authority or a statutory undertaking and the dwelling-house is reasonably required for the purpose of the execution of the statutory duties or powers of the authority or undertaking, and the court is satisfied as aforesaid as respects alternative accommodation ; or

(f) the landlord became the landlord after service in any of His Majesty's forces during the war and requires the house for his personal occupation and offers the tenant accommodation on reasonable terms in the same dwelling-house, such accommodation being considered by the court as reasonably sufficient in the circumstances ; or

(g) the dwelling-house is required for occupation as a residence by a former tenant thereof who gave up occupation in consequence of his service in any of His Majesty's forces during the war ;

and, in any such case as aforesaid, the court considers it reasonable to make such an order or give such judgment.

The existence of alternative accommodation shall not be a condition of an order or judgment on any of the grounds specified in paragraph (d) of this subsection—

(i) where the tenant was in the employment of the S. 5. landlord or a former landlord, and the dwelling-house was let to him in consequence of that employment and he has ceased to be in that employment ; or

(ii) where the court is satisfied by a certificate of the county agricultural committee, or of the Minister of Agriculture and Fisheries pending the formation of such committee, that the dwelling-house is required by the landlord for the occupation of a person engaged on work necessary for the proper working of an agricultural holding ; or

(iii) where the landlord gave up the occupation of the dwelling-house in consequence of his service in any of His Majesty's forces during the war ; or

(iv) where the landlord became the landlord before the thirtieth day of September nineteen hundred and seventeen, or, in the case of a dwelling-house to which section four of the Increase of Rent and Mortgage Interest (Restrictions) Act, 1919, applied, 8 & 9 Geo. 5. became the landlord before the fifth day of March, c. 7. nineteen hundred and nineteen, or in the case of a dwelling-house to which this Act applies but the enactments repealed by this Act did not apply, became the landlord before the twentieth day of May nineteen hundred and twenty, and in the opinion of the court greater hardship would be caused by refusing an order for possession than by granting it.

(2) At the time of the application for or the making or giving of any order or judgment for the recovery of possession of any such dwelling-house, or for the ejectment of a tenant therefrom, or in the case of any such order or judgment which has been made or given, whether before or after the passing of this Act, and not executed, at any subsequent time, the court may adjourn the application, or stay or suspend execution on any

such order or judgment, or postpone the date of possession, for such period or periods as it thinks fit, and subject to such conditions (if any) in regard to payment by the tenant of arrears of rent, rent, or mesne profits and otherwise as the court thinks fit, and, if such conditions are complied with, the court may, if it thinks fit, discharge or rescind any such order or judgment.

(3) Where any order or judgment has been made or given before the passing of this Act, but not executed, and, in the opinion of the court, the order or judgment would not have been made or given if this Act had been in force at the time when such order or judgment was made or given, the court may, on application by the tenant, rescind or vary such order or judgment in such manner as the court may think fit for the purpose of giving effect to this Act.

(4) Notwithstanding anything in section one hundred and forty-three of the County Courts Act, 1888, or in section one of the Small Tenements Recovery Act, 1838, every warrant for delivery of possession of, or to enter and give possession of, any dwelling-house to which this Act applies, shall remain in force for three months from the day next after the last day named in the judgment or order for delivery of possession or ejectment, or, in the case of a warrant under the Small Tenements Recovery Act, 1838, from the date of the issue of the warrant, and in either case for such further period or periods, if any, as the court shall from time to time, whether before or after the expiration of such three months, direct.

(5) An order or judgment against a tenant for the recovery of possession of any dwelling-house or ejectment therefrom under this section shall not affect the right of any sub-tenant to whom the premises or any part thereof have been lawfully sublet before proceedings for recovery of possession or ejectment were commenced, to retain possession under this section, or be in any way operative against any such sub-tenant.

(6) Where a landlord has obtained an order or judg- S. 5.
ment for possession or ejectment under this section on
the ground that he requires a dwelling-house for his own
occupation, and it is subsequently made to appear to
the court that the order was obtained by misrepresenta-
tion or the concealment of material facts, the court may
order the landlord to pay to the former tenant such sum
as appears as compensation for damage or loss sustained
by that tenant as the result of the order or judgment.

6. No distress for the rent of any dwelling-house to Restriction
which this Act applies shall be levied except with the on levy of
leave of the county court, and the court shall, with rent.
respect to any application for such leave, have the same
or similar powers with respect to adjournment, stay,
suspension, postponement and otherwise as are conferred
by the last preceding section of this Act in relation to
applications for the recovery of possession :

Provided that this section shall not apply to distress
levied under section one hundred and sixty of the County
Courts Act, 1888.

The provisions of this section shall be in addition to
and not in derogation of any of the provisions of the
Courts (Emergency Powers) Act, 1914, or any Act amend- 4 & 5 Geo. 5.
ing or extending the same, except so far as those pro- c. 78.
visions are repealed by this Act.

7. It shall not be lawful for any mortgagee under a Restriction
mortgage to which this Act applies, so long as— on calling in
of mort-
    (a) interest at the rate permitted under this Act is gages.
        paid and is not more than twenty-one days in
        arrear ; and

    (b) the covenants by the mortgagor (other than the
        covenant for the repayment of the principal
        money secured) are performed and observed ; and

    (c) the mortgagor keeps the property in a proper
        state of repair and pays all interest and instalments
        of principal recoverable under any prior encum-
        brance,

S. 7.

to call in his mortgage or to take any steps for exercising any right of foreclosure or sale, or for otherwise enforcing his security or for recovering the principal money thereby secured :

Provided that—

(i) this provision shall not apply to a mortgage where the principal money secured thereby is repayable by means of periodical instalments extending over a term of not less than ten years from the creation of the mortgage, nor shall this provision affect any power of sale exercisable by a mortgagee who was on the twenty-fifth day of March nineteen hundred and twenty a mortgagee in possession, or in cases where the mortgagor consents to the exercise by the mortgagee of the powers conferred by the mortgage ; and

(ii) if, in the case of a mortgage of a leasehold interest the mortgagee satisfies the county court that his security is seriously diminishing in value or is otherwise in jeopardy, and that for that reason it is reasonable that the mortgage should be called in and enforced, the court may by order authorise him to call in and enforce the same, and thereupon this section shall not apply to such mortgage; but any such order may be made subject to a condition that it shall not take effect if the mortgagor within such time as the court directs pays to the mortgagee such portion of the principal sum secured as appears to the court to correspond to the diminution of the security.

Restriction on premiums.

8. (1) A person shall not, as a condition of the grant, renewal, or continuance of a tenancy or sub-tenancy of any dwelling-house to which this Act applies, require the payment of any fine, premium, or other like sum, or the giving of any pecuniary consideration, in addition to the rent, and, where any such payment or consideration has been made or given in respect of any such

dwelling-house under an agreement made after the S. 8. twenty-fifth day of March nineteen hundred and twenty, the amount or value thereof shall be recoverable by the person by whom it was made or given :

Provided that, where any agreement has been made since the said date but before the passing of this Act for the tenancy of a house to which this Act applies, but the enactments repealed by this Act did not apply, and the agreement includes provision for the payment of any fine, premium, or other like sum, or the giving of any pecuniary consideration in addition to the rent, that agreement shall, without prejudice to the operation of this section, be voidable at the option of either party thereto.

(2) A person requiring any payment or the giving of any consideration in contravention of this section shall be liable on summary conviction to a fine not exceeding one hundred pounds, and the court by which he is convicted may order the amount paid or the value of the consideration to be repaid to the person by whom the same was made or given, but such order shall be in lieu of any other method of recovery prescribed by this Act.

(3) This section shall not apply to the grant, renewal or continuance for a term of fourteen years or upwards of any tenancy.

9. (1) Where any person lets, or has, before the passing of this Act, let any dwelling-house to which this Act applies, or any part thereof, at a rent which includes payment in respect of the use of furniture, and it is proved to the satisfaction of the county court on the application of the lessee that the rent charged is yielding or will yield to the lessor a profit more than twenty-five per cent. in excess of the normal profit as hereinafter defined, the court may order that the rent, so far as it exceeds such sum as would yield such normal profit and twenty-five per cent. shall be irrecoverable, and that the amount of any payment of rent in excess of such sum

Limitation on rent of houses let furnished.

46

S. 9.

which may have been made in respect of any period after the passing of this Act, shall be repaid to the lessee.

(2) For the purpose of this section, " normal profit " means the profit which might reasonably have been expected from a similar letting in the year ending on the third day of August nineteen hundred and fourteen.

Penalty for excessive charges for furnished lettings.

10. Where any person after the passing of this Act lets any dwelling-house to which this Act applies or any part thereof at a rent which includes payment in respect of the use of furniture, and the rent charged yields to the lessor a profit which, having regard to all the circumstances of the case, and in particular to the margin of profit allowed under the last preceding section of this Act, is extortionate, then, without prejudice to any other remedy under this Act, the lessor shall be liable on summary conviction to a fine not exceeding one hundred pounds, and the court by which he is convicted may order that the rent so far as it exceeds the amount permitted by the last preceding section of this Act shall be irrecoverable and that the amount of any such excess shall be repaid to the lessee, but any such order shall be in lieu of any other method of recovery prescribed by this Act.

Statement to be supplied as to standard rent.

11. A landlord of any dwelling-house to which this Act applies shall, on being so requested in writing by the tenant of the dwelling-house, supply him with a statement in writing as to what is the standard rent of the dwelling-house, and if, without reasonable excuse, he fails within fourteen days to do so, or supplies a statement which is false in any material particular, he shall be liable on summary conviction to a fine not exceeding ten pounds.

Application and Interpretation of Act.

Application and interpretation.

12. (1) For the purposes of this Act, except where the context otherwise requires :

(a) The expression " standard rent " means the rent

at which the dwelling-house was let on the third day of August nineteen hundred and fourteen, or, where the dwelling-house was not let on that date, the rent at which it was last let before that date, or, in the case of a dwelling-house which was first let after the said third day of August, the rent at which it was first let :

Provided that, in the case of any dwelling-house let at a progressive rent payable under a tenancy agreement or lease, the maximum rent payable under such tenancy agreement or lease shall be the standard rent ; and, where at the date by reference to which the standard rent is calculated, the rent was less than the rateable value the rateable value at that date shall be the standard rent ;

(b) The expression " standard rate of interest " means, in the case of a mortgage in force on the third day of August nineteen hundred and fourteen, the rate of interest payable at that date, or, in the case of a mortgage created since that date, the original rate of interest ;

(c) The expression "net rent " means, where the landlord at the time by reference to which the standard rent is calculated paid the rates chargeable on, or which but for the provisions of any Act would be chargeable on the occupier, the standard rent less the amount of such rates, and in any other case the standard rent ;

(d) The expression " rates " includes water rents and charges, and any increase in rates payable by a landlord shall be deemed to be payable by him until the rate is next demanded ;

(e) The expression " rateable value " means the rateable value on the third day of August nineteen hundred and fourteen, or, in the case of a dwelling-house or a part of dwelling-house first assessed

S. 12.

after that date, the rateable value at which it was first assessed ;

(f) The expressions " landlord," " tenant," " mortgagee," and " mortgagor " include any person from time to time deriving title under the original landlord, tenant, mortgagee, or mortgagor ;

(g) The expression " landlord " also includes in relation to any dwelling-house any person, other than the tenant, who is or would but for this Act be entitled to possession of the dwelling-house, and the expressions " tenant ' and " tenancy " include sub-tenant and sub-tenancy, and the expression " let " includes sublet ; and the expression " tenant " includes the widow of a tenant dying intestate who was residing with him at the time of his death, or, where a tenant dying intestate leaves no widow or is a woman, such member of the tenant's family so residing as aforesaid as may be decided in default of agreement by the county court ;

38 & 39 Vict.
c. 87.
60 & 61 Vict.
c. 65.

(h) The expression " mortgage " includes a land charge under the Land Transfer Acts, 1875 and 1897 ;

(i) The expressions " statutory undertaking " and " statutory duties or powers " include any undertaking, duties or powers, established, imposed or exercised under any order having the force of an Act of Parliament.

(2) This Act shall apply to a house or a part of a house let as a separate dwelling, where either the annual amount of the standard rent or the rateable value does not exceed—

(a) in the metropolitan police district, including therein the City of London, one hundred and five pounds ;

(b) in Scotland, ninety pounds ; and

(c) elsewhere, seventy-eight pounds ;

and every such house or part of a house shall be deemed S. 12. to be a dwelling-house to which this Act applies :

Provided that—

(i) this Act shall not, save as otherwise expressly provided, apply to a dwelling-house bonâ fide let at a rent which includes payments in respect of board, attendance, or use of furniture ; and

(ii) the application of this Act to any house or part of a house shall not be excluded by reason only that part of the premises is used as a shop or office or for business, trade, or professional purposes ; and

(iii) for the purposes of this Act, any land or premises let together with a house shall, if the rateable value of the land or premises let separately would be less than one quarter of the rateable value of the house, be treated as part of the house, but, subject to this provision, this Act shall not apply to a house let together with land other than the site of the house.

(3) Where, for the purpose of determining the standard rent or rateable value of any dwelling-house to which this Act applies, it is necessary to apportion the rent at the date in relation to which the standard rent is to be fixed, or the rateable value of the property in which that dwelling-house is comprised, the county court may, on application by either party, make such apportionment as seems just, and the decision of the court as to the amount to be apportioned to the dwelling-house shall be final and conclusive.

(4) Subject to the provisions of this Act, this Act shall apply to every mortgage where the mortgaged property consists of or comprises one or more dwelling-houses to which this Act applies, or any interest therein, except that it shall not apply—

(a) to any mortgage comprising one or more dwelling-houses to which this Act applies and other land if the rateable value of such dwelling-houses is less than one-tenth of the rateable value of the whole of the land comprised in the mortgage ; or

(b) to an equitable charge by deposit of title deeds or otherwise ; or

(c) to any mortgage which is created after the passing of this Act.

(5) When a mortgage comprises one or more dwelling-houses to which this Act applies and other land, and the rateable value of such dwelling-houses is more than one-tenth of the rateable value of the whole of the land comprised in the mortgage, the mortgagee may apportion the principal money secured by the mortgage between such dwelling-houses and such other land by giving one calendar month's notice in writing to the mortgagor, such notice to state the particulars of such apportionment, and at the expiration of the said calendar month's notice this Act shall not apply to the mortgage so far as it relates to such other land, and for all purposes, including the mortgagor's right of redemption, the said mortgage shall operate as if it were a separate mortgage for the respective portions of the said principal money secured by the said dwelling-houses and such other land, respectively, to which such portions were apportioned :

Provided that the mortgagor shall, before the expiration of the said calendar month's notice, be entitled to dispute the amounts so apportioned as aforesaid, and in default of agreement the matter shall be determined by a single arbitrator appointed by the President of the Surveyors' Institution.

(6) Where this Act has become applicable to any dwelling-house or any mortgage thereon, it shall continue to apply thereto whether or not the dwelling-house continues to be one to which this Act applies.

(7) Where the rent payable in respect of any tenancy of any dwelling-house is less than two-thirds of the rateable value thereof, this Act shall not apply to that rent

or tenancy nor to any mortgage by the landlord from s. 12.
whom the tenancy is held of his interest in the dwelling-
house, and this Act shall apply in respect of such dwelling-
house as if no such tenancy existed or ever had existed.

(8) Any rooms in a dwelling-house subject to a separate
letting wholly or partly as a dwelling shall, for the purposes of this Act, be treated as a part of a dwelling-house
let as a separate dwelling.

(9) This Act shall not apply to a dwelling-house erected
after or in course of erection on the second day of April
nineteen hundred and nineteen, or to any dwelling-house
which has been since that date or was at that date being
bonâ fide reconstructed by way of conversion into two or
more separate and self-contained flats or tenements ; but,
for the purpose of any enactment relating to rating, the
gross estimated rental or gross value of any such house to
which this Act would have applied if it had been erected
or so reconstructed before the third day of August
nineteen hundred and fourteen, and let at that date,
shall not exceed—

(a) if the house forms part of a housing scheme to
which section seven of the Housing, Town Plan- 9 & 10 Geo. 5.
ning, &c., Act, 1919, applies, the rent (exclusive of c. 35.
rates) charged by the local authority in respect of
that house ; and

(b) in any other case the rent (exclusive of rates)
which would have been charged by the local
authority in respect of a similar house forming
part of such a scheme as aforesaid.

(10) Where possession has been taken of any dwelling-
houses by a Government department during the war,
under the Defence of the Realm regulations, for the
purpose of housing workmen, this Act shall apply to such
houses as if the workmen in occupation thereof at the
passing of this Act were in occupation as tenants of the
landlords of such houses.

13. (1) This Act shall apply to any premises used for

business, trade or professional purposes or for the public service as it applies to a dwelling-house, and as though references to " dwelling-house," " house " and " dwelling " included references to any such premises, but this Act in its application to such premises shall have effect subject to the following modifications :

(*a*) The following paragraph shall be substituted for paragraph (*c*) of subsection (1) of section two :

(*c*) In addition to any such amounts as aforesaid, an amount not exceeding thirty-five per cent. of the net rent :

(*b*) The following paragraph shall be substituted for paragraph (*d*) of subsection (1) of section five :

(*d*) the premises are reasonably required by the landlord for business, trade or professional purposes or for the public service, and (except as otherwise provided by this subsection) the court is satisfied that alternative accommodation, reasonably equivalent as regards rent and suitability in all respects, is available :

(*c*) The following paragraph shall be added after paragraph (*g*) of the same subsection :

(*h*) The premises are bonâ fide required for the purpose of a scheme of reconstruction or improvement which appears to the court to be desirable in the public interest :

(*d*) Paragraph (i) of the same subsection shall not apply :

(*e*) Sections nine and ten shall not apply.

(2) The application of this Act to such premises as aforesaid shall not extend to a letting or tenancy in any market or fair where the rent or conditions of tenancy are controlled or regulated by or in pursuance of any statute or charter.

(3) This section shall continue in force until the twenty-fourth day of June nineteen hundred and twenty-one.

General

14. (1) Where any sum has, whether before or after the passing of this Act, been paid on account of any rent or mortgage interest, being a sum which is by virtue of this Act, or any Act repealed by this Act, irrecoverable by the landlord or mortgagee, the sum so paid shall be recoverable from the landlord or mortgagee who received the payment or his legal personal representative by the tenant or mortgagor by whom it was paid, and any such sum, and any other sum which under this Act is recoverable by a tenant from a landlord or payable or repayable by a landlord to a tenant, may, without prejudice to any other method of recovery, be deducted by the tenant or mortgagor from any rent or interest payable by him to the landlord or mortgagee.

(2) If—

    (*a*) any person in any rent book or similar document makes an entry showing or purporting to show any tenant as being in arrear in respect of any sum which by virtue of any such Act is irrecoverable ; or

    (*b*) where any such entry has, before the passing of this Act, been made by or on behalf of any landlord, the landlord, on being requested by or on behalf of the tenant so to do, refuses or neglects

to cause the entry to be deleted within seven days, that person or landlord shall, on summary conviction, be liable to a fine not exceeding ten pounds, unless he proves that he acted innocently and without intent to deceive.

15. (1) A tenant who by virtue of the provisions of this Act retains possession of any dwelling-house to which this Act applies shall, so long as he retains possession, observe and be entitled to the benefit of all the terms and conditions of the original contract of tenancy, so far as the same are consistent with the provisions of

S. 15.

this Act, and shall be entitled to give up possession of the dwelling-house only on giving such notice as would have been required under the original contract of tenancy, or, if no notice would have been so required, on giving not less than three months' notice :

Provided that, notwithstanding anything in the contract of tenancy, a landlord who obtains an order or judgment for the recovery of possession of the dwelling-house or for the ejectment of a tenant retaining possession as aforesaid shall not be required to give any notice to quit to the tenant.

(2) Any tenant retaining possession as aforesaid shall not as a condition of giving up possession ask or receive the payment of any sum, or the giving of any other consideration, by any person other than the landlord, and any person acting in contravention of this provision shall be liable on summary conviction to a fine not exceeding one hundred pounds, and the court by which he was convicted may order any such payment or the value of any such consideration to be paid to the person by whom the same was made or given, but any such order shall be in lieu of any other method of recovery prescribed by this Act.

(3) Where the interest of a tenant of a dwelling-house to which this Act applies is determined, either as the result of an order or judgment for possession or ejectment, or for any other reason, any sub-tenant to whom the premises or any part thereof have been lawfully sublet shall, subject to the provisions of this Act, be deemed to become the tenant of the landlord on the same terms as he would have held from the tenant if the tenancy had continued.

Minor amendments of law.

32 & 33 Vict. c. 41.

16. (1) Section three of the Poor Rate Assessment and Collection Act, 1869, shall, except so far as it relates to the metropolis, have effect as though for the limits of value specified in that section there were substituted limits twenty-five per cent. in excess of the limits so

specified, and that section and section four of the same S. 16.
Act shall have effect accordingly.

(2) It shall be deemed to be a condition of the tenancy
of any dwelling-house to which this Act applies that the
tenant shall afford to the landlord access thereto and all
reasonable facilities for executing therein any repairs
which the landlord is entitled to execute.

(3) Where the landlord of any dwelling-house to which
this Act applies has served a notice to quit on a tenant,
the acceptance of rent by the landlord for a period
not exceeding three months from the expiration of the
notice to quit shall not be deemed to prejudice any right
to possession of such premises, and, if any order for
possession is made, any payment of rent so accepted
shall be treated as mesne profits.

17. (1) The Lord Chancellor may make such rules and Rules as to
give such directions as he thinks fit for the purpose of procedure.
giving effect to this Act, and may, by those rules or directions, provide for any proceedings for the purposes of
this Act being conducted so far as desirable in private
and for the remission of any fees.

(2) A county court shall have jurisdiction to deal with
any claim or other proceedings arising out of this Act or
any of the provisions thereof, notwithstanding that by
reason of the amount of claim or otherwise the case
would not but for this provision be within the jurisdiction
of a county court, and, if a person takes proceedings
under this Act in the High Court which he could have
taken in the county court, he shall not be entitled to
recover any costs.

18. (1) This Act shall apply to Scotland, subject to Application
the following modifications :   to Scotland
                                                           and Ireland.

    (a) " Mortgage " and " encumbrance " mean a
       heritable security including a security constituted
       by absolute disposition qualified by back bond or
       letter ; " mortgagor " and " mortgagee " mean
       respectively the debtor and the creditor in a

S. 18.

heritable security ; "covenant" means obligation ;
"mortgaged property" means the heritable subject or subjects included in a heritable security ;
"rateable value" means yearly value according
to the valuation roll ; "rateable value on the
third day of August nineteen hundred and fourteen" means yearly value according to the valuation roll for the year ending fifteenth day of May
nineteen hundred and fifteen ; "assessed" means
entered in the valuation roll ; "land" means
land and heritages ; "rates" means assessments
1 & 2 Geo. 5.
c. 53.
as defined in the House Letting and Rating (Scotland) Act, 1911 ; "Lord Chancellor" and "High
Court" mean the Court of Session ; "rules"
means act of sederunt ; "county court" means
the sheriff court ; "sanitary authority" means
60 & 61 Vict.
c. 38.
the local authority under the Public Health (Scotland) Act, 1897 ; "mesne profits" means profits ;
the Board of Agriculture for Scotland shall be substituted for the Minister of Agriculture and
Fisheries ; the twenty-eighth day of May shall be
substituted for the twenty-fourth day of June ;
the reference to the county agricultural committee
shall be construed as a reference to the body of
persons constituted with respect to any area by
the Board of Agriculture for Scotland under
7 & 8 Geo. 5.
c. 46.
subsection (2) of section eleven of the Corn Production Act, 1917 ; references to levying distress
shall be construed as references to doing diligence ;
the reference to the President of the Surveyors'
Institution shall be construed as a reference to
the Chairman of the Scottish Committee of the
Surveyors' Institution ; a reference to section five
9 & 10 Geo. 5.
c. 60.
of the Housing, Town Planning, &c. (Scotland)
Act, 1919, shall be substituted for a reference to
section seven of the Housing, Town Planning, &c.,
Act, 1919 ; and a reference to section one of the

House Letting and Rating (Scotland) Act, 1911, S. 18.
shall be substituted for a reference to section three
of the Poor Rate Assessment and Collection Act, 32 & 33 Vict.
1869 :   c. 41.

(b) Nothing in paragraph (b) of subsection (1) of the
section of this Act relating to permitted increases
in rent shall permit any increase in rent in respect
of any increase after the year ending Whitsunday
nineteen hundred and twenty in the amount of
the rates payable by the landlord other than rates
for which he is responsible under the House
Letting and Rating (Scotland) Act, 1911 :

(c) Paragraph (d) of subsection (1) of the section of
this Act relating to application and interpretation
shall not apply :

(d) Where any dwelling-house, to which the Acts
repealed by this Act applied, is subject to a right
of tenancy arising from a yearly contract or from
tacit relocation, and ending at Whitsunday nineteen hundred and twenty-one, the year ending at
the said term of Whitsunday shall be deemed to
be a period during which, but for this Act, the
landlord would be entitled to obtain possession of
such dwelling-house.

(2) This Act shall apply to Ireland subject to the
following modifications :

(a) A reference to the Lord Chancellor of Ireland
shall be substituted for the reference to the Lord
Chancellor :

(b) A reference to section fifteen of the Summary 14 & 15 Vict.
Jurisdiction (Ireland) Act, 1851, shall be sub- c. 92.
stituted for the reference to section one of the
Small Tenements Recovery Act, 1838 :

(c) The expression " mortgage " includes a charge
by registered disposition under the Local Regis- 54 & 55 Vict.
tration of Title (Ireland) Act, 1891, and any c. 66.
notice of the apportionment of the principal money

secured by a mortgage, if and when the notice becomes operative under this Act, and the award of any arbitrator with reference to any such apportionment may be registered under the enactments relative to the registration of deeds or titles as the case requires :

(d) The expression "rateable value" means the annual rateable value under the Irish Valuation Acts : Provided that, where part of a house let as a separate dwelling is not separately valued under those Acts, the Commissioner of Valuation and Boundary Surveyor may, on the application of the landlord or tenant, make such apportionment of the rateable value of the whole house as seems just, and his decision as to the amount to be apportioned to the part of the house shall be final and conclusive, and that amount shall be taken to be the rateable value of the part of the house for the purposes of this Act but not further or otherwise :

(e) The following paragraph shall be substituted for paragraph (ii) of subsection (1) of section five of this Act :

(ii) Where the court is satisfied that the dwelling-house is required by the landlord for the occupation of a person engaged on work necessary for the proper working of an agricultural holding ; or

(f) The following subsection shall be substituted for subsection (9) of section twelve of this Act :

(9) This Act shall not apply to a dwelling-house erected after, or in course of erection on, the second day of April nineteen hundred and nineteen, or to any dwelling-house which has been since that date or was at that date being bonâ fide reconstructed by way of conversion into two or more separate and self-contained flats

or tenements ; but the rateable value of any S. 18. such dwelling-house to which this Act would have applied if it had been erected or so reconstructed before the said date shall be ascertained as though the rent for the purposes of section eleven of the Valuation (Ireland) Act, 15 & 16 Vict. 1852, were the rent for which a similar dwelling- c. 63. house might have been reasonably expected to let on the third day of August nineteen hundred and fourteen, the probable average annual cost of repairs, insurance, and other expenses (if any) necessary to maintain the dwelling-house in its actual state, and all rates, taxes, and public charges, if any (except tithe rentcharge), being paid by the tenant :

(*g*) The medical officer of health of a dispensary district shall be substituted for the sanitary authority in section two of this Act and in the First Schedule thereto, and the issue of certificates and the payment of fees in connection with applications by tenants under the said section shall be subject to regulations to be made by the Local Government Board for Ireland :

(*h*) This Act shall not apply to any dwelling-house provided by a local authority under the Labourers (Ireland) Acts, 1883 to 1919, or under any of those Acts.

19. (1) This Act may be cited as the Increase of Rent Short title, and Mortgage Interest (Restrictions) Act, 1920. duration,
and repeal.

(2) Except as otherwise provided, this Act shall continue in force until the twenty-fourth day of June nineteen hundred and twenty-three :

Provided that the expiration of this Act or any part thereof shall not render recoverable by a landlord any rent, interest or other sum which during the continuance thereof was irrecoverable, or affect the right of a tenant to recover any sum which during the continuance thereof was under this Act recoverable by him.

S. 19.   (3) The enactments mentioned in the Second Schedule to this Act are hereby repealed to the extent specified in the third column of that schedule :

52 & 53 Vict. c. 63.   Provided that, without prejudice to the operation of section thirty-eight of the Interpretation Act, 1889, nothing in this repeal shall render recoverable any sums which at the time of the passing of this Act were irre-coverable, or affect the validity of any order of a court, or any rules or directions made or given under any enactment repealed by this Act, all of which orders, rules, and directions if in force at the date of the passing of this Act shall have effect as if they were made or given under this Act, and any proceedings pending in any court at the date of the passing of this Act, under any enactment repealed by this Act, shall be deemed to have been commenced under this Act.

SCHEDULES

Sections 3 and 18.

FIRST SCHEDULE

FORM OF NOTICE BY LANDLORD.

INCREASE OF RENT AND MORTGAGE INTEREST (RESTRICTIONS) ACT, 1920

Date

To

Address of premises to which
   this notice refers

Take notice that I intend to increase the rent of £   s.   d. per   at present payable by you as tenant of the above-named premises by the amount of £   s.   d. per

The increase is made up as follows :

(a) £   s.   d. under paragraph (a) of subsection (1) of section two of the Act, being six [eight] per cent, on £   s.   d. expended by me since

[*insert date*] on improvements and structural 1st Sch.
alterations, and consisting of *

(*b*) £   *s.*   *d.* under paragraph (*b*) of subsection (1) of section two of the Act, on account
of an increase in the rates payable by me from
£   *s.*   *d.* per   to £   *s.*   *d.* per
in respect of the premises.

(*c*) £   *s.*   *d.* under paragraph (*c*) of subsection
(1) of section two of the Act, being   per
cent. on the net rent of the premises.   The
net rent is £   *s.*   *d.*   The standard rent
is £   *s.*   *d.*

(*d*) £   *s.*   *d.* under paragraph (*d*) of subsection (1)
of section two of the Act, being   per cent.
on the net rent of the premises.   The net rent is
£   *s.*   *d.*   The standard rent is £   *s.*   *d.*

The increase under head (*b*) will date from   ,
being one clear week from the date of this notice, and
the remaining increases from   , being four clear
weeks from the date of this notice.

† The increase under head (*d*) is on account of my
responsibility for repairs, for no part [part only] of which
are you under an express liability.

‡ At any time or times, not being less than three
months after the   day of   19 , you are
entitled to apply to the county court for an order suspending the increases under heads (*c*) and (*d*) above if
you consider that the premises are not in all respects
reasonably fit for human habitation or otherwise not in
a reasonable state of repair.   You will be required to
satisfy the county court, by a report of the sanitary
authority or otherwise, that your application is well

---

* Here state improvements and alterations effected.

† Where the tenant is under an express liability for part of the
repairs, the increase under head (*d*) is to be settled in default of agreement by the county court.

‡ This paragraph need not be included if there is no increase under
head (*d*).

47

founded, and for this purpose you are entitled to apply to the sanitary authority for a certificate. A fee of one shilling is chargeable on any application for a certificate, but, if the certificate is granted, you can deduct this sum from your rent. The address of the sanitary authority is

Signed

Address

SECOND SCHEDULE

ENACTMENTS REPEALED

Session and Chapter.	Short Title.	Extent of Repeal.
5 & 6 Geo. 5. c. 97.	The Increase of Rent and Mortgage Interest (War Restrictions) Act, 1915.	The whole Act.
7 & 8 Geo. 5. c. 25.	The Courts (Emergency Powers) Act, 1917.	Ss. 4, 5 and 7.
8 & 9 Geo. 5. c. 7.	The Increase of Rent and Mortgage Interest (Restrictions) Act, 1919.	The whole Act.
9 & 10 Geo. 5. c. 90.	The Increase of Rent, &c. (Amendment) Act, 1919.	The whole Act.

INDEX

48

49

**THIS BOOK IS DUE ON THE LAST DATE
STAMPED BELOW**

AN INITIAL FINE OF 25 CENTS

WILL BE ASSESSED FOR FAILURE TO RETURN
THIS BOOK ON THE DATE DUE. THE PENALTY
WILL INCREASE TO 50 CENTS ON THE FOURTH
DAY AND TO $1.00 ON THE SEVENTH DAY
OVERDUE.

LD 21–100m-7,'39 (402s)

Lightning Source UK Ltd.
Milton Keynes UK
UKHW021323200219
337612UK00006B/510/P